SO-ADS-625

SOVIET AND EAST EUROPEAN STUDIES

Editorial Board

The National Association for Soviet and East European Studies exists for the purpose of promoting study and research on the social sciences as they relate to the Soviet Union and the countries of Eastern Europe. The Monograph Series is intended to promote the publication of works presenting substantial and original research in the economics, politics, sociology and modern history of the USSR and Eastern Europe.

SOVIET AND EAST EUROPEAN STUDIES

Books in the series

The History of Poland since 1863

R. F. LESLIE
ANTONY POLONSKY
JAN M. CIECHANOWSKI
Z. A. PELCZYNSKI

EDITED BY R. F. LESLIE

CAMBRIDGE UNIVERSITY PRESS

CAMBRIDGE

LONDON   NEW YORK   NEW ROCHELLE
MELBOURNE   SYDNEY

Published by the Press Syndicate of the University of Cambridge
The Pitt Building, Trumpington Street, Cambridge CB2 1RP
32 East 57th Street, New York, NY 10022, USA
296 Beaconsfield Parade, Middle Park, Melbourne 3206, Australia

First published 1980
First paperback edition, with epilogue, 1983

Printed in Great Britain at the University Press, Cambridge

Library of Congress Cataloging in Publication Data
Main entry title:
The History of Poland since 1863.
(Soviet and East European studies)
Bibliography: p.
Includes index.
1. Poland – History – 20th century. 2. Poland –
History – 1864–1918. I. Leslie, R. F. II. Series.
DK4382.H57   943.8   78-73246
ISBN 0 521 22645 7 hard covers
ISBN 0 521 27501 6 paperback

Contents

Maps

Thanks are due to the London School of Economics who drew the maps.

Preface to the paperback edition

This history of Poland starts with the disastrous aftermath of insurrection of 1863 which constituted a major watershed in Polish evolution, marking the end of the political and social supremacy of the nobility and the emergence of new forces which made possible the creation of a modern nation. Like history itself it has no end, but an attempt has been made to analyse events up to the present day. Though it is a joint work, the authors take responsibility for their own individual chapters which have been subject to minimal editorship only. R. F. Leslie (Chapters 1–3), Antony Polonsky (Chapters 4–7), Jan M. Ciechanowski (Chapters 8–11) and Z. A. Pelczynski (Chapters 12–17) express opinions which are entirely their own. Nevertheless, all the authors share certain views about the Polish past. They believe that Polish history has too often been written as if it took place in a social and economic vacuum and they have thus stressed the importance of these factors in assessing political developments. They recognize too the merits of both of the principal approaches to the political dilemma in which Poland finds itself and do not therefore align themselves with either the realist/positivist or the romantic/insurrectionary view of the Polish past.

Polish history is full of striking paradoxes. It oscillates between periods of great victories and achievements and abject defeats, between periods of concerted striving for freedom, justice and liberty and periods of humiliating and partly self-engendered decline. The authors have tried to strike a balance between a too optimistic and a too defeatist interpretation of Poland's development. This paperback edition appears at a difficult and grave moment in Polish history when a peaceful popular revolt against the mismanagement, corruption and injustice of the Communist system in the 1970s appears to have failed though not without inflicting a tremendous shock on the Communist Party, which perhaps will prove salutary. Its authors hope that, as before, the resilience, faith and courage of the Polish people will enable them to overcome the defeat and to create, within the stern limits of geopolitics, a future in which, in the words of the Gdańsk shipyard workers' song, 'Poland will be truly itself'.

Abbreviations

AK	Armia Krajowa (Home Army)
AL	Armia Ludowa (People's Army)
BBWR	Bezpartyjny Blok Współpracy z Rządem (Non-Party Bloc for Co-operation with the Government)
CBKP	Centralne Biuro Komunistów Polskich (Central Bureau of Polish Communists)
CKN	Centralny Komitet Narodowy (National Central Committee)
CPSU	Communist Party of the Soviet Union
CRZZ	Centralna Rada Związków Zawodowych (Central Council of Trade Unions)
FRG	Federal Republic of Germany
FSZMP	Federacja Socjalistycznych Związków Młodzieży Polskiej (Federation of Socialist Unions of Polish Youth)
GDR	German Democratic Republic
GL	Gwardia Ludowa (People's Guard)
KOR	Komitet Obrony Robotników (Workers' Defence Committee)
KPP	Komunistyczna Partia Polski (Polish Communist Party)
KPRP	Komunistyczna Partia Robotnicza Polski (Communist Workers' Party of Poland)
KRN	Krajowa Rada Narodowa (National Council of the Homeland)
KSR	Konferencja Samorządu Robotniczego (Conference of the Workers' Self-Government)
KW	Komitet Wykonawczy [Centralnego Komitetu Robotniczego] (Executive Committee of the Central Workers' Committee)
KZ	Komitet Zagraniczny [Centralnego Komitetu Robotniczego] (Foreign Committee of the Central Workers' Committee)
NKN	Naczelny Komite Narodowy (Supreme National Committee)
NKVD	Narodnaya Kommissiya Vevnutrikh Dyel (People's Commission of Internal Affairs)

NSR	Narodowe Stronnictwo Robotnicze (National Workers' Party)
NSZ	Narodowe Siły Zbrojne (National Armed Forces)
NZCh	Narodowy Związek Chłopski (National Peasant Union)
NZR	Narodowy Związek Robotniczy (National Workers' Union)
ONR	Obóz Narodowo–Radykalny (National Radical Camp)
ORMO	Ochotnicza Reserwa Milicji Obywatelskiej (Volunteer Reserve of the Citizens' Militia)
OUN	Organizacja Ukraińskich Nacjonalistów (Organization of Ukrainian Nationalists)
OWP	Obóz Wielkiej Polski (Camp for a Greater Poland)
OZON	Obóz Zjednoczenia Narodowego (Camp of National Unity)
PAX	Stowarzyszenie PAX (Catholic social movement)
PKP	Polityczny Komitet Porozumiewawczy (Political Consultative Committee)
PKPG	Państwowa Komisja Planowania Gospodarczego (State Commission for Economic Planning)
PKWN	Polski Komitet Wyzwolenia Narodowego (Polish Committee of National Liberation)
PON	Polska Organizacja Narodowa (Polish National Organization)
POW	Polska Organizacja Wojskowa (Polish Military Organization)
PPR	Polska Partia Robotnicza (Polish Workers' Party)
PPS	Polska Partia Socialistyczna (Polish Socialist Party)
PPSDGiS	Polska Partia Socjalno–Demokratyczna Galicji i Śląska (Polish Social Democratic Party of Galicia and Silesia)
PPSzP	Polska Partia Socjalistyczna zaboru Pruskiego (Polish Socialist Party of the Prussian Partition)
PSL	Polskie Stronnictwo Ludowe (Polish Peasant Party)
PZL	Polski Związek Ludowy (Polish Peasant Union)
PZPR	Polska Zjednoczona Partia Robotnicza (Polish United Workers' Party)
RJN	Rada Jedności Narodowej (Council of National Unity)
RN	Rada Narodowa (National Council)
SD	Stronnictwo Demokratyczne (Democratic Party)
SDKP	Socialdemokracja Królestwa Polskiego (Social Democracy of the Kingdom of Poland)
SDKPiL	Socialdemokracja Królestwa Polskiego i Litwy (Social Democracy of the Kingdom of Poland and Lithuania)
SL	Stronnictwo Ludowe (Peasant Party)

SN-D	Stronnictwo Narodowo–Demokratyczne (National Democratic Party)
SP	Stronnictwo Pracy (Party of Labour)
SZP	Służba Zwycięstwu Polski (Service for the Victory of Poland)
TKSSN	Tymczasowa Komisja Skonfederowanych Stronnictw Niepodległościowych (Temporary Commission of Confederated Independence Parties)
UB	Urząd Bezpieczeństwa (Security Office)
UNDO	Ukrainskie Natsionalno–Demokratychne Objednianie (Ukrainian National Democratic Union)
WIN	[Zrzeszenie] Wolność i Niezawisłość (Freedom and Independence Group)
WOG	Wielkie Organizacje Gospodarcze (Great Economic Organizations)
ZBoWiD	Związek Bojowników o Wolność i Demokrację (Union of Fighters for Freedom and Democracy)
Zet	Związek Młodzieży Polskiej – ZMP (Union of Polish Youth)
ZHP	Związek Harcerstwa Polskiego (Union of Polish Scouts)
ZISPO	Zakłady Imieniem Stalina, Poznań (Poznań Stalin Works)
ZLP	Związek Literatów Polskich (Writers' Union)
ZMP	Związek Młodzieży Polskiej (Union of Polish Youth)
ZMS	Związek Młodzieży Socjalistycznej (Union of Socialist Youth)
ZMW	Związek Młodzieży Wiejskiej (Union of Rural Youth)
ZPP	Związek Patriotów Polskich (Union of Polish Patriots)
ZRP	Związek Robotników Polskich (Union of Polish Workers)
ZSL	Zjednoczone Stronnictwo Ludowe (United Peasant Party)
ZSP	Związek Studentów Polskich (Union of Polish Students)
ZWZ	Związek Walki Zbrojnej (Association of Armed Struggle)

Triloyalism and the national revival

Poland in the 1860's

The Poland of today owes its frontiers to the discussions between the leaders of the USSR, Great Britain and the United States of America. The shape of the new state was proposed at Tehran in 1943 by Winston Churchill in order to bring an end to the long conflict between Russia and Poland:

It was agreed in the principle that the hearth of the Polish state and people must be situated between the so-called Curzon line and the line of the Oder River, including Eastern Prussia and the Oppeln Province as part of Poland. But the final drawing of the boundary requires thorough study and possible resettlement in some points.[1]

Stalin modified this proposal in order to assign to the Soviet Union the ports of Königsberg and Memel. At Potsdam in 1945 the three powers decided that the western frontier should await the final peace settlement:

The three heads of government agree that, pending the final determination of Poland's western frontier, the former German territories east of a line running from the Baltic Sea immediately west of Swinemünde and thence along the Oder River to the confluence of the Western Neisse River to the Czechoslovak frontier...shall be under the administration of the Polish state...[2]

The new Poland differed substantially from the Polish Commonwealth as it stood before the First Partition of 1772, and from the Polish Republic on the eve of the Second World War in 1939. In compensation for loss of territory to the Soviet Union, Poland took possession of substantial German territories in the west. The irony of the present solution is that it was brought about by diplomacy. In the past Poles thought that diplomacy would produce a solution of their own choosing. This was a solution within the frontiers of 1772. The ultimate reconstruction of Poland cannot be conceived in terms in which the Poles themselves sought their freedom from foreign rule.

It might perhaps seem that the position of Poland in Europe was exceptional. With the unification of the world in the twentieth century the division of Poland by the partitions of the eighteenth century may be regarded as part of the normal experiences of mankind. Many territories in the period of imperialism were occupied by European powers and integrated with the metropolitan economies. What makes Poland exceptional is the fact that the Poles had a developed literature and recorded history of their own. Their experience is therefore illustrative of the outlook of other peoples who have suffered foreign domination, but recorded in greater detail. The Polish Question as it recedes into the background is worthy of study for the examples and insight which it gives us for the understanding of the world beyond Europe. History is not dependent upon the written word. Oral tradition in Africa and elsewhere keeps alive knowledge of the past. In the case of Poland we can understand oppression through the medium of the written word, which is the medium which we in Britain and America understand best. The study of Poland in the modern epoch is not an investigation into developments within a community of second magnitude. It is a study of a problem which is central to a situation which is actual in the world today.

The social structure of Poland up to 1939 was established by the evolution of the Polish Republic before the partitions of 1772, 1793, and 1795. In modern Polish historical writings it is customary to refer to the Feudal Epoch, but this is not a helpful description because it leads to comparisons with the systems which existed in France and England. As Poland emerged as a powerful state in the sixteenth century upon the expansion of the grain trade, the lords of the manor and the great proprietors drew upon the labour of the peasants for cultivation of the demesnes. The nobility looked to the market beyond Poland, while the peasants engaged in a subsistence economy, apart from the minor sales which they might make in local markets, the income from which was absorbed by the manor, which had the exclusive right to brew and distil.

The sixteenth century was the Golden Age of Poland. The expansion of arable farming under the stimulus of rising prices was accompanied by a flourishing of Polish culture. The seventeenth century was by contrast a period of diaster. Prices fell and wars brought destruction. To compensate for their loss of income the estate owners sought to take more of the arable land of the peasants into their demesnes. In the devastation attendant upon war the medium gentry suffered more than the magnates. The magnates could reconstruct one ruined estate from the resources of another outside the theatre of operations, and on occasion they could obtain favourable treatment from invaders on grounds of their potential political importance. The medium gentry were forced either to borrow from the magnates to reconstruct their estates, or even to sell their lands to them and become their tenants. For the petty gentry life was scarcely better than that of the peasants. The real rulers of the state were the magnates and the gentry were reduced to clientage.[3] The period of revival in the second half of the eighteenth century was cut short by the partitions of 1772, 1793 and 1795. Polish society was not allowed to evolve as a normal community. Thus the problem of independence was interwoven with the question of how Poland was to emerge into the world of capitalism, a world in which the law of supply and demand replaced an organic society based upon the rendering of obligations. The Polish struggle between 1815 and 1863 was not only to determine who should rule at home, when independence had been won, but also to decide how Poland should be organized for the future. The magnates had been discredited by the Confederation of Targowica of 1792, which led to the Second Partition of 1793. The insurrection of 1794 brought into existence a radical element which owed nothing to the magnates. The peasants viewed the future with a hostility to the landlords which was of long standing.

The Polish Question was complicated, moreover, by the absence of homogeneity among the population. In the western areas Protestant Germans were intermingled with the Polish population. In the north and east Lithuanians, Byelorussians, and Ukrainians were to develop a sense of their own nationality, distinct from that of the Poles who had formerly been their masters. Even more complicated was the Jewish Question. Within the territories of the former Republic the Jews constituted about 10 per cent of the population, but, since they were for the most part excluded from agriculture, they constituted a substantial proportion of the townspeople, and in the smaller market towns in fact were often in a majority. Because they could not work on the Sabbath, they were unable to work side by side with Christians in industries demanding work for six days a week from Monday to Saturday. Thus they were for religious reasons confined to the handicrafts and the retail trades. They were presented in the nineteenth century with many problems. They were required to decide whether they should continue to identify themselves with their own religion and their Yiddish speech, or to blend with the Christian community. In the latter case, they had a choice between Polish and Russian society, but there were those who were not prepared to regard Eastern Europe as their *Heimat* but rather sought to create a Hebraic society of their own beyond Europe, where they would not be deprived of political rights.

To these national complications must be added the problem of the population of Polish speech settled beyond the frontiers of 1772. Most of the Polish principalities of Silesia ceased to have a connection with the Polish crown in the fourteenth century, but, though the Slavonic aristocracy was germanized and the bourgeoisie of the towns German, a substantial Polish population continued to exist in Upper Silesia, which provided a large proportion of the working class in the expansion of industry in the nineteenth century. Even outside Upper Silesia there were pockets of Poles along the right bank of the River Oder. To the south lay the Duchy of Teschen (Cieszyn), the remnant of Silesia which the Habsburgs had retained and to which the Czechs laid claims as part of the Crown of St Wenceslas. To the north in East Prussia in the Masurian districts there was a Polish-speaking population which had lost its connection with Poland in 1657 when the Hohenzollerns obtained the abolition of Polish sovereignty over the area. Clearly, a Poland reconstructed upon the ethnic principle of giving her areas in which the Poles constituted a majority might appear different from a Poland restored upon historic principles within the frontiers of 1772.

The struggle for independence was rendered more difficult by the determination of the partitioning powers to maintain their control without giving the Poles equality of treatment. External control denied to the Poles the right to promote the well-being of their country in response to the normal impulses of civil patriotism. Poland for practical purposes consisted of three frontier regions of three great states, which were often reluctant to develop them. For strategic reasons, for example, the Russian general staff in the nineteenth century was opposed to the connection of Warsaw and Poznań by a railway. The absurd situation arose that the Poles, who thought of themselves as a nation, were treated as troublesome minorities in three empires. The political systems which were to evolve in the Habsburg empire and in the new Germany were no training ground for Polish statesmanship. The maintenance of the autocracy in tsarist Russia meant that neither Russians nor Poles had any schooling in the politics of government by consent. For this reason the Poles cannot be judged by the sober conventions of the British parliament and the rules of the British cabinet. Fundamental to Polish thinking were the bitterness and humiliation inspired by defeat and partition, which necessarily on occasion erupted in violence. Violence was crushed by superior violence and engendered the desire for revenge. Fear of Polish unrest led to the tightening of controls. In such a society normal political evolution was impossible. The abnormality of this situation made a solution imperative.

The solution adopted in the first half of the nineteenth century was one of open challenge. The Duchy of Warsaw, created by France in 1807 from Prussian territory and enlarged at the expense of Austria in 1809, did not survive the defeat of Napoleon I. Nevertheless, the semi-autonomous Kingdom of Poland, attached to Russia by the Treaty of Vienna of 1815, offered the possibility of a national renaissance. In 1830 the Poles stumbled into a revolt against the Russian connection and were crushed in the defeat of 1831.[4] In 1846 an uprising in the Free City of Cracow and in the western districts of Austrian Galicia met with defeat at the hands of the Austrian army and its allies, the Polish peasants (see below p. 8). In 1848 disturbances offered a fleeting glimpse of autonomy in the Grand Duchy of Posen, but the Prussian military authorities were determined not to permit the movement to gain ground and accordingly disarmed the Polish levies.[5] In Galicia the Austrian army maintained a firm control both in Cracow and Lwów, intimidating the Poles by bombardment, just as it bombarded Prague. The insurrection in Russian Poland during 1863 and 1864 equally was crushed, though with great difficulty.[6] While the humiliation of subjection and resentment at defeat remained, many and varied lessons were drawn from disaster.

The period of the Napoleonic Wars when Legions were raised in the service of France left a tradition of militarism of an amateurish kind. Those Poles who were likely to obtain advancement in the armies of the partitioning powers, more especially the Austrian and Russian armies, were to be promoted for their professionalism, of which loyalty to the régime and correspondingly political conservatism were important constituent parts. Though some Poles, who served in the Russian army in the 1850's and 1860's, did pass over to the side of the revolution,[7] it was unlikely after 1863 that the Poles would be able to raise abroad any force capable of influencing the course of events at home. The effort to raise a force in the Ottoman empire during the Crimean War did not enjoy conspicuous success. There was a flutter of Polish military activity in France during the crisis of 1870–1. Jarosław Dąbrowski died on Montmartre as a general of the Paris Commune. The partisans of a solution by diplomacy, led by Adam Jerzy Czartoryski and after his death by his son, Władysław Czartoryski, maintained from the Hotel Lambert in Paris a long activity designed to give currency to the concept that Poland might once again come into existence as a state, though one of unimpeachable conservative respectability.[8] The Eastern Crisis of 1875–8 and the Congress of Berlin revealed beyond doubt that it was impossible for Poland to be restored within the foreseeable future as a result of international factors. The Poles in emigration grew older and died. France under the Third Republic could not make even a pretence of favouring the restoration of an independent Poland. While Austria, Germany and Russia were detemined to avoid armed conflict even when they were in disagreement, the Polish Question did not exist. Nevertheless, the future of Poland was to be shaped by forces at work at home.

The most powerful attempt at drawing upon the resources of the Polish people as a whole was inspired by the Manifesto of the Polish Democratic Society in 1836.[9] It was proposed that the peasants should be brought into partnership by a donation of the freeholds of their farms. It was believed that this act would win their loyalty to the national cause and secure for it a mass support which hitherto it had lacked. Though this policy was commendable for its desire to make the peasant an equal citizen, it was not populism in the sense that it sought to base the organization of the state upon the peasant community. The peasants were cast in the role of auxiliaries in the struggle for independence. A fundamental error, moreover, was the supposition that partitioning powers had no initiative in the peasant question. In 1848 the Austrian administration cut the ground from under the Polish leaders by granting the peasants their freeholds by imperial decree. In March 1864 the Russian government followed suit by a solution of the agrarian problem on terms more generous than those proposed by the Polish insurgents themselves (see below p. 41). The peasants could thus accept without effort to themselves a solution of the problem which the insurgents invited them to obtain by active participation in the armed struggle. From 1864 a summons to the people at large offered no immediate chance of success. The revolution was in effect put on ice.

In step with the conspiratorial struggle after 1815 there were Polish leaders in all three partitioned areas who argued that the proper course to adopt was open activity designed to strengthen the economic position of Poland, extend the network of communications, improve the quality of agriculture, raise the standard of education and create the conditions essential to the transition from the old society to the new industrial and commercial world which had come into existence in Britain and Western Europe. It was argued that revolutionary activity could bring in its train only further repression and would defeat what ought to be the aim of all Poles, the strengthening of Polish society in order to enable it to speak with greater authority to the partitioning powers. This was a concept which could appeal to powerful elements in the Polish community. The magnates had lost their political power and with it their ability to delay the repayment of debts or even to repudiate them, as they had done under the Republic. For them the urgent necessity of conversion to a new system of farming required conditions of tranquillity. The medium gentry, hard hit by the decline of agricultural prices after 1815, could equally fall into line with such a policy. No landowner had had much sympathy for the left-wing programme of granting freeholds as an essential part of insurgent strategy. The few Polish industrial entrepreneurs, seeking to raise themselves to the level of their foreign counterparts, thought in terms of capital investment for which political stability was vital. Commercial and industrial expansion would provide increased opportunity of employment for the educated classes and men of the professions. A similar point of view may be detected in Hungary and Italy before and after 1848. In Poland the movement went by the name of Organic Work. An early example of this point of view may be seen in the activity of Prince Drucki-Lubecki, who, as minister of finance in the Kingdom of Poland between 1821 and 1830, encouraged trade and industry under a general policy of strengthening Polish resources within a connection with Russia.[10]

To persons outside the machinery of government, and therefore not incurring the accusation of being collaborators with the occupying powers, Organic Work was an attractive alternative to insurrection and revolution. Organic Work invited them to increase their incomes in the name of Polish patriotism. Tomasz Łubieński in the Kingdom of Poland succeeded in co-operating in the foundation of the Land Credit Society and the Bank of Poland, serving as general in the Polish army against Russia in 1831, and afterwards as the managing director of his family firm. His brother and principal partner, Henryk, who was active in promoting sugar production and founding factories in Żyrardów, was vice-president of the Bank of Poland until 1842, but was detected in malfeasance and sent to Russia. In Prussian Poland Dr Karol Marcinkowski founded in 1841 the Society for Educational Assistance in order to provide secondary and higher education for children of petty bourgeois families. His main commercial enterprise was the establishment in Poznań in 1838 of 'The Bazaar', a building housing a hotel, civic amenities and shops, which provided a centre for the larger landlords and substantial middle class.[11] In Galicia Prince Leon Sapieha was active in promoting a Land Credit Society and in constructing railways. Probably the most complex figure of all was Leopold Kronenberg, the Warsaw financier, who in 1863 combined his business activities with an intimate relationship with the insurgent National Government, which he tried to direct along lines of moderation.[12] These were the men who, with their successors, emerged in the 1860's, after the disaster of the insurrection in the Kingdom of Poland, as the most important element in Polish society. They had kept within the bonds of legality and escaped the penalty of enforced emigration or exile. They accepted the fact of partition and were best prepared mentally to reconcile themselves to the impossibility of winning independence. For the majority of the people of Poland the benefits of Organic Work were less obvious. Upon them fell the crushing burden of poverty which there existed no Polish government to attack. Triloyalism, the acceptance of subjection to Austria, Prussia and Russia, was no solution of Poland's problems. Only unification and independence could bring real relief.

Austrian Poland in the second half of the nineteenth century

Austrian Poland consisted of the Kingdom of Galicia and Lodomeria, enlarged in 1846 by addition of Cracow, together with parts of the Duchy of Teschen (Cieszyn) inhabited by a Polish proletariat. The long period of Austrian rule in Galicia from 1772 was marked by economic stagnation and the exclusion of Poles from public office. The government under Joseph II had done something to limit the exploitation of the peasants by the landlords, but agriculture remained backward, being dependent upon labour services. In 1846 the hostility of the peasants took on a savage form. When the gentry of the western regions rose in revolt against the imperial government, the peasants turned upon them and killed about 2,000 persons. The imperial government thought it wise to lay claim to the peasants' loyalties by abolishing through the patent of 13 April 1846 the supplementary duties of carting and the provision of extra days' labour which the peasants owed to the manor.[13] The enforcement of labour services on the arable lands of the demesnes, which the peasants wished to see abolished, was achieved only by a massive military operation in which 55,763 troops with 36 guns took part.[14] So dangerous was the situation in Galicia, aggravated by a famine in 1846 of such severity that instances of cannibalism were reported, and by cholera and typhus in 1847, that the gentry and middle classes succumbed to a political paralysis. Up to the Second World War the peasants would taunt visitors from the towns with the song:

> Do you remember, sir, the year of eighteen forty six
> How on Shrove Tuesday the peasants beat you with their sticks?[15]

The massacre, increased mortality and the subsequent pacification in fact had more serious consequences for the peasants than for the upper classes. In 1847 380,000 persons died in contrast to the previous annual average of 153,000. Nevertheless, the new governor of Galicia, Franz von Stadion, preferred to conciliate the peasantry rather than the gentry. In the troubled year of 1848, on 22 April, he ordered on his own initiative that the peasants should receive their freeholds and the gentry obtain compensation from the state funds. The decree received retrospective approval and was backdated to 17 April.[16] A supplementary law of 7 September 1848 guaranteed the peasants' rights of access to woods, meadows and pastures, known in Polish by the term *serwituty*.[17] Disputes relating to the common use of lands technically owned by the manor continued after 1848 to serve as a cause of discontent between the gentry and the peasants. The game laws, which gave the landlord the exclusive right to hunting, shooting and fishing, were another source of annoyance for the peasants, whose crops were damaged by the wild animals reserved for the sport of the gentry. The exclusive right of brewing and distilling (*propinacja*) was not only a source of income for the manors but also a cause of peasant hostility. It was not until 1889 that this privilege was abolished in Galicia. Though the government tried to favour the peasants at the expense of the gentry, the landlords emerged from the crisis of 1846–8 as strong as they had been before. The overpopulation of Galicia ensured that there was always a reserve of rural labour upon which the landlords could draw. It was not until the 1880's that some improvement in the conditions of the wage-labourers began to appear as a result of seasonal migration or departure to the New World. In general, it is true to say that the lot of the peasant in Galicia was not easy. Indebtedness, land hunger, illiteracy and backwardness were features of the province.

The Austrian government emerged apparently triumphant in 1849–50 from the troubles of the great European crisis. The constitution of 4 March 1849 never came into operation and was formally suspended by the proclamation of 31 December 1851. Thus the Polish upper classes in Galicia had to see the transition from the old economy to the new money economy in a political situation in which they were not masters in their own society. They were torn between two desires, the yearning for national unification within a Polish state and the wish to have control over their own community within the Austrian empire. Within Polish society in Galicia there was equally a conflict between the gentry and the bourgeoisie to decide which party should have primacy in legislation. The government in such a situation could enjoy certain advantages. It could favour the peasants against the gentry, as it did do in disputes concerning rights to woods and pastures, or conversely at the end of the 1850's favour the gentry against the peasants.

During the Crimean War the Ukrainians of the eastern regions looked to Russia, a factor which drew the Poles closer to Austria. The Cracow conservatives favoured an association within a federal Austrian empire. Count Agenor Gołuchowski, who became viceroy in 1849, sought to build up confidence in Vienna by establishing a reputation for absolute trustworthiness. Prince Leon Sapieha and his son Adam continued the policy which had emerged everywhere in Poland before 1848 under the title of Organic Work. This in effect meant the abandonment of political struggle in favour of capital investment in enterprises calculated to promote the economic well-being of the province. Thus the Galician Savings Bank, the Land Credit Society and the Agricultural School were designed to assist the Polish gentry in the task of converting the economy to a more modern system. Leon Sapieha was active in promoting the construction of a railway from Cracow to Lwów between 1856 and 1861. In 1865 it reached Czernowitz in Bukovina and the line was extended to Brody on the Russian frontier in 1869.[18] Useful though railway construction was, there was little investment in industry. The gentry used the compensation which they obtained for the loss of their manorial rights to maintain their own standard of living. The province was dominated by foreign capital, especially the *Kreditanstalt*. The industries of Bohemia, Moravia and Austria were too advanced for Polish enterprise to compete with them. For this reason there was no development of a middle class strong enough to be an independent force in the politics of the province. Franciszek Smolka and Florian Ziemiałkowski were moderate democrats of the Lwów middle class who believed in equality of opportunity and constitutional government, but they lacked a mass following and could not exert much influence in a fundamentally agrarian province.

The Poles had little opportunity to assert their claims until the international crisis of 1859, when failure in Italy discredited the régime of Bach. The Austrian government was confronted with two choices. Either it could ally itself with the local aristocracies, or it could admit the German bourgeoisie to a share in political power. The latter alternative had the advantage of offering some hope at least of saving the system of centralism, but it was Agenor Gołuchowski who was first called to power. On 20 October 1860 a patent was issued promising a system of local diets and a central Reichsrat, which however might have no voice in military or foreign affairs. When these proposals met with the opposition of the Hungarians, Gołuchowski was dismissed and replaced by the centralist, Schmerling. In the patent of 26 February 1861 Schmerling emphasized the power of the central government, but, like other areas, Galicia and the Grand Duchy of Cracow were granted a local assembly. The curial system adopted varied from province to province. In Galicia the diet was to consist of the archbishops and bishops, together with the rectors of the Universities of Cracow and Lwów; 44 representatives of the larger landlords; 22 representatives of the towns; and 74 deputies from the rural communes.[19] The administration was placed in charge of a Regional Commission (*Wydział Krajowy*) presided over by the marshal of the diet assisted by six of its members. Persons without property were excluded from the franchise, but, whereas in the other provinces of the empire the government favoured the landlords and the Germans, in Galicia preference was initially given to the peasants, who were to obtain 50 per cent of the representation. The provincial constitution, which was to remain in force until 1918, caused despair among the educated classes. The gentry were at loggerheads with the peasants as a result of the woods and pastures question, and could foresee no hope of reconciliation. The peasants, moreover, were not only Poles, but also Ukrainians, the latter not sharing the national aspirations of the Poles. The educated and upper classes in Galicia were thus forced to accept the constitution and seek within it to gain control over the local administration by manipulating the political difficulties of the Austrian government to their advantage.

The troubles in the Kingdom of Poland and the uprising in January 1863 gave visions of Polish independence, but the Galician leaders, with the possible exception of Adam Sapieha, limited themselves to expressions of solidarity and sympathy, and were not prepared to offer much practical assistance. Neither the magnates nor the bourgeoisie wished the struggle to extend itself to Austrian Poland. In 1862 the Warsaw Reds did make some headway in establishing their influence in Cracow among the university students and the craftsmen, but in Lwów the committee of Smolka, Ziemiałkowski, Adam Sapieha and Dzieduszycki constituted an alliance of the magnates and the bourgeoisie which offered a centre of opposition to the 'Galician Supreme Council' set up by the Reds. Only a few ineffective expeditions against the Russians were launched from Galicia. The Galician Whites tended to flirt with the Reds with the aim of keeping control over the local situation for themselves. Thus some supplies were given to the movement in the Kingdom of Poland. As a result of the Austrian government's taking into custody leaders of the Whites the direction of the national movement fell into the hands of the Reds, who began to make preparations for a more active participation in the struggle in Russian Poland. The agrarian policy of the Reds in the Kingdom of Poland was sufficiently radical to have an appeal for the Galician peasantry. The leaders of the propertied classes therefore exerted pressure upon the Austrian authorities for preventive measures. On 27 February 1864 the governor, Mensdorff-Pouilly, declared a state of siege and brought the province under martial law.

The Galician reaction to events in the Kingdom of Poland was one of despair. The crushing of the rising proved to the leaders of Polish society that there was in fact no hope of establishing independence and that the only course open to them was to seek a compromise with the Austrian government. In Cracow Paweł Popiel condemned the uprising, while Józef Szujski began to sound the alarm against the Ukrainian movement in the eastern regions. The conviction grew that the Poles ought to devote their energies to the defence of their national interests within the Austrian empire. In July 1865 the government of Schmerling was replaced by that of Belcredi, himself a Pole, who began the task of conciliating the Hungarians and the establishment of a federal system within the empire. In such a situation the Poles could hope to extract some advantage for themselves. The aims of the Polish leaders are apparent from the meeting of the provincial diet. Autonomy for them meant control over the district councils in order to prevent them from becoming the instruments of the will of the peasantry. With regard to the organization of the communes there was some difference of opinion, but the aim of all parties was identical. The Cracow conservatives wished to have a single communal council, but the Podolian party sought to establish a commune for each village, which should be separate from the manor, lest the manor be forced to make contributions for purposes which served the interests of the peasants. It was the Podolian view which triumphed. With the Reds insignificant as a political factor after the failure of 1863–4, the gentry emerged to seek an organization of Galicia in their own interest.

With the onset of the crisis which led to the Austro-Prussian war in 1866 the chances grew that the non-German nationalities would obtain concessions from the Austrian government. The Hungarians could speak from a position of strength which was only increased by the Austrian defeat at Sadowa. It was worthwhile buying the Hungarians off in order that Austria might concentrate upon the task of restoring her power in Central Europe. Beust, who replaced Belcredi in February 1867, quickly concluded the agreement known as the Compromise (*Ausgleich*) of 1867. The Poles in Galicia thought that they would obtain an equal measure of autonomy. Symptomatic of the new situation was the reappointment of the ultra-loyalist Gołuchowski to the post of viceroy in September 1866. On 10 December 1866 the Galician diet drew up an address to the emperor, approved by 84 votes against the 40 votes of the Polish and Ukrainian peasants, demanding autonomy within a federal Austria. It was represented to the emperor that concessions to the Poles would strengthen the monarchy and that they for their part would support Austria:

With no misgivings of departure from our national concepts, with faith in the mission of Austria and with faith in the determination upon changes, which Your Majesty's words have pronounced as your resolved intention, from the bottom of our hearts we declare that we stand with Your Majesty and wish to stand with you.[20]

This declaration of loyalty met with only a cold response in Vienna. The negotiations with the Hungarians meant that the Poles were only a minor element in the general situation and that once the Compromise was concluded with Hungary their position was one of relative weakness. The disappointment of the Poles led in its turn to the resolution of the diet of 2 March 1867 by which it was decided to send a delegation to Vienna to attend the Reichsrat, but to withdraw the address. There followed a long campaign to obtain an extension of Polish privileges in Galicia. On 24 September 1868 the diet laid out its claims for the extension of Galician autonomy.[21] It was proposed that there should be an extension of the powers of the provincial diet and that there should be a responsible ministry for Galicia. The resolution met with no response from the Reichsrat, with a consequent loss of prestige among the leaders of the moderate Left and Centre. The swing to the Left in itself produced fresh energy from the Right, especially among the Cracow conservatives. The Cracow conservatives were particularly anxious to combat the wave of left-wing feeling which spread through the province. Count Stanisław Tarnowski, Stanisław Koźmian, the two Wodzicki brothers, Ludwik and Henryk, and Józef Szujski combined to combat the radical revival. They were associated with the publication of *Przegląd Polski* (The Polish Review). In 1869 they produced a series of pamphlets under the title of *Teka Stańczyka* (The Portfolio of Stańczyk); Stańczyk was a clown at the court of the Polish king, Zygmunt I, whose sage and penetrating advice was left unheeded. The Stańczyk party, as they came to be called, attacked the revolutionary tradition which in their view had brought about the insurrections of the past, especially the rising of 1863. Szujski could declare that:

Just as the *liberum veto* after the constitution of the 3 May [1791] took the form of [the confederation of] Targowica, so the *liberum conspiro* after the self-liberation of the people corresponded to it, only in a more dreadful form. This is not freedom – it is socialism, it is not independence – it is the devouring of us by Moscow.[22]

The view of this school of thought was that radicalism would look to the masses and bring to an end the social predominance of the gentry. Thus Poland ought to be steered away from revolutionary thought and the intelligentsia of Galicia kept out of the influence of Franciszek Smolka, the left-wing liberal leader in Lwów.

In 1870 a change appeared in the general situation. Any hopes that Austria may have had of reversing the defeat of 1866 were dispelled by the collapse of France in the Franco-Prussian war. Germany would henceforth be supreme in Central Europe. At first the Austrian government thought that minor concessions to the Poles could work. A new policy under the government of Alfred Potocki, formed in April 1870, foresaw the conciliation of the Poles and the Czechs. There followed a confused situation in which Hohenwart succeeded Potocki and Auersperg succeeded Hohenwart. In 1871 a ministry for Galicia was established and the University of Lwów was polonized. Gołuchowski, who had been viceroy in the years 1849–58 and 1866–8, once more became viceroy from 1871 to 1875. The failure of the government in Vienna to win over the Czechs caused a reversion to centralization. In 1873 the decision was taken to hold elections directly to the Reichsrat, though on the basis of the curial system, as opposed to taking delegations from the provincial diets. The Galician conservatives took the decision to offer unconditional support to the government in return for a measure of limited autonomy. Gołuchowski remained viceroy, and Ziemiałkowski became minister for Galicia. The local administration, the School Board and the District Councils were placed under Polish control. In short the province of Galicia was placed under the control of landlords. Primacy in legislation was to be given to the agrarian interest.

The years from 1873 to 1889 were a period of stagnation under the rule of the Stańczyk party and the landlords of the eastern region. The bourgeoisie was too weak to challenge the landlord class, which reserved to itself the offices of viceroy and marshal of the diet. The curial system of election to the diet, even when modified, placed commerce and industry at a disadvantage in the diet, but the real struggle was between the large landlords and the mass of the peasantry. The 3,000 large landlords occupied 30 per cent of the seats in the diet, whereas 500,000 peasants held less than 50 per cent. The rural proletariat was excluded almost entirely from a share in political life, because the vote could be exercised only by persons paying 25 crowns in direct taxes annually. There was no vote by ballot, which meant that intimidation was always possible. Constituency boundaries were drawn in a way designed to favour the Poles and place the Ukrainians at a disadvantage. Thus the Ukrainians, who constituted just under half of the population, obtained only a quarter of the seats in the diet. All the tricks of bribery, false return and administrative pressure were employed by the upper classes. At the local level the Poles assumed complete control and the agents of the central government in Vienna concurred with this system, which ensured the peace of what might be a troublesome province. In terms of the general development of the Habsburg empire Galicia was assigned the role of a producer of raw materials and a consumer of the goods of Czech and German industry.

The consequences for Galicia of landlord rule were grievous. Education might flourish in the Universities of Cracow and Lwów and keep alive the traditions of Polish culture and learning, but at the elementary level the School Board did little to encourage the building of schools in the villages, where the extension of education was most needed. The motive of this inactivity lay in the fear of the landlords that popular education would encourage the peasants to engage in radical political activity. Where elementary education was established the general aim was to make provision merely for reading, writing and arithmetic. Thus within the Austrian empire sharp contrasts could appear. In Galicia 77 per cent of the population over school age was illiterate in 1880, falling to 67 per cent in 1890, whereas in the same period in Austrian Silesia the comparable figures were 8 per cent, and in the Czech lands only 4 per cent. In all aspects of higher education Poland gained from the existence of a haven of refuge from the severe restrictions placed upon learning in Prussian and Russian Poland. In Cracow there flourished a school of historians who laid the foundations of scientific history in Poland. In the arts, literature and the theatre the Polish language could enjoy a dignity denied it elsewhere in the Poles' own homeland. A flourishing culture, however, which abounded without a corresponding material welfare among the people who spoke the language which provided the vehicle for its progress, was an achievement of questionable value. For the Ukrainian population of the eastern regions of Galicia polonism was unattractive both as a culture and as an expression of the dominion of the landlord class. Economic and cultural grievances combined to give Ukrainian nationalism an especial bitterness. The Poles chose to speak of 'the Ruthenian question' as if it were a minor problem to be solved within a Polish context. Schmerling could look to the Ukrainians for support, but the reappointment of Gołuchowski in 1871 meant that the government in Vienna transferred its affections to the Poles. The Ukrainians, for their part, could in the beginning look eastwards to Russia, but this movement did not make significant progress because it was too closely associated with the clergy and too conservative in its social outlook. The Ukrainians in the late 1860's and the 1870's were beginning to think of themselves as having a nationality distinct from that of both the Poles and the Russians. The Shevchenko Cultural Society in Lwów began to promote the cause of the Ukrainian literature and historical studies. Only in 1880, however, was the first Ukrainian newspaper, *Dilo* (Work), founded. The extension of Ukrainian cultural and political consciousness was necessarily as slow in the circumstances of the village of eastern Galicia as it was in the Polish villages of the west.

The agrarian problem in Galicia became more and more acute from the time of the reforms of 1848. In the period 1852–66 the large landlords, owning properties defined as noble in the survey of 1780, possessed 42.8

per cent of the arable lands and 90.45 per cent of the woods and pastures, to which the peasants had right of access. The loss of labour services in 1848 meant that the landlords could cultivate their lands only with wage labour. Conversion to modern commercial farming was difficult in view of the lack of capital. The large landlords were therefore under pressure to sell part of their lands, especially when agricultural prices were depressed in the 1870's and 1880's, and at the same time to dispose of part of their woods and pastures in order to end the difficulties caused by the peasants' common rights. By 1889 41.3 per cent of all land (both arable and woods and pastures) was still owned by the large landlords, of whom 161 magnates owned about a half. There was therefore a corresponding increase in the amount of land held by the peasants. In the period from 1852 to 1889 peasant lands rose from a total of 4,478,000 hectares to 4,759,000 hectares. This expansion of peasant farming was not, however, synonymous with the growth of peasant prosperity. In spite of a high death rate the population began to grow, rising from about 6,000,000 in 1880 to 7,300,000 in 1900. Agriculture provided a living for about 80 per cent of the population. It is not surprising that the chief feature of the Galician countryside was land hunger.

Some relief was subsequently to be provided by seasonal and permanent emigration. In the 1880's 7,000 persons a year left Galicia for North America, rising to an annual average of 30,000 in the 1890's and 50,000 in the years after 1900. It is estimated that between 1896 and 1914 433,000 Poles and 146,000 Ukrainians left the province. This tended to create a labour shortage, increase wage rates, and to relieve land hunger. Remittance payments from abroad provided money with which to buy more gentry land. Between 1889 and 1902 some 122,000 hectares were bought. Nevertheless, in 1895 it is estimated that 27.2 per cent of the peasant farmers had less than 2 *morgi*.[23] Holdings of 2–10 *morgi* accounted for 41.08 of the total, and holdings of 10.20 *morgi* amounted to 23.36 per cent. Peasant farms of 20 *morgi* or more were owned by 8.36 per cent of the small proprietors.

It could hardly be said that Galicia was a land of prosperous yeoman farmers. The majority of the peasants could not obtain a satisfactory living from their holdings. In the upland districts peasant farms whose acreages might have seemed satisfactory often did not yield enough to support a family. It is not surprising that farmers easily fell into debt. An index of their poverty is the fact that between 1875 and 1884 no less than 23,649 peasant holdings were put up for auction as a result of debts, often amounting to quite paltry sums. The development of Galician peasant society is the subject of some controversy. The orthodox view is that the richer peasants became richer and the poor peasants became poorer.[24] A contrary view is that the richer peasants became poorer and the poor peasants, where they did not give up farming altogether, became richer. In this way there was a tendency for the size of all holdings to approach a common norm which represented the minimum of land capable of sustaining the life of a single family.[25] Whichever view is adopted, the fact remains that there was a tendency in Galicia at least for the size of holdings to fall to an acreage which was too small to provide for a comfortable living. On the other hand, improved methods of husbandry led in their turn towards the end of the century to increased yields and to the extension of livestock production. The conclusion which must be drawn is that the prosperity of Galicia would have been enhanced if only there had been some development of industry to absorb the growing number of peasants who could obtain only a meagre income from their farms and who needed to supplement their incomes either by wage labour in the countryside or by paid employment in the towns. As long as the peasants of the countryside were poor, their demand for the goods of industry would be slight. Galicia was caught in the same cleft stick as many emergent societies in the modern world.

Industry was not looked upon with favour by the Polish ruling classes in Galicia. An expansion of the urban population would lead in its turn to a shift in the balance of political power and the infiltration of socialist doctrines, which, combined with a shortage of labour in the countryside, would affect adversely the position of the larger landed proprietors. The Galician diet therefore turned its face against any programme of capital investment. Industry could in any case hardly develop in the face of the free trade policy adopted from 1865 onwards, when Galician industry was compelled to compete with the goods of technically more efficient countries, especially Germany.

The turning point was in 1878 when Germany returned to a policy of protectionism. Within Austria–Hungary, protectionism favoured the established industries of Austria, Bohemia, Moravia and Hungary. On the whole railway construction worked to the advantage of the larger proprietors exporting raw materials to the industrialized parts of the empire. Better transport equally admitted more easily the goods of other areas into Galicia. The major developments of Galicia were in the expansion of the mining of coal and salt and the extraction of oil. The first 'oil mania' occurred in 1885, but it brought small advantage to the country. The outstanding problem remained the provision of credit. Pressure exerted by Mikołaj Zyblikiewicz for the expansion of the banking system resulted in the foundation in 1883 of the Country Bank (Bank

Krajowy), but the Galician ruling class did not give this enterprise much encouragement and Zyblikiewicz was compelled to resign his post. In 1881 Tadeusz Romanowicz returned to the battle for the industrialization of Galicia through the periodical *Nowa Reforma* (New Reform) which he founded in Cracow. Drawing upon the inspiration of Warsaw Positivism (see below p. 47), he urged a new outlook on life, independent of the ethos of the old *szlachta* society and orientated upon the world of the industrialist. Such views did not meet with a response from the governing classes.

The most spectacular of all failures to obtain a more positive policy was the case of Stanisław Szczepanowski, who in 1888 produced his pamphlet entitled *Nędza Galicyi w cyfrach-Program energicznego rozwoju krajowego* (The Misery of Galicia in Figures: a programme for an energetic development of the country). The work criticized the backwardness of the province and demanded a policy of capital investment. Szczepanowski succeeded in obtaining the support of the liberal democratic element, but he met with a lukewarm response from the Stańczyk party and opposition from capitalists in Vienna with interests in the oil industry. As a result of injudicious investment Szczepanowski's own business was compelled to go into liquidation. The ruin of Szczepanowski is symptomatic of the domination of foreign capital and the indifference of the landed interest in Galicia to a policy of capital investment.

The supremacy of the upper classes in Galicia, with their emphasis upon loyalty to the emperor and Austria, was not accepted without a murmur. The Eastern Crisis of 1875–8 evoked a traditional response. When war between Russia and the Ottoman empire seemed likely in 1876, Wacław Koszczyc founded the 'Confederation of the Polish Nation' in Lwów with the purpose of encouraging armed struggle against Russia as soon as hostilities began. On the other hand, a group associated with the *Gazeta Narodowa* (National Gazette) established in collaboration with Agaton Giller, a member of the National Goverment in the Kingdom of Poland in 1863, the 'Circle' (Koło), which aimed at setting up a new underground government for all Poland. Some contacts were established with the Ottoman authorities, and Britain showed a mild interest. A 'National Government' was established in Vienna, under the control of Adam Sapieha and others, but it met with no response and was dissolved in December 1877. With the conclusion of the Congress of Berlin in 1878 hopes of outside intervention and assistance faded into the background. The incident was sufficient, however, to induce in the governing classes of Galicia some alarm. The chairman of the Polish Circle in the Viennese parliament deliberately refrained from raising Polish problems for fear of arousing patriotic feelings at home. The upper classes in Galicia instead threw their influence behind every effort to turn the province into a base for a struggle to win independence for Poland at some unspecified date in the future.

From this point onwards there was no question any longer of developments in Galician politics which owed their origin to the interaction of outside events. Within Galicia, however, the antagonism of village and manor would sooner or later give rise to some form of peasant organization designed to protect the people against the pressures of the landlords. The illiteracy of the peasants should not be taken to mean that they did not have social and economic aspirations. They were deeply aware that the government in Vienna in general favoured the landlords in the settlement of disputes arising out of the woods and pastures question. It was equally obvious that the upper classes used administrative pressure to keep the peasant representation in the diet down to a minimum. In the provincial parliamentary sessions of 1877–83, and 1883–9 there were no peasant deputies at all. This was the period of landlord supremacy. The peasants therefore had to find some means of organizing themselves to defend their interests against the class legislation of the diet.

In the 1870's there appeared on the scene Father Stanisław Stojałowski. In 1875 he purchased the periodicals, *Wieniec* (The Wreath) and *Pszczółka* (The Bee), periodicals designed to promote a Christian political movement among the peasants, directed by the clergy, much as elsewhere in Europe attempts were being made to found Christian political organizations among the urban workers. The aim of this movement was to avoid class antagonisms. The masses had to be mobilized behind the church in opposition to the democrats. Nevertheless, even these harmless aims were looked upon with suspicion by the landlords.

In 1877 Stojałowski organized a visit of 100 peasants to Rome. He in effect succeeded in arousing the political interest of the peasants, who began to attend meetings to discuss their problems and vent their discontents. From 1878 agricultural clubs were organized and attempts were made to establish co-operatives to buy demesne lands. This action met with the opposition of the landlords and Catholic hierarchy. The activity of Stojałowski, designed to avoid class antagonism, aroused it in the upper classes. His service to the peasantry lay in providing the foundation for a wider political movement.

A pioneer in the field of peasant organization was Bolesław Wysłouch who founded *Przegląd Społeczny* (The Social Review), which appeared from 1886 to 1887, and afterwards *Przyjaciel Ludu* (The People's Friend). Wysłouch believed that the future of Poland lay with the people and that the intelligentsia should join them. He was a populist rather than a socialist, seeking to obtain normal civil rights for the peasantry through the establishment of a political organization for which the petty bourgeoisie might provide the leadership. The elections to the provincial diet in 1889 proved that no party was particularly interested in supporting the peasants, especially the democrats, who saw in the peasants merely the servants and not the partners of the lower middle classes. In contrast with Wysłouch, Stojałowski, imprisoned for four years by the authorities and suspended by the Catholic hierarchy, established his prestige, and succeeded in getting elected to the diet four peasant deputies who formed a 'Catholic People's Club', who nevertheless quickly aligned themselves with the Galician conservatives. A start had been made however. Thereafter the peasant movement tended to be divided: it took on the one hand the form established by Stojałowski and on the other that inspired by Wysłouch under the leadership of Jan Stapiński.

With the passage of time, even in a country as backward as Galicia, it was inevitable that the peasants should themselves provide leaders like Jakub Bojko and Jan Stapiński.[26] Indeed the authorities themselves realized that the appearance of peasant leaders with an independent following ought to be anticipated by the establishment of organizations controlled by the richer peasants who would show solidarity with the gentry. The Union of the Peasant Party (Związek Stronnictwa Chłopskiego), founded in 1893, attracted to it Stojałowski, but he was soon expelled for his refusal to conform to the conservative direction of the ecclesiastical hierarchy. On the other hand the Polish Democratic Society (Polskie Towarzystwo Demokratyczne), founded as a result of the efforts of Wysłouch and his associates in May 1894, attracted to itself young peasant leaders, who in their turn induced 3,000 peasants to travel to Lwów for a meeting on 25 August 1894 on the occasion of an exhibition organized for the display of the province's achievements. As a result there was established the Peasant Electoral Committee (Ludowy Komitet Wyborczy), which assembled in Rzeszów on 28 July 1895 a conference of its local representatives from which emerged the Polish Peasant Party (Polskie Stronnictwo Ludowe – PSL), the leadership of which lay in peasant hands. The new party offered a direct challenge to gentry control, demanding fundamental changes in the electoral system leading to universal suffrage and the ballot, together with economic concessions to the peasantry and working class and the abolition of the remnants of obligations dating from an earlier epoch. The programme significantly did not include a plan of agrarian reform. The aim was to secure redress of immediate grievances.

The influence which Jakub Bojko, a vice-president, and Jan Stapiński, the secretary, had among the peasantry frightened the propertied classes in the countryside. All the traditional weapons were brought into operation against the people. Father Stojałowski would have liked to have added the words, 'Catholic' or 'Christian' to the name of the party to draw off the anger of the clergy, and as a result of the party's refusal to accept this proposal withdrew from association with it, but the record of the church in attacking Stojałowski was such that it is difficult to perceive what advantage would have been obtained by his proposal. In fact, the bishop of Tarnów, Ignacy Łobos, instructed the clergy in August 1895 to support the Central Electoral Committee of the landlords and middle classes against the popular cause on the grounds of the latter's radicalism. The measure of the popularity of the new PSL was shown in the elections to the provincial diet on 25 September 1895, when 9 peasant candidates, 7 of them actually peasants, were returned, to whom should be added 3 conservatively minded peasant deputies. The peasant movement had clearly come of age and had to some extent shed the tutelage of the clergy which was directed by a hierarchy more reactionary than the landed classes themselves.

The industrial population of Galicia was very small in 1880, being mainly in the coal fields of the Cracow–Chrzanów region, and in the oilfields of the Drohobycz–Borysław area. There were some factories in Cracow, Lwów and Sanok, while the railways employed men in small workshops or in handicrafts. The eleven-hour day was normal in industry, but the hours could be longer in the handicrafts. Pay in general was much lower than in Bohemia, Moravia and Austria proper. Conditions were not good and the workers were liable to corporal punishment. These were not circumstances in which a powerful working-class movement could develop. In 1868 'The Star' (Gwiazda) – An Association of Young Workers for Recreation (Stowarzyszenie Młodzieży Czeladniczej ku Rozrywce) – was founded, composed mainly of printers. In 1869 a fortnightly periodical with socialist leanings began to appear entitled *Rękodzielnik* (The Craftsman), in which Bolesław Limanowski, who had emigrated from Russian Poland, played a prominent part. There followed *Czcionka* (Type) in 1872 and *Praca* (Labour) in the August of the same year, both publications being inspired by the printing works. *Praca* organized the first petition for the grant of the vote to the working class. The socialist movement could hardly have existed independently of other movements in Poland.

In 1877 the Austrian police made a number of arrests among the Galician socialists for the import and distribution of works forbidden by the Russian censorship. Erazm Kobylański and Bolesław Limanowski were put on trial at Lwów in 1878 together with the Ukrainian socialists, Mikhail Pavlik and Ivan Franko. The defendants used the opportunity to address the court in the spirit of socialism and to declare that socialism sought to reconcile Poles and Ukrainians in a common cause. The publicity given to the case created great public interest and, contrary to the intentions of the police, advanced the workers' cause. Even more important was the activity of Ludwik Waryński, who arrived from Russian Poland in September 1878 and to escape arrest went to Cracow, where he began activity upon the basis of the so-called Brussels Programme of the socialist movement in the Kingdom of Poland (see below p. 49). In fact, almost all the members of the Cracow group were arrested between February and October 1879, together with their allies in Lwów and Vienna. Once again, in the trial which took place between 16 February and 15 April 1880, the accused used the opportunity to give currency to socialist ideas. In the end they were found not guilty, much to the annoyance of the conservatives, but most of them, including Waryński, were required to leave Galicia.

In the May of 1881 there appeared 'The Programme of the Galician Workers' Party', calling for a socialist policy based upon the principles of internationalism. In the January of 1889 the Social Democratic Party of Austria was founded, which in 1890 led to the creation of a local organization in Lwów. Eventually, on 31 January 1892, the Galician Social Democratic Party (Galicyjska Partia Socjalno-Demokratyczna) came into existence, joining together Poles, Ukrainians and Jews. In theory the party adhered to the marxist principles of the Austrian Social Democratic Party, but within a few years it descended into being representative of the Polish workers alone and saw its role as seeking to improve their lot by engaging in the conventional politics both of Galicia and Austria generally. The most prominent of its leaders, Ignacy Daszyński, was scarcely a revolutionary. His views were much more in tune with the nationalist views which were held by the right wing of the Polish Socialist Party which arose in the Kingdom of Poland (see below p. 59). In 1897 the party extended itself to Teschen (Cieszyn) and changed its name to the Polish Social Democratic Party of Galicia and Silesia, but this made no difference to its fundamental outlook. The best that can be said of the Galician socialist movement is that it provided an organization for the industrial workers of Austrian Poland to fight for such elementary demands as the twelve-hour day.

By the last decade of the nineteenth century there could be no doubt in the minds of the propertied classes in Galicia that their position was being challenged by the people. The supremacy of the gentry and the

Cracow conservatives was coming under attack from not only the people, but also from the urban intelligentsia. Already Stanisław Szczepanowski had questioned the fundamental concepts of conservatism. In the Kingdom of Poland the National Democrats (see below p. 56) had introduced a new strident note into political debate, which with the collapse of their organization in 1894–5 in Warsaw was transferred to Galicia. In Lwów was established in 1895 *Przegląd Wszechpolski* (The All-Polish Review) under the editorship of Roman Dmowski, which was supported in Cracow from 1896 by the periodical *Polak* (The Pole). The National Democrats were not strong enough to enter directly into Galician politics, but the very nature of their propaganda, emphasizing the ideal of fighting for Polish independence, was a challenge to the narrow views of Galician conservatism and clericalism which had not moved outside the confines of loyalty to Austria.

Not much initiative could be expected from the clergy, who could merely underline the anti-semitism and anti-socialism of National Democracy in a more unenlightened form, any more than the so-called Podolians of eastern Galicia could move forward from their hidebound resistance even to the most reasonable of changes. In Cracow, however, there was always a tendency to yield, though only slightly, in order to meet the pressure of new forces. In the 1890's there emerged the concept of 'Neo-conservatism' with the foundation in October 1896 of the Conservative Club, the aim of which was to find a policy other than the system of management through the instrument of the state machinery. What was sought was a programme of conservative modernization, especially with regard to the organization of the rural communes and to the laws of inheritance.

The reaction of the moderate liberals, who in Galician conditions passed for democrats, was undecided. Some began to lean towards the views of the National Democrats, whereas others inclined towards the socialists or towards the peasant movement. It was clear, however, that the Polish middle classes and intelligentsia were becoming increasingly discontented with the stagnation imposed upon Galicia by the rule of the extreme conservatives. The limited self-government achieved in the 1860's and 1870's had been achieved at the cost of debasing the quality of life.

The government of Galicia technically lay in the hands of the viceroys: from 1877 to 1883, the former prime minister, Count Alfred Potocki, the owner of the great palace at Łańcut, in which he lived in royal state, and from 1883 to 1888, Filip Zaleski, of whom no high opinions were held. In truth the machinery of government was controlled by lesser men in the narrow spirit of Podolian conservatism. In 1888 the first crack in the system

appeared with the appointment of the Galician conservative, Count
Kazimierz Badeni, to the office of viceroy, which he held until 1895, when
he became prime minister of Austria. His appointment indicated a desire
to solve the pressing Ukrainian problem. The seething discontent in the
eastern regions of Galicia had led to a section of the Ukrainian population
being led in the direction of a pro-Russian policy. The object of Badeni
was to secure the loyalty of the Ukrainians in return for minor concessions
in their favour.

On 24 November 1890 the Ukrainian nationalist, Julian Romanchuk,
declared in the Galician diet the fidelity of the Ukrainians to the dynasty.
Some minor concessions were made in the field of education, not the least
of which was agreement to the appointment of Mikhail Hrushevsky to a
chair of Ukrainian history in the University of Lwów. Significantly he
adopted the adjective *ukrainsky* (Ukrainian) in place of the word *rusky*
(Ruthenian) – which the pro-Russian faction identified with the word *russky*
(Russian) – in order to indicate that the Ukraine was distinct from Russia.
There were, however, limits to the flexibility of Badeni's policy. Concessions to the Ukrainians were conditional upon the suspension of radical
activity, but these were too little for the Ruthenian–Ukrainian Radical
Party established in 1890. Failure to alter the bases and essentials of the
system did not endear Badeni to the Polish left wing. All the resources
of the administration were employed to harass the leaders of the Left, to
prevent meetings of the growing peasant movements, and to break up the
nascent Social Democratic Party. The imprisonment of Bolesław Wysłouch
and the Ukrainian radical, Ivan Franko, in 1889, and Father Stojałowski
in 1895 to hamper their electoral activity, together with court cases against
Social Democratic leaders and expulsion of radicals from the university,
merely established the prestige of Badeni's victims. The traditional
methods of administrative pressure discredited the old régime and excited
the appetite for reform.

In common with the rest of the inhabitants of Austria the Poles were
dissatisfied with the curial system of election to the Reichsrat, which was
so heavily weighted in favour of the landed proprietors, who could
influence the curiae other than their own through their control of the
administration and the diet. The ultimate aspiration was the achievement
of universal suffrage and the enfranchisement of the large sections of the
population which had no place in the political system.

The Austrian prime minister from 1879, Count Edward Taaffe, saw
advantages in going part of the way to meet the growing radicalism. On
10 October 1893 the government proposed the extension of the suffrage
to all those who could read and write or who had undergone military

service, but the opposition of the conservatives in the Reichsrat forced the resignation of Taaffe. At length in 1895 Badeni, from the point of view of Vienna eminently safe owing to his resolute methods of governing Galicia, became prime minister, charged with solving the wider problems of Austria. The solution which he found for the problem of electoral reform was a fifth curia with 72 seats, of which Galicia was to obtain 15.

The reform did nothing to alter the fundamental inequalities inherent in the curial system, but the relaxation of qualifications for the vote greatly increased the electorate and gave the underprivileged political parties the chance of widening their support in the elections of March 1897. Because of the prevailing methods of electoral pressure in Galicia, the possibilities of widespread violence were increased. As a result no less than 8 persons were killed, 39 wounded and 800 imprisoned, though these figures represent moderation by comparison with losses inflicted upon Poles in political troubles in the Kingdom of Poland. The Polish parties in Galicia, moreover, did not spare one another. The Social Democrats and the PSL vied for the loyalties of the countryside, the latter descending to anti-socialist abuse and appealing to primitive religious feelings. For the first time the socialists obtained 3 seats, 1 of them held by Daszyński, while the PSL won 3. The most successful group was that of Father Stojałowski, which obtained 6 seats.

On arrival in Vienna the new deputies did not all cover themselves with glory. Stojałowski, returned in February 1898, solved his own personal difficulties, arising from the numerous court cases outstanding against him and his excommunication by the church, by giving his support to the government in joining the Polish Circle and accepting into the bargain a cash payment. From that moment his prestige collapsed and the leadership of the peasantry passed into the hands of the PSL, whose deputies, together with the Social Democrats, remained aloof from the Polish Circle.

The ruling classes in Galicia, moreover, did not accept the appearance of a formidable opposition with resignation. The new viceroy of Galicia, the reactionary Podolian, Count Leon Piniński, used the pretext of anti-semitic riots in six districts to declare a state of emergency in thirty-three districts of western Galicia in order to attack areas in which the Social Democrats and the Peasant Party had influence. The repressions instituted by Piniński taught the Social Democrats and the PSL a salutory lesson by reminding them of their common enemy. Stapiński, who now became the leading peasant leader as secretary of the PSL, could not accept a formal association with the Social Democrats, but he could at least accept the element of socialism as one of the components in the fight against the oppressive system of conservative government.

The elections of 1897 were a turning point in the history of Galicia, bringing into existence a substantial number of Polish deputies in the Reichsrat who did not give automatic support to the government. The taste of success in 1897 encouraged the leaders of the workers and peasants to press still further for reform of the franchise. It is true that they were sucked into the unedifying system which passed for parliamentary life in Vienna, upon which too many hopes were placed, but the desire to extend their influence had the important result of forcing them to attack the narrow system of class rule which had emerged in Galicia. The propertied classes in their quest for autonomy and freedom from the rule of a partitioning power had brought into existence political organizations of other classes who were forced to resist their excessive claims upon the meagre wealth of the province.

Prussian Poland in the second half of the nineteenth century

Galicia was for Austria a province beyond the Carpathians, the loss of which could never have threatened the empire with disruption. For the Germans the Poles were a minority in a frontier area which, though not a dangerous thing in itself, nevertheless represented a certain lack of symmetry. Whereas in Austrian Poland the use of the Polish language in the administration represented no challenge to germanism, in the eastern regions of Prussia the conflicting claims of German and Polish in everyday life called into question what the rulers of Prussia and later the German nationalists considered to have been a permanent conquest. The Poles within Prussia, whether in the Grand Duchy of Posen, in the lower reaches of the Vistula and in Pomerania, in the Masurian districts or in Upper Silesia, were scarcely strong enough to offer a challenge. Correspondingly they seemed weak enough to be eliminated as a factor in German national life. For the Germans the elimination of polonism might be achieved by the slow process of attrition in which the Prussian administration excelled, but, with the appearance of a more aggressive nationalism in the second half of the nineteenth century, opinion on the right moved in favour of even more resolute action to remove this seemingly dangerous foreign element in what ought to be a wholly German state.

Prussia survived the crisis of 1848–50 with more ease than might be supposed. In the eastern provinces of Prussia the crown never lost command of the army, which ensured that the old royal system of control was preserved. Though the Polish districts of Prussia were to enter into the North German Confederation and afterwards into the German empire, the functions of the central government were limited in matters affecting the states joined in the union. It was the Prussian state which dealt with matters most vitally touching upon Polish developments.

The constitution of 1850, which remained in force until the downfall of the Hohenzollern dynasty in 1918, ensured the effective control of the administration over all aspects of life in the kingdom. The Upper House of the diet was virtually nominated by the crown, while the tri-curial system of election to the Lower House ensured a heavy over-representation of the upper classes. The central government of imperial Germany dealt with foreign policy, tariffs, posts and railways, but taxation, education and justice were under the control of the Prussian administration, upon which the Prussian parliament could, even if it had wished, place few checks. Prussia was divided into provinces, regencies and districts, over which were placed the Oberpräsident, the Präsident and the Landrat, appointed by the crown without any limitation being placed upon their powers, except by the government in Berlin.

With the extension of local government, limitations were imposed upon its operation in the Grand Duchy of Posen in order to ensure that the German element in the population enjoyed a disproportionate influence. The excellence of the German system of education ensured that Poles learned German, for which reason it was in time not necessary to employ German officials with a knowledge of Polish. Conscription could be used as a weapon of germanization. Polish recruits were increasingly sent for their period of service to German areas in the west, where upon the outbreak of hostilities they would be employed rather than in the Slavonic east where reliability might be questionable. The pressure of the Prussian administration upon the Poles, however, in the end ruled out docile acceptance of foreign rule.

The provinces of Poznań and West Prussia were basically agricultural in character. Upper Silesia on the other hand was industrial. The agrarian question had been settled for the Poznań area in 1823. There, as elsewhere under the rules of 1816, the purchase of freeholds was limited to those peasants holding 25 Magdeburg *morgi* (6.4 hectares) and spread over a period of 41 years.[27] In 1850 a new law permitted peasants below this limit to purchase their freeholds, but this did not apply to the small peasants who had already been dispossessed. At the same time some manorial rights were abolished. By the end of 1858 all rights of the manor came to an end, except tithes and the privilege of the manor to select village officials, which were abolished only in 1872.

Prussian reforms may have got rid of archaic survivals, but in general they favoured the owners of large estates. In East Prussia and Silesia the large landed proprietors were German, whereas in West Prussia there was a substantial Polish element in the southern districts of the province. In Poznania the Poles predominated. The policy of the government was to favour the German proprietors by the provision of easy credit for the purchase of Polish estates. The system of liquidation of peasant obligations had created a rural proletariat which provided a reserve of labour, but the larger proprietors were quick to adopt new methods and purchase farm machinery. Crops for industrial processing, especially sugar beet, were grown and considerable progress achieved in the rearing of livestock. In such a situation there was every reason to get rid of strip farming and to consolidate holdings, though progress was evident more on German farms than on Polish.

Though conditions varied throughout the regions of Prussian Poland, it is broadly true to say that here the larger peasants with holdings over 20 hectares prospered, whereas the smaller peasants tended to grow poorer and were compelled to supplement their income by wage labour. Below them were the mass of rural labourers, for whom conditions were extremely hard. Only towards the end of the nineteenth century did seasonal and permanent migration improve the situation. To meet any labour shortage, however, there was at hand a reserve of labour in the Kingdom of Poland and Galicia. The authorities were well aware of the political consequences of the influx of Polish labourers and sought to prevent them from taking up permanent residence. The agricultural policy in the eastern provinces of Prussia was one which favoured the larger proprietors and the larger peasants, who supplied the industrial provinces.

By contrast with Poznania and West Prussia, Upper Silesia was the most heavily industrialized region inhabited by a Polish population. While industry did not reach the high technical level of the Ruhr and the Saar, the production of coal, iron, steel and zinc rose rapidly in the second half of the nineteenth century. Coal production rose from 1,352,761 tons in 1852 to 24,815,044 tons in 1900, and iron in the same period rose from 47,163 to 61, 969 tons. The ownership of enterprises rested with the great landlords of the region, and the management was German. The mass of the working class which provided the labour force contained a large Polish element. Whereas between 1864 and 1910 the population rose in Poznania by 35.8 per cent, in West Prussia by 45.7 and in East Prussia by 33.3, the increase in Upper Silesia was 129.1 per cent. In Poznania there was a low level of industrial activity, which resulted in emigration not only to the Americas, but also to the industries of Westphalia and the Rhineland. Upper Silesia by contrast did not suffer as large a loss from emigration. The influx of labour into Upper Silesia from the Kingdom of Poland and Galicia reinforced the Polish element in industry, but the conditions of the workers, while favourable by comparison with those of the workers in the industrial regions of the Kingdom of Poland and Austrian Poland, were poor. Wages were low, accidents frequent and housing primitive. Industrial discontent in Upper Silesia was in the end to turn itself into a national struggle against the German factory owners and management who dominated the life of the region. The development of Upper Silesia, however, had not been associated with that of the Polish Republic. It was rather Poznania which was regarded by Poles and Germans as the centre of the Polish national movement.

The Grand Duchy of Posen in 1815 was not in law part of the Germanic Confederation, but merely a territory attached to the Prussian crown. The Prussian government nevertheless regarded Poznania as an integral part of the Kingdom of Prussia as much as any other province. Oberpräsident Horn acted against Poles who assisted the insurrection of 1863 in the Kingdom of Poland with the severity which earlier in the 1830's had been shown by Flottwell. The trial of Polish leaders between May and December 1864 was a *cause célèbre*. It says something for Prussian liberalism in the 1860's that its protests ensured that sentences of death were commuted and terms of imprisonment limited to preventive arrests. Clemency, completed by the amnesty of September 1866, did not mean however that the Prussian administration relaxed its pressure. In January 1867 Poznania lost its separate status with its formal incorporation into the North German Confederation. In 1871 it automatically became part of the German empire. Poznania was thus most powerfully influenced by the politics of the new Germany.

The furore excited by the Papal Decree of Infallibility in 1870 and the protests of the Old Catholics gave Bismarck an opportunity to launch an attack upon the Roman church. The abolition of the rights of the church in the supervision of education and restrictions upon the persons who might be appointed to church offices were directed mainly against the Catholic areas of the German regions. The *Kulturkampf* was nevertheless waged also against the Catholic Poles in the east. Though this struggle was brought to an end with the shift in the balance of political power in Germany to which formal recognition was given by the anti-socialist law in 1878 and the new tariff policy of 1879, for which the support of the Catholic Zentrum was required, the effect upon Poznania was more permanent.

The archbishop of Poznań and Gniezno and primate of Poland, Ledóchowski, was a cautious conservative, who saw his role as the defence of the rights of the church. With the onset of the *Kulturkampf* he tried to avoid a direct struggle with the state. In 1872 he warned his priests against participating in the movement for popular education initiated by the Society for the Education of the People. When the government issued orders that henceforth religious instruction should be given only in German, he consented upon the condition that teaching in the four lowest classes might be conducted in Polish. The government had nevertheless turned a political issue in Germany into a national issue in Poznania. The closing of the theological seminary in Poznań, and the school of the Sisters of the Sacred Heart and of the Ursulines in Poznań and Gniezno, together with fines upon Ledóchowski, converted the church into a symbol of national resistance. When Ledóchowski was arrested in February 1874 and imprisoned for two years, the Prussian government made a hero out of a man whose enthusiasm for Polish nationalism was lukewarm. The response of the population to the attack upon the church, especially among the peasants, created the mass basis for political clericalism in a Polish province which had after 1848 seen a noticeable decline in left-wing feeling.

In middle-class and gentry circles emphasis was placed upon the need for solidarity among all classes in association with the church. *Dziennik Poznański* (The Poznań Gazette) was an organ devoted to defence of the national interest within a conservative setting. Socialism was regarded as a dangerous doctrine. In fact, the Polish organizations which emerged corresponded very much to the agrarian structure of Poznanian society. The Central Economic Society (Centralne Towarzystwo Gospodarcze), founded in 1861 and reorganized after a period of suspension during the rising in the Kingdom of Poland, sought to raise the level of production in all branches of industry and commerce. The movement to create agricultural societies extended throughout the province and into West Prussia. The stimulus to organize had its effect also upon the richer peasants and the craftsmen of the towns. The promotion of academic studies began with the establishment of the Society of the Friends of Learning (Towarzystwo Przyjaciół Nauk) in 1857, which was followed in 1875 by a similar Learned Society for West Prussia at Toruń. Popular education in Polish, however, met with the opposition of the clergy, who feared a diminution of their influence by the propagation of lay culture, and of the government, which suppressed the Society for the Education of the People in 1879 for its interest in political matters. Nevertheless, the German policy of limiting teaching in Polish to the lower classes of primary schools in itself encouraged resistance, which raised the Polish language in Masuria, Upper Silesia and even in the Kaszubian districts of West Prussia above the level of a mere patois which state education in the course of time could eliminate in favour of German. Some relief from the sense of isolation of being a national minority in a German state was obtained by the proximity of Cracow as a centre of Polish learning and the arts in a culturally more tolerant Austrian Poland.

In the politics of Germany, however, the Poles could scarcely exert influence. The Polish members of the Prussian parliament could seek to ingratiate themselves with the authorities by voting for credits during the struggle for the augmentation of the army, but the Prussian policy towards Poland in 1863 showed that a co-operative attitude would yield nothing. Within Prussia the crucial system of election worked against the Polish interest. With the parcelization of holdings the number of persons who qualified for the first two curiae fell, with a consequent advantage to the German interest. Thus, whereas in the period from 1860 to 1870 there were 22 Polish members in the Prussian Parliament, in the period from 1900 to 1914 there were only 13. Elections to the Reichstag by universal suffrage, however, reflected the growth in the Polish population, but Polish representation was not sufficient to have any influence upon the course of debates. The conservative outlook of the Polish representatives led them in general to throw in their lot with the Catholic Zentrum during the period of *Kulturkampf* and to reject association with any German groups with radical policies. The Polish Circle in the Reichstag was in itself an illustration that Prussian Poland was not an area from which a new Poland was likely to arise. The Polish conservatives conceived themselves as having a defensive role on the one hand against the attempts of the Germans to curtail the rights of the Polish nation, and on the other against the efforts of Polish radicalism to introduce new political creeds which might challenge their position in society.

The change in the political situation in Germany occurred in the second half of the 1870's when the conservatives began to get the upper hand over the National Liberals. The tone of the new phase of German history was set by the anti-socialist law of 1878, which indicated that the government of Bismarck stood firmly upon the defence of the existing social order, and the reversion to a high tariff policy in 1879, designed to protect the interests of the conservative sections of the population, whether the landed interests or the great industrialists of expanding German industry. The factor of egocentric nationalism had been present in Germany since the beginning of the nineteenth century, but now traditional liberalism was less capable of combating its more extreme forms. For this reason the Poles of the east became the target of criticism. The Prussian policy of limiting Polish rights now had obtained the support of ideologists, who represented the German state as being under attack from an advance of the Poles, calling into question the eastern frontier more by sap than by storm. There were even those who could argue that the real interests of Germany lay in pushing the German frontier farther to the east to achieve the position which Prussia had obtained under the terms of the Third Partition of 1795. In that case the frontier would run from Niemen to the south-eastern tip of Upper Silesia, a concept which was to emerge later during the First World War as a solution of the Polish problem approved by the general staff, and actually to be achieved temporarily in 1939 on a slightly wider scale. In the absence of a general war, the German state was compelled to confine itself to administrative measures.

Action began with the decree of 26 March 1885, when the Ministry of the Interior ordered the expulsion from the eastern provinces of all Poles and Jews possessing Russian citizenship, if they did not have permission to live in them, an order which was extended to Polish and Jewish citizens of Austria in the following July. The orders affected about 26,000 persons, who had entered eastern Germany in search of work. Ideology and economic facts did not always mix. The closure of the eastern frontiers to immigrants and the expulsion of those who had already settled in Germany excited some protest from the liberals, but it was the pockets of the great landowners and industrialists which were touched, because they were deprived of a source of docile and cheap labour. In 1890 the orders were relaxed to permit immigrants to come to work provided that they returned home for the winter, when in fact the landowners would have little use for their services.

The speech from the throne in the Prussian parliament on 14 January 1886 foreshadowed measures to extend germanism in the east. In April a bill was presented to parliament proposing the establishment of a fund of 100,000,000 marks to be administered by a Colonization Commission, controlled by the Oberpräsident of Poznań, to encourage the settlement of Germans in the east in the provinces of Poznań and West Prussia. The plan was for the purchase of Polish land upon which substantial peasants could be settled as a bastion of germanism.

In terms of German politics the new policy revealed contradictions. The National Liberals, who gave their support to the colonization measures, thought also that a substantial peasantry would serve as a counterweight to the Junkers, who in their turn believed that the money should be devoted to the creation of smallholdings, which, owing to their inability to support a family, would provide a reservoir of cheap labour. For the Poles the measure was an unpleasant surprise, indicating to them that they were not only second-class citizens, but were also unwelcome intruders in the German Reich. Even more worrying was the fact that many Polish agricultural proprietors, hard hit by the agricultural crisis, were willing to sell their lands.

In fact, the German measures were not always carried out with Germanic thoroughness. Between 1886 and 1890 50,000 hectares were acquired at a cost of 30,000,000 marks, of which only 3,400 hectares belonged to Germans. Indeed the Colonization Commission showed some reluctance to buy lands from Germans and intervened only to prevent German lands being acquired at auction by Poles. The land acquired by the Commission was not in compact masses, but rather distributed among Polish lands, which compelled the German settlers to rely upon Polish labour for the cultivation of their holdings. Of the 690 colonists settled in the first phase of the Commission's activity, 333 came from Poznania and West Prussia and thus did not strengthen the German presence at all. It was clear, however, in the first instance that the Poles could not offer an effective defence. The Polish Land Bank (Bank Ziemski) founded in 1886 could not raise more than 1,200,000 marks. The general financial weakness of the Poles was such that any failure on the part of the Prussian government had its causes in the impracticability of the colonization measure itself.

Hand in hand with it went efforts to abolish the teaching of Polish in schools and substitute German as the language of instruction. Fines were imposed for non-attendance and in 1887 the teaching of Polish as a compulsory subject in Poznania and West and East Prussia was abandoned in favour of English. In the interests of the larger policies of the Vatican Leo XIII appointed a German, Julius Dinder, archbishop of Gniezno in place of Ledóchowski in February 1886, which ensured that the Catholic church would require all religious instruction to be carried out in German, an order for which was issued by Dinder in 1887.

A prospect of relaxation of German pressure came with the death of William I. Frederick III did not live long enough to make any impression upon German policy, but William II was a man determined to make his mark. Bismarck outlived his usefulness in foreign policy which he had handled with increasing lack of certainty since 1887. In the field of domestic affairs his anti-socialist law represented an attack upon an increasingly important section of the German population which gave its loyalties to the Social Democrats, who had by February 1890 become an important political factor in the Reichstag. A young monarch could not place himself at loggerheads with his own subjects so early in his reign. The resignation of Bismarck in March 1890 enabled William II to conciliate his own subjects and begin the campaign to make himself master within the German and Prussian administrations, in order to exercise the real power which Bismarck had wielded in the name of William I.

The appointment of Caprivi in place of Bismarck seemed to the conservative Poles to offer a chance of reaching an understanding. The

Polish Circle for its part supported the military and naval proposals of the government as a gesture of conciliation, and consented to the Russo-German commercial agreement of 10 January 1894, even though it did not meet with the approval of the landed interests generally with whom Polish conservatives normally sided in economic questions. It was argued that the Poles represented a force directed against socialism and revolutionary doctrines. The price of their loyal co-operation was only the suspension of anti-Polish measures. Father Florian Stablewski established such a reputation for respectability by a speech in Toruń in 1891 attacking socialism that he opened the way for his appointment as archbishop in November 1891.

An understanding with the Poles had no place in the general considerations of a German government which was compelled to take account of public opinion within Germany. Concessions could be given to the Poles as an expression of good will, but not as a result of political pressure. All that emerged from the relaxation after 1890 was a trickle of easement which made tolerable the more vexatious ordinances without providing the Polish population with the major concessions necessary for the conduct of normal civilized life. The fundamental hostility of German nationalism remained.

The Caprivi era was merely an interval in which Poles might delude themselves with the possibility of compromise. In 1892 Caprivi surrendered the post of Minister-Präsident in Prussia to Count Eulenberg in order to devote his energies to being chancellor of Germany. Eulenberg interpreted his obligations to the Poles in a narrow Prussian sense. The forces of nationalism were reshaping themselves already in 1891 with the foundation of the Deutscher Ostmarkverein, which was better known as 'Hakata' after the initials of the founders, Hansemann, Kennemann and Tiedemann, and began from April 1894 to agitate for a renewed effort to conquer the Polish districts of the east. With the fall of Caprivi and the advent to power of Prince Hohenlohe the old practice of seeking to dispossess the Poles and submit them to all manner of harassment began again, especially in the conduct of public meetings, a practice which was condemned by German laywers, who, to their honour, drew a distinction between justice and policy whenever they had the opportunity of expressing the spirit of the law.

By 1897 William II had established his mastery over the German administration and the old policy resumed its course when in 1898 a further 100,000,000 marks was granted for the purposes of colonization in the east. The Deutscher Ostmarkverein, founded in 1899 and supported by the historian Treitschke and academics of similar persuasion, revealed that anti-Polish feeling had some popular support, but its power should not be exaggerated. The fundamental opposition to polonism lay in the Prussian administration with its eye upon Prussian *raison d'état* and its fundamental contempt for human rights. The Prussian bureaucracy, however, conducted its policy according to a well-mapped theory. Up to 1900 the Colonization Commission purchased 135,700 hectares, of which over 90,000 were bought in Poznania and 45,000 in West Prussia, but, whereas in the first instance land was acquired from Poles, as time passed by the price of land rose and Germans were willing to sell. In the period from 1898 to 1901 almost three quarters of the land acquired by the Commission came from Germans. Towards the end of the nineteenth century the tide began to turn. Poles began to acquire more land than Germans. The influx of German peasants was insignificant. Up to 1900 3,141 families were settled in Poznania and 1,136 in West Prussia. Thus in fifteen years, if it is supposed that each family contained five persons, some 13,500 persons were settled. This was a small return for so much effort and invited the supposition that the original project had not been pursued with sufficient energy.

The organization of Polish political parties in Prussian Poland never exhibited much vigour before 1900. For practical purposes the climate of opinion among Poles was conservative. The Polish Socialist Party of the Prussian Partition (Polska Partia Socjalistyczna zaboru Pruskiego – PPSzP), founded in 1893, could hardly exert much influence upon a fundamentally agrarian area. Even discontent with the policy of seeking a compromise with the government in Berlin could not excite a nationalist reaction. The National Democrats (see below p. 56) found it difficult to obtain a response.[28] In Silesia the national movement suffered from the lack of a national intelligentsia to give it momentum. Only at the beginning of the twentieth century did the Polish movement in Silesia take on a national outlook, uniting itself with the wider cause of Polish independence. It is difficult to see in the activities of Poles within Prussia a serious threat to the Prussian state, and equally difficult to perceive more than a defensive attitude towards germanization. The challenge of the twentieth century brought new forces to the fore and compelled Polish Prussia to look beyond the narrow confines of traditional conservatism, whether social or religious.

Map 2   The Kingdom of Poland 1815–1914

Russian Poland in the second half of the nineteenth century

The bulk of the former Polish Republic had fallen to the Russian empire by 1815. The Kingdom of Poland was still administered under the Napoleonic *Code Civil*, while the district of Białystok, acquired in 1807, remained a separate unit within the empire. The former eastern provinces were ruled as part of the empire under two governor-generalcies. The governor-generalcy of Vilna consisted of the *gubernii* (provinces) of Kovno, Grodno, Vilna, Vitebsk, and Minsk, and the governor-generalcy of Kiev embraced the *gubernii* of Kiev, Volhynia and Podolia. The relations of Russians and Poles, therefore, extended over a wide area.

Whereas in the west and south the Poles had to contend with Germanic occupying powers, the Russians were Slavs like themselves. However, far from simplifying the relations of Poles and Russians the very closeness of their languages but diverse histories created subtle complications. Poland had emerged with a parliamentary tradition. The subjection of Muscovy to the overlordship of the Khanate of the Golden Horde had led to the evolution of an autocracy, by which alone the Russians had been able to drive back the nomads of the steppes. By the end of the eighteenth century the historic role of the Russian monarchy had been completed. The treaties of Kutchuk Kainardji of 1774 and Jassy of 1795 established the power of Russia on the northern shores of the Black Sea, just as the treaty of Nystadt of 1721 had finally set Russia upon the Baltic. The treaty of Bucharest of 1812 and the defeat of Napoleonic France in 1812–14 were merely confirmation of earlier victories. From 1815 Russia was ready to proceed to a form of social organization in which the power of the autocracy might be modified to permit the population at large gradually to participate in the government of the country, but the great struggle had brought into existence the massive bureaucracy which had organized the empire for victory, accustomed to debate within itself, but not to share power with the subjects of the tsar. The cautious steps taken towards reform by Nicholas I in the early years of his reign were arrested in the 1840's for fear of submitting Russia to the turmoil which appeared in Western and Central Europe in 1848. The shock of defeat in the Crimean War confronted Russia with unpleasant alternatives. The backwardness of Russia was reflected in international politics by the decline of her military power in relation to that of Prussia and even Austria.[29] An increase in Russian power to correct the balance could be achieved only by a programme of speedy industrialization, which would bring in its train unpleasant social consequences. In these circumstances the decision was taken to control development from above and to control all manifestations of dissent from below. The upper classes might be taken into limited partnership, but the ultimate direction of Russia's advancement was to remain in the hands of the tsar and the bureaucracy. From this principle tsarism never deviated in practice until the downfall of the monarchy in March 1917, however much it might have had to make tactical changes of course. Against this background Russo-Polish relations are to be understood.

The leaders of Russia were suspicious of the Poles. The great crises of Russia in the past had been closely connected with Poland. In 1610 the hetman Stanisław Żółkiewski had advanced upon Moscow and installed a Polish garrison, which was not expelled until 1612. In 1708–9 Charles XII had marched into Russia from Poland in an effort to reduce the Petrine state to the frontiers of historic Muscovy. In 1812 Napoleon Bonaparte actually took Moscow, having assembled his army in the Duchy of Warsaw. The Polish revolts against Russia in 1830–1 and 1863–4, especially the latter, revived the fears of Russians. Thus, on the one hand, the tsar and the bureaucracy took the decision to administer the Polish areas as occupied territory in which the inhabitants of Polish speech were to enjoy only a minimum of civil rights. On the other hand, the Poles shared with the mass of the educated Russian population resentment at a system of government which permitted the individual to have no initiative in promoting the welfare of society. A basic problem of Polish nationalism in the modern and contemporary epoch has been the conflict of distaste for the Russian state with consciousness of a common interest with the Russian people. This theme has many permutations, but its existence points to a fundamental difference between Russo-Polish relations and those of Poland with the German states. Within Russian Poland before the First World War, however, Poles of all parties found it difficult to arrive at a satisfactory solution to the problem of Russian domination.

The narrow limits of the tsarist administration's willingness to conciliate the Poles of the Kingdom may be seen at the height of the effort to achieve a *modus vivendi* in 1862. In a letter of instruction of Alexander II to the Grand Duke Constantine Nikolayevich of 18/30 June 1862 upon his appointment to the office of Viceroy, Alexander insisted that Constantine had been sent to Poland to serve the interests of Russia within the general context of promoting reform and conciliation, but there could be no concessions beyond what had already been granted: 'There can be no talk of this, and especially of a constitution and a national army. Neither the former nor the latter will I permit in any circumstances whatever.'[10] It was thus not foreseen that there would be any return to the situation of 1815–30. Alexander II rejected Panslavism, which many ascribed to Constantine, as dangerous for Russia and the monarchical system, likely to lead to the break-up of the empire into separate and hostile republics. Panslavism for him was fanciful, and he declared that 'The union of all Slavs under one state is a Utopia.'

The failure to achieve reform and stability under Constantine and the outbreak of the insurrection in 1863 brought about a revision in Russian thinking even within the narrow confines of instructions given to Constantine. Henceforth the Kingdom of Poland was to become part of Russia, except that the concessions which the régime was ready to make to Russians were not to be extended to Poles. In this manner the Poles suffered the burden of centralization except in as far as their separate status could be used in the interest of Russian *raison d'état*. The decree of 1864 establishing councils in the *gubernii* and districts (zemstvos) of the empire was not extended to the Kingdom of Poland or the western *gubernii*, any more than the decree of 1870 on municipal self-government. The Kingdom of Poland was treated as occupied territory and its inhabitants as citizens of dubious loyalty. The only organization in which the Poles could play any part was the commune, in which they could receive their orders.

In 1866 the separate Secretariat of State was abolished and replaced by the Emperor's Personal Chancery for the Affairs of the Kingdom. In 1867 the Council of State and the Administrative Council were abolished and their functions assigned to Russian institutions. The most important institution was the Executive Committee for the Affairs of the Kingdom of Poland, which was composed entirely of Russians. The Finance Commission became a Financial Chamber on Russian lines. The Bank of Poland was eventually merged with the Russian State Bank in 1885. In every respect, in the administration, justice and education, the Kingdom was assimilated with the Russian empire. Because the Poles could not be trusted, they were submitted to closer supervision.

In 1866 the Kingdom was divided into 10 *gubernii* and 85 districts, whereas before there had been only 5 provinces and 39 districts. The increase in the number of administrative divisions led to the influx of more Russian officials into the Kingdom. The intention of russification was proclaimed by reference to the Kingdom as 'The Vistula Territories' (Kraj Privislansky). When Count Berg died in 1874 the office of viceroy perished with him and henceforth the country was ruled by the governor-general of Warsaw, charged with the supervision of the civil administration and command of the army. In 1861 a state of war had been proclaimed. It was under these conditions in one form or another that the Kingdom of Poland was governed up to the outbreak of the First World War. Control had been strict up to January 1863, but it was in practice often rendered more tolerable by the fact that it was exercised by Poles themselves. The system had been operated by a few Russians at the centre. After the rising, however, there was an influx of Russian officials and schoolteachers to take the place of the Poles. The business of the administration, the courts and even of the communes was conducted in Russian. It was in these conditions that the Kingdom of Poland was expected to achieve that transition from one form of social organization to another necessitated by the agrarian reforms of March 1864.

To the east in the western *gubernii* of the Russian empire the same policy of russification was followed. All business had to be conducted in Russian. Neither Polish nor Lithuanian could be used. Every effort was made to reduce the Polish presence. Exiles returning from the interior of Russia were forbidden to settle in Lithuania, Byelorussia and the Ukraine. Poles were not allowed to purchase land or to acquire it on long leases. The emancipation decree for the governor-generalcies of Vilna and Kiev had been modified by Muraviëv in 1863 to the advantage of peasants, which was a measure designed both to win the loyalties of the common people and at the same time to penalize the Polish landlords.

According to an estimate made in 1867 there were in the six *gubernii* of Grodno, Vilna, Kovno, Vitebsk, Minsk, and Mogilev, the constituent portions of the former Grand Duchy of Lithuania, about 447,000 Poles, and in the Ukrainian *gubernii* of Podolia, Volhynia and Kiev 478,000. Socially the Poles represented the upper classes of the towns and the landlords together with their agents in the country, but there were some settlements consisting of Polish peasants and in Lithuania villages owned by *szlachta zagrodowa*, gentry who had enjoyed the privileges of nobility, but in practice lived merely as free peasants. In no *gubernia* did Poles constitute a majority of the population. In the *gubernia* of Vilna there were 143,288 Poles, amounting to 15.9 per cent of the total, in the *gubernia* of Grodno 89,853 (10.1), in the *gubernia* of Minsk 117,748 (11.8), in Podolia 233,647 (12.5), and in Volhynia 172,405 (10.8). In the other provinces the Poles did not amount to more than 10 per cent of the population. Tsarist statistics are not to be trusted, because anyone who could be counted not to be a Pole was assigned to some other category. Polish influence was probably slightly higher than the bare figures would give us to believe. By the time of the census of 1897 the number of Poles in the Lithuanian and Byelorussain *gubernii* had risen to 563,814, but had declined in relation to the total population. Only in the *gubernia* of Grodno in 1897 did the Poles achieve the figure of 10 per cent with a population of 161,622. Elsewhere the Polish element had fallen below 10 per cent. The tsarist administration could therefore expect, with some reason, that the policy of russification would succeed.

In the Kingdom of Poland, with a population of about 6,078,000 in 1870, the Polish element was according to the official reckoning 64.9 per cent, but this figure was achieved by counting Jews, who had adopted Polish as their language, separately from the Poles. Similarly Uniate Christians in the *gubernii* of Lublin and Podlasie were regarded either as Ukrainians or Russians. In fact the Polish element was nearer 70 per cent in 1870. By 1897 the population had risen to 9,402,253, of whom 6,755,503 were Poles. Because the Russians incorporated their army of occupation into the total population, the Polish element was rather larger than it would appear in relation to the total number of civilians, amounting to 73.4 per cent of the whole. In general therefore it is true to say that in historic Poland under the dominion of Russia the Poles began to lose their influence in the western *gubernii* of the empire, but grew stronger in the Kingdom of Poland. A hypothetical figure for the number of Poles everywhere in Europe and overseas is 17,123,000 in 1900. The largest single element found itself under the control of tsarist Russia.

The crisis in the post-reform period

The reforms of 2 March 1864 initiated a crisis in Polish society of a magnitude not experienced in Prussian and Austrian Poland. The system of compensation for the landlords was scarcely satisfactory to them. For every *mórg* of land surrendered in freehold to the peasants they obtained 15–20 roubles for the loss of labour services. Compensation, however, was paid in the form of bonds, a portion of which was to be redeemed annually over the course of forty-two years. The landlords could sell their bonds, but any return which they might obtain from this source was insufficient to provide them with the draught animals and the implements which hitherto they had relied upon the peasants to provide when they performed labour services. Labour now presented a severe problem, because the peasants were reluctant to serve on the manors in the post-reform period. The landlords were thus compelled to employ farm servants, or enlist seasonal labour from Galicia and the Russian empire, whom they normally paid in kind. Only in time did harvesters and threshing machines reduce the size of this problem, but machinery obviously required money. To some extent the problem was offset by the buoyant grain prices of the 1870's and early 1880's but from 1885 grain prices began to fall as a result of the influx of cheap American corn and the protectionist policies of imperial Germany.

Since the grain crisis equally affected the Russian empire, the state encouraged the export of grain to the Kingdom of Poland, where relatively higher prices prevailed. The increased tempo of industrialization in the 1890's, which brought about a migration of labour from the countryside to the towns, in part helped to sustain demand, but the landlords were compelled to turn their attention to the cultivation of crops other than grain, especially potatoes and sugar beet, and to the raising of cattle and pigs. This conversion brought in its train the rotation of crops and the modernization of Polish agriculture at least on the lands of the larger proprietors, but there were many landlords for whom reform brought hardship and even disaster. Many estates were sold, while indebtedness to the Land Credit Society rose from 68,200,000 roubles in 1870 to 139,900,000 roubles in 1900. The epoch of the old *szlachta* society was over. The bucolic life of the past was never to come again. Before reform life had been able to proceed in an untroubled manner:

And so the young man, settling down on his father's patch, and thus entering into the circle of the gentry, could confidently finish his education in the second or third class, and might have no ideas of spelling and grammar. No one judged him the worse for that. Provided his legs did not give way under a gallon of wine, provided he did not spit in the vegetables, provided he shot straight, rode well and knew the faults of a horse, he could be certain of the respect and assistance of his fellow landlords.[31]

The land could no longer sustain *szlachta* of this kind. A common pattern was for the eldest son to inherit the estate, but to seek education as a form of social insurance. Indifference to methods of agriculture gave way to inquiry into the means of improving yields. The carefree social life of the past gave way to a careworn struggle to make ends meet. The rest of the family went to the towns, a factor which enforced for practical purposes the emancipation of the upper-class woman upon Polish society. The noble suffix of -*ski* of a surname, the equivalent of the French *de* and the German *von*, lost its significance, and the word *Pan*, literally meaning *lord*, descended to being merely a polite form of address, adopted in time by the peasants. The years after emancipation created great mobility among the *szlachta*. Some made fine careers, while others were assimilated into the working class. This was easy enough for the petty *szlachta*, who were already indistinguishable economically from the peasantry, but for the *szlachta* with any pretensions to gentility descent in the social scale was scarcely acceptable.

In a society dominated by Russian officialdom, especially in the stark years of the governor-generalcy of Field Marshal Osip Gurko from 1883 to 1894, who systematically secured the dismissal of even minor Polish officials, there was no hope of a career in public administration. The alternative lay in science, technology and the arts. As the system of reform caused a revolution in the life of the *szlachta*, they in their turn brought about a revolution in the life of the Polish towns, swamping the German and Jewish elements as they converted themselves into an urban intelligentsia. The word *intelligentsia* has a broader meaning in Polish than it has in English, in which it has associations with intellectualism. In Poland it embraced the whole spectrum of literate persons from the white-collared workers to those in the professions and the liberal arts.

The Kingdom of Poland could not provide the opportunities for a *déclassé szlachta*, which constituted about 10 per cent of the population, but the great Russian empire with its slowly evolving industry required a managerial class. The Polish colonies began to expand in all the major Russian cities, especially in St Petersburg, Moscow and Kiev, as a result of the influx of engineers, technologists and commercial representatives, bringing with them a host of tailors, shoemakers, valets and pastry cooks.

The Polish population of St Petersburg rose from 11,157 in 1864 to 70,000 in 1914.[32] There were also the temporary residents of Russia, the Polish students who studied in the Russian universities where they came in contact with Russian revolutionary movements. Military service took thousands of Poles into Russia and some, especially Lithuanian Poles, took service with the Russian army permanently as career officers, their sisters often marrying Russian officers. Some Poles chose to identify themselves with Russia and their children assumed a transliterated but recognizably Polish name. The consequence was that Poles had a much closer relationship with Russian society than they had with German society, understanding its impulses and frequently sympathizing with it, but there was no escaping the fact that they were in their own homeland only second-class citizens. Association did not lessen the desire for national self-determination. The knowledge that Russians themselves were disenchanted by the maintenance of the autocracy had a powerful influence upon Polish attitudes.

The peasants, on the other hand, reacted to their new conditions in their own way. They obtained their freeholds and were liberated from all obligations to the manor, as well as tithes and other dues to the church. They retained the right of access to woods and pastures, the so-called *serwituty*, the abolition of which could be secured only by voluntary agreement and the payment of compensation to the peasants. The rural commune was separated from the manor and the landlord ceased to be by law the mayor (*wójt*). The mayor and his clerk were responsible to a communal assembly for the conduct of affairs. In theory the tutelage of the manor was abolished, but in its place came the Peasant Commissions and the district commissioners responsible to the Executive Committee appointed under the chairmanship of Nikolai Milyutin, which was to supervise the enactment of reform. In theory the peasants paid nothing for their economic liberation, but the government raised the land tax in 1866 in order to cover the costs of compensation to the landlords. The maintenance of the communal administration and courts, together with the cost of the schools and construction of roads, bore heavily upon the peasants. The actual arrangements for conferring freeholds upon the peasants, supervised by Russian officials unfamiliar with local conditions and problems, gave rise to complaints and accusations on both sides. Poorly educated peasants found it difficult to contest the claims of the manor and resented the intervention of incompetent officials. In consequence they frequently took the law into their own hands, removing timber from the woods, placing animals on the pastures without specific agreements, and committing assaults upon the landowners and their agents. The authorities were compelled to use force in support of the landlords and thus earned for themselves the reputation of favouring the upper classes. Discontent and violence were endemic in the countryside. In such conditions it was unlikely that the government's plans for russification would succeed.

According to the figures of the Executive Committee 592,750 peasant holdings were embraced by reform by 1872. Of these 21.8 per cent consisted of holdings of three *morgi* or less, 40.6 fell within the category of 3–15 *morgi*, and 37.0 were over 15 *morgi*, which gave an average of 8.2 per holding. There were, however, considerable variations within the Kingdom. Holdings tended to be larger on the right bank of the Vistula than on the left. By 1889 the pattern of peasant landholding was clearly changing. Holdings had risen to 717,257, but those below 3 *morgi* had fallen to 15 per cent, while the group between 3 and 15 *morgi* had risen to 44.5 per cent and over 15 *morgi* to 40.5 per cent. By British standards a holding of 3–15 *morgi* was a poor basis for prosperity, and in fact arrears in the land tax owed by peasants amounting to 114,500,000 roubles in 1892 indicate that the peasants endured a grinding poverty. The true index of the condition of the countryside and indeed of the whole economy of the Kingdom of Poland was the existence of a class of landless labourers, estimated to have been in 1864 about 200,000, but rising in 1891 to 849,328, and in 1901 to 1,220,333. Neither in its initial stages nor in its long term consequences did the Russian solution of the agrarian problem in the Kingdom of Poland satisfy the broad mass of the Polish peasants.[33]

The development of industry in Russian Poland

The agrarian society of the Kingdom of Poland had contained within itself the seeds of an industrial revolution. In the years from 1827 to 1830 the textile industry had established itself in Łódź to which Ludwig Geyer brought steam power in 1839. In 1851 the abolition of the customs barrier between the Kingdom of Poland and the Russian empire opened an ever expanding market to Polish production. To textiles were added the activities of the brothers Thomas, Andrew, Alfred and Douglas Evans, who founded in Warsaw in 1822 a metal works producing machines and agricultural implements, which developed into a nucleus of an engineering industry, controlled by the firm of Lilpop, Rau and Loewenstein. There were supplies of coal and iron in the Dąbrowa basin, which already in the 1820's offered hope of substantial expansion. The Kingdom of Poland, therefore, differed radically from Poznania and Galicia, because the beginnings of investment in industry had been undertaken. Beyond the Kingdom, but for practical purposes part of the same industrial complex, lay the town of Białystok and its environs, which achieved an importance of their own as an industrial centre.

Because the Kingdom of Poland lay at the western extremity of the Russian empire extending as far as the Pacific Ocean, there was every encouragement to the foreigner to invest in its industry. Polish industry in the past had had no connection with the world market, but the attachment to Russia ensured a development to which a Poland within a purely European context could never have aspired. Expansion, however, occurred with all the worst features of modern capitalism, accentuating the problems of nationalism. There were no substantial capitalists of native Polish origin to provide the funds available to the industries of Britain, Belgium, France and above all Germany. Germans in particular sought to invest in the Kingdom of Poland, because they could shelter behind the tariff barriers which the Russian empire was to impose upon foreign goods especially in 1877 and 1881. The bulk of the workers in the first instance were docile, submissive peasants, especially in the textile industries of the area of Łódź, but foremen and management were Germans, or of Western European origin. Under the Russian system of government the workers had no protection against the employers. When the workers offered resistance, the employers had only to call upon the resources of the state to impose order and maintain their position of economic control. The industrial system of tsarist Russia offered unlimited profits tempered only by the possibility of revolution. The growth of the limited liability company, as elsewhere, meant that the employers measured progress by dividends, and not by the welfare of the human beings employed in production. The impact of industrial expansion, however, brought in its train an improvement of communications. The length of railway lines in the Kingdom of Poland grew from 635 km in 1864 to 1,941 km in 1885, rising to 3,394 km in 1911. Poland was badly served by railway communication, but the linking of the Kingdom of Poland with the other railway networks of Europe assisted in breaking down the isolation of the rural districts and in opening a wider market for the products of the countryside.

Industrialization led to a rapid increase in the population. Between 1840 and 1863 it grew from 4,500,000 to 5,000,000 but from 1863 to 1886 it rose to 7,900,000. By the time of the Russian census of 1897 it had risen to 9,402,000, of which non-agricultural workers and their families, exclusive of the army and persons of independent means, accounted for 2,582,000. The workers employed in factories, mining, railways, building and comparable tasks amounted to 311,050, of whom 115,181 belonged to the textile industry. Hours of work were long, amounting to twelve to thirteen hours a day for six days a week. The great strike at Łódź in 1892 (see below p. 17) secured a ten-hour day, but a law of 1897 fixed the day at eleven and a half hours. Wages were low. A textile worker earned from 209 to 239 roubles a year, whereas a miner might earn from 290 to 435 roubles, a metal worker 294, and a foundryman 403. Payment for women was even lower. The rapid urbanization, proceeding apace in the period of greatest expansion in the 1890's, was not accompanied by the provision of the decencies of civilized life. By 1904 only Warsaw, Łomża, Lublin and Płock had piped water, a privilege enjoyed by Cracow and Lwów in Galicia, but in Prussian Poland in every town of about 25,000. A sewage disposal system was therefore a corresponding rarity. It is not surprising that life in Polish cities was unhealthy. Smallpox, cholera, tuberculosis and typhus abounded. Warsaw in particular was an unhealthy city in every respect. In 1910 out of 235 suicides for the whole of the Kingdom 225 occurred in Warsaw, and 285 of the 354 deaths from violence. Syphilis and gonorrhea were rife, but that may be a reflection upon the number of soldiers present in the garrison. According to the census of 1897, 34.2 per cent of men and 26.8 per cent of women could read and write, an average of 30.5, which compares unfavourably with the 32.6 per cent for the Russian empire. By 1905 37.2 per cent of recruits were literate, but in the empire the figure was 59.7 per cent.[34] Russian rule not only struck national pride. It did nothing to raise the quality of life as it pursued the quest for the enlargement of Russian power by industrialization. The Polish and Russian revolutionary movements were in essence the assertion of the dignity of man.

The politics of a country under such complete domination as the Kingdom of Poland were necessarily limited, but the propertied classes as everywhere had the opportunity to rescue themselves at least from disaster. On the extreme right were the followers of the Marquis Alexander Wielopolski, whose son, Zygmunt, kept alive the cause of reconciliation with Russia upon the basis of the common interest which both tsardom and the Polish upper classes had in staving off the advance of radicalism. To the end of his days Zygmunt Wielopolski faithfully represented the ultra-right attitude to the social changes which were engendered by the industrialization of the country. Only slightly less conservative were those landowners who had followed Andrzej Zamoyski. Ludwik Górski, Tomasz Zamoyski and Tadeusz Lubomirski thought in terms of a policy based on existing Polish institutions, upon which they could build the foundations of a new Poland. In fact, in the course of time there was little difference in practice between Zygmunt Wielopolski and those leaders who had not been closely associated with his father. Theirs was essentially a programme of Organic Work, and there were those who were prepared to transmit the same concepts, though in a new form. The periodical *Przegląd Tygodniowy* (Weekly Review), founded in 1866, rejected the *szlachta* tradition and the outlook of romanticism and stuffy clericalism of the Galician conservatives. Instead emphasis was laid upon the humdrum virtues of thrift and industry. All classes were invited to unite in the common effort to increase the wealth of Poland. The theory, which went by the name of 'Warsaw Positivism', and drew freely upon the writings of Auguste Comte, J. S. Mill, Herbert Spencer, Darwin and Buckle, had its roots in the obvious facts of Polish subjection. Its principal exponent, Alexander Świętochowski, might condemn through the periodical *Przegląd Tygodniowy* the outmoded ethos of the *szlachta* and demand a leading role for the entrepreneur and the industrialist, but theory and practice were unhappy bedfellows. Economic expansion brought new problems in its train. Agrarian discontent and the restiveness of the working classes revealed that the Poland of the future might arise from more fundamental forces than those which the educated classes by themselves could generate. The impending social conflict began to seem more threatening than the nostalgia of the *szlachta* for the idealized concept of the past.

The new situation seemed to call for the solidarity of the propertied and professional classes. In 1879 Alexander Świętochowski left the editorial board of *Przegląd Tygodniowy*, having declared that socialism was a more important enemy than the traditional views inherited from an earlier epoch. In his *Wskazania Polityczne* (Political Suggestions), published in 1882, he laid emphasis upon the need for national unity. Warsaw Positivism arose merely as a movement born of necessity as a tactical deviation in the period of failure. It was a transient phenomenon which left little impact upon Polish national life. The conservatives sought to establish their respectability as the true representatives of Poland. When war broke out with the Ottoman empire in 1877, Zygmunt Wielopolski and 800 landowners drew up a loyal address to Tsar Alexander II, declaring their absolute support for the war effort. Again in March 1884 Wielopolski memorialized Tsar Alexander III upon the dangers of radicalism, evidence of which he could find even among the bureaucrats. In Pope Leo XIII the Roman church had a leader, who, in his encyclical of 28 December 1878 entitled *Quod apostolici muneris*, condemned the apostles of the new creeds, the socialists, nihilists, anarchists and communists. On 24 December 1882 the papacy was able to secure the re-establishment of diplomatic relations with the Russian empire. Though the Russian authorities chose to interpret the agreement as they thought fit, the Roman Catholic church through its hierarchy in the Polish lands exerted its influence until the First World War to preserve the *status quo*. In Cracow Count Jerzy Moszyński drew upon all the arguments of religion to bolster the position of the propertied classes. From the side of the Polish upper classes there would be little initiative for the promotion of the national cause, except if it were designed to serve their own privileged position.

The assassination of Alexander II on 1/13 March 1881 changed the climate of opinion in official circles. The actual assassin, Ignacy Hrynie-wiecki, was a Pole, but the populist movement, 'The People's Will' (Narodnaya Volya), which had planned the deed had given notice that there existed in Russia a revolutionary element which lacked only the support of the masses to achieve its ends. It seemed therefore that there was no place even for the most moderate liberalism in the Russian empire. Discipline, Russian nationalism and extreme conservatism were the declared policy of the government, given formal expression in the confirmation of the privileges of the nobility upon the centenary of Catherine II's charter of liberties of 1785. The government manifested its black-hearted policy by the encouragement of pogroms of the Jews in the Ukraine, Byelorussia and Poland in an effort to divert discontent against an identifiable and often unpopular element in society. In such a situation only the most politically cautious and socially acceptable of Poles could enjoy the toleration of the régime. Only those who could profess absolute acceptance of foreign domination could speak openly for Poland. Antoni Wrotnowski in his *Porozbiorowe aspiracje narodu polskiego* (The Political Aspirations of the Polish Nation since the Partitions) accepted without question association with Russia on behalf of the great proprietors. The spokesmen of professional classes, Włodzimierz Spasowicz, the editor of *Ateneum*, founded in 1876, and Erazm Piltz, the editor of *Nowiny* (News), appearing from 1878, sought to provide a link with Russians of similar standing. In 1882 they founded the weekly *Kraj* (The Homeland) in St Petersburg, which sought to promote understanding upon the basis of an alliance of the propertied classes not only in Russian Poland, but also in Prussia and Austria. Thus one of the most prominent of organs directed its efforts against active struggle for Polish independence. The upper classes in the last quarter of the nineteenth century were concerned more with immediate tactics than ultimate strategy.

The growth of industry in the Kingdom of Poland and the district of Białystok was gradually destroying the bases of the political and economic thought of the upper classes. The advance of rapacious capitalism, drawing upon the submissive and defenceless labourers who flooded in from the countryside, could not go unstemmed for ever. High dividends were secured by the fact that the Russian state did not permit the workers to organize in their own defence. Already socialism was making progress in Germany in the 1860's and in 1875 the Social Democratic Party of Germany was founded. Socialism in Russian Poland might to some extent have drawn upon the inspiration of Germany, but the conditions in which it grew were those which gave rise to the populist movements of 'Land and Liberty' (Zemlya i Volya) and Narodnaya Volya, which flourished in the Russian universities. The Russian movements were fundamentally agrarian in their outlook. The rate of industrial growth in Poland, however, was faster than in Russia. It was for this reason that a socialist movement appeared earlier in Warsaw, Łódź and other cities. The founder of the Polish socialist movement was a Pole from the Ukraine, Ludwik Waryński, though there were Polish intellectuals in Warsaw who were familiar with the theoretical problems of socialism.[35]

The distinctive feature of Waryński's activity was his desire to harness the revolutionary impulses of Russian movements to the aspirations of the Polish working class. It was for this reason that in January 1877 he took employment as a workman in the metal works of Lilpop, Rau and Company in Warsaw, where he was employed for eight months before enrolling in the Agricultural Academy in Puławy in order to obtain exemption from conscription. The earliest form of working-class organization was the Resistance Fund (Kasa Oporu) which enabled the workers to take strike action. The vigilance of the police, however, soon forced Waryński to flee to the more sedate climate of backward Galicia, where he met for the first time Bolesław Limanowski, who was himself born in Polish Livonia and after a period of imprisonment from 1861 to 1868 settled first in Galicia and afterwards in Western Europe[36] (see p. 22). Waryński and Limanowski were to be symbolic of two themes in Polish socialist thought, Waryński being willing to accept internationalism, whereas Limanowski thought in terms of the national struggle for independence by means of socialism. Only abroad could Limanowski's writings appear without the hindrance of the tsarist censorship. Switzerland was a haven of refuge for the socialists and anarchists of all Europe, in which they at a distance from their homelands could discuss the bases of their policies. It was there that in 1879 Stanisław Mendelson, Kazimierz Dłuski, Szymon Diksztajn and Maria Jankowska founded the monthly, *Równość* (Equality), in the first number of which appeared the so-called 'Brussels Programme'.[37] The programme, drawn up by Waryński and declared for reasons of security to have been composed in Brussels, stated that '... active participation in the struggle against the established social order is the duty of every Pole who values the fate of millions of Polish people above the interests of the noble and capitalist sections of our nation'. The revolution was, however, 'general and international', in alliance with the socialists of all countries upon the basis of the concepts of the First International promulgated in Geneva on 3 September 1866.

In November 1880 the editors of *Równość* organized a conference in Geneva on the occasion of the fiftieth anniversary of the uprising of November 1830, which was attended by Russian and German socialists as well as Poles. The Polish socialists defined their attitude to the Polish Question, rejecting the old *szlachta* tradition in favour of a national regeneration based upon the people and in association with the international movement.[38] In common with most movements of the left the Polish socialists were divided on the question of tactics. The anarchist and populist leanings of Waryński and Diksztajn led to disputes which ended the publication of *Równość*, which was replaced in August 1881 by *Przedświt* (Before the Dawn). The internationalism of the early socialists, moreover, was challenged by *émigrés* who thought in terms of a national uprising. In August 1881 Bolesław Limanowski established 'The Polish People' (Lud Polski), nominally a socialist association, but giving greater emphasis to national liberation upon the basis of a federation of Poland, Lithuania, Byelorussia and the Ukraine. The fundamental differences in outlook were revealed at a conference at Chur in Switzerland on 2 October 1881. Waryński and Dłuski upheld the doctrine of international struggle within each portion of partitioned Poland, whereas Limanowski proposed a national uprising throughout Poland by all Poles. There thus appeared a conflict between socialism and patriotism, which was not easy to resolve when the visible manifestation of oppression was the foreigner and its instrument a foreign army. The declaration by the editors of *Przedświt*, entitled 'To our Russian Socialist Comrades', proposed the creation of a Polish socialist party within the Russian empire.[39] The question of national liberation was represented as having been removed from the policies of the privileged classes. What remained was the need for a class war upon the basis of solidarity and a common programme of struggle: 'For us the time for separatism and traditional hatreds has already passed...A common aim must unite us fraternally on the field of battle.' This was a policy which was dictated by political fact, but the elevation of it to a point of principle tended to deprive socialism of support among nationally minded workers.

The socialist cause received an enormous stimulus from the economic crisis of 1881–2, during which the bigger enterprises in Warsaw dismissed large numbers of workers. Symptomatic of the general discontent and at the same time of the low level of political thinking among the mass of the workers were the attacks upon the Jews during the Christmas of 1881.

The aim of the Polish socialists was to give working-class discontent an organization directed at the alleviation of economic conditions. Polish students from St Petersburg, Moscow, Vilna and Kiev in 1880 founded in Warsaw the Polish Commune (Gmina Polska), which after a short existence was succeeded by the Polish–Lithuanian Social Revolutionary Party, set up in St Petersburg in 1881, of which an inner committee, 'The Centre' (Ognisko), was responsible for its general direction. In Warsaw itself there was a small group of journalists with socialist convictions, led by Stanisław Krusiński, Bronisław Białobłocki and Ludwik Krzywicki, who were highly critical of the Positivist doctrines so acceptable to the middle classes. It was in this economic and intellectual climate that Ludwik Waryński returned to Poland in 1881 to found a working-class party. The full programme of the party, which took the name of 'Proletariat', was first announced in its full form on 1 September 1882.[40] It declared itself to be a social-revolutionary party working for the liberation of the working class of both town and country. Simultaneously there was established the Society of the Red Cross in the Kingdom of Poland, which was associated with the Red Cross of Narodnaya Volya, to assist political prisoners and their families. Its relations with Narodnaya Volya were fraternal, based upon an undertaking to work for the common cause of overthrowing tsarism.[41] Narodnaya Volya declared

It would not decide even to take on the responsibility of the direction of affairs in a country so different from Russia, just as it would not agree to handing over its affairs to the influence of any sort of non-Russian party whatsoever. A close connection between the parties of Narodnaya Volya and Proletariat in the interests of the revolution, however, is equally as necessary as their complete independence.

There were in fact considerable differences between the two parties. The Poles placed greater emphasis upon the organization of the working class, whereas Narodnaya Volya was prepared to think in terms of the effectiveness of terror. The socialism of Narodnaya Volya had a closer affinity with anarchism, while the Polish socialists, presented with the practical opportunities of influencing the growing working class, were more concerned to base their success upon solid foundations.

The organization of a working-class movement in the conditions of the police control existing in Russia was necessarily difficult. As activity expanded, so the chances of discovery by the police grew. An early success occurred in February 1883. The chief of police in Warsaw, Buturlin, had issued a regulation ordering the medical inspection of women working in factories and elsewhere as if they were common prostitutes working in brothels. Proletariat organized a protest which compelled Buturlin to withdraw his order. The incident drew attention to the possibilities of leadership by Proletariat, which extended its influence from Warsaw to the textile town of Żyrardów and thence to Łódź. No one knows how far the influence of Proletariat extended, but it is believed that there were several hundred members in Warsaw and that it enjoyed the sympathies of several thousand workers who were not actually integrated in the organization. Certainly it was the first socialist organization which was able to produce within Poland a periodical with a socialist content *Proletariat*.[42] Inevitably arrests begun to break up the leadership. Waryński was arrested in September 1883, and his associates Edmund Płoski and Henryk Dulęba soon followed him into prison, but it was significant that the movement was strong enough for new leaders to appear. Alexander Dębski, Felix Kon, and Bronisław Sławiński took over control, but they were joined by socialists who had closer contacts with Narodnaya Volya: Tadeusz Rechniewski, Bolesław Onufrowicz, and Stanisław Kunicki, who were more inclined to adopt terrorist tactics. Nevertheless further arrests followed in 1884. Several hundred members of Proletariat were arrested, of whom twenty-nine from the industrial areas of Poland were selected as being principally responsible for the direction of the party. The trial of 23 November to 20 December 1885 produced its first socialist martyrs. In the end the Russian Piotr Bardovsky, Stanisław Kunicki, the shoemaker Michał Ossowski and the weaver Jan Petrusiński were hanged on 28 January 1886. Waryński died in the Schlüsselberg fortress in St Petersburg in 1889. The leadership now fell to others, especially Maria Bohuszewicz, who was herself condemned to exile and died on the road to Siberia. Still the party found a new leadership in the person of the locksmith Stefan Ulrych, who in turn was sentenced to exile in Siberia in 1888. The tradition of socialist agitation had now been established. Proletariat II arose in the place of Proletariat I, under the leadership of Marcin Kasprzak and Ludwik Kulczycki, to uphold the cause until 1893. Proletariat did not achieve its ends, but it laid the foundations of Polish socialism. Socialism now took its place as part of the Polish political tradition.[43]

Russian Poland in the 1890's

Russian Poland began to change rapidly in the 1890's in response to the increased tempo of industrialization. Within Russia proper was to arise the Russian Social Democratic Workers' Party in March 1897 at Minsk. In October 1897 the General Jewish Workers' Union (the Bund) was founded at Vilna, a socialist organization, but committed to demands for equal rights for Jews, and therefore in the end to maintain an organization separate from the other parties struggling against tsarism. The Socialist

Revolutionaries, the lineal successors of the populist movement, were somewhat slower to come together to found a party, doing so only in 1901–3. Nevertheless, it was clear that Russia herself was beginning to produce revolutionary parties which would work for the overthrow of tsardom. As Russia began to change from within, the alignment of international forces gave rise to the supposition that the relative stability, which owed its origin to the agreement of Germany, Austria and Russia to concert even when they were in disagreement, was breaking down. The ruin of Bismarck's system was already apparent in 1887, when he was compelled to accept the fact that the Reinsurance Treaty of 18 June 1887 was a poor substitute for the Dreikaiserbund of 1881 and forced to bring Russia to heel by his campaign of financial pressure on the Berlin bourse against acceptance of Russian bonds. The transfer of Russian attention to the Paris bourse found a ready response among the French small investors. The subsequent Franco-Russian alliance of 1891–4, resulting from the political advantages to be obtained by Russia against Britain in the field of colonial conflict rather than from Russian hostility towards Germany, nevertheless had a direct effect upon the European balance of power. The community of interest between Germany and Russia, to which Russia nominally subscribed from the 1860's more out of fear of Prussia than from the conviction that the old friendship could be maintained, began to wear thin. The growth of borrowing from France was accompanied by growing economic hostility on the part of Germany, culminating in the tariff war of 1893. As Russo-German hostility increased, French investment in Russia grew. The last decade of the nineteenth century was the period of most rapid industrial expansion. It was for this reason that Russian opposition movements began to seek a mass basis for their agitation in the towns in contrast with the populist movements of Zemlya i Volya and Narodnaya Volya, which were by the very nature of the Russian economy unable to stir the people of the countryside.

The Polish political reactions were to occur earlier than the Russian. The accepted concepts of Polish society were under attack from both lower-middle-class nationalism and from reinvigorated socialism. The middle-class intelligentsia was growing increasingly weary of control by Russians, acceptance of Russian domination by the upper classes and the theories of Warsaw Positivism which elevated submission to a point of principle. Symptomatic of a more radical attitude was the foundation of the newspaper *Głos* (The Voice) in autumn of 1886, which submitted current attitudes to a more stringent criticism. A significant break with the doctrine of passive acceptance of conquest came from abroad in 1886, when the National Treasury (Skarb Narodowy) was founded by Ludwik

Michalski to raise funds for the promotion of the national cause. In the following year Zygmunt Miłkowski (pseud. Teodor Tomasz Jeż), a celebrated novelist with a distinguished career as a fighter for Polish freedom, founded in Switzerland at Hilfikon the Polish League (Liga Polska).[44] His pamphlet published in the same year and entitled *Rzecz o obronie czynnej i o skarbie narodowej* (An Essay on Active Defence and the National Treasury), as its title implies, demanded a national movement to combat foreign domination and especially russification. The Polish League demanded an end of Triloyalism. By its emphasis upon a national approach the Polish League rejected socialism and international solutions of foreign oppression. This was the resurrection of the spirit of competitive nationalism. The mood corresponded with that of the homeland. Efforts were being made to combat the lamentable educational policy of the Russian government. Circles for National Education (Koła Oświaty Narodowej) and the Union of Polish Youth (Związek Młodzieży Polskiej) generally known as 'Zet', led by Zygmunt Balicki, were to arise to organize classes in Polish language and literature. In April 1893 was founded the National League (Liga Narodowa), led by Roman Dmowski, controlled by a Secret Council and a Central Committee based upon Warsaw. Emphasis was placed upon the traditions of the past and upon the anniversaries of events of national importance. A demonstration on 17 April 1894 to commemorate the part played by the citizens of Warsaw in the Kościuszko insurrection of 1794 merely resulted in arrests, the closure of *Głos* and a decline in the activity of the Union of Polish Youth. The leadership of the National League transferred its activity to Galicia, where in the more backward conditions of an agricultural province it could settle down to the exposition of its narrow principles through the periodical, *Przegląd Wszechpolski* (All-Polish review). Its generalities amounted to little more than a plea for national solidarity against the alien rule of the tsarist government and even against the Russian people. Concentration upon the more abstract postulates of nationalism coupled with an undefined radicalism could win for the National League the reputation of being patriotic without its having at the same time to put forward a practical programme of activity. The evolution of the National League's programme in the end owed more to the possibilities of achieving concessions than to a finely worked out policy for the Poland of the future.

It was only the traditional ruling class of Poland which in the first instance could even so much as approach the Russian government. The 1890's offered the possibility of some relaxation of control. Alexander III died on 19 October/1 November 1894 and his successor, Nicholas II, had the opportunity to change the policy of Field Marshal Gurko, who had been the governor-general of Warsaw since 1883 and pursued in collaboration with the curator of the Warsaw Education District, Alexander Apukhtin, a policy of extreme russification. The new governors-general Pavel A. Shuvalov and Prince Alexander Imeretynsky, revealed more gentlemanly approaches to Polish questions which promoted hopes in the minds of the Polish upper classes that concessions might be possible. In November 1894 the leaders of the Polish salon society presented a loyal address to Nicholas II. In September 1897 the tsar visited Warsaw and received a contribution for charity of a million roubles from his Polish subjects. As ever, Zygmunt Wielopolski emerged to plead the cause of reconciliation. Likewise Count Władysław Tyszkiewicz produced in 1897 his *Zarys stosunków rosyjsko-polskich* (Outline of Russo-Polish Relations), which like other pamphlets of the time suggested moderate reforms such as the solution of contentious questions arising out of agrarian reform, the admission of Poles to the upper ranks of the administration and some relaxation of restrictions upon the use of the Polish language and the practice of the Roman Catholic religion. Leading financiers like the Natansons, Blochs and Kronenbergs would have liked some local self-government on the lines of the zemstvos in the Russian empire proper. All in effect the Polish upper classes wanted was to be taken into partnership with the dynasty. Imeretynsky thought that the Russian government might win the loyalties of the peasants who would become the basis of Russian rule in the Polish regions. There was the danger otherwise that they might become a prey to revolutionary propaganda. The workers too should be the object of official solicitude. Within this context some attempt at the reconciliation of the Polish educated classes might be attempted subject to the understanding that the former Polish territories in north western and south western Russia were to be assimilated and discriminatory legislation within them dropped. The concepts of Imeretynsky were limited no doubt by the knowledge that the mind of the Russian bureaucracy was itself limited in its vision. Unfortunately for the Polish upper classes some of the correspondence of the Russian administration fell into the hands of the Polish socialists, who published it together with the hostile comments of the tsar and the ministerial committee's rejection of the concepts of Imeretynsky's report for 1897.[45]

If the Russian government had accepted the proffered friendship of the Polish upper classes, it might have established a moderate liberal political movement, which, owing to its ability to obtain the amelioration of Polish conditions, could have enlarged its influence in the country. The hidebound inflexibility of thought in the Russian administration with regard to the Polish problem in the end was to bring about the very situation which the severity of control was designed to avoid. It is remarkable that the right-wing leaders of Poland persisted even into the First World War in the belief that conciliation was possible, but the fact remained that liberalism in the Western European sense was never to emerge as a powerful political force in Poland. For practical purposes the upper classes were compelled in the course of time to yield hegemony among the educated classes to the National Democractic Party (Stronnictwo Narodowo–Demokratyczne – SN-D), a political party founded under the auspices of the National League in 1897.

The National Democrats adopted the attitude that in the fight for the rights of Poles the struggle for social justice should take second place, because that would divide the nation by a class war and detract from efforts to obtain independence. The relations of capital and labour could, after the removal of Russian control, best be regulated in an independent Poland in which the spirit of industrial conciliation would prevail. The National Democrats were in fact the leaders of the lower middle class which saw the future in terms of their own prospects in a Polish state created within the frontiers which existed before 1772. They took their stand upon the emotive word *Polskość*, which is difficult to translate into English. It indicates at its worst the standards of ethics to which all Poles should be faithful despite what the commonly accepted precepts of morality might prescribe. Thus the National Democrats could understand no national aspirations other than their own. They attacked any manifestation of internationalism such as socialism. They adopted an attitude of hostility towards the Jews who were so heavily concentrated in the towns as shopkeepers, craftsmen and workers in light industry, and who therefore appeared as the competitors of those sections of the Christian Polish population which aspired to establish themselves in small businesses. National Democracy was a lower-middle-class populism, which bequeathed to the Polish political tradition an unpleasant and increasingly vicious element (see below pp. 71, 192). The logic of its position was that, in basing itself mainly upon the urban middle class and, where it could, on the conservative peasantry, it would come to adopt in time policies at variance with the radical anti-clerical nationalism which it professed at the outset and drift into the policy of compromise with tsarism already proposed by the upper classes, who themselves were to perceive the utility of association with National Democracy as the means of securing the basis for mass support. Those who were most vociferous in their declarations of patriotism were not always those who had the national cause most at heart.

The evolution of Polish socialism in the 1890's revealed a greater maturity as the prospect of mass support from the workers became more probable. Proletariat II had tended to think that terror directed by a conspiratorial organization might obtain political results, but the immediate improvement of the workers' lot was unlikely to be achieved by such means. In the 1890's the possibility arose of converting socialism from theoretical sympathy with the workers into a practical means of creating an organization to achieve redress of their grievances. Early failures could not conceal the fact that the discontent of labour would be a permanent factor in Polish political life. It was for this reason that a group of young socialists founded in the summer of 1889 the Union of Polish Workers (Związek Robotników Polskich – ZRP) in order to give a political form to working-class agitation. May Day was to be celebrated for the first time in 1890 as a festival of the workers in accordance with the resolution of the Second International, a concept which invited open struggle, because such a celebration could take the form of a one-day strike. The ZRP was split between the various views on how the workers' struggle ought to be conducted. Ludwik Krzywicki, who had been influential in Proletariat II, was opposed to the creation of a mass movement while the system of autocracy was maintained by tsarism, a view which argued in favour of terrorism. On the other hand, there were those like Jan Leder and Julian Marchlewski who believed in the strike weapon, which they tended to overemphasize, as a means of securing the workers' demands. Abroad the National Socialist Commune, founded in 1888, in which Bolesław Limanowski was a prominent leader, laid emphasis upon socialism as a weapon in the fight for independence rather than as a creed in an economic struggle. The Commune was in fact close to the views of the Polish League from which it received recognition in 1889.

The arguments of the intellectuals were resolved by the actions of the workers themselves. In May 1892 there occurred the Łódź uprising which demonstrated the capacity of the workers themselves to take action. Discontent at the end of April and at the beginning of May met with resolute police action. On Friday, 6 May, all the workers of Łódź came out on strike. The authorities had recourse to their usual tactics. A pogrom of the Jews was organized as a distraction, but the workers preferred to attack the police and the army, which succeeded in restoring order only on 9–10 May 1892. This was no ordinary disturbance. There were no less than 217 killed and wounded, and 350 persons arrested.[46] There could no longer be any doubt that the Polish workers were militant. The question was now whether Polish socialists could provide effective leadership and an effective programme. There were those who wished to place working-class discontent within a national context. Stanisław Grabski and Stanisław

Mendelson believed in the re-establishment of Polish independence through a war of the European great powers, for which reason the Polish socialist movement ought to maintain its independence of the Russian revolutionary movement and seek to build a new Poland upon the basis of separation and the creation of a democratic federation with Lithuania and Byelorussia. The difference between this kind of approach and that of the National Democrats lay merely in the choice of the force within Polish society which should achieve independence.

It was in the light of this thinking that the so-called Paris Conference took place from 17 to 21 November 1892, which embraced socialists from Russian Poland, representing Proletariat, 'Unification' (Zjednoczenie), which was a splinter group formed from members of Proletariat, the ZRP and the National Socialist Commune under the chairmanship of Limanowski. The decision was taken to form the Union of Polish Socialists Abroad (Związek Zagraniczny Socjalistów Polskich), which would work for the creation of a socialist party at home. The principles adopted by the Paris conference were printed in *Przedświt* in 1893 in the form of an 'Outline of the Programme of a Polish Socialist Party'.[47] Among the demands was

2. The grant of absolute equality to the nationalities entering into the composition of the republic on the basis of voluntary federation.

Though the traditional demands of socialist movements were included in the programme, fundamental to the thinking of the Paris Conference was the establishment of a federal Poland, by implication in the frontiers of the eighteenth century, within which obviously the Poles would be the dominant element. Within Poland the ZRP and Proletariat II joined together to form the Polish Socialist Party (Polska Partia Socjalistyczna – PPS). The PPS did not receive the support of the Union of Polish Socialists Abroad, nor did it accept its direction or take kindly to the disgraceful suggestion that Marcin Kasprzak, who had disagreed with views of the periodical *Przedświt*, was an agent of the Russian police. The perennial difficulty of Poland under foreign control was the belief of Poles abroad that they had a prescriptive right to bring their superior wisdom to the solution of problems at home, while those at home who had to bear the brunt of oppression thought always that their closer acquaintance with the prevailing conditions of the country entitled them to the formulation of policy.

The 'Outline of the Programme of a Polish Socialist Party' was rejected at a meeting on 30 July 1893 and the dissidents established a party which went by the name of the Social Democracy of the Kingdom of Poland

(Socjaldemokracja Królestwa Polskiego – SDKP), which was itself supported by a publication abroad entitled *Sprawa Robotnicza* (The Workers' Cause), edited in Paris by Rosa Luxemburg, Leon Tyszka-Jogiches, Adolf Warski-Warszawski and Julian Marchlewski. The aim of the Social Democrats was to found a party based upon the internationalism of the workers' cause. The new party duly held its first congress on 10–11 March 1894.[48] It is, however, difficult to suppose that in the first years of their activity the Polish Social Democrats were effective proponents of the interests of the working class. The party's base was narrow and arrests deprived it of its leadership. In October 1893 the leadership in Łódź was sadly depleted and in 1894 further arrests were made in Żyrardów and Warsaw. Almost all of the members of the First Congress found themselves in prison and all that remained of the party was a small cadre within Poland and the distinguished group led by Rosa Luxemburg abroad. Rosa Luxemburg enjoyed an undeserved prominence in the affairs of the SDKP as a principal theorist of the party, removed from the actual political struggle at home and drawn more and more into the realm of international and German socialism.[49] It was not until the arrival in Warsaw of Felix Dzierzyński in September 1899 that the remnants of the SDKP could reassemble and join in 1900 with Polish Social Democrats in western Russia to form the Social Democracy of the Kingdom of Poland and Lithuania (Socjaldemokracja Królestwa Polskiego i Litwy – SDKPiL).

Far more important was the Polish Socialist Party which emerged on the right wing of the working-class movement. In February 1894 the so-called Second congress of the PPS was held in Warsaw, on the grounds that the First Congress had taken place in Vilna in June 1893, though this meeting was virtually only a preparatory session. The congress established a central committee, of which the most important members were Jan Stróżecki, the Lithuanian and future ruler of Poland, Józef Piłsudski, and Stanisław Wojciechowski, who was to be the president of Poland from 1922 to 14 May 1926, when Piłsudski's *coup d'état* forced him from office. In fact, the central committee was more powerful than the party itself, because it selected the local representatives who constituted the party congress and at the same time had the support of the Union of Polish Socialists Abroad with its excellent publicity service. Within Poland a new paper, *Robotnik* (The Worker) achieved a wide circulation. The Social Democrats held their own against the PPS until the arrests of 1894–5 which left the country open to the activity of socialists, but there was already within the PPS some hostility to the Union of Polish Socialists Abroad and its view on the national struggle for independence. At the Third Congress in June 1895 internationalist views carried the day and a motion was passed for association with the revolutionary parties of Russia. The congress, moreover, declared that no member of the party could belong to another secret organization, which meant that members could not at the same time join in the efforts of the National League. The leadership of the party, however, maintained its position owing to the arrest of left-wing activists. Piłsudski, Wojciechowski, Stanisław Grabski, Witold Jodko-Narkiewicz, Leon Wasilewski and Władysław Studnicki were a formidable combination which forced upon the party the concept of a national approach to socialism and claimed for the PPS a leading role in the Kingdom of Poland and in the provinces of north western and south western Russia, but concentration upon propaganda against tsarism at the expense of the day-to-day struggle of the workers gave rise to some discontent in the lower ranks of the party. Nevertheless, since the PPS was in effect the only party which defended the interests of the workers after the collapse of the SDKPiL, it continued to attract support. Only in the course of time was the left wing at home able to challenge the leadership.

Abroad the leadership of the PPS succeeded in excluding Rosa Luxemburg from participation in the conference of the Second International at Zurich in 1893. At the next conference in London in July 1896, however, the proposal of the PPS that the International should embody in its programme the demand for the reconstruction of Poland met with opposition, because a call for an offer of support to the cause of one nation alone was inconsistent with the policy of a movement which supported the doctrine of self-determination for all peoples. Rosa Luxemburg, who was admitted to the conference in 1896, had declared in 1895 in her pamphlet *Niepodległość Polski a sprawa robotnicza* (The Independence of Poland and the Workers' Cause) that nationalism was a distraction from the real fight for social justice. The view of the International, therefore, was at variance equally with the policy of both the PPS and the SDKP, but Rosa Luxemburg doggedly persisted in her condemnation of what she termed 'social patriotism' which in her view destroyed the solidarity of the working class by introducing discordant elements into the struggle.[50] Just as the PPS went too far in its refusal to collaborate with the Russian revolutionaries, so the SDKP introduced an unnecessary irritant by insisting upon the doctrine of pure internationalism in circumstances in which Poles in Russian Poland were forbidden to use their own language in their dealings with the administration. Rosa Luxemburg's insistence upon internationalism was as divisive for the solidarity of the Polish working class as the claim of the PPS to speak exclusively for it. As it was, the PPS suffered a severe blow on the night of 21–22 February 1900 when the printing works of *Robotnik* was discovered in Łódź and Józef Piłsudski arrested. The actual direction of the PPS activity tended to move into the hands of the largest single element within the country, the Warsaw district committee.

The achievement of Polish socialism in its broadest sense in the 1890's was that it had begun slowly to give direction to the cause of the workers. The tsarist government itself had come to the conclusion that it too must enter into competition for the respect of the working class. Elementary labour legislation, however, could scarcely disguise the fact that it was brought into existence by the decrees of an autocratic government. The fundamental fact remained that no section of the working class could form an association in defence of its interests without suffering police persecution.

Poland at the end of the nineteenth century

The end of a century in the Christian calendar does not necessarily mean the end of one epoch and the beginning of another, but in the case of Poland there is evidence of change in or around the year 1900. Polish thought and culture developed up to 1900 in a climate of induced stability, when the three partitioning powers had undertaken few steps one against another which might lead to a general conflict, but in the 1890's the first evidence of potential instability began to appear with the transfer of Russian interest to the Far East, where an armed conflict might ultimately be expected, and the rapid expansion of Russian industry which brought into existence a working class capable eventually of challenging the tsarist system of government. In the first instance after the collapse of the rising of 1863–4 there was a strong reaction against the romanticism of the earlier epoch and emphasis was laid upon the mundane virtues of scientific study, but as the century drew to a close the acceptance of foreign domination became less attractive. The arts and literature began to respond to the change of mood under the influence of the movement known as Young Poland (Młoda Polska).

In the early stages of the period after the uprisings, Poland suffered from lack of endowment for a normal cultural life, which caused many talented Poles to leave the coutry to make careers abroad. Among the most famous were Joseph Conrad and Ignacy Paderewski. Like many Polish scientific workers, Maria Curie-Skłodowska made her reputation abroad. Two future presidents of Poland, Gabriel Narutowicz and Ignacy Mościcki, first made their reputations as scientists in Switzerland. The dispersal of talent, however, did not cause very serious losses. The real problem lay in the Polish need to create a system of cultural and scientific patronage for themselves. An important role was played by the Academy of Sciences and

Letters (Akademia Umiętnośći), established in Cracow in 1872–3, covering all branches of learning. The Poznanian Society of the Friends of Learning (Poznańskie Towarzystwo Przyjaciół Nauk), founded in 1876, together with the Toruń Society of the Friends of Learning (Toruńskie Towarzystwo Przyjaciół Nauk), set up in 1876, kept alive Polish academic activity in the hostile atmosphere of Prussian Poland. The Poles in Russian Poland were not so well served, but the Mianowski Fund (Kasa im. Mianowskiego) financed the publication of scholarly works from its foundation in 1881. Galicia provided an excellent university education at Lwów and Cracow, in which teaching was conducted in Polish, but inevitably thought was influenced by the extreme conservatism of Galician politics and the reactionary attitudes of the Roman church. In 1869 the Main School (Szkoła Głowna), which had provided in Warsaw the equivalent of a university education, was suppressed, and in its place was established the University of Warsaw, in which the language instruction was Russian, though at the end of the century it had over 1,000 Polish students. Only in 1898 was the Warsaw Polytechnic founded. In Poznań nothing could be hoped for from an indifferent and hostile Prussian government. Education was good, but it was designed to convert Poles into Germans. When the Prussian government did decide to raise the level of learning in Poznań it was with the purpose of making the town an outpost of germanism. If Poles wished to obtain a higher education, there was good reason not to seek it in Poland but to go abroad either to Russia proper, or to Germany, Belgium and France. So far from destroying Polish learning and culture, the fact of partition gave Poles a deeper appreciation of the culture of other countries in continental Europe and a determination to hold their own against total absorption. It was only Great Britain among the European states which remained relatively unfamiliar to Poles. British culture was appreciated, but the concepts of British society were not understood. The Polish discovery of Britain has been a feature of the second half of the twentieth century.

At the foundations of Polish society there existed a people often deprived of basic education, concerned more with the everyday problems of winning a living in adverse circumstances. At the higher level Poles were conscious of a duty to establish for a country which did not exist in international law an identity which all could recognize. A central position was occupied by the historians, whose first conference took place in Cracow in 1880. Already steps had been taken to emphasize the achievements of Poland in the past. The first volume of *Monumenta Poloniae Historica* appeared in 1864, while *Scriptores Rerum Polonicarum* was begun in 1872. *Kwartalnik Historyczny* (Historical Quarterly) followed in 1887.

Poland was thus abreast of other countries in this field. The schools of history at Cracow and Lwów reflected the views of Galician society. Józef Szujski and Walerian Kalinka assessed critically the insurrectionary tradition and want of statesmanship in the past, thus by implication bestowing upon the Galician régime the accolade of academic approval. Michał Bobrzyński brought to the study of history in his *Dzieje Polski w zarysie* (The History of Poland in Outline), first published in 1879, the concept that the error of the past had been the want of strong government, for which even the church had in part been responsible. The outlook of the Warsaw historians, confronted with daily evidence of foreign rule, was different. They looked back to the state which Poland might have created but for the partitions. Tadeusz Korzon produced his classic work, *Dzieje wewnętrzne Polski za Stanisława Augusta* (The Internal History of Poland under Stanisław August) in 1886, which revealed that Polish society had exhibited a capacity to reform itself which partition had frustrated. A similar point of view was taken by Władysław Smoleński, who in his *Dzieje narodu polskiego* (History of the Polish Nation), published in Cracow in 1897–8, emphasized the signs of a national renaissance in the past which held out hope for independence in the future, in contrast with the Cracow School which perceived virtue in the limited autonomy and national identity achieved in Galicia.

In the field of literature the prolific novelist Józef Ignacy Kraszewski (B. Bolesławita) moved into a position of accepting the outlook of Warsaw Positivism, whereas Zygmunt Miłkowski (T. T. Jeż) emphasized fidelity to the ideals of the insurrections. Literary attitudes responded to the social changes which industrialization and new economic facts brought about. Eliza Orzeszkowa, Bolesław Prus (Alexander Głowacki) and Maria Konopnicka moved forward into the realm of social criticism, declaring against the consequences of the concepts of Organic Work. In the field of the historical novel Henryk Sienkiewicz represented the desire to maintain the patriotic traditions, but in his *Faraon* (Pharoah), first published in 1897, Bolesław Prus used a theme of ancient Egypt to investigate problems of political organization and the need for reform. The Realist movement, as it is called, gave way in its turn to Young Poland (Młoda Polska), emerging in the years from 1890 to 1900, in which some tendency was exhibited to a return to romanticism. While on the one hand the desire for independence remained, on the other interest moved towards universal artistic forms and concepts. To some extent the movement away from the central theme of national liberation indicates that a silent victory had been won. Polish writers, poets and dramatists had preserved a national tradition, from which a shift to normality in the sense that literary criticism, the theatre, poesy, and all forms of artistic expression no longer centred upon the question of national identity, indicated a basic national self-confidence. Foreign occupation could determine political conditions, but the subtleties of culture escaped the officials who controlled what for them was merely territory. Poland was to emerge with its own artistic traditions, invigorated by association with above all the German and Russian influences, but distinct because it drew upon its own inspirations. In the cultural sense Poland existed. In the political sense it was necessary to create it.

Polish politics, however, developed in abnormal conditions. Poles could not grasp at real power to shape the present or future of their own country. All educated Poles sought to play their part in the development of the community. It is noticeable that Polish historians seek to give credit to each Pole who had proved his patriotism, associating with each patriotic activity meaningless lists of names. In a normal society patriotism is taken for granted, and experience of political power eliminates the incompetent and elevates the able. In Poland, however, no one could be elevated to a position of power and there were therefore more contenders for distinction when once political independence had been achieved. The Austrian Reichsrat was a poor training for a politician in anything except interest politics, while the Reichstag and the Prussian parliament offered no avenues to political power. The multiplicity of Polish economic, political, cultural and education associations threw up a political class in which there was a strange mixture of ability and mediocrity, with inherited attitudes towards Poland's neighbours and those national minorities which would fall within the compass of the new Poland. A nation existed, but it was denied the right to rule itself. Its future rulers received their training in the unreal conditions in which few of them ever administered a government department, except in Galicia or Vienna, and in which most of them would not have been surprised to be arrested, deported, or compelled to flee. This was the society in which the future leaders of Poland emerged: Józef Piłsudski, Ignacy Daszyński, Stanisław and Władysław Grabski, Stanisław Wojciechówski, Roman Dmowski, Tomasz Arciszewski, Ignacy Paderewski and others. It is open to question whether any of them would have risen to great distinction in a country with normal constitutional government.

Poland and the crisis of 1900–7

The Polish Question did not exist in 1900, but the Great Powers were gradually edging themselves towards an international crisis which would bring it into existence along with other seemingly dormant problems even older than the problem of Poland. Already in 1891 the beginning of the construction of the Trans-Siberian Railway gave notice that tsarist Russia intended within the foreseeable future to become in fact as well as in theory a great power in the Pacific and no longer acquiesce in a position of inferiority. The Sino-Japanese War of 1894–5 resulted from Japan's determination to anticipate the advance of Russia's real power in the Far East. The German initiative which led to the modification of the Treaty of Shimonoseki in 1895 was a precursor of an interest which became actual in 1897 with the German seizure of Kiaochow. The tentative commitment of tsarist Russia to a forward foreign policy by the seizure of Port Arthur in 1897 and the occupation of Manchuria in October 1900 were followed by a long debate upon the real aims of Russian policy. The *Weltpolitik* pursued by imperial Germany was hardly likely to bring in its train economic and political disasters, but in Russia the Ministry of Internal Affairs was conscious that a policy which put pressure upon the population of the European provinces might cause political upsets likely to call into question the entire system of autocratic government, while the Ministry of Finance knew well that Russia was too weak to sustain an ambitious programme of expansion so far away from the developed areas. The Ministry of Foreign Affairs disliked a policy which it did not entirely shape, while the Ministry of War had doubts about the capacity of the army to hold its own with lines of communication so gravely extended. The ultimate tragedy of the Russo-Japanese War of 1904–5 had its roots in a system of government which did not take the people into partnership. Expectation of automatic obedience and the absence of the corrective of informed and powerful public opinion led tsarism into a crisis which threatened with destruction the system of government which the military monarchy had created. For the peoples of the Russian empire the prospect appeared of relief from the stultifying control of the bureaucracy. For the

Poles of the empire and of the Kingdom of Poland there was hope that the grant of civil liberties normal in constitutional countries would be accompanied by the opportunity to develop their own national institutions. Consciousness of opportunity, however, was to expose the fissures which existed in Polish society.

The Kingdom of Poland and the crisis

The Kingdom of Poland followed the pattern of tsarist Russia in its development and shared in its crises. In 1900 the Kingdom accounted for about 12 per cent of the productive forces of Russia. The rapacious character of capitalism in Russia and its reliance upon foreign investment ensured that in the event of a crisis it would be more severely affected than countries which had experienced an earlier and more leisurely development. The first signs of a monetary crisis appeared in August 1899. Owing to the fixing of the rouble's value in 1897 by the introduction of the gold standard, the government was unable to meet the crisis by the issue of notes. As the foreign banks raised their interest rates, so the State Bank of Russia was compelled to follow suit. In order to meet their own domestic difficulties, foreign banks began to withdraw their capital from Russia. The period of rapid expansion of the 1890's had come to an end and share prices began to fall, especially in the mining and metallurgical industries, but textiles also felt the effect. A curious feature of the crisis, however, was the advantage taken of it by German investors who took the opportunity of strengthening their hold upon Polish industry in the Kingdom of Poland. The Commercial Bank (Bank Handlowy) likewise bought up shares cheaply and extended its control over industry. By 1903 the production of iron ore had fallen to 35.2 per cent by comparison with 1899, while by 1905 the mining of hard coal amounted to only 86.4 per cent of the figure for 1900. In this crisis many small firms went into liquidation, while the larger concerns sought refuge in cartelization. In any reorganization industries in the Kingdom of Poland were bound to suffer to some extent from the Russian government's policy of showing preference to production in the interior of Russia.[1]

The tsarist government was well aware of the troubles which depression might bring in its train. The late 1890's had already shown that the working class in Russia itself was stirring. The answer which the government found was the introduction of factory legislation, combined with a tightening of security, especially in the border regions of the empire. The Finns from 1900 found that relative docility did not prevent the government from attacking their liberties. In the Kingdom of Poland and western Russia generally tsarist policy was more severe. Sentences of hard labour and floggings were the fate of those who voiced their discontents in public demonstrations. In 1900 the Warsaw chief of police had his powers reinforced by the establishment of the Department for the Defence of Order and Public Security, the infamous Okhrana, which extended its tentacles into every aspect of Polish life through its informers and *agents provocateurs*. The death of the governor-general of Warsaw, Alexander Imeretynsky, in 1900 removed a voice of relative moderation. His successor, Mikhail Chertkov, was a man who saw no reason for accommodation with the Poles. It was the common people, especially the working class of the towns, upon whom cynically indifferent employers and heavy-handed bureaucrats pressed so hard.

In the years from 1900 to 1904 the working class of Warsaw, Łódź and the major industrial towns each May Day gave evidence of their rooted hostility to the régime. Here and there in the countryside there were peasant disturbances. The University of Warsaw and the other institutes of higher and technical education were alive with discontent. In a country where normal political associations were forbidden it was difficult to maintain sustained activity. In 1900 the PPS had suffered a major setback when the printing works of *Robotnik* were discovered by the police. Piłsudski and many active leaders were under arrest. It was not until the Sixth Congress of the party in June 1902 that a reorganization could be carried out. The local Workers' Committees were in theory organized by an enlarged Central Workers' Committee. Its meetings were in fact infrequent and real power lay in the hands of the Executive Committee (Komitet Wykonawczy – KW), dominated by the older elements, the so-called 'Seniors' (Starzy). The local organizers, however, the 'Juniors' (Młodzi), resented the directing role of the Executive Committee, which was not always in tune with the feeling within the country. The influence of the Seniors was increased by the fact that much of the theoretical writings of the party issued from the Foreign Committee of the Central Committee (Komitet Zagraniczny – KZ), in which the most active figures were Bolesław Jędrzejewski, Witold Jodko-Narkiewicz and Leon Wasilewski. When the Foreign Committee moved from London to Cracow it came into closer contact with feeling at home, but it associated itself with the Polish Social Democratic Party of Galicia and Silesia (Cieszyn).

The influence of the party now extended throughout the Polish areas of Russia as far as Białystok, Vilna, Grodno, Kiev, St Petersburg and Moscow, but its influence was not uniform. On the whole it was stronger among the industrial workers than among the craftsmen and white-collar workers. The propaganda of the party was directed against Russian domination in all its forms and, therefore, against those elements in Polish society which could see the possibility of a compromise with tsarism, but the party under the influence of the Seniors saw itself as having an essentially national role which excluded the possibility of co-operation with other left-wing parties with internationalist views. The general view of the Seniors was that the PPS should fight for a constitutional system in which socialism could develop as it had elsewhere. Thus the national ends of the party in essence took precedence over the achievement of social justice. The problem of the relationship with the Russian Social Democratic Workers' Party remained unresolved. The concept of Lenin that all parties opposed to tsarism should join in a common struggle was rejected, though Lenin thought that the Poles were entitled to independence. The Seniors were reared in the traditions of armed uprising and war against Russia, which in the circumstances of the early years of the twentieth century was as yet scarcely realistic. The Seniors had little confidence in the ability of the Russians themselves to overthrow tsarism. From their point of view the real problem was relations with the non-Russian inhabitants of the north western and south western *gubernii* of the empire, in other words the pre-1772 provinces of the former Polish Republic. Concepts of a federal system in which the Letts, Lithuanians, Byelorussians, and Ukrainians joined in a common union coincided unhappily with independence within the area of Polish landlordism, which would survive in the constitutional state for which the Polish socialists strove. Even the cultivated Kazimierz Kelles-Krauz could convince himself that Poland and her civilization were attractive to the non-Polish nationalities of the east:

A certain part of the lands, which once belonged to the Republic, even today incline towards Poland as a hearth of civilization, as a link between them and Europe. The development of Polish civilization is identified more and more with the development of Polish socialism. Thus the role of that hearth, of that centre of attraction, and link passes to the Polish Socialist Party. How far the influence of the Polish Socialist Party, in other words of Poland, will extend in the moment of revolution, we do not undertake to draw on the map, but with that limitation this party will try to separate these territories from Russia. It is possible to foresee that this separation will embrace besides Poland, Lithuania, Latvia, Livonia, Courland, perhaps part of White Russia... Most probably Lithuania and Latvia will form with Poland one body politic, based upon the principles of autonomy and the guarantee of completely free national development, while Poland will be joined with Ruthenia in a looser union.[2]

Such ideas contained a degree of presumption which rested ultimately upon the concept of Central as opposed to Eastern Europe being the focal point of the coming revolution.[3]

The position of the PPS would perhaps have been more understandable if it had been the only claimant upon the loyalties of the working class. Already in 1900 Ludwik Kulczycki had led a secession and formed the Polish Socialist Party – Proletariat – commonly known as the Proletariat III, to distinguish it from the two previous organizations which went by that name. Proletariat III was ready to accept the possibility of a revolution in Russia leading either to independence or self-government for Poland, but its influence was limited owing to its emphasis upon the weapon of terror. A more important element in the PPS was the Juniors, who found the exercise of control by the Seniors vexatious, but their opposition was to appear only later under the pressure of events in 1905. An actual competitor of the PPS was the SDKPiL. In 1899–1900 the Social Democrats like the socialists experienced the dissolution of its organization within Poland, especially when Felix Dzierżyński was arrested in Warsaw on 4 February 1900, but it was soon reconstructed with an influence extending to the same area as the PPS. The section of the population to which it had most appeal tended to consist of craftsmen, shoemakers, tanners, and bakers, though it had some influence among the textile workers of Łódź and Białystok. It was less strongly based among the miners, foundrymen and metal workers, and had virtually no support among the white-collar workers. The resolutions of the Third Congress held near Warsaw at Otwock on 28–29 September 1901 revealed the rejection of the concept of Polish independence. Its programme in this respect differed from that of the socialists in one important respect:

The Conference resolves: Standing on the ground of reality the party does not enter into a definition of the hypothetical paths of political development for Poland and Lithuania in the distant future, but in every circumstance it will try to exploit the situation in favour of the widest possible autonomy for the Polish and Lithuanian peoples, declaring its demands for the present in the form of a demand for constitutional democracy on the basis of the complete autonomy of these peoples, as also for all the inhabitants of the Russian state.[4]

The prime enemy of the people was tsarism, which could be fought only by solidarity of which national hatred and chauvinism were the negation. Thus the Social Democrats could propose a federal organization to the Russian, Lithuanian and Jewish Social Democrats, declare that theoretical controversy with the Polish Socialist Party and the Lithuanian Social Democrats was fruitless, even though their tactics might be criticized, and recognize the Jewish Bund as a fraternal organization.

Any working-class organization which sought to extend its influence had to take into account the General Jewish Workers' Union, or Bund, which could appeal to about 52 per cent of the urban population of Byelorussia and Lithuania employed mainly in the crafts.[5] The proportion of Jews was lower in the Kingdom of Poland and Białystok. The Bund, however, did not conceive its policy in terms of union with the other Social Democratic groupings, on the ground that it alone represented the Jewish workers of the Russian empire. The PPS showed some distaste for Jewish movements in western Russia, because Jews there tended to learn Russian and absorb Russian culture, but the pogroms organized by the tsarist administration, especially the massacre at Kishinev of 6–7/19–20 April 1903, in which fifty persons were killed, won for them Polish sympathy. Nevertheless, the Bund could not bring itself to continue its association with the Russian Social Democrats and seceded from the conference of July–August 1903. The Polish Social Democrats adopted the equally unco-operative attitude of Rosa Luxemburg, who sought to establish the correctness of her own position in respect of Lenin's article in Number 44 of *Iskra*, entitled 'The National Question in our Programme', in which he declared that the Poles might declare in favour of a free and independent republic.[6] Rosa Luxemburg instructed Adolf Warski-Warszawski to withhold the party's federal association with the Russian Social Democratic Workers' Party on the grounds that in the light of Lenin's arguments 'the moral value of our joining the Russians (a device against the Polish Socialist Party) is minimal for us, and we are concerned only with the moral factor'.[7] The theory and practice of Rosa Luxemburg's socialism in 1903 bore little relation to the problems of combating tsarism. The left-wing movement in Poland tended to fragment, like left-wing movements elsewhere, with the desire of each revolutionary party to convert the working class to its own exclusive brand of socialist purity. The principal rivals, the PPS and the SDKPiL, who divided upon the fundamental question of whether the class struggle or the national cause should take priority in the working-class programmes, were in fact not well prepared to meet the crisis when it came in 1905. The practical problems of revolution were to some extent to concentrate the minds of the socialist leaders.

The upper and middle classes

The upper and middle classes of Poland were not condemned to under-ground and clandestine activity like the revolutionaries. They could become members of boards of directors or technical specialists in industry. In this way they were absorbed into the Russian economic system. Those of them who lived in the Russian empire proper tended to think in terms of compromise and reconciliation, knowing that they were vulnerable not only to discriminatory Russian legislation, but also were the object of criticism from the non-Polish nationalities of north western and south western Russia. The upper classes of the Kingdom of Poland knew well enough that a revolutionary socialist movement existed all around them in the cities and a traditionally disgruntled peasantry had grown in size to add land hunger to its discontents. The extreme conservative landlords waged a class war with an undisguised display of self-interest, but there were others who believed that timely concessions would secure them from the worst excesses of agrarian violence. The industrialists relied upon the Russian authorities to bring police and troops to their assistance when the workers offered resistance to them. The Catholic church under the leadership of the archbishop, Wincenty Popiel, used its influence in many bad causes, attacking the Jews, condemning strikes and socialism, and pronouncing against any movement which seemed likely to bring enlightenment to the masses.

Real political influence, however, by the beginning of the century lay with the National Democrats, who could appeal to the mass of the *déclassé szlachta* who now constituted the middle class. Through the Union of Polish Youth (Zet) it established an organizational network in the cities and set up the Jan Kiliński Union (Związek im. Jana Kilińskiego), named after the shoemaker hero of the 1794 Warsaw insurrection, to enlist the support of the working class. The Society for National Education (Towarzystwo Oświaty Narodowej) sought to establish a following among the peasantry. As the National Democratic movement increased in strength, so its ideology began to take on a more precise form. The narrow-minded philosophy of the Polish middle classes was summarized by Roman Dmowski in 1902 in his *Myśli nowoczesnego Polaka* (Thoughts of a Modern Pole), and by Zygmunt Balicki in his *Egoizm narodowy wobec etyki* (National Egoism and Ethics) published in 1903. It was they who bequeathed to modern Polish nationalism the concept that the Nation is the pinnacle of all morality. Any feelings of compassion towards other nations was correspondingly immoral: 'An example would be the support of Czechs for German charitable institutions, or the despatch by Poles of gifts for the hungry in Russia.'[8] From this point of view socialism could be condemned as unpatriotic:

A social class which might feel a sense of solidarity with the same class of another nation, a party for which an international community of principles has greater weight than the community of national traditions and interests, a social circle which enters into daily contact and social relations with circles of an enemy society...deserves absolute condemnation from the point of view of public morality...for putting the egoism of their own altruism above the altruism binding upon them in virture of national egoism.[9]

The Russians were the object of the National Democrats' dislike, but it extended also to the Lithuanians and to the Ukrainians, though a voluntary federal union with them might ultimately be possible. In this way the political programme came close to proposing the restoration of Poland within the pre-1772 frontiers. A Polish supremacy was regarded as a natural end for which to aim. The Jews were condemned as an alien element within Polish society, who in the circumstances of economic crisis competed with the Polish lower middle class. Anti-semitism could enlist the support of certain sections of the Polish population, of which the pogrom at Częstochowa of 11 September 1903 was evidence.

The National Democrats attacked the upper classes who sought compromise with Russia, but there were wealthy persons who began to perceive that they did offer the possibility of creating a mass movement which was not socialist, and were therefore deserving of financial support. In theory the National Democrats attacked the Roman church, but they shared with it an anti-semitic programme and attracted members of the lesser clergy. Roman Catholicism was therefore declared now to be an attribute of the Polish nation. The country which the National Democrats most admired was Britain, in their view an imperial and at the same time conservative state. It was even hoped that Britain would favour the creation of a Polish state as a counterweight to Russia, strengthening British policy in Asia. With the deepening of the crisis after 1900 and the opening of war with Japan, the claim by the National Democrats that they alone represented the national cause began to wear thin. The danger of mass action by the Polish working class, on the one hand, and on the other the prospect that the Russian government might make concessions in order to meet the crisis half way revealed the advantages of limiting National Democratic demands to proposals for local government, the use of the Polish language in schools and the administration, and observance of the separate character of the Kingdom of Poland. Spiritually they were chauvinistic nationalists, but politically their attitudes were those of career-minded *déclassé szlachta*. For practical purposes they accepted the political aims of the Polish upper classes. Ludwik Kulczycki bitterly attacked Roman Dmowski for his fundamental lack of culture. In his view National Democracy was an umbrella organization: 'All those who do not wish openly to confess that they have no desire for a positive policy demanding sacrifices, and who fear all kinds of "isms" and want at the same time to appear as and pass for "good Poles", have joined the National Democracy.'[10] For him they were the enemies of the people, dragging along with them the Christian lower middle class with a programme of anti-semitism: 'They are harmful not so much because they are conservatives, but above all because they are barbarians, ignorant people, lowering the level of political education in the nation.'[11] This is not an unperceptive view of politicians whose lineal successors found so much attractive in Mussolini's Italy and Franco's Spain (see below pp. 181, 192).[12]

The Russo-Japanese war and the domestic crisis

The Japanese attacked the Russians at Port Arthur on the night of 8–9 February 1904 without the formality of a declaration of war, but tsarist Russia had adopted an attitude of overt hostility and accepted the possibility of a Japanese attack which would exonerate the ruling circles in Russia from all blame for the outbreak of war. In fact, Russian public opinion revealed no deep attachment to the Far Eastern policy of the tsar and his advisers. There was a flicker of nationalist sentiment in Russia proper, encouraged by the government, but there was a poor response in the non-Russian territories on the periphery of the state. For the majority of the inhabitants of Russian Poland the struggle was meaningless. The Polish Question had been associated with many strange causes, but never with Russia's policy towards Japan. Predictably the Polish upper classes sought to establish their own respectability by demonstrations of loyalty. They had persisted in declarations of solidarity, of which the address to Nicholas II of 7 November 1904 was but another example. In his pastoral letter of 12 October 1904 the archbishop, Wincenty Popiel, had declared against socialism as being subversive of all institutions. The war brought in its train collections for the army, contributions for the establishment of an ambulance unit and prayers for the success of Russian arms in the Cathedral of St John in Warsaw. The war did not in fact prosper. The extended crisis of 1900–3 was deepened in February 1904. The needs of the army diverted industry from normal peacetime production. Shortages led to speculation in conditions of unemployment and declining production. In the Kingdom of Poland floods led to food shortages. Floods in the spring were followed by a severe drought and lack of fodder. The poor performance of the Russian army in the Far East shook the credit of Russia in the international money markets. The cost of the war amounted to 2,000,000 roubles a day, which could be covered only by foreign loans at a ruinous rate of interest. For the year 1905 no less than 30 per cent of the budget was assigned to the costs of the war. Increases in direct and indirect taxation bore heavily upon a population whose capacity to pay was limited by the general rise of food prices and the growth of unemployment. In the Kingdom of Poland the urban middle class converted its savings into foreign currency and deposited them in foreign banks. Polish merchants trading with the interior of Russia suffered from the bankruptcies of their Russian customers, or from their reluctance to honour their debts. In July 1904 23 per cent of the bills of exchange in the Warsaw branch of the State Bank were not honoured. The priority given to the needs of the army resulted in the disruption of rail services. Consignments of goods remained undespatched in the railway sidings. To an unpopular war were added popular discontents.

There was no doubt of the hostility of the Polish peasants and workers to a war in which they had no interest. In common with the workers of the Russian cities the workers of Warsaw declared their opposition to the mobilization, but in the last quarter of the year 1904 demonstrations spread to all the Polish towns. The May Day of 1904 marked the beginning of serious demonstrations, the most drastic of which took place on the Plac Grzybowski on Sunday, 13 November 1904, when workers led by the PPS under Józef Kwiatek and Walery Sławek, among whom some were armed, clashed with the police and army. Hundreds of arrests were made and six persons were killed and twenty-seven wounded. In such a situation something more than expressions of loyalty were required of the Polish upper classes. They were caught between the two forces of tsarism and the working classes. The consciousness on the other hand of an impending crisis whetted the appetite of the propertied classes with expectations that concessions would be made to them. On 15/28 July 1904 the minister of the interior, Plehve, was assassinated in St Petersburg by the Socialist Revolutionary Sazonov. In Plehve's place was appointed the governor-general of Vilna, Prince Piotr Svyatopolk-Mirsky, whose reputation for moderation in contrast with the brutal severity of his predecessor seemed to offer possibility of reform. Indeed his first important pronouncement was a speech to the senior officials of his ministry declaring his conviction that the government must establish conditions of mutual trust between itself and the population at large. The liberal opposition in Russia which had been ignored or disgraced by Plehve was allowed to raise its head. A conference of zemstvo representatives was held from 19 to 22 November 1904. Svyatopolk-Mirsky boiled down their views and presented his own plan of reform on 23 November/6 December 1904, in which he proposed a state council with consultative rather than legislative functions, in which elected representatives of the zemstvos might take part. The special committee which considered this plan could not agree even to this limited concession. Instead an ukase was published on 12/25 December 1904, promising only solicitude for the peasants, state insurance for the industrial workers, revision of laws relating to the Jews, relaxation of the censorship, and minor judicial reforms. Initiative was to rest with the government and no steps were to be taken to limit the powers of the autocracy by any system of representation. The limit of the pressure of Russian liberals upon the government was a banquet agitation, but autocratic governments were not commonly shaken in their resolve by opponents' toasts to reform and their well-fed bellies.

Of greater interest to the understanding of the Polish problem was the conference which took place in Paris in November 1904 of representatives of the opposition parties in Russia. The groups taking part in the discussions included the Liberation Movement (Soyus Osvobodzheniya), which had been established in St Petersburg in January 1904, the Socialist Revolutionaries, Finnish, Georgian and Armenian nationalists, and from Poland the National League, represented by Dmowski and Balicki, and the PPS represented by the Seniors, Piłsudski, Alexander Malinowski, Jodko-Narkiewicz and Kelles-Krauz. No concrete proposals emerged, except that the parties would work for the introduction of universal suffrage and the calling of a constituent assembly.

The participation of Piłsudski and Dmowski in the conference is instructive. Piłsudski, who had escaped from prison in 1901 and returned to political activity, went to Japan with Tytus Filipowicz in July 1904 in order to raise men from Polish prisoners of war and lay the bases of an armed uprising in the Kingdom of Poland, but the Japanese government showed small interest in his plans.[13] Piłsudski's action was symptomatic of his own preference for seeking foreign aid rather than building the foundations of a mass movement at home. That Dmowski should follow him to Japan to advise the Japanese against adopting his plan is indicative both of the low level of National Democrat thinking in the crisis, and also of the determination to avoid the outbreak of an armed struggle. For Piłsudski the Paris conference offered the opportunity to reconnoitre the possibilities of armed struggle, whereas for Dmowski it was a means of aligning the National Democrats with the Russian liberals in order to extract concessions from the government. The upper classes and aristocracy of the Kingdom of Poland sought rather to bridge the gap between themselves and the government. On 10 November 1904 a memorandum was submitted to Svyatopolk-Mirsky by twenty-three leading conservatives representing high finance and the large estate owners.[14] It amounted to a declaration of complete fidelity:

Standing unswervingly on the ground of loyalty to the throne, devotion to the Monarch and the unity of the state, and bearing in mind not only the good of our own country, but also the advantage of the whole state, we regard it as our sacred duty to draw the gracious attention of Your Excellency to those aspects of conditions existing in our country, which in our considered opinion cause harm to the state, and even more at the present time when in view of the external danger the solidarity of the provinces of the Russian state has become so important a matter.

In short, *raison d'état* seemed to prove the case for equality of rights for Poles, religious toleration, and the use of Polish as the official language in the administration and schools, which would be a means of combating those extreme elements within the Polish community which were working not only against the government, but also against the state and reconciliation with Russian society. On 23 December 1904 Count Władysław Tyszkiewicz presented a fresh memorandum more precise in its views than the memorandum of 10 November.[15] The fresh proposals seemed to have owed something to suggestions by Svyatopolsk-Mirsky upon what might reasonably be proposed by himself to the tsar. The ukase of 12/25 December 1904 revealed that the Russian government would not allow even that limited degree of initiative to the Poles. There was therefore small hope for the groups of Warsaw intelligentsia which organized meetings to discuss principles of reform in December 1904, among which they numbered return to the constitutional position of the Kingdom of Poland in 1815. This element, occupying a position half way between that of the National Democrats and the PPS, was in October 1905 to form the Progressive Democratic Union (Związek Postępowo-Demokratyczny), but its constitutional liberalism evoked small response in a country which sought freedom first from national and economic oppression.

Bloody Sunday and the revolutionary crisis of 1905

The war had by the end of 1904 gone badly for Russian arms in the Far East. In theory Russia ought to have been able easily to resist the Japanese attack of 8–9 February 1904. In time of peace Russia had an army of 1,000,000 men, with reserves amounting to 4,500,000, whereas the Japanese army amounted only to 150,000 with 850,000–900,000 in reserve. In the early stages of the war the Japanese were able to bring into the field more men than the Russians owing to the poor transit facilities on the Trans-Siberian Railway and the difficulties of carrying men and supplies over a distance of 9,000–10,000 kilometres. Operations were on a scale of which the military administration had had no previous experience, and conducted in a theatre which had not been adequately studied. Russian soldiers and sailors fought bravely, but each reverse on land and sea called into question the wisdom of continuing the war. The upper and middle classes of Russia at first supported the war effort, but the workers, peasants and students grew more and more discontented. Successive mobilizations of army classes, dislocation of industrial and agricultural production and rising prices brought matters to such a pitch in the closing months of 1904 that only a brilliant victory could save the reputation of the government. On the one hand it dangled the possibility of reform before the growing opposition, while on the other it waited for the generals to rescue the autocracy on the field of battle. On 2 January 1905 Port Arthur capitulated. The military monarchy of the Romanovs had been judged by its own standards in the Crimean War of 1854–6 and the war with the Ottoman empire in 1877–8 and found wanting. Once again in 1905 a failure in a foreign adventure brought discontents to a head, but now in a more acute form.

The crisis occurred in a bizarre manner. The government had taken the decision itself to direct the discontents of the workers into channels which it could itself control. In 1901 Colonel Zubatov, chief of the Moscow Okhrana, had begun the creation of government-sponsored associations of the workers, but by 1903 the so-called *Zubatovshchina*, so called after its inventor Colonel Zubatov, provided a framework for working-class agitation which went beyond the limits intended by its founder or acceptable to the industrialists. A second attempt at controlling the workers was the Assembly of Factory Workers of St Petersburg (Sobraniye Russkikh Fabrichnozavodskikh Rabochikh Goroda St-Peterburga) created with official agreement by Father Georgei Gapon in February 1904, designed officially to make working-class activity remain within the confines of the Christian religion, much as Christian Democracy and Christian Socialism elsewhere sought to compete with materialist creeds like socialism and anarchism. In fact, Gapon's movement provided an umbrella for militant workers to organize within the bounds of legality, which by the beginning of 1905 permitted workers not necessarily committed to Gapon's point of view to use the cover of his organization to promote more radical policies.

On 3/16 January the great Putilov works went on strike in support of four workers who had been dismissed, but the movement soon spread and embraced over 100,000 persons. The strength of the workers gave rise to a plan for presenting a petition to the tsar. The petition demanded a legislative assembly elected on the basis of universal suffrage, an eight-hour day, equality for all classes, nationalities and religions, together with normal civil liberties and an amnesty for political prisoners. Above all, it asked for the end of the war. The petition was to be presented on 9/22 January 1905. The committee of ministers, which met on 8/21 January, was accurately informed of the peaceful intention of the organizers of the demonstration, but it took the decision to deal with it as the Austrian and French armies had dealt with the revolution in 1848 and as the Paris

Commune had been suppressed in 1871. As the peaceful demonstration of 140,000 workers approached the Winter Palace, the army fired into it. The slaughter of the St Petersburg workers did not bring with it the expected subjugation of the masses. Everywhere in the Russian empire there was a spontaneous explosion of wrath. For the Russian people the shootings destroyed the fiction that the tsar was their protector. For the Poles this had always been a myth.

In the Kingdom of Poland the situation was already tense. As in Russia, so in Poland the revolutionary parties emerged to lead the workers. The SDKPiL was already committed to collaboration and solidarity with the Russian workers. The PPS, which had hitherto been less convinced of the value of working with the Russians, soon formed its own strike committee. A general strike was called for 28 January, but the workers of Warsaw in fact left the factories and workshops on the morning of 27 January even before the manifestos of the socialist parties could be distributed among them. The PPS proclamation was not even circulated until 30 January.[16] Warsaw was now transformed into one of the major centres of the revolution in the Russian empire. Clashes with the army, which brought 29 companies of infantry, 5 squadrons of cavalry and 4 cossack hundreds into Warsaw, were inevitable. How many persons died during the strike is not known with any accuracy, but according to official sources 64 were killed and 29 died of wounds. It is suspected that at least 200 persons were killed and that some 270 were wounded.[17] In Łódź the long tradition of the workers' struggle ensured a mass stoppage which embraced the whole of the area. Then the strike spread by 1 February to Częstochowa and to the Dąbrowa basin where about 200 persons were killed and wounded by the soldiery. On 30 January the *gubernii* of Warsaw and Piotrków were placed in a state of alert, which gave the police and army wide powers of search and arrest and for practical purposes suspended the law. In effect, the police were given the power to conduct a reign of terror. This did not prevent the governor-general of Piotrków, Artsimovich, from issuing a high-minded address to the workers of Łódź encouraging them in the name of the Almighty to return to work in the best interests of their families and the economy.[18] In response to his requests for assistance the archbishop of Warsaw, Wincenty Popiel, ordered the clergy to use their influence to prevent disorders.[19] On 4 February the state of alert was extended to *gubernii* of Kalisz, Radom, and Siedlce, and on 27 February to the *gubernii* of Kielce, Lublin, Łomża, Płock and Suwałki. Thus the whole of the Kingdom of Poland was affected by a revolt of the masses including not only the industrial workers, but also the peasants.

The general strike was a phenomenon of immense importance not merely for the Kingdom of Poland and the district of Białystok but for the Polish territories as a whole. For the first time, the entire population and not solely the educated classes demonstrated its desire for social justice and self-government. The deep-seated resentment of the Poles found expression in strikes of schoolchildren and teachers. In the countryside the owners of large properties found that the farm workers demanded higher wages and that the landed peasants invaded the woods and pastures over which the manors claimed control. On 18 November 1904 there had come into existence in Warsaw the illegal Polish Peasant Union (Polski Związek Ludowy – PZL) which emerged on 3 May 1905 with a programme of struggle against tsardom and the demands for a parliament in Warsaw to carry agrarian legislation in which the peasants themselves had a say.[20] Clearly what was at stake in Poland was not only the rule of Russia, but also the social and economic predominance of the upper and middle classes.

The great landowners and the big bourgeoisie were caught by surprise when their comfortable existence was threatened. Some sent their families abroad. The foreign capitalists appealed to the Russian authorities for assistance against the workers. Like the clergy the National Democrats used their influence in a campaign to calm the ferment. Nevertheless, the situation presented all parties with an opportunity. On 22 January/4 February 1905 the tsar appointed Nikolai Bulygin minister of the interior in place of Svyatopolsk-Mirsky and in his rescript of 18 February/3 March instructed him to prepare a constitution with a state duma endowed with consultative functions. On 17/30 April 1905 there followed the edict of toleration. Clearly the government was playing for time and might be pushed even further in the direction of reform in the event of lack of success in the war in the Far East and under pressure of mass discontent. The political groups in Russia proper and in the Kingdom of Poland had therefore to define their attitudes towards the crisis and the possibilities it presented.

For the revolutionary parties in Poland the great strike movement of January–February 1905 was a turning point. What had been illegal conspiratorial groups now had the opportunity of converting themselves into mass parties. New members could be attracted into the SDKPiL and the PPS. Authority now tended to pass into the hands of those leaders who could respond to the expanded party membership. This was a problem which affected above all the PPS.[21] The Warsaw Workers' Committee and the Workers' Regional Committee without the approval of the Central Committee called a meeting which took place in Warsaw on 5–6 March 1905, which converted itself into the PPS Party Congress.

What took place was the capture of the party by leaders within the country, though reliance was placed upon Henryk Walecki (Maximilian Horwitz), a member of the Central Committee who had come forward from Cracow to take part in the meeting. Authority was now vested in the party congress, which was to decide upon all matters relating to the programme, tactics and organization, and to appoint the Central Committee.

The programme was in fact limited. Party policy was defined as the revolutionary struggle to obtain a separate identity for the Kingdom of Poland and the calling of a constituent assembly in Warsaw upon the basis of universal suffrage and equal, secret and direct elections. The party was to seek collaboration with the Jewish Bund, and with the socialist parties of Lithuania with the aim of establishing a constituent assembly in Vilna.[22] The PPS had in effect moved away from a strictly nationalist point of view towards solidarity with the socialist movement within the entire Russian empire. A number of defects in the party's new policy were, however, evident from the beginning. The PPS was in competition with the SDKPiL for the allegiance of the Polish working class. Within the party itself there was a conflict between members who had been active since its inception, the Seniors led by Józef Piłsudski, and the Juniors, who had now in 1905 come to the fore. Unfortunately for the unity of the party the Secret Combat Section (Wydział Spiskowo-Bojowy), established by the party congress in March, was placed under the control of Józef Piłsudski, supported by Alexander Prystor and Walery Sławek. Piłsudski's intention was to use the relative freedom from party control, which the Secret Combat Section would necessarily have in organizing armed action, to establish a core of followers who would form the nucleus of an army to carry out an insurrection in the future. With Piłsudski they were to construct a group of followers who were to provide a substantial section of the Polish political elite after the *coup d'état* of 1926 (see below p. 158) and Sławek was to be prime minister of Poland in 1930–5. The Juniors of the PPS conceded the need for armed action, but wished to keep the direction of the Secret Combat Section's activity in the hands of the party and to use it in large-scale planned actions with a political purpose. The differences in outlook were not resolved by the party council of 15–18 June 1905, which left open the question of mass or individual acts of violence.[23]

Piłsudski's visit to Japan in 1904 had not yielded political results, but it had at least secured the assistance of Japanese officers in the embassy in Paris in training Poles in the making of explosives and the construction of bombs. One of the functions of the combat organization was the elimination of informers and traitors, but its more spectacular activity was attacks upon Russian officials. Not all bombs exploded, and not every armed action succeeded. On 21 March 1905 an attempt to blow up the chief of police, Karl Nolken, failed, but he was severely wounded on 26 March. The most distinguished target was the governor-general of Warsaw himself, General Konstantin Maximovich, who was so shaken by an attempt on his life on 19 May that he thought it prudent to move to the fortress of Zegrze and thence to the fortress of Modlin. When the combat organization began to run out of money, Walery Sławek on his own authority turned its attention to district treasuries, though without great success. Of four actions planned for the night of 5–6 August 1905 only the attack of Montwiłł-Mirecki on the district office of Opatów enjoyed any degree of success. Terrorist activity was bound to come to an end, because the Okhrana succeeded in infiltrating its organization. David Ajzenlist, a section commander, informed the police of everything and in the end Walery Sławek was himself arrested on 10 September, which effectively destroyed the central command for the moment. The taste for violence had been established. The Eighth Congress of the PPS of 12–23 February 1906, held at Lwów, attempted once more to bring armed activity under the control of the Central Committee through its combat section, but Piłsudski, though he did not actually direct personally any action and remained outside the Kingdom until 1909, was a man with a mind of his own, seeking to keep the organization intact as the nucleus of an army. By July 1906 the PPS possessed a combat unit with 752 members, which enabled it to return to the task of harassing the Russian government. In May 1906 a fresh campaign of violence began, contrary to the wishes of Piłsudski. The culminating point of the campaign was the attack on the governor-general, Skalon, on 18 August 1906, but above all 'Bloody Wednesday' of 15 August, when in a series of attacks all over the Kingdom about 80 persons were killed. In the course of 1906 no less than 678 attacks were made on government officials, causing 336 deaths. The lack of control over the actions of the Combat Section led to its suspension and the expulsion from the PPS of its leading members at the Ninth Congress of 19–25 November 1906 at Vienna. Piłsudski and his followers constituted themselves as the Polish Socialist Party–Revolutionary Fraction (PPS–Frakcja Rewolucyjna), the main party adopting the name of PPS–Left (PPS–Lewica). In fact, the Revolutionary Fraction was not revolutionary, but aimed at working for Polish independence by association with an Austro-German alliance in the event of a general European war. Its socialism was that of the programme of 1893, but it did not base itself upon the working class.

The role of the Left in the crisis of 1905 was in part to organize the workers in the struggle for the improvement of their conditions. The primary aim was to maintain pressure and overthrow the autocracy to make way for a democratic republic. Predictably May Day was to be a demonstration throughout Poland of the workers' determination to achieve liberty. The workers took part in demonstrations everywhere in Poland, but it was in Warsaw that the most impressive manifestation of discontent took place. The authorities had, however, already decided to make a show of force. One demonstration organized by Felix Dzierżyński and the SDKPiL, but supported by members of the PPS and the Bund, was fired upon as it turned into the Aleje Jerozolimskie. No less than 37 persons were killed, and 45 wounded. The massacre caused such revulsion that the SDKPiL was able to call a strike in protest on 4 May. The most imposing of all working-class actions was to take place in Łódź, where the textile workers, like their fellows in Russia in the region of Ivanovo–Voznesensk, who came out on strike on 12/25 May 1905, were seething with discontent. On 18 June a party of workers, returning from a Sunday meeting outside the town organized by the SDKPiL, was attacked by cossacks and soldiers. Five workers were killed and several wounded. On 22 June, the Feast of Corpus Christi, an elemental upsurge of anger against the police and cossacks led to the construction of barricades. The uprising again brought about terrible losses. Between 18 and 25 June no less than 151 persons were killed, of whom 55 were Poles, 79 Jews and 17 Germans, according to official figures, but losses were probably even greater.[24] With a working class continuing to demonstrate and accept casualties on this scale it is small wonder that the propertied classes were struck with terror by the prospect of a proletarian revolution. In anticipation of troubles on May Day, about 33,000 persons applied for passports to leave the country.

The propertied classes viewed the situation with a mixture of emotions. On the one hand they feared the people, but on the other hand they perceived the opportunity of using the embarrassments of tsarism to obtain concessions. They could indeed present the case to the Russian government that they were its natural allies in a period of turmoil and that autonomy and relaxation of pressure would be a small price to pay for their aid. The upper classes by themselves lacked influence among the masses, but they had to handle the National League and the National Democrats. At the beginning of 1905 Roman Dmowski and Zygmunt Balicki arrived in Warsaw to give the National Democratic Party (Stronnictwo Narodowo-Demokratyczne) a disciplined organization. Powerful allies were soon found, especially Count Maurycy Zamoyski, the richest landowner in the Kingdom, who could through their local influence and wealth extend the influence of the National Democrats to all parts of the Kingdom. The Kingdom was divided into five regions and the activists in the Association for National Education (Towarzystwo Oświaty Narodowej) became agents of the party. In the towns they brought into existence the National Workers' Union (Narodowy Związek Robotniczy – NZR) to compete with the revolutionary socialist parties of the Left for the workers' loyalties.[25] In a situation as serious as that of 1905 the church could forget the anti-clerical views of the National Democrats in earlier years and lend its support against the revolutionary forces.

The propertied classes and liberal opposition in Russia were themselves seeking to evolve their own political organization in somewhat similar conditions. They professed to see in the tsar's rescript of 18 February/ 3 March 1905 the beginning of a constitutional era, but the reluctance of the government to enlarge upon its promises drove the Union of Liberation further to the left. At its Third Conference in Moscow from 25–28 March/7–10 April 1905 a new programme was drawn up demanding a legislative assembly upon the basis of universal suffrage and direct and secret elections, with the grant of votes for women. A programme of agrarian reform, moreover, was constructed upon the basis of dividing up state lands among the peasants, and, where these would not suffice, the parcelization of private estates with compensation to the landlords. For the working class they asked for an eight-hour day. This was a bolder programme than the propertied classes in the Kingdom of Poland and in north western and south western Russia were prepared to put forward. In May 1905 a conference of representatives of the zemstvos and the towns decided to draw up an address to the tsar, which was couched in somewhat vaguer terms. When the address was presented to the tsar on 6/19 June 1905, Prince S. N. Trubetskoy in his speech toned down its demands and represented its aim as the peaceful transformation of Russia in association with the government. The tsar accepted the address with the condition that he would act in accordance with 'existing Russian principles', which in effect meant the preservation of the autocracy, a point of view which was more to the taste of the emergent right-wing organizations like the Union of the Russian People (Soyuz Russkikh Lyudey) and the Union of the Fatherland (Otechestvenny Soyuz). These were forces which the liberals evidently feared. At a meeting with zemstvos representatives in Moscow on 8–9/21–22 April it was explained to the Poles that the National Democrat programme of autonomy with a parliament meeting in Warsaw was one which no Russian party could accept. There was thus a gap between Polish nationalism and Russian nationalism which might be difficult to bridge. For the Russians the Polish Question was of only minor significance, but for the Poles it was their very existence.[26] The self-centred outlook of National Democracy caused its leaders to seek any solution which might bring Poland benefit. This did not exclude an understanding with the dynasty at the expense of the common cause of fighting against tsarist oppression.

The summer of 1905 was not uneventful in Poland. Hardly a day went past without some manifestation of Polish hostility to the government. The police and the army, for their part, were directed to use all methods of brutality to secure subjection to authority. The depths to which tsarist officialdom could descend were revealed in the pogrom of the Jews organized in Białystok on 12 August 1905, when 38 persons were killed and over 200 wounded. In spite of the the heroic opposition of the Polish workers, the speed of events was in fact determined by events in Russia. The battle of Mukden between 20 February and 9 March ended in Russian defeat. Of greater importance was the naval battle of Tsushima of 27-28 May, after which there could be no pretence that Russia could win the war. Barricades went up in Odessa on 14/27 June and the crew of the battleship *Potemkin* mutinied, though on the Black Sea they had scarcely suffered the demoralization of defeat. The plain fact was that Russia itself was disenchanted with tsarism as it negotiated the Peace of Portsmouth, signed on 5 September 1905. The announcement of Bulygin's proposals for a constitution on 19 August 1905 revealed that the government still did not wish to meet even the minimum demands of all parties. A consultative assembly based upon a three-class franchise according to the electoral procedures for the zemstvos introduced in 1864 could satisfy no one. Russia was no longer the country of 8/21 January 1905, when Gapon had sought to influence the government by a peaceful demonstration of workers, singing hymns and holding aloft sacred banners. The workers were now organized and determined to secure their ends. By the beginning of October 1905 the strike movement had spread to the printers of Moscow, whose example induced other trades to strike. On 8/21 October the railway strike began, which was complete by 12/25 October, and set in motion a general strike throughout Russia. On 13/25 October the first meeting of the Soviet of Workers' Deputies took place in St Petersburg. Street fighting broke out in Odessa, Kharkov, Sebastopol and Kiev. The Poles responded with a general strike in Warsaw lasting until 20 November 1905, which spread to all parts of the Kingdom of Poland. The government had clearly for the moment lost control of the country and its dependencies.

In the crisis of the Russian administration the advisers of the tsar were not united. The deputy minister of internal affairs, Trepov, was prepared to use the maximum force to restore the authority of the government, but the former minister of finance, Sergei Witte, declared that the only way to obtain stability was the introduction of reforms. The problem was put to the Grand Duke Nikolai Nikolayevich, whom the tsar would have asked to introduce a military régime to put into practice Trepov's recommendations, but he pronounced in favour of the policy proposed by Witte. Thus Tsar Nicholas II was compelled to issue the manifesto of 17/30 October 1905 promising Russia a legislative as opposed to a consultative parliament. Witte did not believe in constitutions. The proposed state duma for him had no real significance. It was the promise of reform which had greater political meaning.

There was one section of the liberal opposition which saw itself as participating in the exercise of power. At the end of their consultations of 12–18 October/25 October–1 November 1905 they established the party of the Constitutional Democrats, or Kadets, as they are generally known. There were others who were prepared to accept the direction of the affairs of state by the existing bureaucracy, subject to the condition that laws were submitted to the legislative duma for approval. This group, known as the Octobrists, after the decree of 17/30 October, in effect offered no opposition to the possession of power by the existing bureaucracy. The decree of 17/30 October 1905, officially a concession by the autocracy, was in political terms a measure designed to divide the liberal opposition, which was satisfied that it could obtain within its terms the bases and essentials of a parliamentary state. The limits of the government's concessions were shown by the ukase of 11/24 December 1905 establishing a vague and therefore complicated system of election of deputies to the duma by a curial system similar to that of the Prussian constitution. On 20 February/5 March 1906 the Council of State (Gosudarstvenny Sovyet) was converted into a legislative body, with minor reforms to introduce an elected element, to serve as a second chamber with powers equal to those of the duma. In the international field the reforms paid lip-service to constitutionalism and paved the way for the agreement to a loan of 2,250,000,000 francs, of which French and British banks provided two-thirds, which would not have been granted without the introduction of some form of parliamentary government. Internally the realities of autocratic government were in the eyes of the Left to remain.

The Soviet of Workers' Deputies established in St Petersburg remained in existence for only fifty days until 190 of its members were arrested on 3/16 December 1905. The Social Democratic uprising in Moscow of 7–18/20–31 December established nothing more than a tradition of armed insurrection.[27] The revolutionary parties of the Russian towns therefore declared that they would boycott the elections, which they considered only a sham. The reaction in the Kingdom of Poland was similar. The National

Democrats were ready to accept the new constitutional arrangements, but the left-wing parties showed their hostility to such an extent that the governor-general, Skalon, declared a state of war on 10 November 1905 in the *gubernia* of Warsaw, which was extended on 21 December to the remaining nine *gubernii*. All the resources of the upper classes were brought to bear to maintain order. On 3 December 1905 Pope Pius X issued an encyclical to the archbishop of Warsaw and the Catholic bishops of the Russian dominions to use their influence in the interest of internal peace. The National Democrats pressed the peasants to accept the situation, and on 16 January 1906 threatened armed action against militant members of working organizations in the towns. Between 3 and 5 January 1906 Ignacy Daszyński, the leader of the Polish Social Democratic Party of Galicia and Silesia (Polska Partia Socjalno-Demokratyczna Galicji i Śląska – PPSDGiS), published a series of articles in *Naprzód* (Forwards), condemning association with the Russian revolutionary movement.[28] All the counter-revolutionary forces were brought into action in order to allow the Poles to play the parliamentary game. The Russian revolutionary movement was defeated and the solidarity of the Polish socialist parties, both the PPS and the SDKPiL, did nothing to help the common struggle. The reality was that the National Democrats could contest the forthcoming elections with a reasonable chance of obtaining the sole representation of the Kingdom of Poland unchallenged by the Left. The situation after the elections was unclear, but already on 21 November 1905 Roman Dmowski had approached Witte, now the chairman of the Council of Ministers, with a promise of support in return for regional autonomy. Nothing could then be done owing to the disturbed state of the Kingdom, but the National Democrats were presented with the opportunity subsequently either of associating themselves with the Kadets, if ever they should obtain ministerial offices, or, on the other hand, of selling their support to the administration, if the bureaucracy should retain its essential power within the shell of constitutional government.

Elections to the First Duma

The hopes excited by the tsar's manifesto of 17/30 October 1905 both at home and abroad did not meet with much satisfaction in the electoral law of 11/24 December 1905. The electorate in Russia was divided into four curiae: the large landowners, the peasants, the townspeople and the workers, but as far as the Kingdom of Poland was concerned provision was made for 37 members to be returned to the duma, of which one was to represent the Orthodox population of the *gubernii* of Siedlce and Lublin.

The voting was in three stages for the curia of the workers, and in two stages for the large landowners and the townspeople. The peasants were divided into two groups, those possessing 3–20 *morgi*, who formed the peasant curia, while those who possessed 20–95 *morgi* were assigned to the curia of the large landowners. In the final analysis, out of 850 electors representing the electorate as a whole, 194 came from the peasant curia, 286 from the larger landowners, and 341 from the towns. From the curia of the working class there were only 29 electors.[29] This was a situation which could scarcely meet with the approval of all classes. The Russian bureaucracy had invented a system which made concessions to the upper classes but gave nothing to the workers and the peasants. The boycott of the elections by the SDKPiL and the PPS together with the Polish Peasant Union (PZL) left the National Democrats and the insignificant parties of the middle class to contend the elections unopposed. The National Democrats opened the campaign with the declaration that the party would seek autonomy for the Kingdom of Poland upon the basis of a legislative parliament in Warsaw with powers in the field of internal affairs. The programme for practical purposes was limited and amounted only to a demand for the use of the Polish language in the schools, courts and the administration.[30] When for the most part the elections were completed on 3 May 1906, it appeared that the National Democrats had won substantially. Roman Dmowski, Zygmunt Balicki and Jan Popławski, the leading members of the National Democratic party, were not entered as candidates, on the grounds that they did not then have the right to vote. The Polish members of the duma were selected on the grounds of their mediocrity. They were to be directed from outside the duma and adhere to the party line. The majority of the representatives were great landlords like Count Maurycy Zamoyski, Prince Seweryn Świętopełk-Czetwertyński and Count Władysław Tyszkiewicz, or members of the professions. There were five peasants of whom the most active was to be Nakonieczny, and one worker, Grabiański, who were to be symbolic of the National Democrats' solicitude for the peasants and the working class. The National Democrats obtained 34 seats out of 37, of which two were won by Lithuanians in the *gubernia* of Suwałki and one reserved to represent the Orthodox population.

Though the National Democrats clearly won in the Kingdom of Poland and could be joined by the 19 Poles elected in Lithuania, Byelorussia and the Ukraine, they were a minority in a duma which consisted of 480 members in all. They thus settled down to following the tactics which had yielded results for the Polish Circle in the Austrian Reichsrat: the sale of their support to the highest bidder in return for local concessions. In fact, the National Democrats did not enjoy the unconditional support of the Polish representatives from north western and south western Russia, who feared to give the impression that they had separatist leanings, lest they provoke the government to taking special measures against them. The Poles of the Russian empire were in the duma not to defend the Polish cause, but to uphold the position of the great landlords against the demands of the peasantry. The Polish Circle, constituted by the National Democrats, considered itself to be an embassy in a foreign capital without special need to throw in its lot either with the largest single Russian grouping, the Kadets, or with the substantial Labour Party (Trudoviki) which had emerged with strong backing from the Socialist Revolutionaries. What they were looking for was concessions to the Poles. They were not concerned specifically to fight for constitutional government and reforms within the Russian empire.

On the one hand, the National Democrats showed some sympathy with the Kadets in the duma, but kept the way open for an understanding with the government. The key question was the problem of agrarian reform, which was more divisive for the Russians than the National Democrats, because the agrarian history of the Kingdom of Poland, which had undergone reform after 1864 was different from that of Russia. The Kadets proposed a system of compulsory purchase of part of the lands of the gentry, whereas the Trudoviki declared for the acquisition of all land and its division among the peasants under an administrative system controlled by the peasants themselves. The Polish expert on agrarian questions, Władysław Grabski, declared against compulsory purchase, but the Polish Circle eventually accepted it in principle, provided that it was controlled by a diet in Warsaw, a solution far removed from that of the Trudoviki and even of the Polish peasantry in the Kingdom.[31] The Polish deputies from the Russian empire itself adopted an attitude of complete opposition to compulsory purchase. Whereas the Polish Circle looked at the political situation in the light of what measure of autonomy might be obtained, the Circle of the Borderlands (Koło Kresowe), the Polish organization for the areas of western Russia, was for economic reasons inclined to seek association with the more conservative Octobrists rather than with the Kadets. On issues likely to give offence to the government the National Democrats abstained from voting in order to demonstrate their fundamental loyalty. In order to maintain their position within Poland they were critical of abuses of power and irregularities condoned by officials in the Kingdom. Fundamentally the National Democrats had adopted a policy of conciliation and compromise, which was a far cry from the brave words and defiant attitudes of the 1890's. Unable and unwilling to institute a genuine constitutional government in Russia, the tsar dissolved the duma on 8/21 July 1906. The Kadets and Trudoviki but not the National Democrats assembled in Viborg to discuss the new position on 22–23 July and, with the knowledge that they would not be allowed to continue their meetings, called upon the people to offer passive resistance, withhold the payment of taxes and evade conscription. The Polish Circle dissociated itself from the Viborg declaration and proclaimed it a useless demonstration of hostility. In this way the National Democrats kept the way open for the policy of conciliation with the government in return for concessions in the Kingdom of Poland. They could, however, have few illusions concerning the possibility of obtaining what was claimed to be their right in the declaration of 13 May 1906, which emphasized the separate institutions of the Kingdom of Poland, but which they had never asked to be placed upon the agenda of the duma. On 24 May 1906 there had been formed a group of autonomists, including Poles, Ukrainians, Lithuanians, Tatars, Cossacks and Latvians, amounting to some 125 to 135 members of the duma in all, but the Polish Circle adopted an attitude of reserve, because support of demands for autonomy in north western and south western Russia could mean only surrender of the claims of the Polish minorities in those areas. The closure of the First Duma was an attack upon constitutionalism in Russia and the beginning of the search by the new government under Stolypin for a system of autocracy working under the cloak of respectability which an ineffective parliament could offer. For the Poles it underlined their inability to decide among themselves upon a solution of their fundamental position with regard to Russia.

The situation in the Kingdom of Poland was by no means quiet. In the countryside the farm labourers organized strikes for higher wages in 1906, especially during the period of spring ploughing and during harvest. The National Democrats in alliance with the estate owners and the more affluent peasants threw their influence against the labourers. Groups of strike-breakers toured the countryside intimidating peasant activists. By the second half of 1906 an official counter-offensive was under way. The Russian government in August 1906 introduced a system of field general courts-martial, which meant that the authorities could carry out summary executions upon the slightest suspicion. In the industrial towns the employers had recourse to the weapon of the lock-out. The government had added its own brand of terror by instigating a pogrom at Białystok in June 1906.[32] Protests in the duma had no effect. A fresh pogrom was organized in Siedlce in September 1906. The action of authorities through the field courts provoked a general strike in Łódź on 10 October 1906. Łódź was already the scene of fratricidal strife. The clergy and the National

Democrats entered into an unholy alliance to organize the large element of illiterate workers, who had left the miserable countryside around Łódź to work in the textile industry, as a counter-revolutionary force. Selective assassinations of leaders of the more politically conscious workers were carried out on a scale much larger than the official slaughter executed by the Russian military courts. In December 1906 the employers decided to secure a victory by enforcing a return to the conditions of 1905 by means of a lock-out. The industrial organization of the National Democrats, the National Workers' Union (NZR), threw itself with vigour into support of the employers with its policy of wholesale murder.[33] In the course of 1906 there were, according to official figures, 189 workers murdered and 138 wounded in internecine strife, and these figures obviously do not include those wounded who did not come to the notice of the police. The murders continued in 1907. The struggle came to an end only in April 1907 after about 300 workers had been assassinated. Faced with the determination of the employers supported by the authorities, and the terrorism of the National Democrats, the workers of Łódź, led by the PPS–Left, SDKPiL and the Bund, were obliged to accept the cruel necessity of returning to work after four months of resistance. It is to the credit of the Polish workers that elsewhere in the Kingdom the thugs of the NZR were never able to carry out an action on the scale which was possible in the area of Łódź.

The elections to the Second Duma did not return a Polish representation which was significantly different from that in the First, but the circumstances of the elections were different. For the first time the SDKPiL in alliance with the Bund entered into the struggle, though the PPS–Left and the PPS–Revolutionary Fraction continued with their boycott. The middle- and upper-class parties formed their own electoral organizations. The National Democrats joined with the Party of Realpolitik and the Polish Progressive party to form the Central Electoral Committee, which in effect meant that the National Democrats took command of the Polish Right. Progressive Democracy, from which the Polish Progressive Party was a break-away group, established its own Central Committee for Progressive Unity. There was little doubt that the National Democrats would win the majority of the seats, but it was important for the other parties to demonstrate their numerical strength in the country, even though a ruling of the senate in October 1906 laid down the principle that only persons having their own exit from their homes and their own kitchens were entitled to the vote. This regulation obviously hit the urban voters in the urban curia. The SDKPiL nevertheless obtained 7,000 votes in Warsaw, and in Łódź carried 68 per cent of the working-class curia, but, owing to the curial system, in the end there were returned 16 landowners, 2 priests, 8 middle class, 5 peasants – selected for symbolic reasons – and one real representative of the workers. In the *gubernii* of Russian inhabited by Polish minorities the representation dropped from 19 to 14, owing to the decision of peasants, Orthodox clergy and the Russian landowners in the *gubernia* of Minsk to join in a common block against the Poles.

The most important of the Polish deputies was Roman Dmowski, who now was returned for the city of Warsaw and to take the lead in St Petersburg. The situation he found was somewhat different from that in the First Duma, because the strength of the Kadets had fallen from 179 to 99, whereas there had been some gains by the parties of the Russian Right and of the Left, including 65 Russian Social Democrats and 37 Socialist Revolutionaries. The fluidity of Russian politics makes analysis of the real state of political feeling in the duma difficult to assess, but it is assumed that the Left had about 222 votes at its command, while the Right had 246. In such a situation the Polish Circle, reinforced by the Polish representatives from the north western and south western *gubernii*, counting upon 46 votes, could expect to obtain some concessions if it were revealed that they held the balance. The extreme Right had no interest in keeping the duma in existence. Only the Centre had much desire to seek a compromise with the government in order to keep liberal ideas alive in Russia. The prime minister, Piotr Stolypin, had to obtain a parliamentary majority in order to secure the passage of the budget, which was a condition of obtaining a French loan. Feelers were put out to the Poles to obtain their support, but Dmowski made Polish accession to the government bloc conditional upon the government's accepting the Polish Circle's policy on educational reform in the Kingdom of Poland. This Stolypin was unwilling to accept. Nevertheless, the Polish Circle voted for increased conscription in order to conciliate the government. The policy was explained away by Henryk Konic, one of the Polish deputies, by the statement that 'Poles contend with the government, not with the Russian state'. In other words, the Poles were a loyal opposition in the field of international affairs. If it had not been for the Poles, the government would have failed to obtain a majority for its bill. In this way the Polish Circle voted for the increase of the very instrument of their own subjection. When it came to the vote on the budget the government had other plans. The Russian Social Democratic group was accused on 31 May/13 June 1907 of attempting to undermine the loyalty of the army. On 1/14 June Stolypin demanded the expulsion from the duma of 55 Social Democratic members, and the arrest of 16 of them. This proposal was so obviously based upon fictitious evidence that the government feared that it would no longer be able to secure a majority and might even be faced with a vote for the compulsory acquisition of noble land for distribution among the peasants instead of its own plan of voluntary sale and purchase. On the night of 2–3/15–16 June 1907, the Social Democratic deputies were arrested, and on the morning of 3/16 June 1907 the decree dissolving the duma was published.

The Poles had achieved nothing, nor had they shown significant opposition in important matters. The government in any case was too powerful to feel itself in need of making concessions for Polish support. The methods which deputies and national groupings employed in the Austrian Reichsrat were of no avail. The Poles had sought to represent themselves as useful. Their fundamental error was to assume that the tsarist government had a use for them.

The National Democrats had lost, but Poland had obtained valuable political experience. In February 1861 the accidental killing of five persons in a Warsaw demonstration had provoked a crisis and forced the Russian government into concessions. In 1904–7 Poles died in their scores. Though they had achieved virtually nothing, they had given witness to a capacity and willingness to make sacrifices which in itself was an indication that Polish nationalism had a mass basis in popular sentiment. Industrial workers and the peasants had laid their claim to be independent political forces in the Poland of the present and the future. The PPS and the SDKPiL had established themselves as parties of cities, but perhaps of even greater significance was the emergence of the PZL as a party capable of giving leadership to the peasants, who formed the majority of the population. The national movement was represented by the upper and educated classes which assembled under the banner of the National Democrats. A political revolution within the framework of Russian politics was not achieved, but within Polish society a social revolution had been effected.

Austrian and Prussian Poland and the crisis of 1905–7

Events in Russian Poland in the great crisis of 1905–7 had no direct influence upon Polish policy within either the Austrian or the German empires, but an unheaval of such dimensions indicated that suspicions of a possible Polish revival entertained by the enemies of Poland in Germany had a solid basis in fact. The Prussian policy of buying out Polish landowners was enlarged in 1902 by increasing the colonization fund from 200,000,000 to 350,000,000 marks, together with an allocation of 1,000,000 for the increase in the area of state properties and woodlands in Poznania and West Prussia. A law of 1904 placed restrictions upon the creation of new Polish farms by the parcelization of larger properties. In 1908 a further 125,000,000 marks was allocated to the Colonization Commission, and an extra 25,000,000 given for purposes of acquiring land for the state. In the field of local government every effort was made to exclude Poles both in Poznania and Silesia. The state administration was almost entirely in the hands of Germans. Every effort was made to give Poznań German cultural institutions. The foundation of the Kaiser Wilhelm Library in 1902 was followed by the Royal Academy in 1903, and the Kaiser Friedrich Museum in 1904. The conservative society of Poznania was placed even more on the defensive than it had been in the nineteenth century. The most famous of all events was the revolt of the schoolchildren of Września, where in April 1901 religious instruction in Polish was abolished in the two highest classes. Corporal punishment was used against the children in order to compel them to study the Christian religion through the medium of the German language. The pupils' strike and the barbaric treatment administered to them did little to raise the reputation of the Prussian government at home or abroad, but nothing deterred it from its chosen policy.

The Poznanian conservatives thought that they could hold off Prussian pressure by declarations of unswerving loyalty. The ultra-loyal Archbishop Stablewski was succeeded in 1906 by Edward Likowski who did nothing which might give offence to the government, even in the thorny question of religious instruction in German. The development of industry in Poznania and West Prussia was so inconsiderable that the German Social Democratic Party had to support the weak Polish Socialist Party of the Prussian Partition (PPSzP). In the absence of an active defence of Polish interests there existed a political power vacuum which could be filled by the National Democrats, who had begun to extend their influence in Prussian Poland before 1900. In 1904 they founded the National Democratic Party (Stronnictwo Narodowo–Demokratyczne – SN-D) – though its existence was not formally made public until 1909 – with a programme drawn up by Marian Seyda. Thus the National Democrats were able to provide an umbrella organization which could attract the gentry and the conservative elements and establish a mass basis for resistance.[34] Events in Russian Poland excited immense interest, coinciding as they did with general discontent in Germany in 1905. The National Democrats could provide a programme which was both nationalist and anti-socialist and could therefore pose as a party of respectability in a difficulty situation. The continuation of the school strikes was of great use to the National Democrats in the sense that this action was in defence of a national interest and an established religion, but at the same time had no association with socialism. What happened in Poznania was a pale reflection of the bloody massacres which occurred in the Kingdom of Poland, but the Prussian government held the opinion that the Polish provinces were an area in which revolutionary activity might be expected.

The situation in Galicia was different.[35] The Polish upper classes had control over most aspects of government outside the realm of foreign affairs, the army and finance. The problem of agrarian reform was pressing. Peasant strikes broke out in 1902, especially in the Ukrainian areas of eastern Galicia, which called into question the extreme conservative position of the group of landlords who went by the name of the Podolians, and indeed a system of government which rested upon a provincial diet of 161 members, of whom 92 were the owners of large properties. Pressure for reform was increasing when Count Andrzej Potocki was appointed viceroy in 1903 in place of Count Leon Piniński. Potocki's policy sought to divide the opposition by a modicum of agrarian reform designed to appease the larger peasant proprietors, much as Stolypin was later in Russia to seek a mass basis for tsarism among the farmers with sufficient land to make them defenders of the existing system. The National Democrats established themselves as an independent party in 1904 with a policy which was both anti-semitic and anti-Ukrainian, designed to appeal to the lower middle classes. Christian Socialism appeared to add another element attractive to the lower classes of the towns as opposed to the Social Democrats. There was little in the politics either of Polish Prussia or Galicia to provide the motive power of a social upheaval. The revolution of 1905 in Russia and the repercussions in Russian Poland nevertheless provided the spur for a more energetic action, especially in Galicia, and gave the Polish Question an urgency which it had hitherto lacked.

Events in the Kingdom of Poland could not have failed to excite interest in Galicia, where smouldering discontents were kindled into fire by news of the shootings in St Petersburg on 9/22 January 1905. Demonstrations of solidarity with the Russian workers took place in Lwów, Cracow and all the major towns of the province, but they necessarily took on a national meaning when the workers of the Kingdom of Poland were simultaneously striking and demonstrating against tsarist oppression. As a result of the radicalization of Galicia, the Austrian government was conscious that Polish national feeling was directed also against itself. The struggle for the introduction of universal suffrage now took on a new significance. On 6 October 1905 a vote in the Reichsrat in favour of electoral reform failed to obtain the necessary two-thirds majority and the Polish Circle actually voted against the proposal. The action of the Polish deputies aroused the anger of the working class in Galicia, especially when the provincial diet opened in Lwów on 23 October. A demonstration representative of all elements in Galicia, workers, peasants and students, Poles and Ukrainians alike, gave its support to a petition demanding electoral reform based upon direct, equal and universal suffrage and vote by ballot. This was not a movement peculiar to the Polish territories, but one which affected other areas of the Habsburg dominions, leading to demonstrations in Vienna, Prague, Trieste, Salzburg, Linz and elsewhere. The railway workers in western Galicia, Bohemia and Moravia conducted a work-to-rule strike in December 1905. In the face of what threatened to be a revolutionary movement, the Austrian government capitulated and the prime minister, Gautsch, declared on 28 November 1905 that electoral reform would be treated as a matter of urgency.

The promised widening of the franchise presented the ruling classes of Galicia with a threat to their social supremacy when they viewed it against the background of revolutionary activity in the Kingdom of Poland. Efforts were made to dissociate political agitation from the movement in Russian Poland and to keep it within the framework of an effort to achieve complete regional autonomy. The conservatives, National Democrats and the clergy combined to condemn all forms of revolutionary activity in Galicia, and the provincial diet on 7 November 1905 called upon the Austrian government to take stern measures to maintain public order. The outlook of the upper and middle classes was not dissimilar from their counterparts in the Kingdom of Poland. The Polish Social Democratic Party of Galicia and Silesia (PPSDGiS) found itself confronted with a situation in which it might have to prove that it was no less determined than socialists in the Kingdom in stating the claims of the workers. Ignacy Daszyński was drawn closer to the negative policy proposed by Piłsudski and sought in his 'Open Letter to the Central Committee of the PPS' of January 1906 to dissociate the Polish working-class movement from the Russian (see above p. 86). The Polish Peasant Party (PSL) was pleased to note the appearance of a peasant party in the Kingdom in the form of the PZL, but its leadership viewed with suspicion the presentation of demands for compulsory purchase as a solution of the agrarian problem in Russia, which might have serious repercussions for Galicia. For practical purposes the main political groups in Galicia sought to contain political agitation within its Austrian context.[36]

Both the conservatives and the National Democrats desired to modify the proposal for universal suffrage by securing conditions of eligibility. The conservatives wished to exclude illiterates and persons who were not self-employed, and to require residence qualifications, which in Galician conditions would mean the refusal of the franchise to a very large section of the population. The National Democrats, revealing an attitude of mind which foreshadowed their subsequent sympathy for Italian fascism, sought to base the franchise upon occupational groups. The Austrian government's plan of 2 February 1906 proposed the abolition of the curial system and the introduction of universal suffrage for men over the age of twenty-four. This was more than the conservatives were prepared to concede, for which reason the socialists and the peasants found themselves in the position of being compelled to support the government's project in preference to their own rather wider demands. The Austrian Social Democrats and the PPSD in May 1906 pronounced in favour of a general strike after the conservatives had succeeded in overthrowing the government of Gautsch. In the end the reform of the franchise was achieved in January 1907, though with considerable modifications. Women, soldiers serving with the colours and persons subsisting on public funds were not given the vote. An ingenious modification of the curial system ordained that in a constituency one representative had to obtain 50 per cent of the votes, and the other only 25 per cent. The actual system of voting likewise tended to favour the upper classes. Nevertheless, the representation of Galicia was raised from 78 to 105 members. On the other hand there was no immediate reform of the system of election to the provincial diet and the modifications of it which were eventually agreed did nothing to shift the political balance of power within the province. The elections to the Austrian parliament in 1907 brought about a coalescence of the conservative and middle-class groupings in defence of the existing system against the possible victory of the parties representing the workers and the peasants. The conservative elements suffered a relative defeat in the sense that the Polish Circle was to consist of only 54 of the 105 members for the whole of Galicia, as opposed to 65 out of 78 under the previous system, but the dissident elements were fragmented. The peasants of western Galicia obtained 17 seats, the Christian Democrats 12, and the socialists 6, of which the PPSD had only 4. The Ukrainian parties obtained 27 seats. The Polish Circle constituted the largest single element from Galicia in the Reichsrat, but is opponents had at least demonstrated that they were a force to be reckoned with. The old order was changing and the stultifying conservatism of early years was given notice that reform and change were needed.[37]

Poland on the eve of the First World War

The great crisis of 1905–7 passed away, but it could no longer be contended that the Polish Question had ceased to exist. In fact, events were to give it a greater significance. The crisis in Bosnia-Herzegovina of 1908 left the Poles in no doubt that sooner or later the three great powers of Central and Eastern Europe would be involved in war and that in consequence one side or the other would be required to produce some solution to the problem of their existence. Poland did not exist as a country, because it was merely a frontier area on the periphery of three great empires. It was therefore clearly assigned to be a battlefield when the great conflict came. Since Poland did not herself possess an army to fight for her independence it followed that the Poles speculated upon which of the contending alliance groups they ought to place their hopes. No clearly defined solution could be found. The position of Germany was plain. The Germans had no place for the Poles in a Europe of their making. For practical purposes the choice lay between Austria–Hungary and Russia. The Polish inhabitants of Prussian Poland saw no future for themselves in a German state and were attracted to Russia. The landed proprietors of eastern Galicia, harassed by the Austro-Hungarian government's disposition to support the Ukrainians as a means of putting pressure upon the Poles, thought that they would fare better in a conservative Russian state. On the other hand the relatively mild Austrian régime, tempered by the devolution of control upon the Poles in local affairs, appealed more to the white-collar workers both in Galicia and in the Kingdom of Poland. The policy of russification meant that Poles could never find a career in the public service in the tsarist empire. The hope of association with Austria–Hungary, however, was dampened by the knowledge that she was the junior partner in her alliance with Germany. Any Austrian solution of the Polish Question, therefore, would be subject to German approval. This was a hard reality to which Russian strategic plans seemed to give an added significance.[1]

The Kingdom of Poland formed a salient in the German territories. On the other hand, a Russian army concentrated in the Kingdom was exposed to a pincer movement, from East Prussia and Upper Silesia. The strengthening of fortresses at Modlin, Grodno, Kovno, Brest-Litovsk, Dęblin, Zegrze and Osowiec seemed to point to a policy of defence in depth in which the Russian forces would defend the right bank of the Vistula, or even retreat to the line of the Niemen and Bug, thus leaving a large part of the Kingdom open to Austro-German occupation. The logic, moreover, of the Franco-Russian alliance seemed to point towards a major Russian effort against the German army in order to relieve pressure on the French army in the west. The Russian general staff had two plans. Plan 'G' was directed to meet a major German offensive, while Plan 'A' provided for an attack against Austria–Hungary in Galicia from the region of Lublin, Chełm and Kowel in the north, and from Rovne and Ploskirov in the east, leaving a holding force in the region of Kovno, Grodno and Łomża to watch the Germans. In either case the significance of the old-fashioned fortresses in central Poland was diminished. By 1913 the fortresses of Warsaw, Dęblin and Zegrze were abandoned in favour of modernization of Kovno, Grodno and Brest-Litovsk. Confirmation of a Russian defensive strategy was also found in the reduction of the number of Russian troops in the Kingdom of Poland, which fell from 271,905 in 1904 to 180,019 in 1911, though rising slightly in 1912. The withdrawal of troops took place for both strategic and political reasons. The Russian army would have to concentrate either for Plan 'G' or for Plan 'A' and the stationing of units had to be made with these strategic intentions in mind. The internal situation within the Russian empire, moreover, was an argument in favour of withdrawing troops from Poland for security reasons. Polish opinion tended to place an incorrect interpretation on Russian plans. Russia aimed to place no obstacles in the way of the reconstruction or even the break-up of the Austro-Hungarian empire. It is evident from a memorandum of the Russian foreign minister, Sazonov, of 20 January 1914 that the Poles were seen as possible instruments in an anti-Austrian policy. The Poles could be associated with Russia upon the basis of terms determined by Russia. The concept of Sazonov was that the Kingdom of Poland, granted the use of the Polish language in the schools and the local administration and the abolition of religious disabilities, would form the core of a new Polish state under Russian influence. So far from Russian policy being defensive, as many Poles thought, it was in fact offensive and the Poles merely tools in it. Long-term plans in the event of war were, however, in stark contrast with the actual conditions prevailing in Russian Poland upon the eve of hostilities in August 1914.

Russian Poland, 1907–14

The end of the domestic crisis of 1905–7 in the Russian Empire was marked by a continued policy of seeking to base the power of the state upon the right wing of the propertied classes. The new electoral ordinance of 3/16 June 1907 reduced the number of members of the duma from over 500 to 442 in order that greater representation could be given to the ethnically Russian areas. At the same time a system of indirect election was preserved, with five classes of the population each being given a proportion of the representation. Whereas the large landowners of the first curia elected one representative for every 230 votes, it required 125,000 voters to elect one deputy for the fifth curia of the working class. As far as the Kingdom of Poland was concerned, representation was reduced from 37 to 14 deputies, of whom 2 had to represent Russians resident in the Kingdom of Poland and Uniates in the *gubernii* of Lublin and Siedlce. There was a similar reduction of representation in the nine western *gubernii* of the empire in order to limit Polish representation. The Russian government had clearly aligned itself with the interests of the most reactionary element of the Great Russian population against the mass of the Russian people and the national minorities. The Third Duma was a façade which lent respectability abroad to what was in the Russian empire a savage and mindless autocracy. Whereas the tsar and the bureaucracy ought to have taken the population into partnership, they took the decision to base their rule upon elements which did not represent the real forces in the community. A situation, which was oppressive for Russians, amounting to a complete divorce of the government from the population, was for the Poles completely destructive of respect for civil authority. Systematically the Russian authorities in the Kingdom of Poland suppressed the associations of the workers and trade unions which had arisen in the crisis. Private educational associations were closed. The period from 1908 to 1909 saw the supremacy of a counter-revolution, of which the propertied classes in Poland approved in a negative manner as eliminating competitors for power within Polish society. Elections to the Third Duma seemed pointless.[2] Only the National Democrats under the leadership of Roman Dmowski showed much desire to participate in them, and then only with a programme of preserving Poland from worse disasters.

The Third Duma, which sat from 1/14 November 1907 to 9/22 June 1909, was dominated by the reactionary Right. The Kadets melted away to an insignificant minority and the Octobrists, never distinguished for anything except a stuffy constitutionalism which fell short of demands for a responsible ministry, found themselves as a centre party with 113 members representing the voice of moderation. In such a situation the Poles had no role to play. The Party of Realpolitik, representing high finance, the aristocracy and large landowners, and sitting in the Council of State, took its stand upon the ultra-conservative policy of unconditional co-operation with the government. This was a point of view adopted by the Polish landowners elected from the north western and south western *gubernii*, who feared the compulsory acquisition of their estates for distribution among the peasantry. They had no interest in the autonomy of the Kingdom of Poland and were prepared to accept permanent incorporation within the Russian empire. The National Democrats, who had stoutly proclaimed their programme to be in favour of autonomy for the Kingdom of Poland, now adopted the policy of co-operation with the government in measures of which they approved, but Stolypin was not prepared to make any concessions. The policy of Roman Dmowski was to bring the Polish Circle as near as he could to official Russian policy by adopting an anti-German policy. In 1908 Dmowski published his *Niemcy, Rosja a Sprawa Polska* (Germany, Russia and the Polish Question). He represented Germany as the greatest danger to the Poles and committed Poland to permanent association with Russia. Dmowski was falling into line with the policy of 'Neoslavism', which was designed to turn the Slavs of the Austro-Hungarian empire towards Russia. This movement, of which the high point was the Slavonic Congress in Prague of 12–18 July 1908, was short-lived. The brotherhood of the Slavs might be acceptable to the Czechs, who did not have to endure tsarist oppression, but it was an empty proposition when in fact the Poles were suffering continual suppression of their national organizations. It was not surprising that Dmowski resigned his seat in the duma in February 1909. The working-class wing of the National Democratic movement, the National Workers' Union (NZR), dissociated itself from the official policy. Even within the intelligentsia there was a split and the left wing formed the 'Fronde'.

Nevertheless, the Polish Circle continued to support the government, even in some of the bad causes which the administration so brazenly defended. The tsarist government continued to act more or less as it wished in its dealing with the Poles. For strategic reasons the government proposed to purchase the Warsaw–Vienna railway, control of which was still in Polish hands. In March 1913 the purchase was approved and the Polish workers, who numbered some 16,000, were replaced by Russians. Even more serious was the question of Chełm. In 1907 the Council of Ministers took up the question of separating eleven districts of the *gubernii* of Siedlce and Lublin from the Kingdom of Poland and incorporating them into the Russian empire as the *gubernia* of Chełm. The area was inhabited by a mixed population of Roman Catholic Poles and Uniate Ukrainians. The area had long been associated with Poland, and its separation from Poland met with the general resentment of the Poles, but the Polish Circle did no more than abstain from voting when the matter was put to the decision of the duma. Thus on 23 June/6 July 1912 the *gubernia* of Chełm was taken out of the jurisdiction of the governor-general of Warsaw. Undoubtedly the separation of Chełm from the Kingdom of Poland had the support of the extreme Russian nationalists. It was therefore not surprising that the question of the autonomy of the Kingdom of Poland and the institution of a system of local government met with opposition. In the Second Duma the Polish Circle had proposed that the Kingdom of Poland should be converted into an autonomous region within the Russian empire, with its own parliament, treasury, and judiciary; the Kingdom was to have no control over foreign affairs, military policy, the currency, customs, or any other of the primary fields of activity of the state. For practical purposes the Polish Circle was seeking a Polish administration and the use of Polish as the official language. In the Third Duma the aspirations of the Poles were limited to the promotion of a system of local government in town and country. Discussions began in 1909, but the problem of municipal government remained unsolved in the duma up to the opening of the war in 1914. The plan for introducing zemstvos in the Kingdom of Poland likewise met with delays. Even the law of 23 June/6 July 1912, providing for a system of insurance to cover illness and retirement, was kept under the close control of the bureaucracy and embraced only the workers in the larger factories.

It was small wonder that the elections to the Fourth Duma in the autumn of 1912 were conducted with even less enthusiasm than the elections to the Third. A fresh electoral law reduced the number of voters still further, but on this occasion the parties of the left emerged to test their strength. The years from 1908 to 1909 had seen the power of the working class at its lowest ebb. Arrests, sentences of exile and death, and constant harassment by the police had induced an atmosphere of demoralization. Systematic suppression of trade unions legalized in 1906 placed the workers in a poor position to resist the counter-attacks of the employers, who had recourse to lock-outs and all the other weapons in the armoury of the socially indifferent capitalist class of Central Europe in a campaign to re-establish the supremacy which they had lost in 1906. The peasants fared no better than the workers. The Polish Peasant Union (PZL), which sought to give the people of the countryside a political existence independent of the National Democrats and to promote a programme of agrarian reform, was suppressed in May 1907. The peasant movement, however, revealed a toughness which enabled it to survive repression. The periodical *Zaranie* (Daybreak), published from 1908 to 1915, continued the work of the Polish Peasant Union with a programme of popular education and promotion of co-operative movements. In fact, the growing activity of the peasant movement brought new competitors. The clergy and the National Democrats had always been hostile to the PZL, but in 1912 the breakaway Fronde of the National Democrats entered into the contest by establishing the National Peasant Union (Narodowy Związek Chłopski – NZCh) in order to promote a pro-Austrian orientation. The right-wing Revolutionary Fraction of the PPS set up its own Peasant Union (Związek Chłopski) in 1912 in order to win support for a policy of armed insurrection. Though there was no permanent political organization before the outbreak of war in 1914, it was already clear that the peasants were establishing their position as a political force independent of the tutelage of the National Democrats. It was not until 5 December 1915 that the three elements consisting of the Zaranie Group, the National Peasant Union, and the Peasant Union came together in Warsaw to form the Polish Peasant Party (Polskie Stronnictwo Ludowe) to which was attached the description *Wyzwolenie* (Liberation), after the periodical of that name which appeared in December 1916.

The socialist movements of the cities were slower to revive. The secret police, the Okhrana, infiltrated all Polish organizations as they did in Russia proper. There was nothing as spectacular as the case of Azev, the Socialist Revolutionary Party leader, who in 1908, to the incredulous astonishment of the party hierarchy, was uncovered as a paid agent of the police, or that of the assassin of Stolypin, Bogrov, who obtained entry into the theatre in Kiev to execute his deed in virtue of the trust which the police put in him as one of their own agents within the Socialist Revolutionary movement. Nevertheless, the police had enough agents in all the working-class movements to be able to hamstring their development. The number of strikes in the Kingdom of Poland fell from 2,868, embracing 498,538 workers, in 1906, to as low as 63, involving 4,538 workers, in 1910. May Day was scarcely celebrated at all in 1908 and 1909. To some extent the geographical location of industry in the Kingdom of Poland gave the authorities a tactical advantage. Large-scale industry was concentrated mainly in the two *gubernii* of Warsaw and Piotrków, especially in the major cities of Warsaw and Łódź. It was thus relatively easy to concentrate troops in support of the employers in the event of a strike or a lock-out. Nevertheless, in the years immediately preceding the First World War, as in so many other countries, working-class discontent rose sharply. In 1911 a poor harvest and a consequent increase in food prices brought about a rise in the number of strikes, which were necessarily both economic and political in their intent. As long as the employers called upon the assistance of the Russian state the workers were bound to have the political aim of achieving a political revolution.

The Social Democracy of the Kingdom of Poland and Lithuania (SDKPiL) had kept intact its basic organization in the major industrial areas of the Kingdom of Poland and in Białystok. In its Sixth Congress, held in Prague from 5 to 13 December 1908, the leadership, headed by Leon Tyszka-Jogiches, Adolf Warski-Warszawski, Julian Marchlewski and Felix Dzierżyński, all of whom were compelled to live abroad, conferred with those of their colleagues responsible for the organization of the party at home. The problems which were most prominent on the agenda were those most vital to the Kingdom of Poland. It was proposed that the Kingdom should be given legislative autonomy and its own administration, but the concept of an independent Poland was made dependent upon the general success of the socialist revolution in Europe. With regard to the peasants, the congress recognized that the peasants were emerging as a political force, but Marchlewski thought that the redistribution of land to the peasants after the successful revolution would be politically and economically undesirable. Within the wider context of the Russian revolutionary movement, the party aligned itself firmly with the Bolshevik wing of the Russian Social Democratic Workers' Party against the Mensheviks, though calling for unity, but this desire for unity did not extend to organizational co-operation with the PPS–Left.[3] The prospect of co-operation with the Bund, however, was acceptable. It is difficult to avoid the conclusion that the SDKPiL still had a concept of a certain doctrinal purity ill-matched to the situation actually existing in Poland. In common with many Polish organizations there arose tensions between the leadership actually in the country and leading figures dwelling abroad. The decision that part of the Main Executive should remain in the country, but that it should have the right to confirm party decisions, was evidence of an uneasy situation within the SDKPiL. In fact tensions grew. In December 1911 a conference in Warsaw demanded of the Main Executive an explanation of its activity. The Main Executive replied in kind, calling a new Warsaw Committee and condemning its critics. A revolutionary court called to judge Józef Unszlicht and Mateusz Matusz-ewski found against the Main Executive, and was supported by leading figures at home and abroad. Thus the original Warsaw Committee was able to reject the authority of the Main Executive. From 1911 the SDKPiL was split into two groups, the supporters of the Main Executive and the adherents of the Warsaw Committee which drew its support mainly from within the country. The SDKPiL carried on an extensive agitation in Poland, but the divisions within the party rendered its work less effective. It was not until 1916 that the SDKPiL came together again to form a united party.

The PPS had already split in the autumn of 1906 at its Ninth Congress in Vienna. The PPS–Left at the Tenth (First) Congress, held in Cieszyn (Teschen) in January 1908, thought in terms of a legal struggle on the basis of a united workers' movement in the Kingdom of Poland allied to the Menshevik wing of the Russian Social Democratic Workers' Party, in contrast to the PPS–Revolutionary Fraction which identified the political struggle exclusively with the quest for independence.[4] By the time it had held its Eleventh (Second) Congress in Opawa in April 1912, the tendency towards legal struggle had weakened and opinion had turned in favour of an underground organization of the party's work. On the question of the autonomy of the Kingdom of Poland its position was not much different from that of the SDKPiL, to which in most matters it was very close, but its aspiration to unite all the socialist groups in Poland was not to be realized before the war of 1914. Only on 16 December 1918 did the PPS–Left join with the SDKPiL to form the Communist Workers' Party of Poland. The leading members of both the SDKPiL and the PPS–Left were fearless workers for the socialist cause. Marchlewski and Dzierżyński died respected leaders in the USSR. Rosa Luxemburg and Leon Tyszka-Jogiches were murdered by German counter-revolutionaries in Berlin in 1919. Others were done to death in shameful circumstances. Of the SDKPiL, Bortnowski, Bobiński, Grzeszczalski, Krajewski-Stein, Leński, Próchniak, Radek, and Warski, and from the PPS–Left Bitner, Hempel, Wera Kostrzewa (Maria Koszutska), Królikowski, Ryng and Henryk Walecki (Maximilian Horwitz) were falsely accused and died in Soviet purges. Duracz and Małgorzata Fornalska died at the hands of the Germans in the Second World War. A better fate would have awaited them in a Poland with a happier history.

Galician politics and political groupings, 1908–14

Galicia in the years immediately preceding the First World War exhibited the extreme divisions present among the Poles of the Kingdom of Poland, but with the complication that the Poles were a dominant nationality contending with the Ukrainians for the upper hand in the eastern regions of the province. In the elections to the provincial parliament in February 1908 the conservatives lost ground in the urban and rural *curiae* but their control over the *curia* of the large landowners gave them 43 seats and made them the largest single element. The Polish Peasant Party (PSL) emerged with 20 seats. The party, however, decided in March 1908 to join the Polish Circle in the Reichsrat, and cannot therefore be considered a radical force in Polish politics. The government in Vienna, to ensure the peace of the province, would have favoured a compromise with the Ukrainians by granting them admission to the local administration and educational concessions in return for abandoning their demands that the province should be divided into two parts. When the negotiations conducted between the committees of the Polish and Ukrainian Circles were revealed to the public there was an outcry on both sides which exacerbated relations between the two peoples. On 12 April 1908 the viceroy, Andrzej Potocki, was shot dead by a Ukrainian student, Miroslav Sichynsky, who happened to be a member of the Ukrainian Social Democratic Party, but had acted upon his own initiative. This act excited the worst nationalist feelings of the Polish reactionaries, who demanded rigorous measures against the Ukrainians, who for their part regarded the death sentence imposed upon Sichynsky as adding yet another martyr to the national cause. The impending crisis in the Balkans induced in the Austrian authorities a sense of caution. The new viceroy was Michał Bobrzyński, the distinguished historian from Cracow and a loyalist conservative. His policy was to continue working towards an understanding with the Ukrainians. In fact, he was prepared to go even farther than Potocki and was ready to concede the creation of a Ukrainian university in Lwów. The death sentence on Sichynsky was commuted to imprisonment and a pardon was issued to him in 1909. Discussions continued from 1908 to 1913 on the thorny question of how to satisfy the nation aspirations of the Ukrainians. Bobrzyński in 1913 produced a complicated reform of the curial system, designed on the one hand to strengthen the hand of the administration by increasing the ex-officio members of the parliament, and on the other to give the Ukrainians, who constituted 43 per cent of the population, 62 seats out of a total of 227. This was a small concession indeed, but it aroused the opposition of the Roman Catholic church. On 16 April 1913 the Polish bishops condemned the scheme as encouraging radicalism and at the same time as being unjust to the Catholics.[5] The church, which ought to have worked for conciliation, revealed itself to be the most reactionary and nationalist element in Galician politics. The unfortunate Bobrzyński was compelled to resign and the politics of the province were thrown into disarray, with consequent complications in the Reichsrat where the Ukrainian Club began a campaign of obstructionism. With the support of the central government the new viceroy, Witold Korytowski, revised Bobryński's scheme, which was carried in the provincial parliament by an overwhelming majority. The result of the elections was a weakening of the Polish Peasant Party and of the National Democrats, but the conservative elements, with the exception of those at Cracow, which had been attacked by the church for their flirtation with radicalism, emerged relatively strong owing to their control over the curia of the large landowners. In fact, it was the conservatives of eastern Galicia, numerically the least strong of the Polish population in Galician society, who emerged as the most powerful element in the provincial parliament with 40 representatives. Such a situation could not hold promise of stability for the future.

The alignments of Polish political parties in Galicia underwent considerable evolution during the discussions undertaken by Bobrzyński in the years 1908–13. The Polish Peasant Party (PSL) became less popular as it scented real power and was joined by members of the middle class and even of the aristocracy like Count Mikołaj Rej, an old magnate, and Count Zygmunt Losocki, the prefect (*starosta*) of Tarnobrzeg. When the Polish Peasant Party joined the government coalition, Władysław Długosz became minister for Galicia from 1911 to 1913. In the elections of 1911 the Polish Peasant Party joined with the Cracow conservatives and democrats to support the viceroy Bobrzyński's policy. In the elections of 1913, however, the Polish Peasant Party lost some influence on account of its association with conservatism and failure to represent the interests of the peasants. The leader, Jan Stapiński, came under criticism from within the party. The party broke up in December 1913 into two groups The right wing formed itself into the Polish Peasant Party–Piast (after the weekly publication *Piast*), under the leadership of Jakub Bojko, Długosz, Count Rej and Wincenty Witos, who was to be a growing force in Polish politics and to be prime minister in independent Poland in 1920–1, 1923 and 1926. Stapiński for his part, who seceded from the Polish Circle, formed the Polish Peasant Party–Left (PSL–Lewica) with five of his fellow members of the Reichsrat. The Piast group tended to represent the interests of the larger peasants and to seek an accommodation with the upper-and middle-class groups, especially the clergy. Stapiński tended to look towards the left-wing groups, but his record was suspect. Thus the peasant movement in Galicia found itself in disarray on the eve of the First World War. The leaders of the popular parties paid the penalty for identifying the petty provincial politics of Lwów and subtle adjustments of the parliamentary game in Vienna with the real needs of Polish society.

The significance of Polish politics in Galicia for the future of Poland was slight, but Galicia did offer a refuge for those parties which did not enjoy a legal existence in Russian Poland. In Cracow and in Lwów there were agencies of both sections of the SDKPiL, the PPS–Left and PPS–Revolutionary Fraction. Their publications could be printed without fear of their being confiscated by the Russian police. In June 1912 the Central Committee of the Russian Social Democratic Workers' Party established its Foreign Section in Cracow, as did the Lithuanian Social Democratic Party. Lenin himself lived for a while in Cracow. The Galician conservatives could struggle with the radicalism which threatened them in the province of Galicia, but they did little to combat the radicalism and revolutionary spirit which thrived among those who sought to overthrow the even more conservative forces of tsardom.

The PPS-Revolutionary Fraction had lost its mass following in the Kingdom of Poland, except in the Dąbrowa basin, but sought to compensate for its decline in influence by hitching its fortunes to those of the Austro-Hungarian empire. As early as 29 September 1906 Józef Piłsudski and his closest associate, Dr Witold Jodko-Narkiewicz, established contact with the intelligence officers of the Austrian Tenth Corps, stationed at the fortress in Przemyśl.[6] There is no doubt that Austrian intelligence knew much about the activities of the Polish Socialist Party. Present also at these conversations was a certain Józef Czernecki, a captain in the Austrian reserve, who assisted Austrian intelligence from 1902 to 1912, after which he vanished, probably to Kiev, which would indicate that he was also an agent of the Okhrana.[7] Certainly the Russian authorities would have wished to establish close contacts with the Austrian police, but the worsening international situation after the Bosnian crisis of 1908 caused the Austrians to look, if not with favour, at least with tolerance upon the activities of anti-Russian conspiratorial groups. In 1908 the Revolutionary Fraction established the Association for Active Struggle (Związek Walki Czynnej), under the leadership of Kazimierz Sosnkowski, with a programme of working for the establishment of an independent democratic Polish republic. The socialist content of the programme, however, was soon whittled down, because any attempt to re-establish Poland would be in association with Austria–Hungary. Slogans of solidarity and national unity began to replace plans of social reform, especially when other organizations began to arise. Dissident National Democrats established the Polish Military Association (Polski Związek Wojskowy) in 1908 in Cracow and 1909 in Lwów, with the aim of preparing for an armed struggle by creating the nucleus of an officer corps. Rifle clubs were founded in 1910 by Piłsudski, who set up the Rifleman (Strzelec) in Cracow, and then by Władysław Sikorski, who founded the Rifle Association (Związek Strzelecki) in Lwów. The Polish Military Association established the Polish Army (Armia Polska) with its own legal rifle clubs, the Polish Rifle Teams (Polskie Drużyny Strzeleckie). This paramilitary activity in Galicia gave the Russian government some considerable anxiety. As early as 24 July 1906 the Russian ambassador in Vienna, Prince Urusov, complained of the Polish Socialist Party's military activity in Galicia. Further protests were made on 1 September 1909, 26 November 1909, 7 October 1910, 21 December 1910, 27 June 1911 and 9 March 1912. The frequency of Russian protests is some indication of the laxity with which the Austrian government dealt with this aspect of Polish activity. The intelligence departments of the First, Tenth and Eleventh Corps, based upon Cracow, Przemyśl and Lwów, were prepared to accept the paramilitary organizations' existence with equanimity. Their armament was negligible, but the information they provided about Russian troop dispositions was useful. What the Poles had to do was to prove their own respectability to the Austro-Hungarian government. On the orders of Piłsudski, Marian Kukiel in August 1912 drew up a memorial for the Austrian authorities, in which he represented the Polish Socialist Party as being closer to the socialist parties of Western Europe and as not intending to achieve political ends by means of revolution.[8] In 1913 it was proposed to the Austrian general staff that in the event of a war with Russia the Polish Socialist Party should call a rising in the Kingdom of Poland and set up the skeleton of a Polish administration. The logic of this plan was that the new Poland should be associated with Austria in the same way that the Kingdom of Hungary formed part of the Habsburg empire. There was an element of make-believe in Piłsudski's concepts. The Habsburg empire was likely to have its very existence put to the test in a general European war, and, even if the empire emerged intact from it, Germany was hardly likely to tolerate an enlarged Austrian Poland which would turn Poznania, West Prussia and Upper Silesia into a Polish *irredenta*. Piłsudski had come a long way since he had first joined the Polish socialist movement. The editor of *Robotnik* of 1894 was beginning to move into the realm of cabinets and kings and to exhibit all the signs of his subsequent inordinate conceit.

On 25–26 August 1912 a conference was held at Zakopany attended by representatives of the PPS–Revolutionary Fraction, the Polish Social Democratic Party, the Polish Progressive Party (Polskie Stronnictwo Postępowe), persons connected with the periodical *Zarzewie*, the National Peasant Union (NZCh) and the Independence Organization of the intelligentsia. As a result of their discussions there was established on 10 November 1912 The Temporary Commission of Confederated Independence Parties (Tymczasowa Komisja Skonfederowanych Stronnictw Niepodległościowych – TKSSN), of which the secretary was Jodko-Narkiewicz and the military leader Józef Piłsudski.[9] This broad-bottomed organization, which meant the resignation of many of the constituent parties' political aims, did not meet with the approval of all parties. Its pro-Austrian orientation did not appeal to the Galician National Democrats, or to the reactionary groups in eastern Galicia known as the Podolians who thought that association with Russia offered better security against Ukrainian nationalism. Even within the Commission there were difficulties. The followers of Piłsudski sought to dominate its activity in consequence of which there were substantial secessions in May 1914. The real significance of the paramilitary activity in Galicia lay in its creation of a nucleus of political leaders with pretensions to military ability. Kazimierz Sosnkowski, Marian Kukiel, Felicjan Sławoj-Składkowski, Walery Sławek, Alexander Prystor and Edward Śmigły-Rydz were to achieve prominence in independent Poland. Władysław Sikorski, briefly eclipsed in 1926, when Piłsudski retired him compulsorily, emerged once more in 1939 to become prime minister and commander-in-chief. When the time came they were all to be advanced in rank in the new Polish army. Their promotion owed nothing to their military education, but everything to their conspiratorial past. Just as the Reichstag, Reichsrat and duma bequeathed to independent Poland politicians inexperienced in the exercise of real power based upon the consent of the community, so the legions which Piłsudski and his friends were to raise as the nucleus of a fighting force created an officer class of dubious ability, but with a keen sense of its own importance in the body politic.[10]

Poland in 1914

When the great powers of Europe put their alliance systems to the test in 1914 they unwittingly submitted to the arbitrament of war questions which had lain dormant for centuries. With the advent of the Ottoman empire to the war on the side of the Central Powers the Turkish domination of the Arab world could no longer be taken for granted. The Battle of the White Mountain of 1620, which seemed to have imposed upon the Czechs permanent subjection to, or at the best association with Austria, no longer possessed a final validity. The lands of the Crown of St Stephen, which the Austro-Hungarian ultimatum of 23 July 1914 sought to protect, were now open to partition in the event of an unsuccessful war. Equally Poland, partitioned in the eighteenth century, might in the twentieth once again have an independent existence. The Poles entered the war with some advantages. Their national culture had not been undermined by foreign rule. Their historical sense was strong. They nevertheless suffered from grave handicaps. Separate political existences within three empires had destroyed their own political unity. Among the contending great powers France and Britain had no fundamental interest in promoting the Polish cause. A solution of the Polish Question was not obligatory upon Germany, Austria–Hungary or Russia. Poland was not a European question, nor could its manipulation yield any of the powers particular advantage. The decision to create a Czech state in 1918, and therefore to destroy the political unity of the Austro-Hungarian empire, was made because of its obvious utility in the midst of a bitter struggle. The creation of a new Poland would mean merely the loss of frontier provinces by three states, but did not threaten them with destruction. The Polish Question must be seen in its proper perspective. It was one which existed only for the Poles themselves. The only interest which the partitioning powers had in the Poles was the conscription of 1,500,000 of them to serve in their armies, together with the civilian labour which could be employed in their factories and peasants who tilled the soil to provide food. It is therefore understandable that in the first instance the Poles could not respond to the war as a nation. The war was an opportunity. The problem before the Poles was how to use it. The Poles can therefore be excused for inexperience.

The Russian state, which embraced most of the territories to which the Poles would lay claim, took some time to define its attitude. On 14 August 1914 the Russian commander-in-chief, the Grand Duke Nikolai Nikolayevich, issued a manifesto declaring that it was Russian policy to join Poland together as a state within the Russian system. This statement was in its very essence equivocal. A commander-in-chief had no authority to make such a declaration on policy and could easily be disavowed. A promise as important as this ought to have been issued in the name of the tsar himself. The terms of the manifesto were, moreover, vague in the extreme, offering freedom of religion, the use of the Polish language and local self-government. This proposal fell far short of the independence which remained the ultimate aspiration of most Poles. Nevertheless, the propertied class had already declared their allegiance to Russia. In the duma the National Democrat, Wiktor Jaroński, a landowner from Kielce, pledged Polish support in the name of the Polish Circle for a War of the Slavs against their eternal enemy, the Germans. In their support for the war the pro-Russian party had the adherence of the clergy in the Kingdom of Poland. The clergy in Poznania and the Christian Democrat in Silesia, Adam Napieralski, for their part urged Poles to show their loyalty to the Prussian state and even to say daily prayers to the Lord of Hosts for a German victory. In Galicia most politicians pronounced in favour of Austria. On 16 August 1914 the Polish Circle set up the Supreme National

Committee (Naczelny Komitet Narodowy) in Cracow, which declared its
faith in a victorious war to liberate Poland from the domination of the
tsar. Piłsudski, whose plans for an invasion of the Kingdom of Poland
received approval from the Austrian military authorities on 26 July 1914,
sent a small body of some 200 men, drawn from the rifle clubs, into the
gubernia of Kielce to disrupt Russian mobilization. On 27 July an
announcement was made in Cracow that a 'National Government' had
been established in Warsaw and that Piłsudski had been appointed
commander-in-chief. In that capacity Piłsudski declared that units of the
Polish army had entered the Kingdom of Poland and that all Poles had
the duty to support it. This gasconade had no influence upon events. On
25 November 1914, Roman Dmowski at the head of the National
Democrats, together with adherents of the Party of Realpolitik, founded
the Polish National Committee (Komitet Narodowy Polski) in Warsaw in
order to promote the cause of Poland in association with Russia. The
response of the parties to the war was predictable. The upper classes turned
to the states under whose rule they lived. The major working-class parties
like the SDKPiL and the PPS–Left condemned the imperialist war and
strove to achieve the social revolution. The war which was to present the
Poles with a chance to win their independence found them in disarray. Four
years were to elapse before a satisfactory solution could be found.

The multiplicity of political parties and their splinter groups reveals the
nature of the Polish problem. While all Poles longed for independence they
were not likely to be of one mind when they achieved it. As far as the
socialists were concerned the struggle for economic and social justice
would continue. Independence would not immediately dispose of the
question of land hunger for the peasants. The upper classes who feared
for supremacy before 1914 might contemplate the future with misgiving.
The fight for national self-determination was accompanied, as it had been
before in Polish history, by a contest to determine who should rule at home
when independence had been won.

4

The emergence of an independent
Polish state

The first year of the war

The war began in 1914 with German expectation of a quick victory in the west at least. In fact, the stabilization of the front in France after the Battle of the Marne revealed that the struggle would be a long one. The powers which had partitioned Poland now turned to the question of enlisting Polish support in the conflict which was to extend until 1918. None of the powers had clearly defined aims for Poland at the beginning of the war. The clearest objectives were those of Austria–Hungary, where there was widespread support for the incorporation of the Kingdom of Poland into the Habsburg empire and its union with Galicia as a third constituent portion of the monarchy. The Austrians, however, hesitated to make this aim public. The attempt of the Pole, Leon Biliński, the Austro-Hungarian minister of finance, to persuade the emperor Franz Joseph to issue a declaration in favour of the 'Austro-Polish solution' was unsuccessful. Nevertheless, on 12 August Berchtold, the Austrian Foreign minister, received a general promise from Germany that an Austro-Polish settlement would be looked upon with favour, a promise repeated, though in vague terms, at a conference between Austrian and German representatives at Poznań in January 1915. The Germans were on this occasion more interested in the division of the spoils in the Dąbrowa basin which had fallen into the hands of the Central Powers (Germany and Austria–Hungary).[1] The Hungarians objected to the concept. The plan put forward by the Austrian prime minister, Karl Sturgkh, in 1915 proposed only that the new Polish territories within the monarchy should enjoy the same autonomy as Galicia. Eastern Galicia with its predominantly Ukrainian population was to be made into a separate province.

As far as the Germans were concerned, they were committed to an Austro-Polish solution, but as early as 31 July Kaiser William II had told Bogdan Hutten-Czapski, a leading pro-German figure among the Polish aristocracy in Prussian Poland, that, if Germany were victorious, he would establish an independent Polish state 'linked with us'.[2] The annexationist programme set out in September 1914 by the German chancellor, Bethmann-Hollweg, also affirmed that among the states participating in the 'Central European economic association' would be Poland.[3] A number of factors determined German policy in addition to support of Austria–Hungary. The belief was strong in the German Foreign Office that no decisive actions should be taken on the Polish Question lest it undermine the prospects of a separate peace with Russian or affect the loyalties of Poles in Prussia. The makers of German policy, in particular the military, were increasingly concerned to acquire territory at the expense of the Kingdom of Poland, partly for economic reasons, but also to establish an area for German colonization stretching from East Prussia to Upper Silesia to act as a cordon between the Poles in Prussia and the remainder of the Polish nation.[4]

The Russian manifesto issued by the Grand Duke Nikolai Nikolayevich on 14 August 1914 (see p. 110) encountered strong opposition in reactionary circles in Russia, especially among those who hoped to reach a separate peace with Germany. Dmowski's Polish National Committee did not acquire any measure of popularity and indeed drew its support in Poland only from the National Democrats and the Party of Realpolitik. An attempt to raise a Polish legion to fight on the side of Russia as a competitor of Piłsudski's legions also met with little success. Its commander, Witold Gorczyński, was an obscure figure previously unknown in Polish politics. The Russians kept a close watch on the legion recruited at Puławy and deprived it of any really Polish character. They were, moreover, in no hurry to enlarge upon the promises made in the commander-in-chief's manifesto. The reactionary minister of the interior, Nikolai Maklakov, even explained to the acting governor-general of 'the Vistula Territories' that it applied only to Polish lands outside Russia which would be conquered during the war. Until then the existing laws and regulations were to be maintained in force, though 'with the greatest goodwill'.[5] When the question of Polish autonomy was finally discussed by the council of ministers in November 1914, a distinctly moderate plan proposed by Sazonov, the Russian foreign minister, was accepted, though not without strong opposition from the more reactionary of them. This scheme would have permitted the wider employment of Poles and a greater use of the Polish language in the administration and educational system but would have left military and foreign affairs in the hands of the central government.

In January 1915 Nicholas II gave instructions to the council of ministers to consider how this plan might be carried out. By March a proposal was accepted which whittled down still further the autonomy to be offered to the Poles. In fact, the only significant modification of previous tsarist policy at this time was the extension of Russian municipal law to the Kingdom of Poland, which meant that the Polish language could now be used in local administration. Yet the value of this concession was seriously diminished in Polish eyes by the simultaneous separation from the Kingdom of the district of Chełm, which was now formally incorporated in the Russian empire. Indeed, the inadequacy of Russian measures led to criticism by the pro-Russian Poles and the establishment of a joint Russo-Polish commission on 19 June 1915. It included among others both Dmowski and Zygmunt Wielopolski, but in spite of holding nine sessions it could not reconcile Russian and Polish views. On 1 August, however, the Russian premier, Goremykin, did announce to the duma that the tsar had ordered the cabinet to draft a bill to establish Polish autonomy.

The early efforts of Piłsudski to set up a 'National Government' had failed. The Germans themselves quickly took possession of the Dąbrowa basin, where he might have expected some local support. The incursion into the region of Kielce had proved a fiasco. Such was his situation that he was faced with the difficult alternatives either of disbanding his legions, or subordinating them to Austrian military control, as the Austrians demanded in an ultimatum to him of 13 August 1914. The establishment of the Supreme National Committee (NKN) on 16 August, bringing together not only the TKSSN (see above p. 108), which Piłsudski thought too 'left-wing' to serve as the basis of a 'National Government', but also the Conservatives and the National Democrats, provided a way out of his dilemma. The Supreme National Committee proclaimed its 'Austro-Polish' orientation and the Austrians gave it permission to establish a military force with Polish uniforms and Polish as the language of command, on condition that it swore an oath of alliance to the emperor. Accordingly a Western and an Eastern Legion were authorized, each to consist of 8,000 men. Piłsudski's forces were incorporated as the First Regiment, later to be the First Brigade, of the Western Legion.

The unity of the Supreme National Committee was fragile. The adherence of the Galician National Democrats to an Austro-Polish solution was a matter of expediency rather than conviction. It was completely undermined by the Russian victories in eastern Galicia, which led to the capture of Lwów on 3 September 1914. As a result the National Democrat politicians succeeded in persuading the overwhelming majority of the soldiers in the Eastern Legion to disband in September, while they themselves withdrew from the Supreme National Committee on 8 November.[6] The Western Legion, based on Cracow, soon grew to comprise three brigades. The part played by the First Brigade in the

Austro-German offensives of early 1915 and the renown of its exploits laid the foundation of the reputation of its 'commander', as Piłsudski was known, and did something to dispel the reserve with which he was held in Russian Poland.

Piłsudski's alliance with Austria was always purely tactical in character. Before the war he had made it clear that he believed the war would see first the defeat of Russia by the Central Powers and then their defeat by France and Britain. His desire to act upon the supposition of this sequence of events ruptured what ties he had with the PPS and the Socialist Revolutionaries.[7] He tried continually to emphasize the independent character of the war he was fighting against Russia. The specific features of his brigade showed a difference, ranks not corresponding with those in the Austrian army. All officers were paid an identical salary, while officers and men addressed one another as 'citizen'. He sought to extend his influence by setting up a Polish National Organization (Polska Organizacja Narodowa – PON), which concluded a short-lived agreement with the Ninth German Army, providing for propaganda activity and recruitment to the legions in the Russian areas of Poland. He likewise established a Polish Military Organization (Polska Organizacja Wojskowa – POW) under Adam Koc in the Kingdom of Poland in the hope of creating a diversion in the Russian rear.

The first year of the war proved a serious disappointment to Polish political groupings. Those who placed their faith in the Central Powers, generally known as the 'activists', were disillusioned by the failure of the Prussian government to modify its policy towards Poland and by the savage German bombardment of Kalisz on 2 August 1914 in retaliation for sniping at German troops. German, and to a lesser extent Austrian, economic exactions were severe in the Kingdom of Poland. Faith in the Austrians was undermined by reprisals taken against both Ukrainians and Poles for their alleged collaboration during the Russian occupation of eastern Galicia. Pro-Russian groups were disheartened by the failure to implement the promised self-government, while the crude policy of russification pursued in eastern Galicia and the scorched-earth tactics adopted by the Russians in their retreat in the Kingdom of Poland dismayed those who looked to the east for a solution. The Russian evacuation of the Kingdom led to the displacement of 800,000 persons into the interior of the empire and was accompanied by a pointless wave of arrests in Warsaw before its evacuation in 1915.

July 1915 to the proclamation of a German-controlled state, November 1916

The successful German and Austrian offensives in the spring and summer of 1915 changed the situation radically. On 4 May the Russian front was broken at Gorlice and by 5 August Warsaw was in German hands. At the end of October 1915 the front was stabilized along a line running from Dünaborg in the north to Tarnopol in the south. Though the Brusilov counter-offensive in the summer of 1916 enjoyed some success against the Austrians, the Russians were unable to dislodge the Central Powers from the Polish areas they had conquered. Two occupation régimes were established in the former Kingdom of Poland, a larger German sector with its capital at Warsaw, and an Austrian zone controlled from Lublin. The Germans, hard pressed by the Allied blockade, pursued a policy of systematic economic exaction in their zone, removing not only raw materials, but also machinery and industrial apparatus. At the same time their administration, headed by General Beseler, did make some concessions to Polish national sentiment. They allowed the development of a Polish school system and in November 1915 the University and Polytechnic of Warsaw were reopened. Polish was used as the language of instruction for the first time since 1869. The lower courts were placed in Polish hands, while a system of local self-government was introduced. In the Austrian zone similar concessions were made.

Agreement over what long-term policy should be adopted for the former Kingdom of Poland proved more difficult to achieve. The Germans still hesitated to take any irrevocable steps lest they should make impossible the separate peace which they had hoped their offensive would compel the Russians to conclude. By August 1915, however, they informed the Austrians that they were prepared to consider an Austro-Polish solution, provided they were granted territory in the Kingdom of Poland, closer economic and political links between Germany and Austria–Hungary were established and the position of the Germans in the Dual Monarchy was safeguarded. Subsequently they posed even more severe conditions, demanding the conclusion of a military convention between Germany and Austria–Hungary and guarantees which would make Polish economic and transport systems dependent on Germany.

German policy began to move away from the Austro-Polish solution at the end of 1915. This change was caused by a number of factors. The Germans were dissatisfied with the Austrian response to the demands they had made in relation to the Polish Question and were concerned to safeguard their eastern frontier against a possible Russian resurgence. They were also becoming increasingly interested in the Kingdom of Poland, which before the war took 75 per cent of Germany's exports to Russia.[8] The military were increasingly attracted by the prospect of recruitment from an 'independent' Polish state. The new German policy was rejected in April 1916 by Count Burian, the Austro-Hungarian foreign minister. The German attempt to make it more acceptable by offering the throne of the new state to an Austrian archduke failed to induce him to change his mind. The collapse of the Austrian front in the face of the Brusilov offensive made it more difficult for the Austrians to resist German demands and increased also the need for new sources of recruits. Thus in August 1916 Burian accepted the German scheme of establishing a 'Kingdom of Poland' with a 'hereditary monarchy and constitutional institutions'.[9] The new state was not to have an independent foreign policy and its army was to be under German control. Burian was able, however, to limit German demands for an economic monopoly. The implementation of this policy was for the moment delayed by new hopes of a separate peace with Russia occasioned by the dismissal of Sazonov in July and his replacement as foreign minister by Stürmer.

The Austro-German conflict was paralleled by growing discord among Polish groups supporting the Central Powers. At the root of this problem lay a different assessment of how the war would develop. The leadership of the Supreme National Council was now convinced that the Central Powers would win the war and that the Poles stood to gain most by whole-hearted co-operation with them and above all with Austria. Piłsudski agreed that Russia would be defeated and soon be involved in a revolutionary crisis. He was, however, by no means certain that the Central Powers would be victorious. Even if they were, he thought that the Poles were likely to gain more by adopting an uncompromising position than by yielding too easily. He was convinced, moreover, that the weakness of Austria made an Austro-Polish solution unlikely and was moving towards the idea of co-operation with Germany.

As a result Piłsudski effectively sabotaged the plans of the military department of the Supreme National Committee (NKN) headed by Colonel Sikorski for large-scale recruitment in the Kingdom of Poland after August 1915. The dispute soon widened in scope. With the movement of the Legionary Command to the Kingdom of Poland in April 1915, the autonomy that Piłsudski's First Brigade had enjoyed began to be whittled away by the Austrian general in charge of the Legions, General Durski-Trzaska, and his chief-of-staff, Major Włodzimierz Zagórski. Piłsudski thus began to demand the 'legionization' of the legions and the removal of Austrian officers. He made little progress, though Durski-Trzaska was replaced by another Austrian, General Puchalski. In February

1916 he encouraged the emergence of the Colonels' Council, which in memoranda to the Austrians and the Supreme National Committee in June and August demanded more autonomy for the Legions, which were to be regarded as a Polish army fighting for an independent Poland, the removal of Austrian officers and the dissolution of the military department of the NKN. In addition they called for an agreement between the National Central Committee (Centralny Komitet Narodowy – CKN) which had been sponsored by Piłsudski in December 1915 to unite the various political organizations in the Kingdom of Poland supporting him and the Supreme National Committee. Together they were to create a Polish government which would control the Legionary Command. At the end of July Piłsudski himself resigned from his position in the First Brigade. The Austrians, who were still hoping to use the Legions as an argument against the Germans in favour of the Austro-Polish solution, agreed to the creation of a Polish Auxiliary Corps of two divisions. At the same time they were compelled by German pressure to accept Piłsudski's resignation on 26 September, which increased the turmoil in the Legions, particularly in the First and Third Brigades. The new commander of the Legions, the Austrian general, Stanisław Szeptycki, was, however, able to restore discipline by the end of October. By this stage the Legions numbered approximately 1,000 officers and 20,000 men.

Throughout this period Piłsudski attempted to create for himself a broader political base. He continued his efforts to build up the clandestine Polish Military Organization, sending into it some of his most trusted men from the First Brigade. In addition, he endeavoured to win over the pro-Russian groups in the Kingdom of Poland, now organized in the Inter-Party Political Circle (Międzypartyjne Koło Polityczne), and generally referred to as 'passivists'. He was, however, unable to make of the National Central Committee, established under his auspices in December 1915, a broad umbrella organization similar to the Supreme National Committee (NKN) in Galicia. The National Democrats, in particular, were too suspicious of his radical past and still placed their hopes in an Allied victory. Nevertheless he did induce a number of leading passivist politicians in February 1916 to sign a 'Declaration of the Hundred' drawn up by the National Central Committee, which called for 'the attainment of an independent state, protected by its own armed forces'.

In Russia it still proved impossible to take a decisive initiative on the Polish Question. The speech by the newly appointed premier, Stürmer, in the duma on 22 February 1916 in which he promised the Poles the opportunity to achieve their 'cultural and economic aspirations' even seemed a step back from Goremykin's speech in the previous year.[10] The slowness of Russia to take action caused increasing disillusionment among the pro-Russian Poles and in November 1915 Dmowski thus moved to Western Europe. His view was that only pressure from France and Britain would induce Russia to change her policy. There were a number of signs that France, in particular, was prepared to exert more influence in this respect. Briand, the new foreign minister, mentioned the possibility of a future Polish state in the Chamber of Deputies in November 1915 and did begin tentatively to raise the question with Izvolsky, the Russian ambassador to France. Viviani, minister of justice, and Thomas, minister of munitions, were persuaded only with some difficulty by the French ambassador Paléologue from raising this question during their visit to Russia in May 1916.

As a result Sazonov was determined to take action, both to forestall the Central Powers and to prevent France and Britain from 'internationalizing' the Polish Question. In June 1916 he therefore submitted to the tsar a proposal for autonomy which would have given the Poles control of internal organization, education and the Catholic religion, while leaving foreign, military and most economic affairs in Russian hands. On 12 July Nicholas approved Sazonov's scheme, but matters were again thrown into confusion by Sazonov's dismissal on 20 July. A major factor was the hostility of the tsarina to Sazonov and his views on the Polish Question. On 18 August it was announced that the Polish statute would be proclaimed only when Russian troops entered Poland. This further confirmed the Polish loss of faith in Russia, and the pro-Allied elements now increasingly put their faith in the 'internationalization' of the Polish Question. Already in February 1916 Dmowski in a memorandum had called for a fully independent Poland, though Izvolsky believed he would still accept a dynastic union with Russia.

At the same time war-weariness and the severity of German and Austrian economic exactions were increasing the strength of the anti-war groups in the Kingdom of Poland. Both the PPS-Left and the two factions of the SDKPiL had opposed the war in 1914 and a joint committee to co-ordinate action had been established in Warsaw. It had broken down, however, in March 1915, when the Social Democrats proved intransigently hostile to the municipal self-government introduced into the Kingdom of Poland by the Russians. Both parties had taken part in the Zimmerwald and Kienthal conferences, where the two groups of the Social Democrats came close to Lenin's views on the war as a revolutionary catalyst. Their links became closer in November 1916, when they passed a joint resolution that only the destruction of capitalism and the establishment of socialism could end wars.[11]

From November 1916 to the end of the war

The agreed proclamation of an 'independent' Polish state was made by the German and Austrian emperiors on 5 November 1916. The new state was to be allied with the Central Powers and its frontiers left for subsequent settlement. Its army was to 'embody the glorious traditions of the Polish army of former times and the memory of our valiant Polish comrades-in-arms in the present great war',[12] phrases whose significance was largely explained by the call for Polish volunteers made by General Beseler, governor-general of the German zone of occupation, on 9 November. The Austrians, worried by the impact of an 'independent' Kingdom of Poland on Galicia, had already issued a proclamation on 4 November proposing increased autonomy for that province. On 6 December the two governors-general announced the establishment of a Provisional Council of State composed of twenty-five members to be appointed by the occupying authorities. Its functions were to be purely advisory and in addition it was to co-operate with Beseler in creating a Polish army.

Though the powers conceded to the Council of State were clearly of an extremely limited character, Polish opinion reacted to these develop- ments in a generally positive way. The conservative activists, the NKN and similar groups in the Kingdom of Poland, on whom above all the Germans hoped to rely, greeted the declaration with approval. They were, indeed, strengthened by the defection of a number of leading passivist politicians, of whom the most important was the landowner, Jan Stecki. The left-wing activists in the National Central Committee also approved and attempted not very successfully to widen their political base by creating on 15 November a National Council, to which a number of smaller passivist groups adhered. The reaction of the passivist Inter-Party Political Circle also was not hostile. In a declaration of 27 November it criticized the tardiness of Russia and the Western Allies in relation to the Polish Question. Piłsudski himself responded positively, writing to his *homme de confiance* in the Legions, Śmigły-Rydz, that 'You must now show a justified patience and confidence that the Polish soldier will ultimately find in this world war his Fatherland in the form of his own government, his own army.'[13] His main preoccupation was to achieve the union of all Polish political groupings. He even tried, though in vain, to sponsor an agreement between the newly formed National Council and the Inter-Party Political Circle on the composition of the Council of State. He realized also that he could not while in uniform resist the Germans as he had the Austrians. He thus decided to accept nomination to the Council of State as a representative of the Austrian zone.

The Provisional Council of State met for the first time on 14 January 1917. It had proved impossible to persuade the Inter-Party Political Circle to serve in it. It thus consisted of 6 representatives of the National Central Committee, 9 members of conservative activist groups and 10 non-party representatives. A number of administrative departments were created together with a military board headed by Piłsudski. Disillusion with the limited powers of the Council soon grew among the activist Left and on 1 February the PPS representative resigned from the National Council. At the same time the National Central Committee also split, losing groups more in favour of full co-operation with the Germans.

The Russian revolution of March 1917 caused a major change in the situation. Up to its outbreak the Russian government had been successful in preventing the 'internationalization' of the Polish Question and in March had even obtained the assent of France for 'Russia's full freedom in the matter of determining her western borders' in return for a reciprocal understanding on France's eastern frontier.[14] On 30 March 1917 the Russian provisional government, under pressure from the Petrograd soviet, issued a manifesto promising to set up an independent Polish state composed of all ethnically Polish territories linked with Russia in a 'free military union'. The eastern frontier of this state was to be settled by the Russian constituent assembly. One of the main results of the revolution was the emergence of a Polish military force in Russia. The core of this formation was provided by the Gorczyński Legion, which by March 1917 had grown into a rifle division and now was augmented by many Poles serving in the Russian army. In June 1917 a Supreme Polish Military Council was formed. Although its establishment was most strongly supported by groupings favouring the Western Allies, it made Piłsudski its honorary president. It succeeded in raising the Polish First Corps under General Józef Dowbór-Muśnicki, amounting to 20,000 men stationed at Bobruisk. In theory the corps had to maintain a neutrality in Russian internal affairs, but it was not above coming to the aid of the Polish landlords in western Russia.[15]

The revolution had powerful repercussions in the rest of Poland. In Galicia it took the form of a revolt of the socialist, peasant and National Democrat parties against the conservative leadership of the Polish Club in the Reichsrat. This led to the adoption of a resolution on 16 May calling for a strong and independent Polish state with access to the sea. In the Kingdom of Poland the effect of the revolution was not uniform. Many members of the upper classes, worried by the possible impact of the revolution in Poland, became more sympathetic to co-operation with the Central Powers. Though the Inter-Party Political Circle remained firm in its passivist orientation, it lost a number of its leading adherents, including Prince Zdzisław Lubormirski, who told Czernin of his relief that the trenches which divided Russia from Poland would 'keep the revolution from Poland more surely than the Wall of China'.[16]

At the same time the revolution and the entry of the USA into the war increased demands for a greater degree of independence. The activist Right in the Provisional Council of State feared to lose its influence and demanded on 6 April the establishment of a Regency with powers over the courts and education and the right to send representative to the Central Powers and the neutral states. On 2 May the PPS, which was now calling for a republic with a system of universal suffrage, withdrew from the Provisional Council of State, though its representatives remained unofficially for two months. Similar demands were made by the PSL–Liberation.

Piłsudski was slow to move in opposition. As late as 1 May he argued in the Provisional Council of State 'I believe that the interests of the occupying powers will compel them soon to create a parallel government (*Nebenregierung*)'.[17] What led him to clash with the Germans was control of the enlarged Polish army. Piłsudski wanted an assurance that the Legions and the Polish Military Organization, which now claimed 11,000 members, would be the basis of a reorganized force reflecting his ideas. He also required an assurance that it would be employed only against the Russians. Beseler was not interested in co-operation with Piłsudski, whom he regarded as 'a military dilettante and a demagogue'.[18] When the Supreme Polish Military Council was established, Piłsudski, by now becoming increasingly hostile to the Germans, thought of crossing into Russia and placing himself at the head of its forces. He began also to prepare for underground activity, believing that an uprising against the Germans would fail. His 'Konwent Union A' was successful enough in consolidating his influence over left-wing groups, but his attempt to do the same for the Right through 'Konwent Union B' was much less effective. He tried unsuccessfully to secure an agreement between the National Council and the Inter-Party Political Circle. His encouragement of his supporters to refuse to take the oath of loyalty Beseler required of the Polish forces in July 1917 was merely the pretext for a break made inevitable by his realization of how limited was the independence the Germans envisaged for Poland and of their indifference to working with him. Almost the entire First and Third Brigades refused the oath and 3,300 of their members were interned, while 3,500 from Galicia were incorporated in the Austrian army. Piłsudski was arrested with his principal assistant, Sosnkowski, on the night of 21–22 July and interned in Magdeburg. The

Second Brigade, under Brigadier Józef Haller and Colonel Sikorski, was handed over to Austria as a Polish auxiliary corps. By autumn 1917 Beseler's Polnische Wehrmacht, created from the remnants of the First and Third Legions together with new recruits, amounted to only 2,700 officers and men.

The crisis caused a decline in the authority of the Provisional Council of State from which the whole of the activist Left, now referred to as the pro-independence Left, seceded on 25 August. In order to strengthen the pro-German elements the occupying powers set up on 12 September a Council of Regency and a legislative Council of State with limited powers over the courts and education. The Council of Regency finally established on 15 October was composed of Archbishop Alexander Kakowski, Prince Zdzisław Lubomirski and Count Józef Ostrowski, all conservatives who had previously held passivist views. The prime minister of the new government formed on 7 December 1917 was Jan Kucharzewski, a conservative lawyer who had supported an Austro-Polish solution. At this time, in fact, an Austro-Polish settlement was again emerging as a possibility. Germany was ready to yield on this point in return for a dominant position in the Habsburg monarchy as well as territorial concessions in Poland. The Germans required a free hand in the Baltic, where they had in December 1917 set up an 'independent' Lithuanian state with its capital at Vilna and established their hegemony in Romania. In short, Germany looked at the problem within the context of comprehensive war aims.

In the West the Polish Question had now assumed an international importance. On 4 June 1917 France decided in agreement with the Russian provisional government to form in France a Polish army composed of Polish emigrants and prisoners of war of Polish nationality. Dmowski and his associates created a Polish National Committee in Lausanne on 15 August 1917. Though it did not constitute a government-in-exile, as Dmowski had wished, it requested that the Allied governments should recognize it as an official organization representing Polish interests, especially in matters relating to the proposed Polish army in the West and its welfare. In September it was recognized by France as an intermediary between the French authorities and the Polish army. Recognition by Britain, Italy and the United States came by the end of the year.

At the same time the German position was growing steadily weaker in Poland. Disillusion with the position Germany had achieved in Romania as a result of the Treaty of Bucharest in March 1918 had caused the Germans again to move away from the Austro-Polish solution, while the fears aroused among conservatives by the Bolshevik revolution increased support for the Regency Council and for a compromise with Germany. These feelings, however, were drastically undermined by the agreement concluded at Brest-Litovsk on 9 February between the Central Powers and the nationalist Ukrainian People's Republic, which had established itself in Kiev. This limited the Polish state to its narrowest ethnic limits in the south-east, even conceding to the Ukrainians the Chełm district. In a secret clause, whose contents soon became public, Galicia was to be divided into Polish and Ukrainian areas.

Announcement of the agreement caused a wave of strikes and protest demonstrations in Poland. The Kucharzewski government resigned and on 13 April the Regency Council issued a proclamation bitterly attacking this 'new partition'.[19] The Galician conservatives were particularly angry and the Polish Circle in the Reichsrat made a strong protest as did the Polish Circle in the German Reichstag. The unrest also reached the Second Brigade, fighting as a Polish Auxiliary Corps in Bukovina, and on the night of 15–16 February 1,500 of its members led by General Haller succeeded in crossing the lines into Russia. The remainder of the Corps, including Colonel Sikorski, were interned. Further bitterness was created by German policy in Lithuania, where, as Ludendorff's staff officer, Colonel Hoffmann argued, 'the Lithuanians must be our allies in the struggle against the Poles',[20] and by the disarming in May and June of the three Polish corps which had been established in Russia. The operation had passed off peacefully in relation to the First and Third Corps, but action against the Second Corps, to which General Haller's troops had adhered, caused considerable bloodshed.

It is true that the new government of the Regency, formed in early April by Jan Kanty Steczkowski and in which the leading role was played by the great landowner Janusz Radziwiłł, did try hard to achieve some workable compromise, particularly when the great spring offensives of 1918 made a German victory seem likely. Steczkowski hoped by making minor concessions on the German–Polish frontier to obtain German consent to a return of the Chełm district as well as the area around Vilna. He was encouraged in this course by what seemed to be a change in the attitude of the Central Powers to the Polish eastern frontier. The growing weakness of the Ukrainian People's Republic led the Austrians to abandon the territorial clauses of the agreement of 9 February, while the development of a conflict between the German authorities and Lithuanian nationalists caused the occupying forces to support the Poles as a counterweight. In the Ukraine the new government of the hetman, Pavlo Skoropadsky, established with German assistance in late April, was more favourable to the Polish landlords, as indeed were the Germans in Byelorussia. The continued disagreement of Germany and Austria–Hungary over the future of Poland and the hostility of Ludendorff to concessions prevented any progress towards a solution. An indication of the weakness of pro-German groups, even among the privileged classes was provided by the elections of 9 April 1918 to the Council of State. They were boycotted by the Left because of the restricted franchise under which they were conducted. Of the 55 elected seats, 37 were won by the Inter-Party Political Circle which looked for a solution supported by the Western Allies.

The emergence of an independent state

The Polish Question now seemed to depend increasingly on the Entente. Already in December France had declared in favour of Polish independence. In his speech to the Trade Union Congress on 5 January 1918, Lloyd George gave his support for independence. President Wilson made an independent Poland with access to the sea one of his Fourteen Points on 8 January. It appeared that the Western Allies envisaged a far more radical solution of the Polish Question than the Central Powers. Nevertheless, they hesitated to recognize the Polish National Committee as a government-in-exile, although the French government did concede to it a great degree of control over the Polish army in France as well as some financial support.[21] In June the Western Allies formally rejected the Austro-Polish solution and called for a united and independent Poland with access to the sea. When the war turned in their favour in August 1918 they were still readier to sponsor an independent Poland. On 28 September the Polish army in France, then comprising 17,000 men, was recognized an 'Allied belligerent army', commanded from October by General Haller, who arrived in France from Russia, having deserted the Austrians and crossed over to the Allied side. The army was to consist also of the Polish formations raised in Russia. On 13 November the Polish National Committee was recognized by France as a *gouvernement de fait* in relation to the Polish army, foreign policy and the care of Poles in Allied countries,[22] but it was unable to obtain recognition from Britain and the USA.

In the West the National Democrats thus obtained advantages, but their situation by no means as favourable at home. At the end of August the Steczkowski government resigned in the face of political storm aroused by German revelation of the very limited proposals it had made to the Central Powers in April 1918. It proved very difficult to create a new government at all, although the Piłsudski-ites and the National Democrats were eager for an all-party coalition. Neither of these parties was, however, willing to yield the other a dominant role in such a coalition, to which in any case the pro-independence Left was very hostile. The Council of Regency was alarmed by the strength of the radical parties in the Kingdom of Poland, demonstrated by the growth of the SDKPiL and PPS-Left and the successful strikes against the occupation authorities organized on 14 and 16 October. In an attempt to diminish the appeal of revolution, the regents on 7 October called for an independent Poland consisting of all Polish territories, together with access to the sea. They also announced the dissolution of the Council of State and fresh elections. Although their attempt to form an all-party coalition under Jan Kucharzewski failed, they did on 12 October assert their control over the Polish army in the Kingdom of Poland, which Beseler was obliged to concede at the end of the month. A more satisfactory oath was devised and the army was placed under the command of an Austrian general, the Pole Rozwadowski. The army, now organized on the basis of universal service, grew rapidly, especially when many of the Legionaries released from internment joined its ranks. On 16 October the Polish National Committee, now in Paris, approached political parties at home once more in order to form a provisional government. It had no success with the pro-independence Left, but Józef Świeżyński, the chairman of the Inter-Party Political Circle, did establish a government on 23 October in which the National Democrats enjoyed the dominant position. This government lasted only until 3 November. After disavowing the Council of Regency, in an attempt to establish its popularity, it was dissolved and acquiesced supinely in its defeat.

Events now moved rapidly. On 3 November Austria–Hungary sued for peace. Already on 28 October all Polish parties in Galicia established a Liquidation Committee to take over the government. In the Kingdom of Poland the parties of the pro-independence Left made a bid for power by establishing a 'People's Government' in Lublin on 6–7 November under the Galician socialist, Ignacy Daszyński. In its manifesto it proclaimed a constitutional republic and a programme of radical political and economic reforms. Its authority was limited to the Lublin region, parts of the Dąbrowa basin and Austrian Silesia, where a Polish national Committee had been established at the end of October. It was unable to win over the Galician Liquidation Committee largely because of the opposition of Wincenty Witos, leader of PSL–Piast (see above p. 106), who had connections with the National Democrats. It also seemed likely to come into conflict with the Council of Regency. Poland thus presented a picture of political disintegration in a critical moment.

The German revolution broke out on 9 November. By 11 November the German forces in the Kingdom of Poland had been disarmed, for the most part without a struggle. On 10 November 1918 Piłsudski himself returned to Poland, overwhelmingly popular as a result of internment which had given him the aura of a martyr and the reputation of an indomitable fighter for independence unsullied by compromise. Piłsudski had come a long way since he had been a PPS conspirator. He now saw himself as a national rather than a party leader, maintaining a neutrality in the class struggle and thus willing to accept the co-operation of the Polish conservatives.[23] He was met at the station in Warsaw by a regent, Lubomirski, who clearly saw in him a saviour from social chaos. The Council of Regency submitted and conferred its power upon him on 14 November 1918 as provisional head of state. He had already become the commander-in-chief of the armed forces on 11 November. Piłsudski saw himself in the role of unifier and conciliator. In retrospect the Left was to see him in a counter-revolutionary role, bringing under control the forces of progress which sought to apply the principles of social justice to the new Polish state.

The Lublin government collapsed on 18 November 1918 and Piłsudski applied himself to the task of creating a coalition government. He thought that to deny the pro-independence Left a place in the government at this stage was to run the risk of revolution, but, as he told his supporters in this group on 10 November, Poland was too poor and had suffered too much destruction during the war to undertake radical social experiments.[24] The Left would have to wait the results of experiments in the West to guide its social policy. The Right would not accept Daszyński as prime minister, nor did he find favour with the National Democrats or Wincenty Witos. Piłsudski therefore selected Jędrzej Moraczewski, a right-wing member of the Galician Polish Social Democratic Party with Piłsudski-ite leanings, acceptable to the Right and Witos. The new cabinet consisted of 6 socialists, 5 members of peasant parties including Witos as deputy prime minister, 2 members of the parties of the radical intelligentsia and 2 non-party ministers. In order to give the government a broad character 2 posts were reserved for National Democrats from Poznania and 2 for members of peasant parties. The government's function in Piłsudski's eyes was to prepare for elections as soon as possible. Piłsudski as provisional head of state, commander-in-chief and minister of war was the most powerful figure in Poland, enjoying what he later described as 'almost dictatorial power'. In fact, the government's authority extended only to the Kingdom of Poland, parts of Austrian Silesia and those areas of Galicia which had not come under the control of the Western Ukrainian People's Republic, established after the collapse of Austria–Hungary. To the east of the Kingdom of Poland the authority of the German occupying armies of the *Ober-Öst* was still effective, while in Prussian Poland the overwhelmingly National Democrat leadership, which had formed a Supreme People's Council in Poznań on 3 December 1918, was prepared to wait for the peace conference to decide the future of the area. It was, moreover, hostile to the political complexion of the Moraczewski cabinet.

Indeed, the government soon found itself under attack from both Left and Right. The SDKPiL and the PPS–Left sank their differences on 15 December and united as the Communist Workers' Party of Poland (Komunistyczna Partia Robotnicza Polski – KPRP; from 1925 Komunistyczna Partia Polski – KPP). The party saw the moment as ripe for the seizure of power and the establishment of the dictatorship of the proletariat on the Soviet model. They were aided by the fall in real wages and greatly increased unemployment caused by the war, and enjoyed some success in forming workers' councils, particularly in the Dąbrowa basin. The party's explicit rejection of Polish independence, however, and its call for collectivization rather than the distribution of land among the peasantry reduced its appeal. This intransigent 'Luxemburgist' policy, coupled with government action against communist-dominated workers' councils and their Red Guards, kept the party's influence small and meant that without Bolshevik aid it had no real chance of achieving power.

More serious was the threat from the Right. Neither the National Democrats nor the former activist conservatives were mollified by the appointment of Moraczewski. They greatly exaggerated the radicalism of his government, arguing that the introduction of the eight-hour day was the first stage on the road to Bolshevism and declaring Piłsudski to be a Polish Kerensky. The National Democrats, moreover, believed that Piłsudski's links with the Austrians and Germans would damn him in Allied eyes, for which reason they hoped to see the return to Poland of the Polish National Committee, supported by the Allies and Haller's army. Continual demonstrations were organized against the government. Paramilitary forces were organized by the Right. The upper classes refused to pay taxes or contribute to the national loan, so much so that the Polish Loan Bank, the main source of government finance, was compelled to inform the government that it could make no further advances owing to its lack of ready cash. By this stage the government was even more isolated by the opposition of both Witos' Polish Peasant Party–Piast and the National Workers' Union (NZR) which had supported an activist policy during the war.

Nevertheless, both the Polish National Committee in Paris and Piłsudski himself were eager for a compromise. Dmowski and his associates knew that they were not strong enough to take power on their own, and feared that even if they were able to use Haller's army to establish a new government they would be widely attacked in the West for 'murdering the forces of liberty'.[25] Dmowski was deeply worried also by communist influence in Poland and believed that a coalition was necessary to prevent a Bolshevik takeover. Piłsudski, for his part, was well aware of the need for good relations with the Allies, who did not recognize the Polish government, and directed his emissaries to the Polish National Committee. He himself had little sympathy for the more radical aspirations of the Moraczewski cabinet. He needed aid from the West to equip his army and wished to embody Haller's army in it.

The first real attempt at a compromise was made by Stanisław Grabski, who was sent to Poland for this purpose by the Polish National Committee and had several meetings with Piłsudski between 5 and 10 December. Though no agreement was reached, Piłsudski did declare his willingness to abandon his plans for federal links with the national states which he believed would emerge to the east of Poland and agreed to the establishment of a 'non-political' cabinet of experts.[26] In addition, he tried to dispel the impression that he was pro-German by asking the German diplomatic representative in Warsaw, Count Harry Kessler, against whom the National Democrats had been organizing demonstrations, to leave Poland on 15 December. When an opposition delegation requested him on 16 December to agree to a national government, he replied that 'all parties, without exception, must understand that they must subordinate themselves to the general interest'. He also despatched a delegation to Paris to discuss with the Polish National Committee the possibility of establishing a common front to present the Polish case to the Allies. With this delegation he sent a letter to Dmowski, whom he referred to as 'Respected Sir' (*Szanowny Panie Romanie*), in which he expressed the hope that they both would be able to 'rise above the interests, cliques and groups'.[27]

The deadlock was broken by the famous pianist, Ignacy Paderewski, who undertook a mission to Poland in early January as a result of pressure from Balfour, the British foreign secretary, and with the agreement of the Polish National Committee. The choice of Paderewski was a fortunate one. He belonged to no party, though he had supported the pro-entente policy and was connected with the Polish National Committee. He had at the same time criticized Dmowski's anti-semitism and was thought to be sympathetic to Piłsudski's federalist plans. Agreement was hastened by an unsuccessful coup on the night of 4–5 January 1918 by a small group of army officers led by Colonel Marian Januszajtis, which aimed at establishing a government headed by the conservative, Eustachy Sapieha. The conspirators succeeded in arresting Moraczewski and a number of his ministers, but General Szeptycki, the chief of the general staff, was able to induce the troops under their command to surrender and the coup collapsed without bloodshed. Certain aspects of this incident remain mysterious. It was almost certainly not instigated by the National Democrats, though Januszajtis and his associates did have right-wing links. Paderewski and Grabski may, however, have known of their plans and it has even been argued that Piłsudski himself deliberately provoked the coup in order to facilitate the emergence of a national government.[28] Certainly after its failure he summoned Paderewski from Cracow and, having convinced himself that he had not been involved, rapidly reached agreement with him over the heads of the PPS and Moraczewski on the formation of a new government. The cabinet, which was headed by Paderewski, had a predominantly centre-right character, though most of its members had no party affiliation, a fact which was stressed by the premier when he took office. Five members of the previous cabinet remained in office, but only one of these, Józef Próchnik, had close political ties with the radical group, the PSL–Liberation. He and three of his four former colleagues did not remain in the cabinet for the whole of its life. Foreign affairs were to be dealt with by a commission headed by Paderewski on which all major parties, including the socialists, were represented. The Polish National Committee was to be enlarged by the addition of ten Piłsudski-ite members and was to represent Poland at the peace conference.

The cabinet was described by the National Democrat *Gazeta Warszawska* as 'technical and provisional'.[29] After the elections, it claimed, it would be replaced by a government based on the majority in the sejm (parliament). These elections were duly held for the Kingdom of Poland and western Galicia on 26 January. Eastern Galicia and former Prussian Poland were to be represented by the deputies to the Reichsrat and Reichstag. The elections failed to produce a clear result and revealed a striking difference between the political attitudes of the Kingdom of Poland and western Galicia. In the Kingdom the National Democrats won a major victory. The picture in western Galicia was strikingly different. (See tables 1 and 2.) The elections revealed the real evolution of Poland before 1914 and the coalescence of forces during the war. The activist conservatives were shown to enjoy small popular support.

The problem which faced the political parties in the sejm of 1919 was their alignment one with another in a united Poland. The situation is presented in table 3. There was therefore no real majority for any group in the sejm, with the further elections in parts of Austrian Silesia, Prussian

Table 1. *Elections in the Kingdom of Poland, January 1919*

Party	Percentage of votes
National Democrats	45.48
Polish Peasant Party–Liberation (PSL–Liberation)	21.97
Polish Socialist Party (PPS)	8.65
Polish Peasant Union (PZL)	4.90
National Workers' Union (NZR)	2.32
Polish Peasant Party–Piast (PSL–Piast)	2.16

The Jewish religious parties polled 5.36 per cent, but the Jewish workers obtained only 1.2 per cent. There were other minor groups of no great significance.
Source: J. Jabłoński, *Narodziny Drugiej Rzeczpospolitej*, p. 246.

Table 2. *Elections in western Galicia, January 1919*

Party	Percentage of votes
Polish Peasant Party–Piast (PSL–Piast)	34.01
Polish Peasant Party–Left (PSL–Lewica)	19.36
Polish Social Democratic Party (PPSD)	17.87
National Democrats	10.54
Catholic Peasant Party	8.82

Source: H. Jabłoński, *Narodziny Drugiej Rzeczpospolitej*, p. 250.

Poland and the Vilna and Suwałki areas merely underlining the political divisions in the country. Politics were fluid as a result of the tendency of groups of Right and Left to split off and join a very loosely united Centre. Alignments in 1919–22 are best shown in the form in table 4.

Under these conditions, any attempt to establish a government based on a parliamentary majority was likely to prove very difficult. Indeed, in view of the bitterness of the Left over the collapse of the Lublin government in December 1918, a Right–Centre coalition with a clearly political character was likely to cause social conflict. As Dmowski wrote to Zygmunt Wasilewski on 20 February 1920, 'It is certain that if we formed a government – let us assume with me at its head – we should well and truly cut the throat of Poland'.[30] Thus the Paderewski compromise lasted with no major changes until 9 December 1919, when it fell over parliamentary resistance to the attempt of the last of its finance ministers, Leon Biliński, to place the state's finances on a sound footing and over disputes on the proposed land reform. It was succeeded by a centrist

Table 3. *Results of the elections of January 1919*

	Total percentage	Percentage of vote by parties
Right	37.0	
Popular National Union (Związek Ludowo-Narodowy)		37.0
Centre	15.4	
Catholic Peasant Party (Stronnictwo Katolicko-Ludowe)		1.8
National Workers' Union (NZR)		1.8
Polish Peasant Union (PZL)		3.3
Polish Peasant Party–Piast (PSL–Piast)		8.5
Left	34.0	
Radical Intelligentsia groups		0.5
Polish Peasant Party–Liberation (PSL–Liberation)		17.0
Polish Peasant Party–Left (PSL–Lewica)		4.0
Polish Socialist Party (PPS) and Polish Social Democratic Party (PPSD)		12.5
National minorities	11.5	
Jewish non-socialist parties		9.0
Jewish workers' parties		1.0
German parties		1.5

Source: A. Próchnik, *Pierwsze piętnastolecie Polski niepodległej* [The First Fifteen Years of Independent Poland] (reprint, Warsaw, 1957). Some smaller groups have been omitted, for which reason the percentages do not total 100.

Table 4. *Party alignments 1919–22*

	Feb. 1919	June 1919	Jan. 1920	July 1922
Right	34.2	35.8	18.1	24.8
Centre	30.8	33.2	59.1	53.9
Left	30.3	26.8	17.7	16.5
National minorities	3.5	3.2	3.2	3.9
Non-party	1.2	1.0	1.9	0.9

Source: Próchnik, *Pierwsze piętnastolecie Polski niepodległej*, pp. 50–61.

coalition headed by a member of the PSL–Piast, Leopold Skulski, and supported by the main peasant groups and the Christian Democrats, which lasted until the political crisis created by the Polish–Soviet war. Throughout this period Piłsudski retained the posts of head of state and commander-in-chief which he had resigned to parliament on 20 February and in which he had been unanimously confirmed. Though he lacked a veto over domestic legislation, he played a major though not undisputed role in shaping foreign policy and was clearly the dominant figure in the army. Indeed, one of the most significant developments in the first year of Polish independence was the great increase in the size of the army which grew from barely 30,000 officers and men on 11 November 1918 to over 600,000 by August 1919, organized in the autumn into twenty divisions.

The settlement of the frontiers

The compromise which had led to the formation of the Paderewski government masked deep differences over the form the new state should take. Dmowski and his followers, true to their belief that Germany was Poland's principal enemy, aimed at extending the country as far as possible to the west, in order to make it a 'buttress against the German *Drang nach Osten*'. In the memorandum Dmowski presented to President Wilson in October 1918 on behalf of the Polish National Committee, he made large claims on Germany: Poznania, Pomerania, Upper Silesia and parts of East Prussia. He did not limit Polish claims in the east to those areas where there was a Polish minority, but demanded much of the former Grand Duchy of Lithuania, parts of Volhynia and Podolia and the whole of Galicia. In these areas he believed that Polish cultural influence was dominant and their population could thus be assimilated to the Polish nation in a unitary and centralized state.

Piłsudski continued to regard Russia as the main threat to Polish independence. He opposed far-reaching claims in the west on the grounds that they would make impossible a satisfactory relationship with Germany. He saw in the weakening of Russia, caused by the revolution and civil war, the opportunity to ensure Poland's security in the east by fostering the creation of national Lithuanian, Byelorussian and Ukrainian states which would be federally linked with Poland. Though the Poles were to be the dominant power in this federation, Piłsudski was almost certainly sincere in his claims that he respected the national aspirations of the Lithuanians, Byelorussians and Ukrainians in these areas. The same could hardly be said for the Polish landowners here who saw in these federal schemes a means of safeguarding their estates. Poland lacked the resources to embark upon so grandiose a policy, but it accorded well with Piłsudski's dictum: 'Poland will be a great power or she will not exist.' This was not a point of view which bore any resemblance to the facts of the situation as it existed in 1919, and was in the event to saddle the country with a war with the Soviets it could ill afford.[31]

The settlement of the frontiers of the new state preoccupied political life for the first two and a half years of independence. Indeed, the country only took the form it held for most of the interwar period in March 1922, when the Vilna area was finally incorporated, and it was only in March 1923 that its frontiers were recognized by the Allies. The Versailles treaty, finally signed on 28 June 1919, laid down the western frontiers of Poland. The settlement, partly as a result of Lloyd George's unwillingness to press Germany too hard, did not fully meet the Polish claims.[32] It assigned to Poland the province of Poznania, which had come under Polish control as a result of an uprising on 27 December 1918 which had anticipated the peace treaty, some adjacent areas of Silesia and Pomerania (Pomorze), with access to the sea at Danzig. Danzig itself became a Free City, with Poland entrusted with the conduct of its foreign affairs and granted a customs area within it and use of the port, its railways and waterways. The future of disputed areas in East Prussia and Upper Silesia was to be decided by plebiscite. In Prussia the plebiscite took place in July when the Poles seemed about to be overwhelmed by the Red Army, but of greater importance was the tradition of long association with Germany and the use of administrative pressure. Only 2.2 per cent in Allenstein voted for amalgamation with Poland and 7.6 per cent in Marienwerder. The situation was different in Upper Silesia where the plebiscite took place after two Polish uprisings. The same factors were present as in East Prussia, but 40.3 per cent voted for Poland, against 59.6 per cent for remaining part of Germany. The Poles, however, were in a majority in the more industrialized eastern districts. The fear that they might remain in Germany led to the third Silesian uprising on the night of 2–3 May 1921. Unable to agree among themselves on the future of Silesia, the Allies recommended to the Council of the League of Nations that the province be partitioned. Poland obtained most of the industrial and mining areas with a population of nearly a million, of whom about a quarter were Germans. According to German statistics some 530,000 Poles remained within Germany. In truth the Polish government, being more concerned with the conflict with Soviet Russian and therefore wary of antagonizing the Western Powers, had been slow to support the Silesian insurgents. The special problems of Silesia led to the granting of wide autonomy, including a regional parliament dealing with all matters except foreign affairs, the army, the judiciary and tariffs. Polish Silesia continued to enjoy regional self-government until 1939.

The remaining source of conflict in the west was Austrian Silesia, of which the principal town was Teschen (Cieszyn). A provisional agreement was reached on 5 November 1918 between the Polish and Czech national committees which had sprung up in the area to divide the province on ethnic lines. This would, however, have left the railway from northern

Bohemia to Slovakia in Polish hands, as well as the valuable coking coal deposits and metallurgical factories of the Karwina basin. It was therefore unacceptable to the Czechoslovak government, which took advantage of the Polish–Ukrainian conflict in eastern Galicia to seize part of this area on 23 January 1919. A truce was arranged by the Allies on 1 February with a new demarcation line favouring the Czechs. It was agreed that a final division of the territory was to be made by the Supreme Allied Conference. Polish demands for a plebiscite, accepted by the Allies in September, proved impossible to carry out and in July 1920, at the height of the Polish–Soviet war, the Allies decided at the Spa Conference in favour of Czechoslovakia. As a result the area up to the left bank of the river Olza was incorporated into Czechoslovakia with a Polish minority, over-whelmingly Protestant, amounting to 140,000 according to official Polish claims. This ostensibly minor dispute was to cast a dark shadow over Polish–Czechoslovak relations throughout the inter-war period and after.

It was the settlement of the Polish eastern frontier which was to create most difficulty. Here not only did Piłsudski's federal concepts conflict with the National Democrat policy of a unitary state which would assimilate Lithuanians, Byelorussians, Ukrainians, but also created problems in the mixed-nationality areas between ethnic Poland and ethnic Russia which involved the Russian Whites, the Bolsheviks and the emergent nationalist groups. The Poles first clashed with the Bolsheviks when their troops, moving into the vacuum created by the collapse of the *Ober-Ost*, met one another at the small Byelorussian town of Bereza Kartuska in February 1919. The conflict assumed more serious dimensions in April, when Piłsudski captured Vilna, in his words, 'the key to Lithuanian–Byelorussian affairs'. He failed, however, to win substantial support for his schemes from either the Lithuanians or the Byelorussians. Lithuanian nationalism was fundamentally anti-Polish in character and Polish–Lithuanian relations deteriorated still further in August 1919 as a result of an attempted coup by the Polish Military Organization (POW) aimed at placing a pro-Polish government in power at Kaunas (Kovno). Among the Byelorussians land hunger and hostility to the largely Polish landlord class were stronger than anti-soviet nationalism. Piłsudski also failed in his attempt to obtain the backing of the Allies, and above all Britain, for his eastern schemes. This was largely because of his hostility to the Russian Whites, who in his view would, if they won the civil war, re-establish 'Russia one and indivisible', which would spell the end of his federal schemes. Indeed, all Allied attempts to sponsor an agreement between the Poles and the Whites foundered on this rock. Talks did take place between the two sides in July and again in September 1919, but by October Piłsudski was observing with some satisfaction the increasingly obvious defeat of the Whites. This he thought was a necessary first stage in his plans for an agreement with Britain, but Britain was not in principle in favour of assigning Lithuania, Byelorussia, Volhynia and eastern Galicia to Poland.[33]

The main concern of the Soviet leaders at this stage was to win the civil war and to this end they were ready to conclude an unfavourable peace like that of Brest-Litovsk with Germany even at the price of the collapse of the Lithuanian–Byelorussian Soviet Republic established early in 1919. Thus from the spring of 1919 Soviet Russia, in spite of the opposition of some Polish communists, undertook discussions with the Polish government, which led to formal talks in July. Soviet Russia was represented at them by the veteran Polish communist, Julian Marchlewski, who was prepared to make far-reaching concessions, believing that any frontier settlement would be rapidly overturned by the world revolution. No agreement was reached and Piłsudski continued his advance, capturing Minsk on 8 August 1919, where he issued a manifesto on 19 September to the inhabitants of the Grand Duchy of Lithuania promising to defend their national traditions. The key to the conflict, however, was the Ukraine. Although the Poles were locked in a bitter conflict with Ukrainians in eastern Galicia, over which they gained full control in July 1919, they nevertheless were able, for a time at least, to establish satisfactory relations with the Ukrainian nationalist government in Kiev. The agreement of May 1919 between the two parties was soon repudiated, but the capture of Kiev by the Whites at the end of August soon drove them together again, the Whites having no sympathy for either Polish or Ukrainian aspirations. The Bolsheviks were still determined to buy peace by ceding territory on their western frontiers and made successful approaches to Estonia in August, and to Finland, Latvia and Lithuania in September. In October they began talks with the Poles at the small Byelorussian town of Mikashevichi. There has been some dispute over the reason for their breakdown, which became obvious in mid-December. Some have argued that the Soviet aim was merely to buy time and that by the end of 1919 Lenin was in an expansionist mood. The debate in Soviet circles, it is suggested, 'was not *whether* the Polish bridge should be crossed, but how and when'.[34] Piłsudski's refusal to accept Soviet terms was thus a recognition of the impossibility of reaching a negotiated settlement. On the other hand it could be claimed that, although there was some support for the use of the Red Army to extend the revolution, the Soviet leaders, in view of the exhaustion and war-weariness of Russia, were in fact interested in an agreement. This is not to say that Piłsudski was not willing to reach a settlement. Where he erred was in his overestimation of Soviet weakness and the determination of Allied intervention. He wished to have a free hand in the borderlands and above all in the Ukraine in return for the recognition of Bolshevik rule in Russia. This was too much for the Bolsheviks to accept, convinced as they were that Piłsudski's eastern policy had the support of the Western Allies.

The failure of the Mikashevichi negotiations made an escalation of the conflict inevitable. With the fall of Paderewski's government and the formation of a new cabinet under the more pliable Skulski, Piłsudski's internal position seemed stronger. He took too little account, however, of war-weariness in Poland, where the PPS was leading a campaign for peace.[35] The National Democrats likewise were hostile to his plans and he was still unable to obtain the British support upon which he had reckoned. He nevertheless continued with his policy, concluding in December an agreement for far-reaching political and economic co-operation with Semën Petliura, the Ukrainian nationalist leader. Soviet Russia, while preparing for war, undertook also a peace offensive, making a far-reaching offer of territorial concessions to Poland in the hope of avoiding conflict. The effect of this move on Western Europe was considerable, making Britain even more unwilling to support Polish plans. The Allied Supreme Council declared on 13 December 1919 that it was in the interest of the Allies that there should be a strong Poland, but Britain's position was essentially one of aiding Poland to defend herself rather than of encouraging her to adopt a forward policy in the east.[36] Indeed, The Supreme Council in December 1919 proposed the so-called 'Curzon Line' as the eastern limit of the lands in which they recognized the right of the Polish government to form an administration. This was a line which ran from the Carpathians west of Rawa Ruska to East Prussia, giving to Poland the region of Białystok, but not the northern part of the Suwałki province inhabited by Lithuanians. The Council did add that their decision would not necessarily detract from Polish rights east of the line. In July 1920 Curzon was to ask the Soviet government to halt its forces on this line and undertake negotiations for peace. Piłsudski thus pursued his policy at his peril. He hoped to obtain still better terms from Soviet Russia and in March 1920 proposed a settlement which would have recognized Polish dominance in the Ukraine. Soviet Russia rejected this proposal, whereupon Piłsudski on 21 April concluded a political agreement with Petliura, supplemented three days later by a military convention.

Early in May 1920 the Poles attacked. Piłsudski's aim was to establish an 'independent' Ukraine under Polish influence and at first his efforts were crowned with success, his troops capturing Kiev on 7 May. However, support for the Ukrainian nationalists proved weak and the Poles were soon thrown back by the strong Soviet counter-offensive. As the Polish army retreated a debate took place in Bolshevik circles which in the end resulted in the decision to pursue the Polish forces into ethnic Poland and establish there a Polish Provisional Revolutionary Committee at Białystok under the leadership of Julian Marchlewski which was to set up a Soviet state. Even at this stage the Western Allies showed reluctance to give assistance to Poland, but the Polish victory in the battle of Warsaw on 16 August thrust back the Soviet army in disarray. On 25 August the Bolsheviks decided to seek a peace. Talks began in October and a peace treatry was finally signed in Riga on 18 March 1921 which gave to Poland the western part of Byelorussia and eastern Galicia, which was to the west of a line proposed to Poland by Soviet Russia in January 1920. In October 1920 Piłsudski organized a *coup de main* through one of his followers, Żeligowski, at Vilna, which with the surrounding area was incorporated into Poland in March 1922.

The effects of the war with Soviet Russia on Polish political life were enormous. It revived in a bitter form the antipathy towards Piłsudski among the National Democrats, for whom the advance upon Kiev had been an act of rash and even criminal folly. Piłsudski for his part bitterly resented their attempts to belittle his role in the battle of Warsaw, which they claimed had been won by the French general, Weygand, though some in a spirit of compromise were prepared to ascribe the victory to divine intervention as 'The Miracle on the Vistula'. In fact, modern research has shown that the victory was the work of the professional officers inherited from the Austrian and Russian armies, which served them ill when in 1926 Piłsudski was to retire them in favour of his old associates from the Legions. The war, apart from making difficult Polish–Soviet relations, embittered the Byelorussians, Ukrainians and Jews in eastern Poland, who were subjected to harassment in the course of the military operations and treated as second-class citizens after their becoming Polish citizens. Military expenditure strained an already overburdened treasury. Victory bequeathed to the Polish army a completely false sense of reality. While the Reichswehr in Germany and the Red Army began to consider the techniques of mechanized warfare, the senior officers of the Polish army basked in the glory of 1920 and adhered to the concept of the overriding role of the cavalry. The lack of support from France and Britain induced in the mind of official Poland a belief in their country's capacity to rely upon its own resources. The facts of the case were different. Poland was a state of second magnitude, beset with internal difficulties accentuated by the neglect attendant upon partition. With the temporary eclipse of Germany and Russia, illusion could enjoy the appearance of reality, but the ultimate reality was that Poland lay exposed to grave dangers.

The breakdown of parliamentary government

The new Poland

After over a hundred years of foreign rule the dream of independence had been achieved, but it was no easy task to unite areas which had for so long been integral parts of Russia, Austria–Hungary and Germany, and whose social and economic development had as a result diverged enormously. Thus the mines, textile industry and metallurgical works of the Kingdom of Poland were dependent upon the Russian market, while Upper Silesia's coal mines, iron and zinc foundries and chemical industry had been linked with Germany. The efficient capitalist agricultural system of Poznania and Pomerania had supplied food to the large German towns. It is estimated that of products exported from partitioned Poland 83.3 per cent had gone to the partitioning powers, while 85 per cent of imports came from them.[1] After 1918 this association ceased. The Russian market was virtually closed, while the high tariffs of Poland and the Habsburg successor states hampered trade. Some industries like sugar refining duplicated one another in the different parts of Poland, while others, such as machine tools and armament industries, were almost entirely lacking. The level of agricultural development varied widely from the highly productive farms of the former Prussian areas to the backward estates of the eastern borderlands and the dwarf holdings of Galicia, where in 1921 four-fifths of all farms were less than 5 hectares.[2]

The creation of a single economic system was a slow and difficult process. It was only in 1920 that a single currency was established. Until then as many as six currencies had circulated in the country. As late as 1920 former Prussian Poland still maintained a tariff and a passport was necessary to travel from Warsaw to Poznań. The country lacked a unified transport system. Rail and river communications had been developed in the interests of the partitioning powers. More than fifty Austrian and German railway lines had led to the Russian frontier, but only ten continued beyond it. The railway systems differed in their equipment and methods of administration. Four legal systems existed and their unification

Table 5. *Constituent areas of the Polish state*

	Total (millions)	Percentage of total population
Former Russian Poland		
1. Kingdom of Poland	10.5	30
2. Eastern borderlands	4.8	37
Former Prussian Poland		
1. Poznania and Pomerania	2.9	11
2. Upper Silesia	0.98	0.8
Former Austrian Poland		
1. Galicia	7.6	20
2. Austrian Silesia	0.145	0.3

Source: *Rocznik Statystyki Rzeczypospolitej Polskiej*, III, table 111.

caused such difficulty that codification was still not complete by 1939. The forms of taxation had varied, being largely indirect in Russia, mainly direct in Germany and both direct and indirect in Austria. The quality of education was uneven, being lowest in Russian and highest in Germany. Illiteracy was still widespread in the former Russian and Austrian regions.

War damage increased the state's economic problems. By 1920, when operations came to an end, 90 per cent of the country had been touched directly by war and 20 per cent the scene of heavy fighting. In consequence 55 per cent of bridges, 63 per cent of railway stations, 48 per cent of locomotives and 18 per cent of buildings had been destroyed.[3] Polish industry had been seriously affected by the requisitioning by the occupying powers. The metallurgical industry of the Kingdom of Poland had ceased production. As late as 1922 only 7 out of the 11 furnances working in 1914 were in operation. At the Peace Conference the Polish delegation estimated their country's losses at 73,000 million French francs.[4] No industrial investment had been made outside Upper Silesia, thus increasing Poland's backwardness.

Poland was still predominantly agricultural. Of the country's 27.2 million inhabitants in 1921, 63.8 per cent earned their living from agriculture, a figure exceeded in Europe only by Albania, Yugoslavia, Bulgaria, Romania, Lithuania and Soviet Russia.[5] Apart from the western areas and a few well-run estates elsewhere Polish agriculture was under-capitalized and inefficient. The wheat yield was 40–50 per cent and that of potatoes 30–40 per cent below the German average.[6] One of the main reasons for this was far-reaching fragmentation of peasant holdings. In 1921 one-third of all peasant plots (3.5 per cent of the arable land) were less than 5 hectares. Many of these plots were not self-sufficient and their owners were forced to supplement their earnings by working on larger farms.

A principal cause of this fragmentation was the rate of population growth which in 1921 was still one of the highest in Europe. Before 1914 the pressure which this had caused was somewhat relieved by emigration and by absorption into the growing industries, but after the war, as emigration became difficult and industry failed to expand, the problem of the surplus agricultural population became increasingly serious. By 1935 it was estimated that with no change in agricultural techniques 2.4 million could leave the villages without adverse effect upon production. If one adds the number of semi-employed, the surplus rural population was probably as high as 4.5 million.[7]

Not all peasant holdings were inadequate in size. Farms of 20-50 hectares were rare outside Poznania and Pomerania, but holdings of 5-20 hectares were common everywhere, making up nearly one-third of all holdings and comprising 30.8 per cent of agricultural land. This category had increased significantly in the fifty years before 1914. At the same time large estates remained an important feature of Polish agriculture, amounting to 0.9 per cent of all holdings in 1921, but embracing 47.3 per cent of all arable land.[8] These estates were for the most part well run, producing most of Poland's grain exports, but they were a source of social bitterness, particularly in eastern Poland, where the landowners differed in nationality from the peasants.

After 1918 the favourable conditions enjoyed by agriculture before the war came to an end. The agrarian reforms of 1920 and 1925, which provided for the annual distribution of 200,000 hectares among the peasantry, could do little more than keep pace with the rise in population. The overwhelming majority of peasants lacked the capital to modernize their holdings. As late as 1939 only one tractor was in use for every 8,400 hectares.[9] The peasants likewise suffered from the high price of industrial goods in relation to agricultural products. Their difficulties were further exacerbated by the depression of 1929 and after.

In spite of the largely agrarian economy there had been considerable industrial development before 1914, particularly in the Kingdom of Poland and Upper Silesia. In 1921 15.4 per cent of the population earned its living in mining and industry. In 1927 850,000 people worked in mines and factories employing more than five persons.[10] The largest industries were coal-mining, textiles and metallurgy, followed by chemicals, food processing and timber. A high degree of concentration existed, with 100 factories in 1928 employing one-third of the industrial work force.[11]

Cartels accounted for 40 per cent of production in 1929.[12] At the same time handicrafts embraced 320,000 workshops, according to official figures for 1928, employing 881,000 persons.[13]

The state played a large part in economic life. State direction, a feature common to the economies of the partitioning powers, developed still further during the war. Shortage of capital in independent Poland, together with the need to integrate the economy and build armaments industries, led to far-reaching state action. A substantial part of Polish industry was owned by the state, which exercised wide control over the credit system. Before 1914 much of Polish industrial growth had been the result of foreign investment. After the war the government and its credit organizations absorbed most domestic capital, and private industry was encouraged to seek capital abroad. In 1929 foreign capital made up one-third of equity investment. The proportion was still higher in certain industries like founding and the chemical and electro-technical sectors.[14] France was the largest source of capital, followed by Germany, the USA and Belgium. Industry failed to expand as rapidly after 1918 as it had before the war. By 1928, though most war damage had been made good and some progress in integration had been achieved, the index of production reached only 116.4 before the slump of 1929, whereas it had been 135.1 in 1913.[15] Poland was in fact the only European country whose production remained below the pre-war level. The accumulated problems of partition and reintegration, war damage and a basically peasant economy were aggravated by shortage of capital. There were few native Polish entrepreneurs and many state enterprises were not managed economically.

By 1921 the agricultural revolution of the second half of nineteenth century and foreign competition, especially from the Ukraine, had undermined the position of the landlord class in Polish society. The large and medium landowners nevertheless still numbered with their families about 70,000 persons,[16] and occupied a strong position in agriculture. The ethos of the old *szlachta* society to some extent survived, leading industrialists seeking to buy country estates for the prestige they conferred upon them. Roman Dmowski's supporters were so stung by the hostile comments of his enemies upon his lowly origins – his father having been a roofer – that Jędrzej Giertych wrote in his defence that his family belonged to the lesser gentry of Podlasie.[17] Podlasie in fact had been heavily populated with petty *szlachta* and Dmowski's origins were thus no different from those of others who had moved into the towns in the nineteenth century.

The largest single class was the peasantry, numbering altogether 14.5 million in 1921.[18] The peasants differed noticeably from the townspeople in language, dress and social customs. In spite of much stratification they had a strong consciousness of their own common identity. The centre of peasant life was the farm and the family, 'the expression of the unity of the group in the economic world'.[19] Holdings were subdivided to make marriage possible for the members of the family, the theory being that each partner should bring an equal quantity of land into it. This led to parcelization and often to the fields of a farm being widely scattered. The peasants' concept of the nation was distinctive. Indeed, to this day there remains a subtle difference between the word *naród* (nation) which historically applied to the *szlachta*, and the word *lud* (people), commonly applied to the peasantry. The peasants tended to be more conscious of the village and its locality than of the national community. Religion remained strong in the countryside side by side with strange superstitions. Although emigration and industrialization had done something to break down the closed world of the peasants, change came only very slowly to the villages. A man's worth was assessed by possession of land. The agricultural workers and their families, accounting for about 3 million were held in low esteem.[20] Some with special skills who worked on large estates might be relatively well-off, but the majority were among the poorest people in Poland.

Industrialists and capitalists, who with their dependants numbered about 260,000 persons, did not play an important part in social life.[21] Industry was not highly developed. Indeed, industry and commerce gave employment to a larger number of Germans and Jews which excited prejudice against them, but industrialists were able to exert pressure on the government through the Central Union of Polish Industry, Mining, Trade and Finance, commonly known as 'Leviathan'. The absence of a strong native bourgeoisie explains the role of the intelligentsia, which embraced a far wider group than it did in Western Europe, and totalled 1.4 million persons in urban society.[22] *Świat pojęć*, a popular pre-war encyclopaedia, defined the intelligentsia as follows:

The intelligentsia in the sociological sense of the term is a social stratum made up of those possessing academic higher education. Typical representatives of the intelligentsia...are professors, doctors, literary figures etc. The social position of the intelligentsia does not mean that its members have a rigidly defined social or ideological position. Members of the intelligentsia can identify with the most varied social and political trends. In fact, they occupy the leading role in all political groupings.[23]

Membership of the intelligentsia was not in fact to be identified strictly with the possession of a high school diploma. It was more important that a man's manners should be those of the educated classes and that he should have some familiarity with the humanities. In spite of many differences of income and status the intelligentsia had a markedly strong feeling of solidarity and responsibility. Descended from *szlachta* who had migrated to the towns in the 1870's and 1880's (see above p. 42), they saw their careers as an alternative to a way of life which had collapsed. The intelligentsia saw themselves as representatives of the nation, the keepers of its conscience and its directing force. A post in the service of the state enjoyed great prestige, while a certain disdain for trade and industry led some to develop pretensions to wide cultural interests. Respect for culture and knowledge was often that of the dilettante and not of the specialist. An overproduction of 'literary intellectuals' had much to do with the right-wing radicalism prevalent in the universities.[24]

There were other significant urban groups, 1.3 million people deriving their livelihood from trade. Petty trade was primitive, but it was adapted to existing conditions of economic development. The government tried without much success to replace private tradesmen with peasant co-operatives. Trade was concentrated in Jewish hands. In 1921 62.9 per cent of persons employed in trade and industry were Jews, but of those 88.9 per cent were engaged in retail trades.[25] It is difficult to estimate the number of people owning handicraft workshops, because many were not registered with the authorities. The figure of 1.1 million for such workers and their families is therefore hypothetical.[26] Most workshops were small, often employing only members of the owner's family. Many were owned by Jews, especially in tailoring, leather work, baking and bookbinding. Jews were correspondingly not numerous in heavy industry. Industrial workers and their families amounted to 4.6 million. Of these 1.8 million were employed in handicrafts or cottage industries, while 2.8 million worked in heavy industry and mining.[27] Standards of living varied widely among the working class. Workers in government monopolies were among the better-off, enjoying higher wages and relative security. Unskilled workers were often very poor as were those employed in cottage industries, especially in and around Łódź, Białystok and Bielsko-Biała. The majority of industrial workers were Poles, but many skilled workmen in Upper Silesia and Łódź were German. In common with other under-developed countries, industrial workers in Poland were better-off than the peasantry.

The new Poland was a multinational state. In 1921 69.2 per cent of the population gave their nationality as Polish, while in 1931 69.8 gave Polish as their mother tongue.[28] The national minorities were of two kinds. There were those who constituted a majority in certain regions, and others who were dispersed throughout the country. The largest of the territorial minorities were 5–6 million Ukrainians living in the provinces of Lwów,

Stanisławów, Tarnopol and Volhynia and to a lesser extent of Lublin and Polesie. In eastern Galicia they were overwhelmingly Uniate by religion, but in the former Russian areas they were largely Orthodox. The majority were peasants, but almost all the landlords were Poles. The towns were inhabited mostly by Poles and Jews, with Ukrainians employed in the less well-paid and unskilled jobs. There were virtually no Ukrainian industrialists, though at the turn of the century a small intelligentsia had arisen, including priests, teachers and managers of the extensive Ukrainian co-operatives. A similar position was occupied by the 1.5 million Byelorussians who formed the bulk of the population in the provinces of Polesie and Nowogródek, as well as a large minority in the province of Vilna and a small element in the Białystok province. Most of them were Orthodox, but there was a sizeable Catholic element. Byelorussia was the least developed part of Poland and most of its inhabitants were peasants or agricultural labourers.

The 1.1 million Germans, however, were dispersed throughout the community. In no single district (*powiat*) did they constitute a majority, though there were some villages which were predominantly German. Even after the emigration which followed independence they continued to be an important element in Poznania and Pomorze (Pomerania), making up a significant part of the large landlords and prosperous peasants. In the towns some German officials had remained, while many agricultural processing plants were in German hands. In Upper Silesia almost all the larger landowners and industrialists were German. Here many Polish workers and peasants themselves had been subject to considerable germanization. Elsewhere Germans played an important part in the textile centres of Łódź and Bielsko-Biała. There were long-established peasant communities in the Kingdom of Poland, Galicia and the eastern borderlands.

The Jews were mainly urban, with three-quarters of them living in towns in 1931. They made up one quarter of the population in towns with over 20,000 inhabitants and nearly 30 per cent of those with less than 20,000.[29] In Galicia, however, where the granting of civil rights had enabled Jews to buy land, a class of Jewish landowners had grown up, together with some Jewish peasants and market gardeners. Jews were an important part of the intelligentsia, including in 1931 49–50 per cent of all lawyers and 46 per cent of doctors.[30] They were important also in literary life. There were some large Jewish industrialists like the Łódź factory owner, Oskar Kon, but the typical Jewish capitalist was either the owner of a small factory or a master craftsman with a large workshop. The largest single occupational group among the Jews in 1921 was those engaged in trade and insurance, accounting for 34.1 per cent.[31] Most Jews were extremely poor and their advancement was retarded by the slow recovery of industry. They were concentrated in the less modern sectors of the economy and the traditional outlet of emigration was now closed to them. The anti-semitism of the Polish state and community was an additional handicap. There were altogether 3.0 million Jews in Poland, dispersed throughout the country, though not so much in former Prussian Poland. The majority of them still held to Jewish religious orthodoxy, many observing to the letter the 613 commandments and declaring themselves followers of one of the great rabbinical courts. Yet urbanization and industrialization, particularly in the Kingdom of Poland, drawing able men and women away from the stifling atmosphere of small towns to the freedom of the big cities, had brought about an internal upheaval in the closed world of Judaism.

Political life in reborn Poland

The constitution of the new state was finally adopted in March 1921. After much dispute it was modelled on that of the French Third Republic, in part because the war was seen as the victory of democracy over autocracy. A far more practical factor, however, was the National Democrats' desire to limit as far as possible the functions of the presidency in order to prevent Piłsudski from again exercising the power he had enjoyed in the years immediately after 1918. Thus the most important element in the new political structure was the lower house of parliament (sejm), elected by universal suffrage with proportional representation. It could compel governments or individual ministers to resign by votes of no confidence and had the right to question the administration on its policies and actions. It enjoyed in addition the ultimate right of decision in many financial and military matters. The powers of the senate and president, on the other hand, were much more limited. The president, elected for seven years by the sejm and senate sitting together, had no right of veto over legislation. Though he was nominally the highest-ranking military officer, he could not be commander-in-chief in time of war. The senate, elected by universal franchise, but with a higher age qualification for voters than for the sejm, could only delay legislation by demanding that bills required an eleven-twentieths' majority in the lower house. To dissolve the sejm the president required the support of three-fifths of the members of the senate.

In local government, in spite of a constitutional provision that 'the principle of decentralization shall be introduced', a highly centralized system on the French pattern was established. A departure from this rule was the wide self-government enjoyed by Upper Silesia under the law of 15 July 1920 and the terms of the Geneva convention between Poland and Germany of May 1922. In addition, before east Galicia was definitely assigned to Poland, a law was passed in September 1922 conferring considerable autonomy on the provinces of Lwów, Tarnopol and Stanisławów. It was intended to influence the Council of the League to accept the incorporation of east Galicia into Poland, but once this was accomplished in May 1923 its provisions were largely disregarded.

This sophisticated political system did not work well in Poland. The long years of partition had created very different political traditions among those who had lived in areas administered by semi-constitutional Germany and Austria and those which had been ruled by autocratic Russia. In no sphere more than in politics, claimed Stanisław Thugutt, a radical peasant leader, was it so important: '...whether one become active under the Russians or under the Austrians, with the tradition of armed uprisings and mole-like conspiratorial work in the blood or with the habit of small struggles for the achievement of very limited aims.'[32] Thugutt spoke with some feeling, for this divergence of outlook affected particularly the various peasant parties were a characteristic feature of Polish political life, as in a number of other East European countries. They were all committed to democratic principles, but at the same time upheld the interests of the peasants and claimed for them, as the majority of the population, the leading position in the state. In the words of one of the most remarkable of their leaders, Wincenty Witos, the self-educated peasant from Galicia, 'Poland fell as a state of the nobility...Poland rises again as a state of the peasantry and as such can and must survive...'[33] Yet the differing levels of development and contrasting political traditions of Russian and Austrian Poland hindered the co-operation of peasant groups. Only in 1931 was a united Peasant Party created (Stronnictwo Ludowe – SL).

Indeed the variety of political experience combined with proportional representation and the exuberance of the Polish intelligentsia playing a leading role in all political parties led to far-reaching fragmentation. In 1925 there were no less than 92 registered political parties, of which 32 were represented in the sejm and organized in 18 political clubs. Political atomization made it difficult to establish stable and lasting administrations. Between the achievement of independence in 1918 and Piłsudski's coup of May 1926 there were 14 different cabinets. The Polish Circles in the Austrian, German and Russian parliaments had been minority pressure groups, concerned almost exclusively with Polish problems and seeking to obtain redress of specific grievances. This was a poor background for parliamentary life in independent Poland. As Thugutt wrote, 'everyone wants to be in opposition. On no account will anyone accept responsibility.'[34] Faith in the parliamentary system was further undermined by the scale of corruption in public life, inherited partly from Russia and Austria, and partly as a consequence of political immaturity. Widespread poverty and ignorance increased the temptation to indulge in demagogy. As late as 1931, after twelve years of compulsory education, only 70 per cent of the population could read and write.[35]

The long preoccupation with national survival obscured for many Poles the need to accord fair treatment to Poland's national minorities. Germans, Jews, Ukrainians and Byelorussians constituted a third of the population and were all to some degree dissatisfied with their position. The highly centralized administration, based on the French system, gave no scope for self-government to the territorially compact Ukrainians and Byelorussians, who were embittered by the failure to introduce a significant measure of land reform. The Germans resented attempts to undo the effects of 150 years of germanization in former Prussian Poland, while the large Jewish population was conscious of discrimination and harassment. The neglect to deal fairly with the national minorities was in some measure due to the pervasive air of national insecurity. Poland had emerged not so much through her own efforts, but rather as a result of the simultaneous collapse of the partitioning powers. Germany and Soviet Russia were dissatisfied with their frontiers with Poland. As their strength recovered, calls for a revision of the Polish borders, particularly those with Germany, found a sympathetic hearing in Western Europe, above all in Great Britain. Relations with the smaller neighbours, Czechoslovakia and Lithuania, were likewise unsatisfactory. Only on the narrow frontiers with Latvia and Romania was there no threat to Poland's security.

Daunting problems faced Poland. The ravaged economy, poverty, inflation, the strain of the military operations of 1918–21 all imposed an immense strain upon the country. To meet the deficits attendant upon the collapse of the taxation systems of the three partitioning powers, the government resorted to the printing press. The amount of money in circulation in Poland rose from 1,024 milliard Polish marks in 1918 to 793,437 milliard in 1922.[36] The conviction that independence would bring about an automatic improvement made it difficult for the government to exert discipline in the economy. The socialists were unwilling to impose sacrifices upon the urban workers. The peasant parties opposed the freezing of agricultural prices. The Right was not prepared to sacrifice the interests of industry. Inflation took on a momentum of its own. Wage earners demanded pay rises in advance of price increases. Factory owners held back the repayment of loans and taxes, aware that they could thus reduce in real terms the amount they had to pay. Whereas in December 1918 the exchange rate for the Polish mark was 9.8 to the dollar, by the end of 1920 it had reached 579.3, and by December 1922 17,808.3.[37] Hyperinflation proceeded with a vengence, the dollar being worth 2,300,000 marks by November 1923. The political consequences were serious. Workers and agricultural labourers were more disposed to go on strike. As the intelligentsia and middle classes saw their savings disappear their political attitudes became more extreme. Confidence in the parliamentary system was eroded by the way in which speculators, often connected with members of parliament, profited from the rise in prices. A notorious example was the Dojlidy affair. Dojlidy was an estate in Podlasie, bought in August 1921 from the government land office by the Polish–American Peasant Bank, an organization in which prominent members of the PSL–Piast were involved. The bank paid 14,400 Polish marks a *mórg* (55 ares). Two months later farms were offered to peasants at 120,000 a *mórg*. The land was eventually sold to the Lubomirskis, a family of large landowners, for several times the purchase price.[38]

The greatest threat to political stability was the now largely artificial conflict between the followers of Dmowski and Piłsudski. The National Democrats had sought to curtail Piłsudski's power under the constitution of 1921. Piłsudski and his followers never accepted the limitation on the power of the Head of State. There was indeed little exaggeration in the statement with which the journalist, Stanisław Mackiewicz, prefaced his account of Polish history between 1918 and 1939: 'The history I am writing could be called "Dmowski and Piłsudski". The history of my generation is the struggle of these two men'.[39] There is an element of simplification in this view. The conflict related above all to the composition of the officer corps. Some officers were members of the Legions or members of the Polish Military Organization (POW), who lacked formal military education, but considered that, because of their part in the struggle against Soviet Russia, they were entitled to special consideration.[40] In the grandiloquent words of one of their spokesmen 'The Legions, through the genius of their creator and leader, were not only the heirs of the national chivalric spirit, but also the heirs of the great historic mission of Poland – the Jagiellonian tradition based on modern methods of realization.'[41] Amateurism conflicted with professionalism in terms which were essentially political. Officers from the Legions were at odds with those who had served in the Austrian imperial army, with whom they had clashed during the war and whom they had reproached for their long servility to Austria. They disliked also General Haller, who had commanded the Second Brigade of the Legions and the Polish army in France, led originally by a small number of French officers of Polish descent and non-commissioned officers from the German and Austro-Hungarian armies, which had returned to Poland in 1919. Officers of the old Russian army were for the most part neutral in this dispute, but some were sympathetic to Piłsudski, having been born like himself in the eastern borderlands. The conflict in the army did not relate to problems of military doctrine. It was essentially a quarrel related to credentials established in the struggle for independence and bore no relation to the questions of military planning for the future.

According to the Constitution the president was the head of the armed forces, but its parliamentary affairs were in the hands of the minister of war, always an army officer, who was responsible to the sejm for all acts of the military in time of peace and war. This arrangement was to be the shield of the commander-in-chief, who was not responsible to parliament, and who was nominated by the president on the recommendation of the minister of war. Piłsudski was opposed to this degree of civilian supervision which he believed would make the army the tool of politicians and detract from his own control over it. He tried to anticipate the Constitution by issuing a decree in January 1921, which established for the army the independence he required. While he was commander-in-chief his influence prevented the introduction of a bill to put into effect the provisions of the constitution, but his position was under continual attack from the National Democrats and their supporters in the army. Piłsudski's concept of the army was one which would never for a moment have been tolerated in Great Britain or the United States. His were the traditions of the armies of the partitioning powers. Thus far had the socialist editor of *Robotnik* come on the road to the etatism of the conservative powers which had divided Poland.

The breakdown of parliamentary government

The unsatisfactory functioning of the parliamentary system was evident almost from the beginning. The new constitution was brought into operation only in November 1922. This was in part the result of the need to set up the new electoral system and of a belief that certain laws would be easier to pass in an assembly in which the number of the representatives of national minorities was small. Even more it reflected the fear of two centre groups, the Polish Peasant Party–Piast and the National Peasant Union, which had been strengthened by secessions from the left-wing Polish Peasant Party–Liberation and the National Democrats, lest their influence be diminished in a new parliament. From January 1920 the Centre, with 60 per cent of the seats, enjoyed an absolute majority over the Right and the Left, which had about 18 per cent. This situation persisted until the elections of 1922. The groups which made up the Centre lacked real cohesion, ranging from the National Peasant Union (which still had links with the National Democrats) and the Christian Democrats to the Polish Peasant Party–Piast and the National Workers' Party, and including some former Cracow conservatives, the Club of Constitutional Work, who sat in the sejm by virtue of having been members of the Austrian parliament. Though the government of Leopold Skulski established in December 1919 had an apparently secure parliamentary majority, it was unable to reach agreement among its supporters on the details of land reform, of which the general principles had been laid down by the sejm in July 1919. It fell on 9 June 1920 as a result of the threatening military situation caused by the successful Soviet counter-offensive after the Polish capture of Kiev. It was succeeded by a non-parliamentary cabinet under the respected National Democrat, Władysław Grabski. Grabski's government was able to settle the question of land reform with the passage on 15 July of a bill which the Right was more willing to accept in view of the advance of the Red Army. The law provided for the distribution of holdings in excess of 180 hectares, including woodlands on the large estates, to landless labourers and small peasants, with a higher limit in the east and a lower limit in industrial areas. Compensation was to be paid at half the market price. The law was not in fact to be put into operation after the retreat of the Red Army.

The threat to Warsaw induced a mood of national unity. When the Grabski government was unable to obtain any real support from the Western Powers at the Spa Conference of 5–16 July, it was replaced by an all-party coalition headed by Wincenty Witos, with the socialist, Ignacy Daszyński, as vice-premier. Once the threat of a Soviet victory had passed, agreement between the parties proved difficult to maintain. In November the National Democrat ministers withdrew from the cabinet to be followed by the socialists in December. The Polish Peasant Party–Liberation seceded in January 1921 and the National Workers' Party (formed in May 1920 from the NZR and the NSR – Narodowe Stronnictwo Robotnicze) in May. By this time the government had evolved into a Centrist coalition like the Skulski administration, coming under increasing fire from the Right, which persuaded the Christian Democrats and part of the National Peasant Union to withdraw their support. In consequence the government lost its majority and resigned on 13 September 1921.

An attempt by the National Democrats to set up a cabinet under Stanisław Głąbiński failed and another non-party administration took office on 20 September under Antoni Ponikowski, the rector of the Warsaw

Polytechnic, relying upon support from the Centre and the Left. Its minister of finance, Jerzy Michalski, tried with a programme of drastic economies and new taxes to reduce the budget deficit and bring inflation under control. The Polish mark did in fact rise against the dollar from 4,550 in December 1921 to 3,957 by June 1922,[42] but the deflationary policy aroused opposition among the working class and led to a wave of strikes. The government's fall was precipitated by a clash with Piłsudski, who was strongly opposed to the policy of the foreign minister, Konstanty Skirmunt, who thought that the state's security, dependent as it was on the alliance with France of February 1921, was being undermined by Poland's international reputation for irresponsibility. He thus tried to improve relations with the Soviet Union, Czechoslovakia and Great Britain. Piłsudski was of the view that too many concessions were being made. After the agreement between the Soviet Union and Germany at Rapallo in April 1922, Piłsudski summoned the government to him and declared it to be too weak to resist foreign pressure. The cabinet thus resigned on 6 June 1922.

A major crisis now ensued, because the National Democrats were determined to establish a government sympathetic to themselves, believing that this would strengthen their position in the coming elections. The motion of no confidence in the government established by Piłsudski under his supporter, Artur Śliwiński, the historian, was carried. Piłsudski threatened to resign when the National Democrats tried to set up a government under the Silesia leader, Wojciech Korfanty. The National Democrats now overreached themselves. Their motion of no confidence in Piłsudski was defeated by 207 votes to 187. The crisis was finally resolved by the creation of a non-party government under the Cracow conservative, Julian Nowak, who enjoyed the support of the Centre and Left, whose links with Piłsudski had been strengthened by these events. Nowak's cabinet included almost all the ministers of the Śliwiński government, including the minister of war, General Sosnkowski and the foreign minister, Gabriel Narutowicz, whose appointments Nowak had specifically left to Piłsudski. It was this government which supervised the elections of November 1922.

Far from resolving the political crisis, the elections merely made it more acute. No political group gained a clear majority in the sejm. The Right, composed of the National Democrats and the Christian National Club, the principal landowners' party, had 125 seats out of 444. The Centre, comprising the Christian Democrats, the National Workers' Party and the PSL–Piast, had altogether 132 seats. The Left, principally the PPS and the radical peasant parties, had 98 seats, while the national minorities, most

Table 6. *Elections to the sejm, November 1922: state of the parties at the polls*

	Percentage of vote
Right	*30.1*
Christian Alliance of National Unity	29.1
(National Democrats, Christian Democrats, Christian National Party)	
National–State Union	0.4
State Alliance of the Borderlands (Kresy)	0.6
Centre	*21.0*
PSL–Piast	13.2
Polish Centre (Catholic Peasant Party and counterpart in the former Kingdom of Poland)	3.0
Bourgeois Centre	0.3
National Workers' Party	5.4
Left	*25.2*
PSL–Liberation	11.0
PPS	10.3
People's Councils	0.5
PSL–Left	0.7
Radical Peasant Party (Fr. Okon) (Chłopskie Stronnictwo Radykalne)	1.3
Communist lists	1.4
National minorities	*21.6*
National Minority Bloc	16.0
East Galician Zionists	2.0
West Galician Zionists	0.9
Jewish Populists (Folkists)	0.6
Chliborobi (pro Polish Ukrainians)	1.0
Bund	0.9
Zionist Workers' Party (Poalei Sion)	0.2

Source: Próchnik, *Pierwsze piętnastolecie Polski niepodległej*, p. 133; 'Statistique des élections à la Diète et au Sénat effectuées le 5 et le 12 Novembre', *Statystyka Polski* VIII (1926). The total does not add up to 100 owing to the omission of minor parties. The names of parties changed frequently in this period.

of whose political groupings had stood on a common list, had 89. The main consequence of the election was thus to strengthen the Right, the Left and above all the national minorities at the expense of the previously dominant Centre.

Under these conditions, only three parliamentary governments were possible: a Centre–Right coalition, a Centre–Left, or an all-party coalition such as had been formed during the Polish–Soviet war. This last was

Table 7. *The sejm in December 1922: alignment of parties*

	Seats	
	No.	Percentage
Right	*125*	*28.0*
Popular National Union (National Democrats) –	98	22.0
Związek Ludowo-Narodowy		
Christian National Club	27	6.0
Centre	*132*	*29.9*
Christian Democracy	44	10.0
National Workers' Party	18	4.1
PSL–Piast	70	15.8
Left	*98*	*22.1*
PSL–Liberation	48	10.9
PSL–Left	2	0.4
Radical Peasant Party	4	0.9
PPS	41	9.3
Communists	2	0.4
Non-party	1	0.2
National minorities	*89*	*20.0*
Ukrainians	20	4.6
Byelorussians	11	2.4
Ukrainian Peasant Party	5	1.1
Russians	1	0.2
Germans	17	3.8
Jewish Club	34	7.7
Jewish People's Party	1	0.2
	444	*100.0*

Source: Próchnik, *Pierwsze piętnastolecie Polski niepodległej*, p. 135.

unlikely, however, except in a situation of grave national crisis. A Centre–Right coalition would not include the Christian Democrats (who were still closely linked to the National Democrats) but would require the support of the national minorities. A Centre–Right coalition was for the moment impossible because of disagreements between the National Democrats and the PSL–Piast, above all over land reform. Though the National Democrats had accepted the principle of land reform, they wished to modify some provisions of the 1920 law, particularly those relating to compensation. The PSL–Piast, for its part, insisted on the law's implementation in full. A Centre–Left coalition was difficult for two reasons. Because it was impossible to include the Right–Centre Christian Democrats, the government would need the support of the national minorities. This would lay it open to strong attack from the National Democrats. It was feared, moreover, by some of the Centre party leaders as an electoral liability. In addition, relations between the two large peasant parties, the PSL–Piast and the PSL–Liberation, were very strained, particularly after the bitterness of the recent election.

A crisis immediately arose over the election of a new president. Piłsudski refused to stand for the office, holding that its prerogatives had been diminished with him specifically in mind. The National Democrats provocatively nominated Maurycy Zamoyski, who with an estate of 191,000 hectares was the largest landowner in Poland. This ruled out a compromise with Witos. The PSL–Piast nominated instead Stanisław Wojciechowski, one of the organizers of the co-operative movement in Poland, a former socialist who enjoyed the support of Piłsudski. There were several nominations from the Left, but the serious candidate was Gabriel Narutowicz, foreign minister in the Śliwiński and Nowak cabinets. He was anathema to the Right because of his co-operation with Piłsudski between July and November 1922 and because of his role in steering through the sejm the law conferring autonomy on the provinces of east Galicia.

According to the constitution the president was to be elected by an absolute majority, and on each successive ballot the candidate with the fewest votes was eliminated. Though Zamoyski won most votes on the first ballot, Narutowicz was elected on the fifth ballot by the votes of the Left, the national minorities and the PSL–Piast, whose candidate, Wojciechowski, had been eliminated in the fourth ballot. The political situation at once became exceedingly tense and violent. The Right, which had emerged somewhat strengthened from the elections, thought that it had been cheated of its electoral victory by a conspiracy of the national minorities, in particular the Jews. Deputies were attacked outside parliament by nationalist mobs and this unrest culminated in the assassination of the president, two days after his inauguration, by a nationalist fanatic, Eligiusz Niewiadomski, on 16 December 1922.

Civil war seemed near, especially because some of Piłsudski's associates saw this as the right moment for reaching a final reckoning with the National Democrats. However, the leadership of the PPS refused to go along with these plans and the crisis was resolved by the formation of a non-parliamentary Cabinet of Pacification under General Sikorski, who was still on relatively good terms with Piłsudski in spite of the clashes during the war over the command of the Legions. This cabinet rested on a Centre–Left majority, enjoying the support of the PSL–Piast, disgusted by National Democrat complicity in the assassination of Narutowicz.

The government was immediately faced with a major economic crisis: between July and December the rate for the mark had fallen from 3,957 to 18,075 to the dollar.[43] Sikorski summoned a conference of experts to draw up a reform programme and was able to persuade the highly competent Władysław Grabski, who had earlier broken with the National Democrats, to accept the post of minister of finance. Grabski proposed an increase in state revenue by reform of the tax system and heavy cuts in expenditure. Loans would be sought to balance the budget. He had some success in reducing the rate of inflation, but the implementation of his programme was cut short by a somewhat unexpected event, an agreement between the PSL–Piast and the National Democrats.

The two parties, in what was known as the Lanckorona pact, accepted a compromise on land reform, which paved the way for a government headed by Witos and based on a secure parliamentary majority. This cabinet was, however, hated and feated by the Left and the national minorities and found itself faced with the open hostility of Piłsudski. General Sosnkowski, Piłsudski's close associate, refused to serve as minister of war and on 29 May the marshal himself resigned as chief of staff. A month later he gave up his post as president of the Inner War Council. His resignation was followed by the weeding-out of a number of his supporters in the army. This does not mean that Piłsudski abdicated his role in Polish politics.

The government also ran into very serious difficulties as the inflation continued to accelerate, partly under the impact of the German hyperinflation. Since the cabinet hesitated to take action which would hurt its peasant and industrialist supporters, the dollar rate for the mark fell drastically from 52,000 in May to 6 million in December.[44] The fall in real wages caused by inflation provoked a wave of strikes. When the railwaymen struck in October, the government conscripted the strikers and forced them to work, on pain of punishment for desertion. Violence and bloodshed increased, culminating in a general strike on 5 November, during which the workers, led by the PPS, took over the town of Cracow after clashes with the police. Again on this occasion the Piłsudski-ites wanted to act against the Right, but when the government reached a compromise with the strikers, Piłsudski became convinced that he could no longer rely upon his old socialist allies. The riots gravely weakened the Witos government which fell on 14 December, after the secession of a group within the PSL–Piast who feared that the prime minister was making excessive concessions on the question of land reform.

The new cabinet of Władysław Grabski was non-parliamentary and was granted special powers by the sejm. It lasted from December 1923 to November 1925, the longest government after independence, and made a brave attempt to reform the finances of the state. Grabski created in April 1924 a new central bank and a new currency, the *złoty*, resting on the gold standard. The old currency was called in and the budget was to be balanced by cuts in expenditure, increases in taxation, and foreign and domestic loans.

This programme had some initial success, and Grabski was able to resolve some other pressing political problems. In February 1925 he concluded a concordat with the papacy and in July 1925 he secured a compromise on land reform with the sejm. This provided for an annual voluntary distribution of 200,000 hectares, for which full compensation was to be paid. The government could not, however, induce Piłsudski to return to the army, and its minister of war, General Sikorski, soon became involved in an acrimonious controversy with the marshal. In relation to the national minorities it was also not very successful. Stanisław Thugutt, who entered the cabinet in November 1924 with special responsibility for minority affairs, was unable to improve relations with the Byelorussians and Ukrainians and resigned in May 1925. His resignation was followed by an upsurge of communist and nationalist terrorism, particularly in the Byelorussian areas. The attitude of the the Germans remained hostile. Though Grabski did reach an agreement with Dr Leon Reich, the chairman of the Jewish Club in the sejm, this soon collapsed with accusations of bad faith on both sides.

By the middle of 1925 it was clear that reform was failing. Grabski was unable to balance the budget or obtain large foreign credits. The balance of trade remained highly unfavourable, while price control and wage restraint would not be maintained. The Grabski programme finally collapsed under the impact of the German–Polish tariff war which began in June 1925. Between June and August the *złoty* depreciated from 5.18 to 5.98 to the dollar. When the director of the Bank of Poland insisted in November that the new rate could not be maintained, Grabski resigned.

The Grabski government was succeeded by an all-party coalition under Alexander Skrzyński, a former Austrian diplomat. By now the economic situation was very serious. Unemployment rose to 250,000 and the exchange rate of the *złoty* against the dollar fell. The new minister of finance adopted a programme of substantial cuts in expenditure, coupled with tax reliefs to encourage industry and action against speculation in an attempt to combine the policies of the Right with those of the socialists. The programme had little immediate impact and Skrzyński decided in mid-April that further deflationary measures woulds have to be introduced. This was too much for the socialists, who withdrew their support, so that the government was compelled to resign on 5 May.

At this time the army issue was becoming acute. On the fall of Grabski over 400 army officers had demonstrated at Piłsudski's house at Sulejówek near Warsaw, and this probably secured the appointment of General Żeligowski, known for his sympathy towards the marshal, as minister of war in the Skrzyński cabinet. By April Żeligowski had succeeded in drafting a new army bill, which would have made possible the return of Piłsudski to active service. This however ran into strong opposition in parliament. In the course of the discussion the National Democrat marshal (speaker) of the senate, Wojciech Trąmpczyński, went as far as to say on 5 May that he regarded the idea that Piłsudski might again be commander-in-chief as a 'disaster' for the country 'because I believe that Mr Piłsudski has not the military education which this position requires. Like many others, I have had this conviction since 1920.'[45]

The international situation was also increasingly threatening. The basis of Polish security appeared to be seriously undermined by the 1925 Locarno agreement which seemed to consider the Polish western border a matter for negotiation. Although the nature of this political defeat was disguised by the Franco-Polish guarantee of October 1925, by December the country's new and perilous position had become apparent. The atmosphere of crisis was further intensified by the Soviet–German Neutrality Pact of April 1926 which seemed explicitly directed against Poland. It was in this situation that President Wojciechowski after some hesitation agreed to the establishment of a government under Witos on 10 May. This was a disastrous error, stirring up memories of the ill-fated first PSL–Piast and National Democrat coalition of 1923. Witos' cabinet was totally unacceptable to the Left, which feared it would be the prelude to the introduction of a more authoritarian system of government. Indeed, in February 1926 Witos had asserted that if the sejm did not embark on a large-scale programme of political reform 'it will destroy itself, and Poland not wanting to collapse will be compelled to seek another way out'.[46] The appointment of the Witos cabinet also outraged Piłsudski who, in retreat at Sulejówek, seemed to many Poles the one man, untainted by the incompetence and corruption of the politicians, capable of restoring the state to equilibrium. Piłsudski had long planned some action against the constitution and had made use of General Żeligowski's tenure of the war ministry greatly to strengthen his influence in the army. On 12 May 1926 he called an armed demonstration in an attempt to induce his old friend, Wojciechowski, to rescind the establishment of the Witos government. However, when Wojciechowski refused to submit to the marshal's demands, fighting broke out between government and rebel troops. The PPS supported Piłsudski, though it had not been informed of his plans in advance, by calling a strike of railway workers and preventing the transfer of government troops to the capital. After three days of fighting, in which over 500 people were killed and 1,000 wounded, Piłsudski was master of Warsaw and, in effect, of Poland.

6

Piłsudski in power, 1926–35

'A government of labour'

Piłsudski came to power with no definite aims. His main interests were in the army and in foreign policy. Though he had strongly criticized the 1921 constitution, he had few clear ideas of what should be put in its place. Indeed, he had only with extreme reluctance decided to order the armed demonstration which had overthrown the Witos cabinet, and the belief that he was a spent force politically had much to do with the decision of the politicians of the Right to set up a new Centre–Right coalition. He was studiously vague about his intentions after the coup, declaring grandly, 'My programme is the diminution of robbery and the pursuit of honesty',[1] and arguing that a strong executive was required to unite the diverse elements in the state. In spite of his former links with the Left, he had no intention of embarking on a radical policy. Poland in his view, as in 1918, was too poor to embark on social experiments. As a result, he resisted demands from the left-wing parties to hold new elections, because they could only return a new parliament strongly conscious of its rights and demanding major social changes. At the same time he criticized the Polish right, which he claimed, unlike the Right elsewhere, was an opponent of a strong executive and lacked political responsibility, as had been shown in the agitation which had preceded Narutowicz's assassination.

Piłsudski still thought of himself as a democrat. After the coup he affirmed that Poles could not be ruled 'with a whip',[2] and in August 1926 stressed to one of his associates his 'intention of still maintaining what is called parliamentarianism. It is the basis of democracy, for which there is always a place in Poland, even directly in governing.'[3] Attempts have been made to claim for him some conscious design for a new political system. This seems an exaggeration because he generally worked from day to day in politics. Insofar as he did have conception of the most suitable political system for Poland, it was one in which parliament could criticize and even to some extent modify the actions of the government, though the government could not be overthrown by a vote of no confidence as under the 1921 constitution. He was, in fact, a curious combination of an old-fashioned military dictator and a political manager on the lines of Giolitti in Italy before 1914 or Taaffe in Austria–Hungary.

It was because of these views that Piłsudski, to the surprise of some of his more zealous supporters, did not establish a dictatorship after the coup. He allowed Rataj to organize the election of a new president and, though he stood for this office in order to legitimize his seizure of power, he resigned as soon as he had been elected. His successor as president was the largely apolitical figure of Ignacy Mościcki, who before 1914 had been an obscure member of the PPS. The constitutional changes passed by the sejm in August 1926 did not amount to an abrogation of parliamentary government, although they did strengthen the power of the executive. The president was granted the right to dissolve parliament and, in addition, if a budget was not passed by parliament during the requisite five-month session, the government's proposals were to have the force of law. If they were rejected, parliament could be dissolved and the previous year's budget was held to be enacted. The president's power to issue decrees was widened, though these had to be presented to the sejm for ratification within fifteen days of its reassembling. The sejm lost the right to dissolve itself.

The changes in the civil service and army after the coup were not as far-reaching as might have been expected. Some of the most irreconcilable opponents of the *Sanacja* (literally 'purification'), as the new government styled itself, did lose their positions. The personnel of the president's chancery and the prime minister's office was changed entirely, while several generals, including Rozwadowski, Jaźwiński and Kukiel, were dismissed, but no real attempt was made to initiate a drastic purge.

This is not to say that Piłsudski was well-disposed towards parliament. As he stressed privately, 'I am determined on a final showdown, and that of a brutal type, if they [the deputies] want to return to their former habits'.[4] He had already gathered round him his inner group of advisers, including Walery Sławek, Józef Beck, Kazimierz Świtalski and Adam Koc who had all been active in the legions or the POW. What united them was an absolute faith in the political wisdom of the marshal. To them he remained the commander of legionary days to whom unquestioning allegiance was owed. In this circle only Sławek could speak to Piłsudski as an equal. The rest were his 'boys' (*chłopcy*) and he was to them more like a stern and omniscient father than a political leader. Their attitudes were strongly elitist, deriving from their view that Polish society had been corrupted by foreign rule and that they alone raised the banner of independence. They could not forget the bitter experience of their political isolation before and during the war. Many of them were to prove inadequate to the political and administrative tasks entrusted to them.

For the moment, however, Piłsudski was content to exercise his influence behind the scenes. Although some members of his inner circle were attached to various ministries, their role was still small. Piłsudski did take the office of prime minister from October 1926 to June 1928 and again from August to December 1930, but he played little part in day-to-day government. During his first period as prime minister, for instance, he attended only 19 of 66 cabinet meetings.[5] Indeed, the only office he held continuously after the May coup was that of minister of war.

Piłsudski had the insight to realize that, irascible and moody as he was, he was not the man to co-operate successfully with parliament. As a result, in his desire to retain some semblance of constitutional government in Poland, he entrusted the running of his administration in its early years to Kazimierz Bartel, a self-educated locksmith, who had become professor of mathematics at Lwów Polytechnic. Bartel was prime minister between May and October 1926, and June 1928 and April 1929, holding the post of deputy prime minister in the intervening period. He had no close links with the Piłsudski-ites and had not been a member of either the legions or the POW. A former member of the PSL–Liberation, he had resigned in March 1925 on the issue of the party's call for land reform without compensation and had been a founder of the small radical Party of Labour. Bartel was well-known and respected in parliament, particularly on the Centre and Left, and he went out of his way in speeches to the sejm and senate in late July 1926 to reassure the deputies as to the character of the 'blank cheque' they were signing in accepting the government's constitutional proposals. While he stressed that his 'government of labour' would not embark on doctrinaire experiments in social and economic matters, it would attempt to make the governmental machinery function more effectively in order that the economic crisis could be overcome and the administration made more accessible to the general public. A friendlier policy towards the national minorities was to be adopted and the land reform was to be implemented fully. Like Piłsudski, Bartel envisaged for parliament only the limited role of critic of the government with no real control over its principal lines of policy.[6]

Bartel placed stress on the improvement of government efficiency. He was able to establish a dominant position for the prime minister within the cabinet and reorganized the prime minister's office to make it operate more effectively. The functioning of a number of ministries was improved, while the control of the minister of the interior over local authorities was firmly asserted. At the same time the government steadily diminished the power of local elected bodies, granting, instead, wide-ranging functions to the local administration.

The government was not particularly effective in its campaign against the corruption it claimed had been rife before 1926. The Special Commission to Combat Financial Abuses, established in 1927, found it difficult to amass evidence of financial malpractice. Only one successful prosecution was brought, against General Żymierski, who was sentenced to five years' imprisonment for irregularities in the purchase of gasmasks. A leading figure in the National Workers' Party, Karol Popiel, was strongly attacked in the government press for his role in this affair. When he resigned his parliamentary seat, the government found that it lacked sufficient evidence to prosecute him. Wojciech Korfanty was similarly criticized for his financial dealings by a parliamentary court, but no charges were in the end brought against him.

In some other fields the government did achieve a fair measure of success. This was particularly true in relation to the economy. Piłsudski himself was not much interested in economic problems, so much so that Świtalski, one of his close associates, remarked on his 'quite blatant disregard for economic matters'.[7] Indeed, persons with real competence in economic affairs were unusual in Piłsudski-ite circles. Bartel, who expressed especial concern for the economy, was fortunate in being able to recruit two highly able men, Gabriel Czechowicz, who was minister of finance until April 1929, and Eugeniusz Kwiatkowski, minister of trade and industry until May 1930. The policy they pursued did not differ radically from that of Zdziechowski before them, stressing the need for balancing the budget and stabilizing the currency. The government was, however, able to eliminate one cause of inflation. The automatic linking of the salaries of government officials to the cost of living index was ended and tighter control was exercised over government expenditure.

An economic recovery was evident almost immediately. It is true that the economy had shown signs of a revival even before the coup. The government was aided by the British coal strike which opened new markets for Polish coal, particularly in Scandinavia. The increased political stability did, however, affect business confidence. Between 29 May and 7 July the dollar rate for the *złoty* rose from 11 to 9.15,[8] while unemployment declined and production increased. The government attempted not very successfully to attract foreign capital. It was able to arrange in October 1927 a large loan with a group of European and American banks to stabilize the *złoty* and link the Polish credit system with world capital markets. The index of industrial production rose from 79.96 in 1926 to

116.4 in 1928,[9] real wages rose and unemployment continued to fall. The improvement in economic conditions affected agriculture also. The profitability of peasant farms increased, while large landowners took advantage of rising values to sell land, with the result that the land reform law's annual target of 200,000 hectares was exceeded in these years. The revival was not complete. The economy was to a considerable extent dependent on short-term foreign credit and vulnerable to the fluctuations of the world economy. Yet, for the moment, the government could claim to have dealt successfully with a problem which had proved too much for earlier cabinets.

The government attempted to introduce a new policy in relation to the national minorities. This policy, as proposed by the competent minister of the interior, Młodzianowski, declared that the goal of assimilation was to be renounced and that conditions were to be created to secure equality of treatment.[10] Though Młodzianowski was replaced in October 1926 by the far less effective Felicjan Sławoj-Składkowski, an attempt was still made to put into practice his policy. The need to deal fairly with the minorities was impressed upon local government, but it remained true that liberal initiatives in Warsaw were often frustrated by the poor quality and inexperience of regional officials. The government was most successful in dealing with the Jews. In October 1927 it introduced a decree extending and reorganizing the Jewish communal organization (Kahals), which won it a good deal of support, above all from Orthodox Jews. Steps were taken to revive Jewish trade, which was benefiting from the economic revival, while the *numerus clausus* was prohibited in institutions of higher learning.

It proved more difficult to make progress in relation to the other minorities. The government tried to implement the land reform in eastern Poland in the interest of the Ukrainians and Byelorussians and does seem to have reached some understanding with the main Ukrainian organization in east Galicia, the Ukrainian National Democratic Union (Ukrainskie Natsionalno–Demokratychne Objednienie – UNDO). Yet no real changes were made in the much-resented bilingual school system here, which was seen as an instrument of polonization. It proved impossible to overcome the obstacles placed by both Polish and Ukrainian chauvinists in the way of the establishing a Ukrainian university. In the Byelorussian areas political developments hindered a major change in policy with the emergence of the communist-dominated Hromada as a mass movement in late 1926. Though the strength of the communist movement had to some extent waned by the end of 1927, partly as a result of government repression, Polish rule was at best grudgingly accepted.

The position of the German minority in Poznania and Pomerania improved after 1926, but in Upper Silesia the situation became increasingly tense. Here the new Piłsudski-ite provincial governor, Michał Grażyński, a former PPS member, attempted both to tighten the links between Silesia and the rest of Poland and to bolster the strength of pro-government political organizations. In an effort to counter the influence of Korfanty, he began to outbid him in Polish chauvinism and brought himself into conflict with the German minority, particularly on the question of the right of parents to determine whether to send their children to Polish or German schools.

The government did succeed in achieving satisfactory relations with the Catholic church, in spite of the strong anti-clericalism of many Piłsudski-ites and the church's close links with the National Democrats. In foreign affairs the position of Poland improved, largely as a result of the reduction of tension in Europe after Locarno. No major changes of policy were introduced and the alliance with France was retained, though relations were not as close as they had been. Piłsudski did achieve some improvement in relations with Germany, though this had definite limits because Piłsudski wanted to obtain confirmation of the existing frontier while the aim of the German chancellor, Gustav Stresemann, was its revision. Some vexed question between the two countries were settled. In March 1930 a trade agreement ending the tariff war was concluded, though it was never ratified because the depression led to a hardening of the German attitude. Relations with the Soviet Union improved after some initial tension, while Anglo-Polish ties became closer.

One of the less successful areas of the government's activity was the army. After the coup, the principles of military organization for which Piłsudski had fought for so long were finally adopted. The army was nominally controlled by the minister of war, who was responsible to parliament, but real power lay with the inspector-general of the army who was empowered to deal with all matters relating to the preparedness of the army and defence in time of peace, and who was commander-in-chief-designate in the event of war. Both these posts were conferred upon Piłsudski. He did not exercise well the vast power over the army he thus acquired. He lacked the staff training and technical expertise which would have allowed him to absorb and apply the rapid advances in military thinking after 1918. His remoteness and the absence in his immediate entourage of anyone with whom he could converse as an equal exaggerated his belief in his own omniscience in military matters. His ideas became increasingly out-of-date. He continued to believe that any future war would be a repetition of the Polish–Soviet conflict of 1920. This view led him to exaggerate the importance of infantry and cavalry at the expense of artillery, tanks, aircraft and communications. His contempt for the 'know-alls' of the general staff led to its importance being downgraded, which further impeded serious thinking about strategic and tactical problems. Piłsudski was in fact largely responsible for the virtually unchallenged acceptance in the army of the slogan 'Eyes east'. This concept rested on the assumption that the alliance with France and the Versailles treaty would contain Germany, for which reason a serious threat to Poland could only come from the Soviet Union. This remained the orthodox view, not only in the 1920's when it had some justification, but also in the early 1930's, when the rearmament of Germany made it more and more questionable.

A Piłsudski-ite past, moreover, became an important factor in promotion in the army. By 1928, of the 10 army inspectors (designate divisional commanders) 8 had actively supported the May coup and 6 had served in the legions. At a lower level the transformation went even further. Whereas in 1926 only 10 per cent of army officers had served in the legions, by 1939 legionaries made up 70 per cent of infantry divisional commanders and of cavalry and armoured motorized brigades. These officers generally lacked formal military training and had in many cases won their advancement in the Polish–Soviet war. For the most part they remained dominated by their experience in that war, which led them to overrate the significance of the cavalry as a decisive factor in a war of movement and fail to perceive the growing significance of armour and aircraft.

The government and parliament

Piłsudski did not for the moment establish a political organization to support his government, but did inform one of his associates that he regarded it as essential 'to create a single front with the broadest party span'.[11] He made a number of approaches to the conservatives among the large landowners, with whom he had co-operated before and during the war and whose backing would, he thought, give a wider basis to his régime and also deprive the National Democrats of some of their support. He attempted unsuccessfully to persuade a prominent conservative to stand for the presidency in May 1926, but two other leading conservatives, Alexander Meysztowicz and Karol Niezabytowski, did enter the cabinet in October. The alliance was sealed by Piłsudski's presence at a banquet at the Radziwiłł estate of Nieśwież in late October, which was attended by many principal landowners. By the end of 1926 two of the main conservative organizations had come out in favour of the government, while the third, the Christian National Party, was divided between those who wished to support Piłsudski and those who still held to the Party's traditional links with the National Democrats. The government was also successful in winning the support of the principal Polish industrialists' organization.

These links with landowners and industrialists were an indication that the régime did not intend to embark on radical policies. Yet at the same time the government did hope to win some support from the parties of the non-communist Left, the PPS, PSL–Liberation and the Peasant Farmers' Party (Stronnictwo Chłopskie) in all of which Piłsudski-ites held prominent positions. In October 1926 Jędrzej Moraczewski of the PPS entered the cabinet, as did Bogusław Miedziński of the PSL–Liberation in January 1927. A section of the National Workers' Party seceded in June 1926 to found a new pro-government party. Attempts were made to rally support for the government among radical opinion by the League for the Reform of the Republic, the Party of Labour and the group of politicians linked with the journal *Droga* (The Way).

Relations between the government and parliament did not develop smoothly. Although Piłsudski was probably sincere in his declared intention of retaining a constitutional system, he had small understanding of co-operation with parliament. His political experience had been in conspiratorial techniques and he was extremely intolerant of parliamentary criticism and party politics. He was, moreover, not above violating the spirit, if not the letter, of the constitution. Conflict arose almost immediately parliament re-assembled in September 1926, when the National Democrats, angered by the purges in the army and civil service, were eager to cut the budget. The government's heavy-handed response won the National Democrats some support, as did the brutal physical assault upon Jerzy Zdziechowski, the former finance minister, by pro-government zealots. Resistance was also aroused by a decree in November 1926 limiting significantly the freedom of the press. The parties of the Centre and Left were nevertheless not eager to press their hostility to the government to the breaking point. The budget was thus passed without difficulty in March 1927. The situation deteriorated again with the sudden prorogation of parliament at the end of March, which drove the PPS and PSL–Liberation into stronger opposition. Almost all the political parties were now determined to restore to parliament its right of dissolution in order to force the government to hold elections. Tension grew also as a result of the rumours about the fate of General Zagórski who had fought on the government side in May 1926. He had almost certainly been murdered, perhaps accidentally and probably without the direct authorization of Piłsudski. Faced with this growing opposition, the government reconvened parliament only to present the budget as it was legally obliged to do. Parliament was then adjourned immediately until its mandate expired at the end of November.

The government hoped that the elections of 4–11 March 1928 would produce a more amenable parliament. After some delay it established in January a Non-Party Bloc for Co-operation with the Government (Bezpartyjny Blok Współpracy z Rządem – BBWR), which lacked any more definite programme than its name suggests. Its core was made up of former legionaries and POW members. Its membership ranged from landowners and industrialists to radical supporters of the *Sanacja* in the Party of Labour and the League for the Reform of the Republic, and included some pro-government Jewish, Ukrainian and Byelorussian personalities. Its main attack was directed against the National Democrats, both because they were regarded as the irreconcilable opponents of Piłsudski, and because this might win left-wing support. Indeed, the parties of the non-communist Left hesitated to attack Piłsudski directly and often claimed during the campaign that they were more truly representative of his views than the BBWR.

The government intervened actively in the election, making use of the local administration to support its candidates and using funds from both private and public sources to finance a large-scale campaign. It also exploited its influence on the Electoral Commission to invalidate a number of lists, mostly communist in character, though it must be stressed that the actual voting took place without significant administrative interference. The results were a qualified success for the régime, whose lists won over 25 per cent of the votes against 8.6 per cent for the Right, 10 per cent for the Centre and over 26 per cent for the Left. The communist list also did well, winning almost 7 per cent of the votes. The national minorities did not present a single list: nationalist groupings among them won 18 per cent of the votes against 3.4 per cent for the socialist parties.

In the new sejm the BBWR and the parties of the Left enjoyed a clear majority, and the government believed that this would make possible a more satisfactory relationship with parliament. As a pledge of the sejm's willingness to co-operate, Piłsudski demanded that it accept Bartel as the speaker. The parties of the Left were not unwilling to accede, but resented Piłsudski's peremptory orders, and, as a result, to the great irritation of the government, the socialist leader, Daszyński was elected to this office. This did not lead to an outright clash with Piłsudski, though relations remained uneasy and were exacerbated by disputes over parliament's attempts to repeal the government's press decree in May 1927 and its resistance to a number of proposed taxes. At the same time none of the

Table 8. *Results of the elections to the sejm, 1928*

Parties	Percentage of votes (100)
Pro-government lists	*25.2*
BBWR (including Silesia)	21.0
Catholic Union (Katolická Unia)	1.7
Bloc of Labour (Blok Pracy)	1.3
Peasant League (Związek Chłopski)	1.2
Right	*8.6*
Monarchists	0.5
Catholic National list	8.1
Centre	*9.9*
Christian Democrats and PSL–Piast	6.7
Silesian Christian Democrats	1.2
National Workers' Party	2.0
Non-revolutionary Left	*26.3*
Peasant Farmers' Party (Stronnictwo Chłopskie)	5.4
PSL–Liberation	7.3
Radical Peasant Party (Fr. Okon)	0.4
PPS	13.0
Independent Socialist Party of Labour (Niezależna Socjalistyczna Partia Pracy)	0.2
Communist and pro-communist	*6.7*
Communist lists	2.4
Peasant Self-Help (Związek Samopomocy Chłopskiej)	0.2
White Russian pro-communist lists	1.2
Sel–Rob (Ukrainske Selansko–Robotnyche Sotsialistychne Obyedannia) [Ukrainian Peasant–Worker Socialist Alliance]	1.7
Sel–Rob Left	1.2
National minorities nationalist lists	*17.9*
Bloc of National Minorities	12.6
Ukrainian Party of Labour	0.4
Ukrainian National Alliance	0.1
Ruthenian (Russian)	1.2
Galician Zionists	2.1
Orthodox Jews	1.5
National minorities: socialist and radical lists	*3.4*
Bloc of Ukrainian Socialist and Peasant Parties	2.4
Bund	0.7
Poalej Sion	0.3

Source: T. and W. Rzepecki, *Sejm: Senat, 1928–33* (Poznań, 1928), p. 229. As some splinter groups have been omitted, percentages do not total 100.

Table 9. *Composition of the sejm, 1928*

Parties	Deputies (total: 444)	Percentage (100)
Pro-government	*130*	*29.3*
BBWR	122	27.6
National Workers' Party–Left	5	1.1
Peasant League	3	0.6
Right	*37*	*8.4*
Popular National Union	37	8.4
Centre	*54*	*12.1*
Silesian Christian Democrats	3	0.6
Christian Democrats	16	3.6
National Workers' Party	14	3.1
	21	4.8
Non-communist Left	*129*	*29.2*
Peasant Farmers' Party	26	5.9
PSL–Liberation	40	9.1
PPS	63	14.2
Communist and pro-communist	*19*	*4.1*
Communists	7	1.5
Peasant Self-Help	1	0.2
Sel–Rob	4	0.9
Sel–Rob Left	2	0.4
White Russian Worker-Peasant Club	5	1.1
National minorities: nationalist parties	*65*	*14.7*
Ukrainian/White Russian Club	30	6.8
Ukrainian Party of Labour	1	0.2
Non-party White Russians	1	0.2
Russians	1	0.2
Germans	19	4.4
Jews	13	2.9
National minorities: socialist and radical parties	*10*	*2.2*
Radical Ukrainians	8	1.8
German socialists	2	0.4

Source: Próchnik, *Pierwsze piętnastolecie Polski niepodległej*, p. 282, table XVIII.

parliamentary groups were prepared yet to push their opposition to extremes and the budget was again passed easily in June 1928.

Another source of tension was Piłsudski's growing irritation with the deputies, which was probably increased by the worsening state of his health. When he resigned the premiership in June 1928, he gave vent to his bitterness in an interview, in the course of which he declared, 'If I had not overcome my inclinations, I would have done nothing but beat and kick the gentlemen-deputies without ceasing'.[12] The defects of parliamentary government could, he claimed, be done away with only by constitutional reform. The interview, with its threat of a more authoritarian constitution, increased significantly the hostility to the government on the Left, above all in the PPS. This led to a growing rift within the party which culminated in the secession of most of its pro-Piłsudski politicians and the foundation in November 1928 of a new party, the PPS–Former Revolutionary Fraction, named after the organization led by Piłsudski before 1914, when he had resisted those in the PPS who had wished to place more emphasis on social rather than national issues. However, its secession to the government side brought it no substantial increase in strength.

During the new parliamentary session, which began in late October, Piłsudski again attacked the deputies as 'men without a past or a future'.[13] The belief that constitutional government was endangered led to increasing co-operation on the left. On 14 November 1928 the PPS, PSL–Liberation and the Peasant Farmers' Party united to form a Consultative Committee of left-wing parties for the Defence of the Republic and Democracy. Conflict soon arose over the government's failure to present for ratification its supplementary credits not authorized in the budget, the removal from the courts of a number of prominent judges and its demands for constitutional reform. Increasingly Piłsudski's inner circle of legionaries and POW members, often referred to as the 'Colonels' group', began to urge the government to take a harder line in relation to parliament.

The constitutional issue became pressing when the BBWR presented its proposals to parliament on 6 February 1929. These were totally unacceptable to the Left and were denounced in the socialist paper *Robotnik* as constituting 'in practice the liquidation of parliamentary democracy'.[14] It was soon clear, moreover, that the government lacked the necessary majority for their acceptance by parliament. Nevertheless, the clash between the government and parliament came not over the constitutional issue, but on the question of its supplementary credits. The minister of finance, Gabriel Czechowicz, wished to present these to parliament for ratification, but was prevented from doing so by Piłsudski, who seems to have feared that budgetary scrutiny would reveal that he had obtained from the treasury an extraordinary credit of 8 million zł. (£180,000) for the BBWR election campaign.[15] He must have been aware how ridiculous and compromising such a revelation would appear after his innumerable attacks on parliamentary corruption.

At the end of February the sejm voted to establish a special committee headed by the socialist, Herman Lieberman, to investigate Czechowicz's responsibility and on 14 March this committee voted to impeach him. Piłsudski's reaction was to place more weight on his inner circle of advisers, which now tended to take over from the cabinet the formulation and discussion of policy. In 1929 there were only 17 cabinet meetings 4 of which Piłsudski attended, and in 1930 20, of which he attended 5.[16] He was resigned to a conflict with parliament which he was convinced he would win. On Czechowicz's resignation he again launched into a violent tirade against the deputies, claiming that he alone was responsible for the failure to submit the credits and attacking Czechowicz's accusers as people 'who cover themselves with their own excrement'.[17]

One of the casualties of the new hard-line was Bartel who resigned as premier on 13 April. He was succeeded by the first of the 'colonels' cabinets', headed by Piłsudski's close collaborator, Kazimierz Świtalski, and including several prominent members of the marshal's inner circle, among them, Colonels Ignacy Matuszewski, Alexander Prystor and Ignacy Boerner. Of the 14 members of the cabinet 6 were military. At the same time the three parties of the non-communist Left established a permanent Consultative Committee. A collision seemed inevitable.

The clash

The worsening of relations between the government and parliament coincided with a serious deterioration of the economic situation. In spite of the revival after 1926 the Polish economy, dependent as it was on agricultural exports and largely short-term foreign credits, was extremely vulnerable to the collapse of international trade and investment which began with the Wall Street crash of October 1929. The impact of the slump in Poland was very harsh. It has been estimated that Polish national income fell 25 per cent between 1929 and 1933 compared with the 4 per cent fall in Britain.[18] The index of industrial production dropped from 116.1 in 1929 to 71.2 in 1932, a decline exceeded in Europe only in Germany, Austria and Czechoslovakia.[19]

The government's response to this crisis was slow and fumbling, partly because the resignation of Czechowicz in April 1929 and of Kwiatkowski in May 1930 robbed it of its most able economists. Its policy, like that of almost all governments faced with the slump, was to resort to orthodox deflationary measures. Since the régime was determined to maintain the parity of the złoty, which it regarded as one of its major achievements, this policy was particularly rigidly implemented in Poland. As a result recovery was delayed until late 1935, as Polish exports priced themselves out of world markets. All sections of the population suffered severely from the depression. Unemployment rose rapidly, affecting over one-quarter of the labour force in 1931, according to one estimate,[20] and hurting not only industrial workers but also members of the intelligentsia. Peasants were harshly affected by the steep fall in agricultural prices in comparison with those of industry. In 1931-2, the worst year of the crisis, it has been calculated that the net return on 1 hectare of land on farms of 2-50 hectares was only 8 zł.[21] As a consequence peasant indebtedness increased substantially.

The economic crisis had a generally radicalizing effect on the political situation and seriously reduced the chances of a compromise settlement of the constitutional conflict. Though a clash appeared imminent with the formation of the Świtalski cabinet, another seventeen months were yet to pass before the issue was finally resolved. Neither side wanted to push the situation to extremes. Piłsudski, as in the years immediately before the coup, hesitated to take the final step, while the parties of the Left still hoped that some acceptable compromise could be reached. Thus Świtalski, on taking office, attempted to calm public opinion and allowed the trial of Czechowicz to take place before the Tribunal of State, a body composed of the president of the supreme court and 12 members chosen by the sejm and senate. Its verdict, announced on 29 June, was basically unfavourable to the government. It upheld the right of the sejm to ratify supplementary credits, but claimed that in the resolution impeaching Czechowicz, there was no judgement on the merit of the credits he had contracted. The tribunal thus decided to 'postpone its proceedings' until the sejm made such a judgement. In view of the anti-government majority in parliament this was almost certain to be unfavourable to Czechowicz.

This decision brought a conflict nearer and defeated those on the Left, like Daszyński, who still hoped to reach an accommodation. On the Right, too, the mood was aggressive. In October 1928 the main National Democratic grouping, the Popular National Union, was re-formed as the National Party and began to cooperate closely with the near fascist Camp for a Greater Poland (Obóz Wielkiej Polski) formed under Dmowski's *aegis* in December 1926. Its leaders were eager to regain their lost influence by demonstrating their hostility to the régime. The government was also in a hostile mood. On 17 October Miedziński, who probably reflected Piłsudski's own views, told a meeting of BBWR parliamentary representatives that the opposition had become hysterical and lacked real support outside the intelligentsia. Piłsudski, he claimed, would choose the right moment to act.[22]

A move against the sejm was widely expected when the parliamentary session reopened on 31 October. Piłsudski himself shrank back. Though over 100 army officers assembled at the parliament, perhaps in an attempt to cow the deputies and perhaps even to disperse them, they withdrew when Daszyński refused to open the session. This incident strengthened the determination of the six parties of the Centre and Left, the Centrolew, (the PPS, the three peasant parties, the Christian Democrats and the National Workers' Party) to resist the government. The PPS was now calling for the 'total liquidation of the post-May system',[23] and on 6 December a vote of no confidence was passed against Świtalski's government, with opposition only from the BBWR and its allies.

Piłsudski was at first undecided as to how to deal with the situation. He had already almost made up his mind that it was not possible to co-operate with the existing parliament, but did not believe that this was the right time for new elections, because the economic situation had deteriorated and the budget had not yet been passed. He may also still have hoped to reach a compromise and may have been swayed by Daszyński, who told the president on 9 December that the majority which had defeated the Świtalski cabinet did not aim at forming a government.[24] Piłsudski thus persuaded Bartel to form a government. The new premier, who declared in an interview that he favoured the 'therapeutic' rather than the 'surgical' methods,[25] certainly aimed at reaching an accommodation with parliament and excluded from his cabinet the most unpopular members of the previous government.

The chances of such a compromise, however, were small. Most of Piłsudski's inner circle did not believe Bartel could succeed and were eager for a confrontation, while by the beginning of March it was clear that the majority of the sejm was strongly opposed to the constitutional changes the government favoured. The Czechowicz affair was another obstacle to a compromise, because it was to be expected that, once the budget had been passed, the opposition could use the budgetary committee to make an assessment of the credits in the case. The course of the session made it clear to Piłsudski that no agreement on his terms was possible. Thus when the PPS proposed a vote of no confidence in Colonel Prystor, the minister of labour, who had attempted to diminish the socialist control of local sick funds, he acted. The PPS did not intend a direct challenge to the government, but Piłsudski saw their motion as a useful pretext and compelled Bartel to make the vote against Prystor a vote of confidence in his government. When it was passed, Bartel resigned on 15 March.

On 29 March a new government was formed by Piłsudski's close friend and confidant, Walery Sławek. It was universally regarded as signifying the victory of the advocates of a hard line. On 5 April the parties of the Controlew responded by calling for the dissolution of parliament, so that the nation could chose between Piłsudski and the sejm. Piłsudski had also decided on elections, but needed time to prepare for them. As a result, he made use of a number of dubious constitutional pretexts to prevent the reassembling of parliament as was being demanded by the opposition. This aroused strong resentment both in the National Party and in the Centrolew, which on 20 June demanded the 'removal of the governments of the dictator Józef Piłsudski' and their replacement by a constitutional cabinet.[26] To support their demands, they called a special congress of the Centrolew in Cracow on 29 June, which, attended by about 1,500 delegates and over 25,000 supporters, again called for the ending of Piłsudski's 'dictatorship' by constitutional means. The leaders of the Centrolew believed that their pressure would induce the president to resign or to dismiss Sławek so that a new compromise government could be formed. At worst, there would be new elections. They were also considerably encouraged by the deterioration in Piłsudski's health which they believed would compel him to withdraw from politics.

They underestimated Piłsudski. As Witos wrote later, 'they forgot that no speeches could topple Piłsudski's government'.[27] Already, on 11 August, he instructed Sławoj-Składkowski, the minister of the interior, to assemble evidence so that charges could be brought against the Centrolew's leaders. Two weeks later he took the post of prime minister. On 30 August parliament was dissolved and new elections announced for 16 and 23 November. At the same time the government was faced with a serious deterioration of the situation in east Galicia, where the Ukrainian Military Organization, formed in February 1929, embarked on a campaign of sabotage from mid-1930. The régime responded by holding villages collectively responsible for sabotage committed in their vicinity and succeeded with considerable brutality in ending the violence. Nevertheless, it was able to exploit the situation in east Galicia by accusing the Centrolew of being in league with those who aimed at the destruction of the Polish state. This propaganda proved effective despite the fact that relations between the Centrolew and even moderate Ukrainian organizations were poor, the Ukrainians suspecting the Centre groups of Polish chauvinism.

On the night of 9-10 September, eleven of the Centrolew's leaders were arrested. They were not, for the most part, its most important figures, but were all men against whom Piłsudski had a personal grudge or who were known for their radicalism. Arrests continued throughout the electoral period and by mid-October several thousand people were in custody, including sixty-four deputies, many of whom were confined in the fortress of Brześć and allowed no contact with the outside world. To the last the Centrolew refused to resort to radical methods of protest, convinced that the electoral confrontation would prove decisive and its result would be accepted by the government. Its leaders were shocked by the scale of the régime's repressive measures and were well aware of the difficulty of organizing a general strike in conditions of mass unemployment.

Table 10. *Results of elections to the sejm, 1930*

Parties	Percentage of votes
Pro-government	*47.4*
BBWR	46.7
PPS–dawna Frakcja Rewolucyjna	0.7
Right	*12.7*
National list	12.7
Monarchists	—
Centre and Left	*22.1*
Centrolew	17.3
Christian Democrats	3.8
Socialist bloc (i.e. PPS in Silesia)	0.4
Left socialist bloc (Bund and Independent Socialist Party of Labour)	0.6
Communist and pro-communist	*2.5*
Communist lists	2.1
Peasant Self-Help	0.2
Sel–Rob	0.2
Minorities	*14.5*
Ukrainian and Byelorussian electoral bloc	6.4
Ruthenian Peasant Organization	0.1
German electoral bloc	2.7
Grunbaum Zionists	2.2
Galician Zionists	1.6
Orthodox	1.3
Poalei Sion	0.2

Source: *Statystyka Polski*, series C, no. 4, 'Statystyka wyborów do Sejmu i Senatu z dnia 16 i 23 listopada 1930 roku'. As some minor splinter groups have been omitted, percentages do not total 100.

The government was, however, not prepared to leave the election to chance and intervened on a much larger scale than in 1928, invalidating electoral lists and using administrative pressure, above all in eastern Poland. These measures, coupled with the belief the government was bound to win the confrontation and the indifference of much of the population to the complicated constitutional issues involved, led to triumph for the régime in the elections. The government lists obtained over 47 per cent of the vote against 13 per cent for the Right and a disappointing 17 per cent for the Centrolew. The communist vote fell to 2.5 per cent and the various minority groups won 14.5 per cent. The government's power was now unchallengeable. As Piłsudski told his inner circle on 18 November, 'We [have] 5 years of the most perfect quiet and we must know how to make use of it.'[28]

Table 11. *Composition of the sejm, 1930*

Parties	Deputies (Total: 444)	Percentage (100)
Pro-government		
BBWR	247	55.6
Right		
National Party	62	14.0
Centre	40	9.0
Christian Democrats	15	3.4
National Workers' Party	10	2.2
PSL–Piast	15	3.4
Left	57	12.9
Peasant Farmers' Party	18	4.0
PSL–Liberation	15	3.4
PPS	24	5.5
Communist and pro-communist	5	1.1
Peasant Self-Help	1	0.2
Communists	4	0.9
Minorities	33	7.4
Ukrainian–Byelorussian Club	18	4.0
Radical Ukrainians	3	0.6
Germans	5	1.2
Jews	6	1.4
Orthodox Jews	1	0.2

Source: Próchnik, *Pierwsze piętnastolecie Polski niepodległej*, p. 395.

After Brześć

The government did not take especial advantage of the freedom it obtained, and indeed lost much of the dynamism it had previously possessed. Piłsudski himself, suffering from arteriosclerosis and, unknown to his entourage, cancer of the liver and stomach, tended increasingly to withdraw from political life. He had been deeply depressed by his need again to have recourse to unconstitutional measures in the dispute, believing that 'force does not educate, it destroys'. he was convinced that he 'cast too big a shadow on Polish life'.[29] Though major decisions were ultimately referred to him, he tended to exercise even less control over the government than he had previously. He became ever more isolated and increasingly lost touch with those outside his immediate circle. In the words of his close associate, Kazimierz Świtalski, 'My impression is that the commander is a solitary individual. He cuts himself off from people and is thus the prisoner of the opinions and even the chance intrigues of those with whom he speaks and who give him a distorted view of the political situation'.[30]

The day-to-day conduct of government was thus the responsibility of Piłsudski's inner circle, the veterans of the Legions and the POW, whom alone he trusted. They in turn tended to place army officers in prominent positions in the apparatus of state. In the cabinet of Sławek of December 1930 to May 1931 9 ministers were drawn from the army and only 6 civilians. Under Alexander Prystor (May 1931 to May 1933) the ratio was 8:5, but under Janusz Jędrzejewicz (May 1933 to May 1934) it was intended to restore a measure of civilian rule with officers holding only 5 out of 12 posts. The government of Leon Kozłowski (May 1934 to March 1935) saw a fresh attempt at appeasing the opposition by adopting a radical posture. Kozłowski, who had been a moderately successful minister of agriculture between 1930 and 1932 was a former legionary, though not closely linked with Piłsudski. Yet even in his cabinet there were 7 soldiers to 5 civilians. Military men also became increasingly important in the foreign ministry and in the ministry of the interior. By the early 1930's the majority of provincial governors and a sizeable proportion of sub-prefects were officers, as were most heads of provincial departments dealing with the nationalities and security. They were also prominent in the state sector of the economy, which increased significantly in size at this time as the depression caused many firms to become insolvent and as the state became more involved in armaments production. Many of them were not competent to perform the functions with which they were entrusted, and in addition some were not above making full use of the perquisites of office. Piłsudski's claim to have ended the corrupt rule of the 'sejmocracy' began to appear ill founded.

The government became increasingly authoritarian. It now possessed a secure majority in the sejm which it used to wind up the Czechowicz affair to its own satisfaction. Yet it remained extremely suspicious of any real co-operation with parliament, where debate was limited as far as possible. Moreover, from March 1932 the government was granted vast powers of legislation by decree, which it used to the full. Laws were also passed restricting the right of railwaymen to strike and restricting the freedom of assembly. Press censorship was intensified in the period after the election and in addition the government acted to remove its opponents in the universities, dismissing about fifty university professors when the autonomy of the universities was curtailed in March 1932.

The régime had little positive to show for the vast array of power which it had acquired. Its greatest failure was in dealing with the economy, where it was able to do little to alleviate the effects of the slump. It is undeniable that there were no easy solutions and that Poland, a largely agricultural country, overpopulated and short of capital, could not do much on its own to restore prosperity and confidence. Yet none of the ministers responsible for the economy in this period exhibited more than a superficial understanding of the problems facing the country and none was prepared to consider any kind of radical experiment. They all held to the maxims of a balanced budget and a stable and convertible currency which had been set out at the onset of the crisis. In order to balance the budget, drastic cuts in government expenditure were made at considerable social cost. Yet so great was the decline in revenue that even these draconian measures did not significantly reduce the deficit. An attempt was made to cut down the power of the cartels which were held to be largely responsible for the way the price scissors had worked to the disadvantage of the peasants. By 1935, for instance, in order to purchase the industrial goods he had bought in 1929, a farmer had to sell double the amount of agricultural produce.[31] Little success was achieved in reducing cartelized prices, because the government hesitated to antagonize industry excessively. Cartels were, moreover, necessary to the government's economic strategy. They were encouraged to sell abroad at a loss, in order to obtain much-needed foreign currency and had to be allowed to recoup their losses on the domestic market. The adjustment of agricultural debts was also on too small a scale to help most peasants.

Thus, the harsh effects of the depression continued to be felt. The net income per hectare of farms of 2–50 hectares was still only 18 zl in 1934–5,[32] while this situation was even worse on plots of less than 2 hectares which made up one-third of all holdings. Industry, too, remained depressed and the index of industrial production was still only 92.2 in 1934.[33] Unemployment increased still further, and between 1933 and 1935 was probably as high as 40 per cent of the labour force.[34] An important consequence of the depression was to increase still further the role of the state in the economy when much of private industry became unprofitable and was taken over by the government. In 1935, for instance, of the total capital of joint-stock companies in Poland, 52 per cent was in foreign hands; of the remainder, 42 per cent was owned by the state,[35] which held a strong position in the banking and credit system.

In the army, too, these years saw an intensification of those defects which had marked Piłsudski's administration after 1926, the downgrading of the general staff, resistance to technical advances, favouritism shown to former legionaries in promotion, and the marshal's own extreme inaccessibility. Part of the failure to modernize the army was the result of Poland's poverty and the impact of the depression, but fundamentally it was Piłsudski's out-dated views which delayed the acceptance of armoured warfare and the modernization of the air force and anti-aircraft defence. Communications remained in a primitive state, while the number of engineer battalions was reduced because of Piłsudski's view that, since any future war would be a war of movement on the 1920 pattern, trenches would not be required and, as a result, there was no need for sappers. The advancement of poorly qualified legionary officers affected the quality of the officer corps. Piłsudski seems to have been aware of this, and Świtalski noted after a meeting with him in January 1934 that 'critical remarks often of an extremely unfriendly type were recorded by the commander concerning our highest-ranking legionary officers'.[36] Even if this was his view, he did little to act on it.

The government did introduce a number of important legal reforms, making use of its powers of decree to unify the criminal codes of the various regions of Poland on 11 July 1932 and the codes of civil procedure on 1 December 1932. At the same time, ostensibly in order to facilitate the introduction of the new codes, it suspended for a period the immovability of judges and used the opportunity to remove more of its opponents on the the judiciary. The restructuring of primary and secondary education introduced in March 1932 was intended to make access to secondary education easier for children from poorer families and rural areas. The legislation, however, was not adequately prepared and failed, in fact, to achieve its objectives. A uniform pattern of local government at the lower level was introduced in March 1933, but this also reduced still further the role of elected bodies and retained indirect election in some areas.

The régime was, moreover, faced with the difficult problem of what to do with the politicians arrested during the electoral campaign. Ugly rumours soon leaked out of the brutal treatment they had been subjected to in the fortress at Brześć. Here they had been forced to perform humiliating tasks such as cleaning lavatories. They had been beaten and given inadequate food and had been subjected to mock executions to break their spirit. By January 1931 detailed descriptions of their experiences had received wide circulation and caused a revulsion against the government even among those who had little sympathy with the aims of those arrested. The régime decided to brazen out the situation and even rewarded those responsible for the maltreatment of the prisoners. After some delay, eleven people were brought to trial in Warsaw in October 1931 charged with planning a 'coup' to remove the government 'by force'.[37] The accused did not include the leaders of the parties which had made up the Centrolew, or the members of Centrolew consultative committee. Among their number were Herman Lieberman, the main prosecutor in the Czechowicz affair, and five other members of the PPS as well as Witos and Kiernik of the PSL–Piast and politicians from the PSL–Liberation and the Peasant Party. The trial was intended to justify the Brześć arrests, but its course demonstrated that the Centrolew had never intended to go outside the framework of the constitution in its attempts to dislodge the government. Nevertheless, all except one of the accused were found guilty and their sentences, which were increased on appeal, ranged from three to five years. Rather than face imprisonment Witos, Lieberman and three others went into exile. their conviction was followed by other political trials directed mainly against the PPS and by the use of summary courts against Ukrainian nationalists. In July 1934 the government established a concentration camp for political offenders at Bereza Kartuska in eastern Poland. Most of those detained were right-wing extremists, communists or Ukrainian nationalists. Altogether about 5,000 people were imprisoned in this camp, which remained in existence until the outbreak of the war.

The issue of the Brześć arrests and trial hung over the politics of the thirties. Poles had experienced too much at the hands of the partitioning powers not to be sensitive to the government's brutality. Thus the popularity of the exiles, above all Witos living in Czechoslovakia, rose to almost legendary proportions, while the failure of the government to issue an amnesty prevented any real rapprochement with the parties of the Centre and Left. In the words of the writer, Maria Dąbrowska, 'The moral links between the government and the majority of the population were shattered. From now on all attempts to restore them, however well-intentioned, were to prove vain'.[38]

The government's own ranks were badly shaken by the affair. Bartel made a personal protest to President Mościcki. Three BBWR deputies and a former minister, Witold Staniewicz, left the bloc, while even the president confessed to being 'left with a disagreeable impression'.[39] Partly as a result the BBWR became increasingly weak and ineffective. It proved even more difficult to win support by the propagation of the vague cult of Piłsudski which made up the *Sanacja's* only real ideological content. The clash between the conservatives and radicals in the block became much more bitter. The failure of the bloc was most evident in its inability to attract the younger generation, which Piłsudski and his followers had believed would prove more responsive to their appeals on the grounds that it had not been corrupted by foreign rule. In practice the young were largely bored by the stale debate about pre-war orientations and saw the government as tired, repressive and without any real solutions for the country's pressing problems. At the universities, the great majority of the non-Jewish students supported the National Party or the various fascist groups which sprang up at this time, but a minority were adherents of the different parties of the Left. The universities were thus the scene of frequent disturbances of an anti-government and also anti-Jewish character.

The Centrolew did not survive 1930. Criticism of the alliance was voiced in all parties, but was strongest in the PPS, which had suffered most in the elections and whose strength certainly diminished in the early thirties. The party tended to move to the left, as members criticized its devotion to legality, which they held responsible for the debacle of 1930. As a result, relations with the communists again became a live issue. After Hitler's seizing of power, the communist party abandoned the intransigent leftist line which it had upheld since 1928 and which had led it to describe the Centrolew as one of the 'different factions of Polish fascism'.[40] Though a popular front was not established, the two parties agreed to stop polemics against each other.

The PPS continued to maintain its support for the peasant groups which united to form a single Peasant Party (Stronnictwo Ludowe) in March 1931. The united party overcame the divisive tendencies within its ranks and tended to become more radical as the slump persisted. Calls for expropriation of large estates without compensation became more frequent, and in 1932 and 1933 there were rural 'strikes' when peasants refused to allow agricultural produce to be transported to the towns. The party remained divided between those who saw its main ally as the PPS and those like Witos who looked rather to the Centre and Right.

The Christian Democrats and the National Workers' Party maintained their opposition to the government, but struck out on their own, away from the other parties of the Centrolew. They failed to acquire much support and the principal right wing group remained the National Party. This was still plagued by the division between the older parliamentary politicians and the young radicals of the Camp for a Greater Poland (OWP), who, supported by Dmowski, grew in influence at this time. The party became increasingly hostile to capitalism as such and markedly more anti-semitic. As the Left revived its members, more and more took the view that the real enemy was not the *Sanacja*, but the Popular Front, often referred to as the 'Folks Front' to underline its allegedly Jewish character. The government, alarmed by the rapid growth of the OWP, banned it but this was followed by the emergence of the openly fascist National Radical Camp (Obóz Narodowo–Radykalny – ONR), which, however, soon split into a number of small groups, some of them hoping to co-operate with the government.[41]

Relations with the national minorities were not good. The 'pacification' of eastern Galicia, which led to the arrest of nearly 1,800 persons, cast a shadow over Polish–Ukrainian relations after 1930. The government did make attempts to come to terms with the main Ukrainian group, the UNDO. They were assisted by growing distrust among Ukrainains of the Organization of Ukrainian Nationalists (OUN), a fascist party supported by Germany. The increasingly repressive policy pursued in the Soviet Ukraine strengthened the willingness to compromise. From later 1933 the UNDO decided to seek autonomy for the Ukrainian areas in Poland and sought an accommodation with the government on this basis. Indeed the assassination of the minister of the Interior, Bronisław Pieracki, on 14 June 1934 by a member of the rival OUN, hastened an agreement. This act was strongly condemned by the UNDO and its executive began negotiations with the government with a view to an understanding. In the Byelorussian areas pro-Soviet feeling had been strong, but collectivization and suppression of Byelorussian cultural organizations within the USSR induced some disenchantment. The German minority presented different problems because it was more susceptible to extreme nationalist views and was distrusted while Germano-Polish relations remained tense. Upper Silesia in particular was a centre of conflict. Education presented a problem, while administrative pressure in the national and local Silesian elections gave cause for resentment. The Jews likewise were discontented. This was not so much a result of government policy as a consequence of the slump, which affected Jewish traders severely as well as Jews employed in the handicraft industry at a time when emigration was virtually impossible. The government resisted demands for anti-semitic measures, particularly the restriction of the number of Jews in universities. These demands, however, gained in strength as the depression persisted. The Nazi régime in Germany showed how action could be taken with impunity against the wealthiest and most assimilated Jewish community in Europe. Clearly the policy of the Polish state towards its national minorities, while not presenting overwhelming difficulties, nevertheless left problems which were related to the conduct of foreign policy.

Poland's relations with her neighbours were subject to review in the light of the Locarno agreements of 1925. Piłsudski was the architect of Poland's foreign policy, but its execution lay with Colonel Józef Beck, who was a legionary who had risen to importance as a result of devotion to Piłsudski. He was to be minister of foreign affairs from 1932 to 1939. In defence of Beck, it may be said that the initial decisions to make a departure in Poland's foreign policy were not his own but those of Piłsudski. Nevertheless, he accepted uncritically the view that the Franco-Polish alliance was of small value and that Poland should rely upon her own strength in foreign affairs. In this view it was important to establish good relations with her neighbours. he believed that the weakening of the Versailles system would enable Poland to deal with a number of 'unsolved problems', of which the most important were 'Danzig, the minorities treaty, Lithuania and the Cieszyn area'.[42] In January 1932 Poland was able to conclude a non-aggression agreement with the Soviet Union, which was highly alarmed by the Japanese forward policy in Manchuria. There has been some dispute concerning Polish policy towards Germany in these years. It has frequently been asserted that Piłsudski responded to the coming to power of Hitler by proposing a preventive war to France. The failure of France to respond, it is argued, led Piłsudski to seek an accommodation with Hitler. It is true that Piłsudski did make informal soundings in Paris early in 1933 and again in October, but he was already convinced that no action could be expected from France. There is a strong suspicion that his approach to France had no serious intention in the first place, but was designed to establish an excuse for the policy upon which he had already decided. He was not particularly worried by the Nazis, whom he regarded as 'nothing but windbags'.[43] They appeared to him less hostile to the Poles than old-style Prussians like Schleicher. The German government responded favourably to his approach for an understanding and concluded with Poland the non-aggression agreement of 26 January 1934. The Poles, however, resisted German pressure to convert it into an anti-Soviet alliance. Polish policy was myopic. The agreement with Germany was to last only ten years. Germany was not in a position in 1934 to adopt an overtly hostile foreign policy. It was safer to press for an *Anschluss* with Austria, which would seem merely to be giving expression to the principle of self-determination, uniting two parts of the German nation. Union with Austria would thus place Germany in the position of holding Czechoslovakia in a vice. It is small wonder that the Czechs regarded the Germano-Polish pact with grave misgiving. Piłsudski thought of Hitler as an Austrian concerned mainly with South German problems. He did not realize that Hitler intended first to establish his mastery over Germany by the elimination of potential sources of opposition and then to establish a German hegemony in Central Europe and beyond. The agenda of his policy of conquest had Austria merely as its first item. The *Anschluss* was the prelude to the destruction of Czechoslovakia and then of Poland. By the agreement of January 1934 Poland stood aside from efforts to create a system of collective security. Piłsudski launched Poland upon this policy. Józef Beck was only his executor, just as the other colonels pursued his policies in other fields.

In the first instance the agreement of 1934 seemed to yield substantial advantages to Poland. Pressure for revision of the frontier with Germany lessened. The agitation of the German and Ukrainian minorities died down for the good reason that Germany did not regard the problem as having immediate priority. Indeed, Germany exerted her influence to keep the Ukrainians under control after the assassination of the minister of the interior, Pieracki. As Germany grew in strength Poland pursued the aims of small-power imperialism. Poland renounced unilaterally the minorities treaty in September 1934. Territorial demands against Czechoslovakia in the Cieszyn area were revived. Poland seemed to behave as if she would be a partner of Germany in the reshaping of Central Europe. France in particular resented Polish opposition to Barthou's plan for an eastern guarantee pact. Piłsudski and Beck set their face against any agreement which would allow the USSR to play any part in Central European affairs. The Franco-Soviet pact was signed on 2 May 1935 and Laval decided for internal political reasons to go to Moscow, stopping on 10–11 May in the hope of seeing Piłsudski, but Piłsudski was then on his deathbed. In a moment of consciousness he asked his doctor: 'What is that madman going to Moscow for? This will end up badly for France.'

As Piłsudski's health began to deteriorate it became obvious to his entourage that some action would be necessary to ensure that the *Sanacja* retained power after his death. They managed by a clearly illegal manoeuvre to have a new constitution adopted by parliament on 23 April 1935, by a simply majority instead of the two-thirds required by law. This constitution was intended to give lasting form to the principles of government under Piłsudski after the coup of 1926. The dominant position was occupied by the president, elected for seven years by universal suffrage from two candidates, the one chosen by the outgoing president and the other by an electoral college composed for the most part of members chosen by parliament. The president had powers of legislation by decree and of veto on measures passed by the sejm. He appointed the prime minister, who was responsible to parliament, and nominated the commander-in-chief. In theory there may have been something to say for a strong executive combined with an element of popular representation, but the aim of the April constitution was to perpetuate the tenure of power by the Piłsudski-ite faction. For practical purposes the constitution established a collective dictatorship and dispensed with the safeguards common to normal parliamentary states.

Piłsudski did not long survive the adoption of the constitution. His health had worsened from the end of 1934 and he died on 12 May 1935, the ninth anniversary of the coup of 1926. His death caused genuine grief and anguish in Poland and he was given a hero's tomb in the Wawel cathedral in Cracow. Though the régime had become increasingly isolated from public opinion, Piłsudski had been widely respected as an honest, far-seeing and noble man. There was a corresponding sense of shock when he died, his illness having been carefully concealed from the public. It remained to be seen how his successor could cope with the many pressing problems of Poland, which in the last years of his life seemed to threaten disaster.

7

Poland without Piłsudski

Political changes after 1935

The death of Piłsudski created a major crisis for the régime he had created. Although ill and unable to take any real part in government in the last years of his life, Piłsudski personified an ultimate authority which could settle all disputes over the direction of policy and which could preserve the unity of the heterogeneous groups which supported him. His death thus forced into the open the deep divisions within the *Sanacja*, because there was no one among his followers who could assume his mantle. This was immediately evident in the crisis over the succession. On a number of occasions Piłsudski had informed his entourage that the office of president, with the vast powers it enjoyed under the new constitution, was to be held by Walery Sławek, who had again become prime minister at the end of March 1935. Sławek, the marshal's closest confidant, was not a happy choice. A man of irreproachable honour and decency, he was politically naive and quite unfitted for the heavy responsibilities of power. He was accustomed to implementing Piłsudski's instructions without question and was shattered by his idol's death. Alexander Prystor, who was deputed by the inner group of colonels to rouse him from his inactivity in the tense period after Piłsudski's funeral, remarked that he believed even then that 'Walery at a moment's notice would reach for the telephone to ask the commander for an appointment'.[1]

Sławek's obvious incapacity caused President Mościcki to resist the pressure of Piłsudski's inner circle to resign his office. Indeed, the president, who had displayed during Piłsudski's lifetime an almost servile compliance with the marshal's demands, now emerged as a politician of some skill and resource. He was further encouraged in this course by the prompting of a number of his associates, notably Eugeniusz Kwiatkowski and Wojciech Stpiczyński. Kwiatkowski, who had been a successful minister of trade and industry until May 1930, had lost his post as a result of a clash with Piłsudski, who distrusted his radical views. He knew that he had no chance of returning to office if Sławek, with his desire to follow the marshal's directives, established himself in power. Stpiczyński, an able but emotional and demagoic journalist, had also clashed with the inner circle and had been deprived of his post as editor of *Głos Prawdy*, when that newspaper had been transformed into *Gazeta Polska* in 1929.

Piłsudski's instructions were followed more closely in relation to the army. General Tadeusz Kasprzycki, deputy minister of war since 1934, was to be made minister, while the more important post of inspector-general of the armed forces, the designate commander-in-chief, was conferred on General Edward Śmigły-Rydz. Śmigły-Rydz, one of Piłsudski's closest military collaborators before 1914, had been a senior officer in the Legions and commander of the POW after Piłsudski's internment. He was minister of defence in the short-lived popular government headed by Daszyński in November 1918, and between 1919 and 1921 had held various senior posts in the army, attaining the rank of army inspector (designate army commander) in 1921. He was not one of the inner circle of Piłsudski-ites and had taken no part in any of the major political decisions between May 1926 and Piłsudski's death.

In designating Śmigły-Rydz Piłsudski seems above all to have been motivated by his desire to keep the army out of politics. Śmigły-Rydz, though a reasonably competent soldier, had little gift for politics. He had been criticized by Piłsudski for accepting office in Daszyński's government and had not subsequently been entrusted by him with political duties. Piłsudski thus passed over the much more able General Kazimierz Sosnkowski, who had been his chief of staff between 1914 and 1916 and minister of war between 1920 and 1923, and again in 1924. This decision was taken partly because of Sosnkowski's failure to support the May coup, but was more the result of Piłsudski's belief that Sosnkowski would have an important role to play in politics. This was a major miscalculation. Śmigły-Rydz, who would have made an able if not highly imaginative divisional commander, was neither intellectually nor temperamentally fitted to hold the post of inspector-general. Moreover, in spite of Piłsudski's belief that by his reorganization of the high command he had removed the army from politics, the powers of the inspector-general were so wide and the prestige of the army so great that he was bound to play an important political role. For this Śmigły-Rydz was to show himself quite unsuitable.

Not only was there no one among the Piłsudski-ites who could take over the marshal's role and thus make the new constitution function effectively, but its residual parliamentarianism was soon undermined. The first inroads were made by the new electoral law adopted on 8 July 1935 in spite of the strong resistance of the opposition and even some sections of the government camp. The law made virtually impossible a free selection of candidates and increased enormously the control of the régime over elections. In elections for the sejm proportional representation was abandoned and the country divided into 104 two-member constituencies. Candidates were to be nominated by a special assembly in each constituency, composed of local government bodies, economic organizations such as chambers of commerce, and professional associations. In addition, any group of 500 candidates was entitled to one representative. If only four candidates were presented to the assembly, all could stand for election. If more than four were nominated, only those who received a quarter of the votes of the assembly, each member having four votes, could stand. Elections for the senate also were organized on an indirect basis.

The first election under the new law was held on 8 September 1935. Because of the many possibilities of administrative interference the opposition parties refused to participate, with the exception of some groups from the national minorities and a break-away section of the Peasant Party, which reached special agreements with the régime. This boycott of 'the plebiscite which the government had organized against itself',[2] was fairly successful. Whereas in 1928 78.3 per cent of the population had voted and 74.8 per cent in 1930, the proportion now fell to 46.5 per cent. The number of abstentions was particularly high in western and central Poland where the government could exert less pressure on the electorate. Thus in Warsaw and Poznania only 23 per cent of the electorate voted, while in the Łódź province the figure was 27 per cent and 30 per cent in Pomerania.[3]

The unhappy results of the election widened still further the political divisions within the *Sanacja*. Mościcki was now convinced that he should under no circumstances yield office to Sławek, whose faulty political judgement had, he thought, been clearly demonstrated. He was moreover fully persuaded that the government's unpopularity was the result of the continuing slump. He was determined in co-operation with Kwiatkowski to embark upon a more radical economic policy. This he was aware would be unacceptable to Sławek, who shared the general ignorance of the 'Colonels' in economic matters, but who knew that the marshal had been opposed to Kwiatkowski's views. The president thus took the initiative and was able to force Sławek to resign. He also succeeded, in spite of the opposition within the inner circle of the 'colonels', in persuading one of the younger Piłsudski-ites, Marian Zyndram-Kościałkowski, to form a cabinet on 11 October. Kościałkowski had gained a reputation as a liberal while governor of the Białystok province and as minister of the interior. His appointment was thus welcomed by parties of the Centre and Left as making a return to a more civilian style of government.

Sławek's defeat was followed on 30 October 1935 by the dissolution of the BBWR, which further weakened the Piłsudski-ite system. This took place partly because Sławek believed that the new electoral system made parties superfluous and partly as a consequence of the bloc's unpopularity and the growing conflict of the radicals and conservatives within it. Sławek was motivated also by a certain pique at the way his authority was being undermined. In dissolving the bloc he again demonstrated his political incapacity, depriving in this way the government of an organized body of support and creating a serious political vacuum. Indeed, the appointment of the Kościałkowski government and the dissolution of the BBWR marked an important stage in the evolution of political life after Piłsudski's death. These two events signified the virtual disappearance as a coherent political force of the 'Colonel's Group', the inner circle which had run the country under Piłsudski's orders since 1929. The 'colonels' were united in their hostility to the new cabinet above all because of the way Sławek had been slighted, but they were at odds with one another on most other major issues and some were becoming doubtful of Sławek's own political ability. Miedziński, for instance, the editor of the semi-official *Gazeta Polska*, was thinking increasingly in terms of a political role for Śmigły-Rydz as a counterweight to the influence of Mościcki and Kwiatkowski. Miedziński was not alone in seeing Śmigły-Rydz as the most suitable candidate in what Mościcki referred to as the Piłsudski-ites' 'search for a Pope'.[4] The cult of Śmigły-Rydz was now being sedulously propagated also by Stpiczyński in his paper, *Kurier Poranny,* where the special role of the army and 'its leader' in Polish national life was stressed, while 'Śmigły-Rydz's desire for radical social change was equally underlined.[5] In fact, there was little truth in the claim that Śmigły-Rydz favoured a 'left' orientation within the government. A man of few political ideas, he inclined rather to a simple-minded nationalism and distrusted radical change. Yet, since he had not been one of the inner circle, he did not share the unpopularity of the government. His refusal to make a clear statement of his political views, moreover, allowed his influence to increase rapidly even in opposition circles.

The growing power of Śmigły-Rydz, who had been strongly opposed to the formation of the Kościałkowski government, was a clear threat to the president. In an attempt to neutralize this danger, Mościcki proposed to Śmigły-Rydz in December 1935 that they should reach an understanding. The Kościałkowski government was to be allowed to remain in office until the budget had been passed and was then to be replaced by a new cabinet formed by the president and the inspector-general in close co-operation. Kościałkowski, however, was not informed that the fate of his administration had been settled and embarked upon an attempt to win at least the tacit support of the Centre and Left. The left-wing parties were quite willing to respond, but were quickly disillusioned by the half-hearted character of the government's measures. Thus, though an amnesty for political prisoners was proclaimed in January 1936, it did not apply to the political émigrés after the Brześć trial, or to those detained in the Bereza Kartuska camp. The persistence of the slump, moreover, greatly increased working-class radicalism and the government was faced with a serious outbreak of labour unrest in the spring of 1936. Sit-in strikes led to violent clashes between police and workers in Cracow, Częstochowa and Łódź in which at least fourteen people were killed.

The labour unrest finally convinced Śmigły-Rydz that the Kościałkowski government was too weak to deal with the country's problems. The formation of a new cabinet, however, was delayed by disputes over the position of the premier. The appointment to this office on 15 May 1936 of Felicjan Sławoj-Składkowski, one of the least competent members of Piłsudski's entourage, was intended to be no more than a stopgap. Sławoj-Składkowski, who had been minister of the interior in the years 1918–29 and 1930–1 and minister of war between 1931 and 1936, lacked any real desire for power and was therefore acceptable to both Śmigły-Rydz and Mościcki. As often is the case in politics, however, this provisional solution proved more durable than might have been expected. Składkowski remained prime minister until the fall of the Polish state in 1939. The remaining posts in the cabinet were distributed among the supporters of Śmigły-Rydz and the president.

The following months saw a further increase in the influence of Śmigły-Rydz, whose role as the successor of Piłsudski was strongly emphasized by the new premier. In his first speech in parliament Składkowski affirmed that 'we now have a leader whom the commander designated as the guardian of the Republic and who at the same time keeps a careful watch over the spirit of the nation'.[6] Śmigły-Rydz began to seek support outside the government camp. At the Congress of Legionaries on 24 May 1936 he made a widely publicized appeal for national unity, which, with its absence of legionary phraseology and its stress upon the external dangers facing Poland, was well received in the country as a whole. His attempt to exploit his peasant origin by attending a mass rally of the Peasant Party on 29 June 1936 was less successful. Śmigły-Rydz was so irritated by the repeated cries of 'We want Witos' that he left the meeting early.

In mid-June, however, Mościcki tried in the cabinet to challenge Śmigły-Rydz's position, but he was unable to assert himself. He was persuaded by Kwiatkowski that the way to win over Śmigły-Rydz was to make an explicit recognition of his special role. Accordingly he informed Śmigły-Rydz early in July that all members of the government were to treat the inspector-general with the greatest respect because he had the most important function in the country after the president, that of the country's defence.[7] In implementing these instructions Składkowski went far beyond Mościcki's intenstions, issuing a circular to all ministers and provincial authorities on 15 July, which recognized Śmigły-Rydz as 'the first person in Poland after the president'.[8] Strictly speaking, this had no legal force, because the constitution could not be altered by a ministerial circular, but it did mark a further break with its principles. In place of Piłsudski's ideal of a parallel obedience of the prime minister and the inspector-general to the president the authority of the latter was now clearly recognized to be superior.

The years after 1935 saw important changes in the opposition also. The PPS believed that the collapse of the government bloc, which had long been predicted, was now imminent and that the real danger was an agreement between the National Party and the right wing of the régime. It thus attempted to maintain its contacts with government circles in the hope of fostering a leftward movement there, in spite of the party's bitterness at the new electoral law. The formation of the Kościałkowski government had been seen as a particularly hopeful sign. As a result the PPS argued then against too militant a line during the labour troubles in the spring of 1936 for fear of provoking a right-wing reaction. At the same time relations with the communists, with whom the PPS concluded a 'non-aggression pact' in July 1935, became closer. Calls for a popular front, however, were undermined by the PPS's resistance to the communist desire to exploit the labour unrest in 1936 in order to provoke a major clash with the *Sanacja*. The purge of Kamenev and Zinoviev together with their supporters in the Soviet Union and communist attempts to infiltrate PPS organizations caused relations to become cool. For this reason the 'non-aggression pact' was renounced in November 1936. Relations with the Peasant Party and the socialist parties of the minorities, above all the Jewish Bund, remained fairly close. In general this period saw an increase in socialist strength, which reached its high point in the Łódź municipal elections of September 1936. The PPS and Bund, with communist support, won an absolute majority of seats on the city council. For its part the Peasant Party likewise grew in influence and became notably more radical. Calls for more determined action against the régimes were strong among the youth section of the party, but were still resisted by the leadership, above all by Maciej Rataj, who believed that such a confrontation could end only in defeat. Nevertheless, there were violent clashes between striking agricultural labourers and blacklegs in the summer of 1936, while transport of produce to market was again prevented in the area of Zamość and in Volhynia. Demands for a national peasant strike gained much wider currency.

The National Party saw in the decline of the *Sanacja* after Piłsudski's death the chance to make its bid for power. To a large extent it was now controlled by the younger followers of Dmowski, whose fascist sympathies became more marked. The party attempted to exploit the Jewish question as a means of gaining support and embarrassing the government. There was recourse to violence. In the single month of December 1935 the police recorded 26 cases of assaults by nationalist vigilantes on Jews, one of whom was killed, while 34 incidents of breaking windows of Jewish houses and 6 cases of destroying Jewish property were reported.[9] Criminal methods however, were opposed by the more responsible members of the party, whose leadership was increasingly split on questions of tactics, some elements entertaining hopes of an accommodation with the government. During the labour unrest in the spring of 1936 the party executive instructed its activists not only to avoid clashes with the police, but even to assist them in dealing with the Left. The divergent tendencies of the small fascist groups persisted after 1935. One section of the ONR tried at the end of 1936 to reach an agreement with the executive of the National Party, while others made approaches to the government. Most successful in this respect was the ONR–Falanga of Bolesław Piasecki, which began to co-operate with the régime in 1937. None of these groups, however, was able to win substantial popular support.

The growing extremism of the National Party caused great unease among the more responsible section of right-wing opinion. One consequence was an agreement reached at Morges in Switzerland in February 1936 between the former prime minister, Paderewski, General Józef Haller and Witos. They aimed at the establishment of a broad Centre–Right alliance which would restore the democratic system and abandon Beck's foreign policy in favour of a more pro-French orientation. The 'Front Morges', however, did not win a large following in Poland. It was attacked by the Nationalists, who held that its liberal character would make it susceptible to 'Masonic and Jewish influences'. In the Peasant Party there was some suspicion of it for being insufficiently radical. Nevertheless, some eminent figures like General Władysław Sikorski and Wojciech Korfanty supported it. It received the backing also of the Christian Democrats and the National Workers' Party, which in October 1937 united to form the Party of Labour (Stronnictwo Pracy–SP).

The Camp of National Unity

In the face of the obvious weakness of the government calls for a political organization to replace the BBWR became increasingly frequent. The creation of a new party may have been part of the agreement between Śmigły-Rydz and Mościcki in December 1935. Its establishment was certainly given a boost by the rise in the power of the inspector-general which followed the creation of the Składkowski cabinet in May 1936. Indeed, the speech which Śmigły-Rydz made on 24 May calling for greater national unity certainly carried the implication that this unity was to take an institutional form under the banner of the needs of 'national defence'. Śmigły-Rydz entrusted the formation of the new grouping to Adam Koc, one of the younger Piłsudski-ites, who had been a leading figure in the POW and, as a regular officer, one of Piłsudski's principal links with his supporters in the army between 1923 and 1926. From 1928 he had been a deputy to the sejm and between 1928 and 1930 editor of *Gazeta Polska*. In 1930 he became under-secretary in the Ministry of Finance and in 1936 deputy-director of the Bank of Poland. Koc was not a fortunate choice. A man of restricted outlook, his political views were naive, the product of his now strong conservatism and his belief that the government should broaden its base by reaching an understanding with the younger Nationalists. He was moreover plagued by a war injury which contributed much to his almost pathological inactivity. Thus the first months after Śmigły-Rydz's appeal were spent in protracted disputes over the drafting of the new organization's programme and in attempts to win opposition backing mostly on the extreme Right. Koc returned much impressed from a visit to the training ground of Piasecki's ONR–Falanga and as a result decided to delegate the running of his youth section to this group, entrusting its establishment to Piasecki's deputy, Jerzy Rutkowski. An attempt to reach an agreement with the Peasant Party foundered on the government's refusal to yield to demands for a change in the electoral system, the acceleration of land reform and an amnesty for Witos.

The programme of the new grouping was finally made public on 21 February 1937 after a long delay caused both by Koc's procrastination and clashes between Miedziński's more radical views and Śmigły-Rydz's conservatism. It was vague, somewhat conservative and nationalistic, and unspecific on the question of whether a totalitarian system was to be introduced. The virtues of the 1935 constitution were stressed as was the special position in the state of the army and national defence which were to 'unite all subjects and silence their sterile and demoralizing discords'. The sections dealing with the economy tended to reflect Śmigły-Rydz's outlook, the question of land reform being passed over with anodyne phrases. In relation to the national minorities some important concessions were made to the National Democrat viewpoint. While anti-Jewish violence was condemned, the desire of Polish society to 'defend its culture' and establish 'economic self-sufficiency', euphemisms for anti-Jewish measures, was applauded.[10] Subsequently Jewish membership of the new organization was made virtually impossible.

In the following months the membership of the Camp of National Unity (Obóz Zjednoczenia Narodowego–OZN, or OZON as it came to be called) grew rapidly. It absorbed several Piłsudski-ite organizations: the National Christian Alliance of Labour in Silesia, the various pro-government secessions from the Peasant Party and the National Workers' Party, the Union of Young Nationalists, which had broken with the National Democrats in 1934, and, with some reservations, the radical League for the Reform of the Republic. A number of semi-political Piłsudski-ite groups and some non-political bodies proclaimed their accession also. As significant was the list of groups which refused to support the Camp. No major party outside the *Sanacja* joined, while even within its ranks there was much dissatisfaction. This was strongest in left-legionary circles and in the pro-government trade-union movement, while the conservatives, now divided into liberal and nationalist groups, were equally reserved about the Camp.

Its relationship to the government remained undefined. Mościcki did make a declaration on 19 May in support of Śmigły-Rydz's campaign for national consolidation, but the question of whether the OZON was to be the first stage in the creation of a one-party system was not settled, in spite of the clear sympathy of Koc and his 'chief of staff', Colonel Jan Kowalewski, for totalitarian models. Support for the introduction of a fascist régime was also voiced in the 'Club of 11 November', which enjoyed the patronage of the Ministry of Justice under Witold Grabowski, the prosecutor in the Brześć trials, and by Śmigły-Rydz himself and the OZON youth group, dominated as it was by Piasecki's followers. Attempts were made to win over the nationalist Right, of which the most notable was Śmigły-Rydz's acceptance of an invitation to attend a banquet of the old-established student fraternity, Arkonja, long the preserve of the National Democrats and their offshoots.

An open clash between the totalitarian and liberal elements in the régime, of whom the most important figures were Mościcki and Kwiatkowski, was precipitated by two events. The first of these was the ten-day strike called by the Peasant Party on 15 August 1937, in which peasants refused to allow agricultural produce to be transported to the towns. The aims of the strike were openly political, the manifesto issued at its commencement demanding the 'liquidation of the *Sanacja* system', an amnesty for the Brześć exiles, the re-establishment of democracy and a change in foreign policy. The decision to make a frontal challenge to the authority of the government was the consequence of the growing radicalism of the party and of the increasing influence within it of Witos' protégé, Stanisław Mikołajczyk. The strike was fairly widely observed, above all in Galicia. It was for the most part peaceful, but attempts by the police to break down peasant barricades led to considerable violence. According to the offical figures, 42 people were killed and 1,000 were arrested, of whom 500 received prison sentences. One-day strikes in sympathy were organized by the PPS in a number of towns.

The régime was severely shaken by this outbreak of peasant radicalism which seemed even to moderate observers to be the first stage in a civil war.[11] The divisions within the government were further widened by Składkowski's suspension on 30 September of the executive committee of the Piłsudski-ite Union of Poland Teachers and his placing its affairs in the hands of a government commissioner, Pawel Musioł, a leading member of the ONR–Falanga. Składkowski's action was largely the result of promptings by Koc, who was angered by the growing strength of left-wing elements on the executive. It aroused a storm of protest not only from the opposition but also from the radical wing of the *Sanacja*. In February 1938 Składkowski was compelled to give way and allow the original executive committee to be re-elected. For the moment, however, Koc's initial success seems to have led him to attempt more far-reaching action. At two cabinet meetings in early October he demanded the curbing of the left-wing opposition and the establishment of a more totalitarian régime. Faced with the resistance of Mościcki, he seems even to have thought of a new coup at the end of October.[12] His behaviour aroused strong opposition also within the left wing of the government bloc, which was able to rally considerable support. Mościcki further strengthened his hand by receiving a PPS delegation on 13 November, which presented him with a detailed memorandum on the political situation. The PPS leadership had come more and more to see a fascist coup as the principal danger in Poland, and hoped to avert this by maintaining contact with the more democratic elements within the *Sanacja*.

This view, though illustrative of PPS unwillingness after the defeat in 1930 to risk a frontal attack on the régime, did have some justification. From later 1937 Śmigły-Rydz himself became ever more uneasy concerning Koc's management of OZON, and in particular about the manner in which its youth organization had fallen into fascist hands. Unable to persuade

Koc to terminate the Falanga's control over this body, he gave way to Mościcki's demands that Koc be compelled to resign, which he did on 10 January. He was succeeded as head of OZON by General Stanisław Skwarczyński, the brother of a well-known radical Piłsudski-ite. His appointment was seen widely as a shift to the Left on the part of the Camp. Skwarczyński did in fact end the fascist monopoly in the government youth organization, which caused the Falanga members to withdraw from OZON in April 1938. As a regular army officer, however, he saw matters above all in military terms and deprived OZON of any clear political character, making it above all a means of mobilizing civilian support for the army's plans for national defence.

Koc's resignation did not end the divisions within the *Sanacja*. From the spring of 1938, however, in an atmosphere of increasing international tension, the intensity of conflict within the government camp, and between it and the opposition, tended to decline. Questions of national security came to play a larger part in political life. Beck's questionable triumphs in the field of foreign policy and the improvement of the economic situation increased the government's popularity. Parliament now became the main arena of the power struggle within the government. There was much dissatisfaction among the OZON deputies with the régime's apparent abandonment of the nationalists and conservative character of the Camp. This led to a number of secessions from the OZON parliamentary group in February and April. The government's lack of support in parliament was clearly revealed when, after the death of the speaker of the sejm, Sławek was elected to this office by the convincing margin of 144 votes to 30 with 32 abstentions. Sławek's election posed a real threat to both Mościcki and his supporters and to Śmigły-Rydz, because a presidential election was due in 1940 and the successful candidate would be chosen by the sejm and senate jointly. Śmigły-Rydz and Mościcki therefore agreed, to the complete surprise of the opposition and some sections of the government camp, to dissolve parliament and call new elections for 6 and 13 November.

The electoral campaign revealed once more the divisions in the régime. Mościcki and Kwiatkowski both stressed their commitment to the introduction of a new electoral system and their desire to co-operate with the opposition. Składkowski for his part bitterly attacked the political parties, who again decided to boycott the election, comparing their action to that of the *szlachta* before the partitions. The boycott was far less successful than in 1935. Altogether 67.3 per cent of the electorate voted and only 4.2 per cent of the votes cast were invalid. There were various reasons for the government's undoubted success. The régime was determined to avoid the debacle of 1935 and exerted strong pressure on the electorate to vote. The apparent triumph of Colonel Beck in acquiring the Trans-Olza area of Cieszyn (Teschen) from Czechoslovakia after the Munich Agreement may have won the government some popularity among uncritical voters. The opposition parties had good reason to be half-hearted on the question of the boycott. Both the PPS and the Peasant Party attempted to reach agreement with the government on participation and were both influenced by promises to introduce a more democratic electoral system if the turnout of voters was reasonably high.

One of the main consequences of the election was political extinction of Sławek, who failed to obtain re-election in Warsaw and found that he had far fewer supporters in the new parliament. Deeply hurt by this rebuff, fearing for the future of Poland and believing that he had failed his beloved commander, he committed suicide in March 1939. In spite of promises during the campaign, the period after the election was one of further intensification of government repression, with the introduction in November of a more rigorous press law and a decree 'protecting certain interests of the state' which was so vaguely worded that the government could ban all serious opposition. At the same time Masonic organizations were proscribed, an ominous gesture to the extreme Right which believed that Poland was threatened by a 'Judaeo-Masonic conspiracy'. This legislation even led the new OZON chief-of-staff, Zygmunt Wenda, to make an attempt unsuccessfully to overthrow Kwiatkowski and reduce Mościcki's power.

In view of the delicate balance of forces within the régime, the decision to allow the holding of long overdue local elections from late 1938 assumed special importance. The cabinet promised that it would not be subject to administrative pressure and the opposition was thus eager to use this opportunity to show its strength, conscious that the fall of Primo de Rivera in Spain in 1931 had followed defeat in local elections. Over the country as a whole the results seemed to favour the government. According to official figures, OZON and its allies won 48.1 per cent of the seats in the 394 towns where elections were held against 15.6 per cent for the National Party, 10.8 for the PPS, 17.4 for the Jewish parties and 8.1 for others.[13] Many of these towns, however, were little more than villages, where the régime, in spite of its assurances, was able to exert considerable pressure. A clearer picture of political allegiances can be gained from the results in the 160 larger towns where the PPS put forward candidates. Here OZON and its allies won about 30 per cent of the seats, the PPS about 25 and the National Party 17.[14] The PPS fared still better in the 48 towns with a population of over 25,000 (see table 12). By this

Table 12. *Elections of November 1938: votes in 48 towns with more than 25,000 inhabitants*

Party	Percentage
PPS	26.8
OZON	29.0
National Party	18.8
Bund	9.5
Party of Labour	1.6
National Radicals	1.2
Others	13.1
	100.0

Source: J. Żarnowski, *Polska Partia Socjalistyczna w latach 1935–39* (Warsaw, 1965), p. 331.

time calls for a popular front of the Left had become anachronistic. In August 1938 the Polish Communist Party (KPP) was dissolved. The party, it was claimed, had been infiltrated by agents of the Polish Government's agents, but the real reason for this action was probably its Luxemburgist past and links with Trotsky. There was perhaps also a belief that its mere existence might hinder a rapprochement between Poland and the Soviet Union. Nearly all of its leaders were executed in the Soviet Union or were to die in camps there. The cause of Polish socialism lay very much in the hands of the PPS. A union of the opposition parties against the government, however, was not to take place.

The moderate success of the opposition in the local elections did lead to renewed calls for reform of the electoral system, to which the government was in no hurry to respond. By the end of 1938 it was evident that Nazi Germany was threatening Polish independence. It was this issue which overshadowed all else. Already in January 1939 the Peasant Party declared its support for the 'slogan of the unification of society around the defence of the state'.[15] From February the leadership of the National Party, weakened by the death of Dmowski in the previous month, began to seek an understanding with the government. This new climate of national solidarity was used by the régime to float a highly successful domestic loan for military purposes, which won the support of all the main opposition parties. The problem of the political exiles was now settled. With the German occupation of Bohemia and Moravia, Witos and his associates returned to Poland to be arrested, but they were released after a few days of nominal imprisonment. The government was ready to talk of national reconciliation and consolidation, but it had no intention of sharing power with the opposition. The PPS calls for changes in the electoral system were rebuffed and a campaign was launched to discredit Witos for his alleged links with the Gestapo after the annexation of Bohemia. There was no real basis for these highly compromising allegations. As *Robotnik* pointed out, the campaign was hardly the way to achieve national unity.[16] In June Śmigły-Rydz and the principal members of the government decided not to widen the bases of their support or establish a national coalition. As a result Poland entered the war with the régime jealously guarding its political monopoly, a fact that was to assume great significance after the rapid defeat of the Polish army.

The economy, national minorities, foreign policy and the army

The death of Piłsudski removed the main obstacle to the abandonment of the orthodox economic policy which had been pursued since the onset of the slump. Even with drastic cuts it had not been possible to reduce the state deficit, while the social costs of the policy, most clearly demonstrated in the wave of labour unrest in the spring of 1936, were now thought by many in the government, including the president himself, to be too high. In addition, the determination of the administration to maintain the convertibility of the *złoty* at a high fixed rate was diminished by the failure of foreign capital to invest in Poland and by the slow recovery of international trade, which it was hoped would stimulate the domestic economy. At the same time, the use of deficit financing and programmes of public works to achieve an economic revival in the United States, Germany and elsewhere and the five-year plans in the Soviet Union had undermined faith in *laissez-faire* principles.

The appointment of Eugenuisz Kwiatkowski as minister of finance in the Kościałkowski cabinet in October 1935 did not, however, immediately herald the adoption of a new policy. Kwiatkowski, an able administrator, whose economic views were not particularly radical, continued with greater success the policy of balancing the budget and also acted more vigorously against the cartels. The financial crisis in France from early 1936, which seriously affected the *złoty*, forced him to introduce a strict system of exchange control in Poland and suspend cash transfers for the service of foreign debts. Controls over foreign trade were also established. These measures, which were strongly criticized by the more economically orthodox members of the government, including Koc, who resigned as deputy director of the Bank of Poland in March 1936, were intended by Kwiatkowski at first to be purely temporary expedients to deal with a crisis situation. They provoked a further dispute within the administration between the military, led by Śmigły-Rydz, who now wanted to abandon entirely orthodox budgetary financing and embark on a course of expansion based on planned inflation on the German model, and the more cautious views of Kwiatkowski. Kwiatkowski's rather limited four-year plan adopted in July 1936 was, however, expanded in scope as a result of the French loan to Poland of £12,500,000 in autumn 1936. This enabled larger targets to be set and also stimulated the concentration of the government investment in a new Central Industrial Region, remote from the country's frontiers. By March 1939 the plan's investment objectives had been realized and new and more ambitious goals were set, the achievement of which was cut short by the war.

Kwiatkowski's policies were followed by a significant economic upturn, though there has been some dispute about how far this was the result of the world economic revival in these years. The index of industrial production rose to 142.2 by 1938 (1925–9 = 100),[17] while the indexed output of goods produced increased even faster from 103.1 in 1936 to 156.8 in June 1939.[18] At the same time unemployment remained extremely high, with the understated official statistics showing 456,000 jobless in 1938.[19] Polish foreign trade was still below the 1928 level, while agriculture likewise did not share in the revival. The government did attempt to speed up the pace of land reform and to limit the burden of debt on the small farmers, but its measures were no more than palliatives. The price scissors continued to work against agriculture, while the rise in the rural population more than outweighed the effects of land reform. Indeed, the annual increase in the surplus rural population in the late 1930's was perhaps 100,000. By 1939 the number of persons who with dependants could leave the countryside with no adverse effect upon production was probably as high as 8,000,000.[20]

The problem of the national minorities remained urgent after 1935. The government was able to reach an agreement with the Ukrainian National Democratic Union (UNDO), the main nationalist group in Eastern Galicia. In return for respecting Polish 'state needs', the UNDO was allowed to propose candidates for the 1935 election, of which 13 were elected to the sejm and five to the senate. Most Ukrainians held in Bereza Kartuska were released. Credits were now granted to Ukrainian economic institutions in eastern Galicia and Ukrainian language rights in the schools were more fully recognized. This rapprochement aroused much opposition in Ukrainian political circles and it did not prove lasting. Good intentions of the régime were often frustrated by local officials, while, as the international situation grew more threatening, policy towards the

Ukrainians came to be determined by the local military, for whom the prime consideration was the maintenance of 'security'. Acute bitterness was aroused by the army's attempt to foster the separate identity of a number of small ethnic groups in the Carpathians in south eastern Galicia and by efforts to claim as Polish the large number of mostly Ukrainianized petty gentry in the region. Pro-Polish sentiments in Volhynia were undermined by the attempt to prevent the local Uniate population from returning to Orthodoxy, and by closure of Orthodox churches or their transfer to Catholics and Uniates. By the beginning of 1939 the increasing dynamism of Nazi foreign policy, which made it seen that the Ukrainians could look to Germany to achieve their aims, had largely destroyed the rapprochement. Though considerable disillusion was caused by Germany's support for the Hungarian annexation of the Ukrainian 'Piedmont' of Sub-Carpatho-Ruthenia in March 1939, the revival of pro-Polish sentiment did not have a firm base. Equally unsuccessful were Polish efforts to find a solution to the problems of minorities in the north east. The Byelorussians were subject to increased pressure from the régime during this period. A number of Byelorussian cultural organizations were banned for alleged communist connections, including the main political group, the Byelorussian National Committee. Politically the region remained quiescent and there was no resurgence of the terrorism of the mid-1920's. The government's attempts to foster economic development in this area, however, were largely unsuccessful.

The principal feature of the German minority's history between 1935 and 1939 was its almost total conversion to National Socialism. This development did not lead, as in Czechoslovakia, to the emergence of a single dominant party. Instead a right-radical movement grew up alongside an old-established nationalist group, and, though relations between them were not always harmonious, both looked to Nazi Germany for the achievement of their goals. The government's policy following the Polish–German Non-Aggression Pact was to reduce sources of conflict as far as possible. In November 1937 a further agreement was reached on the general question of the two states' respective minorities. Although agreement did now try to meet German grievances, tension remained, especially in western Poland and Upper Silesia. With the deterioration of Polish–German relations after March 1939 many Poles feared that the German minority could be used for espionage and subversion. As a result many Germans were arrested, or fled to the Reich, claiming to be victims of 'Polish terror'.

The position of the Jews deteriorated seriously in the last years before the war. Anti-semitism began to play an ever-increasing role in the political attitude of the régime, both as a means of winning over the younger nationalists and of diverting attention from other social problems. The campaign to persuade peasants to boycott Jewish shops and stalls in small market towns took more violent forms and led to incidents in 1936 and 1937 which can be described only as pogroms. Though the government condemned anti-Jewish violence, it failed to see anything objectionable in the boycott as such. In the universities Jewish students were subject to harassment. In the academic years 1935–6 and 1936–7 most of the universities had to be closed for short periods on account of anti-Jewish violence. In October 1937, in an attempt to placate students, special 'ghetto benches' were established in most universities and polytechnics. Calls for the reduction of the number of Jews in the professions, above all in law and medicine, grew in strength. It should be stressed that Poland did not see the emergence of a mass anti-semitic movement similar to the Arrow Cross in Hungary or the Iron Guard in Romania. The government came to see the solution of the Jewish problem only in large-scale emigration and accordingly supported both Zionism and other schemes, such as the migration of Jews to places like Madagascar. By such actions as refusal to grant a moratorium on traders' debts when measures were introduced for peasants in 1933, or the virtual exclusion of Jews from their prominent position in the timber trade, the government hoped to put pressure on Jews to emigrate. This approach was too moderate for the more zealous supporters of the régime. It seems that only the coming of the war prevented the adoption of an anti-Jewish law presented to parliament in January 1939. The consequence of rising anti-semitism and government policies was the progressive economic ruin of the Jewish community. Emigration did not increase, because the flood of refugees from Germany, Austria and Czechoslovakia, to say nothing of the rest of Eastern Europe, caused more and more countries to close their doors to Jews. By the outbreak of the war, perhaps one third of the Polish Jews were almost entirely dependent on relief provided largely by private Jewish organizations financed from the United States.[21]

After 1935 Polish foreign policy remained under the exclusive control of Piłsudski's designated successor in this field, Józef Beck. Beck ostensibly continued to uphold the Piłsudski-ite principle that Poland should strive to keep a balance between her two powerful neighbours. In fact, however, the emphasis of the policy changed and its key now became the maintenance of the improved relations with Germany which had followed the Non-Aggression Pact. Beck believed that this rapprochement had greatly increased Poland's freedom of manoeuvre and he was prepared to make considerable concessions to preserve it. This was most clearly reflected in his policy on Danzig, where he co-operated with the Reich in reducing the power of the League Commissioner and acquiesced in the rapid nazification of the free city. At the same time he was not prepared to contemplate an alliance with Germany and rejected German suggestions for common action against the Soviet Union or for Polish adhesion to the Anti-Comintern Pact. To some extent Beck ran with the hare and hunted with the hounds. Beck did not believe that Nazi Germany constituted a threat to Polish security because of the irreconcilable antagonism between Nazism and Bolshevism. German expansion, in his view, would first take a south-easterly direction, towards Austria and Czechoslovakia, and would then be directed against the Soviet Union. At least in its initial stages, this development would work in Poland's favour. The disappearance of Czechoslovakia would enable the satisfactory settlement of the Cieszyn (Teschen) question and would allow the creation of a common Polish–Hungarian frontier and the emergence of an independent Slovakia, which would also act as a bridge between Poland and Hungary. On the other hand Poland was to maintain her position in the French alliance system. He thought of the Franco-Polish alliance as a counterweight to the association with Germany, though he had little faith either in the willingness or in the ability of the French to honour their commitments in Eastern Europe. The improvement in relations which followed the Rambouillet agreement of September 1936 had, as a result, little substance. Beck did attempt to maintain correct relations with the Soviet Union in accordance with the Non-Agression Pact of November 1932. However, he continued to regard the USSR as Poland's principal enemy and opposed attempts to build up a system of collective security, which he regarded as a pretext for the increase of Soviet influence in Europe. He criticized the Franco-Soviet and Czechoslovak–Soviet alliances as making these countries tools 'in the hands of the Comintern'.[22] Under these conditions. Polish–Soviet relations remained cool. The Polish foreign minister aimed also at achieving 'great power status' for his country, which meant that Poland should participate in any future schemes for the establishment of a European directorate on the lines of Mussolini's four-power pact of March 1933. A 'Third Europe' composed of the states from the Baltic to the Black Sea was to create a force capable of withstanding the USSR and Germany. The truth of the situation was that, if Poland were to receive Soviet support in the event of a conflict with Germany, the lines of communication of the Red Army would extend across the Polish territories in Byelorussia and the Ukraine. The USSR would come into possession *de facto* of the provinces which she had ceded *de jure* by the Treaty of Riga of 1921. The climate of opinion prevailing among the rulers of Poland, most of whom had made brilliant careers in the Polish–Soviet War of 1919–20, was not conducive to the realistic consideration of policy. The low level of thinking is illustrated by the celebrated remark of Śmigły-Rydz: 'Avec les Allemands nous risquons de perdre notre liberté; avec les Russes nous perdrons notre âme!'[23]

The state of the Polish army was such that Poland had more to lose than her liberty and soul. Piłsudski's death, it is true, made possible a new approach to military problems. The general staff under the direction of General Stachiewicz regained its proper position in decision-making. A plan was presented for the modernization of the army to Śmigły-Rydz between August 1936 and December 1937. A radical reorganization was not foreseen, but rather a rationalization of existing resources and the provision of those weapons which had been neglected under Piłsudski. To support the army it was proposed to build up the Polish armament industry with a six-year plan, which was actually adopted in July 1936. Moderately heavy investment was made, but the plan could not significantly alter the strength of Poland relative to that of her neighbours in the short time which was left with the onset of the crisis. The paper strength of the army was 30 infantry divisions rising to 39 on mobilization, supported by 11 cavalry brigades, 10 armoured battalions and 10 air-force regiments. Equipment, however, remained in short supply. Piłsudski's concepts of mobile warfare were in theory sound enough, but by 1939 mobility was measured in terms of tanks, lorries and aircraft, in short, in terms of the internal combustion engine which had given a new dimension to warfare since 1918. To problems of matériel were added problems of planning. Convinced that the principal enemy was the Soviet Union, the general staff prepared its plans upon the assumption that operations would take place in the east. Plans for a war in the west were at the best rudimentary. Colonel Beck's belief that Poland's security rested not upon a system of collective security, but upon Poland's own strength, lay upon flimsy foundations. Poland was not a great power and could not afford to adopt an egocentric attitude when the peace of all Europe was at stake. Beck's policy may be defended on the grounds that the weakness of Britain and France left him with no alternative but to seek an accommodation with Hitler, but that is only to say that he did not understand the nature of German policy. Caution in dealing with Germany was a necessity, but there was no excuse for associating Poland with the German pressure on Czechoslovakia in 1938.

The tragedy unfolded with unpleasant speed. The Munich agreement of September 1938 was to destroy the essence of the French alliance system in Central Europe. Czechoslovakia, already held in a strategic vice after the German occupation of Austria in March 1938, lost the frontier areas inhabited by Germans and thereafter lay absolutely at the mercy of Germany. On 15 March 1939 Bohemia and Moravia were occupied by German troops and a protectorate established. Slovakia obtained its independence. All the conditions for founding the 'Third Europe' of Beck's imagination were established, but the truth proved otherwise.[24] Poland appeared almost as the ally of Hitler. The Germans occupied the Sudetenland on 1 October. The Polish army moved into Trans-Olza on 2 October 1938, stripping Czechoslovakia of that portion of former Austrian Silesia to which Poland had laid claim since 1920. The common frontier with Hungary was not achieved. Germany had no interest in a 'Third Europe'. Her object was to fragment Central Europe and thus make German domination easier. Almost immediately the German government began to seek a settlement of questions outstanding between Poland and Germany. When the Polish Ambassador, Lipski, met Ribbentrop on 24 October 1938, he discovered that Germany required the retrocession of Danzig, extra-territorial rights in Polish Pomerania to give unimpeded access to East Prussia, and Poland's accession to the Anti-Comintern Pact. The implication was obvious. Poland could if she wished become a satellite state of Germany, but there could be no thought of Poland's being a great power. Even more ominous was the attitude of the Soviet Union. The USSR had no reason to regard international politics except in the light of Soviet *raison d'état*. The conversion of the the Soviet Union to a policy of collective security in 1933–4 in the face of the coming to power of the Nazi party in Germany never excluded the possibility of reversion to the entente with Germany arranged at Rapallo in 1922. The Locarno agreements of October 1925, which seemed to leave the frontiers of Germany with Poland and Czechoslovakia open to revision, appeared to point the way to the acquiescience of Britain and France to the ultimate establishment of a German hegemony in Central Europe. The Munich agreement of September 1938, in which the USSR had not taken part, seemed to show an equal indifference on the part of Britain and France to Soviet interests. Too many battles of historic importance had been fought in Bohemia and Moravia for the strategic significance of the Czech lands not to be understood. In October 1938 Soviet officials began to drop hints that the USSR might have to contemplate another partition of Poland in order to avoid German hostility. To reinforce hints, Stalin, at the Congress of the Communist Party of the Soviet Union (Bolsheviks) on 10 March 1939, declared that it should not be assumed that the USSR would automatically adhere to a policy of collective resistance. Stalin was commonly referred to in Soviet official circles as the *khozyain*, the boss.

If he made a public statement of this importance, it clearly indicated that Soviet policy had become more flexible. Flexibility took the form of economic discussions with Germany in 1939, which could be expanded in the event of need into conversations of a political nature.

The German occupation of Bohemia and Moravia called into question the validity of Chamberlain's policy with regard to Central Europe. Two days later on 17 March 1939 Chamberlain, in a speech in Birmingham, condemned German aggression, but in the final paragraph equivocal sentences implied that there was still the possibility of a negotiated settlement. The pressure of public opinion in Britain forced Chamberlain to enter into negotiations with the USSR, but clearly he showed no sense of urgency. On 31 March 1939, however, Chamberlain announced in the House of Commons a guarantee of Poland's independence. A guarantee was also to be offered to Romania. The aim of British policy was to stiffen the morale of Poland and Romania in the face of German pressure.[25] It was realized that Britain and France could not render effective military assistance to either of them. The USSR, on the other hand, proposed on 18 April 1939 a treaty of mutual assistance. France, Britain and the USSR were to be bound to assist one another not only if Germany were to attack any one of them, but also if Germany were to attack the Baltic states on the one hand, or the Low Countries on the other. Britain was reluctant to enter into so comprehensive an agreement, preferring to create a 'peace front', which other powers might be unwilling to join if Britain and France were bound in an alliance to the USSR. The negotiations for an alliance were conducted with the USSR by a junior official, William Strang, and not by a senior minister of political rank. The negotiations for a military convention were placed in the hands of relatively junior officers and not the chief of the imperial general staff. What the Soviet Union required was 'reciprocity', the formal recognition of Soviet vital interests and, therefore, the recognition of the USSR as a great power. Basically Britain wanted a deterrent alliance that would prevent a war with Germany: the Soviet Union, believing such a conflict inevitable, wanted an alliance which would make it possible to fight the war. In the end the impossible happened. Germany and the USSR composed their differences in the Germano-Soviet pact of 23 August 1939, and agreement to recognize one another's spheres of interest and, if Poland were to collapse, to partition her once again. Britain momentarily shook Hitler's confidence by the announcement on 25 August 1939 of the Anglo-Polish alliance. Nevertheless, on 1 September 1939 Germany attacked Poland and brought about the collapse of the Polish state.

The history of Poland between the wars is indeed disheartening and at no point more depressing than in 1939 when Poland once more became a battlefield. The Polish government of Piłsudski and his successors must bear full responsibility for a foreign policy which took for facts the figments of their imagination. Poland was neither a great power, nor even a prosperous country. There had been signal failures in dealing with the economy, the minorities, and even the institution of normal civil rights. Nevertheless, all was not failure. The taste of independence and its problems gave the Poles a new sense of nationality. Cultural life had blossomed in the new republic, an impressive educational system had been set up and some successes were also achieved in the economic field, above all in the building of Gdynia. Independence had brought a much wider political consciousness and had stimulated collective responsibility. The war of 1939–45 differed from the conflict of 1914–18. Poles knew that they were fighting not so much for independence as for existence. They knew also that they had the capacity to live together as a political community.

Map 3 Poland in 1939

8

Poland in defeat, September 1939–
July 1941

The collapse of Poland, 1939

Poland was the first country to resist German aggression. The pretext for the invasion was the ill-treatment of the German minorities in Poland, but there are no grounds for suggesting that Germans were in fact an under-privileged element in Polish society. The German motive was the desire to proceed to the total domination of Eastern Europe and the subjection of the continent to German rule. The invasion of Poland began on 1 September 1939. The bulk of the German army and air force was thrown into the struggle. The Germans were aware that they were taking a serious risk, but, though Britain and France declared war on 3 September, it was Poland which bore the brunt of Nazi aggression. Only massive and immediate support from Britain and France on the Western Front could have saved her from destruction, but no offensive was forthcoming despite Polish hopes and demands. The British and French declarations of war were for the time being merely diplomatic gestures.[1] Britain did not expect to save Polish independence at the beginning of the war, indeed, it was believed that nothing could be done to assist Poland. France for her part did nothing more than launch a probing attack upon the German Siegfried line, which was little more than a token gesture and gave no relief to Poland.[2] General Jodl, the head of the *Wehrmachtführrungsstab*, stated after the war: 'If we did not collapse in 1939, that was only because the approximately 110 French and English divisions in the West, which during the campaign in Poland were facing 25 German divisions, remained completely inactive.'[3]

The situation in Poland was catastrophic. By 2 September Colonel Jaklicz, the deputy chief of the Polish general staff, came to the conclusion that the situation was lost.[4] The Polish army, badly deployed, only partially mobilized and desperately short of modern equipment, was no match for the formidable German military machine. Hitler engaged in Poland 65 large formations, including all his armoured and motorized divisions, altogether 1,850,000 men with 10,000 guns and mortars, 2,800 tanks and over 2,000 aeroplanes.[5] Fifteen panzer and motorized divisions with powerful air support were the spearhead of the German advance. With this mobility, fire-power and air support the Germans could conduct a war of movement and for the first, but not the last, time display their mastery of Blitzkrieg tactics. Hitler's plan was simple. Assuming that Britain and France would remain inactive, he concentrated his efforts upon destroying Poland as soon as possible. Two army groups, the southern group in Silesia and Slovakia under General von Rundstedt and the northern group under General von Bock in East Prussia, were to launch simultaneous attacks enveloping Warsaw and the area a little to its east, with the intention of encircling and destroying the Polish armies deployed in the bend of the Vistula before they could retreat behind the lines of the rivers Vistula, Narew and San. They planned a second wider encircling movement east of those Polish formations which might evade the jaws of the inner trap.[6] The geography of the German–Polish frontiers favoured this strategy, allowing the Germans to deploy their forces from the outset in such a way as to make encirclement possible. The Polish army could not hope to defend itself successfully in such a situation. In fact, the Polish plan was sketchy and incomplete, covering only the initial stages of the campaign. It was based upon the assumption that the Germans would deploy against Poland the bulk of their forces and that the Poles would have to adopt a defensive position, preventing their troops from being destroyed until the Anglo-French offensive in the west, which they assumed would begin on the fifteenth day of French mobilization. The aim was to inflict heavy losses on the Germans in the hope of holding a defensive position and preventing undue loss of territory and, above all, of the important industrial areas west of the Vistula. The chances of this imprecise plan succeeding were slender. Although Śmigły-Rydz realized that the Germans had a numerical and material superiority, he failed to recognize its true extent. He failed likewise to envisage the possibility of Soviet intervention in Poland, although some Polish commanders considered it a foregone conclusion after the signing of the Germano-Soviet pact and were fully aware that Poland would be the loser in her first encounter with Germany. Śmigły-Rydz trusted in the Anglo-French offensive in the west, believing that the war would be long and arduous, but would end with a final victory for Poland and her allies. The German plan in fact succeeded beyond all expectations. Within a week the Germans occupied the industrial areas of Silesia and the so-called 'Polish Corridor' in Pomerania. On 9 September the Fourth Panzer Division attempted to take Warsaw, but was beaten off by a hastily improvised Polish defence force. The Polish army was now in full retreat. On 6 September Śmigły-Rydz had realized that the battle for the frontier region was lost and ordered a general retreat to the line of the rivers Vistula, San and Narew. Śmigły-Rydz's concept of defending 1,500 kilometres along the German–Polish frontier was an operational absurdity. His troops were spread out too thinly and the Germans could easily penetrate their defence lines or simply by-pass them altogether. The Germans exploited their initial successes by driving wedges with their mechanized forces between the mainly horse-drawn Polish armies. The Poles could therefore not stabilize a front, being cut off from their rear. Śmigły-Rydz's withdrawal to the Vistula, San and Narew came too late. The German panzer divisions pierced the Polish defences and reached the line of the middle Vistula south of Warsaw from Góra Kalwaria to Sandomierz sooner than the slow moving Polish formations. Almost simultaneously the Germans crossed the Narew and made further Polish withdrawals in the north essential. The plan of defending the Vistula, San and Narew thus came to nothing. The Germans could now encircle the main body of the Polish army in a double pincers movement. The four Polish armies in the bend of the Vistula, *Pomorze, Poznań, Łódź* and *Prusy*, were doomed and their destruction only a matter of time. The counter-attack on the Bzura undertaken by the *Poznań* and *Pomorze* armies was at first successful, but success was not exploited and the balance not redressed. The battle on the Bzura was lost because of lack of co-ordination in the high command. Within the first week Śmigły-Rydz lost operational control. The Polish army was defeated in a piecemeal fashion by the Germans, despite the customary heroism of the Polish soldiers and the tactical skill of their officers in the field. Most Polish front-line units fought well, but bravery and tenacity could not avert disaster.

On 10 September, having learned that the Germans had crossed the Vistula and Bug, Śmigły-Rydz ordered a general retreat into eastern Galicia, where he intended to organize a new line of defence based on the Romanian and Hungarian frontiers, with the Polish troops supplied from Romania. Once again his plan was hardly possible in view of the exhaustion of the Polish army. On 12 September the Germans reached Lwów and three days later were at Brześć. On 14 September Warsaw itself was encircled and the campaign reached its final stages. The Germans themselves were now compelled to reduce the tempo of their advance owing to supply difficulties and the battle fatigue of some mechanized formations, but it was too late for the Polish army to exploit this situation. At this stage the Germans considered the campaign as good as won and consequently began to transfer troops from Poland to the Western Front.

On 17 September they had begun to counter-attack on the Bzura and within a few days crushed the Polish forces there by a combination of armoured and air onslaughts. Only a few Polish units were able to avoid destruction and break through to besieged Warsaw or Modlin. The Polish army was 'simply cut to ribbons'.[7]

On 17 September the Red Army entered Poland and the Polish government and high command left Poland for Romania. The Soviet invasion occurred when the campaign was already effectively lost, but it did hasten the collapse of Polish resistance and prevented many Polish units from escaping abroad. Warsaw fell on 28 September, though some Polish units did continue to resist until 5 October, when they finally capitulated.[8] The entire campaign had lasted thirty-five days. For the Poles it was a shattering and bitter defeat, leading to the *de facto* disappearance of Poland from the map of Europe. The overwhelming German superiority meant that the outcome of the campaign was never in doubt. The best that can be said of the campaign is that it bought time for the Western Allies to prepare themselves for their own encounter with Germany.[9] For the Poles it was destructive of the prestige of the commander-in-chief, Śmigły-Rydz, who had lost control of the operations at an early stage. As Mikołajczyk was to write, the campaign was 'a bitter rout...which became an endless succession of bombings, retreats, sickening sights of broken cities and strafing and blasting of roads clogged with defenceless people fleeing from one gaping jaw to another.'[10] Many sensed that they had been badly served by the high command.[11] The Germans lost about 45,000 men, about half the losses they were to sustain from the outbreak of the war to the attack on Russia in June 1941. In material they lost 697 aeroplanes, 993 tanks and armoured cars, about 370 guns and mortars and 11,000 military vehicles. Polish losses were very much higher, amounting to 200,000 killed and wounded and 420,000 taken prisoner. Only some 90,000 Polish soldiers managed to escape abroad to Romania, Hungary and Lithuania. The Red Army captured about 200,000 officers and men.[12]

Defeat for Poland was a tragedy. The deeper causes lay in Poland's economic weakness and inability to create and sustain a modern army. If Poland had been allied with the USSR, Hitler might have been deterred from attacking her, but association with Russia, whether communist or not, was a psychological impossibility for the rulers of Poland in 1939. Thus the Poles were to suffer partition as a result of the Germano-Soviet pact of August 1939. The Soviet Union improved its political and strategic position substantially by regaining control over almost all the territories lost in the years 1917–21. All the Byelorussians and Ukrainians now came under Soviet control. The Soviet motive was clearly to prevent Nazi

Germany from using the mixed nationality areas of Poland as a base for promoting discontent in the Byelorussian and Ukrainian areas within the USSR. The Soviet Union was in 1940 to occupy the Baltic states and Bessarabia and incorporate them as Soviet Socialist Republics. The Soviet Union claimed that there was 'nothing sentimental' in the Germano-Soviet rapprochement. It was argued that 'in the jungle the strangest animals got together if they felt their joint interests made this advisable'.[13] Moreover, in October 1938 Potemkin, the deputy soviet commissar for foreign affairs, had told the French ambassador that the Anglo-French abandonment of Czechoslovakia at Munich had left Russia no choice but to strive for the 'fourth partition of Poland'.[14] Probably Stalin's basic motives for entering into an agreement with Hitler were his desire to regain the territories Russia had lost in the years 1917 to 1921, and a wish to keep her out of the war, which he knew would break out in Europe, for as long as possible. It is also probable that only after the fall of France in 1940 did he realize that he faced a situation of immense gravity. The USSR was faced by a victorious Germany in control of almost all Western and Central Europe with their economic and industrial resources. As a matter of pure precaution the USSR sought to maintain the outward appearance of good relations with Germany up to the very outbreak of hostilities in June 1941. For this reason Soviet relations with Great Britain from the fall of France to June 1941 were correspondingly cool, Stalin fearing even to appear willing to consider British propositions for closer association. For the Poles, Soviet intervention in 1939 was an act of treachery. They were now convinced that they were faced by two mortal enemies, Germany and the Soviet Union, and thought of themselves as being in a state of war with the USSR until 1941. Hitler, for his part, had to review German policy after the Battle of Britain and the failure to bring about a British submission. Neither Pétain in France at Vichy nor Franco, freshly victorious in the civil war in Spain, was prepared to assist Germany in extending the war in the Atlantic theatre by offering bases in their colonial territories. The logic of the situation was to attempt to knock out the USSR before the USA intervened actively in the European war, since it obviously favoured Britain, having provided war materials in the crisis of 1940–1. In 1939 Hitler had attacked Poland to remove the danger of an eastern front, but the destruction of Poland brought into existence 'a second front that was ultimately to destroy him'.[15]

Poland under German rule, 1939–41

Poland was to endure almost six years of intense suffering and upon a scale surpassing anything ever experienced before. The country was divided by the German–Soviet agreement of 28 September 1939 into two parts or 'zones of interest'. The territory west of the line of the rivers Pisa, Narew, Bug and San was occupied by Germany, while the areas to the east were allocated to the USSR. The demarcation line known as the Ribbentrop–Molotov line, approximated roughly to the Curzon Line of 1919–20. Germany acquired territory amounting to almost 189,000 square kilometres, which were primarily ethnically Polish with a population of 21.8 million, while the Soviet Union occupied about 200,000 square kilometres inhabited by about 13.2 million people of whom 5 million were Polish, 4.4 million Ukrainian and over 1.2 million Byelorussian. The German and Soviet governments agreed not to tolerate 'Polish agitation' in their occupation zones. By the end of October 1939 it became obvious that they had no intention of establishing a rump Polish state in any form or shape. Their policy was to be one of partition and annexation pure and simple. From the outset both parties set about strengthening their hold on Poland by establishing an administrative structure to control their zones. For the Poles there could be no question of collaborating with the occupying powers. Poland was the one country under German domination or influence which did not produce a figure of the character of Quisling or Pétain.

On 8 October 1939 Hitler annexed the northern and western regions of inter-war Poland and created out of them two new administrative districts of Germany, the Reichsgau Danzig and the Reichsgau Wartheland. On 12 October he established a German administration for the remainder of Polish territory west of the demarcation line, which was given the name of the Government-General. The incorporated areas, which included Polish Pomerania, Upper Silesia, the Dąbrowa basin, parts of the provinces of Łódź and Cracow and the Suwałki salient, covered an area of 91,974 square kilometres with a population of over 10.1 million, of whom 8.9 million were Poles, 603,000 Jews and 600,000 Germans. These territories were earmarked by the Nazis for complete germanization as part of the Reich and were turned into a German outpost in the east. The Polish character of the area was to be obliterated. Poles who were considered by the Germans to be a threat to the Reich or unfit for germanization were destined for deportation either to Government-General or to the Reich and ultimate extermination. This in effect meant the overwhelming majority of the Polish population, whose place was to be taken by German colonists from the USSR, the Baltic states and elsewhere. The execution of this policy was entrusted to Heinrich Himmler, the head of the SS and Gestapo. Those Poles who remained were to be a source of cheap labour, deprived of basic human rights and reduced to the status of helots. Mass killings, arrests and deportations began almost as soon as the German administration was established and continued unabated to the end. The first to suffer were prominent citizens and the intelligentsia, who were either shot, sent to concentration camps or deported to the Government-General. This action was designed to rob the Polish communities in the annexed provinces of their elite. The aim was to transform the mass of the Polish population into an enslaved people exploited in the interest of the Reich. At the same time the Germans assumed control of all Polish enterprises, whether industrial, commercial or agricultural. The dispossessed Poles were compelled to work as the menial employees of their German masters. The standard of living of Polish workers was reduced to a level much lower than that of their German counterparts. All Polish cultural and educational institutions were closed and the Poles allowed only the most rudimentary forms of primary education. They were not allowed to speak their own language freely or move without restriction. The annexed areas were used for the benefit of the German war effort and thus integrated completely with the economic system of the Reich. In the second half of 1940 the German authorities turned their attention from the towns to the countryside, where the peasants' farms were sequestrated and the peasants turned into labourers to work for their new 'landlords'. Many younger peasants were sent to Germany to work in industry or agriculture, while others were set to work in neighbouring towns or deported to the Government-General. The aim of these measures was the settlement of Germans in their place and to ensure a supply of cheap foodstuffs and labour for the German war effort.[16] By the end of 1944 some 750,000 Germans had been settled in the annexed provinces, while more than 330,000 Poles in these regions had been murdered and a further 860,000 deported to the Government-General or the Reich. The remaining Poles existed under appalling conditions and, indeed, many were declared to be Germans and made liable for military service. The result was predictably to produce in the Poles a most profound hatred and a thirst for revenge.

In the Government-General, embracing central and southern Poland including Warsaw and Cracow, events were equally sinister. The Poles were regarded as an 'inferior people' who should accept the facts of their new status. The intelligentsia and the Jews were destined to be exterminated. The rest were subjected to merciless exploitation in the interest of Germany. The area of Government-General was originally a quarter of the pre-war territory, but in 1941, after the invasion of Russia, it was enlarged to 142,000 square kilometres by the inclusion of eastern Galicia, increasing the population from 12.3 million to 16 million. The other parts of pre-war Poland were administered separately from the Government-General. On 12 October 1939 Hitler appointed Hans Frank, a leading Nazi lawyer, governor-general. Frank was directly responsible to Hitler, controlling an administration which was almost entirely German. The remnant of the Polish administration was allowed to function only at the level of town or village. From the outset the Government-General was policed by Germans, though the Polish ordinary police continued in existence under strict German supervision.

It was the German intention that the Government-General should eventually be germanized. In the meantime the population was subject to severe pressures and reduced to the level of semi-starvation. In the years 1939–44 1.3 million people were deported to Germany.[17] Frank employed the most ruthless and brutal methods to keep the Poles under control. His main consideration was the maintenance of military security and ensuring that 'the backbone of the Poles is broken for all time'.[18] It is estimated that during the war Poland lost 45 per cent of her doctors, 57 per cent of her lawyers, 15 per cent of teachers, 40 per cent of university professors, almost 50 per cent of qualified engineers, 30 per cent of technologists and technicians and 18 per cent of the clergy.[19] This dismal catalogue of losses among the educated classes and professional elite and the terrorization of ordinary workers and peasants show that the Poles were indeed involved in a struggle for survival. The Jews were assigned to immediate or eventual extermination. This policy was carried out in two stages, the first being a campaign of minor terror lasting from September 1939 to the attack on Russia in June 1941, and the second being the period of the 'final solution' from 1941 to the end of the war. At first the Germans introduced a number of anti-Jewish measures. By a decree of 26 October 1939 compulsory labour was imposed on all Jews between the ages of 16 and 60. Their property rights were restricted by a decree of 24 January 1940, supplemented by a further decree authorizing confiscation on a wholesale scale. A decree of 26 January 1940 restricted the Jews to their place of residence and deprived them of freedom of movement. As a result the Jews were concentrated in the ghettos, which were in effect temporary concentration camps isolating them from the Poles. They were guarded by police who checked exit and entry. No food or goods could be brought in from outside. nearly 500,000 people were incarcerated in the Warsaw ghetto alone. The ghettos were administered by German-appointed

'Jewish Councils' (*Judenräte*) with the help of Jewish police, responsible for the execution of German orders and the function of supplying Jewish forced labour. Each ghetto formed an isolated Jewish community cut off from other ghettos and the rest of society.[20] Simultaneously the Germans organized forced-labour camps for able-bodied Jews, who worked under appalling conditions. By 1944 over 300 such camps existed in Poland. On 4 March 1941 the Germans issued a decree outlawing Jews and Gypsies and depriving them of legal protection, and at the same time classifying the Poles living in the incorporated areas as second-class citizens. From October 1941 the penalty for leaving the ghettos or the labour camps could be death. Poles who sheltered or helped Jews risked their lives, being liable for summary execution. Because the Jews were not protected by law, Germans were not liable for prosecution if they robbed, injured or killed them. The Jews were allotted even smaller rations than the Poles.[21] In 1941 the daily food ration for a Warsaw Jew was 184 calories compared with 669 for a Pole, whereas the entitlement of a German was 2613.[22] Frank declared that he was simply not interested in whether the Poles had 'anything to eat or not'. The Poles were to receive whatever was to spare after feeding the Germans.[23] Thus food smuggling became a large and highly organized business. All Poles were underfed, but the people in the ghettos were starving, with a consequent high mortality rate among the very young and aged. Jews were forced to pay high tributes in money, gold, silver and furs. Pogroms in which hundreds died were common occurrences. In the years of 'minor terror' of 1939–41 about 100,000 Jews perished at the hands of the Germans.

The inhumanity of these years gave way in 1941 to a policy of mass extermination, which continued unabated until the end of German occupation. During this period the Germans liquidated almost the entire Jewish population, murdering about 2.7 million Polish citizens of Jewish origin.[24] Only 40,000–50,000 survived, of whom 5,000 were children.[25] About 1 million non-Polish Jews were brought to Poland by the Nazis and exterminated in death camps on Polish soil. Those who escaped owed their lives to the help of Poles. As Lucjan Blit has emphasized, 'every Jew who survived in Nazi-occupied Poland did so only because Gentile Poles risked their lives to hide them'.[26] Under the challenge of Nazi occupation, all Poles but a few extremists of the near-fascist elements on the extreme Right responded stoutly to the protection of the Jews, but the Germans were present in overwhelming force and were determined to destroy them. Poland seemed to Hitler a good testing ground for the 'final solution' of the Jewish problem.[27] The total Polish losses during the years 1939–45 amounted to 6,028,000 people, almost one-fifth of the entire pre-war population. Most of them were deliberately done to death by the Germans. Only 664,000 people were killed in the course of military operations.

As the war progressed the pressure on the Poles increased. Higher education was suppressed and the lower levels of instruction strictly controlled. In the summer of 1940 alone some 3,500 intellectuals and politicians were killed.[28] Attempts were made also to control the Catholic church. After the fall of France, however, an effort was made to revive the Polish economy and improve communications in preparation for the coming attack upon Russia. The Government-General became an important staging area and base for operations in the USSR. Food prices rose very rapidly and the poorer sections of the community suffered from malnutrition and starvation, because the Germans froze wages at pre-war levels. The section of the community which did profit was the peasantry, who could charge high prices for their products. Even their relative prosperity soon came to an end when the Germans demanded deliveries of large quantities of produce at low prices. It was German policy to drive a wedge between the intelligentsia and the masses in town and country, but their efforts failed. In the face of German brutality and exploitation the Poles maintained a national solidarity. The German security forces considered all Poles to be members of the resistance. Indeed, the Gestapo believed that by May 1941 there was 'not a single Pole who would come forward and really work' for Germany. The Germans were to complain that it was impossible to subdue the Poles because of their 'fanatical faith' in the 'resurrection of Poland'.[29]

Soviet policy in the annexed areas

The USSR was anxious to justify and legalize its annexation policies in eastern Poland. Soviet entry into Poland was represented as the result of the virtual collapse of the Polish state and government and arising out of a need to protect Ukrainian and Byelorussian 'blood brothers'.[30] In November 1939 the occupied territories were incorporated into the USSR. It was claimed that this step was based on the right of the 'Western Ukrainians' and the 'Western Byelorussians' to self-determination. They constituted the majority of the population and demanded through 'democratically' elected assemblies assimilation with the Soviet Union. At the same time the large estates were confiscated and banking, heavy industry and mining nationalized. In July 1941 Latvia, Estonia and Lithuania were incorporated into the USSR, with Vilna being ceded to Lithuania. The Polish government refused to accept this disposition of the eastern provinces, which it continued to regard as an integral part of Poland, questioning the legality of annexation and dismissing as fraudulent the elections which preceded it. In fact, the case of the Polish government was not strong by the standards of the Atlantic Charter of 1941. There were in the areas annexed by the Soviet Union over 4.5 million Ukrainians, about 1.2 million Byelorussians, over 1.1 million Jews, and other nationalities amounting to over one million. Nevertheless, when the Germans attacked the USSR in June 1941 there were grounds for a serious dispute. The Polish government-in-exile took its stand upon the frontiers of 1939, whereas the Soviet government insisted upon the frontiers as they existed in 1941. From 29 November 1939, the Soviet authorities considered all Polish citizens domiciled in the annexed provinces now to be Soviet subjects as distinct from those normally resident in the German zone, whose civil rights were accordingly restricted. 'Politically and socially dangerous elements' were deported to Siberia and Asiatic Russia. Well over a million people suffered deportation, including not only landlords, capitalists, politicians, officers, civil servants, teachers and policemen, but even peasants, poor shopkeepers, foresters and artisans, together with their families.[31] The majority of the exiles were Polish. The pre-war opposition and left-wing politicians, including members of the Polish Communist Party (KPP), disbanded on Stalin's orders in 1938, were treated with the same suspicion and distrust by the Soviet authorities.[32]

The annexed territories were administered by Soviet officials with little knowledge of local conditions, who tried to impose Soviet models and solutions upon a sceptical population. Until the second half of 1940 the government tried to secure the support and co-operation of the Ukrainians and Byelorussians and convince them that the USSR had come to liberate them from Polish oppression and exploitation. It was declared that Polish rule would never return. Molotov declared that 'Nothing is left of Poland, this ugly offspring of the Versailles Treaty'.[33] Most Poles were dismissed from official positions and reduced to second-class citizenship. Ukrainian and Byelorussian were made official languages, while Russian became a compulsory language in the schools. The teaching of religion was forbidden. These measures were resented by the Poles, even the Polish communists.[34] In the second half of 1940, however, Soviet policy began slowly to change in respect of the Poles as a result of growing awareness after the fall of France that the USSR was now directly threatened by Germany and needed the support of the staunchly anti-German Polish population. At the same time the Ukrainians and Byelorussians were showing signs of hostility to enforced collectivization and high taxation introduced in the spring of 1940. In November 1940 the 85th anniversary of the poet Mickiewicz's death was solemnly observed in Lwów. There was talk of establishing an autonomous Polish region in the Białystok province, inhabited by over a million Poles, and even of a 'Polish government' under the premiership of Kazimierz Bartel, who travelled to Moscow for talks. In the autumn of 1940 conversations took place with a number of Polish officers, including Lieutenant Colonel Zygmunt Berling, who had been captured by the Red Army, about the possibility of forming a Polish division attached to the Soviet forces.

The Polish communists, under the leadership of Wanda Wasilewska and Alfred Lampe, tried to persuade Stalin to change his attitude towards the Poles and allow them to re-establish the Polish Communist Party (KPP). Probably as a result of these representations, some members of the KPP were from the spring of 1941 admitted to the Communist Party of the Soviet Union. In January 1941 a Polish monthly, *Nowe Widnokręgi* (New Horizons), began to appear in Lwów under the editorship of Wasilewska, publishing articles by both communist and non-communist writers. As relations with Germany began to deteriorate, the attitude of the Soviet authorities began to mellow, but the first encounter of Poles with Stalin and stalinism was far from pleasant, even for communists and their sympathizers. When Germany attacked the Soviet Union in June 1941, Poles and Russians were united by their having a common enemy, but the experience of Poles at the hands of the German and Soviet authorities tended to confirm the Polish belief that independence could best be achieved by reliance on the Western Powers.[35]

The Polish resistance

The nucleus of a Polish resistance leading to the creation of the Home Army (Armia Krajowa) and the Polish underground state was created in Warsaw in September 1939, when General Michał Tokarzewski established a clandestine military organization, 'Service for the Victory of Poland' (Służba Zwycięstwu Polski – SZP). The leaders of SZP tried to organize a force capable of day-to-day resistance to both Germany and the USSR, in preparation for a national insurrection in the last stages of the war in Poland. From the outset they tried to formulate a plan of general resistance embracing intelligence, sabotage and subversion, together with reprisals against military and administrative personnel, in preparation for a general insurrection. In Poland there was long tradition of insurrection and revolt: 'The Poles rose in revolt against foreign domination in 1794, 1830, 1846 and 1863. Poland was the country of classic insurrections just as France was the country of model revolutions.'[36] The leaders of resistance could draw upon a common tradition of revolt which gave an instinctive disposition to underground discipline. Poles were perhaps more united under foreign occupation than they were under governments of their own election. Confident in the moral support they could expect from the population, the leaders of the resistance sought to establish a force capable of assuming far more than military functions. It had to ensure the continuity of the state and the honour and morale of the nation. To realize these aims Tokarzewski appealed for help to those sections of the army which had avoided capture and to the leaders of the opposition parties, the PPS, the Peasant Party (SL), the National Democrats and the Party of Labour (Stronnictwo Pracy – SP). The army was to provide the resistance with its military cadres, but the opposition was to furnish its political base. This concept revealed a subtle change in the alignment of political forces in Poland. The officers of the army of 1939, closely aligned with the régime of Piłsudski and his successors, were ready to share authority in the future with the régime's opponents, who would now provide the political base of the resistance.[37] The pre-war opposition represented the majority of the nation and disliked the *Sanacja*. The opposition therefore continued, in spite of its support of the resistance, to entertain reservations with regard to the military, which it suspected of maintaining Piłsudski-ite views on the future organization of Poland. Opinions differed also on the social and economic problems which would face Poland at the end of war. In fact, the debate was to change its course under the challenge of communism advancing side by side with the victorious Red Army. Tokarzewski was anxious to dissociate the resistance from the *Sanacja*, because the opposition had the network of contacts necessary for the creation of a mass resistance. For the moment the conflict of forces within the Poland of 1939 remained unresolved, but an uneasy coalition was established.

In December the leaders of the resistance proclaimed their intention of fighting against the invaders and continuing until the day of liberation within the pre-war frontiers, when the army could be re-established and a provisional government set up. From the point of view of the resistance, Poland was to be a constitutional state, its constitutional system to be determined by a freely elected parliament and all totalitarian ideologies abandoned. In the first instance no problem of Polish communism arose, because the communists showed no sign of political activity on a national scale. The leaders of the resistance began to extend the authority of the SZP throughout Poland and establish contact with the Polish government-in-exile. By the end of 1939 a network of organizations existed in both the German and the Soviet zones of occupation.[38]

The government-in-exile and the army

On 30 September 1939 a new Polish government was formed in Paris under the premiership of General Władysław Sikorski, the government having been interned in Romania. The new government came into existence as a result of President Mościcki's assigning under the constitution of 1935 his powers to Władysław Raczkiewicz, an administrator associated with the *Sanacja*. There were certain essential differences from the pre-war system. Sikorski was not only prime minister, but also, from 7 November, commander-in-chief of the armed forces. Sikorski was therefore, in name at least, the dominant figure within and without Poland. In November 1939 Sikorski established an official underground organization, the Association of Armed Struggle (Związek Walki Zbrojnej – ZWZ), of which General Kazimierz Sosnkowski, one of the close collaborators of Piłsudski, was to be the commander. The government-in-exile divided the political and military functions of the resistance, which covered both the German and the Soviet zones. Tokarzewski was appointed to command the ZWZ in the Soviet zone, while his chief of staff, Colonel Stefan Grot-Rowecki was to take charge of the German zone. In July 1940 Grot-Rowecki's command was extended to cover the whole of Poland. Though he had served with Piłsudski's legions in the First World War and taken part in the Russo-Polish war in 1920, he regarded himself primarily as a soldier and tried to avoid political involvement. With other resistance groups, subordinating themselves to the ZWZ, the government-in-exile hoped to enjoy undisputed control over the underground at home. In theory the *Sanacja* had lost control, but there were still enough of the pre-war government's supporters in high positions to create difficulties in moments of crisis. Sikorski's Government of National Unity was recognized by France, Britain and the USA as well as most neutral countries. It was situated first in Paris and, after a short stay in Angers from November 1939, moved to London with the fall of France. A parliament-in-exile, composed of the four main political parties – the SL, PPS, National Democrats and Party of Labour, together with the Jewish national minority – was set up in the form of the National Council (Rada Narodowa – RN), the members of which were appointed by the president on the recommendation of the prime minister. Paderewski was appointed chairman, but owing to his ill-health the deputy chairman, the leader of the SL, Stanisław Mikołajczyk, presided over its proceedings. Sikorski tried to deal with France and Britain on equal terms, but his position was weak when his government depended upon them for support not only for itself, but also for the equipment of the Polish army-in-exile. Polish troops raised in France in the winter of 1939–40 were short of uniforms and equipment, which were to be supplied by the French government. In June 1940 the Polish forces of all arms amounted to 84,500 in the west, composed largely of men from the Polish forces who had escaped from Poland, and Polish citizens living in France.[39] The army consisted of four infantry divisions, two infantry brigades and one armoured brigade. The air force, stationed partly in France and partly in Britain, consisted of 9,171 men, and the navy, operating from British ports, of 1,400. The Western Allies were willing to help the Poles reorganize their forces and were pledged to restore an independent Poland, but they were not prepared to antagonize the USSR in support of Polish claims. It was doubtful whether they would be able to restore Poland within her pre-1939 frontiers. Britain thought that Poland's claim to territories east of the Curzon line was questionable. Indeed, in October 1939 Lord Halifax stated that the Russians had advanced their boundary to what was 'substantially' the frontier recommended by Britain for Poland in 1919–21.[40] Already Britain was trying to improve relations with the USSR and persuade the Poles that the loss of the eastern provinces was the necessary price for a rapprochement. The problem of the Soviet–Polish frontiers was to be one of the most acute questions which the Allies had to face in the years 1939–45.[41] The Poles were reluctant to relinquish their claims, but as early as November 1939 Sikorski himself had doubts of Poland's ability to recover the areas lost to the USSR and believed that Poland should be compensated at the expense of Germany.[42] In his messages to Poland Sikorski called for national solidarity in the fact of the German and Soviet threat and assured Poles at home that post-war Poland would be a democracy in which justice would prevail. Sikorski's ideal Poland would be a constitutional state with a primarily capitalist economy, but the frontiers of the new Poland remained to be defined.

The collapse of France and the exiled government in Britain

On 10 May Germany attacked the Netherlands, Belgium and France. With the beginning of the Battle of France, Winston Churchill became prime minister in Britain, upon which the Polish government would have to depend for support after the collapse of France in June. The fall of France was a severe blow to all Poles believing in the victory of the Western Allies supported by the USA, but no one dared to think of capitulation.[43] The Polish troops in France had fought well and hard, but suffered heavy losses. Most of their front-line units were destroyed or interned in Switzerland. After the French capitulation an Anglo-Polish agreement provided for the evacuation of the government and the remnants of the army, about 19,000 men, to Britain.[44] The transfer was not effected without a minor Polish crisis. On 18 July 1940 President Raczkiewicz actually dismissed General Sikorski from his position as prime minister. Raczkiewicz thought that the flexible views of Sikorski with regard to future relations with the USSR were unacceptable and appointed in his place August Zaleski, but representatives of the Army, including General Sosnkowski, declared against placing the government-in-exile in the hands of members of the *Sanacja*. The way was kept open to a compromise with the USSR.[45] Polish policy was thus kept in line with the British aim of winning over the USSR for a joint struggle against Nazi Germany. In June Sikorski had told Churchill that he regarded the defeat of Germany as Poland's main task and that he was prepared to seek a rapprochement with the USSR. Sikorski survived the criticism of the politicians in exile, but in 1940 he was still a long way from coming to an agreement with Soviet Russia. On 18 June 1940 the ZWZ was ordered to prepare itself for a long struggle and therefore limit its immediate operations to an essential minimimum, for fear of incurring unnecessary losses which would allow the Germans to destroy the resistance long before the ultimate insurrection. The actions of the Poles in 1940 were not insignificant. Polish fighter pilots played an honourable role in August–September 1940 in the Battle of Britain, constituting the largest single foreign element in Fighter Command, with the Polish 303 Squadron in particular distinguishing itself by its outstanding success in shooting down German aircraft.[46]

In July 1940 Churchill assured Sikorski that he could count on him for 'ever' and that 'England will keep faith with the Poles'.[47] It was not on Britain alone that Sikorski sought to base Poland's cause. In March 1941 he visited the USA to enlist American support for Poland's war effort and obtain permission to enlist volunteers among Americans of Polish descent. He drew American attention to the atrocities committed by the Germans in Poland and the plight of Polish Jews. Sikorski informed Roosevelt of his efforts to promote the establishment of federal unions in Central Europe, especially the Czech–Polish plans for post-war co-operation. A Polish union with the Czechs, it was hoped, would make these countries independent of both Berlin and Moscow. Sikorski's plans were as ambitious and far-reaching as those of Colonel Beck, but the Czechs, wary of any plans for the future which might not find approval with the USSR, upon which they intended to base their security, were to dissociate themselves from the Polish venture. Sikorski, a few days before the German invasion of Russia, came to the conclusion that an improvement in Soviet–Polish relations was essential. On the one hand he was compelled to move with care in the light of the distrust of the USSR entertained by Poles at home and those holding posts in the government-in-exile in Britain. On the other hand, to reach a satisfactory understanding with the Soviet Union he would have to solve the thorny problems of the Soviet–Polish frontiers and the citizenship of Poles deported to Russia.[48] The restoration of diplomatic relations was therefore fraught with difficulty. On the Soviet side there lingered a traditional distrust of the Poles nurtured by memories of earlier national crises and conflicts in the disputed borderlands. If at times the diplomacy of Sikorski was to appear equivocal, he had many unpleasant alternatives with which to contend.

The German–Soviet war: Soviet–Polish relations, 1941

On 22 June 1941 Germany launched Plan Barbarossa and invaded the Soviet Union. The whole course of the war in Europe was changed. Great Britain obtained a reprieve from a desperate situation. The possibility of German defeat brought new hope of final victory to the peoples of occupied Europe. In Poland the news was greeted with joy and jubilation. The fact that Poles and Russians were fighting against a common enemy opened the way to a temporary understanding. The British government, in the interest of promoting harmony, played an important part in bringing about a Soviet–Polish rapprochement by giving Sikorski's critics within his government to understand that he had its support. On 30 July a Soviet–Polish agreement was signed in London, though not without protest from General Sosnkowski, August Zaleski and Marian Seyda, all three members of the Polish cabinet, who acting in concert with President Raczkiewicz ostentatiously refused to attend an all-party reception at the Savoy Hotel designed to effect a reconciliation.[49] The treaty provided for the restoration of diplomatic relations, military co-operation, the raising of a Polish army in the USSR and an amnesty for all Polish citizens detained in Russia. Significantly the question of the future frontiers between the two countries was passed over in silence, but the USSR recognized that the Germano-Soviet agreements of 1939 with regard to Poland had 'lost their validity'. For the meantime both parties agreed to differ in face of the immediate issue of fighting Germany. Sikorski's failure to settle the frontier problem in 1941 left open the future course of Soviet–Polish relations. In 1941 the diplomatic position of the USSR was weak when the German forces had made deep penetrations into Russia. Again in 1942 the offensive in the direction of Stalingrad made the Soviet Union a suitor for aid, but with the successful counter-offensive in November 1942 the tide of battle turned in favour of the Soviet Union.

The repulse of the German offensive at Kursk in July 1943 meant that the Soviet forces would eventually drive back the Germans into Central Europe. Soviet diplomacy was thus weak in the course of 1941–2, but spoke with strength from the end of 1942 and in the course of 1943. Churchill and Roosevelt succeeded in bringing Stalin to the conference table at Tehran in November 1943, hoping that by agreement they could limit the gains which would probably fall to the USSR. As far as the Polish government-in-exile was concerned, it had secured the British agreement to the principle of non-recognition of the territorial changes which had taken place in Poland since 1939, but at the same time Britain denied that this constituted 'any guarantee of frontiers'. The British attitude clearly contained many serious reservations. Men like Sosnkowski, Zaleski and Seyda required an explicit Soviet recognition of the frontiers established by the Treaty of Riga in 1921 as essential to an understanding, arguing that this point should be pressed while the Red Army was staggering under the massive German assault. They maintained that it would be impossible to obtain guarantees when once the Soviet military position began to improve.[50] The majority of the Poles greeted the Soviet–Polish agreement with satisfaction, their 'tempered sympathies' lying with the Soviet Union.[51] Sikorski and Stanisław Mikołajczyk nevertheless took their stand upon the pre-war frontiers, their views being expressed in the Polish newspaper in London, *Dziennik Polski* (The Polish Daily), on 1 August 1941, which called forth a retort in the official Soviet newspaper, *Izvestia*, on 3 August, rejecting the terms of the Treaty of Riga of 1921. In the end Churchill was bound to defer to Soviet wishes in the desire to maintain Soviet determination to stay in the war. The USA was not to enter the war until December 1941 when Japan attacked Pearl Harbour, but the crisis in the Pacific was likely to make the US administration cautious of offending the USSR, upon whose aid it might wish ultimately to call to bring the war in Asia to an end. The Polish diplomatic position could not be strong in the light of the global policies of the powers.

9

The ill-fated alliance, August 1941–
April 1943

The uneasy partnership: Sikorski, Anders and Stalin

In spite of the conclusion of the Soviet–Polish pact acute problems bedevilled co-operation. Serious arguments arose connected with the size, equipment and deployment of the Polish army in Russia under General Władysław Anders, which led finally to its withdrawal to the Middle East in the summer of 1942 in an atmosphere of mutual recrimination. The evacuation of the Polish army was a severe blow to the alliance. Sikorski originally intended that Anders' troops should eventually enter Poland together with the Red Army. Indeed it would have been a political asset of great importance if the former were to occupy Poland and re-establish the organs of the civil administration in the name of the Polish state and owing allegiance to the government-in-exile in London, but now this advantage was thrown away. A second cause of conflict was the question of about 8,000 officers captured by the Soviet forces in 1939, whose disappearance Stalin could not explain. To this problem was added dispute about the citizenship of all persons of Polish nationality domiciled in the territories annexed by the USSR in 1939. The main bone of contention, however, was the unresolved frontier dispute. Sikorski visited Moscow in December 1941, when Stalin suggested to him that an agreement might be reached, but Sikorski declined to discuss the matter. The conversation with Stalin on 3 December of Sikorski, Anders and the ambassador, Stanisław Kot, was soured by Sikorski's proposal to remove the Polish army to the Middle East. However, on 4 December Stalin nevertheless turned to the all important question of Soviet–Polish relations in the future, declaring that he desired a friendly and stronger Poland, but Sikorski took his stand upon the frontiers of 1939 and asked to be excused from discussing this delicate matter. All that emerged from the meeting was a declaration of solidarity in the struggle against Germany. It has been argued that Sikorski missed an opportunity of tying Stalin to an agreement at a difficult moment when the Germans were at the gates of Moscow. In fact, the Red Army was about to drive the Germans back 100 kilometres and stabilize the front, the first time a German army had been halted since 1939. The almost simultaneous opening of the war in the Far East with the Japanese attack on Pearl Harbour on 7 December 1941 placed international relations in a new dimension. On the one hand the entry of the USA into the war placed the immense resources of the Americans at the disposal of the Allies. On the other hand the United States would welcome the assistance of the USSR in Asia when the war in Europe had been won. The policy of Sikorski, however, after his visit to Moscow, rested upon the concept that the agreement with the Soviet Union of 30 July 1941 was a temporary expedient in a difficult period of the war. Sikorski foresaw the weakening of the USSR in the conflict with Germany and sought to base Poland's future upon association with Great Britain and a confederation of Poland, Czechoslovakia and Romania, linked with a Balkan confederation of Greece and Yugoslavia. Sikorski wished to have good relations with the USSR. In this lay the essential difference between his policy and the disastrous policy of Beck in 1934–9. The essential error of Sikorski was to believe that his plans of confederation in Central Europe should be realized before an agreement had been reached with the USSR.[1]

In 1942 Polish–Soviet relations were far from friendly. The departure of Anders' troops led to a serious deterioration of the status of Poles remaining in Russia. In July 1942 the Soviet government began to close down the network of agencies which had been set up by the Polish embassy to deal with the welfare of Poles in the Soviet Union. The Soviet authorities claimed that this network was used for spying and arrested a number of the local Polish delegates. The situation deteriorated even further in January 1943 when the Soviet government decided that all Poles from the annexed territories were to be regarded as Soviet citizens. It was clear therefore that Stalin would be willing to look to other sources of support in Poland than those offered by the official government-in-exile in London, but in the first instance he was to approach this task with caution for fear of the diplomatic complications it might cause with the Western Allies. While the USSR remained in diplomatic relations with the Polish government-in-exile it would have been unwise to support other elements in Poland which were in conflict with it. This above all meant the Polish communists.

Stalin and the Polish communists, 1941–2

In 1938 the Comintern had suppressed the Polish Communist Party (KPP) on the grounds that it was 'contaminated by hostile elements' and its leadership infiltrated with 'agents of Polish fascism'. Almost the entire leadership of the KPP was liquidated in the purges of 1937–8. The safest place for a Polish communist at that time was ironically in a *Sanacja* prison. It was precisely because they were political prisoners that the future leaders, Władysław Gomułka, Marceli Nowotko, Paweł Finder and Edward Ochab, managed to survive. Stalin's motives in purging the KPP are difficult to divine. Perhaps the deaths of Polish communists in the USSR were a by-product of the purge of the Soviet party, but it is possible to argue that Stalin was clearing the way for a new Polish party more suited to leading the Polish proletariat during a time of mounting international crisis. The liquidation of the KPP was symptomatic of Stalin's great distrust of all Polish political parties regardless of their colour.[2] Hitler's invasion of Poland in 1939 caused the political internees of the *Sanacja* to be released, the communists taking refuge in Białystok and Lwów in the Soviet zone. Until the German invasion of Russia began in 1941 there could be no thought of reviving the KPP, but the war changed Stalin's mind. The Polish communists had emerged and demanded recognition, but to resurrect the KPP would have been a confession of error in the past. An 'Initiative Group', consisting of Marceli Nowotko, Paweł Finder and Bolesław Mołojec were parachuted into Poland in December 1941 to bring together the Polish communists and establish a Polish Workers' Party (Polska Partia Robotnicza – PPR).[3] The name in itself is significant. The task of the new party was to stress the need for an anti-Nazi alliance of the communist and bourgeois forces. The essential aim of all communist parties in occupied Europe was to establish broad anti-German fronts. The new party was to be free of the sectarian strife which had plagued the KPP and be able to participate in the government of post-war Poland, though with the ultimate aim of striving for a social revolution. Meanwhile, the PPR was to call for the democratization of life in Poland.

The Polish Workers' Party was founded in January 1942. Its first manifesto called for a national front to struggle for an independent Poland based on a democracy free from economic exploitation. The party was open to all who might wish to join it irrespective of previous political affiliations. In spite of the connection of the PPR with Moscow, the party was at pains to stress that it was not a member of the Comintern.[4] At first the PPR was prepared to co-operate with Poles owing allegiance to the government in London, hoping by this means to enter into the mainstream of politics as the representative of the Left. The PPR pursued a broad-bottomed policy to make itself attractive to many shades of political opinion. It wished itself to prepare for a national insurrection and to help in the organization of guerrilla warfare. The PPR wished to co-ordinate its activity with the Red Army, but this became a major source of conflict between it and the pro-London forces. It created a People's Guard (Gwardia Ludowa – GL), which in 1944 became the People's Army (Armia Ludowa – AL). In June 1942 the PPR had 4,000 members and had recruited 3,000 men to the People's Guard.

The activity of the PPR gave rise to growing concern among the pro-London circles, which accused the PPR of planning a communist take-over at the end of the war, attempting to discredit the official ZWZ by claiming that only the People's Guard was fighting the Germans and thus calling upon the people to rise prematurely against them, while at the same time fomenting class war. The propaganda of the PPR was effective especially among the young people anxious to fight and impatient with the restraint called for by the government-in-exile. The timing of the insurrection was becoming a major cause of dispute between the pro-London and the communist forces. The government-in-exile planned an insurrection during the German collapse, but the PPR proposed intensification of operations against the Germans to assist the Soviet war effort. The government-in-exile sanctioned only 'limited warfare' in spite of demands for a more active policy, fearing lest premature involvement lead to unnecessary losses and endanger long-term plans. In the second half of 1942, however, Grot-Rowecki realized that, owing to the German terror, the policy of limiting the ZWZ's operations was becoming untenable and was helping the communists to win more followers. He maintained that the German application of the doctrine of collective responsibility and mass terror was causing heavy losses, despite Polish efforts to avoid reprisals by limiting armed resistance to a minimum, while concentrating instead upon sabotage and intelligence work. This policy was causing more active members to join the PPR. He therefore advised the London government-in-exile that a defensive attitude might erode the offensive spirit of his men and suggested that he be allowed to intensify his operations and in eastern Poland to begin guerrilla warfare.

At the end of 1942 the Germans began to expel Polish peasants from the Lublin and Zamość areas and replace them with Germans. The eviction of the Poles was accompanied by the worst kind of atrocities, which led to a mass flight of the young people to the woods. Grot-Rowecki ordered his troops in those regions to retaliate by attacking German lines of communications and destroying the farms made vacant, but the London government-in-exile instructed him to keep retaliatory operations to a minimum, and prevent the outbreak of a national insurrection. He received orders also to resist the demands of the masses for more drastic action. These orders gave rise to articles in the government underground press desiged to cool the general demand for active resistance. The government had consistently stated that the resistance was to act decisively only at a suitable moment in the closing phases of the war. In February the Germans stopped the evictions. The first major Polish operation was successful, showing that determined resistance could have some effect on the German terror. The Germans were reluctant to provoke an insurrection in Poland when their main communication lines ran through the country to their heavily committed forces in Russia. An outbreak of serious fighting was bound to affect the flow of supplies and reinforcements to the Eastern Front. The communists exploited this success in accusing the ZWZ of undue timidity. They continued to argue that the German terror must be met with counter-action. Differences of political attitudes were thus combined with different views on the strategy to be employed in occupied Poland.

Sikorski's policy, 1942-3

Sikorski tried to strengthen his position by seeking agreement with President Beneš to construct after the war a confederation of Poland and Czechoslovakia. The essence of the difficulties which Sikorski met in his dealings with Beneš lay in his attitude to the USSR.[5] Sikorski in February 1941 insisted upon Poland's claim to the frontiers of 1939, but Beneš maintained a reserved attitude. Beneš was convinced that Czechoslovakia would not have been partitioned in 1938 if the USSR had played her full part as a European Great Power. Beneš had even before the outbreak of war between Germany and the USSR made it clear that he thought Czechoslovak independence would be restored ultimately by the USSR. The Soviet–Czech agreement of 18 July 1941 presented by no means as difficult a problem as the Soviet–Polish agreement of 30 July 1941. Restoration of Czechoslovakia to the frontiers of 1939 was a matter of relative simplicity. Between Czechoslovakia and Poland lay the problem of Trans-Olza, taken by Poland in October 1938. The Czechs therefore could use this matter as an excuse to dissociate themselves from the plan of confederation which they had agreed in principle with the Poles in a declaration of 11 November 1940. A Polish–Czech Co-ordinating Committee began consideration of the details of union on 4 November 1941. Sikorski had, in addition, ideas of associating with it Romania, Hungary and the Lithuanian Republic, which was to be separated from the USSR. The final agreement of Poland and Czechoslovakia of 19 January 1942 was vague in the extreme, not departing from generalizations. Much the same can be said of the Yugoslav–Greek agreement of 15 January 1942. Sikorski consulted the representatives of all the governments-in-exile in London and made approaches to the Council of Lithuanian Deputies in

Berne. All he succeeded in doing was to irritate the Great Powers.[6] After the victory of the Soviet Union before Moscow in December 1941 he was convinced that the USSR would emerge victorious in the war in spite of possible reverses in the campaigns of 1942, but he drew from this conclusion no concepts of altering his policy. Essentially his policy was one of aligning Poland with Britain and the USA, without consideration of the effect his claims had upon Soviet thinking.

The aim of the British government was to give a closer definition to the Anglo-Soviet partnership. For this purpose Eden visited Moscow in December 1941 after the departure of Sikorsko. Among the subjects discussed was the question of the Polish frontiers. Stalin wished Britain to recognize the frontiers of 1941, but he was willing to postpone a final decision in respect of the Polish frontier until direct talks had been held between the Polish and Soviet governments, provided that the frontier between the two states conformed more or less to the Curzon line of 1919–20. The British government was reluctant to agree to the Soviet proposition in respect of Poland without a clear expression of the United States' views, but was usually wary of giving offence to the USSR. Sikorski for his part objected to concessions to the USSR, even in respect of the Baltic states and Bessarabia. On 11 January Raczyński went as far as to give an interview to *The Sunday Times* and declared against the Baltic states remaining in the Soviet Union, even going as far as to extend the hand of friendship to Hungary. The Polish government-in-exile put pressure on the United States. Sikorski visited the United States on 24–30 March with the aim of thwarting the Anglo-Soviet treaty. In public he declared his support for the USSR, but in his conversations with Roosevelt and American officials he drew attention to the consequences for Central Europe of the advance of the Soviet forces. American policy was one of postponing all questions of frontiers until the conclusion of hostilities. The British policy was one of 'non-recognition', from which it could depart when necessary. In short, US policy was one which would leave all difficult questions to the moment when the USA could speak with the full authority of accumulated might. In these circumstances the USA leaned slightly to the side of Sikorski, but made no specific statement of policy. Molotov arrived in London on 22 May 1942 to settle the question of the Anglo-Soviet treaty and press for the opening of a Second Front by the Western Allies. Molotov entertained no great hopes of obtaining recognition of the frontiers of June 1941. In the end the British government agreed in vague terms to launch a Second Front, but the question of frontiers was passed over in the treaty of alliance signed on 26 May 1942. In Washington Molotov succeeded in obtaining the promise of a Second Front in 1942, which the British government did not believe could be begun in that year.

Apparently the policy of Sikorski had triumphed, but it was of little concern to the USSR that the frontier problem had not been solved. If the USSR were to drive the Germans back into Central Europe and Germany itself, the matter would be solved by the fact of Soviet conquest. Sikorski obtained the impression of his having played an important part in international affairs, but the Great Powers retained the final decisions in their own hands. The government-in-exile might have served its aim of returning to Poland at the end of the war better if it had explored the possibility of closer co-operation with the USSR more carefully. In almost a year of diplomacy Sikorski had not advanced the cause of Poland from the position on which it stood at the conclusion of the agreement with the Soviet Union of 30 July 1941.

The politics of the resistance in Poland

The resistance movement owing allegiance to the government-in-exile in London was guided by the 'doctrine of two enemies', Germany and the Soviet Union. This in effect meant that they thought of preparing action against the Germans, but also of opposing the USSR, lest it try to sovietize Poland. Like the leaders in exile they saw the alliance of 30 July 1941 as a temporary arrangement imposed by the fortuitous circumstances of Hitler's attack on the USSR. They saw in the exhaustion of both their enemies in the armed conflict an essential condition of the establishment of their ideal Poland with the assistance of the Western Powers, who would in consequence be the undisputed masters of Europe. They looked back to the circumstances of 1917–18, when Germany and Russia were faced with internal upheaval. In such a situation Poland would emerge as a fully sovereign state independent of its two powerful neighbours. Between 1939 and 1944 repeated efforts were made to unify resistance in Poland, but despite its large following the pro-government movement failed to bring all the resistance forces under its control. Failure led to a struggle between the rival resistance groups during the last years of the war when German defeat was clearly approaching. The fundamental cause was the existence of extremist resistance forces of both Left and Right. The communist-controlled People's Army (Armia Ludowa – AL) and the ultra-nationalistic National Armed Forces (Narodowe Siły Zbrojne – NSZ) differed so widely from the pro-government groups in their political and ideological outlooks that they could not be brought together under one organization. Their irreconcilable differences made complete national unity impossible and foreshadowed the struggle for power between the London Poles and the communists at the end of the war. In the summer of 1943 the communists began a campaign to win the allegiance of the Left, while the NSZ embarked on a similar effort to establish a dominance over the extreme Right. The pro-government forces were left in the centre of the political spectrum. When the Germans appeared in 1944 to face imminent defeat before the Soviet advance, the three groups pursued their own distinct policies. The leaders of the pro-government resistance formulated a policy for military action against the Germans and political opposition to the Soviet Union and the PPR in the hope that, with Western help, they would be able to secure power for the government-in-exile. The communist AL were fighting the Germans and with the help of the Soviet Union intended to instal their own administration in the Polish territories as they were liberated. The NSZ spread confusion and civil strife by concentrating their efforts against the PPR and the left wing generally. They were so extreme in their views that they considered the pro-government movement to be almost a pro-Soviet organization. The NSZ intended to liquidate as many of their opponents as possible in an attempt to weaken the forces which in their opinion were ready to collaborate with Moscow. The long-term policies of the NSZ were coloured by their anticipation of a conflict between the USSR and the Western Powers.

The pro-government resistance force which had evolved from the ZWZ, the Home Army (Armia Krajowa – AK), was the largest underground organization in the country. By 1944 the strength of the AK was at least 200,000, which in the existing conditions of occupied Poland was a great achievement, even though most of them had no weapons.[7] Its operational effectiveness therefore was limited by shortage of arms rather than by the number of men at its disposal. In 1944 the AK had arms for only 32,000, which meant that the mass insurrection envisaged in earlier plans was not a practical proposition. In Warsaw, shortly before the insurrection of 1944, the AK was about 50,700 strong, including 4,300 women, but it was lamentably short of weapons. On 1 August 1944 there were arms for only one-sixth of its members. The AK soldiers were divided into three groups. The first and most important group consisted of full-time members, the 'professional conspirators', who formed the hard core of the resistance and remained underground 'under false identity with forged documents and labour permits'. All the AK senior officers belonged to this group. The 'professional conspirators' received no payment other than small monthly allowances to cover their living expenses. The second category of AK personnel consisted of those who served in the partisan units, living in uniform mainly in the forests and fighting the Germans openly. Until 1944 this group was equally small. In 1943 it consisted of about 40 partisan units in the field with strengths varying from 30 to 100 men. The largest group consisted of the part-time resistance members, leading, as it were, 'double lives'. In their day-to-day existence they differed little from ordinary civilians, working in offices and factories, on the railways, on farms and elsewhere, but every one of them was in touch with his unit commander, from whom he received his orders on the tasks to be carried out. Often a whole unit was used for a major task, but the ultimate aim was always to husband resources for the national insurrection. After an action these units would return to 'normal life'. The majority of the AK belonged to this category and received no payment for their services.[8]

Politically and socially the AK was broadly representative of the nation, being recruited from all social classes and parties, with the exception of the PPR. Many of its units had originally been para-military organizations of the National Democrat, Peasant, Socialist and Labour parties and were therefore of divergent political outlooks. In May 1944 the commander of the AK, General Tadeusz Bór-Komorowski, stated that it was impossible to eliminate political differences and transform the secret army into an apolitical force. He admitted that his officers were too conservative in outlook and were out of touch with the far more progressive ideas of their men and society at large. To remedy this defect Bór-Komorowski began a campaign to spread democratic and progressive ideas among his right-wing supporters. He was apprehensive of the attitude his troops might display towards the Red Army if it should enter Poland. He was certain that they would fight enthusiastically against the Germans, but uncertain of their reaction to the Soviet forces, especially if they should try to act as champions of social progress in Poland. He felt that in this case his more left-wing units would become unreliable. Fears of this kind influenced his determination to prepare for an insurrection against the Germans in 1944. He pressed the government to announce plans for radical reform after the war, being convinced that this would be a popular move which would strengthen the loyalty of his troops. It was strange indeed that requests for radical reform should be made by a military commander rather than the civil authorities of the resistance. The civil leaders were hampered in their discussions by their differences of political outlook. The underground state was a coalition of diverse political forces held together by the need to preserve a modicum of national unity in the face of foreign occupation and the communist 'menace'. All its declarations were the result of compromise between the conservative National Democrats, the anti-Soviet socialists and the moderate Peasant and Labour parties. Political aims were expressed in terms too mild and vague for the increasingly radical masses to appreciate. Bór-Komorowski's desire for a broad policy of reform was based on sound military reasons. A consensus of opinion on the post-war reorganization of Poland would give cohesion to the insurgent movement. The division of authority between the civil and military branches of the resistance, however, was designed to strengthen the authority of the government-in-exile and prevent the emergence of unified civil and military command in Warsaw, rivalling the cabinet abroad. In practice this meant that, although the military commander was expected to act in consultation with the government delegate in Poland, the AK was never subordinated to the civil authorities. This system functioned adequately under Sikorski, who combined in his own person the offices of premier and commander-in-chief and could give orders to both branches of the resistance. After his death in July 1943 these offices were separated and in consequence the unity of command disrupted. Relations between the new prime minister, Stanisław Mikołajczyk, and the commander-in-chief, General Kazimierz Sosnkowski, were strained from the outset, owing to their differences on the question of Poland's attitude to the Soviet Union. In theory the commander-in-chief could not issue orders to the AK without first consulting the cabinet, but in practice he could, as Sosnkowski often did, try to inspire the commander at home to disregard government directives without actually ordering him to do so. These differences, moreover, not only detracted from the government's authority among the resistance leaders in Warsaw, but even encouraged them to act upon their own initiative without prior discussions with their superiors abroad. Indeed, the resistance leaders believed that the government-in-exile was often out of touch with conditions in Poland and in no position to issue directives. On the one hand the authorities in London lacked clear understanding of internal conditions, while the underground leaders at home had only a partial appreciation of the international situation. The result was frequent confusion.[9]

The two main channels of communication between London and Warsaw were wireless and couriers. Owing to German counter-measures only a limited exchange of ideas and information was possible. Attempts were made to improve liaison by the establishment of special agencies intended to serve as channels of information. The government delegate and his staff, the Delegatura Rządu, acted as the representative of the government in Poland and the link between home and abroad. Its task was to co-ordinate policies and prepare the necessary administrative machinery for the assumption of power after liberation. The Delegatura was even able in the closing stages of the war to assemble an underground parliament. A secret administration organized education courses at both the secondary and higher levels, the publication of journals and books, underground theatres, clandestine lectures, exhibitions and concerts. Even protection of works of art came within its orbit.[10] The delegate was the deputy prime minister and with two other ministers formed the underground Council of Ministers. The Delegatura acted in close co-operation with the Political Consultative Committee (Polityczny Komitet Porozumiewawczy – PKP), which was the deliberative body of the resistance.

The parties forming the PKP were the National Democrats, the Peasant Party, the PPS and the Party of Labour, representing the majority of the population. In August 1943 the four parties decided to enter into closer co-operation. They pledged themselves to support the government and assist in the preparation of the forthcoming insurrection, announcing their intention of administering Poland in the immediate post-war period. The parties also published a joint programme. They stated that the government would strengthen Poland's ties with her Western allies and secure her 'sovereign rights and territorial integrity', especially the 'absolute' integrity of the 1939 frontier with the Soviet Union. The dangers of growing Soviet influence on Allied diplomacy was to be stressed by pointing to the dangers inherent in 'Russo-Communist totalitarianism'. Territorial compensation was to be sought at Germany's expense, while a Central and East European federation of states could offer security against the domination of the area by any one single power. The parties stated that after liberation the government would ensure civil freedoms, introduce land reform, nationalize certain sections of industry and combat unemployment. The programme was essentially a compromise between the conservative National Democrats and the moderately progressive Peasant Party, Party of Labour and the PPS, for which reason it exhibited a vagueness and absence of detail.[11] Nevertheless, the PKP recognized the need for a fundamental reconstruction of the country after independence had been regained. Intransigence towards the USSR revealed their inability to realize that a *modus vivendi* was essential for Poland. The main difference between the coalition and the PPR lay precisely in the field of foreign affairs. Both sides agreed on social and economic reform, but the PPR looked to an association with the Soviet Union.

In March 1944 the PKP was transformed into a Council of National Unity (Rada Jedności Narodowej – RJN), which acted as a quasi-parliament of the resistance with the socialist, Kazimierz Pużak ('Bazyli') as chairman. The RJN declared that post-war Poland was to be a parliamentary democracy with a strong executive. In the west Poland's frontiers were to embrace East Prussia, Danzig, western Pomerania and

Silesia, but in the east they were to remain unchanged. Friendly relations with Moscow were welcomed, provided that the USSR recognized the frontiers of 1921 and did not interfere in Poland's internal affairs. The RJN enlarged upon the joint programme of the four parties in August 1944. Though Poland was to continue to have a mixed economy, a radical land reform was proposed. All private estates over 50 hectares would be confiscated and one-family farms of 8–15 hectares created. Existing holdings were to be expanded to that norm. All forests were to be nationalized. The state was to have the right to nationalize public utilities, key industries and banks where it was in the public interest. The object was to provide full employment in a welfare state. Like the earlier programme the RJN's declaration was an uneasy compromise. The National Democrats regarded some of its provisions, especially the land reform proposals, as too radical, while the Peasant Party and the PPS thought them insufficiently far-reaching. They favoured outright national-ization of key industries and the expropriation of all private and ecclesiastical estates over 50 hectares, though leaving the question of compensation open. The absence of radical solutions in the RJN pro-gramme reduced its attractiveness to growing left-wing elements among the population and gave the communists ample material for counter-propaganda.

Relations between the government forces and the communists, 1942–3

The relations between the pro-government forces and the communists were tense and unhappy from the beginning. At first the growing rivalry found expression in a propaganda battle, but at the end of 1942 the communists approached the delegate with a proposal that all resistance forces should be unified. This decision coincided with a change in the leadership of the PPR. On 28 November 1942 the leader of the PPR, Marceli Nowotko, was murdered in obscure circumstances at the instance of Bolesław Mołojec, another of the founders of the PPR and the People's Guard (Gwardia Ludowa – GL). It is suggested that Mołojec had personal motives for instigating Nowotko's assassination, wishing himself to become the leader of the party, but some authorities believe he acted on orders from Moscow. Whatever the truth of this episode, Pawel Finder, the new head of the party, empowered Władysław Gomułka, a member of the new party leadership, to open negotiations with the delegate, Professor Jan Piekałkiewicz, a member of the Peasant Party. He favoured an understanding between the government and the pro-communist forces. The outcome of the negotiations between Piekałkiewicz and Gomułka, however, depended largely upon the attitude of Grot-Rowecki, the commander of the AK until his arrest in Warsaw on 30 June 1943, who, though a soldier, exercised considerable influence over the political affairs of the resistance.

Negotiations began in January 1943. The PPR leaders believed that in view of the victory of the Western Allies in North Africa and of the Soviet forces at Stalingrad the question of an insurrection in Poland had become a pressing issue, for which reason preparations for it would demand the creation of a national front and the intensification of guerrilla warfare as a prelude to an uprising. Grot-Rowecki held similar views, but, unlike the communists, had no desire to shape his strategy in accordance with the needs of Moscow. In May 1943 he was to decide, in view of the acute state of relations between Poland and the USSR, to reduce the scale of his operations against the Wehrmacht and German lines of communication with the east and to concentrate his efforts against the German security forces and administrative organs. Differences of attitude towards the Soviet Union prevented the development of joint operations by the AK and the communists. By the beginning of 1943 the PPR had at its disposal, under the command first of Marian Spychalski and from August 1942 of Franciszek Jóźwiak, the Gwardia Ludowa consisting of about 8,000 men, and was not in a position to create a viable national front without the help of the pro-London forces. Gomułka hoped to establish an alliance of all Polish parties, with the exception of the *Sanacja* and the right-wing NSZ, which would establish a government in the country and in time replace the authorities in exile. Gomułka presented the PPR as an independent marxist–leninist party, without affiliations with the Comintern, striving for national independence and the establishment of socialism by constitutional means. The PPR declared its good will towards the Soviet Union and supported the Soviet–Polish understanding of July 1941, believing that the question of the frontier could be solved upon the basis of national self-determination. The PPR called for the democratization of post-war Poland and the introduction of far-reaching reforms. The PPR attitude to reform was very close to that of the Peasant Party and the PPS. On the other hand, Gomułka stressed that rejection by the delegate of the communist offer of collaboration would amount to giving the PPR 'a free hand' in its future activities. The PPR was in effect trying to secure for itself a place among the organizations of the pro-London underground and to present itself as the champion of both liberation and social progress.

The negotiations were conducted in unfavourable circumstances, coinciding with a deterioration in Soviet–Polish relations and the arrest of Piekałkiewicz by the Germans. His successor, Jan Jankowski, although a member of the Party of Labour, was a competent administrator rather than a politician able to grasp the advantages of co-operation with the communists. Grot-Rowecki, moreover, suspected that the PPR's offer of collaboration with the AK was a communist strategem to infiltrate its ranks and gain recognition as a leading resistance force. He maintained that the possibility of co-operation with the PPR should be considered only if it declared openly that it was not a member of the Comintern and undertook to be absolutely loyal to the government, recognizing the integrity of the 1939 Soviet–Polish frontier. Against the background of suspicion and the approaching severance of Soviet–Polish diplomatic relations the chances of an understanding between the Gomułka and Janowski were virtually non-existent. On 26 April 1943 the USSR broke off diplomatic relations with Poland. On 28 April Jankowski replied to Gomułka's offer of collaboration. He insisted upon an undertaking from the PPR to fight against the Soviet Union if demands should be made for frontier changes. Predictably the PPR found this stipulation unacceptable. In 1943 no communist could have agreed to such a condition. The negotiations were therefore broken off, but unofficial contact between the two sides continued to be maintained.[12] In the summer of 1943, however, the PPR began to consider the formation of a 'democratic national front' as a rival to the government organizations. This marked the beginning of a struggle for power between the pro-London and communist forces.[13] The government leaders probably made a mistake in refusing to reach an understanding with the communists, because an accommodation might have assisted them to re-establish the military co-operation with the USSR which was to be so lacking in 1944. Jankowski believed, however, that his declining to make common cause with the PPR would isolate it from the public. He was soon to realize that this was not the case. The London government-in-exile, for its part, hoped that by increasing action against the Germans and so maintaining the loyalty of the masses more and more frustrated by the spectacle of Nazi oppression, it would prevent the communists from gaining ground.

Sikorski and the resistance

Sikorski's instructions were that the resistance should take decisive action only in the final stages of the war, when it would assume the role of representative of a sovereign state in the face of the advancing Russians when they entered Poland. Sikorski forbade resistance to the Soviet forces in the hope of deriving political advantage from Soviet–Polish co-operation. In the event of a Soviet failure to respond, the AK was to ask for Anglo-American mediation. The essential aim of the ultimate insurrection was the 'forestalling of the Russians' in the liberation of Poland by the assumption of political power by the resistance. Sikorski was opposed to using the insurrection as an opportunity for initiating a social revolution, lest this course give the Soviet Union an excuse to interfere in Poland's internal affairs. He ordered the authorities in Warsaw, if the Soviet forces should be 'clearly hostile' to the London government, to reveal the existence in the eastern Polish territories of the civil administration only and to withdraw military units into the interior of the country to save them from destruction. He warned Warsaw not to expect help from the West during the fighting, because it would be very difficult to co-ordinate supporting operations. These instructions were not well received by Grot-Rowecki, who was urging his commander-in-chief to revise his policy towards Moscow and adopt what he euphemistically described as a 'defensive' attitude, in other words a hostile attitude, towards the Soviet Union, but Sikorski stood his ground and refused to change his instructions. The AK was to treat the Soviet forces as allies.[14]

In the meantime the Germans were continuing their policy of seeking to break the spirit of the resistance by intensifying their terror. The methods and scale of German operations might vary, but the principle of ruthless persecution never changed. The Poles for their part responded with counter-terror directed mainly at the Gestapo and their agents. The Germans normally maintained some 400,000–600,000 troops and policemen in Poland. Though the Polish counter-terror never matched the total of 5,384,000 Polish citizens killed by the Germans, the resistance nevertheless killed about 150,000 Germans. About 10,000 operations were carried out, of which 2,300 were undertaken against railway lines and transport installations. Industrial sabotage, assassinations of notorious German officials and collaborators and attacks on military transport were the order of the day. Above all, the resistance operated an excellent intelligence service, providing the Allies with valuable information on German movements.[15] Until the Warsaw uprising of 1 August 1944, the largest and longest operation was the heroic, but hopeless, insurrection in the Warsaw ghetto. On 16 February Himmler ordered its total destruction. On 18 April Nazi troops under the command of SS-Brigadeführer, Jürgen Stroop, moved in to evict the remaining inhabitants. Armed units of the Jewish underground organizations met them with fierce resistance, which developed into a protracted struggle street by street and building by building of the ghetto. Fighting continued until 16 May when the last pockets of resistance were crushed. Stroop was then able to report to Himmler that 'the Jewish quarter no longer exists'. About

57,000 people were killed or captured by the Germans and the ghetto left as a pile of rubble.[16] The extermination of the Polish Jews had a deep effect upon other Poles. It was a clear indication of the lengths to which the Nazis would go in pursuit of their pseudo-scientific theories of German racial superiority and consequently stiffened Polish determination to fight.

The breakdown of Soviet–Polish relations

By the beginning of 1943 it was evident that Soviet–Polish relations were at breaking-point. The diplomacy of Sikorski was running into difficulties in the second half of 1942. Beneš on 12 November asked for the suspension of talks on Central European federation until the agreement of 'certain' Great Powers had been obtained. This in effect meant the agreement of the USSR. The views of Beneš were reinforced by the great Soviet offensive which on 23 November 1942 surrounded the German Sixth Army at Stalingrad. Henceforth Soviet diplomacy would speak from a position of strength. There could no longer be any supposition that the USSR would collapse. The problem now was to convince the USSR of the Western Allies' desire for sincere co-operation, of which the promotion of a Central European federation, which in Soviet eyes appeared to be much the same as a *cordon sanitaire*, would not be an example. The object now was to bring Stalin to the conference table in order to have firm agreements to which the Western Allies could hold him in the future, but in December 1942 Stalin expressed reluctance to come to such a meeting on the grounds that he could not leave the Soviet Union while important military operations were in progress. There was no doubt some truth in Stalin's excuse,[17] but it was equally evident that with the successful conclusion of the winter offensive USSR would speak with greater authority, especially in view of the inability of the Western Allies to launch a Second Front in Northern Europe during 1943. It was against this unfavourable background that Sikorski paid a third visit to the United States from 1 December 1942 to 10 January 1943. Sikorski was opposed to pushing the Polish frontier as far forward in the west as the line of the Oder and the Lusatian Neisse because this would include in the new Poland a large number of Germans, fanatically opposed to polonization and ready always to act as a fifth column in the future. A similar moderation did not appear in his memorandum of 23 December 1942, which took its stand on the frontiers of the Treaty of Riga of 1921, including[18] as it had done up to 1939 discontented Byelorussians and Ukrainians. To this proposal Sikorski added the concept of the Central European federation aligned with a Balkan federation. In the military sense this policy called for an invasion of south eastern Europe as a preliminary to its execution, whereas the American generals favoured an invasion of Northern Europe. In the political field Roosevelt favoured a better understanding between the USA and the USSR and adopted an attitude of reserve towards Sikorski's concept of a solution designed to contain the advance of communism. He was more favourable, however, to the extension of Poland's frontiers to the west. Sikorski offered to go to Moscow to discuss Soviet–Polish problems, provided that he obtained the support of Roosevelt in the form of a letter upholding the Polish position, to which Roosevelt agreed, on condition that the text of the letter was consonant with the principles of the Atlantic Charter. Because the Charter called for respect for sovereignty of states and the restoration of sovereignty to peoples who had been deprived of it, the American government could not bind itself to specific frontiers. Sikorski convinced himself that ultimately he could rely upon the support of the Western Powers, but he had obtained nothing from his discussions in Washington.

On his return to London Sikorski was faced with a difficult situation. The Soviet government had taken the view that the frontier of 22 June 1941 should remain in existence, but minor modifications might be made in areas to the east of it where Poles constituted a majority. Sikorski for his part had made public statements in the USA claiming for Poland the frontiers of 1939. As a warning to Sikorski the Soviet government on 16 January 1943 withdrew the modifications of laws governing the citizenship of Poles resident in the annexed territories contained in the decree of 29 November 1939. On 16 January the Polish government-in-exile requested the restoration of exceptions in favour of the Poles. By now leaks to the press and attacks upon Sikorski by members of factions on the extreme Right in the USA and Britain brought the difficult problem of Soviet–Polish relations out into the public. The Ukrainian writer, Alexander Kornyeychuk, published in the periodical *Radyanska Ukraina* (Soviet Ukraine) an article entitled 'The Unification of the Ukrainian People in their own State', which was repeated in *Pravda*, claiming the right of self-determination for Ukrainians. The Polish government considered itself called upon to make a reply. On 25 February it published a resolution accepted by the National Council restating the Polish claim to the Western Ukraine and Western Byelorussia. To this Soviet news agency, TASS, on 1 March replied by stating that the Ukrainians and the Byelorussians had rights which could not be denied by the Polish government. It stated that Poland was splitting the united front of the Slavs against the German invaders and questioned whether the Polish government really enjoyed the support of public opinion in Poland. In spite of intense pressure by the

Polish government on the USA and Britain, no statement of support was forthcoming from those quarters. The USA and Britain were more concerned to conciliate the USSR than support what they thought was a not very good Polish case. When Churchill saw Sikorski on 15 April 1943, he refused to intervene until the completion of the campaign in North Africa, but he suggested that a solution could be found in making cession of territory to the USSR in the east in return for compensation in the west at the expense of Germany. This was the first time that Churchill had indicated his conversion in principle to drastic frontier modifications, though he did not suggest the extent of the changes.

The strain upon Soviet–Polish relations was evident to all and especially the Germans. On 12 April 1943 the German government revealed the discovery in the Katyn Forest near Smolensk in Soviet territory of a mass grave containing the bodies of thousands of Polish officers captured by the Soviet forces in 1939. The Soviet government replied on 15 April that the German accusation laying responsibility at the Soviet door was another example of Nazi propaganda designed to sow discord in the Allied ranks. Such a statement could find wide acceptance because the Germans themselves had committed so many atrocities that responsibility could be attributed to them. The fact remains, however, that at Nuremberg in the prosecution of war criminals after the war, no German was ever brought to trial in connection with Katyn.[19] In 1943 the German revelation created grave difficulties for the government-in-exile. A formal protest by the Polish government would seem to be acceptance of the German accusation. It was decided therefore to request the International Red Cross in Geneva to make an investigation of the affair, but the German government, informed of the Polish intention, simultaneously made an identical request on its own behalf. The Soviet Union retorted by accusing the Polish government of consorting with the enemy. In his letter to Churchill of 21 April, Stalin declared that the Polish government was hostile to the USSR, for which reason he had come to the conclusion that the Soviet Union must break off relations with it. Churchill on 24 April appealed to Stalin to delay an announcement until all efforts to seek a reconciliation had been exhausted.[20] Eden put pressure on Sikorski to induce him to withdraw the appeal to the Red Cross, but all that Sikorski could do was to agree not to press further for an inquiry. On 25 April the USSR broke off diplomatic relations with the Polish government. The Soviet Union declared that the Polish government had taken advantage of German propaganda in pursuit of a policy of obtaining territorial concessions at the expense of Lithuania, Byelorussia and the Ukraine.

The crisis in Soviet–Polish relations was a turning point. The relations of Poland with Czechoslovakia had been cool in 1942, but Beneš had not given up hope of an understanding. In January 1943 he proposed a Soviet–Czech alliance with provision for the accession of Poland to it, but Sikorski had not responded favourably. Sikorski's concept had been that Poland and Czechoslovakia should first come to an agreement and then jointly approach the USSR. The breaking-off of diplomatic relations between Poland and the Soviet Union placed Polish–Czech relations in a new perspective. On 20 February 1943 Sikorski had in a note to the Czechoslovak government laid claim to the frontiers of 1 September 1939, which included Trans-Olza, taken by Poland in 1938. On 15 May the Czechoslovak government replied, complaining of Polish claims to Czechoslovak territory. The British government did not recognize the Munich agreement, which placed Czechoslovakia in a stronger position than Poland. In effect, Poland had lost the support of Czechoslovakia and thus the cornerstone of the proposed Central European federation. The Polish government was thus isolated and had no policy other than its own pretensions. The Czech government was to seek a basis for security in an alliance with the USSR. The USSR by breaking off diplomatic relations with the Polish government-in-exile had obtained a free hand in dealing with the problems of the frontiers which had bedevilled relations between the two states. Britain and the USA continued to recognize the Polish government-in-exile and the USSR for its part trod warily in its policy towards Poland, but there could be no real doubt that the independent and ambitious policy pursued by Sikorski was founded upon unreality. Before 1939 Beck's policy had been unrealistic. Though Sikorski had little political sympathy for the views of Beck, it is difficult to argue that his view of the place of Poland in the post-war world was any more practical.

The years of Tempest, May 1943–
December 1944

Changes in London and Warsaw

In 1943 the war entered a new phase. The Soviet forces held the last serious German offensive in the battle at Kursk on 12–15 July and themselves went over to the offensive, liberating large areas of the Soviet Union. North Africa was cleared of the Axis forces and for practical purposes fascist Italy was knocked out of the war by the Allied landings at Salerno in September 1943. In the Far East the American forces were to go over to the offensive and drive back the Japanese. It was no longer a question of whether the war would be won, but when it would be won. As the end approached, the situation of the Polish government-in-exile was difficult. Neither Britain nor the USA cared to look after its affairs in the USSR. In the end it was Australia who undertook to represent Polish interests. The London government continued to take its stand upon the frontiers of 1 September 1939, but Stalin expressed his view that a strong and independent Poland might be created at the end of the war. This gave Sikorski to hope that diplomatic relations might be resumed shortly. He continued to believe that the Western Allies would sooner or later bring the weight of their influence to bear upon the side of Poland. His tour of the Near and Middle East in June 1943 had the purpose of reassuring diplomatic representatives and military commanders and requesting them to preserve a stoic calm for the meantime. On 5 July 1943, however, Władysław Sikorski died when the aircraft carrying him crashed in the moment of take-off at Gibraltar. The normal testimonies of respect for Sikorski followed, but he left behind him a difficult situation, which was not made any easier by the appointment of his successor. On 14 July a new government was formed under Stanisław Mikołajczyk, the leader of the Peasant Party. On the other hand Kazimierz Sosnkowski was appointed commander-in-chief. In this way the two functions exercised by Sikorski were separated, Mikołajczyk continued to hold to the policy of Sikorski in foreign affairs, hoping to reach an understanding with Stalin which would allow the government-in-exile to assume power in Poland at the end of hostilities. Mikołajczyk as the leader of a substantial political party thought that with the support of the peasant masses at home and a policy of friendship with both the Western Powers and the USSR he could establish a stable political system in Poland. Sosnkowski on the other hand, whose nomination Mikołajczyk had opposed on the grounds of his anti-Soviet outlook, was unlike him in both personality and political views.[1] For many years he had been closely connected with Piłsudski, which made him unpopular in left-wing circles. In 1941 he had resigned from Sikorski's cabinet, in which he had served as minister responsible for the ZWZ, in protest against the agreement of 30 July 1941 with the USSR on the grounds that it failed to bind the Soviet Union to recognition of the 1939 frontiers. Sosnkowski believed that a more resolute attitude on the part of Poland during the negotiations would have produced better results. He was to advocate a similar course during Mikołajczyk's attempt to reach an understanding with Stalin. As commander-in-chief he believed that he was entitled to play an important role in politics. His relations with Mikołajczyk therefore were strained and unhappy.

On 30 June 1943 the commander of the AK, Grot-Rowecki, was arrested in Warsaw by the Gestapo, to be executed on Himmler's orders in 1944. In his place Sosnkowski appointed General Tadeusz Bór-Komorowski, a cavalry officer of noble origin with political sympathies close to those of the National Democrats. He was not an officer with high professional qualifications or a career to suggest that he was qualified for high command. With regard to internal questions he in fact had a keen appreciation of political realities in the light of the radicalization of Polish society under the impact of German oppression, but his chief-of-staff, General Tadeusz Pełczyński, believed that it might be necessary to 'prop up' Bór-Komorowski by 'helping' to take the right decisions.[2] As commander of the AK he held a responsible position and upon him rather than the authorities in London might rest the power of decision at a crucial moment in the war.

Mikołajczyk believed that he must seek to establish cordial relations with the USSR and abandon the 'demagogy of intransigence', considering that the calculations in some Polish circles based on a possible conflict between the Western Powers and the Soviet Union were 'illusory and dangerous'. He was aware that the Western Powers were not prepared to fight for the Polish eastern frontiers and that in the event of a crisis they would not support Poland. He hoped nevertheless that, in the event of a Russo-Polish understanding, Britain and the USA would be ready to guarantee the settlement. There was an element of exaggeration in his thinking, which made light of the difficulties of conciliating the USSR and inducing the

Western Powers to take Poland's side. Sosnkowski, on the other hand, was convinced that the government must defend the territorial integrity of Poland 'in spite of all and against all'. He was opposed to making concessions, because in his opinion they would merely lead to the gradual 'sovietization of Poland'. Like many Poles in exile he was convinced that the Western Powers sooner or later 'might be compelled to face a showdown with Russian imperialism', for which reason there was no need to adopt a conciliatory attitude towards the USSR. He maintained that the London Poles could influence neither Soviet policy nor the outcome of military operations and were therefore left with no alternative except to defend their interests and 'demand the same from the Western Powers'. He wished to turn the Polish Question into a 'problem for the conscience of the world', a test case for the future of European nations. More mundane views prevailed elsewhere. Churchill expected the Poles to co-operate in his work of improving relations with the Soviet Union for their own and the common benefit. His plan was simple. By encouraging the Poles to make territorial concessions he intended to bring about a rapprochement between the two parties and persuade Stalin to allow the exiled government to return to liberated Warsaw. Mikołaczyk showed no immediate desire to open negotiations with Stalin because 'Russian victories' were creating a bad climate for talks with the USSR. He hoped that better conditions would develop when the voice of the Western Allies might 'carry more weight' as the successes of their forces brought them closer to Central Europe. Poland was only one of the many problems which arose in 1943 in a more acute form. As far as Poland was concerned, Stalin expressed the view that the USA, Britain and the USSR ought to take joint action to secure a change in the composition of the Polish government as a preliminary to the resumption of diplomatic relations. Because any Polish government in diplomatic relations with the USSR would have to accept an eastern frontier running approximately along the Curzon line, the Western Powers began to consider more seriously the problem of compensation for Poland in the west, which would involve the separation of Poles from Germans by population transfers. President Beneš in May 1943 was to seek, in Washington, support for the transfer of Germans in Czechoslovakia to Germany proper. It followed that a similar solution might be applied to Poland with the aim of constituting a state with no internal nationality problems. By the summer of 1943 it became obvious that the Great Powers would settle the affairs of the smaller states with or without their leave in the interests of maintaining their own unity.

Roosevelt and Churchill met in Quebec from 14 to 24 August 1943, when among many matters of common interest discussed was the problem of relations with the USSR. Stalin in fact was to complain that the Western Powers consulted among themselves and merely informed the USSR of their decisions. From the point of view of the Western Powers it was necessary to bring Stalin to the conference table in order to get his agreement to solutions of practical problems. To the suggestion of a meeting Stalin on this occasion agreed, but insisted upon a place convenient to himself. The choice eventually fell upon Tehran, though this was not especially convenient to Roosevelt. The fact that he inconvenienced himself shows that the need for a conference and direct contact with Stalin overrode other considerations. As far as Poland was concerned, the problem of the frontiers would be considered at the highest level by the Big Three. Polish affairs had been taken up by the American ambassador to the USSR, William Standley, and the British Ambassador, Sir Alexander Clark Kerr, in an interview with Stalin and Molotov on 11 August, but Stalin delayed his reply until 27 September. In it the Soviet Union dismissed minor matters relating to Poles in the USSR and their citizenship and the question of evacuation from the Soviet Union to the Middle East. The most important question for the Soviet Union remained the claims of the Polish government to parts of the Ukraine, Byelorussia and Lithuania. Until the Polish government withdrew these claims there could be no question of a resumption of diplomatic relations. Stalin was now clearly speaking with the voice of one confident of victory.

The Polish communists and the USSR

The Red Army's victories and the growth of the German terror brought about a change in the attitude of many Poles towards the USSR. The hope grew that the war would soon end and that Poland would be liberated, in which case the USSR might play an important part in the country's development. Some were alarmed by the prospect, but others were ready to compromise with the USSR and accept the inevitable. There was a general demand for the intensification of the struggle against the Germans. The communists, who were constantly proposing a more active policy against the occupying forces, profited politically from this feeling and began to attract more support from the mass of the population. By 1944 they were thought capable of launching an insurrection on their own account. The leaders of the pro-London underground, who assumed that they would control the timing of the insurrection, were worried lest the communists take control and lead the impoverished population into a conflict with the Germans. They believed that the PPR was bent on promoting a social revolution leading to the creation of a pro-Soviet government. The policy of the underground government was to maintain 'law and order' in the liberated areas, by force if necessary. The programme of social reform which they proposed was an attempt to anticipate the actions of the PPR. In fact, their preoccupation with the possibility of internal 'anarchy' suggests that the insurrection they planned was to frustrate communist attempts to win power as much as to combat German occupation. Relations between the government parties and the communists deteriorated still further when in September 1943 Bór-Komorowski issued orders to the AK to 'combat brigandry'. The PPR regarded this order as a threat to itself rather than an instruction to free the country from bandits, who were at that time a serious problem. The cause of this misgiving was the ambiguous wording of Bór-Komorowski's order.[3] The communists secured a copy of the order and published it in their press, informing the Great Powers also of its contents. The affair caused disquiet in Poland and forced Bór-Komorowski to state that his instructions referred to brigandry as such. He claimed that only the near-fascist NSZ was 'liquidating' communists, but he admitted that his order had provided the PPR with an opportunity to discredit the AK. In April 1944 he was to give orders that 'a negative but unaggressive' attitude was to be adopted towards the communists. In July 1944 he instructed his units to avoid conflict with them, while the communists for their part stated they would refrain from fratricidal strife.

The PPR during 1942–3 had been considering the formation of a people's government, but, until the breaking-off of diplomatic relations between the London government and the USSR, made no public pronouncement. With the death of Sikorski and the appointment of Sosnkowski as commander-in-chief, it appeared that the *Sanacja* had got the upper hand in London. Already before Sikorski's death they had condemned his government's policy in the May Day address. In October 1943 the PPR began to establish in Warsaw, in co-operation with other parties where possible, the nucleus of a National Council of the Homeland (Krajowa Rada Narodowa – KRN), which was to organize a 'democratic national front' in rivalry with the government authorities. The task of establishing the KRN fell to Władysław Gomułka, who became secretary of the Central Committee of the PPR after the arrest of Pawel Finder on 14 November 1943. The PPR declared that the task of building democracy in Poland could not be entrusted to the government-in-exile, but should be assigned to a provisional government set up by the 'national democratic front'. The provisional government would introduce social reforms and solve the agrarian problem on the basis of expropriating private estates over 50 hectares without payment of compensation to the owners. The land would be distributed among the peasants and agricultural workers, who would be allowed to take possession during the interim period. This was a determined bid for peasant support and therefore a claim to lead the nation. The PPR declared that the supporters of the *Sanacja* were entrenched in senior posts abroad and were pursuing policies hostile to the Soviet Union. The PPR, according to Gomułka, intended to cultivate good relations with Poland's neighbours and at home to secure the co-operation of the Peasant Party and the PPS for a programme of social justice. Nevertheless, Gomułka failed to win over the parties of the Left and form a 'democratic front'.

While these developments were taking place at home, Poles in the Soviet Union were seeking to establish their own organization. On 4 January 1943 Wanda Wasilewska, Alfred Lampe and Stefan Jędrychowski approached the Soviet government for permission to found a Union of Polish Patriots (Związek Patriotów Polskich – ZPP). As a result of the agreement of the Soviet authorities, a weekly periodical, *Wolna Polska* (Free Poland), began to appear from 1 March. Ostensibly the ZPP appeared to constitute the nucleus of a future government of Poland. A foundation conference took place in Moscow on 9–10 June, which drew up a declaration of intent. It pledged itself to work for a Poland based upon the sovereignty of the people and reform of the social system. In the field of foreign affairs its object was to insure Poland against the possibility of renewed German aggression. The frontiers established by the Treaty of Riga of 1921 were declared to be inconsistent with the rights of the Ukrainians and Byelorussians. The basis of Polish security was to be an alliance of the Soviet Union, Poland and Czechoslovakia. The reforms it proposed were those common to the Polish parties at home, but the programme was closest in detail to that of the PPR. The ZPP's activities were not co-ordinated with those of the PPR owing to a breakdown of radio contact with Warsaw between November 1943 and January 1944. Some ZPP members associated with the Polish military formations being raised under General Zygmunt Berling were prepared to exclude the PPR from their plans for assuming power after the Soviet entry into Poland. They favoured the creation of a non-party government in Warsaw, backed by the army. These plans conflicted with the official policy of the ZPP, because their realization would have led to the establishment of a left-wing military dictatorship rather than a parliamentary democracy or 'the dictatorship of the proletariat'. The ZPP was clearly not united and in January 1944 a Central Bureau of Polish Communists (Centralne Biuro Komunistów Polskich – CBKP) was established in the USSR to control all the activities of the ZPP, both civil and military, and serve as a link with the Soviet authorities. On 28 April 1943 the ZPP had issued a call for the formation of Polish military units and on 8 May the USSR began to raise the Kościuszko Division, named after Tadeusz Kościuszko, the hero of the uprising of 1794. By July 1943 some 15,700 men had been enlisted, officered by Soviet soldiers usually of Polish descent. The rank and file were moved by a concept of Polish patriotism, but they were not always clear about the political programme which they were supposed to represent. Their confusion had to be dispelled by a programme of indoctrination by education officers, some of whom were to achieve political prominence after 1944–5.[4] The ZPP thus began to create an army alternative to the regular forces of the government-in-exile, the bulk of which was to be committed to the Italian front in cooperation with the Western Allies. The Polish army raised in Russia would serve as a nucleus for a much larger army when the Soviet forces entered Poland and recruits from the liberated areas were embodied in it. The ZPP had every appearance of serving as the basis of a new Polish government backed by forces of its own, but this was not to be.

On 31 December 1943 the PPR set up in Warsaw the National Council of the Homeland (KRN). When the ZPP learned of the creation of the KRN in January 1944, it abandoned its own plans for establishing a National Committee in Moscow and eventually on 28 May 1944 recognized the KRN as the only legal representative of the Polish nation. In spite of the refusal of the Peasant Party and the PPS to join with the PPR, Gomułka had established the KRN in the hope that it would attract to itself many supporters of the left-wing parties, but the abstention of the leaders of the Left meant that it was to be controlled almost entirely by communists. Its relatively narrow political base did not prevent it from declaring itself to be the 'actual representation' of the nation for the duration of the war, aiming at uniting all Poles in a common struggle against the Germans and making co-operation with the Soviet Union the cornerstone of Polish foreign policy. The formation of the KRN was a warning to the government-in-exile that, unless it changed its policy towards the Soviet Union, Stalin might refuse to negotiate with it, having at his disposal a native Polish authority which might take over the administration of the country. Stalin in fact treated the KRN with some reserve in the first instance in view of the complicated diplomatic situation. On 16 March 1944 a delegation of the KRN left Warsaw for Moscow, consisting of Edward Osóbka-Morawski – a member of the splinter group of Polish socialists which had seceded from the PPS – Marian Spychalski and Jan Stefan Haneman. It was not until 16 May that it arrived in Moscow after a long and difficult journey through the marshes of Polesie and the Pripet. Only then did Stalin make first-hand contact with them. The Central Bureau of Polish Communists itself had been wary of the KRN, believing that its political basis was too narrow and suggesting an effort to create a wider national front by the inclusion of the Peasant Party and the PPS. In its view the PPR should liberalize the social and economic proposals in its programme. Gomułka for his part, however, declared that the principal bone of contention was not the reforms the PPR proposed, but the continued hostility of the London government to the USSR and the question of revising the eastern frontiers. It was not until the weeks before the opening of the Soviet summer offensive of 1944 that the KRN established a common policy with the ZPP and the Soviet government.

The government-in-exile and the resistance

The formation of the KRN met with a storm of protest in pro-government circles. It was described as an 'act of treason' against Poland, perpetrated by a 'foreign communist agency' parading in national colours. In the last quarter of 1943 the pro-government forces had to consider their strategy for 1944. On 27 October 1943 Mikołajczyk and Sosnkowski issued the resistance with new directives to guide its activity during the approaching German defeat. In their approach to the Soviet Union they represented a distinct departure from earlier directives sent by Sikorski. The government stated that it might at some future date order the resistance to stage an anti-German 'rising', or alternatively to promote an 'intensified sabotage subversion' operation according to the strategic and political situation.[5] It was intended to launch an insurrection either if it were possible to co-ordinate it with Allied strategy, or in the event of a German collapse in the east. In the latter case the rising was to be undertaken even if it proved impossible to secure Anglo-American support for it. The object of the rising was to free Poland from the Germans and assume political power on behalf of the government, of which an important condition would be Anglo-American help. The government, however, was in a quandary because it was unable to inform the resistance what form, if any, such support would take. In fact, from 1941 to 1945 the AK received only some 600 tons of supplies from Anglo-American sources at a cost of 70 aircraft lost.[6] On the one hand Britain wished to help the Poles, but not at the price of antagonizing the Soviet Union, which was opposed to the AK. On the other hand Poland was almost beyond the operational range of the British and American air forces. The government directives stated that, if it should prove impossible to co-ordinate the insurrection with Anglo-American strategy, or if the Germans managed to avoid complete collapse, it would order the resistance to stage the 'intensified sabotage–diversion operation' with the object of making a political demonstration.

The policy to be adopted towards the advancing Soviet forces was complicated. The instructions laid down the principle that, if Soviet–Polish relations were still not restored at the time of the Soviet entry into Poland, the AK should act only behind the German lines and remain underground in the areas under Soviet control until further orders from the government. The Delegatura was likewise to remain underground. In the meantime the government would protest to the Western Allies against violations of Polish sovereignty and announce that the resistance would not co-operate with the Soviet forces. In the event of the arrest of members of the underground and reprisals against Polish citizens, it would issue a warning that the AK would resort to defensive measures. The adoption of this policy would have led precisely to that direct Soviet–Polish confrontation which Sikorski had sought to avoid. The decision to conceal the AK from the Soviet forces was in itself a dangerous proposition, because in all probability it would have led to an open clash with tragic consequences. The instructions contained a contradiction of which its authors appeared unaware. The 'intensified sabotage–diversion operation' was intended to be a political demonstration, but, if the Soviet Union entered Poland, it would have to be carried out as a clandestine action, with units which had been involved in fighting the Germans going underground again. The government was demanding that the AK first perform an active role and then disappear, a course which invited the hostility of both the German and the Soviet forces.

It is not surprising that the leaders of the resistance expected specific and realistic orders and received these instructions with dissatisfaction. The passive role prescribed for them met with opposition and they decided to disregard the government's orders. Bór-Komorowski ordered his men engaged in action with the Germans to reveal themselves to the Soviet forces and 'manifest the existence of Poland'. He believed that otherwise all the AK operations against the Germans would be credited to the communists. In any case, for practical reasons the concealment of a mass organization under conditions of Soviet occupation would be impossible. He intended, however, to restrict to a minimum the number of units which did reveal themselves. The remainder of his forces he hoped to safeguard by demobilization. In the event of permanent Soviet occupation he was preparing the nucleus of a new secret organization to be placed at Sosnkowski's disposal, separate from and unconnected with the AK, the network of which, however, was known to the PPR. Essential to the plan of the resistance was war against the Germans, but only limited co-operation with the Soviet Union. The AK would act as hosts and, if necessary, renew active resistance. Internally the AK intended to undertake large-scale operations against the Germans in order to prevent the communists from assuming the leadership of the resistance. They believed that the communists would attempt a rising at the moment the Red Army entered central Poland and would be joined by many AK members if they were restrained from taking action by their own organization. The political intent of Bór-Komorowski's decision was clear: 'By giving the Soviet minimal military help we are creating political difficulties for them.' Operations were to be undertaken militarily against the Germans and politically against the USSR and the communists.

The AK was to stage either a 'general and simultaneous insurrection' or an 'intensified diversionary operation' which received the code name of 'Tempest' (Burza). The state of the German forces was to determine which of these alternatives was to be adopted. The insurrection was to be undertaken in the moment of German collapse, whereas Tempest was to be launched during a German general retreat from Poland, consisting mainly of attacks on German covering troops and lines of communications. Tempest was to begin in the east and move westwards as military operations moved into Poland. The decision to include in the Tempest plan the eastern regions was illogical, because the AK units in those areas were too weak to undertake effective action without external help. The essence of the Tempest plan was a number of consecutive uprisings initiated in each area as the German retreat began, rather than a synchronized operation beginning in all areas simultaneously. No operations were to be taken against Soviet forces, but on no account were AK men to be embodied in the Soviet forces or the Polish army raised in the USSR. The AK was to conduct its operations independently of the Soviet forces in view of the suspension of diplomatic relations. The success of Tempest depended above all on timing. Premature engagement with the Germans unassisted by the Soviet forces could turn attack into disaster. The AK had to wait for the last hours of German withdrawal. Tempest was a simple plan fraught with hazards and dangers in its execution. Its chances of success would have been greater if it could have been co-ordinated with Soviet military operations, but in the nature of the situation this was not possible. Initially large towns were excluded from the Tempest in order to spare their populations suffering and loss of property, but in July 1944 Bór-Komorowski reversed his decision, ordering his men to occupy large towns before the arrival of the Soviet

Map 4   The Oder–Neisse Line and East Prussia

troops, because he had finally realized that the capture of towns was essential to the policy of acting as hosts to the Soviet authorities.

In February 1944 Bór-Komorowski's decision to reveal the AK to the Soviet forces was approved by the government. From this moment the die was cast. The London government-in-exile believed that the AK operations would result either in securing political power for itself in Poland, or the intervention of the Western Allies on its behalf, and would defend the cause of Poland against the USSR. This view contained a strong element of wishful thinking. It was to fly in the face of the evidence of Western policy which they had already obtained.

The Big Three and Poland

Polish problems were discussed during the Tehran conference of 28 November–1 December 1943, but it had been preceded by a conference of the foreign ministers, Eden, Cordell Hull and Molotov, in Moscow in October 1943. Eden did what he could to solve the diplomatic difficulties of Poland with the USSR. Molotov agreed to a resumption of relations, provided that Poland ceased to follow an anti-Soviet policy, which was the policy expressed in the Soviet note of 27 September. On the question of territorial compensation it was agreed in principle to assign East Prussia to Poland, which gave Eden at least some bargaining power in his dealings with the Polish government, but the question of a Central European federation turned out less well for Eden. In June 1943 he had stopped Beneš from going to Moscow to sign a treaty of alliance between Czechoslovakia and the USSR, which would in effect have placed the future of Central Europe in the hands of the USSR and prevented any form of federation independent of Soviet influence. On 24 October the matter was raised at the meeting of foreign ministers. Cordell Hull was opposed to any form of regional associations anticipating post-war arrangements, while Molotov opposed an association reminiscent of the *cordon sanitaire* policy. Eden was compelled to withdraw his objection to the signature of a Soviet–Czech treaty, though the way was left open to the accession of Poland to it. The Polish policy of a Central European federation linked with a Balkan union was in ruins. The British government for its part became reluctant to renew the Anglo-Polish treaty of 1939, due to expire on 25 August 1944, which had lost its significance in view of the Anglo-Soviet alliance of 26 May 1942. For practical purposes the hegemony in Central Europe in the future was to belong to the Soviet Union. This was a momentous decision for Poland taken in advance of the meeting at Tehran. The seal was placed upon it by the signature of the Soviet–Czechoslovak treaty on 12 December 1943.

Before the Tehran conference Mikołaczyk sought in an interview with Eden on 12 November once more to press the Polish case, but it was now Eden who put pressure upon Mikołajczyk. Eden complained that he had gone to Moscow with no clear indication of the Polish views on the issue of compensation in East Prussia, Upper Silesia and Pomerania. He revealed that the concept of a Polish–Czechoslovak federation was no longer a possibility and advised Mikołajczyk to consider acceding to the Soviet–Czechoslovak treaty.[7] Cordell Hull advised the Polish ambassador in Washington, Ciechanowski, that an essential condition of progress was a change in the policy of the Polish government in London.[8] Mikołajczyk appealed to Roosevelt and Churchill in a memorandum of 16 November 1943, but neither was prepared to discuss matters further with him before the Tehran meeting.

The Polish problem was discussed at Tehran on 28 November and 1 December 1943, but within the context of containing German expansionism, for which an essential condition was a strong Poland, guaranteed by the USSR. Roosevelt took little part in the details of the discussions, leaving to Churchill the task of settling the principles upon which the frontiers of Poland were to be drawn. In the east the Curzon Line was to be accepted as the frontier between Poland and the USSR, while in the west the Polish frontier was to be extended to the line of the Oder, including Stettin, and the Lusatian Neisse. East Prussia was to be assigned to Poland, with the exception of Königsberg which was to be incorporated in the USSR. These provisions did not form part of the official protocol of the conference. It was left to Britain to obtain Polish acceptance of the Great Powers' proposals, Roosevelt being unwilling openly to commit the United States in view of the forthcoming presidential election in November 1944 when the 6–7 million 'Polish' vote would be an important factor. Both Churchill and Stalin desired a strong Poland, but their motives were different.: Churchill saw a Poland re-established under the London government, with which the USSR would restore diplomatic relations, but Stalin entertained doubts about Polish acceptance of the Tehran conditions. If the London government-in-exile would not accept the Curzon Line, it would be open to the USSR to seek an alternative solution by promoting a government in Poland which would. For the moment Stalin could do nothing until Churchill had sought agreement from the Polish government-in-exile. Accordingly Stalin was prepared to stay within the decisions reached by the concert of the Great Powers.

During the weeks which followed, Churchill was delayed in Marrakesh by illness and Eden was deputed to seek an understanding with the government-in-exile in London. Events were to overtake his efforts at reaching agreement. On 3 January 1944 units of the Red Army crossed the 1939 frontier of Poland. The response of the Polish government-in-exile was to propose the resumption of diplomatic relations with the USSR, but on the basis of the frontiers defined by the Treaty of Riga in 1921. The Soviet government replied predictably through the news agency TASS on 11 January 1944 that it was ready to establish a frontier on ethnographical lines between the USSR and Poland, and invited Poland to associate herself in an alliance to contain Germany, for which the Soviet–Czechoslovak treaty already provided a basis. Soviet readiness to extend Polish frontiers to the west was likewise revealed, though not in as precise terms as had been agreed in principle at Tehran. The Soviet statement was well received by Britain and the USA, but above all by the communist KRN in Warsaw, which saw in it a declaration of support for its policy. Mikołajczyk and the rest of the 'London' government however were less than enthusiastic and abided by the policy which they had declared throughout. Equally, the leaders of the pro-government resistance in Poland insisted upon the 'inviolability' of the pre-war frontier and required the USSR to respect Polish sovereignty in eastern Poland. There was an illogicality in the resistance views. The underground leaders asked Mikołajczyk to perform the impossible task of withstanding Soviet territorial demands and at the same time encouraged him to seek agreement with Stalin, who had demanded the frontier based on the Curzon Line.

British efforts at reaching an understanding met with such difficulties that at one stage Eden threatened to withdraw support from the government-in-exile if it made no effort at compromise. Throughout, the Soviet government stood firm upon the decisions of Tehran and once more began to suggest that the Polish cabinet should be reconstructed. Churchill at length arrived in London on 18 January 1944 and on 20 January summoned Mikołajczyk, Tadeusz Romer, the minister of foreign affairs, and the ambassador, Edward Raczyński, to Downing Street. Churchill brought the full weight of his authority to bear upon the discussions in order to obtain a speedy decision. The Polish government shifted its ground slightly and sought a guarantee by Britain, the USA and the USSR of the new frontiers with Germany, but, since this would involve further consultations with the USSR, both Britain and the USA declined to agree. On 15 February 1944 the Polish cabinet in London agreed to two resolutions, the first being not to accept the resumption of diplomatic relations upon the basis of recognizing the Curzon Line, and the second not to accept proposals for the reconstruction of the government. It was proposed that a demarcation line should be established east of Vilna and Lwów, with Polish territory to the west administered by Poland and to the east by the Soviet Union, with foreign observers. By now the government-in-exile had strained Churchill's patience to the utmost and complicated Anglo-Soviet relations. On 22 February 1944 he made a public statement in the House of Commons to the effect that the British government supported the USSR on the question of the Curzon Line, which had been a line of demarcation supported by Britain in 1919–20. The declaration called forth excited protests from the Polish government and citizens abroad, but a statement in the House of Commons represented a firm commitment on the part of the British government from which there could be no going back. Churchill continued to represent Polish views to Stalin and sought his understanding of the difficult position in which Mikołajczyk found himself in his own cabinet. Churchill feared that, if the Polish government accepted the Curzon Line at once, it might lose the support of its followers at home and that in consequence a communist-controlled government might be imposed upon the country. He therefore tried to induce Stalin to soften his attitude, but in his letter of 3 March Stalin rejected all co-operation with the government of Mikołajczyk which laid claim to Vilna and Lwów in its resolutions of 15 February. In a stinging letter of 23 March Stalin indicated that he thought Churchill to be acting in a manner unbefitting an ally and asked him whether or not he stood by the Tehran decisions.[9] The advice Churchill received from the Foreign Office was that the Polish Question should be seen in the light of the general interests of Britain, which Stalin in his letter of 23 March clearly hinted that it should. Frank Roberts, then head of the Central Department, in a minute of 27 March pointed to the long tradition of Russian foreign policy of preferring an independent Poland unaligned with Russia's enemies to a Poland actually incorporated into Russia: 'Despite Polish arguments to the contrary, there is nothing inconsistent with British interests in the existence of such a Poland under strong Soviet influence, provided there is some reality of independence and the Russians behaved themselves in Poland.'[10] The War Cabinet discussed Stalin's letter of 23 March and decided to delay a reply. On 1 April Churchill told Eden that the correct course for Britain was to 'relapse into a moody silence as far as Stalin is concerned'. His advice to Mikołajczyk on 9 April was that further exchanges would lead nowhere and that he should present his case to Roosevelt. Churchill did not wash his hands of the Polish cause, but he was not prepared to risk the wider interests of Britain in what was to him a relatively minor matter.

Mikołajczyk hoped that practical military considerations would induce Stalin to come to terms with the London government-in-exile. There appeared to be signs of Soviet–Polish military co-operation at a local level in Volhynia in April 1944, when the 27th division of the AK seemed to have established cordial relations with the Soviet commanders.[11] It appeared as if the plan Tempest was about to succeed. In the meantime Mikołajczyk sought to enlist the more active aid of Roosevelt in the hope that he could be more successful than Churchill. Roosevelt on the one hand had no wish to antagonize Stalin, but on the other in an election year had to watch the activities of Americans of Polish descent who were organizing themselves to support Mikołajczyk. During his visit to the USA from 5 to 14 June, Mikołajczyk was well received, but on the vital question of Soviet–Polish relations Roosevelt was studiously vague. He indicated that Churchill rather than himself had initiated conversations on Poland at Tehran, and that though he himself was unable to approach Stalin at the moment, he was opposed to the settlement of territorial problems before the end of the war. He said that he would support the retention by Poland of Lwów, Drohobycz and Tarnopol, as well as the acquisition of East Prussia, including Königsberg, and Silesia. Roosevelt's advice was that Mikołajczyk should reconstruct his cabinet to make it more acceptable to Stalin. He thought that Mikołajczyk should make direct contact with Stalin himself and promised to write to Stalin to secure an invitation to Moscow for him. Mikołajczyk gained the impression that he had obtained more from Roosevelt that he had from Churchill. General Stanisław Tatar, who had accompanied Mikołajczyk, enjoyed little success with the representatives of the combined chiefs of staff. His exposé of the state of the AK was received politely, but he did not obtain recognition of the AK as a belligerent force.[12] Sosnkowski informed Bór-Komorowski that in his view Roosevelt had treated Mikołajczyk's visit as an exercise in electoral strategy rather than as an opportunity to discuss real issues of foreign policy.

On his return to London Mikołajczyk resumed his contacts with the Soviet ambassador to the exiled governments in London, Viktor Lebedev, with whom he had had inconclusive discussions in May before his visit to Washington, Mikołajczyk told Lebedev that his government wanted immediate resumption of diplomatic relations and the establishment of military and administrative co-operation. Questions of frontier changes, however, should be postponed to the end of the war. Lebedev reported the discussions of 20 June and requested instructions from Moscow. On 23 June he presented the Soviet demands, that the government-in-exile should recognize the Curzon Line, cease attacks upon the USSR in reference to the Katyn affair, and reorganize itself. Lebedev demanded the removal from office of President Raczkiewicz, the commander-in-chief, Sosnkowski, the minister of national defence, General Kukiel, and the minister of information, Professor Kot. The Soviet government could not have expected acceptance of these terms. It would appear that it was intended to use the talks of 20–23 June to show that the Soviet Union had explored all avenues in search for a settlement with Poland, but had failed owing to Polish opposition. Roosevelt had written to Stalin on 19 June proposing a visit by Mikołajczyk to Moscow, but on 24 June, the day after the final conversation of Mikołajczyk and Lebedev, Stalin replied that there was no point in such a visit, Mikołajczyk not having modified his position.[13] Stalin was cautiously approaching a different solution of Soviet–Polish difficulties.

Stalin and the KRN

The delegation of the KRN, consisting of Osóbka-Morawski, Spychalski and Haneman, had begun their conversations with Stalin on 19 May 1944.[14] The conversations were by no means easy, because the KRN, in addition to asking for arms, which Stalin could easily give, asked for Soviet recognition and support for its programme. It asked also for association with the Polish army in the USSR. Stalin clearly wavered. On the one hand he declared that he would not accept the Polish government in London in its existing form, but on the other he knew that recognition of the KRN might create political difficulties with the Western Allies. A solution by diplomacy was preferable to an open break. In the meantime the KRN was to occupy its time with visits to the Polish army, which raised no political difficulties. When the delegation visited the Kremlin on 22 June Molotov was able to acquaint it with the conversations of Lebedev and Mikołajczyk in London. The demands which Lebedev made on 23 June fit into a pattern. On the one hand they were a prologue to a shift in the policy of Stalin towards Poland and a necessary preliminary to a more positive attitude towards the KRN. On the other the Polish Question was to assume dimensions of paramount importance when on 23–24 June the great Soviet summer offensive undertaken by the First Baltic Front and the First, Second and Third Byelorussian Fronts began and within six days broke the German army group 'Mitte'. The prospect was that the Red Army would soon enter Poland. On 28 May the Union of Polish Patriots (ZPP) had recognized the KRN as 'the only representation of the Polish Nation' and denounced the London government. On 23 June the executive of the ZPP placed itself under the authority of the KRN. There were still some political difficulties, the socialists of the ZPP being more radical in their approach to social and economic problems than the communists, who were advised by Stalin to adopt a policy of moderation with the aim of winning wider support within Poland. On 6 July a fresh delegation arrived in Warsaw, led by General Michał Rola-Żymierski, armed with plenary powers from the KRN to discuss the creation of an executive. At a meeting on 15 July Stalin expressed his view that the KRN should create a 'Committee of National Liberation', which was a compromise solution preferable in his eyes to the Polish provisional government pressed upon him by Osóbka-Morawski and Wanda Wasilewska, who feared that otherwise the Soviet entry into Poland would be represented by their opponents as the beginning of a Soviet occupation. Stalin, however, had to consider the complications which might be created in relations with Britain and the USA if it appeared that the USSR was acting unilaterally. By giving his support to a 'Committee of National Liberation' Stalin implied the way was still open to an understanding with Mikołajczyk if he would recognize the Curzon Line and agree to the reconstruction of his government. On 19 July Stalin told the Poles that as soon as a Polish executive was established he would conclude with it an agreement defining the demarcation line between the Soviet and Polish administrations. While these discussions were proceeding in Moscow, the KRN in Warsaw decided to send a representative to establish an administration in the area of Lublin. This decision resolved the problems facing the KRN delegations and the ZPP in Moscow. On 21 July the formation was announced of the Polish Committee of National Liberation (Polski Komitet Wyzwolenia Narodowego – PKWN) under the chairmanship of Edward Osóbka-Morawski. Its manifesto was published the next day, on 22 July, proclaiming an end to all conflicts with Russia and a foreign policy based upon an alliance with the USSR and Czechoslovakia. Recognition by the USSR of the Committee as the 'temporary organ of executive power in Poland' followed on 26 July. From this moment onwards there were two rival organizations, the PKWN which established itself in Lublin backed by the USSR, representing a provisional government in embryo, and the London government-in-exile, supported by the Western Powers, competing one with another for control of Poland. The 'London' government took its stand upon the frontiers of 1939. The PKWN accepted the Curzon Line and the extension of the Polish frontiers to the west of the line of the Oder and Neisse. The way was nevertheless open for an understanding with the London government-in-exile because the PKWN was not yet formally a provisional government recognized as such even by the Soviet Union.

Gomułka was still striving for an understanding with the government-in-exile. On 1 July 1944 the PPR once more appealed to the Peasant Party and the PPS to join it in forming a broad national front. The PPR stated that, while it opposed the government-in-exile and its representatives in Poland, it accepted its prime minister, Mikołajczyk, as a possible popular leader in a reconstructed government. The PPR recognized that Mikołajczyk was moving towards an understanding with the USSR, but argued that the presence of anti-Soviet elements in his cabinet made his task impossible. The PPR appealed to the Peasant Party and the PPS to assist in the restoration of Soviet–Polish relations and a reconciliation of the government-in-exile with the USSR, towards which a welcome step would be the elimination of 'reactionary' generals from the AK. To achieve this end Gomułka was prepared to dismantle the KRN if it were an obstacle to wider understanding. Gomułka's appeal remained unanswered and at the end of July 1944 the leaders of the PPR left Warsaw for Lublin to join the PKWN. By now the PPR had about 20,000 members, with a hard core of former members of the Polish Communist Party (KPP), but with others recruited from the left-wing sections of the Peasant Party and the PPS. The People's Army (AL), it is claimed, was about 50,000–55,000 strong with operational units numbering 22,000.[15] Its strength was not as great as the AK, but the Polish army returning from Russia on 1 June consisted of 77,932 men, and its numbers were to be doubled in the course of the next two months.[16] The Polish army, led by General Berling, his deputy, General Karol Świerczewski, and its officer in charge of political affairs, General Alexander Zawadzki, was a regular force organized in four infantry divisions, an armoured brigade and a cavalry brigade, supported by artillery and engineers, but it was also a political force. The balance of power was thus tilted in favour of the PKWN. As the Polish army advanced into Poland it would enlist more men and become a school training Poles in new attitudes and outlooks.

Plan 'Tempest'

The position of the government-in-exile was becoming desperate as a confrontation with Stalin and the communists appeared imminent. At this stage only direct negotiations in Moscow resulting in an understanding could retrieve the situation and lead to the establishment of a common front. On 20 July Churchill asked Stalin to invite Mikołajczyk to Moscow, but on 23 July Stalin replied that he had asked the PKWN to act as a temporary administration because he had found no other forces capable of controlling the country. The PKWN was not to be considered to be a government, but it might become 'the core of a provisional government made up of democratic forces'. On 25 July Mikołajczyk told Eden that the PKWN was a body of usurpers and the government-in-exile demanded an immediate British protest against its formation. On 26 July, however, after 'some hesitation' and consultation with Churchill, Mikołajczyk left London for Moscow. Churchill assured Stalin that 'Mikołajczyk is most anxious to help a general fusion of all Poles on the lines which you and I and the President are, I believe, agreed'. He warned Stalin that it would be 'a disaster if the Western democracies find themselves recognizing one body of Poles and you recognizing another'.[17] Churchill now wished to bring about a union of the Lublin and the London Poles in order to save Poland from civil war which might disrupt Allied unity. He had in effect modified his position and was now prepared to see the communists taking part in the new government of Poland. The London Poles believed that Mikołajczyk's visit to Moscow was the final attempt to reach a political and military understanding with the USSR.

Mikołajczyk, accompanied by Tadeusz Romer, spent almost a fortnight in Moscow from 29 July to 10 August. During his stay he became partially convinced that it was not Stalin's intention to 'communize' Poland, although he thought that this was the intention of the PKWN. In his opinion Stalin realized that he would not be able to ensure a united Poland behind the Red Army without the co-operation of the London government-in-exile. He found in fact that Stalin was not prepared to withdraw support from the PKWN and he directed Mikołajczyk to undertake discussions with it. On the question of the frontiers Stalin stood firm on the Curzon Line on the grounds that 'all nations, great and small, have the same rights', for which reasons he had to adopt an impartial attitude towards Poles, Lithuanians, Byelorussians and Ukrainians. On 6–7 August Mikołajczyk conferred with representatives of the PKWN, Bolesław Bierut, the chairman of the KRN, Osóbka-Morawski, Wanda Wasilewska and others, who proposed to him the formation of a government of national unity, with 4 members of the London government-in-exile and 14 members of the PKWN, with Mikołajczyk as premier. To this proposal Mikołajczyk would not agree, nor did he accept the return to the constitution of 1921 in place of the April constitution of 1935. At this stage Mikołajczyk decided to return to London with the purpose of consulting with his colleagues, but he had been overtaken by events. A rising had broken out in Warsaw on 1 August and he was reduced to the role of a suppliant begging for Soviet help to a stricken city. The AK commanders believed that the rising would help Mikołajczyk in his negotiations with Stalin. In fact it added yet another complication to Soviet–Polish relations.

Bór-Komorowski's decision to bring his troops out into the open under the Tempest plan met with mixed reactions in London. Mikołajczyk accepted the decision as realistic, hoping that it might lead to the establishment of Soviet–Polish military co-operation as a preliminary to a political understanding with the USSR. He believed that Stalin would for strategic reasons accept the AK's offer of collaboration, but he was to over-estimate the usefulness of the AK to the Soviet forces as they advanced into Poland. He seems not to have considered the possibility that Stalin might refuse to accept the AK as allies before a final solution of the Soviet–Polish dispute had been reached. For his part Sosnkowski was disturbed by Bór-Komorowski's decision to stage Tempest and sought to cancel it, or at least to minimize its possible consequences. He feared it would lead to a tragedy for Poland, but was unable to declare himself against it. The Tempest plan in his opinion contained many dangers if prior agreement were not reached with the Soviet Union. Nevertheless, the London government gave its assent to Tempest on 18 February 1944.

The Tempest began first in February in Volhynia when an AK unit of about 6,000 men began its operations against the Germans. The Tempest took the form of large-scale guerrilla operations rather than a number of small-scale actions against German rearguards. Very soon important departures from the original plan took place. In March 1944 the AK group assumed the name of the 27th Volhynian Infantry Division, which had been stationed in the region before the war. On 20 March this force under the command of Lieutenant Colonel 'Oliwa' (Jan Wojciech Kiwerski) established its first contacts with the advancing Soviet forces. At first relations were cordial in spite of the fact that the Soviet Union regarded Volhynia as an integral part of the USSR. Indeed it appears that the local Soviet commanders were willing to accept the AK as allies in a common struggle and provide them with arms. An essential condition, according to the reports of 'Oliwa', was the acceptance of Soviet operational control and the disbandment of all Polish units behind the Soviet lines. These local arrangements of a purely military nature left the problem of the recognition of the London government-in-exile unsettled.[18] Soviet commanders in the field had no powers to commit their government on questions of state policy, but co-operation nevertheless seemed welcome even if the AK units continued to maintain their connection with London. Colonel 'Oliwa' entered into an association with the Soviet forces lest otherwise his division be disbanded by them, and anxiously awaited Bór-Komorowski's instructions. For his part Bór-Komorowski gave orders which went far beyond the limits of a military convention, stressing the need for political agreement and recognition of the 1939 frontiers. It was out of the question for the Soviet commander, Sergeyev, to take important decisions, and there is doubt whether Bór-Komorowski's views were ever presented to him.[19]

Reactions in London to events in Volhynia were conflicting. Mikołajczyk greeted them with enthusiasm in the belief that the Tempest had begun to pay political dividends and pave the way for a broader understanding with the USSR, providing the Western Allies with good reasons to intervene on Poland's behalf, because the AK had demonstrated its good will. He though that, if the AK failed to collaborate, the 'Anglo-Saxon World' would think it favourably disposed towards the Germans. Sacrifices in a common struggle, on the other hand, would lay claim to Anglo-American support. Sosnkowski, however, was opposed to military co-operation without previous political agreement. He hoped that the Anglo-American invasion of continental Europe would bring about the liberation of Poland by Western rather than Soviet forces. In his opinion informal military co-operation between the Polish and Soviet forces without authorization by the London government-in-exile was politically harmful. Indeed, he was hinting to Bór-Komorowski that he should adopt a policy of resistance to the USSR. His fears met with a ready response in Warsaw. The resistance leaders regarded the Tempest as one aspect of an approaching confrontation with the Soviet Union in accordance with the doctrine that they were fighting militarily against the Germans, but politically against the communists in defence of Poland's right to independence as they understood it. The Tempest was part of a struggle for power, and inactivity was tantamount to political suicide.

In Volhynia military action settled the matter. On 14–20 April the Germans surrounded the 27th Division and the regiment of Soviet cavalry co-operating with it. 'Oliwa' was killed and his successor, Major 'Żegota' (Tadeusz Sztumberg-Rychter), with difficulty broke out of the encirclement. Part of the division was eventually able to reach the Lublin area, while another part was incorporated in the Polish army formed in the Soviet Union. The episode therefore did nothing to clarify Soviet–Polish relations, but it did reveal the pattern which events were likely to take as the Red Army advanced. The AK would first fight the Germans and co-operate with the Soviet troops, but would then be embodied in the Polish army under General Berling. For this reason Bór-Komorowski decided that, if his forces were to act as hosts to the Soviet troops, they must capture large towns before their arrival. On 12 June Bór-Komorowski decided that the AK forces from the Vilna and Nowogródek areas under the command of Colonel 'Wilk' (Alexander Krzyżanowski) must seize Vilna as the Soviet troops approached. On 7 July Sosnkowski advised him that in addition to Vilna he should try to capture Lwów and other important centres.

On 23–24 June the Soviet army opened its massive offensive in

Byelorussia. By the beginning of July they were approaching Vilna. The Tempest now entered its main phase. AK units numbering about 5,500 men attacked the German garrison in Vilna on the night of 6 July, but the first assault failed to dislodge it. On 7 July Soviet forces joined in the battle. Once again cordial relations were established and maintained during the fighting until the fall of the city on 13 July. The Soviet forces, however, refused to admit other Polish units concentrated in the area into the city. Colonel 'Wilk' was convinced that the Soviet authorities were determined to disband his force and asked Bór-Komorowski to arrange for an Allied mission to be sent to Vilna. Discussions took place on 15 July on the role which the Poles could play, but when Colonel 'Wilk' and other officers went to discuss the question with Soviet staff officers on 16 July they were arrested. When this news reached the AK units outside Vilna they began to march under Lieutenant Colonel 'Strychański' in the direction of the Rudnicki forest, but the majority of them were arrested and interned. Some were incorporated in the army of General Berling. Others did offer a token resistance to the Soviet forces. Mikołajczyk on 18 July asked Churchill to intervene in the affair and pressure was put upon his chief-of-staff, Hastings Ismay, and upon Eden. Churchill reacted angrily and strongly criticized the Poles for taking up the struggle in the area of Vilna and in Volhynia. The matter, moreover, excited no comment in the British press.[20]

The battle began for Lwów on 23 July and lasted four days. AK units, 6,000 strong, took part in the fighting under the command of Colonel 'Janka' (W. Filipowski). While the battle was in progress Soviet–Polish relations were again formally correct, but on 28 July Filipowski was told that Lwów belonged to the Soviet Union and that his units must 'lay down their arms in two hours and disband', his men being given the opportunity of joining the Red Army or the Polish army. Filipowski ordered his troops to disarm and he himself left Lwów for talks with General Rola-Żymierski, the commander of the PKWN troops. The resistance leaders in the Lwów area intended to co-operate with Żymierski provided that an agreement between Mikołajczyk, then in Moscow, and the PKWN could be reached. They considered this to be the only realistic position to adopt, but on 31 July the Soviet authorities arrested some AK officers in Lwów, even though they were trying to reach an understanding. Bór-Komorowski for his part ordered his forces east of the Curzon Line to enlist in the Polish army under Berling if faced with compulsory enlistment. Thus the Tempest as an anti-Soviet demonstration in the east ended in disarray. This disastrous epilogue to Tempest in the east did not lead to its abandonment or to revision of its aims and methods. Failure convinced the AK leaders that an even greater effort was needed. General Leopold Okulicki, one of the authors of the Warsaw insurrection, wrote 'An effort was needed which would stir the conscience of the world...[and] display our extreme good will to Russia and which would even more strongly accentuate her behaviour towards us. The battles which our units fought in Volhynia, Vilna and Lwów could not accomplish this task...'

At the end of July three AK infantry divisions, the Third, Ninth and Twenty-seventh, staged Tempest operations in the Lublin area, west of the Curzon Line, but the pattern of events was the same as before. Some officers and men were arrested, while others were incorporated in Berling's army. In short, Bór-Komorowski's decision to launch the Tempest had led to the liquidation of the AK in Soviet-occupied areas.[21] It is against this background of disappointment that the Warsaw rising of 1 August is to be understood.

The Polish forces abroad, 1939–45

In the years 1940–5 the Polish armed forces in the west played a distinguished part in campaigns against the Germans in North Africa, Italy, France, the Low Countries and Germany. The Polish Carpathian Brigade under General Stanisław Kopański fought with distinction at Tobruk. The Polish air force in Britain grew into ten fighter and four bomber squadrons and had a strength of 14,351 in May 1945. Between August 1940 and May 1945 it flew a total of 86,527 sorties in 198,000 flying hours, losing 1,669 men. Polish airmen destroyed at least 500 enemy planes and 190 V-1 flying bombs and dropped 14,708 tons of bombs and mines on enemy targets. Many Poles served in Transport Command, adding 15,959 flights in 92,853 hours to the Polish contribution. The Polish air force was the largest single foreign unit in British service, with the exception of the French who were able to add the North African units to their air force after 1942.[22]

The Polish army was divided into two parts. The Second Corps, consisting of two infantry divisions and an armoured brigade under the command of General Władysław Anders, played an important part in the Italian campaign, taking Monte Cassino in an heroic effort to break the German Gustav Line and liberating Ancona and Bologna in the closing stages of the war. The Polish First Armoured Division took part in the invasion of France in 1944 and the pursuit of the Germans in 1944–5. The Polish Parachute Brigade took part in the ill-fated battle at Arnhem. Altogether there were about 220,000 men serving in the Polish army under British command in 1945, while Poles resident in France played their part in the French resistance.

In a political sense the London government-in-exile regarded its armed forces as the nucleus of a regular army when it returned to Poland. The British government thought in terms of using the Polish Second Corps in support of its plans for the Balkans and Central Europe. Its employment in Italy served to counter Soviet suspicion that the soldiers evacuated from the USSR would remain inactive. The Second Corps lost 3,783 men, killed, wounded and missing, proving that it too made its contribution to the final victory.[23]

The Polish army under Soviet command had its part to play. From October 1943 Poles were fighting on the eastern front. In the spring of 1944 the First Polish Corps established in August 1943 was transformed into the First Polish Army. The First Army, initially under the command of General Berling, co-operated with the Red Army in the liberation of Poland and took part in the successive Soviet offensives culminating in the storming of Berlin. On 12–13 October 1943 the Polish troops raised in the USSR received their baptism of fire. The first Division of Infantry, named after Kościuszko, with a supporting regiment of tanks and other units, under the command of General Zygmunt Berling played a distinguished role in breaking the German resistance in a bloody battle at Lenino near Mogilev. In September 1944 the Second Polish Army was created and went to the front in January 1945. Both Polish armies, amounting to 185,000 men, took part in the battle for Berlin. By May 1945 the Polish army under Soviet command had risen to 400,000. Its commander-in-chief was General Rola-Żymierski, an ex-Legionary who had served in the Polish army until his disgrace in 1926. Owing to a shortage of Polish officers, reliance was placed upon Soviet officers, often of Polish descent, amounting to 16,000 altogether.[24]

The Polish contribution to the common struggle against Nazi Germany was thus not negligible. The essence of the Polish situation lay not in the want of courage, but in the absence of political agreement. Nothing was to be more tragic than the Warsaw uprising of 1 August 1944 and the legacy of misunderstanding it left behind.

The Warsaw uprising, 1944

The Soviet offensive on 23–24 June 1944 was a decisive point in the Second World War. On 6 June the Western Allies had landed in Normandy, where they were locked in combat with the Germans until their breakout from their bridgehead at the beginning of August 1944. The Byelorussian offensive destroyed thirty German divisions and inflicted immense losses on the Germans, amounting to 500,000 killed, wounded and taken prisoner. The First Byelorussian Front under Marshal Rokossovsky and the First Ukrainian Front under Marshal Koniev made rapid progress in the centre and the south. The object of the Soviet commanders was to reach the Vistula and secure bridgeheads over the river. Warsaw did not feature in the plans of the Soviet army. On 21 July the Soviet forces crossed the Bug and Chełm fell on 22 July. By 26 July they had arrived on the Vistula and on 27 July a bridgehead was established at Magnuszew. On the right flank the Soviet Third Armoured Corps pushed northwards in the direction of Mińsk Mazowiecki and the suburb of Warsaw on the right bank of the Vistula, Praga. The movement in the direction of Praga from the Soviet point of view was of secondary importance. Owing to the lack of contact between the AK and the Soviet commanders Bór-Komorowski was in no position to gauge Soviet intent. German strategy was equally obscure. On 20 July 1944 Colonel von Stauffenberg attempted unsuccessfuly to assassinate Hitler. In consequence General Guderian was appointed chief of general staff. The German high command could either defend the line of the 1914 frontier of Germany or seek to stabilize the front on the Vistula. The latter alternative had advantages of a political nature in the sense that it would cloak the collapse of Hitler's policy in the east. The shorter line from East Prussia to Upper Silesia would be less expensive in men. The Germans chose the latter course. Whereas Warsaw was a matter of secondary consideration for the Soviet commanders, for the Germans it became the centre of the defence system they intended to establish. The German command had at its disposal units of the Herman Göring Division, the SS Viking Division, the SS Totenkopf Division and other elite formations. There is no doubt that on 3 August 1944 the Soviet forces on the right bank of the Vistula opposite Warsaw were severely mauled. There had been some evidence of German panic on 23–24 July in Warsaw, when women employed in the German administration began to leave the city and the remaining German personnel began to fight to board the trains to escape to Germany. The arrival of German reinforcements, however, had a steadying effect.

On 1 August 1944 the AK rose in revolt against the Germans in Warsaw in a battle which was to last until 3 October. The political motives were those which had been apparent in Volhynia, Vilna and Lwów. Bór-Komorowski wished to prevent the communists from establishing themselves in Warsaw and compel Stalin to recognize the Polish government in London. In the diplomatic sense he hoped to assist Mikołajczyk in his talks in Moscow with Stalin and induce Britain and the United States to support the London Poles. In fact, no serious diplomatic preparations for the insurrection had been made either in London or in

Washington, let alone Moscow. Ideologically the authors of the insurrection were guided by the doctrine of two enemies, the Germans and the Russians. The rising was directed militarily against the Germans and politically against the USSR and the PKWN established in Lublin. The decision to fight was based on the belief that the Germans were defeated decisively on the Eastern Front and that the Soviet forces were about to enter the capital. Bór-Komorowski and Jankowski issued their final order for the insurrection when it was erroneously reported to them that Soviet tanks were entering the suburb of Praga on the right bank of the Vistula. They assumed that the battle for Warsaw was approaching its climax and presented them with an opportunity to capture the capital shortly before the Soviet forces entered it. In fact, the decision to call the uprising coincided with the German counter-attack against the Soviet forces on the right bank of the river. The Germans regained the initiative and held it for some days.[25]

There is no doubt that the Soviet failure to take Warsaw in early August was due to military obstacles. This does not, however, explain why Stalin did not act upon Marshal Konstantin Rokossovsky's suggestion that he should renew the offensive on Warsaw after 25 August. It is probable that, preoccupied with the offensive in the Balkans begun on 20 August and its political problems sufficient to require the presence of Marshal Zhukov, Stalin was disinclined to press home the attack on the Vistula. There may well have been sinister motives in his thinking. It is possible that Stalin decided to abandon Warsaw to its fate and thereby avoid a confrontation with the London Poles, leaving to the Germans the task of crushing his Polish political opponents. His refusal at first to allow planes of the Western Allies carrying supplies to Warsaw to land in the Soviet Union seems to support this supposition. On 9 September, however, Stalin did agree under strong pressure from Churchill to allow planes of the Western Allies to land on Soviet airfields. On 13 September Soviet planes reappeared over Warsaw, bombing and strafing German positions and dropping supplies to the insurgents. On 18 September the Americans sent over 100 bombers to drop supplies upon Warsaw from very high altitudes, but supplies from the air for the most part fell into German hands.[26] A second American mission to Warsaw planned by the US air force failed to take place, partly because of bad weather and then because of the capitulation of the insurgents on 3 October.

After the occupation of Praga by the Polish First Army under Berling, Polish troops made an attempt to cross the Vistula and establish a bridgehead in the city. These attempts, lasting from 16 to 21 September, came too late and failed to save Warsaw. The absence of Soviet–Polish military co-operation turned the insurrection into a tragedy, because the Germans used it as an opportunity to carry out the destruction of Warsaw. Himmler assured Hitler on the day of the rising that

Historically, what the Poles are doing is for us a blessing... After five or six weeks Warsaw will disappear, Warsaw the capital, the head of 16–17 million Poles, a people who blocked the East to us for 700 years... will be no more. Then, historically speaking, the Polish Question will no longer present a problem for us, our children, and for all those who will succeed us.[27]

The rising had been ignored by the German military authorities in the early stages, but with the stabilization of the front the Germans and their Russian and Ukrainian auxiliaries set upon Warsaw with a senseless fury and committed appalling atrocities.

For the Western Powers the insurrection was a cause of acute embarrassment, because they were unable and, in the case of Roosevelt, even reluctant to help Warsaw themselves or to persuade Stalin to do so. The supplies parachuted into Warsaw were woefully inadequate,[28] and were dropped more to prevent the fall of Mikołajczyk's cabinet than to help the insurgents. The Soviet appeals calling upon the people of Warsaw to rise against the Germans had little effect upon the authors of the insurrection, except in as far as they strengthened their conviction that the Soviet forces were on the point of taking Warsaw and therefore induced a sense of urgency. In the last days of July the leaders of the pro-'London' resistance knew that only in Warsaw did they have enough men to stage a major operation and carry out a coup in the face of the Soviet advance. With these attitudes it was morally easier for the resistance leaders to order an insurrection than to refrain from doing so, believing as they did that failure to act would amount to political suicide. By acting without co-ordinating their plans with the Soviet commanders, however, they greatly contributed to the tragedy of Warsaw and its people. All important decisions were also taken without prior consultation with the government-in-exile. Mikołajczyk and his cabinet, it is true, seemed to welcome the plans of the resistance leaders, while General Sosnkowski, until the actual outbreak of the insurrection, was undecided whether to approve it or to try to prevent it. His indecision is reflected in his absence with the Second Corps in Italy in the moment of crisis.[29] In January 1945 the Soviet forces were to enter a city of ruins and graves, the only Allied city to become a battleground in the Second World War. Nearly 200,000 Poles were killed during the fighting. The Germans deported the 800,000 survivors from the capital either to other parts of Poland or to Germany. The Germans for their part lost 17,000 dead and missing and 9,000 wounded. A heavy price was paid for what was basically a political venture.

The destruction of Warsaw had a traumatic effect on the entire nation. National romanticism, so strong before 1944, was superseded by political realism. As a result of the insurrection many Poles became aware of the need for close alliance with the USSR, but the memory of the rising was to scar the relationship between the Soviet Union and Poland for years to come.[30] For the London Poles the failure of the rising was a political and psychological defeat from which they never recovered. After the fall of Warsaw the London government's position began to deteriorate rapidly. The AK never recovered. Many of its best soldiers were killed or captured in Warsaw, while many of the remaining units were afflicted by the defeatist feelings permeating not only their own ranks, but also Polish society at large. Soon after the insurrection the last AK commander decided to demobilize many of its units because he feared that they might become completely demoralized or join the communists. For practical purposes the operation Tempest had come to an end.[31]

The insurrection and its aftermath helped rather than hindered the communist assumption of power. The Poles thought that their allies, Great Britain, the USA and the USSR, had treated them more harshly than they treated Hitler's satellites. Many blamed the London leaders for their misfortunes. In the meantime the PKWN began to assume power in the liberated areas. The Committee took immediate steps to strengthen its position in the country. On 26 July agreements had been signed with the USSR concerning the frontiers and the transfer of the civil administration to the Committee.[32] Nevertheless, supreme power in the theatre of operations was vested temporarily in the Soviet commander-in-chief, which meant that Stalin and the Red Army were the real masters of Poland. The Committee's administrative structure was based partly on a network of local national councils established by the PPR and partly on pre-war institutions, but the PPR tended to put its own trusted men in key positions.[33] The Committee set about organizing life in the liberated areas, publishing newspapers, re-opening basic public services, enacting land reform, beginning the process of nationalization and setting up courts to try war criminals. The underground state and the AK were considered by the Committee and the Soviet forces to be illegal and their leaders, who in accordance with the instructions of the Tempest presented themselves to the Soviet authorities, were arrested. The Committee took immediate steps to develop its military and security forces. On 15 August the PKWN proclaimed a general mobilization in the liberated areas. By the end of 1944 160,000 men, including 4,203 officers, were conscripted into the army. A special effort was made to develop military education. By the end of 1944 there were 21 military schools in which 13,000 officer cadets were undergoing training. In addition, 11,513 Soviet officers were assigned to the Polish army. By the end of the year the army had risen to a strength of 290,000 men, of whom 180,000 were serving in the front line units.[34] In November 1944 in order to strengthen its control over the army, consisting mainly of conscripted peasants, the PPR established a military department of the Central Committee, headed by Gomułka, and assigned to it 500 of its activists.[35] The communists were in fact very weak in the army. Even by the end of 1945 only 2,000 officers belonged to the PPR, while the rank and file were not even allowed to join the party. There were nevertheless other ways of winning the soldiers' loyalties than by indoctrination. Agrarian reform, designed to satisfy the land-hungry peasantry and destroy the landlord class, was begun in 1944.[36] By 1945 212,084 hectares were distributed among 109,899 peasants and landless labourers. Once this important step had been taken no régime in Poland could have gone back on it.[37]

Churchill, Mikołajczyk and Stalin

Churchill was encouraged by Stalin's adoption of a less hostile attitude towards the Warsaw rising, which he had on 16 August described as 'a reckless and fearful gamble' and on 22 August as the work of a 'handful of power-seeking criminals'.[38] By 9 September Molotov was drawing a distinction between the Polish people engaged in the rising and the authors of it, who had failed to give the USSR warning of their intentions.[39] On 23 September Stalin told the Western Allies that the Poles had good reason, after all, to rise against the Germans and declared his sympathy for the insurgents. He admitted that he had misjudged their motives and realized why the rising had started prematurely. In his opinion the insurrection had been provoked by the German threat to deport all the male population from Warsaw on the approach of the Soviet forces.[40] This statement can be interpreted either as showing that Stalin was not fully informed about developments in Warsaw at the end of July,[41] or as an attempt to justify his change of attitude towards the rising, from which in August he had dissociated the USSR.[42] Churchill was much encouraged by Stalin's change of heart which he saw as a success for British diplomacy and suggested to Eden that a fresh attempt should be made to solve the Soviet–Polish problem. Under pressure from the British government President Raczkiewicz agreed to dismiss the commander-in-chief, Sosnkowski, who in a speech of 1 September had declared that the British had deserted Poland as they had in 1939. The dismissal of Sosnkowski was seen by Churchill as the removal of an obstacle to Soviet–Polish reconciliation. In his place

Raczkiewicz appointed Bór-Komorowski on 28 September, which gave annoyance to the USSR and to the PKWN, but he was taken prisoner on 5 October by the Germans.

Churchill went to Moscow with Eden in October 1944 with the intention of solving the difficulties of the Polish problem, but before his departure the Polish government-in-exile had stated its position in a memorandum of 29 August. Once more it stood firm on the frontiers of 1939, but did modify its outlook to the extent of consenting to a cabinet reconstruction upon the basis of the equal representation of the Peasant Party, the National Democrats (Stronnictwo Narodowe), the Party of Labour, the PPS and the PPR. The Soviet government did not reply directly to this proposal, but announced through the press agency TASS, on 6 September, that it has been transmitted to the PKWN on the grounds that it dealt with a Polish matter in which the USSR had no standing. The USSR had other problems to face as a result of the success of Soviet forces. In September 1944 Bulgaria, Romania and Finland withdrew from the war. For their part the USA and Britain began to give closer definition to the post-war settlement in the second Quebec conference of Roosevelt and Churchill on 10–16 September. It was agreed that a western frontier on the Oder should be awarded to Poland, but Roosevelt later declined to take an active part in the Moscow discussions, conceding only that the US ambassador in Moscow, Harriman, should attend as an observer. Churchill departed from London entertaining hopes, as he said in the House of Commons, that he would be able to secure the establishment of a united Polish government. On 9 October he obtained the agreement of Stalin to invite Mikołajczyk to Moscow and in the meantime began to discuss with Stalin the division of the Balkans into spheres of influence. On this score Churchill found that no real problems arose. Though no actual agreement was signed, it was assumed that Britain would have a predominant influence in Greece, where in any case there was no Russian tradition of seeking influence. Churchill conceded to the USSR a predominance in Romania and Bulgaria and suggested an equal division of influence in Hungary and Yugoslavia. It is open to question whether in fact an understanding was reached, but the conversations undoubtedly left Churchill with the impression that he had much to lose if the Polish government-in-exile should act in a manner likely to disrupt Anglo-Soviet relations.

After some hesitation Mikołajczyk left London for Moscow on 10 October. Once again he arrived in Moscow with little room for manoeuvre, being bound by the terms of a cabinet memorandum stipulating that post-war Poland must have as much territory as in 1939, including 'in the east the main centres of Polish cultural life and sources of raw materials'. The Polish government held to the concept of equal representation for the five political parties in the new government to be established.[43] Churchill and Eden, for their part, were fully aware of the weakness of their own position and that of the London Poles. They thought that the issue was no longer a question of the frontiers, but of Poland's independence, knowing as they did that Stalin held most of the trump cards in Poland. They believed that they had to act quickly to bring about a fusion between the government-in-exile and the PKWN before the London Poles' situation deteriorated still further. They used all their powers of persuasion to make Mikołajczyk come to an agreement with Stalin. Stalin in the first conversations of 13 October made it clear that he stood by the PKWN and would not accept the composition proposed for the new government in the Polish memorandum of 29 August. On the question of the Soviet–Polish frontier Stalin was equally adamant in his insistence upon the Curzon Line. In this he was supported by Churchill who pointed to the great advantages which Poland would obtain in Silesia, in East Prussia and on the Baltic coast. Mikołajczyk reverted to the concept of a demarkation line, claiming the support of Roosevelt for it. At this point Molotov cut him short and informed him that President Roosevelt had expressed his agreement to the Curzon Line at the Tehran Conference, but had preferred at the time not to let his opinions be known. This was certainly not the impression which Mikołajczyk had obtained during his visit to Washington in June 1944, but Churchill confirmed what Molotov had said. Churchill tried to secure the acceptance of the Curzon Line as a *de facto* frontier to be reviewed at the peace conference, but Stalin would not give his consent and insisted upon the Curzon Line, though with possible minor changes of up to 6–7 kilometres one way or the other. On 14 October Churchill and Eden saw Mikołajczyk and his colleagues alone and exerted very great pressure upon them. Mikołajczyk was told that he could not apply the *liberum veto*, but must accept the decision of the Great Powers. Churchill threatened to wash his hands of the government-in-exile, hinting that the British government might cease to recognize it. On 15 October Mikołajczyk shifted his ground and accepted the Curzon Line (B) as the basis of discussion. Under this variant the frontier would be drawn to include eastern Galicia together with Lwów. At this point Churchill threatened to break off the discussions, but Mikołajczyk refused to change his position, fearing that he would be disavowed by his colleagues in London. Churchill left the room without bothering to say goodbye. Eden renewed the conversations later in the day when tempers had cooled. On 16 October a draft proposal submitted by the British delegation was discussed. Mikołajczyk insisted that the Curzon Line should be understood to include Lwów, but Stalin refused to allow this interpretation, nor would he allow it to be a line of demarcation. It was to be 'the basis of the frontier between Russia and Poland'. All that Mikołajczyk could do was to return to London to seek to convince his colleagues that they must yield to necessity.[44] On the subject of the formation of a new Polish government equally little progress was made. The PKWN delegation insisted upon two-thirds to three-quarters of the posts in the reconstructed government being allotted to themselves, but it was agreed that Mikołajczyk should be prime minister.[45] While the communists had in August been in favour of an immediate understanding with Mikołajczyk, they now sought to postpone agreement as long as possible.[46] Stalin at a dinner after Mikołajczyk's departure did agree for a moment to a fifty-fifty division of cabinet posts, but he quickly corrected himself and amended the division in favour of the PKWN.

Mikołajczyk held to the view that acceptance of the Soviet terms would allow his cabinet to return to Poland and prevent the communists from emerging as the dominant force in the country. He found the task of convincing his colleagues of the need to accept Stalin's demands more difficult than he had expected. To make his suggestions more palatable he once again asked the British government whether it favoured the extension of the Polish frontiers in the west as far as the river Oder and Stettin, and whether it was prepared to guarantee the independence and integrity of the new Poland even if the USA should be reluctant to give its guarantee. Although the British reply was reasonably reassuring, it failed to satisfy the Polish cabinet, which refused to accept Mikołajczyk's solution. Mikołajczyk hesitated to inform Churchill of the outcome of the Polish discussions and in a fresh attempt to convince his cabinet he sought assurances from the USA on three basic points: whether the US government would favour the westward expansion of Poland, protect Poland's 'real independence', and provide large-scale economic aid to Poland. Though Roosevelt's answers were less vague than the Poles had feared,[47] it was becoming increasingly obvious that Mikołajczyk had the support of only his own Peasant Party for his policies. The majority of his cabinet, consisting of the PPS, National Democrats and Party of Labour ministers, refused to support him. In view of their opposition he had no option but to resign on 24 November.

Mikołajczyk believed now that after his withdrawal from the government he should keep himself available for some future attempt to reach agreement with the Soviet Union. He was still convinced that the PKWN, even with full Soviet support, would not be able to control Poland and that 'some day some compromise may be found which will give a chance for the expression of Polish nationalism'. On 29 November a new Polish government was formed under the veteran socialist, Tomasz Arciszewski, but the Peasant Party refused to join it. His government had no chance of being more than a 'Government of National Protest'. For all practical purposes the Western Allies ignored it completely, while the Soviet Union simply dismissed it as a reactionary and unrepresentative body. With the withdrawal of Mikołajczyk and the Peasant Party its authority was severely diminished. It was never again to play a part in Polish affairs. On 31 December 1944 the PKWN announced that it had become the provisional government of Poland, with Osóbka-Morawski as its prime minister. Gomułka became one of the two deputy premiers and Bierut the head of state. On 5 January 1945 the government was recognized by the USSR, because, as Stalin said, the Soviet Union had a greater stake than any other country in 'a democratic Poland' and because 'the Polish problem is inseparable from [its] security'. He claimed that the Lublin Poles had made great progress and accused the London Poles of fomenting civil strife. The Western Allies, however, still gave formal recognition to the government-in-exile and remained for the time being on a different footing from the USSR.

Post-war Poland

The formation of the Provisional Government of National Unity

On 12 January 1945 forces of the First Ukrainian Front followed by the
Third Byelorussian Front and then the First and Second Byelorussian
Fronts and finally the Fourth Ukrainian Front opened a gigantic offensive
which in the course of a few weeks was to liberate the rest of Poland. To
the soldiers of the Polish First Army fell the honour of liberating Warsaw
on 17 January. By the spring of 1945 the Polish armies amounted to 400,000
men, a not inconsiderable achievement in so short a time and a valuable
contribution to the conclusion of hostilities. By the middle of March the
provisional government was in control of what was to become post-war
Poland. The communists, supported by the Red Army, began the task of
rebuilding national life, whereas the pro-London forces were in a state of
near collapse. The presence of Soviet military forces in the country meant
that they were powerless to act. Indeed, by October 1944 Stalin had told
the PKWN that the Soviet forces themselves would suppress AK activity,
which they saw as a threat to their rear. He assured the Committee that
the unity of the Grand Alliance would not suffer as a result of differences
between the Western Allies and the Soviet Union with regard to Poland.
He even criticized them for their lack of 'revolutionary methods' in
dealing with their opponents. As a result the PKWN began a virulent
campaign against the AK. The conflict between the anti-communist forces
and the provisional government created conditions of civil war. As the
Red Army moved westwards some Polish underground organizations
began to revive and regain their freedom of action, but this invited Soviet
reprisals. On 19 January General Okulicki, Bór-Komorowski's successor,
ordered the dissolution of the AK, but he nevertheless continued to
develop his purely anti-Soviet organization, which went under the name
of Independence (Niepodległość – Nie).

The provisional government might act as if Polish sovereignty extended
to the line of the rivers Oder and Neisse, but the war did not end in Europe
until 8 May and there had as yet been no formal agreement between the

USA, Great Britain and the USSR on the Polish Question. The forthcoming conference of the Big Three in the Crimea at Yalta was therefore of great importance for Poland. Preliminary conversations were held on Malta on 1–2 February between Eden and Stettinius, the new secretary of state. They were agreed that the London government-in-exile had no part to play in the solution of Polish problems and that any attempt to seek a fusion of it and the provisional government would be fruitless. A better solution seemed to be the creation of a new government composed of Poles at home and abroad, which in effect meant the inclusion of Mikołajczyk and moderates like Professor Stanisław Grabski. The purpose of the new government would be to hold free elections. In their discussions of the new Polish frontiers it is clear that the Americans were departing from the policy of partition proposed for Germany under the Morgenthau plan of 1944. For this reason the Western Allies were prepared to limit the expansion of Poland at the expense of Germany. Agreement was reached on the cession of East Prussia, Danzig, a small part of Pomerania and the whole of Upper Silesia, but the Americans wished to leave the question of the retention of Lwów by Poland open to discussion. In Eden's view the Western Allies need not make as large a territorial provision for the Lublin government as they would have made for Mikołajczyk. The Yalta Conference of 4–11 February had much to discuss and it was not until the third plenary session of 6 February that the Polish Question was considered. The Curzon Line was accepted as the frontier in the east and Roosevelt, though mentioning the possible inclusion of Lwów in Poland, did not press this point. No final agreement, however, was reached on the exact extent of territorial compensation in the west, except that it should be substantial. Stalin insisted on the Oder frontier and added that, of the two Neisse rivers, he had the Western or Lusatian Neisse in mind, which meant that a shorter line would be drawn and the whole city of Breslau (Wrocław) would be included in Poland. Equally troublesome was the formation of a Polish government, but on 10 February it was agreed that the present provisional government should be reorganized as the Polish Provisional Government of National Unity by the inclusion of democratic leaders from home and abroad and pledged to hold free elections as soon as possible. A commission was to be established in Moscow, consisting of Molotov and the US and British ambassadors, Averill Harriman and Sir Alexander Clark Kerr, to decide upon the composition of the new government.[1] Arciszewski's government in London denounced the Yalta agreement on 13 February 1945 as a fifth partition of Poland, but it was powerless to secure a reversal of the decision of the powers.[2] As a result of the Yalta decisions many Poles began to come to terms with the fact that the Soviet Union and the communists would be the architects of the new Poland. On 22 February the leaders of the pro-London resistance expressed their willingness to accept the Yalta decisions as the basis for discussions aimed at regulating Soviet–Polish relations and indicated their desire to come out into the open and help in organizing the Government of National Unity. The Peasant Party in particular was anxious to end underground activity and return to normal political life. Bad feeling was, however, created when, on 27–28 March, sixteen leaders of the pro-London resistance, including the delegate, the commander-in-chief, Okulicki, and members of the Council of National Unity, were trapped and arrested by the Soviet military authorities, who deported them to Moscow where they stood trial on charges of supporting an illegal organization, collaboration with the Germans and endangering Soviet security. The USSR sought to discredit the pro-London movement in Polish and world opinion and deprive it of experienced leaders at a time when the composition of the new government was being negotiated in Moscow. Many AK members were arrested by the Soviet authorities, or by the Polish security forces operating under Soviet direction. These actions placed the members of the pro-London resistance in a desperate situation and made anti-Soviet and anti-communist outbursts inevitable. In the meantime the conversations on the formation of a new Polish government were running into difficulties in Moscow owing to the Soviet insistence upon its members being acceptable to the USSR, and recognizing the Yalta agreement, which meant a promise not to revive claims to the eastern territories of 1939. At length Mikołajczyk announced his acceptance of the agreement on 15 April. The problem, nevertheless, was still acute enough for the new US president, Harry S. Truman, to speak in terms so undiplomatic to Molotov when he met him in Washington on 23 April that his language astounded his entourage. Truman insisted upon the terms of the Yalta agreement being honoured, but in view of Mikołajczyk's acceptance of it Soviet reservations had in part been overcome. Truman was considering the future course of US–Soviet relations and was determined to resist Soviet claims more resolutely than Roosevelt. On 24 April the secretary of the army, Stimson, warned Truman that an atom bomb was shortly to be exploded and the diplomacy of the future placed in a new dimension. For this reason Truman should not quarrel with the USSR for the moment, but wait until US diplomacy spoke with a stronger voice. Truman accepted this view and sought to conciliate Stalin for the moment. Harry S. Hopkins, the confidant of Roosevelt, was sent to Moscow to bring about agreement on the composition of the Polish government with Stalin. As a result of US–Soviet agreement a new government was formed on 28 June and on 5 July was recognized by the Western Powers. Of 21 ministerial appointments 16 were held by Poles who had owed allegiance to Lublin. Osóbka-Morawski remained as premier, but Mikołajczyk became deputy prime minister and minister of agriculture.

The USSR had concluded a treaty of friendship with the provisional government on 22 April which included provisions for mutual assistance and post-war co-operation, which was an indication of Stalin's determination to support a communist-dominated system in Poland, but the communists for their part had problems of their own. The liberation of Poland presented them with formidable problems of administering the country and feeding the population and at the same time of putting into effect land reform in a country devastated by war and German occupation. Poland's losses are assessed at 38 per cent of the national wealth. In 1945 grain production had dropped to 39 per cent of the 1938 figure. Malnutrition had been so widespread that there were 1.5 million cases of tuberculosis.[3] In the spring of 1945 food shortages caused strikes in several Polish cities. The trade unions strongly criticized the government, which, being preoccupied with the absorption of the German provinces, had little time for organized political activity. The PPR was itself passing through an acute crisis. Its membership had increased from 30,000 in January 1945 to 300,000 in April, which meant the infiltration of its ranks by 'undesirable and opportunist' elements which were later to be purged. Some sections of the party suffered from 'sectarian' and leftist 'infantile disorders', and were becoming 'dizzy with success'. They believed that with the help of the Red Army they would be able to transform Poland immediately into a communist state without the support of other parties. In May 1945 Gomułka complained that reactionary propaganda accusing the PPR of trying to introduce collectivization and turn Poland into the seventeenth Soviet republic owed its origin to the activities of some party members. To dispel such impressions he declared that the incorporation of Poland into the Soviet Union was desired by neither Poles nor Russians and that the PPR stood firmly on the maintenance of Poland's sovereignty and independence.[4] Some PPR leaders in fact resented the fact that they had to rely upon Soviet support to govern Poland. They were irritated by the behaviour of Soviet troops and 'advisers' which they feared might provoke a civil war in Poland. They were worried also by the fact that the security forces were becoming a state within a state and were controlled by Soviet advisers rather than the party leadership. They knew that the masses tended to dismiss them as Soviet agents and were determined to prevent the party from becoming a tool of the NKVD. They were in a dilemma. Most of them knew that without Soviet support they would not be able to remain in power, but their reliance on Soviet backing branded them in popular eyes as agents of the USSR. In May 1945 Gomułka insisted that the masses should consider the PPR as a Polish party. The party was in fact split: there were those who favoured the creation of a Poland organized on the Soviet model and subservient to the USSR, but there were others like Gomułka who believed in a 'Polish road to socialism'. This division remained concealed and was not to become serious until 1948.[5] Meanwhile, divisions were overshadowed by the problems of reconstruction and preparations for the formation of a new government.

When Mikołajczyk returned to join the government agreed upon in Moscow on 28 June, he realized that there was no sense in offering resistance to the USSR. He could not expect the Western Allies to fight the Soviet Union on the issue of the loss of eastern Poland. He thought that his presence in Poland might at least modify communist rule. There was at least the provision in The Yalta agreement for the conduct of free elections, which he was confident he could win. By emphasizing the need for the maintenance of close relations with the USSR he was hoping for some degree of non-interference in Polish internal affairs. On his return to Poland Mikołajczyk became the main hope of the non-communist parties. He enjoyed the support of most peasants as well as large sections of the intelligentsia and the former propertied classes. Although at this stage the communists behaved correctly towards the church, it nevertheless supported Mikołajczyk and his party. The political influence of the church at this juncture was not strong, but it increased rapidly in the period of stalinization.[6]

The Potsdam Conference opened on 17 July 1945. The British attitude was that the western frontier of Poland should be fixed on the Oder and should not be extended as far as the Lusatian Neisse. The British argument was related to fears of the complications attendant upon repatriation of Germans to Germany proper. Truman for his part was inclined to treat the areas occupied by the Poles as a fifth occupation zone, but Stalin rejected all arguments concerning the need to feed Germany and extract reparations which might be used against Poland advancing to the western Neisse. Stalin took as the basis of his claims the need for Poland to be able to resist German aggression in the future. After complicated discussions in which a Polish delegation headed by Bierut took part, it was agreed on 2 August to place under Polish administration German territory east of the Oder and the Lusatian Neisse, but including the town of Stettin, and East Prussia with the exception of a small belt of territory in the north assigned to the USSR in which Königsberg was situated. The final delimitation of the frontier was to await the decisions of the peace conference. The Polish government for its part committed itself to free elections as soon as possible, Mikołajczyk as a member of the Polish delegation having impressed upon Attlee and Bevin, representing Britain after the British general election of July 1945, the need to establish conditions in the country which would enable his Peasant Party to emerge victorious at the polls and thus halt the advance of communization.[7] In fact, the growing disunity of the Great Powers after Potsdam and the postponement of a final decision on the peace treaty with Germany meant that the Oder–Neisse frontier was not to receive recognition immediately. This factor was to increase the dependence of Poland upon the Soviet Union, which was certainly not the aim of Mikołajczyk.

The new Poland of 1945

As a result of the Potsdam agreement Poland was moved some 150 miles to the west. It was represented that the Poles recovered provinces which over the centuries had been lost to the Germans. In the middle ages these territories had formed part of the Poland of the Piast rulers. Now the German population was to be transferred to Germany under 'Operation Swallow', which was in effect to recognize *de facto* that the former German territories would belong to Poland.[8] On 26 July 1945 Poland came to an agreement with the USSR concerning the transfer of Poles from the Ukrainian and Byelorussian Socialist Soviet Republics, which was expanded in a further agreement of 16 August.[9] With regard to the vexed question of Trans-Olza and relations with Czechoslovakia the provisional government conducted negotiations with the Czech premier Fierlinger and the vice-premier Gottwald in Moscow in June 1945. While the Polish government did not approve the policy of Colonel Beck in 1938, it clearly thought there should be some adjustments in the Cieszyn (Teschen) area. On 10 March 1946 the Polish and Czechoslovak governments signed a treaty of amity and mutual assistance, with provision for the Cieszyn question to be solved within two years. The dispute was not solved until the agreement of 13 June 1958. Trans-Olza has remained part of Czechoslovakia, though many Poles still live in the area.

Poland was transformed by the territorial adjustments. The migration of millions of people from the east and to the western territories acquired from Germany led to the creation of a homogeneous state. Poland was to be ethnically Polish and predominantly Roman Catholic by religion. During the years between the wars over 10 million of the population had belonged to the national minorities, but they numbered now a mere 500,000. With the loss of Vilna and Lwów and the eastern provinces Poland

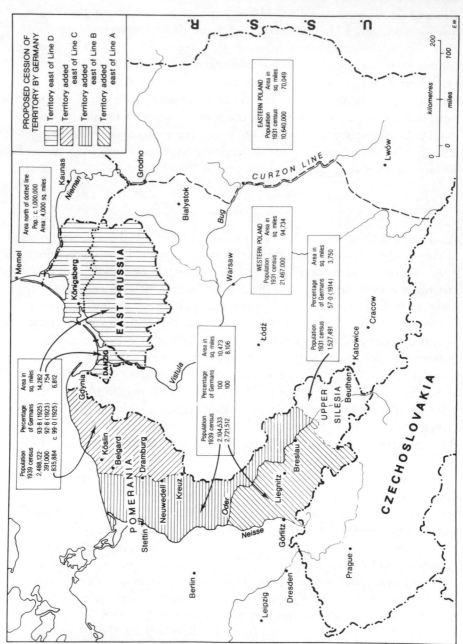

Map 5 Population changes attendant on Polish occupation in 1945

was one-fifth smaller than in 1939, her total area being reduced from 390,000 to 312,000 square kilometres, of which gains from Germany represented slightly less than one-third. Poland's population was reduced to 23.9 million, which was about one-third less than the pre-war figure. Losses as a result of Nazi atrocities were severe. There was scarcely a family which did not mourn the loss of some of its members. Nevertheless, post-war Poland was geographically more compact and potentially richer economically. The areas acquired from Germany included highly developed industrial regions rich in raw materials, concentrated mainly in Silesia, of which pre-1939 Poland possessed only a part. The well-developed agricultural regions along the river Oder were likewise a valuable acquisition. Poland's gains offered an opportunity for rapid economic modernization. One result was a rapid increase in the population. Families reunited after the separation of war were now able to produce children, but even more important was the fact that land reform and the availability of land in the western territories made earlier marriage possible for many peasants who would otherwise have delayed it. The result was a soaring birth rate. By 1955, ten years after liberation, the population had reached 27.5 million, reaching 31.4 million in 1965. Modernization and industrialization were in fact necessities if full employment were to be provided for the new generations of young Poles who would require work.

For some Poles the Potsdam agreement was an unhappy event. Poles in the west were encouraged to return to Poland, but, though all wished to return home to be reunited with their families and play their part in the reconstruction of Poland, the majority feared that they would be regarded by the communists as potential enemies and treated as suspects. Many, especially those who had been domiciled in the provinces ceded to the USSR, had no homes to which to go. The centres of their cultural life in Vilna and Lwów were no longer open to them. Though Poles in the west knew that life in exile was bound to be hard, especially for those who had no trade or profession other than the army, they chose to remain abroad rather than face the uncertainties attendant upon their return. Some thought that their stay abroad would be only temporary and that they would return at some future date once the situation was clarified. Eventually about 105,000 returned to Poland. The remainder settled in the West, mainly in Great Britain, or migrated to the USA and Canada. They have formed the hard core of the second great Polish political emigration.

Post-war political and economic problems and reforms

The new government was nominally a coalition of five parties, the PPR, PPS, the Peasant Party, the Democratic Party and the Party of Labour, but it was in practice dominated by the Communists, who controlled the key ministries of Defence, Public Security, the Western Territories, Industry and Foreign Affairs. In effect they had at their disposal a vast patronage system which gave them the power to distribute farms and jobs to the needy in return for their political support and loyalty. The powers enjoyed by the government were matched by the magnitude of the tasks which faced it. The integration of the new provinces with the old, the completion of land reform and the reconstruction of the devastated areas presented grave difficulties. The new provinces had suffered greater destruction than the old. As a result of military operations and their aftermath their productive capacity was less than 40 per cent of the pre-war level. The Soviet Union in the interim period had stripped much of the area of its industrial machinery and even its railway lines. In addition Poland faced an unprecedented upheaval in the resettlement of millions of Poles from the eastern and central provinces, who were to replace the Germans who left the country. Some 3 million Germans were expelled from Poland in the years 1945–50, but about 3.6 million had either fled, or had been evacuated by the Nazi authorities before the arrival of the Red Army in 1945. Besides the million Poles already settled in the annexed territories, millions of Polish settlers, including 1.5 million repatriated from the USSR, made their homes there.[10] Agrarian reform, initiated by the decree of the PKWN and supplemented by the decree of 18 January 1946, involved the appropriation of all farms exceeding a total of 100 hectares and in the case of arable land only over 50 hectares. This led to the distribution of 6 million hectares of land among the peasants and farm labourers and to the disappearance of the land-owning nobility and gentry. Reform in the older provinces resulted in the proliferation of non-viable smallholdings, but in the former German areas to the creation of medium-sized farms, of which 60 per cent were 5–10 hectares. About 1.5 million hectares were placed under state or collective ownership. Land reform appeased and consequently neutralized the peasantry politically in the years 1946–8. Until the middle of 1948 the PPR was opposed to collectivization. Reform produced the curious paradox of the peasants supporting Mikołajczyk in the hope that he would protect them against collectivization, while the landowners supported him in the hope of modifying the expropriations.[11]

During the years 1945–7 great efforts were made to rebuild the devastated economy and to complete the process begun in 1944 of nationalizing all large-scale and medium-sized industrial concerns. Nationalization was effected without opposition, because by 1943 all major parties had accepted it in principle. There were, however, disagreements between the PPR and the non-communists on its scope and the question of compensation. At this time the communists were insisting that Poland should follow her own road to socialism, distinct from that of the USSR, and have an economy based on three different sectors, the state, private and co-operative. The Nationalization Law of 3 January 1946 provided for the acquisition with payment of compensation of all industrial undertakings 'capable of employing more than fifty workers a shift'. The law gave sanction to the existing state of affairs, but in fact compensation was not paid to small proprietors dispossessed by it. It created the powerful state sector of industry, which by the end of 1946 employed workers producing 91.2 per cent of all goods and materials, while the private sector contributed only 8.8 per cent.[12] By 1946 the commanding heights of the economy were controlled by the state.[13]. Nevertheless, the Three-Year Plan of Economic Reconstruction introduced in 1947 emphasized once again that the economy was based on the coexistence of three sectors, the public, private and co-operative. The plan aimed at rebuilding the consumer goods industry and agriculture and raising the standard of living of the working class above the pre-war level. In fact, the plan during the course of its operation showed a considerable growth of industrial production and a rise in the standard of living by comparison with the immediate post-war years. The worst ravages of war were made good and the new provinces integrated economically with the old. Six million Poles, who had previously lived in other parts of Poland, were resettled. The rebuilding of Warsaw proceeded rapidly. The foundations of an industrial network were laid at Nowa Huta, near Cracow, indicating a willingness to industrialize areas formerly primarily agrarian in character. In June 1948 real wages of manual workers had risen above pre-war levels, although the general standard of living was still below the 1937 level. The expansion of industrial production led to a marked increase in the number of factory workers. In 1938 2,733,000 persons were employed outside agriculture, but by 1946 this figure had risen to 3.5 million. In 1938 wage-earners formed 8 per cent of the working population, but by 1948 they amounted to 14.8 per cent.[14] Poland was thus going through a period of rapid social and economic change.

It was clear, however, that Poland's stability was threatened by the continued existence of a number of anti-communist organizations unwilling and unable to come out into the open and the revitalized Polish

Peasant Party (Polskie Stronnictwo Ludowe – PSL). By 1946 the PSL had a membership of over 600,000, which was almost as many members as all other parties combined. At this stage the PPR had about 235,000 members, the PPS some 165,000 and the communist-inspired peasant party, 'Voice of the People' (Wola Ludu), 280,000. Indeed, the communists were concerned about the growing strength of the PSL and determined to oppose it by all means short of terror. They managed to prevent the total collapse of their own 'Wola Ludu' and maintain their influence over the socialists. Furthermore, they were determined not to allow the formation of other political parties. For this reason they refused to legalize the existence of the National Democrat party,. which was compelled to remain underground. The PPR was losing ground in the villages and its hold over other parties was diminishing. The PPR leaders were concerned about the possibility of a united front of the PPS and the PSL. In order to win the support of the workers for their policies the PPR sought a merger with the PPS. At the same time the PPR was undergoing its own crisis. Its membership fell in the summer of 1945 with the formation of the Polish Government of National Unity and the return of Mikołajczyk.[15] Between April and December 1945 it fell to as low as 65,000. This decline was attributed to the purge of unreliable elements and the return of previous peasant and socialist party members to their old allegiances. In fact, it was due mainly to the anti-communist propaganda campaign carried out by the PPR's political opponents and the terror of the wartime resistance movement which still remained in existence.[16] The liquidation of the AK was long and complicated because some units had still not received Okulicki's order disbanding them, while others decided to ignore it. The anti-communist organization, 'Nie', failed to materialize and its leader, General Emil Fieldorf, 'Nil', was arrested by the Soviet authorities in February 1945. In May 1945 Colonel Jan Rzepecki informed his superiors in London that 'Nie' had ceased to function altogether. From now on only the so-called Delegatura of the armed forces under Colonel Rzepecki existed. Rzepecki intended to dissolve the remaining armed units and conduct his anti-communist struggle mainly by political means. The Delegatura disbanded on 6 August, four days after a declaration of an amnesty by the government, of which 42,000 people took advantage. After the dissolution of the Delegatura, Rzepecki began to organize a new group under the name of the Freedom and Independence Group (Zrzeszenie Wolność i Niezawisłość – WIN), which was to act as an underground political party. WIN was not opposed to the social and economic reforms introduced by the communists, but it called for the holding of free elections under the supervision of the Great Powers. WIN condemned the terrorist activities of ultra-right-wing resistance groups, as well as those of the communist-controlled security forces. The object of Rzepecki was to force the communists to hold free elections and then negotiate from a position of strength, but at the end of 1945 the original leadership of WIN, including Rzepecki, was broken up by the security forces. After Rzepecki's arrest Colonel Niepokólczycki took command of the remnants of WIN, placing himself at the disposal of the government-in-exile. He sought also to establish contact with the British and American ambassador in Warsaw in order to induce their governments to intervene in Polish affairs. In the autumn of 1946, however, Niepokólczycki and his staff were arrested.[17] Communist sources were to claim that 158 armed underground units with a total strength of 25,000 men operated in Poland after the amnesty of August 1945.[18] The PPR tried to connect these units with the PSL, which it accused of helping the terrorists and thereby fomenting civil war in Poland. To what extent these accusations were true it is difficult to say. It seems that the relations between the resistance groups and Mikołajczyk and his party were more complex than the communists suggested and, indeed, were often marked by mutual suspicion rather than the co-operation suggested in PPR propaganda. The fact remains, however, that in the second half of 1945 there were still several thousand men in hiding in the forests. Some of them had originally belonged to the disbanded AK, but the majority of them were members of the near-fascist NSZ which never belonged to the AK. There were also large bands of criminals, deserters, marauders and the Ukrainian partisans of the Ukrainian Insurrectionary Army. These miscellaneous groups were often lumped together with the AK and PSL. Undoubtedly the activities of these disparate and desperate groups were directed against the communists and the security forces,[19] but, as one leading communist put it, the civil war in Poland was conducted at the 'county level'. Indeed, it is surprising that not a single senior officer on either side was killed or wounded during the course of operations, with the exception of General Karol Świerczewski, the deputy minister of national defence, who died at the hands of Ukrainian partisans at Bialigród in the foothills of the Carpathians in the province of Rzeszów on 28 March 1947. The existence of terrorists was convenient for the communists, because it gave them a good reason to strengthen the security forces and to postpone holding elections until they had tightened their hold on the country.

The elections of January 1947 and Mikołajczyk's escape to the West

In spite of their attack upon the PSL the communists were ready to co-operate and form an electoral bloc with it. It was the strength of the PSL which prompted them to try to persuade Mikołajczyk to enter into an electoral arrangement with them by offering him 20 per cent of the seats in the future sejm. In reply the PSL demanded the fulfilment of the Moscow agreement of 1945, under which the PSL was to receive one-third of all cabinet posts and parliamentary seats, together with the abolition of the ministries of Public Security, Propaganda and Food. The PSL asked for 75 per cent of all seats for representatives of the peasants on the grounds that they formed the overwhelming majority of the nation. The communists were prepared to offer the PSL and the Wola Ludu about 200 seats out of 444. Mikołajczyk's refusal to join the 'democratic bloc' composed of the PPR, PPS, the Wola Ludu and the Democratic Party was the signal for a campaign of intimidation against the PSL. The PSL was accused of associating with terrorists, fomenting industrial strife, calling upon the peasants to stop compulsory deliveries of foodstuffs and by so doing spreading famine and unemployment. PSL members were intimidated, the circulation of the PSL press restricted, local government officials belonging to the PSL dismissed and PSL members of the cabinet increasingly ignored. In view of administrative pressure, Mikołajczyk demanded that the elections should be held in July. For its part the 'democratic bloc' proposed conducting a referendum in June to approve or reject the incorporation of the new provinces, land reform, the nationalization of industry and the abolition of the senate as proposed originally by the KRN. The communists believed that in putting these basic questions they could achieve considerable majorities regardless of political affiliations. Mikołajczyk decided that the PSL should vote against the abolition of the senate as a sign of its independence from and opposition to the PPR, but this decision split the PSL. A left-wing group under Tadeusz Rek decided to vote with the communists and was expelled from the PSL. This group set itself up as the PSL–New Liberation, but it failed to attract much support among the peasants. The situation of the PSL was nevertheless critical. The referendum resulted in a victory for the communist bloc, although considerable administrative pressure and even terror was used by the PPR to secure it. The communists realized that they would be faced by a powerful opponent in the forthcoming elections.[20] Simultaneously many of the PPS leaders, including Osóbka-Morawski, started a new campaign for an understanding with the PSL, offering it 25–40 per cent of the parliamentary seats, if the PSL would agree to join the bloc.

Many of the socialists believed that failure to create a common 'democratic bloc' would lead to the establishment of one-party rule. Feeling against the PPR was growing in the PPS. A majority of the socialists wished the PPS to become with the aid of the PSL the leading force, maintaining that their party was well fitted for such a role, as the most radical and 'patriotic' force in the country, independent of foreign connections and pledged to uphold Poland's sovereignty and represent Polish *raison d'état*. Moreover, they demanded from the PPR 50 per cent of all posts in the state and economic administration and the security and police forces. The pro-PPR minority among the socialists considered these demands unrealistic and irresponsible.[21] The opposition of the PPS to the PPR caused great alarm among the communists, who knew that they had been successful only because they had so far been able to prevent the formation of a common front between the socialists and peasants. Mikołajczyk suggested that a united electoral bloc should be formed in eastern and western Poland, mainly for the sake of appearances. Free elections should be held in central Poland on the condition that the three independent parties, the Polish Peasant Party (PSL), the PPS and Party of Labour, received 51 per cent of all seats. This solution, Mikołajczyk believed would allow the PPR to have more seats in the sejm than if truly free elections were held. It would at least safeguard the principle of free elections in part of the country. The condition that the majority of seats should be given to the Polish Peasant Party, PPS and the Party of Labour would provide some guarantee that the agreement would be respected. Whether this proposal was seriously considered by the PPS is impossible to say. In any case Mikołajczyk announced in October that the PSL would not join in an electoral bloc.[22] For their part the PPR and the PPS signed a 'unity of action' pact on 28 November 1946 and were joined by two other parties, the Wola Ludu and the Democratic Party (Stronnictwo Demokratyczne – SD). The PSL–New Liberation and Party of Labour were left outside the bloc. Thus the political forces were realigned and the PPR renewed its attack on the PSL. The communists sought to underline the links between the terrorists and the PSL by arresting its leaders together with leaders of the resistance, with whom many local PSL organizations were accused of co-operating.

The new electoral law was passed in September 1946. Although in principle it was highly democratic, it left the authorities scope for manipulation and was designed to diminish any potential support for the PSL. During the election campaign about a million voters were disfranchised and in 10 out of 52 electoral districts the PSL candidates were struck off the ballot lists. These ten districts, containing about a quarter of the total population amounting to 5,342,000 out of about 24,000,000, were

mainly areas in which the PSL influence was strong. In addition thousands
of PSL members were arrested, including 142 candidates, while troops
were used to assist the PPR campaign. The counting of votes was equally
irregular. The PPR was helped to win the elections by statements made
by Western politicians that Poland's right to the new provinces was
questionable. On 16 September the US secretary of state, Byrnes, declared
at Stuttgart that the Oder–Neisse Line was not the permanent frontier
between Poland and Germany. This statement was badly received in
Poland and had repercussions for the PSL, which was generally considered
to be the pro-Western party. The PSL counter-attacked as best it could.
It secured some support from the Catholic church, which in October urged
the faithful to vote against the communists. In its electoral propaganda
the PSL warned against the forthcoming collectivization and condemned
the continuation of police terror. It demanded the restoration of civil
liberties, but it was careful to stress its good will towards the USSR.

Voting took place on 17 January 1947. The official results gave the
'democratic bloc' over 80.1 per cent of the votes and the PSL only 10.3
per cent. When the seats were allocated the 'democratic bloc' received 394
out of 444 and the PSL only 28. This decisive defeat meant the end of
the PSL's role as an effective opposition party in Poland.[23] The sejm met
on 4 February 1947 and on the next day Bierut, who had been head of
state under the provisional government, was elected president of the
Republic. On 19 February the sejm enacted a new constitutional law, the
so-called 'Little Constitution', which defined the powers of the sejm, the
government, the president and the newly created Council of State. The
sejm was to be the sole legislative body, but when it was not in session
the government could issue decrees with the force of law, which required
the approval of the Council of State and the subsequent endorsement of
the sejm when it reassembled. The Council of State, a small executive body
presided over by the president, was charged with the task of supervising
local national councils which in turn would supervise the organs of the
local administration. On 20 February Bierut appointed Józef Cyrankiewicz
prime minister in succession to Osóbka-Morawski who had lost favour
because of his attempts to establish closer co-operation with the PSL in
the period after the referendum. The new government, which ceased to
use the title of 'provisional', was even more closely controlled by the PPR
than its predecessor, Mikołajczyk and the other PSL ministers being
excluded from it. Its leading figures, moreover, belonged to the politburo
of the PPR. Among them Gomułka acted as deputy premier and minister
of the regained territories. Jakób Berman, the under-secretary of state in
the prime minister's office and *eminence grise* of the régime, exercised a

leading role in ideological matters, foreign affairs and security. Hilary Minc, minister of industry, controlled economic affairs, while Stanisław Radkiewicz, minister of public security, exercised a strict control over public order. On 22 February the government announced a fresh amnesty for the members of the resistance, of which 52,965 people took advantage. About 25,000 persons were released from prison. The amnesty led to the final liquidation of the anti-communist resistance and put an end to the conditions of civil war, during which about 30,000 Poles and 1,000 Soviet soldiers lost their lives, the Red Army having sometimes been used to suppress armed opposition.[24]

The electoral defeat of the PSL caused an immediate crisis within its ranks. By the summer of 1947 the PSL was reduced to a small and insignificant group of deputies still loyal to Mikołajczyk. The great popular support of the previous year had vanished as a result of the loss of confidence in the party and its leader, who had proved powerless to prevent the communists from becoming the dominant force in Poland. Thus in the first half of 1947 the communists eliminated from the political arena two of their main adversaries, the PSL and the resistance. In October 1947 Mikołajczyk, realizing that he and his movement were a spent force, escaped from Poland.[25]

The Gomułka affair

Gomułka was a communist who tried to remain loyal to Moscow, as the centre of the communist movement, but combined with this loyalty was a conviction that the independence of Poland was a 'supreme consideration', to which all others should be subordinated. He always stressed that close Soviet–Polish co-operation was essential to Poland's existence, but he rejected the idea that she should become a replica of the USSR, believing that the Poles should pursue their own road to socialism, because the application of Soviet methods without taking into account the sensitive feelings of the Polish people and peculiarities of the country's economic structure would produce disastrous results and consequently weaken the position of his own party.[26] He fought remorselessly against the narrowly nationalistic 'forces of reaction' which he blamed for Poland's defeat in the war, but he himself sought to convince his fellow countrymen that the PPR was not a Soviet agency, for which reason they should regard it as a national party. He knew that without Soviet support it would be impossible for the PPR in the meantime to govern the country, but he wished to make it less obvious and even in the long run to dispense with it in view of the Poles' anti-Soviet feelings. His attitude towards Stalin was coloured by the dissolution of the KPP and the purge of its leadership.

The Nazi–Soviet pact of 1939 showed that Stalin was guided by his own *raison d'état* in questions of international policy. The collectivization of agriculture in the USSR did not offer a pattern for Poland, where there was a strong concept of individual land tenure as opposed to the collective concepts inherited from the system of repartitional tenure which had existed in Muscovy proper. He was critical of the KPP, which he considered to have been dogmatic and sectarian. Its lukewarm attitude to Poland's independence, derived from the doctrines of Rosa Luxemburg, had prevented it from becoming a major force in the country. He maintained that the PPS had a better record on this score than the KPP. Thus he argued that the PPR must prove that it was a political party free from the shortcomings of the KPP, but able to pursue a revolutionary policy as well as acting in the best national interests of Poland.

In the years 1944–7 Gomułka had a chance to pursue his policies, while Stalin was prepared to leave East European communists with considerable freedom of action internally. In 1947 the international situation changed. In March 1947 the Truman Doctrine showed that the USA, precisely at a moment when the Council of Foreign Ministers was conferring in Moscow, was preparing to offer stronger resistance to Soviet policies. The Marshall Plan of June 1947, designed to promote European economic recovery (which the USA never intended to extend to the USSR, though a formal invitation was issued to the Soviet Union to discuss it), seemed a mere extension of the Truman Doctrine. Poland and Czechoslovakia would have accepted American aid, but they were quickly brought to heel. In September–October the USSR set up the Communist Information Bureau, the Cominform, as an instrument of Soviet foreign policy. Its theory was that the world was divided into two camps, the capitalist and the socialist, and that countries belonged to one or the other. The existence of Cominform implied that there should be a rigid discipline within the countries of the Soviet bloc, which in effect meant the acceptance of Soviet methods. Gomułka stood by his concept of the Polish road to socialism.[27] He refused to accept the concept of collectivization of agriculture as having a universal application. He thus adopted an attitude of defiance of Stalin, whose supporters within the PPR began to consider Gomułka as unreliable and guilty of nationalist deviation when communist solidarity was required. Opposition to Stalin was soon to appear in Yugoslavia, where Tito was in a much better position to offer resistance, having a popular movement of some strength behind him.[28] On 3 June 1948, when the Soviet–Yugoslav dispute was coming to a head, Gomułka once again told his party to cultivate and cherish the best Polish patriotic traditions and follow the socialist road to independence. He warned the PPR that abstract revolutionary ideas and a dogmatic approach to Marxism would fail to produce a marxist revolution.[29] The meaning of his address was clear. To gain the support of the masses the party must reject sectarian solutions, even though the USSR was the best guarantor of Poland's existence in the face of international dangers.[30]

Gomułka failed to carry the PPR leadership with him. His earlier efforts to co-operate with other parties were denounced. He was accused of accepting the heretical doctrines of Tito and even of entertaining dictatorial ambitions.[31] On 3 September Gomułka was dismissed from his post as secretary of the PPR and replaced by Bierut. These developments marked the beginning of a new era in Poland's post-war history, leading to stalinization and the ascendancy of the 'Muscovites' in the PPR. On 4 September 1947 collectivization of agriculture was announced, and a purge followed of the 'nationalists' in the party who had resented Stalin's interference and tried to make the party more independent of Moscow. Gomułka and his followers had committed the cardir ι sin of refusing to place the interests of the USSR before those of Po.and.

The formation of the Polish United Workers' Party (Polska Zjednoczona Partia Robotnicza – PZPR)

After the defeat of the PSL in 1946–7, the absorption of the still independent PPS became a major objective of the PPR. The merger followed a long communist campaign calling for 'unity of action' between the two parties as the first step towards 'organic unity' of the whole working class. The communists used many devices to secure their ends. They tried to prevent a united front between the peasants and the PPS and sought to inspire a belief in socialists that the only alternative to their co-operation with the PPR was the return of the reactionary forces to power. They were not above using the tactics of intimidation. In the summer of 1947 they staged a number of show-trials of right-wing socialists. The charges, normally of espionage and subversion, served as warnings to the socialist leaders that refusal to collaborate with the PPR might be equated with treason.

Questions of co-operation and eventual unification were hotly discussed in the press of both parties.[32] As a result relations between the PPR and PPS became tense. Not long before the elections representatives of both parties had been called to Moscow in November 1946 and induced to sign an agreement to set up a united front, which stated that, although the two organizations were independent of one another, they would co-operate to imbue their members with the spirit of working-class unity and combat the anti-Soviet tendencies and activities of right-wing socialists. They undertook to support the security forces in their attempts to establish law and order and to work against the PSL. After the elections of January 1947 the communists intensified their campaign for amalgamation. On 1 May Gomułka called for unification, but the socialists received his plea badly, rejecting it as premature and accusing the communists of trying to turn Poland into a one-party state. The communists dismissed this charge, maintaining that they merely sought ideological unity. Only skilful manoeuvring within the PPS by Cyrankiewicz and Karol Rusinek prevented serious recriminations. On 26 July the PPR and PPS leaders decided to purge the 'reactionary' and 'hostile' elements in their parties and compose their mutual differences. The PPS leaders in fact called for a speedy merger and carried out a purge of 'rightist deviationists'. In March 1948 Cyrankiewicz, after a visit to Moscow, declared the readiness of the PPS to effect a union, which it was believed would take place in June 1948, but the Yugoslav dispute intervened and unification was delayed until December. In the meantime 'nationalist' and 'right-wing' deviationists were purged from the PPR and the PPS. It is probable that Stalin feared that the Gomułka group in the PPR would join forces with like-minded members of the PPS in their insistence upon upholding Polish national interests.

The formal union between the communists and the socialists took place in Warsaw on 15 December 1948. The Polish United Workers' Party was created, of which Bierut became the leader and the communists the dominant force. For all intents and purposes Poland became a one-party state.[33] Poland entered upon a new period of its history. The process of stalinization of which Gomułka was subsequently to complain in October 1956 was to discredit the rulers of Poland in the eyes of their compatriots.[34]

The rise and ebb of stalinism

The first years of communist rule in Poland differed in important respects from the subsequent period. The power of the PPR, backed by an efficient political organization controlling the apparatus of government, including the security police and the army, and backed ultimately by the might of the Soviet army stationed to the east and west of Poland, was overwhelming. The Party was not yet the only organized political force, nor did it control society completely. Mikołajczyk's PSL, before its collapse in 1947, and the PPS, despite its name not a continuation of the pre-war Polish Socialist Party but a new pro-communist organization, exercised considerable influence. Industry was mostly state-owned, but private enterprise in trade, handicrafts, the services and, above all, peasant farming still played an essential role in the economy. In education, art and intellectual life the communists and their sympathizers were a minority incapable of changing the character of the national culture according to a predetermined marxist pattern. The Party's rule was superimposed on a society still shaped largely by its non-communist past. While the grip of the Party steadily tightened in the first four years, it was not yet all-powerful. The concept of 'the Polish road to socialism', which the PPR officially accepted until the fall of Gomułka, implied that traditional outlooks might be tolerated for some time at least. This situation depended upon the attitude of the USSR. Up to 1948 Stalin was ready to accept something short of Soviet-type communism on his doorstep for various reasons. Perhaps he did not wish to antagonize the West while the German problem remained unsolved, but once the Cold War had begun he had nothing to gain by delaying the sovietization of Eastern Europe. The elimination of all independent political forces outside, and unreliable leaders within, the East European communist parties was the first stage. As the international situation worsened other developments took place.

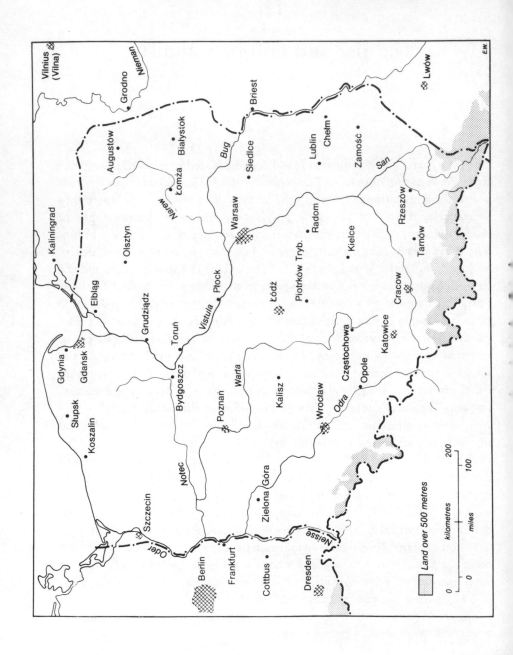

The turning point of 1949

The congress which created the Polish United Workers' Party in December 1948, and suppressed the last independent political force in Poland, took place in the first phase of stalinization. In the period of tension resulting from the imposition in 1948 of a blockade on Berlin by the USSR in response to the Western Allies' project of currency reform in Germany, which was relaxed only in 1949 in the hope of delaying the creation of the Federal Republic of Germany, the leadership of the PZPR sought to make the new party more stalinist in character. A meeting of the Central Committee in April 1949 ordered a new purge aimed at reducing the influence of former PPS members in the lower levels of the party. The party shrank by 100,000 members during 1949. Because almost a quarter of its 1,367,000 members now held responsible office, it became more elitist in character.[1] The aim of the purge was also to eliminate inactive members, especially in the countryside, who had been recruited in the years of competition with other parties to increase left-wing party membership.

The next stage was the purge of the trade unions, in which the PPS influence had always been strong. Socialists were weeded out in the course of selecting delegates to the trade-union congress summoned for 1 June 1949. Alexander Zawadzki bluntly told the congress that the traditional role of unions as defenders of workers' interests ceased to exist in a people's democracy controlled by the working class. Their function was now to mobilize their members in an effort to increase production, upon which economic progress and their own standard of living depended.[2] A new trade-union structure was adopted and wide powers vested in the Central Council of Trade Unions (Centralna Rada Związków Zawodowych – CRZZ). A law passed by the sejm on 1 July 1949 gave them an official standing as independent institutions enjoying many privileges, but in practice they were bureaucratized and subordinated completely to the PZPR. They thus lost their important function of protecting their members' standard of living. The CRZZ's first chairman was Zawadzki himself, but in 1950 he was succeeded by Wiktor Kłosiewicz, a hard-line stalinist, who remained in office until 1956. Another ruthless purge followed. Only 18.5 per cent of the old members of district trade-union committees and 13 per cent of those on provincial committees were re-elected after the congress.[3] The purge was so thorough that the Party leadership and the government had no trouble with the unions after the autumn of 1950 when the industrialization policy got under way.

The new structure and role of the trade-union movement were copied from the Soviet Union. Trade unionists and delegations of Poles from all walks of life, from peasants to poets, went to the Soviet Union during 1949 to study 'Soviet experience'. Festivals of Soviet arts and films, competitions for the best translations from the Russian, exhibitions of Soviet architecture, and other events occurred every month. The PZPR Ideological Declaration of December 1948 had laid down that there was only one way of building socialism. The Party leadership now submitted the country to a crash course in Soviet socialism. Continuous manifestations of gratitude to the Soviet Union and its leadership were staged. The country celebrated Stalin's seventieth birthday on 21 December 1949 as if it were a national holiday. A special train loaded with gifts was despatched to Moscow. Such servile manifestations of admiration for the USSR and Stalin were, however, not enough as the international situation worsened in the autumn.

On 7 September 1949 the German Federal Republic came into existence. On 7 October the Soviet zone of occupation was converted into the German Democratic Republic. After Otto Grotewohl, premier of the GDR provisional government, had declared its acceptance of the Potsdam agreements and the Oder–Neisse line, Poland recognized it on 18 October. The frontier of the two countries was recognized by the treaty signed on 6 July 1950 at the border town of Zgorzelec. It was declared to be a major step towards the security of the Polish western and northern territories, but a treaty with a country without general international recognition was of questionable value. Because the Federal Republic of Germany was declared by the Western Powers to be the only legally constituted government in Germany, only its recognition of the western frontier of Poland could have any validity. The creation of the Federal Republic of Germany, however, cemented the connection between Poland and the USSR. The Bonn government insisted on the legality of the 1937 frontiers of Germany and claimed to represent the whole of Germany. It persisted in referring to the GDR as 'the Soviet zone of occupation' and to the territories to the east of it as being 'under Polish administration'. The so-called Hallstein doctrine laid down the principle that any country which recognized the GDR could not have diplomatic relations with the Federal Republic. In such a situation the Soviet Union could justify the maintenance of forces in Eastern Germany and bases along Poland's western frontier. From the Polish point of view only Soviet military assistance could protect Poland from German revanchism. Poland was unique among all the countries of the Soviet bloc in depending upon the USSR for her survival.

The implications of developments in Western Germany became apparent on 6 November 1949 when Bierut announced that the Soviet Union 'at his request' had placed Marshal Konstantin Rokossovsky at the disposal of the Polish government.[4] Rokossovsky, a Pole by origin, but long domiciled in Russia, was a Soviet commander of a great distinction, but, when he was made a marshal of Poland, minister of defence, deputy chairman of the Council of Ministers and a member of the PZPR politburo, he inevitably became a symbol of Soviet domination and was even regarded by some as the real ruler of Poland. There is no evidence that Rokossovsky was cast in that role by Stalin or had personal political ambitions. He confined himself to military affairs and did not interfere in other matters. It is probable that he found his position in Poland uncongenial.[5] Nevertheless, his appointment marked a change in Polish–Soviet relations amounting to open intervention by the Soviet Union in Poland's domestic affairs.

Rokossovsky began to reorganize and modernize the Polish army. His first task was to create a new officer corps, technically competent and politically reliable, which could staff a new and enlarged army. Eighteen per cent of Polish army officers in 1949 were still pre-war professionals.[6] They were now dismissed and replaced or supplemented by Soviet officers, usually with Polish or Polish-sounding names like Korczyc, Popławski or Kieniewicz, who held all the higher appointments. At the same time efforts were made to train a Polish officer corps in Soviet and Polish military academies. In order to safeguard political loyalty almost 90 per cent of the younger officers were selected from the sons of workers and peasants.[7] Compulsory national service was introduced on 4 February 1950, but until 1952 the Polish army was only a cadre. It was expanded quickly only after the Federal Republic of Germany was allowed to raise an army. By 1953 the Polish armed forces, including security troops, may have amounted to 650,000 men.[8] The Polish army was by far the largest in the countries of the Soviet bloc and could mobilize forty divisions. The navy was of no great significance, but the air force grew steadily. The bulk of the army consisted of motorized infantry, well supported by tanks and artillery. Equipment, training and organization were based upon the Soviet model with even uniforms similar to those of the Soviet army. This modernized army placed heavy demands upon the Polish budget and required investment in an armaments industry.[9] To supervise the needs of the armed forces General Piotr Jaroszewicz, a former political officer of the Kościuszko Division, was made the military vice-chairman of the Planning Commission, from which relatively modest position he was to rise to become prime minister in 1970.

Conscription gave an opportunity to make up for ideological short-comings in the schools. Recruits were inculcated with an enthusiasm for the socialist system and instilled with sympathy for the USSR as Poland's friend and patron of all oppressed, democratic and peace-loving people in the world. Propaganda and indoctrination were assigned to an expanded political section, headed by Edward Ochab, after Spychalski's dismissal, then by Naszkowski and from October 1951 by Witaszewski. Political education, however, was not considered a sufficient means of ensuring the loyalty of the officer corps. The so-called Military Information, responsible for intelligence and security, became virtually an extension of the corresponding Soviet institution, and operated independently of the civil authorities, conducting purges within the army, arresting and trying civilians before military courts for espionage and diversion. At one time it seemed to have terrorized even the upper ranks of the PZPR.[10] Its most spectacular achievement was the show trial in July–August 1951 of Generals Tatar, Kirchmayer, Mossor, Herman and other high-ranking officers who had served in the West on charges of being British spies, for which they received sentences of life imprisonment. Even more sinister was the secret trial and execution of nineteen less senior officers at about the same time. Prominent communists who had fought in the Spanish Civil War, like General Komar, were imprisoned, while many others were summarily dismissed. For practical purposes the Polish armed forces became part of the Soviet army and were virtually outside the control of even the PZPR politburo. They were thus the most obvious sign of Poland's subordination to the USSR.

The Party and the state

November 1949 was no less a turning point for the PZPR and for Poland itself. The Third Plenum of the Central Committee, which met from 11 to 13 November, was concerned with the political sins of Gomułka before 1948. In his opening address Bierut recalled Stalin's theory that capitalist circles always sought to destroy proletarian parties and régimes from within by trying to infiltrate them with secret agents and provocateurs. Gomułka as secretary general of the PPR was said to have shown an inexcusably cavalier attitude to these dangers. By his concept of a wide mass party he was alleged to have encouraged the influx of actual and potential agents or at least of anti-communist and anti-Soviet elements. Bierut declared that Gomułka's proposal for a merger of the PPR and PPS upon the basis of equality and his rightist–nationalist concept of 'a Polish road to socialism' played into the enemy's hands. Therefore he called for an inquiry into the past of all men in responsible positions, for a purge of unreliable elements from the PZPR, for recruitment to the Party from among the workers and peasants, and for constant vigilance of Party members against the class enemies in their midst.[11] Gomułka, Spychalski and Kliszko were expelled from the Central Committee and deprived of the right to hold posts of authority in the Party. Their treatment was unfair, because the harmful recruitment for which they were condemned had been the official line of the Party. Their punishment was, nevertheless, mild by comparison with that meted out to communist leaders in other people's democracies, who were put on trial and executed for similar political crimes.[12] Spychalski and Gomułka were in due course arrested in 1951. Material for their trial was prepared by the security service, but neither they nor other deviationists were brought to trial. Other wartime associates of Gomułka were not even arrested.

The call for vigilance, nevertheless, did have far-reaching effects. The third massive purge of the Party since the autumn of 1948 now began. In two years the membership of the PZPR, including candidate members, fell from 1,301,000 to 1,138,000, although 100,000 new members were admitted during the same period. This 'permanent purge' was halted in December 1951 by a decision of the Central Committee, which called for a more careful examination of each case and ordered a new recruiting drive. It was afterwards admitted that the purges had lost the Party the services of many able and dedicated men and lowered the quality of the leading personnel.[13] Despite emphasis on the 'correct' past and social origins in recruitment there was a deterioration in the social composition of the Party. Ordinary workers and peasants left the Party faster than new recruits from these classes could be enrolled, but the percentage of white-collar workers, mainly officials, rose steadily. In 1950 there were 30,000 full-time Party officials, whose numbers continued to rise steadily. By 1953 the state and other officials in the PZPR accounted for almost 40 per cent of the membership. The continual bureaucratization of state and Party life by replacing unpaid activists with full-time officials meant frequently that a Party card was little more than a ticket of admission to an administrative career. The small number of workers and peasants joining the Party was due to the intense unpopularity of its economic policies and general disillusion with the way in which socialism was being built in Poland.

The purge did not stop at the Party. The army, central and local administration, industrial and other economic enterprises, and co-operative and social organizations lost thousands of competent men because their background aroused suspicion as to their loyalty. Gentry, bourgeois or prosperous peasant origin was fatal. Anybody connected with the pre-war régime, one of the pre-war parties, the London government-in-exile or the pro-'London' underground was automatically disqualified. Family ties with someone who had once offended the Party or lived in the West were often enough to disqualify a man from holding a responsible position, but those purged were usually allowed to earn a living in a menial job. Many places were filled by Party activists who had no formal qualifications for them. In May 1950 Bierut boasted of the appointment of 17,000 workers as factory directors and called for workers to be appointed to even more responsible posts in industry.[14]

The loss of so many competent and honest people was harmful and unnecessary. They were already closely supervised and could be dismissed if they tried to oppose the new tough policies now being adopted in all areas. A more rational policy would have been to retain their services until fresh cadres of properly qualified young men, either communists or at least not anti-communist, were ready to take over. This had been the Party's policy before the fall of Gomułka. The speed in rebuilding the administration, the settlement of the former German territories and the economic recovery under the Three Year Plan was largely due to this liberal policy. Gomułka's successors might have continued this policy on grounds of expediency in spite of strong 'sectarian' sentiments in the PZPR *aktiv*, who welcomed the post-1949 purge for ideological reasons. The crucial decision was in fact taken in Moscow. No doubt it was due in part to Stalin's suspiciousness,[15] but he was moved more by Soviet *raison d'état* than by consideration for the long-term interest of communism in Poland. It semed dangerous in a country as vital to Soviet security as Poland to leave in important posts non-communists, who in the event of war with the West might become a 'fifth column'. For this reason harsh treatment was meted out to former members of the Home Army, who with their experience in the resistance might perhaps be tempted to organize an anti-Soviet underground working for the Western powers. Not only were they hounded out of their jobs, but were also vilified by the PZPR propaganda apparatus for 'fascism', collaboration with the Gestapo and other alleged crimes during and after the war. The campaign against them alienated from the régime hundreds of thousands of people by its virulence and injustice.

The campaign of 'vigilance' and the theory that the capitalist world sought to subvert communist systems from within led to a vast increase in the size and activity of the security police after November 1949. It was an organization of full-time professionals skilled in uncovering spies and saboteurs. There is no evidence that espionage or subversion increased in Poland after 1949. The cases brought to light by the security police were based upon fabricated evidence or confessions extracted by torture. When once the security police were expanded they acquired a vested interest in magnifying dangers to the system in order to enhance their own role and influence. After 1950 there were indeed domestic reasons for increasing the security police. As the Six Year Plan began to erode living standards and pressure on the peasants was intensified, discontent with the system and dislike of its policies rose sharply. Recourse was had to terror to prevent open manifestation of discontent and discourage passive resistance. Because neither 'vigilance' nor terror could be carried out by the Party, the importance of the security police in relation to the Party was greatly increased. In a sense the police rather than the Party became the backbone of the régime. For its part the Party was downgraded and relegated to less important functions.

Nominally the security police was part of the Ministry of Public Security, which was an agglomeration of the ordinary police, prison administration, frontier, railway and factory guards, as well as the Security Office proper (Urząd Bezpieczeństwa – UB). The head of the UB and the minister of public security, Stanisław Radkiewicz, was a member of the politburo and a number of his subordinates were also in the Central Committee which was a reflection of their importance in the political system. The UB underwent a huge expansion between 1947 and 1950, building up a large territorial apparatus of provincial and district offices controlled from Warsaw.[16] A network of secret agents, often disguised as 'personnel officers' in factories and offices, was constructed, supplemented by a large number of unpaid informers recruited by blackmail or ideological appeal. The scope of UB operations expanded continually as such terms as 'public security', 'sabotage' and 'hostility to the people's régime' were interpreted more widely.

The power of the UB was further strengthened in January 1952 by the creation of a special Tenth Department whose Soviet adviser acted as a link with the Soviet security apparatus headed by Beria. The existence of the department was disguised from all but a few politburo members and the Ministry of Public Security. While the other UB departments covered all sections of the population regarded as potentially dangerous to the socialist system, the Tenth Department extended its activity to the PZPR itself, including the top Party and government leaders, with the exception of Bierut and Rokossovsky.[17] It was the Tenth Department which arrested Gomułka and Spychalski and was preparing their trial. It watched all elements in the Party considered not wholly reliable, like the PPR members who had served in the underground, members of the People's Army, veterans of the Spanish Civil War, communists who had lived in the West and former members of the PPS. Incriminating material for possible future use was collected, but few important Party members had been arrested by 1953. The Tenth Department, being beyond the control of the PZPR leadership, made the UB as a whole a state within a state.[18] Only the army with its own security and intelligence was immune from its attention.

In the new political climate after 1949 there seemed little place for parties supposed to represent the peasantry and independent urban artisans and craftsment. Nevertheless, they were retained, though reduced to two by amalgamations. The United Peasant Party (Zjednoczone Stronnictwo Ludowe – ZSL) was established by the Peasant Movement Unity Congress of 27–29 November 1949. It was dominated by the SL which had supported the communists faithfully since 1944. The rump of the former PSL led by Mikołajczyk supplied only one-tenth of its members. The other party which survived was the Democratic Party (Stronnictwo Demokratyczne – SD), which after an internal conflict reorganized itself at a congress in September–October 1949. The SD absorbed the small Christian Democratic SP (Party of Labour), which dissolved itself in July 1950. The latter's role of representing progressive Christians had by then been taken over by the Catholic social association PAX (Stowarzyszenie PAX). Internal purges eliminated the more independent-minded party leaders, officials and members. Their revised programmes committed them to the building of socialism in Poland under PZPR leadership. This meant ZSL support for collectivization and SD support for craft co-operatives, both of them highly unpopular. Not surprisingly their membership shrank, although in 1950 craftsmen temporarily flocked into the SD in large numbers in the hope of escaping harassment. The extra-parliamentary activity of both parties declined, the SD retaining only a skeleton organization, while their newspapers and publications were cut down in number and circulation. Their share of posts in the central government virtually vanished. Their deputies in the sejm and the people's councils voted unanimously with the PZPR deputies, and on other matters carried out the Party's instructions.[19] They had no political influence whatever in the system and merely served to keep up the fiction of a national front. The decision to retain in Poland, as elsewhere in East Europe, the semblance of a multi-party system must have been taken in Moscow. Perhaps Stalin thought he could thus deny Western claims that he had imposed the Soviet system on his satellites. It was also useful in justifying the leading role of the Soviet Union as the only mature socialist society. The only East European country which had challenged the ideological supremacy of Stalin and the CPSU, Tito's Yugoslavia, was a one-party state like the Soviet Union and claimed to be a socialist, not just a people's republic.

These ideological nuances did not prevent the Polish leaders from embarking on the wholesale remodelling of the legal, administrative and constitutional structure of the country on the Soviet pattern. The politburo member in charge of the institutional changes and cadre policy in the state apparatus generally was Roman Zambrowski, who was later to be criticized by his political enemies for favouring other Jews in his appointments. The Jewish intelligentsia was certainly well represented in the administrative and intellectual elite of the PZPR during and after the stalinist period, which was a cause for suppressed resentment among the proletarian elite of the Party which came to the surface in 1956 and 1968. The institutional reforms were without functional significance. The Party and the UB were the effective rulers of Poland even if the façade of pre-war government institutions had remained. The population would have preferred them to remain and would have felt less alienated from the system, but adoption of Soviet institutions, especially the constitution of 1936, was a form of flattering Stalin and the easiest way of promoting 'socialist construction'. The sejm, intimidated and depleted by expulsions and arrests in 1948–9, obediently passed a series of enactments which removed most of the remnants of pre-war 'bourgeois' institutions from the state structure. On 20 March 1950 local government was based on a three-tier system of people's councils corresponding to the administrative divisions of the country: *województwo* (province), *powiat* (district) or *miasto* (town) and the village commune (first *gmina*, then *gromada*). The appointed representatives of the central government were abolished, and all power was nominally vested in the council of each level, which was to be directly elected by the people, although no elections took place for over four years. The council's executive functions were exercised in each case by a presidium, nominally elected by the whole council, which directed and supervised the permanent officials of the council. The presidia in fact performed all the functions of the councils, under day-to-day supervision of the local party *apparat*. They were also controlled and bound by orders of higher councils and government departments which made all the important decisions. It was a system which permitted the ordinary citizen no initiative or influence whatsoever.

In June and July 1950 the whole judicial system was recast on Soviet lines. The courts now contained, beside professional judges, lay assessors nominally elected by the people's councils. The control of the supreme court over the lower courts was greatly strengthened, and the role of the public prosecutor in the judicial process enhanced. Both judges and prosecutors regularly took their orders from Party authorities. The bar lost its autonomy and its members could do little but plead for leniency on behalf of their clients. The rule of law, at least between the individual and the state, practically vanished. Illegalities on a massive scale, committed by officials or managers of industrial or trade enterprises, could not be remedied because the prosecutors refused to take action against the offenders. Over and above this there was the dreaded UB with sweeping powers to arrest, interrogate, torture, imprison or send to a labour camp.[20]

The coping stone of the institutional changes was a new constitution, enacted on 22 July 1952, which was closely modelled on that of the Soviet Union. Great powers of legislation and appointment were vested in the sejm, but both could be exercised by a small Council of State if the sejm was not in session. The office of president of the Republic was abolished and replaced by that of chairman of the Council. The Council of Ministers was given wide powers of issuing orders with the force of law, but was declared an administrative rather than governmental authority. It was a large body because the constitution confirmed the profusion of economic ministries created when the Ministry of Industry and Commerce was split in 1950. A smaller body, not recognized by the constitution, with the name of the Presidium of the Government and consisting of its chairman and deputy-chairmen, in practice worked out the details of policies decided by the PZPR politburo and gave them a legal form.[21] The constitution not merely defined the political system, which continued to be called 'people's democracy', but also described the economic and social system and declared Poland to be a country building socialism. Various political, economic, social and cultural rights were guaranteed, as well as the rule of law and the independence of the judiciary, but most of these provisions were vague and no method of enforcing them was laid down. The official designation of the country became the Polish People's Republic (Polska Rzeczpospolita Ludowa).

The adoption of the constitution was followed by a general election on 26 October 1952. There was only a single list submitted by a 'National Front for Peace and the Six Year Plan', which embraced the PZPR, the two other parties, the trade union movement, the Union of Polish Youth (Związek Młodzieży Polskiej – ZMP) and other 'social organizations'. The National Front temporarily acquired an elaborate organization, consisting of committees at various levels, officials and premises, but after the election fell into inactivity except when it issued or supported appeals, promoted good causes and graced solemn national and local occasions. There were 425 deputies elected in large multi-member constituencies and the party composition of the new sejm was as follows: PZPR – 273, ZSL – 90. SD – 25, and non-party – 37. The percentage of the electorate which voted was 95.03 and the Front's list received 99.8 per cent of votes under conditions of open voting and administrative pressure. The counting was not public and the figures may have been falsified. The new marshal of the sejm was Professor Jan Dembowski, one of the few committed Party scientists. The government was reconstructed on 21 November. Zawadzki became chairman of the State Council. Bierut, retaining his Party post, replaced Cyrankiewicz as chairman of the Council of Ministers, the latter becoming one of eight deputy-chairmen. The others were W. Dworakowski, T. Gede, P. Jaroszewicz, S. Jędrychowski, H. Minc, Z. Nowak and K. Rokossovsky. There were altogether 31 departmental ministers, including a newly created minister of state control who replaced the Supreme Chamber of Control, a body responsible to the sejm for checking the accounts of governmental departments.[22] The new sejm seldom met and passed virtually no laws until 1956. Its chief task was giving formal approval to decrees of the Council of State, which became the main source of legislation in this period, although even the decrees were dwarfed by the vast volume of the resolutions of the Council of Ministers.[23]

The Six Year Economic Plan

It was announced just after the November 1949 Plenum of the Central Committee that the Three Year Plan had been fulfilled in two years and ten months. Between 1946 and 1949 national income rose by 219 per cent, investment by 192 per cent and consumption by 226 per cent. Real wages rose by 33 per cent, and the main objective of the Plan of reaching pre-war consumption levels was achieved. Industrial production increased by an impressive 33 per cent in 1947, 37 per cent in 1948 and 22 per cent in 1949. It was with handicraft production 48 per cent higher in 1949 than in 1938 although agricultural production in 1949 reached only 86 per cent of the 1938 level.

The Plan had been prepared in 1946 by the Central Planning Office, staffed by a team of able economists consisting mainly of PPS members under the chairmanship of Professor C. Bobrowski. Their method assumed a desired level of consumption as the fundamental datum, worked out the necessary investment in light industry, handicraft and farming, and then projected investment in heavy industry. This approach, radically different from the Soviet scheme, which gave priority to heavy industry, came under the increasingly strong attack of Hilary Minc, the minister of industry and trade and the chief PPR economic expert. In February 1948 the Planning Office was taken over by the PPR and on 4 February 1949 replaced by the State Commission for Economic Planning (Państwowa Komisja Planowania Gospodarczego – PKPG) headed by Minc. Simultaneously the Ministry of Industry and Trade was divided into several specialized ministries, both developments being in line with established Soviet

Table 13. *Proposed increases on the 1949 levels*

	1948 version	1950 version
National income	70–80	112.3
Industrial production (socialist sector)	85–95	158.3
Agricultural production	35–45	'above 50'
Consumption per head	55–60	50–60

Source: Speeches of Minc to the Unity Congress, December 1948, and V PZPR Central Committee Plenum, July 1950.

practice. Minc, assisted by E. Szyr and S. Jędrychowski, was the virtual dictator of the socialist sector of the economy and Bierut's right hand man in the PZPR leadership. The agricultural sector of the economy, which remained predominantly private, was controlled by Zenon Nowak. It was a sector where toughness rather than economic expertise mattered most.

The Commission prepared the main targets for the new economic plan, covering the years 1950–5, in time for the Unity Congress. They were ambitious but still reasonably realistic and aimed at a balanced economic growth. As the international situation worsened in 1950, these targest were raised drastically under Soviet pressure.[24] The main differences between the two versions of the plan are shown in table 13. On 16 July 1950 the new targets, which were to prove wholly unrealistic, were approved by the PZPR Central Committee plenum and five days later enacted by the sejm as part of a comprehensive 'Law concerning the Six Year Plan of Economic Development and the Construction of Socialism in Poland for the years 1950–55'. The law laid down specific targets not only for industry and agriculture but also for housing, services, consumption, culture and education.[25]

The success of the Three Year Plan and the good economic situation of 1949 justified a general mood of optimism. The Six Year Plan was greeted with particular enthusiasm by the militants of the PZPR, and the initial enthusiasm probably touched many workers and the younger strata of the population.[26] The vision of large modern factories going up all over the country, the backward rural areas acquiring industry and towns, the whole country changing character from a predominantly agricultural to a predominantly industrial one, and the promise of a higher standard of living, education and culture fascinated and attracted many people. The press, by dwelling on the Plan, reporting progress and applauding successes, contributed to the euphoria. Literature, theatre and cinema, as

Table 14. *Proportion of accumulation (gross capital formation)*
in the national income

Year	In 1961 prices	In 1950 prices
1949	15.8	22.7
1950	21.2	29.4
1951	20.7	28.8
1952	23.2	32.0
1953	28.5	38.2
1954	23.6	32.8
1955	22.7	31.2

Source: *Rocznik Statystyczny (1969)*, p. 38.

well as the visual arts, crudely but often sincerely joined in the propaganda campaign. It was the younger journalists and the younger artists who most sincerely felt and reflected the sense of adventure, battle, and a 'new frontier'. The Union of Polish Youth (ZMP) became an enthusiastic propaganda machine for the Plan among its members and helped recruit volunteers for the most difficult pioneering work and for sectors of the economy, such as coalmines and state farms, which suffered from severe labour shortage.

As time went on, only a small minority retained something of the original enthusiasm. The confrontation with economic realities produced by the Plan killed it dead in the rest. The rate of capital accumulation after the 1950 revision of the Plan was so high that it created total imbalance in the economy. Its growth is shown in table 14, and in the opinion of leading Polish economic historians the 1950 prices rather than those usually quoted for 1961 give a more accurate picture of the situation.[27] The 1953 figure is particularly striking. The amount of national income available for consumption, housing, social and communal services, welfare and recreation drastically diminished; only education and culture retained high priority. As industrialization proceeded, huge uncontrolled migration from the countryside and small towns to the old and new industrial centres took place. It is estimated that about 250,000 people migrated from country to town each year between 1950 and 1953. This, according to an authoritative study of the Plan, led to the employment of about 500,000 more men than was strictly necessary for production.[28] The growth in the labour force was the result of faulty planning owing to a need for labour reserves to meet targets at the last moment and the acute shortage of fixed capital in production.[29] It had unfortunate consequences. Peasants were self-sufficient in food and made minimal claims on the state for housing and public services, but by migrating to towns they became a state responsibility and depressed the standards of the old urban population.

The massive expansion of wage earners created great inflationary pressure and required deflationary counter-measures. The first was the currency reform of 30 October 1950, which hit peasants and private entrepreneurs particularly hard. In June 1951 a National Development Loan of 1,200 million *zł.* was launched. It was aimed at the workers and other state employees who were urged by Party and union activists to subscribe to it. In 1950 the situation of the consumer was still tolerable because many investment projects had not then begun, but in the middle of 1951 great shortages of both agricultural and industrial consumer goods became noticeable. Rationing, abolished in January 1949, had to be reintroduced in September 1951, and was only abolished for good in January 1953, when a general price increase introduced as a deflationary measure brought a reasonable equilibrium between goods and purchasing power. While Western Europe was entering 'the age of affluence', Poland like the rest of Eastern Europe was going through a period of severe austerity. Although the Plan had promised the lowering of prices, in fact they rose faster than incomes until the end of 1953. Nominal incomes in that year were only 203.7 per cent above 1949, while prices of consumer goods were 222.2 per cent higher in the socialized shops, and up to 270 per cent higher in the open peasant markets. Consumption in real terms increased by 16.5 per cent during 1948–50, but the increase between 1951 and 1953 was only 2.8 per cent.[30] The fundamental problem, which continued until 1956, was that huge resources, amounting to almost 40 per cent of national income in 1953, were withdrawn from immediate consumption or from consumer goods industry and tied up in long-term industrial projects, which remained unrealized during the six years of the Plan and sometimes for many years after. When they did finally operate at full capacity they produced mainly raw materials and goods for the further development of heavy industry, energy or raw material base, and did not directly benefit the consumers. The creation of a defence industry after 1951 aggravated the problem by withdrawing additional resources from civilian consumption and production.[31] This enormous gap between consumption and production, which formed the dominant feature of the Six Year Plan, was precisely what the socialist planners who had framed the Three Year Plan had feared and sought to avoid.

The allocation of capital resources between different branches of production was determined by a system of priorities dictated largely by political considerations and emergencies. Deliveries to the USSR and the needs of rearmament and the army had the first claim. Then came heavy and medium industry with their demands for iron and steel, industrial machinery and rolling stock. Light industry, agriculture and handicraft trailed at the end. The last three notoriously lagged behind the rest of the economy in development, and their planned targets were not reached by a wide margin. The proportion of investment in light and consumer goods industry to investment in producer goods declined from 23.77 to 13.87 between 1950 and 1953. Moreover, the planners had a preference for new, large, costly plants in undeveloped regions of the country, rather than for increasing production of old factories or developing the existing industrial centres. The most gigantic project of the Plan, the Lenin steel works in Nowa Huta near Cracow, lay far from the Silesian coalfields on which it depended. Embarking on too many projects at once led to new factories standing idle or operating at one-tenth of their capacity or lacking proper roads, houses or shops for workers. Constant shortages throughout the economy disrupted production and required the regrouping of resources, which further complicated the situation.[32]

The co-ordinator of the system was the vast, ubiquitous and all-powerful State Economic Planning Commission. It became responsible for all economic decisions, all use of resources, all wages and prices. The yearly, quarterly and monthly targets the Commission worked out for every enterprise under its control became more and more detailed and rigid, leaving in the end no scope for any managerial initiative and independence. The Plan was the supreme law of the country and the directors of enterprises were legally responsible for the execution of the part that applied to them. This effectively set them above the trade unions and even factory and territorial Party organizations, whose role in industry, apart from political propaganda campaigns, became mainly the stimulation of workers to greater effort for the same pay. Since the enterprises, in order to maximize Plan fulfilment premiums, concealed their resources and capacities from the planners, the Planning Commission worked to a large extent on guess-work and did not know the exact state of the economy. The Commission's targets also were quantitative and invited evasion by the lowering of quality, the reducing of size and other devices. To all this must be added that prices and wages were fixed without much analysis of costs. They were generally kept low as a matter of policy, and no charge at all was made for the use of capital invested in production. There was thus no economic calculation and no rational pricing according to cost or scarcity, which created a built-in propensity to over-invest with enormous possibilities of error, waste and inefficiency. Any idea of economic cost or interest on investment was rejected as a bourgeois heresy without place in a socialist economy. Here, as in so many other spheres, the mechanical copying of Soviet models and dogmas produced consequences defying all common sense.

While the whole country suffered from the one-sided implementation of the Six Year Plan, the class that was most directly hit by it was the workers. Theoretically they were the chosen people, the pillar of the whole political and economic system, the class that was building socialism under the leadership of the PZPR and with the support of other classes. In practice, their position, especially the position of their solid pre-1950 core, deteriorated beyond all recognition. Within individual factories trade-union branches and works' councils were unable to prevent the rapid deterioration of working conditions and the large-scale violation of health and safety regulations.[33] The national trade unions after the 1949 purge and reorganization became powerless to demand wage increases. Wage rates were fixed by the government without any consultation with trade-union representatives and the wage structure seldom adequately reflected factors such as skill, training, experience and quality of work.

The wage system, copied from the USSR, was based on 'work norms' for various jobs, and was supplemented by a graduated premium when the norm had been exceeded.[34] The norms were difficult to calculate accurately in the light of the productive possibilities of the whole factory and their fulfilment depended on conditions beyond the workers' control. To raise norms the Soviet stakhanovite system and 'socialist competition' were employed. The working week was lengthened and Sunday working, overtime and night shifts introduced when it suited the management, irrespective of the workers' wishes. Special rates of pay legally applicable to such work were frequently ignored in practice. While the management could with impunity take liberties with the law, the latter bore severely on the workers. A series of labour laws, passed in March, April and May 1950 and backed by heavy penalties, tied workers to their jobs, enforced punctual arrival and regular attendance and introduced strict discipline within the factory. To cap all there was a system of 'confidential opinions' about every employee, which accompanied him every time he wished to change his job, and which he was not allowed to see and therefore question. The factory personnel officers were normally UB agents.

The workers lacked both political and economic means of self-defence against the system and its abuses. Strikes were never legally banned but became impossible in practice. When some strikes did occur in the Dąbrowa basin coal mines in spring 1951, caused by extremely hard working conditions, the authorities did not hesitate to use force against the strikers who were treated as 'enemies of the people'.[35] What remained, then, was passive resistance against pressure. There was large-scale absenteeism and illegal changing of jobs. In 1951 the percentage of employees who left the industry for other jobs was 39 in heavy machine construction, 42 in the coal-mining and 66 in branches of chemical industry.[36] Orders were evaded, returns falsified, work done badly, equipment and materials treated carelessly, and anything that could be was stolen and sold on the black market. The abuses, as well as the absurdities and mistakes of the planning system, were a bitter disappointment to the older workers with strong and genuine left-wing convictions, who discovered that the socialism they had hoped for turned out to be a soulless, wasteful and corrupting system. A campaign against social democracy in June 1951 was probably meant to suppress those sentiments.[37]

In fact there was only one solid gain which post-1949 changes brought to the working class as a whole, and that was greatly increased opportunities for the social advance of its individual members. The expanding bureaucracy of the Party, the state and trade unions, as well as the army and police-officer corps, drew new recruits primarily from the workers. Workers' children had privileged entry into secondary schools, technical colleges, military academies and universities, and received their education at the state's expense.[38] But with the education and the promotion to the bureaucratic, technical and managerial strata came either partial assimilation to the values of the old bourgeoisie or the absorption in the exclusive caste of Party or police functionaries. In either case the members of the new elite ceased to count as workers, to share and express their point of view and to show special sensitivity to workers' problems. Sometimes they were more brutal than the old bosses and enjoyed less respect and authority.

The economic policies after 1950 hastened the decline of other classes. The nationalization of industry and the liquidation of private industrialists as a class were completed already in 1948. Before the war handicrafts had played a decisive role in the economy. There were about 343,000 workshops and they contributed half of industry's share of the national income. After 1948 the craftsmen were forced to join co-operatives, subjected to strict regulation and heavy taxation and inadequately supplied with raw material. As a result the number of workshops declined from about 171,000 in 1949 to only about 90,000 in 1953,[39] and a chance was lost to use them to offset the dwindling state supply of consumer goods. Cottage industry, which had played an important role in some regions, was also virtually liquidated during the Plan. As a result of the so-called 'battle for trade' launched in May 1947, the socialist sector absorbed in 1949 98 per cent of wholesale-trade turnover and about half of retail trade.

Table 15. *Gross investments in agriculture (in milliard zł. at 1956 prices)*

Type of ownership	1950	1951	1952	1953	1954	1955
All farms	3.3	2.1	2.9	3.3	4.1	5.8
Socialized	2.1	1.8	2.1	2.6	3.2	4.2
Private	1.2	0.3	0.8	0.7	0.9	1.6

Source: J. Tepicht, *Doświadczenia a perspektywy rolnictwa* (Experiences and Perspectives of Farming) (Warsaw, 1961), p. 120; quoted in Ryć, *Spożycie a wzrost*, p. 65.

After that the proportion of private retail-trade turnover declined to 17 per cent in 1950, 7 per cent in 1952, 3.9 per cent in 1953 and vanished from the statistics in 1954.[40] The place of private shops was taken by state, municipal or co-operative shops and in the countryside by the Peasant Self-Help organization, like all other co-operatives wholly controlled by the state. As their network was not nearly as wide as the old private system, shopping became very arduous owing to shortages and queues. The liquidation of private handicraft and trade hit especially the Western Territories where they had played a vital role up to 1948, and where the failure to replace private businesses by a reasonable number of socialized shops was particularly glaring. Dogmatic socialism once again defied common sense.

Private farming, on the other hand, remained predominant during the whole six years of the Plan, and it was on the work of these individual and mostly small and inefficient farmers that the national economy depended for the supply of food and other raw materials. The Plan set a very high target for agricultural production, a 39 per cent increase in crops and 68 per cent increase in animal products, altogether a 50 per cent increase in the value of agricultural production by 1955. It promised substantial capital outlay on farming to achieve these goals. It also announced that 'the state will create conditions for the inclusion of a considerable part of farms in the socialist co-operative production' and that the already numerous but badly run state farms would become model socialist farming enterprises. None of the objectives were in fact achieved.

In 1951 supplies to agriculture went down sharply and continued to lag behind the Plan by about a quarter till 1954. The lion's share of them went to collective and state farms and state tractor stations, although the private sector produced the great bulk of the foodstuffs and agricultural raw materials. Table 15 illustrates the neglect of private farming. The position of the private farmers worsened rapidly. In July 1951 compulsory deliveries of grain were imposed, and in 1952 extended to pork, beef, milk

Table 16. *Collectivization of farms, 1949–55*

Year	Percentage share of arable land	Number of members	Number of production co-operatives
1949	—	—	243
1950	0.8	23,300	2,199
1951	3.2	77,400	3,056
1952	3.4	85,200	4,478
1953	6.7	158,500	7,772
1954	8.2	192,400	9,322
1955	9.2	205,200	9,750

Source: *Rocznik Statystyczny (1956)*.

and potatoes. The prices the state paid were fixed below production cost. A land tax was introduced in 1950 and raised progressively. The tax together with compulsory deliveries amounted to a confiscation of 20 per cent of net farm production. The burdens were progressive, amounting to 10 per cent on small farmers to 37.5 per cent on large ones. This was in accordance with the Party's declared leninist policy of winning over the poor peasants, neutralizing the middle ones, and liquidating the rich 'kulaks'. In practice all efficient and prosperous farmers, whatever the size of their holdings, were treated as kulaks. The so-called regulation of prices in January 1953 hit the peasants hardest by steeply raising prices of goods and services bought by them. As a result of all these hostile measures they stopped investing in their farms and allowed their equipment and buildings to decay. They sub-divided their farms or simply surrendered to the state some of their land to escape taxation. The area of land under cultivation decreased. With bad harvests in 1951, 1952 and 1953 the average crop yields fell below the 1950 level instead of rising by 10 per cent per year as planned. The livestock situation was better, but the Plan was only partially fulfilled.[41] The exaction of deliveries often had to be backed by force, and in 1951 in the two northern districts of Drawno and Gryfice brutality was so great that the Party leadership had to step in and condemn it publicly. Nevertheless, some use of force went on until the end of 1953, both to exact deliveries and to further collectivization. It is said that 30,000 peasants were imprisoned for resistance.

Collectivization was introduced in 1949 with the formation of 243 collective farms or 'production co-operatives'. Its subsequent progress is shown in table 16. Collective farms were of four different types, of which only 60 per cent were of the advanced type dominant in the Soviet Union.[42]

Over half were located in the former German territories where farmers were post-war settlers and did not have a strong sense of attachment to the land. Often they did not even hold the legal titles to their farms. They were economically weak and needed subsidies or concessions, but even here administrative pressure had to be used on an increasing scale to make more peasants join them, and the superior deliveries to socialized farms were intended to act as incentives. Although expansion was slow, the mere commitment to collectivization produced general uncertainty and inhibited production. Much more force could have been used but the Party authorities seemed as reluctant to force the pace as they originally had been to introduce collectivization.[43] The reason was that the authorities needed food to feed the growing town population and to export it to pay for essential imports from capitalist countries. Apart from coal, meat products were the chief source of foreign currency earnings during the early 1950s.[44]

The attention of Western observers and scholars has naturally focused on collectivization as the most distinctly stalinist aspect of communist policies in Eastern Europe, but for Poland this exaggerates both its political and economic significance. In the USSR collectivization was adopted as a means of making the peasants bear the cost of industrialization as well as securing a steady supply of cheap grain and other farm products for the growing urban population and expanding industry. In Poland the function of squeezing the private farmer was fulfilled by compulsory deliveries, the land tax, high prices of goods supplied by the state and starving the countryside of necessary resources. It was these policies, rather than collectivization, which hit the average peasant hardest and led to large-scale repressive action to enforce his obligations to the state. Economically collectivization was wasteful because farms were inefficient and heavily subsidized.[45] Collectivization in Poland was pursued cautiously and without conviction for political rather than economic reasons, because this was the Soviet way to build socialism in the countryside and perhaps simply because Stalin had ordered it.

Nevertheless the peasants benefited from the other aspect of the Plan, industrialization. Sometimes they could commute and supplement their earnings by doing construction or unskilled factory work in a developing area. The rural over-population, the scourge of pre-war Poland, was alleviated in some areas by migration into industry. Despite difficult conditions, factory work and urban life represented social advance for the peasants. Peasant children now enjoyed better access to education at all levels and a far better chance of reaching intelligentsia status than they had had before the war. If they were not kulaks' children and were prepared to join the PZPR, they could rise rapidly in one of the bureaucracies.

Individual farmers lacked any organization through which they could act jointly or defend themselves against oppression. Their strength, however, was in their numbers, the importance of agriculture to the economy and the possibility of passive resistance by simply producing less and less.

The Soviet contribution was crucial to the industrialization process. Under a long-term agreement with the USSR, signed in Moscow on 29 June 1950, Poland was given credits and was guaranteed for eight years the supply of raw materials and industrial goods necessary for her economic development, and the sale of surpluses of the Polish economy. She was also promised a great quantity of investment equipment, including whole plants for dozens of factories and mines, together with technical advice and personnel training necessary for their design, assembly and initial operation. As a result, new branches of industry, quite unknown in pre-war Poland, were brought into existence. After 1951 a sophisticated defence industry, producing tanks, guns, munitions, aeroplanes and radar, was added to the others. Help on that scale could not have come to communist Poland from the West, least of all the United States which, as the Cold War developed, imposed a strategic embargo on exports to East Europe and withdrew from Poland the most favoured nation treatment in 1952. The reliance on the Soviet Union had, however, serious adverse consequences. Soviet equipment was technologically inferior to the Western, and in many cases obsolete. It used up more resources than was necessary and brought poorer returns. A good example was the motor car factory at Żerań in Warsaw, which produced a Soviet copy of a 1940's American car, large, ugly and uneconomical in petrol.[46] The Soviet Union nevertheless frowned on economic as well as other relations between the West and her satellites, and enforced the myth of superiority of Soviet industry, technology and science over their bourgeois equivalents. Between 1950 and 1953 imports from non-communist countries fell from 35.7 to 25 per cent, and exports to those countries fell from 39.7 to 27.3 per cent.[47] There are doubts whether the price Poland paid to the Soviet Union for her imports, and those she received for her exports were fair. Many people in Poland at the time, and afterwards, believed they were not, but there was no doubt about coal. From 1946 to 1955 Poland exported to the USSR about 8 million tons of coal per annum at a nominal price, which bore little relation to the cost of extraction and even less to the price of coal then in great demand on the world market. In this way Poland lost a large amount of Western currency which could have been used to buy foreign industrial equipment. In November 1956 the losses thus incurred, estimated by the Polish authorities and agreed by the Russians, amounted to 5,000 million dollars. It was equivalent to the value of all Polish imports from the West for 1952 and 1953. One result of this huge unprofitable export was that the Polish government invested no capital in coal-mining and extracted coal by more intensive use of labour, under appalling conditions. This was the reason for the strikes of 1951 already mentioned, Sunday and overtime working and the employment of soldiers and convicts.[48] Since coal was needed also for domestic consumption and industry and for paying for such Western imports as were inevitable, private consumers suffered great deprivation and industry operated for years near to breaking point.

There was another aspect of Soviet influence. The pattern of industrial development was decided by Soviet priorities, strategically important considerations determining industrial investment, whereas Poland itself would have sought a more balanced development. The Korean War provides an example. Its outbreak placed grave pressure on the Polish economy. The Soviet Union, for its own reasons of state, demanded an increase in the tempo of industrialization. The planners tended to seek an over-investment in heavy industry even when the Korean emergency had passed. Directly and indirectly the political subordination of Poland to the USSR, which reached its peak during the Six Year Plan, profoundly influenced the Polish economy for years to come. The over-centralized system of planning and management, which emerged in the course of the Six Year Plan, left a legacy of difficult problems for the future. These difficulties were largely of Soviet creation.

Culture and religion

Already at the end of 1948 the PZPR leaders began to insist that Polish culture and art had to become truly socialist in character and follow the example of the Soviet Union. The leader of the marxist offensive in culture and science and the controller of the so-called 'ideological front' until 1956 was Jakub Berman. Under Bierut's leadership of the politburo, Berman exercised just as much power in his sphere as Minc did over the economy or Zambrowski over the administrative machinery. The three men stood out among their politburo colleagues for intellectual ability and skill in reinterpreting and explaining changes in the Party's general course from a soft to a hard line between 1948 and 1950 and then back to a somewhat softer line after 1953. Throughout 1949 pressure on the intellectuals mounted but was strongly resisted, particularly by the Writers' Union (Związek Literatów Polskich – ZLP). The Party's call for socialist litera-ture, issued at the January 1949 congress of the ZLP, produced much self-criticism among writers but little literary achievement. A high-level conference of writers and Party and government leaders tackled the problem again in February 1950. It was alleged that there was 'a paralysis of creative will' among writers and that the enormous socialist achievements of the last five years found no reflection in literature or indeed art in general. A new ZLP congress met on 29 June 1950 and at last refashioned the organization. From a predominantly professional body and public mouthpiece of the literary community the Union was changed into 'a creative ideological centre for forming the ideological consciousness of writers'.[49] The vague concept of progressive and socially committed literature was replaced by Soviet 'socialist realism' as the official guiding line in literature. The Union organized lecture tours, tours of industrial areas and collective farms and visits to the USSR to help their members steep themselves in social reality, and through so-called 'creative sections' sought to discuss and mould work in progress. The authorities of the Union were purged of non-communist survivals and came under complete PZPR control. The chairman and general secretary of its presidium, Leon Kruczkowski and Jerzy Putrament, were members of the PZPR Central Committee. The latter also headed the powerful basic party organization within the Warsaw branch of the Union. The old literary weeklies (*Kuźnica* and *Odrodzenie*), tainted with opportunism, were abolished and replaced by a militantly marxist *Nowa Kultura* (New Culture), which was the Union's official mouthpiece.

The theatre, cinema, music, painting, sculpture and architecture underwent a similar transformation after 1949. Their professional associations became ideological, acknowledging socialist realism as the only correct style, determined by Party men. Surprisingly strong opposition to the change came from some visual artists who, although PZPR members, passionately believed that many *avant-garde* Western trends in painting and in sculpture were socially progressive and better expressed the spirit of the socialist revolution than the official Soviet style. They were silenced and prevented from propagating their 'incorrect' views by word or deed. The Ministry of Culture and Art became another powerful instrument for promoting socialist realism, through its control over museums, exhibitions, theatres and concerts, state subsidies and commissioning of work. Its advisory body, the Council of Culture and Art, and its weekly periodical, *Przegląd Kulturalny* (Cultural Review), represented the narrow official orthodoxy instead of the whole spectrum of the artistic community. Under the impact of these agencies, some younger artists became genuine social realists and spontaneously produced crude and naive work. Such conversions were rare among the older generation, some members of which conformed for opportunistic reasons, while others chose to earn a living without compromising their artistic consciences.

Compared with the immediate post-war period, the number of active artists shrank considerably and so did the quantity of new work of artistic merit. The official acceptance of socialist realism by the writers and other artists did not produce a flood of socialist realist art. Some good novels and short stories inspired by the Party's ideology or contemporary problems were published by the middle generation and younger writers such as K. Brandys, B. Czeszko and J. Stryjkowski, but very few of them were judged by the critics to be successful examples of the official style. Although often sympathetic to communism, able writers such as J. Andrzejewski, T. Breza, Z. Nałkowska, I. Newerly and A. Rudnicki published little or nothing after 1951. The situation in poetry was even worse. J. Tuwim and A. Słonimski, distinguished pre-war left-wing poets, published little. Younger poets produced little that could qualify as socialist realism. K. I. Gałczyński, perhaps the ablest of them, and procommunist, published nothing in the new style. When a group of young, aggressively 'socrealist' poets, such as W. Woroszylski and A. Mandalian made a debut in 1951, their poetry was mercilessly criticized by the so-called Cracow group of independent literary critics, but even the commanders of the Party's cultural front, Berman, Sokorski and Putrament, expressed dissatisfaction with the 'schematism' and low quality of current literature.[50] In order to publish some good prose and poetry, publishing houses and literary journals had to lower their ideological standards. The situation in the theatre was broadly the same. What kept it flourishing was the classical repertoire of Polish, Russian and Western European plays.

The shortage of acceptable first-class contemporary literature and drama led to a boom in translations, which were of high quality and came from a wide range of languages. As an example, in the year 1951 484 foreign translations of literary works were published, the bulk from the Russian (275) but many from the French (53), German (44) and English (35). The rest were from twenty-nine other languages.[51] The publishing policy was selective, but included most great nineteenth- and twentieth-century writers, and as much contemporary Western literature as was 'progressive' or critical towards its own society. The preference for Russian literature, drama, ballet and music was not an unmitigated disaster because these included much that was great, and Russian standards in the performing arts were very high. The intellectual horizon of the educated Pole in some ways became broader than it had ever been. Cheap books, large editions and numerous libraries created a mass market for literature. Opportunity to study art or to learn it as an amateur also increased greatly. The lavish state expenditure on culture in the widest sense made it available to the masses, especially in the towns, although the chief beneficiaries were white-collar workers, petty officials, the new professional classes and the *déclassé* old bourgeoisie.

A lasting and positive result of the 'culture offensive', or 'cultural revolution' as it was often called, of the stalinist years was the state patronage of popular or folk culture, which was intensively studied, protected and encouraged. There were competitions and exhibitions of folk art together with the promotion of regional song and dance ensembles. The first Festival of Polish Folk Music was held in spring 1949. The impulse behind the patronage was frankly ideological. Popular art was described as 'the inexhaustible source of realistic and national art',[52] and regarded as a salutary antidote to the 'formalistic' and 'cosmopolitan' or Western tendencies of professional art. Its flourishing supported the claim that in People's Poland the masses, and not just the elite, had wide opportunities to contribute to cultural life. The educative effect on professional artists was negligible, but the ordinary public acquired a taste for folk art, which has lasted to this day. It is unlikely that under the impact of industrialization and political turmoil popular culture would have survived, let alone prospered, in the countryside without help from the communist state.

In the field of higher education, research and science in the widest sense, comprising natural, social and humanistic studies, the equivalent of the socialist realist offensive was that of marxism–leninism–stalinism. The institutional conditions were created by the reform of universities and polytechnics and the foundation of the Academy of Sciences, accomplished between 1950 and 1952. The universities became mainly teaching institutions while research came to be concentrated in the Academy. After the reform it was possible to give marxism–leninism–stalinism the monopoly of scientific approach by administrative means rather than through ideological struggle. Representatives of undesirable tendencies could be barred from teaching and their place taken by Party men, or at least professors prepared to toe the line in lectures. Certain subjects disappeared from curricula altogether. Others, copied from the Soviet Union, were introduced, and marxism–leninism and the history of working-class movements, above all of the Soviet Communist Party and Polish communism, became compulsory for all degree courses. New textbooks, generally produced collectively and carefully vetted ideologically, replaced existing ones. The Academy had the right to grant research degrees and, apart from training the young academic cadre, it promoted research from correct ideological positions and prevented unorthodox research being done or published.

In the realm of higher education and science, even more than art, appearance was more impressive than reality. In some fields, such as philosophy, mathematics, economics, sociology and biology, Poland had a tradition of excellence that made it exceedingly difficult to persuade scholars to give up their approaches and to embrace marxism as the only valid scientific methodology. Moreover, it was not an 'open marxism', interpreted freely by each scientist, which had a long tradition in Poland and was officially favoured until 1948, but the rigid, petrified system of thought, which years of stalinism had perfected in the Soviet Union, that the Polish scientists were expected to embrace. The Party had very few adherents among the older and middle-aged generation of academics and scientists and could not afford to scrutinize political beliefs too closely under conditions of rapid expansion of higher education and research. Only the most politically dangerous academics and scientists were excluded from contact with students, and these, paradoxically, often found haven in the Party-dominated Academy of Sciences, where they could earn a living by editing, translating or researching into relatively harmless subjects. Partly because they had been decimated during the occupation, partly because they traditionally enjoyed great prestige among the intelligentsia, the creative intellectuals were treated with great mildness in Poland compared with other communist countries. There was an extraordinary contrast between the speed and ruthlessness with which the Party, the trade-union movement and the state apparatus were purged after 1949 and the slow and humane methods applied to the creative intelligentsia.

The demand for lecturers in marxism–leninism, communist history and marxist economics outstripped the possibilities of the universities and the Academy. An Institute for the Training of Scientific Cadres, later renamed the Institute of Social Sciences, was created in 1950 directly under the PZPR Central Committee and was also given the right to award degrees. Its director, Professor Adam Schaff, was a Central Committee member and the Party's chief expert in philosophy and social science. Through lectures, courses and publications the small but growing cadre of marxist teachers, researchers and scholars associated with the Institute conducted a clamorous campaign against survivals of bourgeois ideology in Poland and contemporary non-marxist trends abroad. They were also following, assimilating and publicizing 'the achievements of Soviet science', which were magnified out of all proportion.

Secondary and primary education was reorganized in 1950 and 'ideologically reorientated' in the same way. Courses were altered, textbooks replaced and political indoctrination intensified. The general tendency was to expand above all technical rather than general education and to sacrifice standards for the sake of rapid increases in numbers of pupils, especially of worker and peasant origin. The key positions of headmasters and school inspectors were mostly in the hands of Party men, but there was a serious shortage of PZPR teachers, especially in primary schools. Although teachers were badly paid, they traditionally enjoyed a high social status and thus teaching attracted many educated middle-class women to whom other openings were denied. Here and in secondary schools the Union of Polish Youth was used to supervise teachers and to report any hostility to the political system. Political indoctrination of school children was carried out also through the two mass organizations, 'Service to Poland' and the Polish Scout Union, but it is doubtful whether all the methods of indoctrination seriously undermined the traditional influence of the home and the church.

The ideological offensive reached the mass of the adult population mainly through the radio and the press and partly through trade unions, professional bodies, basic party organizations in factories and offices, and mass organizations such as the Women's League or the Polish–Soviet Friendship Society, for which membership and attendance at meetings were often semi-compulsory. The Polish Radio and all but a handful of periodicals had Party men as directors or editors-in-chief and a high proportion of Party men on their staff. They were bound by specific directives of the Central Committee's Department of Agitation and Propaganda, and the general line of the press at any given time, such as an accent on 'the struggle for peace', was laid down by the Association of Polish Journalists, also Party-dominated and militantly ideological.

As the Cold War intensified, the press and the radio, like the artistic and scientific 'sector', became virulently anti-capitalist, anti-Western and anti-American and whittled down the amount of news about the West. They were also concerned, together with the universities, schools and historical publications, to reassess recent Polish history and national traditions, to separate 'healthy', 'progressive' and 'democratic' currents from 'rotten', 'backward' and 'reactionary' ones. Developments in the USSR and other communist countries were given detailed and enthusiastic treatment, as were struggles against war, imperialism, colonialism and capitalism everywhere in the world. The general tone of the press was heavily political and economic. Party and government speeches, resolutions and communiqués, the progress of the Plan and the production achievements of mines, factories or collective farms were given great prominence and reported in full. The amount of news and articles of popular interest shrank to a small proportion of that of the pre-1949 period. The mass media very largely ceased to reflect public opinion, and became the mouthpiece either of official bodies or of a mythical 'society building socialism', whose interests and opinions were creatures of the Central Committee Agitprop Department and bore no relation to reality.

An independent and powerful Roman Catholic church, with an elaborate national organization, a larger number of bishops, priests and members of religious communities than before the war, and its own means of influencing public opinion through sermons, pastoral letters, newspapers and publications, was obviously an anomaly in the system after the 1949 turning point. So was the policy of peaceful coexistence between church and state and an ideological dialogue between Catholicism and the progressive camp led by marxists. The immediate cause of worsening of relations was a Vatican decree barring Catholics from supporting or participating in communist parties and reading communist press or publications. The Polish government responded by passing on 5 August 1949 a decree about the liberty of conscience and political opinion, which made any application of the Vatican decree by the church in Poland a punishable offence. This was followed by the suppression of many existing privileges. Church land, previously exempted from reform, was now nationalized and the income from it used to pay state salaries to priests and bishops. The church's welfare and charitable organization 'Caritas', the last survival of the wide pre-war network of Catholic social organizations, was taken over by a lay body with the assistance of the authorities. Catholic press and publications were restricted in number and confined almost wholly to religious and ecclesiastical matters by means of censorship. Religious instruction was discontinued in schools and chaplains were removed from prisons, hospitals and army units.

The second prong of the communist leaders' policy against the church was to sponsor an association of 'patriotic priests' prepared to collaborate politically with the Party and to favour the Catholic social movement, PAX (headed by Bolesław Piasecki, an extreme nationalist leader before the war). The object of PAX was to sow confusion and disunity among Polish Catholics. Through its press PAX solidly supported all the current government decisions and the foreign policy of the communist bloc, and maintained that there was no conflict between Catholic faith and the communist system in practice. Only the atheist and materialist philosophy of marxism–leninism was unacceptable to the believing Catholic. The Vatican eventually declared the views of Piasecki on Catholic–communist collaboration heretical and placed his books and the PAX's periodicals on the Index. Paradoxically the publishing activities of PAX made a wide range of Western Catholic literature, which could not have been published by the state, available to Polish readers. After 1952 both the 'patriotic priests' and PAX became represented in the National Front, and PAX acquired some deputies in the sejm. When about this time the state conferred on itself the right to approve ecclesiastical appointments and regulate church administration in the former German territories, still officially regarded as German by the Vatican, some of the 'patriotic priests' were appointed to bishoprics and other church offices by the government.

The third prong of the anti-church offensive was a propaganda attack on the Vatican as the capitalists' ally in the Cold War and on the allegedly 'anti-Polish' and 'reactionary' record of the Vatican and the Polish hierarchy and clergy in the past. The reluctance of church leaders to support the PZPR-sponsored 'peace campaign' and to sign anti-nuclear appeals increased the virulence of the propaganda campaign against the church, but there was no interference with the purely religious activities of the church, the religious instruction of children by the parish priests and the functioning of convents, monasteries and seminaries. Likewise the Catholic University of Lublin, unique in the whole of Eastern Europe, was allowed to continue. As it accepted academics purged from state universities and students whose social origins barred them elsewhere, it softened the impact of the Party's policies in higher education.

To replace the concordat renounced by the government in 1945 and to put the state–church relations on some kind of legal footing, an agreement was secretly negotiated by a committee of bishops and government representatives, and signed on 14 April 1950. The church acknowledged the supreme authority of the state in all secular matters in exchange for a guarantee of its autonomy in the religious sphere and a confirmation of the remaining privileges. The episcopate apparently hoped the agreement would reduce friction, and the Party leaders were perhaps eager to create a favourable atmosphere for the Plan and collectivization. The agreement failed to improve relations. The church accused the state of breaches of the agreement, while the government and the Party complained that the church was acting against its spirit. An uneasy truce persisted for a year and a half, but after the sejm elections a renewed anti-church offensive broke out.

In October 1952 three bishops of the Katowice diocese were arrested, followed a month later by the arrest of a group of priests working in the Cracow archbishopric office. In January 1953 the latter were tried before a military tribunal as spies working for the American intelligence service and given sentences ranging from death to six years in prison. On 9 February the State Council issued a decree conferring on the government the right of approving all ecclesiastical appointments and removing from their posts clerics breaking the law or undermining public order. Another turn of the screw came in September when Bishop Kaczmarek of Kielce and three of his priests were tried for organizing an 'anti-state and anti-people' centre. They received heavy prison sentences, the bishop one of twelve years although he had been under arrest since January 1951.

Under mounting pressure the conference of the episcopate condemned the activities of 'the Kaczmarek centre', but as the primate of Poland, Archbishop Stefan Wyszyński, remained silent, he was on 29 September 1953 forbidden by the government to exercise his functions and compelled to retire to a monastery. By the end of December all priests and bishops had taken the oath of loyalty to the People's Republic, which the February decree made a condition for holding church office.

The repressive measures and the virulent propaganda campaign which accompanied them did not, however, succeed in undermining the traditional loyalty of the Catholic masses to the church. In the past persecutions had tended to strengthen its hold, and in this case repression and attack won the church some sympathy even in the non-practising and indifferent strata of the population. The political prestige of the papacy, the hierarchy and the clergy might have suffered, but the influence on mass attendance, religious practices, church weddings and christenings was slight. Even Party members secretly married in church and had their children baptized, confirmed and instructed in religion, yielding to tradition and social pressure rather than to the Party's orders. Much more significant than deliberate efforts of the Party were the long-term social consequences of industrialization and urbanization. The young peasants migrating in their thousands from the country often became slack and indifferent in the new urban environment. The lack of churches in the new suburbs or close to the hostels where they lived encouraged laxity in religious practice, but the full impact of these circumstances become noticeable somewhat later.

The minority Christian churches and sects, claiming the allegiance of some 5 per cent of the population found it easier to establish a *modus vivendi* with the state. They were in some ways even favoured as a counter-weight to the Roman Catholic church. Those, however, that had strong links with the United States, like Jehovah's Witnesses, became subject to considerable political persecution.[53]

Stalin's death and the New Course

Stalin died on 5 March 1953, perhaps on the eve of a new mass purge to which the so-called 'doctors' plot' seemed to be a prelude. For the younger generation of PZPR members, brought up in the Stalin cult, his death was a shock. Old communists, who remembered the liquidation of the KPP, were probably less sorry to see him go, as were those who joined the PPR during the war and found themselves discriminated against after 1948. His death must have brought particular relief to the many Jews in the PZPR elite. Since the Slansky trial in Prague in November 1952 they had good reason to believe that Stalin had become an anti-semite and was planning a purge of Jews from leading positions.[54] Nevertheless, Stalin and communism had been almost synonymous for a quarter of a century; his death was bound to make all communists uneasy about the future. Stalin's absolute personal rule was replaced by a collective leadership in which at first Malenkov, chairman of the Council of Ministers of the USSR, played the most important role. The other leading members of the CPSU presidium were Beria, the minister of internal affairs and chief of the security police, Molotov, the minister of foreign affairs, Bulganin, the minister of defence, and Khrushchev, one of the secretaries of the CPSU Central Committee. These men were the new masters not only of the Soviet Union but of the whole Soviet bloc, and their decisions were to have profound consequences for Poland.

Officially, the passing of Stalin was deeply mourned in the Soviet Union and throughout the communist world. In Poland the industrial capital of the country, Katowice, was renamed Stalinogród to honour his memory, and Bierut publicly pledged the PZPR's fidelity to 'the immortal teachings of Comrade Stalin', but soon it became clear that the Soviet leaders were by no means happy about the legacy of the Stalin era. They extolled the virtues of collective leadership, stressed the role of the masses in the building of socialism and advocated the restoration of 'leninist norms of state and Party life'. They also set about easing the burden of stalinist policies for the Soviet people and the peoples of the Soviet bloc. This took the form of a programme of relaxation known as the New Course, which was decided in Moscow some time in May 1953. The rate of industrialization and collectivization had brought the economies of the people's democracies to breaking point. The Soviet leaders, burdened with grave problems at home, were in no position to supply aid to their satellites. The effects of the New Course showed themselves earliest in Czechoslovakia, East Germany and Hungary. In Czechoslovakia temporary concessions were made to consumers after a wave of strikes on 30 May. In East Germany, incipient concessions were interpreted as a sign of weakness by the population, and an abortive uprising, quickly suppressed by Soviet occupation forces, took place on 16–17 June. In Hungary, after intense manoeuvring behind the scenes, in which Soviet leaders were heavily involved, the all-powerful Party secretary, Matyas Rakosi, yielded the premiership to Imre Nagy, and agreed to the introduction of the New Course on 4 July. Its main features were drastic cuts in the investment programme, the breaking up of collective farms, the rehabilitation of Rakosi's victims and a far-reaching cultural thaw. In the Soviet Union, probably because of the struggle against Beria and the upheaval in the security apparatus, Malenkov formally announced the New Course only on 8 August. A series of measures was adopted to alleviate the plight of collective farmers, stimulate farming, and increase the production of consumer goods. The security police was downgraded and brought under Party control, and an amnesty was granted for political offenders. Freer popular criticism and stricter observance of rules began to be insisted on, and there was a 'thaw' in the arts, literature and science. Simultaneously the Soviet leaders sought a détente with the West, beginning with the armistice in Korea signed on 27 July 1953. The occupation of Austria was ended on 15 May 1955 and a four-power summit meeting, the first since 1945, was held in Geneva in July 1955. Soviet diplomacy, however, failed to prevent West Germany agreeing to join NATO in October 1954, and the Soviet response was the creation of a formal military alliance of the European communist states named the Warsaw Treaty Organization, after the Polish capital where it was signed on 14 May 1955.[55] The domestic reform process was only temporarily halted in the USSR after Malenkov resigned on 8 February 1955 and was replaced by Bulganin as chairman of the Council of Ministers. But elsewhere in the Soviet bloc the conservative leaders used Malenkov's fall as an excuse to put a brake on reforms. In Hungary Rakosi promptly branded the New Course as 'right-wing opportunism' and had Nagy expelled from the government and Party.

Poland was the last people's democracy to embark on its version of the New Course. Bierut launched it at the Ninth Central Committee Plenum on 29–30 October, and reaffirmed it at the Second PZPR Congress held between 10 and 17 March 1954, where, as a gesture towards collective leadership, he passed on the premiership to Cyrankiewicz and became simply first secretary of the PZPR Central Committee. There is no evidence that the Polish leaders, like the Hungarian, had to be pressed by the Kremlin into initiating reforms. Strains in the economy caused by the exigencies of the Six Year Plan clearly dictated some relaxation. They probably felt that the situation in Poland, being less desperate than elsewhere in the bloc, required less radical remedies, but the concrete measures adopted were exceedingly modest. Investment was stabilized at the 1953 level so that the proportion of the national income available for consumption could rise from 75 to 80 per cent. In fact, the rate of accumulation declined only by 5.4 per cent in 1954 and 1.7 per cent in 1955, and the effect on the standard of living of the urban population was slight. Agricultural production was to rise by 10 per cent in two years through reduced compulsory deliveries and taxes and increased credits and state investment.[56] Although most of the investment went into the inefficient collective and state farms, grain and meat production of private farmers did improve in 1954 and for the first time exceeded the 1949–50 level. While 1953 saw an intensification of the collectivization drive, the use of 'administrative measures' to further collectivization was now denounced and strictly forbidden. As a result, only half of the 3,000 planned new farms were set up in 1954 and the number dropped to 423 in 1955. The expected improvement in productivity, administrative economies and deliveries of industrial goods to the countryside failed to materialize. No change occurred in Party work during 1954, despite a campaign of criticism and self-criticism. The same could be said of the Party's 'transmission belts' to the masses, such as the ZMP, trade unions or people's councils, where centralization, bureaucracy, Party domination, irregular functioning, social discrimination and 'soulless attitude' to the needs of the masses were vigorously denounced.

There was, however, marked improvement in the press and in cultural life. The so-called social–cultural weeklies and some 'non-party' dailies initiated discussions of marriage and divorce, family life, sexual promiscuity, juvenile delinquency and poor standards of school instruction. Their causes were not probed deeply, but disturbing phenomena were fully and vividly described. The glib official optimism of previous years that socialism solved all problems and the avoidance of embarrassing questions gave way to a mood of frankness, criticism and disagreement. In the treatment of economic, political or international issues, however, the old restraints still applied. Nevertheless, the liveliness of the press reflected a ferment in the Warsaw artistic and intellectual milieux. This ferment represented the widespread discontent with socialist realism and dogmatic marxism and the way they had been imposed on the creative intelligentsia. At the first sign of 'thaw' the fragile façade of conformity to the Party line crumbled away, never to appear again.[57] In April 1954 the minister of culture and art, Sokorski, confessed that there had been deterioration in the whole area of art in the last few years, and blamed it on the false interpretation of socialist realism as a set of prescribed styles and subjects. The artists heartily agreed and pointed out the impossibility of finding a resting point between the artists' personal interpretation of what socialism and realism were and an authoritarian conception of these terms. A minor literary revival followed the liberalization of the Party line. In the poems of Hertz, the short stories of Andrzejewski and the weekly literary column of Rudnicki a mood of dissatisfaction with the absurdities of the stalinist system, though carefully disguised, began to communicate itself to the readers. Some realist non-Party writers such as M. Dąbrowska or J. Iwaszkiewicz began appearing in print again, and earned official praise for their objectivity in dealing with the current problems of Polish life. The relaxed cultural policy had a similarly stimulating effect on the theatre, cinema, visual arts and architecture. The dogmatic interpretation of marxism in the social sciences had already in mid-1953 been challenged by the sociologist J. Chałasiński, who had refused to recant even when rebuked by the Party's chief spokesman in this field, Adam Schaff. Critical thoughts about marxist economics were voiced in December 1953. From the Institute of Social Sciences, up to now a bastion of stalinist orthodoxy, came demands for serious study of non-marxist theories and current Western philosophical trends, the resumption of empirical research of social problems and more genuine academic polemics. The artistic and intellectual ferment went beyond the intention of the Party leaders and in a way was a kind of 'court rebellion', in which the courtiers showed their disapproval of the way they had recently been treated by their royal masters. It was also the first indication that, in some fields at least, the Polish Party leaders were losing their unquestioned authority.

The New Course renewed

It will be remembered that in 1952 Bierut had agreed to the setting-up of a secret Tenth Department within the UB to watch over the political reliability of the top Party cadre. After Beria's arrest, the deputy head of the Department, Colonel J. Światło, defected to the West. In September 1954 he began broadcasting to Poland on Radio Free Europe and the text of his talks, *Behind the Scenes of the UB and the Régime*, was printed as a pamphlet and dropped by balloons sent from Munich over Poland.[58] Full of lurid details about Soviet interference, security-police methods and the life and personalities of the top Party leadership, Światło's broadcasts opened the eyes of the PZPR elite to the extent to which they themselves had come under surveillance of the secret police. Anticipating trouble, the politburo drew up a self-critical resolution about the lack of collective leadership in the Party and the government, and about the mistakes of the security police, and called a central *aktiv* meeting in November to discuss them. A storm of criticism of the leadership's isolation, security matters, economic policy, the imprisonment of Gomułka and the false charges against the KPP by the Comintern in 1938 broke over Bierut's head and, because nobody was willing to defend the leadership, 'it found itself in complete isolation'.[59] Bierut's prestige never fully recovered after that, and he was obliged to make important concessions to his critics. A large number of political prisoners, including Gomułka, but also many anti-communist politicians and resistance leaders, were released without publicity. The security police were severely criticized in the press, and Radkiewicz, its head since 1944, was demoted and excluded from the politburo. Although the UB was only partially purged at this stage, its influence in the Party ended and its role in the country began shrinking rapidly.

Between 21 and 24 January 1955 the Central Committee's Third Plenum met and revealed a deep cleavage.[60] A minority of die-hard stalinists, the nucleus of the later 'Natolin group', proposed a show trial of Berman as a scapegoat for the UB abuses and a sweeping wage rise to win working-class popularity. Bierut resisted this and sided with the majority, who preferred to popularise the system by further policy changes and institutional reforms. The result of the elections to the people's councils at the end of December 1954, the first since they were set up in 1944, during which no harm was caused by allowing voters to nominate some candidates, strengthened the case for general 'democratization' of the whole system. The plenum passed three resolutions.[61] The first dealt with security matters and the need to strengthen the rule of law. The second criticized bureaucracy in the Party work and called for reforms in the mass organizations, propaganda and the press. The third resolution concerned some reforms of the planning and management system in industry and the strengthening of the Party supervision over the economic aparatus. The philosophy behind the reform programme, the first of three comprehensive programmes of 'democratization', was clearly spelt out in the last resolution. As investment could not be seriously cut without jeopardizing industrialization, the extra output needed to raise the standard of living had to come through greatly increased productivity, achieved at shop-floor level. The mass of workers, technicians and managers had to be freed from regimentation and encouraged to show initiative and extra effort. A new political climate had to be created in the country and especially in industry. The task of supervising this process was assigned to two relatively young men with reformist reputations, Władysław Matwin and Jerzy Morawski, who were added to the Central Committee secretariat.

The victory of the reformists in the Party elite proved illusory. The political and economic reforms outlined in the programme were so modest that it is doubtful whether they would have achieved their objectives. In any case they were not implemented. In April 1955, after the fall of Malenkov in the Soviet Union and Nagy in Hungary, the politburo sent out another 'Central Committee letter' to Party authorities, which drew attention to cases of anti-Party activity, especially in literature, and urged 'the struggle on two fronts' against 'dogmatism' and 'sectarianism', but also against 'revisionism' and 'eclecticism' towards Party principles. This immunized the Party *apparat* against criticism of its methods and inhibited the advocates of radical reform. All earlier promises of reform remained unfulfilled. The Central Committee was powerless to discuss the change of front. Although it met briefly twice in June 1955 and February 1956, the agenda was confined to details of agricultural policy. While the leadership showed serious concern to improve agricultural production, its spokesman, the conservative Zenon Nowak, stressed the need to speed up collectivization.[62] It became clear that Bierut was moving steadily towards dogmatism. The Writers' Union and the Council of Culture and Art became platforms for polemics against 'ideological sabotage' in art, disguised as a critique of errors and distortions of socialist realism. A storm broke out when *Nowa Kultura* published Ważyk's *Poem for Adults*.[63] It was a call of a sincere party writer for struggle against the evil apparently inherent in socialism, but the furious Party leaders denounced it as 'slanderous' and dismissed the editor of the journal. Berman addressed a meeting of the Party's leading cultural and ideological activists in September, but the attempt at restoring discipline misfired. The activists, led by K. Brandys, a respected communist writer, turned furiously on Berman and criticized him and the politburo for introducing discredited controls and concealing from them the economic state of the country. The meeting revealed a virtual loss of authority of the Party's 'ideological dictator' and indirectly of Bierut himself.[64]

Apart from the writers' rebellion, three events in 1955 reduced Bierut's prestige. The first was a 'silent rehabilitation' of the KPP. After the January Plenum, a committee went to Moscow to enquire about the fate of the KPP leaders, whose deaths in the late 1930s had never been made public. The committee was informed that they had been executed on Beria's orders on trumped-up charges. Pictures of Warski, Walecki, Wera Kostrzewa, Brun, Ryng and Leński appeared in the Warsaw May Day Parade, and without a word of explanation they and their party began to be freely mentioned in the press. Bierut, a former Comintern official, had in the past supported the false charges against the KPP, and was now made to look foolish. The second embarrassing event was the resumption of relations between the Soviet Union and Yugoslavia and the withdrawal of the bitter charges once made against Tito by Moscow and repeated in Warsaw. The third event was a secret session of the CPSU Central Committee in July, at which Stalin's treatment of Tito and some of the Soviet wrongs against the people's democracies were strongly criticized. This strengthened the case for the rehabilitation of Gomułka, one of whose crimes in 1948 had been to take a pro-Titoist line. To stop the pressure for Gomułka's rehabilitation and demonstrate the politburo's power the authorities, in autumn 1955, staged a belated show trial of a non-communist ex-Minister who had been arrested to discredit the Gomułka group at the Third Central Committee Plenum in 1949.

At the end of December 1955 the PZPR politburo changed its mind again about reforms. A letter from the Central Committee about 'stronger ties with the masses' sounded an ideological alert. The persecution of national minorities was admitted and condemned. The government, having done little in the previous six months, took up such matters as alcoholism, extensively discussed a year before, the state of the retail trade, and poor working conditions in the coal mines. The draft of a new, less repressive, criminal code was published and judicial procedure in criminal cases reformed. A congress of the Union of Polish Lawyers was allowed to hold a stormy debate on the infringements of the rule of law. The ex-chief of the UB investigation department was sentenced to five years in prison for applying illegal methods in his work. In January 1956 the Party leadership in effect capitulated to the artists and in a leading article on art in *Nowe Drogi* (New Paths) renounced again any form of pressure, promising to accept the artists' own interpretation of socialist art. It was the death of the stalinist art dogma in Poland, and a clear indication that Bierut had again decided to appease the reformists in the Party elite. This was all the more remarkable as only on 21 December, the anniversary of Stalin's birth, he was resurrected from the relative obscurity of the last two years and commemorated as a leading theoretician of the communist movement in the Soviet Union, Poland and the rest of the Soviet bloc. The zigzags of Polish policy between January 1955 and January 1956 must surely have been caused by the complicated manoeuvres in the Soviet politburo, which eventually resulted in the victory of the anti-stalinist tendency at the next CPSU congress.

It was due partly to the small marxist section of the intelligentsia that the year 1955 was a turning-point in post-war Polish history. Socialist realism vanished from the artistic scene. In the theatre there was a revival of Brecht and Mayakovsky and an increased emphasis on the classics, foreign and national. The centenary of Mickiewicz's death was celebrated by the staging of his play *Dziady* (The Forefathers), which had vanished from the repertoire in the late 1940s. Young poets, born either in the 1920s, such as M. Białoszewski, Z. Herbert and W. Szymborska, or in the 1930s, such as J. Harasymowicz, S. Grochowiak and J. M. Rymkiewicz, made their début on the literary scene. Through some of them a type of poetry, non-realist as well as non-political, appeared after a five-year interval. Abstract painters, who had been driven underground in the early

1950s, began showing their work again. Contemporary Western music and jazz, banned for over five years, were now given official *imprimatur*. The cultural ferment affected also students and young graduates. Students' satirical theatres sprang up. Discussion groups were formed in universities and technical colleges, while 'clubs of the young intelligentsia' to counteract cultural stagnation and political apathy opened in the big towns and cities. Even the ZMP was influenced by the ferment, although its rigid structure made adaptation to new demands of its members difficult. The mood of the younger generation, the future elite of People's Poland, was well summed up in the manifesto of the reformed student weekly *Po Prostu* (Plain Speaking), which was soon to become that generation's leader: 'We are a group of young hotheads, students and graduates. We are people who cannot stop meddling with all that happens around us. We are a group of the discontented. We want more things, wiser things, better things'.[65] Another group of intellectuals, the economists, entered the stage at the end of 1955 with a discussion of the achievements of the Six Year Plan. Just as the boldest artists had questioned whether anything culturally valuable had been achieved in People's Poland, so now some of the economists began wondering aloud whether the economic results of the six years of rapid industrialization were worth the heavy price paid in other sectors of the economy. The discussion concerned mainly the years 1950–4; in 1955 a modest improvement in consumption, light industry and agricultural production did take place as planned. Nevertheless, the situation of the working class and the urban population in general was still very difficult and contrasted unfavourably with the modest new prosperity of the peasants.

The end of the Six Year Plan

The returns for the various parts of the economy coming in at the end of 1955 enabled Minc to claim that the standard of living of the population during the Six Year Plan had increased by 26 per cent. The figure contradicted the general impression that the standard of living had deteriorated, and it was strongly challenged by some economists. In July 1956 Ochab claimed a 13 per cent increase in real earnings during 1950–5, but this seemed incredibly high. As the Plan ended in December 1955, it seems legitimate at this point to raise the question of what exactly it had achieved.

The best private Polish analysis of the Plan summed up its main results in a table which clearly shows the gap between aims and achievements (see table 17). In most respects the Plan fell short of its aim. Consumption per

Table 17. *Unofficial analysis of the Six Year Plan*

	Level 1949	Plan 1955	Fulfilment 1955	Difference
National income	100	212.3	173.5	− 38.8
All investments	100	240.0	236.0	− 4.0
Industrial production	100	258.3	271.7	+ 13.4
Agricultural production	100	150.0	113.0	− 37.0
Real earnings	100	140.0	104.0–113.0	− 36.0 to − 27.0
Employment	100	160.0	156.0	− 4.0
Consumption per person	100	150.0–160.0	130.0–144.0	− 20.0 to − 16.0

Source: Jezierski, *Historia gospodarcza*, p. 150. (The lower figures for real earnings and consumption are the more probable.)

head, which was still very low in 1949, rose by less than one-third. Employment and investment were more or less as planned, but there was a huge disparity between the planned and actual size of the national income. During the years of the most intensive effort, 1951–3, it rose by only 8 per cent per annum, while the average annual rise during 1947–50 had been 20.7 per cent.[66] Not surprisingly, only the targets for industry were surpassed, because it was for the sake of industrial growth that everything else was sacrificed.

These figures do not tell the whole story. It is estimated that the whole of the industrial growth occurred in the factories already established before 1950, by their extension or more intensive working. Most of the new investment, because of its slowness or suspension during the final two years, brought results only some years later. Of the 210 biggest industrial enterprises planned, only 131 (62 per cent) had begun functioning (and then below capacity) before 1956, 12 (6 per cent) were still under construction, and 67 (32 per cent) were not even begun. The situation with medium-size and small enterprises was even worse. Most of the 630 planned were not built.[67] The greatest effort was made in heavy industry. Iron and steel absorbed over 20 per cent of all investment, fuel industry 18 per cent, machine building 17.5 per cent, and chemical industry 12.5 per cent. What was largely neglected was the development of electrical energy and the extraction of minerals. At the end of six years their capacity had increased only 35 per cent, while the capacity of the processing industries rose to 350 per cent. These figures illustrate the Soviet desire to build up in Poland, in the shortest possible time, the industrial potential useful for war. Even more striking was the neglect of consumer goods and light industry during the six years. The former obtained only 8 per cent and the latter 5 per cent of investment, while in Britain in the mid-1950s the corresponding figures were about 15 per cent and 13 per cent.[68] This under-investment greatly limited the possibility of improving the standard of living in later years.

The Plan almost, but not quite, solved the rural unemployment problem, but did little to even out the economic development of the country. The projects which were abandoned were exactly those to be located in economically backward areas of the country and in the Western Territories. Industrialization also created a large group of peasant–workers (1.5 million), who worked in industry, mostly on building sites, but continued to farm inefficiently. The Plan modernized the social structure of the country. About 2 million people migrated permanently from country to town.[69] The proportion of urban to rural population changed in six years from approximately 36:64 to 44:56. The number of people employed in state enterprises or state-controlled co-operatives increased approximately from 4 to 6.5 million. The size of the working class rose from 2.5 to over 4 million, but the new workers were mostly unskilled and working and living under very difficult conditions. The social structure of the peasantry changed little. The proportion of large farms declined from 6 to about 4 per cent of all farms, a phenomenon welcomed on ideological grounds, but which was, in fact, inimical to agricultural production because the large farms were more efficient and had the largest surpluses for sale. The number of people working on collective farms was 410,000, instead of the 4 million people forecast in the Plan for 1955.

There was a considerable expansion of education at all levels, although the Plan's target for secondary technical education was reached only by shortening the period of studies by one year. By 1955 primary education became universal in towns and near universal in the country, amounting to 83.3 per cent compared with 44.3 per cent after the war and 65.5 per cent in 1949–50. The number of pupils in vocational schools in 1955–6 was over 500,000 and the number of graduates over 100,000, but the percentage of working-class children in both was still modest. Higher education expanded rapidly. The number of schools went up from 59 in 1948–9 to 84 in 1954–5 and the number of students from 103,000 to 155,000, while higher-school teachers increased from about 3,000 in 1948–9 to 16,600 in 1955–6, and this became a foundation for a great expansion of higher education in the 1960s. The number of graduates in technical subjects, agriculture and medicine, rose at the expense of law, economics and the humanities, and brought about a change in the character of the intelligentsia, previously dominated by the latter subjects. The 'cultural revolution' aspect of the Six Year Plan can be illustrated by the increase in book titles from 4,600 in 1949 to 7,200 in 1955 and in the number of copies printed per annum from almost 73 million to 95.7 million, with a record 119 million in 1950. A large proportion must have been simply political propaganda. Between 1951 and 1955 the total number of books translated from Russian or one of the other Soviet languages was 5,181. In 1955 749 titles of books in Russian or one of the Soviet languages were translated into Polish and published in over 10 million copies. This was more than one-tenth of all published books that year and illustrates Soviet 'cultural imperialism' during those years. The number of such translations dropped dramatically after October 1956.

Polish history before the end of the Second World War unfolded in the shadow of the Soviet Union. At no time, however, has the impact of Poland's eastern neighbour been so great, intense, and direct as during the four years between the end of 1949 and the end of 1953. These were years of the sovietization of Poland, both in the sense of overt Soviet domination and exploitation of the country and of the wholesale copying of Soviet policies and institutions. Since Stalin was the chief architect of the Soviet type of socialism, we are right to describe these years as the period of the stalinization of Poland.

It is clear in retrospect, though it was less clear at the end of 1955, that the impact of stalinism on Poland was far less than one might have expected. Much of it proved superficial, almost a theatrical set which could be taken down without much trouble. This was especially the case in the realm of culture in the wide sense of the word. Other features, like the commitment to economic growth at the expense of consumption and welfare and the promotion of heavy industry over all other forms of production, proved more enduring. They could be modified in periods of crisis but reverted to the old tendency when difficulties were over. The most enduring part of all proved to be the heavily centralized and bureaucratic political and economic system. In the Party and the state, the economic administration and the trade unions, the system resisted all attempts to delegate authority to lower levels or to introduce some positive scheme of power-sharing between officials and unofficial activists or to create an institutional form of mass influence from below.

The reasons why stalinism, in at least some respects, proved to be superficial are not difficult to see. There was the obvious difference of time scale. Stalin's impact on the Soviet Union lasted some twenty to thirty years, depending on when one regards his influence to have been paramount. His impact on Poland lasted at most nine years, and, in a brutal and unrestrained way, just over three years. When Stalin died, Poland was only in the fourth year of forced industrialization, at an early stage of collectivization, still predominantly Roman Catholic and Western-orientated. Moreover in Poland, unlike the Soviet Union and some of the other people's democracies, when stalinism was established between 1949 and 1953, its ideological opponents in the political and social elite were silenced and relegated to obscurity, at most imprisoned, but not physically liquidated. Conformity to the Party's stalinist line was strictly enforced only in public at stage-managed meetings of official bodies and in publications of all kinds. 'Backstage' doubts, criticism and disagreements never quite disappeared. They were merely confined to groups and milieux where people trusted each other. In other words, spying and denunciation, though widespread, had a limit. Much of Polish stalinism was extremely superficial, not merely because it was introduced too hastily, but also because it was not really necessary to the system. In the USSR, stalinist institutions, policies and ideas were responses to crises of the system or peculiar problems facing the Soviet leadership or challenges to Stalin's personal authority, but Poland's relation to the USSR ensured that there was no danger from inside or outside to the régime. The need to prepare for a possible armed conflict with the West in the worsening international situation justified only some of the policies followed in Poland after 1948. It was the Soviet desire for the security of their western flank which explains the extent of the sacrifices and controls actually imposed. Thus Polish stalinism was a product of Soviet rather than Polish needs, when something far less drastic would have suited the requirements of the Polish situation much better, and would no doubt have been followed without Soviet pressure.

It is inconceivable that, left to themselves, the Polish leadership, for all their isolation from the rest of the nation, would have adopted all the policies and the institutional structure which they did adopt between 1949 and 1953. Rapid industrialization, collectivization, and struggle against capitalist elements and bourgeois influences, although a matter of principle to Bierut, would have been pursued with a good deal of caution, as the period from the middle of 1948 to the end of 1949 suggests. National traditions would have been flouted less ruthlessly and Soviet models copied more critically. Loyalty to Stalin and to the Soviet Union would probably have stopped short of 'inviting' a Soviet marshal to take over command of the Polish forces. Part of the reason was that Polish stalinists were on the whole much less brutal than stalinists elsewhere and less inclined to go to extremes. Another partial explanation is that, unlike the Czechs or the Romanians, they had to govern a country severely ravaged by war and the Nazi terror, where human resources were extremely scarce. Yet another possible reason is that like most rulers they preferred to interpret situations and take decisions themselves instead of having them imposed from outside. They probably felt that they knew the situation better than the Kremlin and its 'advisers' and should be trusted to do their best. They did of course have a margin of discretion, but it was slender.

In the end Soviet domination and exploitation, although it fulfilled short-term Soviet objectives, worked against the interest of communism in Poland. The resentment against harsh government policies was increased by the hatred of subordination to a foreign power. National pride led people to dismiss the Party leadership as 'Soviet agents' and the system of government as a 'Soviet occupation'. Thus the chances of a free acceptance of the system by the bulk of the population, a pre-condition of stability and viability of any régime, became more than ever remote. Of course the number of those who had a direct stake in the system, the swollen *apparats*, the new technical intelligentsia and the peasants turned workers, grew steadily, but they shared popular attitudes to the Soviet Union and their own commitment to communism was weakened. Even the Party elite must have shared in the anti-Soviet feeling, though for other reasons. They were the men who experienced the presence of Soviet superiors most directly and found their sphere of influence and chances of promotion restricted. The Soviet leaders and their local representatives wore kid gloves after 1953, but the iron fist was still there. Until the Polish communists gained full internal autonomy, they could not hope to be regarded as legitimate rulers of their country. In 1956 they found the courage to demand that autonomy.

The October turning point

The Twentieth CPSU Congress

The Twentieth Congress of the Communist Party of the Soviet Union had been expected for some time, and it is known that on 27 and 28 January representatives of the people's democracies were forewarned that the congress would be critical of Stalin,[1] but well before that date the agenda must have been circulated to the East European leaders, and it must have made clear that the congress would be a continuation of the New Course. The congress took place in Moscow between 14 and 25 February and was attended by foreign communist leaders. The Polish delegation consisted of Bierut, Berman, Zawadzki, Cyrankiewicz and Morawski. In his speech Bierut spoke of the deep love of Poland for the Soviet Union and the willingness of the PZPR to be guided by the experience of the CPSU. The main themes of the congress speeches and debates were already familiar ones of the New Course. The doctrine of different roads to socialism, invoked by Khrushchev in the summer of 1955, was endorsed and the possibility of a peaceful establishment of the communist system was also admitted. Otherwise the congress had little to say about communist parties or their relations with the CPSU. The past exploitation of the people's democracies was not referred to even indirectly. Nevertheless, the moribund Cominform, once Stalin's tool for imposing Soviet wishes on the people's democracies, was dissolved not long after the congress, on 17 April 1956. An important event for the PZPR was the formal rehabilitation of the pre-war Polish Communist Party (KPP), announced in *Trybuna Ludu* on 19 March. A communiqué, issued in the name of the Central Committees of the PZPR and of those communist parties whose representatives on the Comintern executive had dissolved the KPP in 1938, stated that the alleged penetration of the KPP by enemy agents 'was based on materials which were falsified by subsequently exposed provocateurs'. The reaction in Poland was one of shock rather than satisfaction. Letters and articles published in the Party press asked why such a tragic mistake had been made and remained unrectified for seventeen years. The shock had not quite subsided when a far greater one, caused by Khrushchev's denunciation of Stalin, rocked the Polish Party a month or so later and raised even more fundamental questions.

On 25 February, at a closed session of the congress, from which foreign delegates were excluded, Khrushchev delivered a report in which he scathingly denounced the 'cult of personality' established by Stalin, his despotic and suspicious mentality, his policy mistakes and the numerous crimes he committed after 1934 to establish his personal dictatorship.[2] Khrushchev by no means rejected the whole of Stalin's work, but he said more than enough to shatter Stalin's prestige and his claim to be a political genius equal to Lenin. Bierut, who stayed behind after the congress, was probably the first Polish leader to read the full text. One can imagine what a great blow it must have been to him after the many eulogies of Stalin he had delivered. Bierut had been seriously ill for some time.[3] It is not improbable that the shock of reading the speech contributed to the heart attack from which he died in Moscow just before midnight on 11 March. He was buried with great ceremony in Warsaw four days later and praised in Poland and throughout the Soviet bloc as a fearless communist. Towards the end of March the text of Khrushchev's speech, possibly somewhat edited, was sent to the leaders of the people's democracies. The conjunction of those two events, the political death of Stalin and the natural death of Bierut, increased the ferment in the PZPR and speeded up the trend towards democratization.

Bierut left no obvious successor and there appeared to be a number of contenders. According to subsequent rumours, Khrushchev, who came for Bierut's funeral and stayed on to attend the PZPR Central Committee Plenum on 20 March, opposed Zambrowski because he was Jewish, and canvassed support for Zenon Nowak.[4] This interference with the leadership issue was probably deeply resented by the Polish Central Committee. Khrushchev's apparent anti-semitism must also have caused dismay among the large Jewish group in the PZPR elite, who began to associate Khrushchev's influence with the prospect of a purge of Jews. Although the Jewish problem burst openly on the Polish political scene only twelve years later, it powerfully influenced events already in 1956. It may partially explain why the same men who had faithfully carried out Soviet instructions for over ten years were later that year prepared to defy them. In supporting the autonomy of the PZPR they were preserving their political future. The man the PZPR Central Committee actually elected as its first secretary was Edward Ochab, already one of the Central Committee secretaries and a leading member of the Polish communist group in the USSR during the war. Two additional Central Committee secretaries with contrasting background were elected at the same time, Jerzy Albrecht and Edward Gierek. For the latter this was an important promotion, which eventually led to his becoming first secretary at the end of 1970.[5] Ochab was known for his past toughness in pursuing stalinist policies, but now showed great willingness to promote in Poland the directives of the Twentieth Congress. He made his position clear at a joint meeting of the Warsaw City and Province Party *aktiv* conference on 6 April, and the fact that his speech appeared in full in *Pravda* was a sign that the Soviet leadership approved it. Ochab strongly criticized the reform programme of the Third Central Committee Plenum as too timid and inadequately implemented. He announced the setting up of a Central Committee commission, with co-opted *aktiv* members, to prepare a more radical programme of democratization for approval by the next Central Committee plenum. He also promised a number of immediate measures including a rise in wages and salaries, some industrial decentralization and a political amnesty. These were soon after put into force by the Council of Ministers and the sejm, which had a somewhat longer, livelier and more productive spring session than was usual. The amnesty was a sweeping measure because it applied even to anti-communist leaders of the resistance movement and socialist and populist politicians. For a decade there were to be no political prisoners in Poland. At the conference, however, Ochab made public only the release of prominent communists arrested during stalinism and, though absolving Gomułka of all criminal charges, insisted that he had caused the Party great political damage. Radkiewicz and Dworakowski, past and present ministers of public security, Świątkowski, the minister of justice, the procurator general and the chief military procurator were all dismissed from their posts. Fejgin, the head of the Tenth Department, and Romkowski, deputy minister of public security, were arrested, tried and given prison sentences.

Simultaneously with the Warsaw *aktiv* conference, the text of Khrushchev's secret speech was released by the Central Committee secretariat in a large edition of copies. In the USSR and the other people's democracies the speech was read out only in closed meetings of communist officials and activists. In Poland it was read out to the rank and file of the PZPR and ZMP members at meetings to which also non-party men were often admitted. The effect on the younger Party members was shattering. The hero they had been trained to worship was now shown up as a bungler and murderer. The Party intelligentsia threw itself into a vehement campaign of criticism. At the 24–25 March meeting of the Culture and Art Council the literary critic, Jan Kott, scathingly criticized the Party's cultural dictatorship in the past. A month later Sokorski resigned as minister of culture and art, and on 6 May the resignation from the politburo of his patron Berman was announced. From then on Party control over the activities of the Writers' Union ceased and for some years the Party leadership stopped concerning themselves with culture altogether. Urged by the poet Słonimski, the writers now joined a more general struggle for civil and political freedom, recognizing that the freedom of creative activity was secure only in the context of a liberalized political system.[6] Other sections of the intelligentsia followed in their footsteps. The lawyers and the journalists at a joint conference attacked blatant illegality and the lack of judicial independence. The Polish Academy of Sciences and the Polish Economic Association held stormy congresses in June, condemned the consequences of stalinism and removed its more compromised exponents from positions of authority. The scientists insisted that the successful 'construction of socialism' was incompatible with a dogmatic interpretation of marxism and its enforcement by 'administrative means', and blamed the politicians for having retarded scientific progress and impoverished national culture. At the April conference Ochab had criticized the press for straying into anti-party positions in their otherwise laudable zeal for democratization, but this criticism had little effect. The sharpness and independence of press criticism rose markedly after the secret speech, especially in two Warsaw dailies, *Życie Warszawy* (Life of Warsaw) and *Sztandar Młodych* (The Standard of Youth), a ZMP newspaper, and three weeklies, *Przegląd Kulturalny* (Cultural Reviews), *Nowa Kultura* (New Culture) and *Po Prostu*.[7] Led by the last, which became the most sought-after paper in Poland, all these newspapers became aggressively political in tone and ventured into hitherto forbidden territories. Their favourite instrument was the so-called 'unmasking reportage', which frankly exposed scandals, abuses and incompetence in various institutions, and mercilessly pilloried all kinds of *apparatchiki*, especially in the provinces. *Po Prostu*'s reporters roamed the country striking fear and hatred in the local officials, trying to break the conspiracy of silence which generally met them, and making contact with people, mainly young and from the intelligentsia, who cared about democratization and were prepared to do something to further it. The literary equivalent of the journalistic reports were short stories of writers such as Marek Hłasko, who specialized in portraying the brutality of everyday life in Poland with stark realism, a sort of 'anti-socialist realism'. 'Politicization' after the Twentieth CPSU Congress affected particularly strongly students and young graduates, who were a link between the older generation of intellectuals and the ZMP and the mass of unorganized young people. The thriving students' theatres turned to explicit political

satire, and the young intelligentsia clubs became forums for the discussion
of political and economic issues, rather than social and cultural ones, as
was the rule in 1955. On a small scale the clubs reproduced something of
the heated atmosphere and ideological ferment of the capital in the
otherwise calm provinces. The ZMP was in turmoil and uncertain of its
future. Many of its national leaders and activists more or less abandoned
the hope of regenerating the huge, all-embracing organization, and
favoured the concept of a smaller, more elitist and ideological body, in
the revolutionary marxist-leninist tradition, to fight for the achievement
of a truly socialist democracy in the country at large. Meanwhile,
impatience with the ZMP's immobility and disbelief in its radical reform
led to the spontaneous formation of 'revolutionary committees' as the
nuclei of the revolutionary youth organization of the future.

There was a semblance of a spontaneous development in that remarkable
ideological ferment and political militancy which occurred in Poland after
the Twentieth CPSU Congress, but the system of communist rule known
as 'democratic centralism' was still intact in the first half of 1956. It was
simply that certain newspapers, publications, institutions and organizations
had the usual controls relaxed or suspended as a deliberate policy, broadly
sanctioned by the politburo, but interpreted in detail by the Central
Committee secretariat. It is here that the role of the secretariat was crucial.
It had radically changed in composition since 1954, and was far more
reformist than the politburo. Ochab, Morawski, Matwin and Albrecht
were clearly 'democratizers' and Gierek was at least not opposed. Only
Mazur was a stalinist by reputation and he controlled the territorial Party
bureaucracy. This explains why most of the country, which was still under
the thumb of the PZPR *apparat*, lagged so far behind Warsaw in political
excitement. On the other hand, the politburo's composition was still
largely the same as in the spring of 1954, when Bierut was in charge. Its
members were sufficiently loyal to Moscow not to oppose the decisions
of the Twentieth CPSU Congress, but they were inclined to accept only
a minimum of change, in short to follow Bierut's policy towards the New
Course. Most of the powerful provincial Party secretaries, of much the
same background as their politburo colleagues, fully shared this attitude.
Only in Warsaw, where Stefan Staszewski was secretary of the City Party
Committee, and in three other large cities, Łódź, Wrocław and Cracow, were
there reformist tendencies in the Party *apparat*. Below the level of
provincial organization the hierarchy of district, town, village and factory
apparatchiki remained unwilling to change their style of work. Recruited
and trained largely during the years of the 'stalinist cadre policy', generally
badly educated and of working-class or peasant origin, the lower officials

were best at giving and receiving orders in a chain of command without any discussion or consultation with their subordinates. The Party *aktiv* welcomed democratization because it promised them more influence and less tutelage by the Party *apparat*. The *apparat* saw democratization as a threat to its position in the system and was angry with the reformers in the Central Committee secretariat for allowing them to become the favourite target of journalists and sundry intellectuals, when all they had done in the past was to carry out the unpopular decisions of the leaders. The *apparat* also feared for their jobs as well as influence. Copying the decision of the Twentieth CPSU Congress, Ochab announced at the April *aktiv* meeting that the Party *apparat* would be reduced by one quarter in size, and the posts filled by unpaid activists. On the other hand, the press campaign and the 'politicization' of the youth movement were the means by which the reformist Central Committee secretaries tried to bring pressure on the lower Party *apparat* and on the people's councils and the trade unions which they controlled.

In the spring and early summer, political developments were confined almost wholly to the Party. The country as a whole had of course benefited from the reform measures taken since 1954, but at this stage it viewed with indifference and scepticism all the talk of democratization. The peasants reaped the benefits of the agricultural measures, and some of their nearly moribund organizations were beginning to stir a little, but as a mass they did not become politically involved until October. The workers had had some wage increases and tax reductions. Labour discipline and production pressure were relaxed. Illegalities such as overtime without extra pay or breaches of health and safety regulations were condemned in the press, but they were still rife while the plan remained sacrosanct. The trade unions did nothing about the situation, but workers began to be affected by the propaganda about democratization and conscious of the gap between promises of better things and the harsh realities of their everyday life and work. At the end of June they became a force of tremendous importance, changing the whole political situation in the Party, the country, and in Polish–Soviet relations.

The Poznań events

In December 1955 the workers of the Poznań Stalin Works (Zakłady Imieniem Stalina, Poznań – ZISPO) discovered that through some bureaucratic error they had not benefited from a tax allowance introduced in the previous year.[8] ZISPO, before 1939 known as Cegielski Works, was then the largest industrial enterprise in Poland, employing 15,000 workers and specializing in the production of rolling stock. As the local Party and trade union *apparat* showed no interest in their case, the ZISPO workers, through elected delegates, tried to get the error rectified by direct representations to the factory management, the branch administration and finally the ministry in Warsaw. The matter dragged on for six months without any result, and finally the exasperated workers, goaded by other grievances and dissatisfaction with their standard of living, decided to demonstrate in protest. Early in the morning of 28 June, a day before the end of the annual International Trade Fair, which brought numerous foreign businessmen to Poznań, the ZISPO workers marched to the city centre and were joined by workers from other Poznań factories. They carried banners with the slogans 'Bread and Freedom'. The crowd would not listen to a local Party secretary and demanded talks with Premier Cyrankiewicz. When neither he nor any other government or Party spokesman materialized for four hours, the crowd became violent. Shops and a radio jamming station were demolished, prisoners released from the local jail, and the city UB headquarters unsuccessfully attacked with firearms seized from police stations. In the afternoon army units arrived and dispersed the demonstrators with rifle and machine-gun fire, but sporadic exchanges of fire continued for two more days. The official figures were 53 people killed and about 300 wounded, and 323 arrested for taking part in the riots or on suspicion of organizing the demonstration. It was the first incident of this kind in People's Poland and the third working-class demonstration in the communist bloc since the death of Stalin, the others being in Pilsen and East Berlin in 1953.

The Poznań events, as they came to be euphemistically called in Poland, could be interpreted in two diametrically opposed ways, and used as an argument for or against democratization. They could be viewed as an example of the Party's loss of contact with the masses and the separation of the rulers from ordinary people by a thick wall of bureaucracy, which proved that further and more radical democratization was urgently needed, but they could also be considered as an attack on the socialist system, which no workers could possibly have attempted unless provoked by some elements hostile to socialism. The success of the provocation could be blamed on the excessive freedom of press criticism, the weakening of the security police and the unsettling effect of the whole policy of democratization. The PZPR leaders at first chose the second interpretation. Broadcasting to the nation on the evening of 28 June, Cyrankiewicz branded the events as a provocation staged by foreign agents,[9] and threatened to chop off the sinister hands raised against the 'people's power'. The Party's propaganda apparatus simultaneously unleashed a virulent campaign of condemnation through newspapers, radio and mass meetings. Given the composition of the Warsaw politburo it is not surprising that its majority reacted in such a stalinist way, all the more so as this was also the reaction of the Moscow CPSU presidium. It has been shown that the Soviet press,[10] which had up to then been propagating destalinization, abruptly changed its tone after the Poznań riots and began defending the Soviet system against criticism. On 30 June a specially summoned CPSU Central Committee passed a resolution which stressed the tremendous achievements of 'socialist construction' in the USSR and the positive effects of Stalin's leadership. The majority which had supported Khrushchev since the Twentieth Congress broke up as a result of the Poznań upheaval. No attempt was made to remove Khrushchev from his post of first secretary until July 1957, but he was now the prisoner of a new, conservative majority clearly anxious to put a brake on destalin-ization in the USSR and the Soviet bloc. Yet on 1 July, the day after the CPSU resolution, the Polish Radio broadcast a revised judgement on the Poznań events, which showed that the PZPR leadershp had changed its mind. Without quite abandoning the 'enemy agents' theme, the emphasis was now put on the legitimate grievances of the workers and the responsibility for the riots placed on state, Party and trade-union officials who had callously ignored the grievances. With the support of the Central Committee, now in the final stages of preparing the second democratization programme through its various sub-commissions, the Polish politburo decided to defy its Soviet counterpart. For the first time since the communist régime was established in Poland the Polish Party leaders disagreed with their Moscow superiors on a major issue of policy. It was a historic step towards the PZPR's autonomy in internal matters.

The Polish Central Committee met for its Seventh Plenum on 18 July, and Ochab's opening address confirmed that democratization was to be the Party's policy, despite Poznań. Soon after, the Soviet government delegation of Marshals Bulganin and Zhukov, chairman of the Council of Ministers and the minister of defence, arrived in Warsaw, ostensibly to take part in the twelfth anniversary celebrations of People's Poland. Already at the airport Bulganin warned against attempts to separate Poland and the Soviet Union, criticized the Polish press and repeated the Soviet thesis about the 'imperialist provocation' in Poznań. On 24 July *Pravda* supported him with an article warning communist parties against reform-ism and revisionism, and urging them to maintain the 'monolithic unity' of the 'countries of the socialist system'. These attempts at cajoling the Polish leaders failed. The Central Committee plenum adjourned without inviting the distinguished guests to attend, and reconvened after they left the country on 27 July. On 28 July the democratization programme was formally adopted, together with new directives for the 1956–60 economic plan, the decision to summon the Third Party Congress in March 1957, and certain personnel changes in the politburo.[11] The Central Committee also annulled that part of the November 1949 Central Committee Plenum resolution which concerned Gomułka, Spychalski and Kliszko as based on 'untruthful accusations', and readmitted them to the Party.

The second version of the democratization programme[12] was much more detailed and radical than the first in February 1955, but covered the same ground: there was to be a 'fundamental restructuring of Party work' to reduce the domination of the *apparat*, great autonomy for the ZMP, the trade unions and other organizations, more power to the sejm and the people's councils, decentralization of industry and consultation with workers over production, the strengthening of the rule of law, the preservation of cultural freedom and freedom of the press, and an end to discrimination against various groups. Kulaks, private craftsmen and small businessmen, ex-members of the Home Army and the Polish forces in the West, and ethnic minorities were mentioned specifically in this connection. The economic resolution of the plenum strongly criticized the results of the Six Year Plan – neglect of light industry, farming and consumption – and for the first time admitted that real earnings of workers and employees in the socialist sector had fallen during the period. In the new plan investment was to be cut by 43 to 47 per cent, making it possible to raise real earnings by 30 per cent. More resources were to be allocated to the neglected branches of the economy and to housing, social and community services, and cultural amenities. The sum earmarked to improve the standard of living of the poorest working people in 1956 was increased from 5 to 7 milliard *zł.*

Agreement on democratization was not achieved easily. Ochab wrote afterwards that 'the debates, the discussion in the commissions before the VII Plenum and at the Plenum itself were long, sometimes stormy and difficult'.[13] The reformist majority of the Central Committee got their way on the fundamental point, the continuation of the democratization course. But the conservative majority of the politburo insisted on inserting in the resolution a warning that 'the indispensible, revitalizing democratization process in our country cannot be carried through spontaneously, without taking into account the fact that it is taking place in a country in which socialism is still being constructed and in which there are and operate class antagonisms, bourgeois reactionary and nationalist ideological influences, supported and exploited by the class enemy and the alien, imperialist *agentura*'. The democratization course was hence to be another 'struggle on two fronts', against 'the consequences of the personality cult' on the one hand, and against spontaneity, anti-socialism and anti-Soviet sentiments on the other. The trouble was that the rival wings of the Party elite continued to have very different views on the relative importance of the 'two fronts'. Provincial Party committees paid lip service to the July Central Committee resolutions, but did little to change their methods. Trade unions remained passive, though there was at last some self-criticism at the top. In the armed forces democratization was not even allowed to be discussed. The knowledge that the Party leadership was divided in its views and that the Soviet leaders now opposed democratization inevitably encouraged passivity in the conservative wing of the Party.

In Warsaw, however, the Seventh Central Committee Plenum stimulated the reformist wing to greater struggle for democratization. The government dismissed the chairman of the State Planning Commission, Eugeniusz Szyr, and replaced him by Stefan Jędrychowski. When the sejm met in September to hear the governmental programme, Professor Julian Hochfeld sharply criticized the government for continuing to treat the sejm with contempt, and obtained a promise of reform from Cyrankiewicz. The trial of the participants in the Poznań riots, which also opened in September, set a new standard in judicial impartiality. The defence had complete freedom of action, and pleaded the diminished responsibility of the accused, with the help of expert witnesses and theories of crowd psychology. Foreign observers were freely admitted to the trial and the sentences were extremely light.[14] Just after the trial began the ministers who had refused to listen to the grievances of the ZISPO workers were dismissed. Some unpopular people's councils chairmen were spontaneously dismissed by their councils, but the most striking case of spontaneity was the setting up in September of a 'workers' council' in the Żerań motorcar factory in Warsaw by the factory Party committee. With the tacit support of the Warsaw City Committee, other Warsaw factories began setting up such councils, elected by a secret ballot and claiming the right to supervise the management and share its functions. The working-class reformists saw in the councils a break with the stalinist system of management, which was causing the workers' alienation from socialism. The idea was welcomed enthusiastically by the Party intelligentsia and the 'revolutionary' youth movement, and promptly denounced by the stalinist chairman of the CRZZ as a 'blind imitation of the Yugoslav model'. Poland normalized relations with Yugoslavia after the Twentieth Congress, after a gap of eight years, and Yugoslav developments began to be known in Poland through the articles of Polish journalists visiting the country and the visits of Yugoslav social scientists to Poland. Workers' Councils had long been advocated by Western socialist theoreticians as a counterweight to state bureaucracy, and set up spontaneously in Poland just after the occupation, so that it is not certain that the Yugoslav example was decisive. Faced with this initiative from below, the Party leadership consulted a conference of the central economic *aktiv* and then welcomed the councils with some caution and passed a law which provided a basis for their general introduction into state industry. At the same time a Party–Government Commission, which included the economist Michael Kalecki, prepared a number of measures which increased the autonomy of enterprises in some respects and were a modest step towards the decentralization of the economic system.

The Polish October

The PZPR had a definite political and economic programme, wrote Ochab after the Seventh Central Committee Plenum in *Nowe Drogi*; its paramount need was now 'the unity and cohesion of the Central Committee, and the uniting and rallying of the whole Party round the Central Committee'. But in fact after Poznań the leaders of the PZPR became so deeply split that the consistent pursuit of the July programme was quite impossible. Only a new politburo, composed of men sincerely committed to the programme, had any hope of carrying it through, restoring unity and reasserting strong leadership at the top. If Poznań and the change in Soviet attitude to destalinization had not taken place, some kind of 'showdown' with the conservatives might have happened at the Seventh Plenum and the more die-hard of them dropped from the politburo. Now they had to be edged out more gently, by argument and compromise, and this was bound to be slower and more difficult. The process was complicated further by the decision to include Gomułka, readmitted to the Party after the plenum, in the new politburo, and to negotiate with him the terms of his entry. The negotiations with Gomułka did not remain secret for long, and support for his return to the politburo began to be expressed with increasing urgency. Also the rumour gained wide circulation in Warsaw that a group of stalinist die-hards were opposing him and the July programme. They were nicknamed 'Natolinites' after the Party elite country house at Natolin near Warsaw, where they began meeting in the summer of 1956.[15] On the eve of the Eighth Central Committee Plenum the press denounced 'the enemies of democratization' in the Party and demanded the publication of their names. The demand was taken up by the 'revolutionary' groups in the youth movement, the factory Party committees which supported the workers' councils, and other Party organizations, particularly among the intelligentsia. Meetings and rallies all over Warsaw demonstrated their support for democratization and for Gomułka's return to the politburo. Had the die-hards attempted a *coup d'état*, as was widely feared, the youth of Warsaw and sections of the working class would have without doubt taken to the barricades to defend the safety of the Central Committee plenum. The Warsaw City Party Committee, which permitted and encouraged this turmoil, was breaking a fundamental communist convention that disputes within the Party leadership should be settled *in camera*, without the participation of the rank and file. The 'Natolinites' were, however, themselves guilty of breaking the convention which had more recently become established, that the Soviet leaders should be kept out of internal Polish Party conflicts. They seem to have alarmed the Kremlin by their reports on the situation in Poland so much that the Soviet leaders decided to intervene. A warning that this might happen came from an unexpected quarter, the head of the PAX movement, Piasecki, in an article in the newspaper under his control.

On the day the Eighth Plenum began, 19 October, a high-powered Soviet politburo delegation, including Khrushchev, Mikoyan, Molotov and Kaganovich, arrived uninvited in Warsaw and asked for talks with the Polish leaders.[16] Simultaneously Soviet troops began advancing from their bases towards Warsaw with the clear intention of intimidating the Poles. After proposing the co-option of Gomułka, Kliszko and Spychalski to the Central Committee the politburo suspended the proceedings for talks with the Soviet leaders, in which Gomułka also took part. The Russians complained about having been kept in the dark and made objections to impending changes. The Poles suggested discussions in Moscow and asked that Soviet troops return to their bases. After some bitter recriminations, Khrushchev and his colleagues were persuaded that the Polish leaders could keep the situation under control. They therefore returned to Moscow, having ordered the Soviet forces to withdraw. When the Central Committee resumed its meeting, Gomułka delivered a long speech, which was remarkable for its scathing condemnation of stalinism and its political and economic consequences in Poland. He described as 'clumsy' and 'very politically naive' the blaming of the Poznań events on imperialist agents and saboteurs, and called the events a painful lesson given by the working class to the Party leadership and the government. He called for an enquiry into security-police activities in the past. He accepted the programme of the Seventh Plenum as a correct solution to the country's difficulties, but assessed much more critically the results of the Six Year Plan and the agricultural policy of the Party during the period.[17] He nevertheless warned that the Party would not allow democratization to be exploited for anti-socialist purposes or to weaken Poland's friendship with the Soviet Union. Polish–Soviet relations had left something to be desired in the past, but were now re-established on the basis of equality and independence. The Party and the whole governmental and economic system needed thorough reform, but the Party had above all to be united and function according to democratic centralism in order to control the process of democratization. The speech, simultaneously relayed by radio to the country at large, won Gomułka instant personal popularity. It was debated by the Central Committee for the rest of the second and the third day of the plenum, and those who were not called upon to speak sent in written statements. Most of the speeches and statements dealt with the responsibility for the past, and were strongly critical or self-critical.[18] At the end of the third day of the plenum the Central Committee unanimously approved a resolution based on Gomułka's speech.[19] It was the third version of the democratization programme, which at last stood a good chance of implementation. In a secret ballot the Central Committee elected Cyrankiewicz, Gomułka, Jędrychowski, Loga-Sowiński, Morawski, Ochab, Rapacki, Zambrowski and Zawadzki members of the new politburo. Gomułka was elected first secretary of the Central Committee, but the other members of the secretariat were largely the same as before, except that Zambrowski replaced Mazur.[20] Zambrowski is reputed to have played a key role in winning the support of the conservative provincial Party secretaries and top governmental officials for the changes in the politburo. The 'Natolinites' made a proposal to add Rokossovsky to the politburo but he received only 23 out of 70 votes. Roughly the same number of votes were cast against Morawski and Zambrowski, for different reasons *bêtes noires* of the die-hard stalinists. The figures revealed the strength of this group in the Central Committee: one third of its full members.

The 'October turning point', as it came to be called, had profound consequences for both the external and internal situation of Poland. It was received coolly by the communist leaders of Bulgaria, Czechoslovakia, East Germany and Romania because they feared that the Polish example might generate pressure for democratization in their own countries. It was greeted with pleasure by Yugoslav leaders, who saw Poland moving towards their position with regard to the USSR and the Soviet model of socialism. In Hungary the reaction was dramatic.[21] Exasperated with the conservative leadership of Erno Gero, Rakosi's successor, the students of Budapest publicly demonstrated their sympathy for Polish developments on 23 October. When they were fired on by the security forces, a popular revolt against the Gero régime broke out in the capital. A Soviet military intervention transformed the nature of the protest, which became increasingly violent, anti-communist and anti-Russian, until the Hungarian Workers' Party and the whole political system disintegrated, multi-party democracy was proclaimed, and Hungary declared neutrality and withdrew from the Warsaw Pact. A renewed Soviet intervention on 4 November stifled the revolt and enabled a new pro-Soviet government of Janos Kadar to establish itself in power. The handling of the Hungarian crisis strained once more relations between the Soviet Union and Yugoslavia, and left Poland isolated in the Soviet bloc. The possibility of a Warsaw–Budapest–Belgrade axis of reformist communist states, which the Poles would have welcomed warmly, collapsed.

The Hungarian drama was tensely followed in Poland. Medical supplies and blood for transfusion generously volunteered by ordinary people were sent to Budapest, and the PZPR Central Committee called on the Hungarian communists and people to stop fighting and to rally to the original Nagy–Kadar government formed on 24 October.[22] The Polish leadership openly deplored the Soviet intervention and instructed the Polish representative in the UN to abstain in a vote on an anti-Soviet resolution in the General Assembly, which was the first and only time Poland fell out of step with the USSR in that body, but, as the slide to the right continued in Hungary, the necessity of the Soviet action was reluctantly accepted. The course of events in Hungary influenced Polish developments. It discredited the 'Natolinites', whose attempt to involve the Soviet leaders in the proceedings of the Eighth Plenum were seen as brinkmanship which might have led to a national tragedy. It vindicated the reformist leaders who, with Gomułka's aid, skilfully executed a difficult political manoeuvre without any disaster to the system of communist rule. Even the Soviet leaders, faced with the Hungarian debacle, must have been grateful that they did not have to contend with Poland at the same time and were more willing to accept the *status quo*. A simultaneous popular revolt in Hungary, Poland and possibly again in East Germany might have upset the whole post-war settlement in East-Central Europe. The strangling of an independence movement in a country for which the Poles had traditionally felt strong friendship inflamed anti-Russian feelings. On the other hand the spectre of Soviet invasion put a damper on the public expression of those feelings. The failure of the Hungarian revolt thus calmed and stabilized the situation in Poland, and enabled the new leaders of the PZPR to maintain control, despite the breakdown of its normal power apparatus. But the developments in Hungary also starkly showed how fragile this power apparatus was and how weak was the popular support for communism. The movement for a humane type of socialism and the democratization of communist institutions and policies in Hungary was all too easily transformed into a movement against communism. This probably made the Polish Party leaders, and especially Gomułka, even more apprehensive of political experiment and more inclined to rely on traditional instruments of power than they already were.

The talks about Polish grievances against the USSR were delayed by the Hungarian revolt, and the Polish delegation, with Gomułka at the head, arrived in Moscow only on 15 November. The way had been paved by the Soviet government on 30 October issuing a declaration of principles of co-operation between the USSR and other socialist states, defined as 'complete equality, respect for territorial integrity, state independence and sovereignty, and non-interference in one another's internal affairs'. The Soviet government admitted that violations of these principles had occurred in the past, and declared its readiness to discuss such matters as the presence of Soviet economic and military advisers and military bases in other countries.[23] The declaration was in a sense a sequel to the Twentieth CPSU Congress, which had ignored the whole subject of Soviet-bloc relations, and it was the October Polish and Hungarian events that forced the issue into the open. The Polish–Soviet talks, which lasted four days, brought the following results.[24] The policies of the Eighth Plenum were agreed to be compatible with the Soviet declaration and the Polish–Soviet alliance. The Soviet Union cancelled all outstanding Polish debts in compensation for the coal supplied by Poland between 1945 and 1953 at an artificially low price, and for the non-payment of transport and other service costs incurred by the Soviet army on Polish territory. The Soviet government agreed to sell Poland grain and other goods on long-term credit. The stationing of Soviet troops was accepted as necessary by the Polish side, but its conditions were to be regulated by treaty and its cost taken over by the USSR. Finally the Soviet government agreed to facilitate the repatriation of Poles still remaining in the USSR, including men held in captivity. Altogether almost a quarter of a million people returned,[25] but a large proportion of them were Jews who went straight on to Israel. On his return journey from Moscow, Gomułka received a hero's welcome, and was showered with flowers at every railway station between the frontier and Warsaw. The material gains of the talks were substantial, but what is more, were seen as a moral victory for Poland and the end of the era of Soviet irregularities.

The November talks established a reasonable *modus vivendi* between the two governments, but in no way healed the wounds in Party relations caused by the clash during the October Plenum. Through articles in the Soviet press the Kremlin clearly showed its displeasure with decollectivization and other policies. It also condemned the concept of 'national communism', but *Nowe Drogi* promptly denounced it too as an invention of the US State Department which had no application whatever to Poland. For their part the Polish leaders gave prominence to the concept of 'polycentric communism', first introduced by the Italian communist leader Togliatti. In official pronouncements they refused to acknowledge the leading role of the USSR in the socialist camp, or 'commonwealth' as it became called about this time, and emphasized China's importance as the largest communist state in the world.[26] This was in spite of Chinese wishes, and the Chinese prime minister, Chou En-Lai, visited Warsaw in January 1957 in a vain attempt to make the Polish leaders accept the 'leading role' formula. Although evidence is lacking, it is probable that the Chinese communist leaders had played a certain role in the Soviet–Polish conflict and had used their influence in Moscow to restrain the Russians. The Chinese warmly supported the Eighth Plenum changes and the Soviet government declaration of 30 October. But after the collapse of the communist system in Hungary they became outspoken enemies of 'revisionism' and advocates of orthodoxy and unity within the socialist bloc.[27] The ideological sniping in the Soviet and Polish Party press ceased after Khrushchev's defeat of the 'Anti-Party Group' of Molotov, Kaganovich and Malenkov in June 1957, and was followed by complete reconciliation of the two communist parties. The ideological subtleties were lost on the ordinary Pole, but, while the dispute lasted, the vague knowledge that the Polish communism was disapproved of by the Russians increased its popularity among the Polish people.

The election of the new politburo and Central Committee secretariat was greeted with tremendous enthusiasm in Warsaw, where the support for democratization had always been strongest. The journalists, students and workers mobilized by the Warsaw City PZPR Committee regarded the outcome of the Eighth Plenum as their own victory over the Natolin group, and a decisive stage in the struggle against all 'conservative' and 'reactionary' forces in the Party. Rallies were held all over Warsaw, culminating on 24 October in one outside the Palace of Culture and Science, addressed by Gomułka and attended by a crowd estimated at between 300,000 and 400,000, the largest gathering of its kind in Polish history. The wave of meetings and demonstrations spilled over to other cities and towns, accompanied by extraordinary conferences of Party committees at which officials opposed to democratization were forced to resign. Fifty secretaries of provincial committees were said to have resigned in this way.[28] The purge spread to districts and small towns or even lower. Sometimes whole executive committees resigned and were replaced by new ones, but where the democratizing elements were weak many of the old officials retained their posts. The new politburo at first welcomed the purge as a convenient way of getting rid of their political opponents, but soon became concerned at the disorganization it was causing and sought to contain it.

'The purge from below' took a particularly violent form in the armed forces. The dead weight of Soviet officers, headed by Rokossovsky, and the political apparatus controlled by the 'Natolinite' General Witaszewski, had stifled all political stirrings among soldiers, airmen and sailors and their officers between the Twentieth CPSU Congress and the end of the October Plenum. Now at stormy meetings military units pledged support for the new Party leadership and programme, denounced the Soviet tutelage and forced hard-line political officers to resign. On 26 October Witaszewski was replaced by Spychalski, who thus resumed the post he lost seven years before. Rokossovsky went first on leave and then resigned. On his return to Russia he was made vice-minister of defence of the USSR. The host of other high-ranking Soviet officers were thanked for their services, decorated with medals and repatriated to the Soviet Union in November, together with 'Soviet advisers' in the security police and other institutions. Poles were appointed to the vacant posts and the armed forces came under full control of the Polish government. The removal of the visible signs of Soviet domination was immensely popular with the nation as a whole and reinforced the feeling that the new Party leadership was sincerely committed to the defence of Polish national interest.

In the trade-union movement the Eighth Plenum brought about the long-delayed change of leadership and heart, after sharp criticism of the old leaders at meetings all over the country. Loga-Sowiński became the new chairman of the CRZZ. Far-reaching changes also took place in the individual unions. The new union executives sought popularity by demanding independence from Party and state control and pressing for higher wages, but they were eclipsed by the new workers' councils, spreading rapidly after October, which were free from the legacy of the past and could claim to be true democratic representatives of factory crews. The Eighth Plenum deepened the chaos in the youth movement and eventually caused its disintegration. The ZMP found itself disowned for its immobility by the politicized students and the 'revolutionary committees' which spread like wildfire after the Eighth Plenum. Also less ideological 'worker youth committees' began springing up, especially in Silesia, and in the countryside there was a spontaneous revival of the traditional peasant youth movement 'Wici'. On 6 December a national committee of peasant youth activists resolved to create a new organization in the countryside, to be called Union of Rural Youth (Związek Młodzieży Wiejskiej – ZMW). When on the same day a national conference of delegates of 'revolutionary committees' declared strong support for an avant-garde youth organization, the main board of the ZMP surrendered and in January 1957 formally dissolved the organization. The PZPR leadership suppressed an embryonic non-socialist youth organization affiliated to the SD, but was unable to prevent the collapse of the ZMP. It had just enough influence to bring about a unification of the 'worker youth' and 'revolutionary youth' movements into one Union of Socialist Youth (Związek Młodzieży Socjalistycznej – ZMS). Radical changes took place also in the scout movement, where non-communist traditions, methods and activists were spontaneously reinstated in a bid to popularize the movement. Many other organizations changed in a similar fashion. The Union of Fighters for Freedom and Democracy (Związek Bojowników o Wolność i Demokrację – ZBoWiD), the veterans' and resistance members' organization,[29] was almost taken over by the AK, the Peasant Battalions (Bataliony Chłopskie – BCh) and other London government-in-exile supporters, who joined the organization *en masse* and proceeded to vote the existing officers out of office. Professional organizations of academics, journalists and lawyers held plenary meetings of their committees or full congresses and replaced discredited officers with men who had been victims or early critics of stalinism. The writers, as might have been expected, went furthest. At a congress in Warsaw on 29 November, they repudiated the political character of the ZLP and changed it into a non-political professional organization looking after the material interests of writers. Antoni Słonimski described the change as 'the end of the Red Salvation Army'. Other artistic organizations followed suit. The Teachers' Union stopped ideological training within the organization, and the universities abolished the compulsory teaching of marxism–leninism to all students, and reinstated professors who had been dismissed. The national authorities of the ZSL and SD promptly welcomed the result of the Eighth Plenum, but their leaders were discredited by years of servility. New men, more in tune with the Gomułka leadership, came to the fore and undertook overdue reforms. Many former members were rehabilitated and readmitted.

Important changes also took place in the Party's relations with the Catholics.[30] Although Piasecki's support for the Natolin group had discredited PAX and led to the formation of a splinter group, the organization survived a storm of public criticism. Contrary to expectation, Gomułka refused to suppress PAX or strip it of its privileges, perhaps because of its potential future political utility. A major development was a public declaration of support for Gomułka by a group of Catholic intellectuals, which included J. Zawieyski, S. Stomma, J. Turowicz and J. Woźniakowski, men who were close to the episcopate and not compromised by previous collaboration. Recognizing that *raison d'état* forced Poland to remain communist, they accepted the programme of the Eighth Plenum as a basis for co-operation with the new leadership. In exchange they were permitted to organize clubs of the Progressive Catholic Intelligentsia in the large cities and to resume publishing activity, which included the Cracow weekly *Tygodnik Powszechny* (Universal Weekly), the control over which had passed to PAX in 1953 after the old editorial board had refused to print a eulogistic obituary of Stalin. This was part of a remarkable détente between the Party and the Roman Catholic church. Cardinal Wyszyński was freed from arrest on 26 October and assumed his former ecclesiastical duties, as did all other bishops and priests released from prison. After a secret meeting with Gomułka a joint government–episcopate commission considered the church's demands and reported an agreement on 8 December. The 1953 decree was revoked and the church recovered its freedom in making ecclesiastical appointments. Members of religious orders were allowed to return to the Western Territories. Religious teaching in state schools and facilities for the practice of religion in hospitals and the army were restored. In fact, in sermons and pastoral letters the church quickly resumed criticism of government policies which conflicted with the Vatican's teaching.

The policy of restoring socialist legality continued. Political pressure on judges and lawyers ceased and sentences became mild as the courts responded to the mood of public opinion. The supreme civil and military courts instituted a process of trial reviews, exonerating those who had been unjustly sentenced during stalinization. The remaining political prisoners were released. The committee for Public Security Affairs was abolished, the UB placed under the Ministry of the Interior and its size cut by half. Its activities became even more narrowly confined and discreet. Confidential opinions were abolished and the widespread breaches of the law by economic organs finally stopped. With regard to economy, the new leadership proceeded more cautiously. A small measure of decentralization was conceded, but further steps were to await discussion among planners, managers and economists. On 21 December an Economic Council, consisting of a team of distinguished economists under the chairmanship of Oskar Lange, was set up to advise the Council of Ministers. Regulations concerning handicraft and small-scale private enterprise were relaxed to stimulate the production of consumer goods. After consultations with the ZSL leadership, a new agriculture programme emerged in the middle of January 1957. Compulsory deliveries of grain and potatoes to the state were retained, but those of milk and meat abolished. Prices paid by the state for agricultural products purchased under contract were raised, and increased deliveries of all sorts of goods to the countryside were promised. The programme said nothing about collectivization, and with good reason. Immediately after Gomułka's speech to the Eighth Plenum, in which he strongly criticized the practice of collectivization, four-fifths of the 10,000 collective farms were spontaneously dissolved by their members, without official approval and without counter-action by the disoriented rural Party *apparat*. The breaking up of the collective farms, so laboriously built up over seven years, in a matter of some seven days, was a massive demonstration of their unpopularity. It made it impossible to advocate collectivization in the foreseeable future if the PZPR were to retain a minimum of the peasantry's good will.

The collapse of collective farming was the first and most spectacular instance of mass spontaneity. Gomułka never questioned the principle of collectivization as such and probably contemplated only the dissolution of some weak, economically unproductive farms and a reform of the others.[31] The peasants' action showed that the masses were not prepared to stay within the limits of changes approved by the Eighth Plenum. During the three months between the plenum and the sejm elections spontaneity was rife in all sections of Polish society. The peasants stopped paying taxes and fulfilling delivery obligations. In some areas they revived pre-war co-operative institutions known as 'agricultural circles'. Over most of the countryside Party and ZMP activity came to a standstill and the ZSL in many villages and districts came under the control of the former activists of Mikołajczyk's PSL. The priest became once again a political leader of the village community. The workers raised claims against the state which escalated from one to 40 milliard *zł.* for earnings they had been cheated out of during stalinism. Managers disobeyed government directives and paid unauthorized wage supplements to pacify their employees. Absenteeism was common and production dropped through the time wasted by numerous stoppages, political meetings and demonstrations. In some areas, especially Upper Silesia, unpopular directors, foremen and Party secretaries were booted out by workers. Serious street disturbances occurred in December in Wrocław, Bydgoszcz and Szczecin. Indeed at Szczecin the Soviet consulate building was attacked. The intelligentsia revived clubs and associations suppressed in the late 1940s. They began to publish unauthorized periodicals and loudly criticized stalinism. Writers, journalists, lawyers and students in practice interpreted 'democratization' far more widely than the Party leadership. Schoolteachers yielded to parents' pressure and allowed prayers and crucifixes in the classroom.

Gomułka took a lead in condemning many of these activities in meetings with the workers, journalists and Party officials. He was in effect the pillar which propped up the tottering structure of the Party at this time. At an important meeting with Party officials held in Warsaw on 4 November, while he criticized bureaucracy in the past, he called for order and discipline.[32] Having started with a good deal of prejudice against the *apparat*, he realized that there was no substitute for it as an instrument of rule. At a meeting with journalists after their congress early in December, Gomułka strongly defended the officials and pointedly asked: 'Who will replace them today. Who? The revolutionary committees?'[33] If the Polish experience were not enough, the collapse of the Hungarian communist régime served as a terrible warning how unreliable the rank and file of a communist party could be. The Central Committee secretariat and the government found that the sullen *apparatchiki* carried out orders at the best half-heartedly and often not at all. Without the customary pressure the Party *aktiv*, however well-disposed towards the Eighth Plenum changes, shrank from unpopular agitation and action. Some of them saw the continued fight against stalinism as the only worthwhile activity. It is almost possible to say that the Party as such ceased to function.

The need to restore discipline in the PZPR had become absolutely imperative at the end of 1956, but the Party had first to attend to the sejm election, fixed for Sunday, 20 January 1957. Politically there was no need for the election. The old sejm, elected in 1952 in a thoroughly stalinist way, had proved remarkably pliable. At its two sittings after the Eighth Plenum it enacted much reformist legislation, approving large-scale changes in the government and through its commissions discussed critically the new legislation. An election, however, had to be held to comply with the 1952 constitution, and an attempt was made to make it less of a formality than is normal in communist countries. The new electoral law, enacted on 24 October, introduced a limited freedom of choice by allowing more candidates to be nominated than there were seats to be filled in each constituency. Since the National Front established before the previous election proved to be moribund, it was replaced by a 'Front of National Unity', acting through 'consultative committees of political parties and social organizations'. The electoral programme of the front, based closely on the resolution of the Eighth Plenum, was approved at a conference in Warsaw on 29 November. Under pressure of the independently-minded electors, who submitted no less than 60,000 names for consideration, the consultative committee had to revise the provisional lists of candidates extensively and provide for far more local men and non-communists than they had originally intended.[34] There was some danger that the electorate, especially in the countryside, might boycott the election. To counteract such an event the episcopate was induced to issue a statement on 14 January that it was the voters' 'duty of conscience' to take part in the election. A far greater danger appeared in the last few weeks of the electoral campaign in the form of massive deletions of PZPR candidates, especially the national and local leaders who had been prominent in the stalinist period. It grew out of a spontaneous mood of revenge for the past, which was fed by a whispering campaign apparently organized by both the 'Natolinites' and rabid anti-communists. As Party activists seemed to be doing nothing to counteract the campaign and press propaganda appeared ineffective, Gomułka decided to turn the election into a referendum for or against the Eighth Plenum. On 9 January he launched an appeal for the electorate to cast their votes without deletions, repeating it on 14 January, and again in an eve-of-poll broadcast. On this last occasion he used the strongest argument he could muster, the threat of Soviet invasion as in Hungary. 'The appeal to cross PZPR candidates off the ballot paper is tantamount not only to the appeal to cross out socialism. Crossing off our Party's candidates means crossing out the independence of our country, crossing Poland off the map of European states.'[35] It was due to this argument and to Gomułka's enormous prestige and popularity that the appeal succeeded. Although 10.6 per cent of the voters disobeyed Gomułka's call for non-deletion, only one communist candidate, in the Nowy Sącz constituency in the Cracow province, failed to be elected owing to deletions. Of the 18 million people entitled to vote, 94.1 per cent actually voted and 93.8 per cent of them cast valid votes. The Party composition of the new sejm was as follows (figures in brackets refer to the 1952 sejm for comparison): PZPR 239 (273), ZSL 118 (90), SD 39 (25), non-Party 63 (37). Only 12 per cent of the deputies had served in the previous sejm.

Although Gomułka's pre-election appeal smacked of blackmail, it touched a deep chord in the nation's soul. There was a universal awareness of the need to preserve the measure of independence won in October 1956 and to regard the new PZPR leadership as its guarantor. Communism, in its stalinist version, had been regarded by the ordinary Pole as an alien, Russian system, and the PZPR, particularly its ruling elite, as an instrument of foreign domination and exploitation. The events of October 1956 changed this attitude dramatically. The Party's resistance to Soviet pressure, the rehabilitation of Gomułka and the concept of a Polish road to socialism, combined with a stress on national sovereignty and democracy in the mass media, created the feeling that the Party was now at one with the nation, sharing its aspirations and expressing its interests. In a country were historically politics and nationalism are interwoven, a régime to be regarded as legitimate must be seen to express at least some facets of that nationalism. In this sense it would be no exaggeration to say that as a result of the October events the communist system in Poland achieved for the first time a measure of genuine legitimacy. Many, probably most, Poles would have preferred communism to be replaced by a parliamentary system, but it was obvious, after the Hungarian tragedy, that the Soviet Union would not tolerate a Western-type constitutional system in Eastern Europe. All that could be reasonably hoped for was a communist system with a wide margin of autonomy and policies unencumbered by dogmas, respecting popular feelings and national traditions. The PZPR under Gomułka's leadership seemed in a favourable position to fulfil such hopes and deserved a vote of confidence, which it got in the January election. The idea that Poland's *raison d'état*, survival as a sovereign state, necessitated the continuation of a communist régime was most clearly expressed by the Catholic intellectuals who offered Gomułka their support after the Eighth Plenum. In a less intellectual form it became a strong conviction of all thoughtful people in Poland.

14

'The little stabilization'

The six years from the beginning of 1957 to the end of 1963 were a period of comparative stability. The upheaval caused by the twin processes of destalinization and desatellization subsided rapidly after 1957, and the country settled down to life under Gomułka. Polish–Soviet relations and the internal situation fell considerably short of the hopes awakened by the October plenum, and many Poles felt that the PZPR was definitely in 'retreat from October',[1] but for some years the retreat was slow. Many of the 1956–7 reforms remained in force, while the memories of the grim years of stalinism and the Six Year Plan remained fresh in people's minds. Nor were Poles unaware how very different the situation continued to be in the rest of Eastern Europe. Gomułka's pragmatic approach to the task of 'building socialism' in Poland produced an uneasy equilibrium between Party aims and national aspirations. The two were to subside into a state of peaceful coexistence, marked by absence of serious conflict and tensions, and aptly nicknamed *mała stabilizacja* (the little stabilization). This stabilization proved short-lived. It was to be undermined by harsh economic policies to which Gomułka resorted when the political crisis was over. These in turn were caused by the inefficiency of the unreformed economic system, which was incapable of achieving high growth rates and rising living standards at the same time. Nevertheless the years 1957–63 represent the relatively successful half of Gomułka's rule in contrast with the far less happy seven years that followed. They earned him and Poland strong admiration in the West, expressed in numerous books sympathetic to him.[2] Press coverage was favourable, while gestures of goodwill were made by Western governments. What seemed in Western eyes a particular feat of statemanship was the continuation of relaxation at home even though Poland became again fully integrated into the Soviet bloc whose members practised far less liberal forms of communism.

The Party and other organizations

The electoral victory did not automatically improve the situation in the Party, which was analysed frankly in a confidential politburo letter sent to all Party authorities and basic organizations in February.[3] The Party was said to be demobilized in the countryside and inactive in many working-class areas. Elsewhere it was split by revisionists, particularly influential among the intelligentsia, and dogmatists and conservatives whose strength was among the bureaucratic elements in the Party. Gomułka painted the same picture in public at the Ninth Plenum in mid-May, and even more strongly at the Tenth Plenum, a year after the October turning point. In a scathing speech he branded the revisionists as 'liquidators' of the communist system and a tool in the hand of reactionaries who wanted to restore bourgeois democracy and break Poland's ties with the Soviet Union. He likened revisionism to consumption and dogmatism, which he also condemned, to influenza, which was weakening but not fatal.[4] The need to restore unity and discipline in the Party was paramount and an essential precondition of tackling the serious economic problems that lay ahead. The Central Committee ordered a 'verification' of Party membership, a screening process to remove from the register all inactive members, and to expel those with a record of anti-Party activity.

There were foreign as well as domestic reasons for the tough new line. Throughout 1957 both the Soviet and the Chinese communist parties intensified their campaign against revisionism in the communist bloc.[5] Gomułka, who was about to attend a grand gathering of communist leaders in Moscow to celebrate the fortieth anniversary of the Bolshevik revolution, naturally wanted to come more into line with the rest of the bloc. He was also exasperated by the unwillingness of revisionists in Poland to abandon their campaign against stalinism, and enraged by the reaction to the closing of Po Prostu. This outspoken weekly, which had fought a losing battle against censorship during 1957, was not allowed to reappear in October. Warsaw students protested by demonstrating in the streets and, after violent clashes with the police, were disbanded. This was a foretaste of the more serious disturbance of March 1968. It was the first public manifestation of discontent with the policies of the new leadership. The Po Prostu editorial board were promptly expelled from the Party. A meeting of editors of other newspapers was summoned and Gomułka sternly demanded a radical change of heart in the press.[6] The suppression of Po Prostu, the Party purge, and the branding of revisionism as the Party's main danger marked the end of the campaign for democratization, which began at the end of 1954, after the Światło debacle and the 'November uprising'. It was the end of a search for a radical alternative to stalinism within 'the system of the dictatorship of the proletariat' and for checks and balances which would prevent a possible reversion to stalinism in the future. By banning *Po Prostu* and outlawing revisionism, the Gomułka politburo effectively terminated the three-year-long debate on the best model of socialism for Poland. The traditional political and economic model, purged of the gross stalinist distortions, was declared to be perfectly serviceable, at least at the present stage of socialist construction. 'The Polish road to socialism' and 'socialist democracy' were merely the programme of the Eighth Plenum as interpreted by the politburo.

The 'verification of membership', decreed by the Tenth Plenum, lasted until May 1958. About 28,000 members or candidates were expelled for 'revisionism' or 'dogmatism', but a far larger number, amounting to 175,000, were simply deleted from Party records for inactivity or at their own request. A further 80,000 members and candidates left the Party shortly afterwards, but, although this was almost made good by new recruitment, the PZPR had only just over 1 million members and candidates by the end of 1959, the lowest number since the Unification Congress in December 1948 when the membership stood at 1,460,000. Afterwards, owing to a massive recruitment drive, membership rose steadily, but there was a tendency for disillusioned working-class members to leave in large numbers and to have to be replaced constantly by new recruits. Despite the impressive figures the results of the 1957–9 purges were superficial. Deep differences about the ends and means of 'building socialism' remained under the surface of conformity to the current Party line. The mass media, the universities, the professional organizations, and the intelligentsia generally remained overwhelmingly reformist at heart, while the party and state bureaucracy, both central and local, continued to be conservative in their sympathies. This harboured the possibility of a future conflict, such as indeed occurred in March 1968. The situation did not seem to worry Gomułka, who was a pragmatist not an ideologist by temperament. As long as they carried out loyally the decisions of the Party leadership he tolerated men with diverse views. He hoped that the Party would rally behind him in the new economic offensive he was preparing. He had in any case no choice but to balance different groups in the Party elite. Apart from a handful of friends from the underground days, he had no personal following through whom he could dominate the Party and the government. His position in the PZPR rested on his own personal qualities, the success with which he coped with the critical situation in the autumn and winter of 1956–7, and his acceptance as a major communist statesman by the leaders of the CPSU. Between October 1956 and March 1959 he was able to lead the Party perfectly well with the support of a Central Committee chosen in March 1954 in the days of Bierut's ascendancy.

There were few changes in the composition of the Central Committee, the secretariat and the Political Bureau when they were reconstituted by the Third PZPR Congress.[7] The congress was originally to meet in March 1957, but was postponed three times and finally held in March 1959. This long delay was a measure of the extreme disorganization of the PZPR caused by the Eighth Plenum. Apart from the addition of Gierek and Spychalski to the politburo and Kliszko to the secretariat the composition of the two bodies remained the same as in October 1956. The Central Committee was purged of unregenerate stalinists like Kłosiewicz, Mijał and Mazur, but most of the conservatives kept their places, while a few of the more radical reformists of 1956 were not re-elected. But Gomułka's bias against the reformists showed itself more clearly after the congress. In 1959 Morawski left the politburo. Albrecht left the secretariat to take up the less important position of minister of finance. Matwin lost his post in the secretariat and the post of first secretary of Wrocław. The congress nullified all previous strictures against the 'rightist–nationalist deviation', adopted revised Party statutes, approved the measures taken against 'revisionism' and 'dogmatism', declaring itself satisfied with the achievement of 'socialist democracy' in various areas, but the main thrust of its debates and resolutions was economic. The crucial task of the Party in the next seven years was declared to be a great economic offensive, during which a simultaneous and harmonious growth of industry and agriculture, investment and consumption were to be achieved, mainly through increased labour efficiency and a better use of existing equipment. The congress upheld the socialization of agriculture as the Party's long-term aim, but insisted that it had to be wholly voluntary and gradual. The cultural aim of the Party was defined vaguely as art and literature which was intelligible to the working people and expressive of their socialist faith, and which the Party once again promised to promote through ideological, rather than administrative means. In fact, the Party had really no definite policy towards the arts and culturally Poland leaned much more to Western than to Eastern Europe for a decade after 1956.

The congress confirmed and legitimized the tendency, noticeable before the end of 1957, to make economic progress the chief goal of the Party. After the beginning of 1958 most of the Central Committee plena had the character of economic conferences, to which outside experts, even non-party men, were sometimes invited. The idea behind the economic orientation was to make the Party's elite and bureaucracy the promoters of economic growth and efficiency. There was some incongruity in this. In Poland the core of the ruling elite at the end of the 1950s still consisted of pre-war revolutionaries, war-time resistance members and political officers of the Polish army in the USSR. Their knowledge could not match that of the highly trained industrial managers and technical experts with whom they were expected to co-operate closely. They lacked both the outlook and professional training to be controllers of an increasingly complex economy, although they were now required to improve their qualifications by evening courses in economics, technology or agronomy. Only in the lower echelons of the Party and state bureaucracy were men with proper academic qualifications able to play an important part. The main problem, however, was that for many young people religious beliefs ruled out PZPR membership as long as the Party officially maintained its marxist–leninist ideology. There was a large pool of able and enthusiastic men who never achieved the promotion they deserved because they did not hold a Party card.

The reorientation of the Party towards economics inevitably affected the trade unions. At the Fourth Trade Union Congress in April 1958 Gomułka and Loga-Sowiński, who was reconfirmed as chairman of the CRZZ and continued in the post until 1971, told the delegates bluntly that increased productivity took priority over the promotion of their members' material interests, to which they had lately given far too much attention. Gomułka chose the congress to propose a merger of workers' councils, factory councils recruited from the unions and factory Party committees into a new institution, the Conference of Workers' Self-Government (Konferencja Samorządu Robotniczego – KSR). The KSR became nominally a superior body which discussed and decided matters put on its agenda by any of its three constituent bodies, but it executed its decisions through a standing committee, on which the workers' council representatives were in a minority. Thus, without abolishing the workers' councils, the PZPR leadership brought them effectively under the control of the reliable trade-union and Party committees in factories. After the usual 'mass discussion', a bill on workers' self-government was drawn up by the CRZZ and passed by the sejm at the end of the year. In this emasculated form, workers' councils were declared to be an essential part of the Polish road to socialism and extended to all nationalized industries. The 1956 attempt to build into the centralized industrial system a measure of genuine shop-floor democracy was destroyed, and with it also a chance to build into the system of a barometer of working-class opinion.

The urban youth organization ZMS also received the leaders' attention.

The 'revisionist' elements in the old ZMP, although thwarted in their attempt to set up a militant political organization, had much influence within the ZMS, and ideological unrest within it continued until it was purged of some 25,000 members in 1958. After this politics were abandoned, and production, social work, protection of young employees' rights and cultural and educational activities became the ZMS's main concern. It was at first almost a wholly working-class organization, with little activity in schools and none in universities and polytechnics. This changed and the early 1960s saw a quick expansion of membership from a mere 111,000 in 1958 to 900,000 in 1965, but the ZMS continued to lack the mass appeal and influence of the ZMP in its early years. The rural youth organization (ZMW) also grew steadily, but it was largely non-political and concerned with the cultural activities and further education, especially in farming methods. Political education was perfunctory and its socialist character diluted by the influence of the ZSL and the old *Wici* activists.

The Party until 1959 had no concrete programme about how to bring about 'the socialist transformation of the countryside' to which it was committed. Collective farms were extremely unpopular and despite the Party's support remained insignificant in number. Gomułka countered lack of progress with his scheme for an Agriculture Development Fund, announced in June 1959. The farmers associated in 'agricultural circles' were to have the difference between the 'free contract' price and the compulsory delivery price of their produce credited to the account of their village circle. With the funds the circle could acquire farming machinery to be used on their members' land. After obtaining the Central Committee's and the ZSL's approval, the proposal was enacted by the sejm in 1960. In this way the spontaneous development of the loose Western-type rural co-operatives was steered into institutional channels under state and Party control. The reorganized agricultural circles, in theory, rounded off the new structure of socialist democracy in Poland. In practice, they did not work out quite like that. The peasants were suspicious that they might be a step towards collectivization and were very reluctant to join.[8] Those who joined them found that, since there were not enough tractors and other machinery to satisfy the demand, the money was merely accumulating in their accounts. In practice the state and collective farms, now at last beginning to be reasonably productive, continued to have absolute priority in receiving machinery. Neither production nor socialism seemed to benefit much from the scheme. It made little difference to the life of the peasants.

The United Peasant Party (ZSL) took even longer than the PZPR to overcome its own political crisis, created by the capture of many village and district branches by the former PSL members. Its Third Congress took place only in November 1959 and its post-October leadership was reconfirmed. The consultative status which it had achieved since October made it somewhat more popular and its membership rose after 1956. The functions, programme and leadership of the ZSL remained much the same throughout the 1960's. The Democratic Party sorted out its political difficulties by the time of its Sixth Congress in January 1958. In that year the PZPR ceased to regard private enterprise with suspicion and wound up the social commissions to combat corruption and speculation. To prevent any future attempts by undesirable elements to capture the party from within, its new ideological declaration clearly stated that the SD represented only those sections of the urban population who accepted the goal of a socialist Poland and who did not further their interests at the expense of the rest of the people. Its membership was still very small, drawn largely from the artisans, but rarely from among the intelligentsia.

The PZPR's relations with the intellectuals were the least satisfactory. No attempt was made to meddle with art, but the PZPR tried to recapture its influence in artistic organizations. The Writers' Union flatly refused to become involved in a political campaign or ideological debate and insisted on being simply a professional organization. Gomułka's personal appearance at the 1960 Lublin Congress of the Union failed to change its attitude. The Party retaliated by reducing the size of editions and stopping the appearance of new literary periodicals. The cultural periodicals were harassed by censorship and purges of their editorial boards. Inevitably they became dull and lost readership.

The same was true of the Warsaw daily press which had been so lively and controversial in 1956 and 1957. The weekly *Polityka* (Politics) fared better. It was launched by the Party leadership to reflect official Party attitudes to culture and current affairs, but under the editorship of M. F. Rakowski it was transformed into a periodical which managed to remain within the bounds of orthodoxy, but still to publish reports and discussions of topical issues almost as frank and lively as those of the suppressed *Po Prostu*. Eventually it became the leading socio-cultural weekly in the country. The radio and the infant television under the control of the discredited ex-minister of culture, Sokorski, also became politically safe. Television, with the help of local initiative in some large cities, developed much faster than was planned by the authorities. It gave an able cadre of producers and actors, who had already established very high standards in the theatre, a chance to do the same in the new medium.

In 1958 the political truce between the Party and the church came to an end. The press complained that priests had interfered in local elections in the countryside and were using the pulpit for anti-communist propaganda. In July the police raided the Jasna Góra monastery in Częstochowa and confiscated unregistered duplicating equipment and pamphlets with political propaganda. The prior of the monastery was subsequently given a suspended prison sentence. One result of the worsening situation was the imposition of taxation on the income of all church institutions, including the Catholic University in Lublin, in early 1959. In 1959, a year in which the Party line hardened in many areas, Władysław Bieńkowski, the popular minister of education with well-known reformist sympathies, was dismissed from his post. In a growing campaign against alleged clerical influences, parents were induced to demand the end of religious instruction in some state schools, and eventually the school system became secularized again. Instruction continued at 'catechism points' attached to parish churches, but these in turn became a source of friction. Priests were required by a law of 1961 to register the 'catechism points' with the local authorities. The episcopate forbade them to comply on the ground that the matter was solely within the church's jurisdiction. The law was not strictly enforced, but some priests were prosecuted and fined. Another major grievance of the church was that the authorities continued to refuse building permits for churches in new towns and housing estates. This led to many clashes with the police, the most violent being in Nowa Huta in April 1960.[9] In response to this persecution, non-party deputies in the sejm made gestures of sympathy with the church's attitude, such as voting against a bill to municipalize church cemeteries in 1962, but were unable to sway the government. The group in the sejm which went by the name of Znak sometimes criticized general government policy and put forward its own proposals, which were ignored in the press, except the group's own *Tygodnik Powszechny* (Universal Weekly). In revenge the church refused to support Party-sponsored campaigns against the pilfering of state property, and vigorously opposed birth-control and any policy which conflicted with its own doctrine. Since 1957, when a nine-year campaign of prayers to commemorate the approaching millennium of Christianity in Poland was launched by the church leaders, the church's opposition was clearly manifested.[10] Nevertheless, until the mid-1960's the conflict of the two organizations remained muted, and each seemed unwilling to provoke a large-scale confrontation with the other. Late in 1962 the Polish government even made tentative contacts with the Vatican about the possibility of a concordat. Had Pope John XXIII, who had shown himself unusually conciliatory towards communism, not died, it is possible that an agreement might have been concluded.

The state and the economy

The newly elected sejm met on 20 January 1957 and elected its presidium and the Council of State. The new sejm speaker was Czesław Wycech (ZSL). The chairman of the council and head of state was again Alexander Zawadzki. Its vice-chairmen were two reformist PZPR deputies, Jerzy Albrecht and Oskar Lange, and the new leaders of the ZSL and the SD were B. Podedworny and S. Kulczyński respectively. Among the council's other members were Gomułka, Loga-Sowiński and the Catholic writer Jerzy Zawieyski; the latter's inclusion symbolized the modest new place of Catholics in the state. A week later the sejm approved the new Council of Ministers. Its chairman was again Józef Cyrankiewicz and the PZPR dominated it as before. Its two vice-chairmen were P. Jaroszewicz and Z. Nowak, while the chairman of the Planning Commission was S. Jędrychowski and nineteen ministers were from the PZPR, among whom the important portfolios of national defence were held by M. Spychalski, internal affairs by W. Wicha, and foreign affairs by A. Rapacki. The minister of agriculture was Edward Ochab, although the ZSL might have expected the ministry to go to one of its own members. The ZSL had a vice-chairman, S. Ignar, and two ministers. The SD had also two ministers and there were two non-party ministers. The sejm was less of a rubber stamp than its predecessor. Its internal structure was revamped, and the number and powers of its commissions enlarged. The ministers kept in close touch with the sejm through the commissions, and when the Supreme Chamber of Control was recreated later in the session, the sejm's supervision over the administration was further strengthened. The government continued the practice of keeping public opinion closely in touch with its activities, through regular announcements and press interviews. In 1957 the sejm sat for more days than the old assembly during its four-year life. The practice of legislation by decree virtually ceased; between 1957 and 1961 the Council of State issued only two decrees, while the sejm enacted 174 statutes. Although non-party deputies sometimes abstained or voted against the government, the PZPR, ZSL, and SD deputies supported the government monolithically. In an interview in *Trybuna Ludu* in January 1959, Kliszko, chairman of the PZPR deputies' club, a Central Committee secretary and a rising man in the Party leadership, could proudly assert: 'There is now no sphere of economy or [national] life into which our parliament may not look and which is beyond its legislative competence'.[11] The reform of the people's councils began just after the Eighth Plenum with a grant of some economic powers to the provincial councils. In January 1958 the sejm passed a more comprehensive law which made the provincial councils the main planning and co-ordinating authorities in their areas, and allowed districts to take on new functions on an experimental basis. The proportion of state budget spent by the people's councils grew steadily after 1957. After the Eighth Plenum of June 1961 the provincial councils were further strengthened by being charged with preparing comprehensive development plans for state industry in their areas. More powers were devolved on the district councils, which in theory became the main organ of local administration, although in practice all important decisions continued to be made by the voivodship council. Politically the reform strengthened the territorial Party *apparat*, especially the provincial secretariats, which dominated all administration and most economic life in the province. The new law on regional and local elections, modelled on the 1956 sejm's electoral system, allowed 50 per cent more candidates to be nominated than there were seats to be filled. The elections to the people's councils took place in February 1958, but the atmosphere, though free from administrative pressure, was different from the critical, tense and uncertain political atmosphere of January 1957. This time the local committees of the Front of National Unity functioned under strong leadership of local Party officials and had little trouble in getting favourite candidates nominated or elected. The elections were a triumph for the Party machine and demonstrated that it could once again achieve results. The new councils met more regularly than the old and exercised more control over the local bureaucrats. They also tended to be more responsive to the views of the local populace, whom they consulted through periodic meetings and a well-developed committee system with a large proportion of co-opted members. Just under half of all the elected council members were non-party, while of the rest 38 per cent were PZPR members. In 1961 the sejm and people's councils elections coincided and it was decided to hold them on the same day that year and in future at four-year intervals. The proportion of extra candidates which could be nominated for the sejm was brought down from 66 to 50 per cent, but in practice even the smaller quota was not filled. There was little enthusiasm and no excitement during the electoral campaign preceding the April poll. Nearly 95 per cent of the electorate voted, of whom about one million abstained, and more than half a million deleted at least one name and about 300,000 crossed out all candidates. The representation of the PZPR in the new sejm increased by 16 seats, largely at the expense of non-party candidates. The number of Znak deputies, which had increased to 9 after 1957, was reduced to 5 and there were again 5 PAX deputies. The PAX leader Piasecki and some well-known former stalinists, excluded in 1957, found themselves again in the sejm, while a few prominent reformists disappeared. There was little change in the new sejm's authorities, the Council of State and the government.

While democratization resulted in some reforms of the legislative and administrative institutions, much less progress was made with the economic system. The all-powerful State Commission of Economic Planning set up in 1949 was abolished soon after the October Plenum and replaced by a Planning Commission of the Council of Ministers, but this, like the later creation of the Economic Committee of the Council of Ministers, did not change the planning mechanism at all. Nor was the management system changed substantially. The Central Boards, abolished in May 1958, were replaced by looser groupings of enterprises called Industrial Associations, which in practice functioned much the same. In July 1958 the Advisory Economic Council listed the reforms already carried out and suggested several others. The model put forward by the Council was tempered by political expediency. The leading Polish economists were virtually unanimous that the weaknesses of the Soviet-type economic model could not be successfully eradicated without the adoption of a radically decentralized model in which production responded to the laws of supply and demand and the planning commissions influenced the economy through the level of prices, wages, interest rates and profits, rather than laying down precise quantitative targets. The Party and government leaders showed no hurry in implementing the recommendations of the council. They argued that the state of the economy was still rather precarious and that large-scale changes of the economic model would require long preparation. The economy was in fact stabilized during 1958, with the vital help of a loan from the USA, agreed in Washington on 7 June 1957. Poland initially obtained a $30 million credit, and farming surpluses worth another $20 million, repayable in Polish currency. The help continued and Poland received economic aid worth altogether $529 million from the United States between 1957 and 1963.[12] The PZPR congress in March 1959 ended all hopes for a fundamental reform. Gomułka was too cautious and traditionalist to embrace any form of 'market socialism' and in any case was unwilling to prejudice his growing friendship with the Soviet leaders by radical experiments.

The government certainly faced some serious economic problems. Its most urgent task was to prevent inflation, because 16 milliard $zł.$ of extra purchasing power had been injected into the economy during 1956 through wage and salary increases and concessions to farmers. The extra demand was met by encouraging state industry to develop marketable side-lines, permitting the expansion of private trade, handicraft and small industry, but above all cutting down the export of consumer goods. Many other economic tasks remained. The state was faced with enormous claims for compensation for earnings illegally reduced during stalinism and the first unpopular enactment of the new sejm in 1957 was a bill cancelling these liabilities. Labour discipline was non-existent, absenteeism was rife and many strikes occurred. As late as the summer of 1958 there was a serious strike of city tram workers in Łódź. In many factories the workers managed to extract wage rises from the management, often met from the new enterprise fund intended for other purposes. The farmers had to be pressed hard to fulfil their tax and compulsory delivery obligations. The upsurge of private enterprise led to large-scale illegalities and some businessmen made quick fortunes. At the end of February 1958 'the tidying up of the economy' was declared to be the most important Party task. A merciless war was declared on unauthorized wage rises, lax work attendance, the non-fulfilment of plans and other economic evils. In one *Nowe Drogi* article Party committees in the factories were bluntly told that 'production, not pure politics' was their business, while in another the purpose of 'workers' democracy' was defined as 'the struggle for the achievement of economic ends'. A further turn of the screw occurred in the middle of 1959, when lack of fodder, due to bad weather conditions, caused a severe meat shortage. In October the Party leadership took the highly unpopular decision of raising meat prices by 25 per cent, and convened a special Central Committee meeting to justify it. The leaders blamed the meat crisis on the laxity of economic controls and demanded the strengthening of central planning and a halt to decentralization. Among those reappointed to responsible government and Party positions was a group of hard-line planners and administrators, Szyr, Tokarski and Witaszewski, dismissed in 1956. Supporters of fundamental reforms lost positions or influence in the government, and the advisory Economic Council effectively ceased to function in 1960. Also in 1959 there was a reorganization in the security police, caused by the defection to the West of another important official, Colonel Monat.[13] Gomułka put in charge of the police a leading wartime communist partisan commander, General Mieczysław Moczar, who had a reputation for toughness. The 1960's were to be a period of increasing political influence of Moczar and his associates.

Gomułka showed himself a traditionalist also in respect of economic priorities. He regarded the slowing down of industrialization for the sake of consumption after 1954 as a tactical retreat, not a permanent economic strategy, and as soon as the political situation became stable the politburo authorized a new investment drive. In October 1958 investment targets for the last two years of the 1956–60 plan were considerably raised and remained high in the new 1961–5 plan. The main targets for the seven-year economic offensive, laid down by the Twelfth Plenum and confirmed by the Party congress in March 1959, were as follows: national income was to rise by 40 per cent, industrial production by 50 per cent, investment by 49 per cent, farm production by 30 per cent, and real wages by 33–35 per cent. The key to the achievement of these goals was increased labour productivity brought about by better organization and use of reserves and a stricter control of employment. The ambitious offensive got out of hand and led almost to a breakdown of the economy at the end of 1963. Between 1959 and 1962, investment, primarily in the producer-goods industry, grew by an average of 11 per cent per annum (17 per cent in 1959) and the import of machinery and equipment by 18 per cent per annum (27.6 per cent in 1962).[14] Employment in the socialist sector of the economy, which was to rise by about 700,000 between 1961 and 1965, exceeded that figure already by 1963. The average yearly increase of industrial output per employee, which was 7.5 per cent during 1956–60, dropped to half that rate between 1961–3. Real wages, which grew by 15 per cent in 1956 and 12 per cent in 1957, declined in the subsequent six years to 1.6 per cent per annum, which was three times less than the planned rate. Exceptionally bad weather conditions aggravated the defects of the plan. Agricultural production, which lagged behind because of lack of investment, dropped by 13.5 per cent in 1962 and forced the reduction of food exports to the West, the main source of hard currency needed to pay for imports of machinery and raw materials for light industry. National income grew by only 2 per cent in that year, compared with the 7 per cent average envisaged in the plan. The winter of 1962–3 was the most severe for a century and dislocated transport and industry so much that industrial production increased by only 5 per cent in 1963, the lowest annual increase in the history of People's Poland.[15] At the Central Committee plenum in November 1963 the plan was drastically revised, and investment for 1964–5 scaled down by one-fifth, but the main cuts were in the so-called non-productive investment, which included houses, shops and communal and social services, which was to depress the standard of living in future years.

While the economic consequences of the breakdown were obvious, the political consequences, though not immediately apparent, were equally serious. The economic offensive was a test of Gomułka's managerial ability in the eyes of the ruling elite, and he failed dismally to pass it. His undoubted political skill in overcoming a serious crisis in the Party, the country and Soviet–Polish relations was obviously not matched by equal skill in handling the economy. The planning and control mechanism, which he believed would work without any significant reform, clearly did not. Foreign trade and agriculture proved insuperable obstacles to growth. The strategy of developing primarily raw material resources, such as sulphur, copper and lignite, was costly and slow in producing results, although it paid handsome dividends in the 1970's. Private farming, starved of resources, seemed incapable of expanding production quickly. Consumption and the standard of living, not only of the blue- and white-collar workers, but also of the intelligentsia and the bureaucracy, remained static. Gomułka's prestige in the Party had suffered a severe blow by the end of 1963, and a process of erosion of his authority began. Such a process does not immediately lead to a loss of power. A decrease in spontaneous, voluntary obedience in a political system may be, and often is, compensated by an increase in coerced compliance. The repressive features of the second half of Gomułka's rule seem to bear out this generalization.

Foreign relations

Gomułka travelled to Moscow in November 1957, at the head of the PZPR delegation, to take part in the celebrations of the fortieth anniversary of the Bolshevik revolution. The journey marked the end of Poland's isolation from other communist states and parties. He was warmly received by Khrushchev, since July 1957 the undisputed leader of the CPSU, and quickly established a personal rapport with him which was to last until the end of Khrushchev's career. The official expression of the new spirit in the Polish–Soviet relations was a series of 'friendship visits'. Voroshilov came to Poland in April 1958, Gomułka, Zawadzki and Cyrankiewicz went to the USSR the following October, Khrushchev to Poland in July 1959. All ended with communiqués stressing the 'basic unity' of the two parties and governments on all international and inter-bloc affairs. Similar visits to the countries of the Soviet bloc, and return visits of their leaders, followed as a matter of course. Meetings and consultations at the highest level became frequent after 1958, particularly to co-ordinate foreign and economic policies.[16] The great ideological issues of 'peaceful coexistence' with capitalism and 'revisionism' within the communist movement tended to be debated and decided in large and solemn gatherings, such as the two Moscow conferences of November 1957 and November 1960. The new programme of the League of Yugoslav Communists offended the Soviet bloc by its unregenerate revisionism and put Tito once more beyond the pale, while China with Albania, embarked on a course that led to their break with the Soviet bloc. This made Poland the most important loyalist communist state after the Soviet Union. Gomułka seemed to be an eager participant in the conferences, and with Khrushchev's backing became an eminent communist statesman, eventually approaching something like the position of first importance after Khrushchev. The Polish Party abandoned its flirtation with 'polycentrism' and by degrees acknowledged the leading position of the CPSU. Gomułka's influence in communist counsels gave him some power. It was probably on his insistence that the necessity to struggle against 'dogmatism' as well as 'revisionism' was endorsed by the Soviet bloc. He is also reputed to have been a moderating influence on Khrushchev in his dispute with Mao Tse-tung, and to have delayed the public Soviet condemnation of the Communist Party of China, but these were insubstantial gains compared with the practice of once again falling into line with the CPSU on every foreign issue, including the defence of the necessity of Imre Nagy's execution.

The acceptance of Poland as a legitimate member of the 'socialist commonwealth' helped to improve trade relations. Particularly important was the Czechoslovak capital assistance in developing newly discovered Polish suphur deposits, and similar aid from East Germany in exploiting rich new lignite resources along the Western frontier. Polish industrial development was greatly hampered by the shortage of investment capital and foreign exchange with which Western equipment could be bought, but the creation of the EEC seemed to make trade with the West even more difficult. Gomułka turned to the Comecon as a possible radical solution of the problem,. He criticized the organization at a meeting of the PZPR Central Committee, which took place just before the Thirteenth Session of the Comecon in June 1960. 'There is no co-operation whatsoever in the important sector of investment. Everyone peels his own turnip – and loses by it.'[17] Gomułka succeeded in winning over Khrushchev to his point of view, and it was as a Soviet proposal that the initiative for the integration of Comecon was in fact launched. Khrushchev proposed a scheme for a central allocation of investment within the organization so that the needs of members could be better met by specialization in certain lines of production by individual countries which had favourable conditions to develop them. Logically this scheme would have led to the co-ordination of long-term national plans and large-scale capital lending, and ultimately to the creation of a supra-national Comecon planning authority. An agreement in principle was reached after three years of negotiations and institutional reform, but then the scheme foundered because Romania, with Chinese support, opposed it on the ground that the setting up of a supra-state planning body would undermine national sovereignty. Poland's first major international move was thus stymied by a fellow-member of the Soviet bloc, who from now on pursued a more independent and nationalistic course in foreign policy than Poland had ever attempted. Equally unsuccessful was the Polish disarmament initiative, known as the Rapacki Plan, which postulated the creation of a Central European zone, consisting of the two German states, Czechoslovakia and Poland, from which nuclear weapons were to be banned. The plan was first suggested at the UN by the Polish foreign minister in October 1957. It went through a number of modifications and elaborations, and Gomułka himself put forward its extended version at a session of the UN General Assembly in September 1960.[18] It was the first, and only, time that Gomułka visited the United States or for that matter any capitalist country. The Rapacki Plan was politely received in the West, but had no more success than the various disarmament proposals of Khrushchev, with which it was in any case wholly in line. But greater Polish involvement in international affairs was reflected in Poland becoming a member of the Ten States' Disarmament Committee in 1959, of the UN Security Council for 1960, and of the Korea and Indo-China Supervision and Control Commissions. In all these bodies she followed the line of the Soviet bloc. In Europe Poland continued to condemn West German 'revanchism' and 'militarism'. Following the establishment of diplomatic relations between Bonn and Moscow in 1955, Poland began trading with the Federal Republic of Germany on the basis of annual agreements. Discreet Polish feelers, however, about a political settlement on the basis of the recognition of the Oder–Neisse Line met with no response.[19] Nevertheless, a further step towards normal relations with the Federal Republic was taken in March 1963 by concluding a three-year trade agreement and establishing a West German trade mission in Warsaw. A trade agreement was concluded with France and the existing Anglo-Polish one extended, and this led to a considerable increase in academic and cultural exchanges with those countries. There was an attempt to establish closer relations with the Labour Party, whose leaders, first Gaitskell and then Wilson, were invited to Poland. The United States continued its friendly attitude and granted Poland additional credits for the purchase of farm surpluses, unblocked Polish wartime bank accounts, and extended to her the most favoured nation clause. American foundations offered numerous grants to Polish academics and graduate students wishing to travel to the USA. The Canadian Government at last agreed to return the Polish art treasures which the government-in-exile had deposited there in 1940. Polish international contacts, through high-level visits, trade agreements or both, spread out to many countries in Asia and to Africa and Latin America. Even wider were Polish cultural exchanges, which extended to countries of all the continents. Although one cannot really speak of Poland becoming influential in world affairs, her presence at least became felt in the world at large on an unprecedented scale, a fact which at least members of the ruling elite and the professional intelligentsia appreciated. It was an irony of history that Polish cultural successes in this period, especially the films which won awards at international festivals, had been made possible by the heavy outlay on culture during the obscurantist stalinist years.

The political changes following the October turning point altered the attitude towards their native country of Polish exiles in the West. One might say that for many members of the Polonia Poland under Gomułka became a legitimate state. Some decided to return. Among them were prominent émigré politicians such as J. Poniatowski and Stanisław Mackiewicz and in addition a number of well-known pre-war intellectuals and younger Western-educated professional people who believed they could now make a significant contribution to the welfare of their country. Thousands of people of Polish origin but foreign nationality began visiting Poland, some of them coming for regular holidays. Intellectual groups and cultural magazines sprang up in the West to act as bridges between the émigré communities and the homeland, though most had a short-lived existence. The influential *Kultura* (Culture) magazine, published in Paris since the war and specializing in exposing the darker sides of life in Poland, welcomed the programme of the Eighth Plenum, although its enthusiasm for Gomułka waned after his attack on revisionism. *Kultura*'s editors believed that it was unrealistic to expect more than a relatively liberal communist régime in Poland, and now aimed at giving support to those forces within the PZPR and the Polish intellectual elite which advocated or defended reform, autonomy and pluralism within the system. This attitude was probably shared by many of *Kultura*'s readers in the West.

The decline of Gomułka

In July 1964 People's Poland celebrated its twentieth anniversary. Nine months later it was as old as the Second Polish Republic when it collapsed in September 1939. The comparison between these two periods of Polish history and their relative achievements was a common theme of the anniversary celebrations. Industrial progress during the period of People's Poland was particularly emphasized.

Industry's production potential at present is nine times that in bourgeois Poland...The gap between Poland and the highly industrialized countries of Europe has been reduced by half... Industrial output per capita in Poland has now risen to more than 60 per cent of the average for Great Britain, France, West Germany and Italy, whereas in the years of bourgeois Poland the figure was a mere 17 to 18 per cent... Could anyone have supposed in 1939 that Poland, despite the terrible war destruction, would – twenty years after the worst war in history – have an industrial potential per capita not much different from that of France in 1938 with 150 years of industrial development behind her?[1]

Other achievements could be added. Chronic unemployment had been abolished, and both urban and rural population had secured a steady, if still by West European standards very modest, level of earnings. There was greater social equality than before the war, better educational opportunities and chances of advancement for workers and peasants. Benefits of cultural life were also rather more widely shared, although creative intellectuals suffered more from political constraints than before the war. The outstanding national problem, which had to wait another five years or so for a solution, was the recognition by West Germany of the territorial changes in the west and north of the country, but even without formal recognition the western frontier seemed safe because of the alliance with the USSR. This safety was purchased at a price. To keep Soviet good will Poland had to forego an independent foreign and defence policy, and internally to accept a communist political system with priorities divergent from those of the broad mass of the people.

When Gomułka returned to power in October 1956 the gap between the Party and the nation had become the narrowest in post-war history, although it soon began widening again. During the second half of his rule the gap widened dangerously. A conflict with a section of the intellectuals on cultural policy combined with differences with students on the limits of permissible dissent gave the Gomułka leadership its first shock, but Gomułka's fall was in the end to be brought about by the working class, weary of years which saw no rise in their real wages and enraged by measures proposed in December 1970 which threatened their immediate standard of living.

Political repression and dissent

The political structure of the Polish state changed little in the second half of the 1960's. Elections to the sejm and the people's councils were held in May 1965 and June 1969, producing largely the same distribution of seats among the PZPR, ZSL, SD and non-party deputies. The legislative activity of the sejm is illustrative of its decline. The sejm of 1957 passed 174 laws, but this figure was reduced to 93 in the sejm elected in 1961. The sejm of 1965 passed only 60 laws. That of 1969, which did not run its full term, passed only 36. There was an appearance of political inertia. Recruitment to the ZSL and the SD slowed down after 1964. The PZPR membership rose steadily from just over a million at the end of 1959, accounting for 3.4 per cent of the population, to 2,320,000, or 7.1 per cent, in 1971. The youth organizations, the ZMS and ZMW, more than doubled their numbers, while the Union of Polish Scouts (Związek Harcerstwa Polskiego – ZHP) and the Union of Polish Students (Związek Studentów Polskich – ZSP) almost trebled, but these increases were not synonymous with expanded political activity and awareness.[2] The events of March 1968 were to reveal clearly how little influence the PZPR had over university students.

Beneath the surface of political life the situation was by no means stable. The late 1950's saw the rise and fall of 'revisionism' in the PZPR, but in the 1960's there emerged a hard-line group which went by the name of the 'Partisan Faction', under the leadership of General Mieczysław Moczar, though he perhaps was not its principal strategist.[3] Moczar had been a regional commander of the underground People's Army and had been associated with Gomułka, but he had suffered an eclipse after 1948, when Bierut had taken control. He emerged again in 1956, and in 1959 was appointed deputy minister of the interior and chief of the UB. A second deputy minister was F. Szlachcic, himself a minor partisan leader during the war. By the early 1960's Moczar and his wartime associates dominated the security police and military intelligence. The army's political education system was controlled by General G. Korczyński, who was believed to be another leader of the 'Partisans'. The security police curtailed severely contacts with Western journalists and the import of émigré publications. Ideological unorthodoxy within the Party was kept under close surveillance. Control over judges and lawyers made it easier for the security police to act with impunity. The influence and range of the security police was extended when the PZPR accepted a new interpretation of revisionism in July 1963 at the Central Committee plenum, which was devoted to ideology, and at the Fourth Party Congress between 15 and 20 June 1964.[4] In the past revisionism had been criticized as an ideological deviation in both the Polish and the international communist movement, but now it was declared to be capitalism's means of weakening the communist system from within in an effort to replace it with a bourgeois democracy. The example of Hungary in 1956 seemed to substantiate this view, which was to be confirmed by subsequent events in Czechoslovakia. This new interpretation revived the stalinist theory that deviation inevitably degenerated into subversion. Paradoxically it had been Gomułka and his group against whom it had been invoked in 1949. The security system had been expanded in order to enable it to act as the guardian of socialism in Poland until the collapse of 1954–5. Once again the security police were on the ascendant within the political system, which seems to point to cyclical tendencies within it and an oscillation between relaxation and repression.[5]

After the resignation of Zambrowski from the politburo and the secretariat before the congress in 1964, Ryszard Strzelecki, a chief-of-staff of the communist partisans during the war, became head of the cadre department of the Central Committee's secretariat. With Zawadzki's death later in the year he was promoted to full membership of the politburo. His appointment strengthened the influence of the 'Partisans' in the Party's regional organization, but Gomułka seems to have been concerned to limit their power in its higher echelons. Two new members of the politburo elected at the congress were followers of Bierut, Szyr and Waniółka, who had been rehabilitated after making their peace with Gomułka. Nevertheless by the mid-1960's there was a growth in the Partisan Faction's strength. Under the patronage of Moczar, the ZBoWiD, an association of veterans and former political prisoners, expanded to serve as a bridge between his group and members of the wartime non-communist resistance and Polish forces in the West. Between 1960 and 1968 he trebled the membership of the auxiliary militia, the Volunteer Reserve of the Citizens' Militia (Ochotnicza Reserwa Milicji Obywatelskiej – ORMO), who reinforced the ordinary police and could serve as a link with the working class. The 'Partisans' first drew attention to their ideas by the publication of a book, written by Colonel Z. Załuski, entitled *The Polish Seven Deadly Sins*, which excited immense controversy.[6] It was a vindication of the romantic tradition in Polish history, exalting the insurrections and the struggle, of which the working class revolutionary movement and the communist resistance in the war were said to be outstanding examples. A group of writers and journalists emerged to elaborate this theme, with the aim of promoting the cult of heroism and patriotism. The glorious exploits of the resistance were contrasted with life-styles and cultural outlooks prevailing in the West. Revisionism in philosophy and the social sciences was submitted to severe criticism. A positive aspect of this activity was the rehabilitation of the Home Army as a patriotic and heroic force, but the rewriting of history led sometimes to grotesque distortions. Its stridently nationalist tones were to some extent reminiscent of pre-war right-wing extremism. On the other hand the Partisan Faction was unable to produce anything approaching a political and economic programme capable of solving current problems. The gospel of greater discipline and harder work in the spirit of self-sacrifice and idealism was not attractive to the peasants and the workers of the towns. The creative intelligentsia abhorred the 'Partisans', who in turn questioned the loyalty of many intellectuals to the socialist system. Many prominent intellectuals were Jews, which caused the 'Partisans' to be regarded as anti-semitic and resentful of influence enjoyed by Jews in public life generally. Anti-semitism, however, did not come out into the open until June 1967 after the Six Day War between Israel and Egypt.

The first expression of discontent appeared in March 1964 in the so-called 'Letter of the 34', delivered to the prime minister by Antoni Słonimski. In it a group of writers and intellectuals protested in relatively mild terms about restrictions imposed by the scarcity of newsprint, difficulties in starting new periodicals and the stifling cultural effect of censorship. Political pressure had increased, while trials of minor intellectuals inhibited contacts with abroad. Complaint was made of the closure of the celebrated discussion club in Warsaw, Klub Krzywego Koła, and the suppression of two 'revisionist' weeklies, *Nowa Kultura* and *Przegląd Kulturalny*, which had taken place in 1962. The writers' protest by itself gave the Party leadership less resentment than its publication in the West and its broadcast by Radio Free Europe. Those party members who had signed the letter were expelled from the PZPR. Pressure was placed on 600 loyal intellectuals to sign a second letter defending the government against the 'Letter of the 34' and condemning its signatories for contacts with a hostile foreign agency. To some extent the government modified its restrictive policy towards publishing, but a cold war developed between the Party authorities and the creative intelligentsia which was to last until the end of Gomułka's rule. The intellectuals' hostility played into the hands of those elements in the PZPR elite who were demanding greater discipline and ideological conformity. Radio Free Europe, which eagerly seized upon all signs and rumours of political opposition, and the émigré *Kultura*, which strongly supported the intellectuals, were branded in official propaganda as tools in the service of Western imperialism seeking to subvert the socialist system in Poland.

An equally serious conflict was to erupt in 1965. The Polish bishops attending the Vatican Council, in which on most issues they adopted conservative attitudes, made unofficial contact with the German hierarchy. They now decided to respond to earlier German gestures for reconciliation by composing 'A letter to the German bishops', published on 18 November. The letter proposed forgiveness for wrongs suffered by both nations at one another's hands. The West German bishops were invited to the celebration of the millennium of Christianity in Poland to be held in 1966. The letter's conciliatory tone gave the PZPR leaders intense annoyance, while even many non-communist Poles considered it to be in bad taste. The Party considered it an incursion into the realm of foreign policy, which was thought to be a government preserve. A virulent campaign was launched against the Catholic hierarchy, in which the PAX press joined with gusto, in conformity with its greater commitment to political involvement which lasted throughout the 1960's.[7] Cardinal Wyszyński was denied a passport for some years and could not travel abroad.[8] The incident embittered relations between church and state more seriously than at any time since October 1956. Animosity persisted throughout the celebrations of the millennium in 1966, which the government refused to allow the pope and foreign churchmen to attend. The episcopate for its part refused to support official functions and despite state harassment conducted its own programme of celebration. There followed an unedifying spectacle of rival functions supported by church or state, sometimes held simultaneously in the same place, as occurred in Poznań on 17 April 1966. The Catholic church refused to come to terms with the communist state, the existence of which it regarded as a mere episode in the long history of the Polish nation. The small and declining Znak group was powerless to mediate.

The attitude of the Gomułka leadership to the intellectuals and church was relatively moderate. When opposition arose within the Party, recourse was had to political trials. At the end of 1965 two junior lecturers of the University of Warsaw, J. Kuroń and K. Modzelewski, distributed an open letter among members of the PZPR and ZMS working in it. It criticized the Polish model of socialism in all its aspects, blaming the ubiquitous bureaucracy with its unlimited power for the deterioration in the situation.[9] The inspiration of this neo-marxist critique was drawn from Trotsky and Djilas. It had appeared earlier in 1956 and had subsequently been suppressed by censorship, but it manifested itself again in the mid-1960's. Kuroń and Modzelewski were put on trial for endangering the socialist order of society and sentenced in 1967 to three and a half years' imprisonment. Three senior academics were put on trial at the same time and imprisoned for spreading trotskyist views. These trials provoked an indignant protest from the Polish-born historian, Isaac Deutscher, who published an open letter to Gomułka in the British press. There were many expulsions from the Party, the most famous of which was that of Professor Leszek Kołakowski, the revisionist marxist philosopher, who on the tenth anniversary of the plenum of October 1956 spoke critically at a meeting of Warsaw University students of developments in the past decade. Kołakowski's views were well-known and frequently expressed in private, but a semi-public declaration was now treated as a political offence. His international reputation did not save him from Party sanctions, even though he kept his chair and continued to publish books. Wrath could be visited upon authors of academic works even when they were members of the Central Committee. At the end of 1967 Adam Schaff's *Marxism and the Individual*, which argued that alienation did not automatically disappear in a socialist society, but exhibited itself in Poland with the persistence of anti-semitism and over-centralized planning, was roundly condemned by Kliszko in a discussion specially arranged by the periodical *Nowe Drogi*.

These symptoms of a deteriorating political climate in the mid-1960's were as nothing compared with the storm which broke early in 1968. The play of Mickiewicz, *Dziady* (The Forefathers), showing at the Warsaw National Theatre, was closed down by the authorities on the grounds that it provoked anti-Soviet outbursts among the audience. On the occasion of the last performance on 30 January, some Warsaw University students staged a street demonstration. When its organizers were arrested, a protest meeting was called without the permission of the rector of the university. At the same time the Warsaw branch of the Writers' Union, attended by well-known figures like Słonimski, Jastruń, Andrzejewski, Kołakowski and Jasienica, denounced the decision to close *Dziady* as yet another example of Party obscurantism and censorship which threatened creative activity. On 8 March a student meeting within the university precincts was broken up with brutality by the police and their auxiliaries, the ORMO. Disturbances spread to other academic institutions in Warsaw and spilled out into the streets. Students were arrested in large numbers and the mass media was used to counter their actions, but criticism of the lack of normal freedoms and the stagnation in the economy persisted.[10] Support came from students in Cracow, Lublin, Łódź, Wrocław and Gdańsk. The episcopate likewise expressed its sympathy and the Znak group protested in the sejm against police brutality. When the chairman of Znak, Jerzy Zawieyski, came under attack from the prime minister, he resigned from the Council of State, in which he had sat as a token representative of the independent Catholic movement since January 1957. The intelligentsia showed sympathy for the students, but the workers, no doubt influenced by official propaganda, showed signs of prejudice against them. About 1,200 students were arrested, but few were tried and sentenced to terms of imprisonment. Some were expelled from the university and readmitted only after an examination of their cases. A group of university professors, Bauman, Brus, Maria Hirszowicz, Kołakowski and Morawski, were declared by Gomułka to have been the ideological instigators of the riots and were dismissed from their posts without legal authority. The purge extended to other academic institutions, including the Higher School of Planning and Statistics in Warsaw, where dozens of teachers lost their jobs and whole departments were disbanded. Subsequently a law was passed by the sejm which gave retrospective legal sanction to the dismisssals and gave the government greater control over academic institutions. New men were appointed for their political reliability rather than their academic merit. The wide academic autonomy enjoyed since October 1956, unprecedented under communism, came to an end. An atmosphere of intellectual repression and hostility towards intellectuals, reminiscent of the worst period of stalinism, prevailed in the world of learning until the end of Gomułka's tenure of power. Intellectual opposition and public dissent ceased. The suspicion is invited that the closure of *Dziady* was an act of provocation on the part of the authorities. If this is true, it was a tragic miscalculation with unfortunate consequences.

Revisionism of the marxists and 'liberal oppositionism' in the Writers' Union receded into the background, but a fantastic interpretation of the student unrest began to appear. On 10 March the PAX daily newspaper, *Słowo Powszechne*, alleged that there existed an anti-Polish alliance of Israel and the German Federal Republic which was responsible through 'Zionist elements' for the student riots. This charge was repeated on 13 March by the new Warsaw City Party secretary, J. Kępa, at a meeting of Party activists. He blamed the riots on a group of Jewish students, manipulated by discredited party leaders like Zambrowski and Staszewski, acting in the interest of the international Zionist movement in order to besmirch People's Poland. At the same time Party organizations and committees denounced the 'Zionists' in their midst and expelled Jews from the Party and any posts in which 'national affirmation' was declared to be essential. The press, television and radio, with the notable exception of *Polityka*, weighed in with enthusiasm. The purge degenerated into a witchhunt in which personal envy and animosity often played a large part. This 'purge from below' with much less publicity struck at non-Jewish revisionists not only in Warsaw, but throughout Poland. Even powerful men like Gierek thought it prudent to fall into line. At a meeting of Katowice on 14 March he condemned 'Zionism', while Gomułka in a speech of 19 March, though discounting the existence of many 'Zionists' or disloyal Jewish members in the PZPR, nevertheless offered emigration permits to Jews who preferred to live in Israel. Unnerved by the anti-Zionist campaign and fearing that their careers were shattered, persons of Jewish origin took advantage of the offer and left Poland for Israel, Western Europe and North America. It is estimated that two-thirds of the 25,000–30,000 Jews still living in Poland at the beginning of 1968 had emigrated by the end of the year. The plan for 'the ethnic regulation of Party cadres', first formuated by die-hard stalinists in the PZPR elite twelve years earlier, was thus carried out long after they had lost their power. A historical and ideological justification of the purge appeared in *Miesięcznik Literacki* (Literary Monthly) in June 1968 in an article written by A. Werblan, a high Party propaganda official, and once a PPS leader. He attributed to Jewish communists 'cosmopolitan' and unpatriotic attitudes throughout the history of the Polish communist movement. Leading Jewish members of the post-war Party were accused of following a deliberate policy of favouring Jews in many sections of the Party apparatus, irrespective of their qualifications. In Werblan's view 'Zionism' in the 1960's was the logical outcome of these tendencies.[11]

The anti-Zionist campaign had its roots in the Arab–Israeli war of 1967, when Poland like the rest of the Soviet bloc, with the exception of Romania, broke off diplomatic relations with Israel. In a speech to the Polish trade-union congress on 19 June Gomułka alleged that some Polish Jews who had sympathized with Israel during the war were a potential Fifth Column. The speech unleashed the first anti-Zionist campaign in the press, in which publications associated with the Partisan Faction took an active part. Because some student leaders in the events of March 1968 were Jewish, it was easy to attribute the riots to a 'Zionist plot' and thus justify a purge. There is no evidence that Gomułka authorized the purge. After 19 March he had attempted to put a brake upon it, attributing the troubles to anti-socialist intellectuals in Warsaw and revisionist professors. At the plenum of the Central Committee in July 1968 he criticized abuses in the purge and the creation of an atmosphere of distrust of the Jews, but abuses remained uncorrected. At the same meeting two prominent Jews, Billig and Schaff, and Żółkiewski, were expelled, while Albrecht, who had ridiculed the absurdities of the anti-Zionist propaganda at the end of the plenum, was promptly dismissed from his post of minister of finance. Ochab's resignation from the chairmanship of the Council of Satate was widely interpreted as an act of protest.

There is little doubt that the 'March Events' undermined Gomułka's authority and paved the way for his fall in December 1970, but the Partisan Faction under Moczar had failed in its objective, which was presumably to reduce Gomułka to the position of a figurehead and exercise power in the Party in his name. On the other hand, it had demonstrated its ability to organize action without the approval of the politburo. It was clear that Gomułka no longer was in full control of the Party and that his policy of securing a balance of power within it was failing. Gomułka was a pugnacious man not easily intimidated. At the Fifth PZPR Congress of 11–16 November 1968 the 'Partisans' controlled 600 out of the 1,600 delegates,[12] but he refused to make concessions to them. Moczar, elevated to secretariat and made a candidate member of the politburo at the July plenum, received no advancement, while members of his group obtained only a small number of places in the new Central Committee. At the same time the followers of Gierek, widely favoured as Gomułka's successor among the PZPR, made little progress within the Party organization. Gomułka promoted instead younger men belonging to the post-war generation of youth leaders, two of whom, Józef Tejchma and Stanisław Kociołek, were made full members of the politburo over the much more senior Moczar. The Rzeszów provincial Party secretary, W. Kruczek, a man with a die-hard stalinist past and strong Soviet sympathies, was unexpectedly promoted from the Central Committee to the politburo, a step probably designed to allay the fears of the Kremlin, which felt disquiet at the nationalism of the 'Partisans' and their criticism of communist leaders who had spent the war in the Soviet Union. After the invasion of Czechoslovakia in August 1968 Gomułka's standing in the Kremlin was high and Soviet leaders went out of their way to show their support of him plain. At the November Congress, contrary to custom, Brezhnev did not depart after the beginning of the proceedings, but remained until the new Central Committee and secretariat were chosen. It was ironical that, having come to power in defiance of the Soviet leaders in 1956, Gomułka was to some extent now dependent on their support. This was evidence that his standing with the PZPR elite was on the decline.[13]

International relations

In October 1964 Khrushchev was ousted from the Soviet Party presidium and the collective leadership, virtually unchanged under Leonid Brezhnev as first secretary and Alexei Kosygin, the chairman of the Council of Ministers, took control. It is probable that Gomułka was not sorry to see Khrushchev depart, because his policies had given him cause for concern. At the Twenty-Second Congress of the CPSU in October 1961 Khrushchev embarked on an anti-stalinist campaign in both the USSR and the Soviet bloc, which Gomułka refused to implement, no doubt because he did not wish to encourage revisionism at home. The Cuban missiles crisis of October 1962 resulted from an act of political recklessness which raised the spectre of a third world war and frightened not only Gomułka. The Sino-Soviet conflict dragged on and became more bitter. Before his fall Khrushchev was attempting a rapprochement with Western Germany which gave Gomułka cause for concern.[14] Khrushchev was clearly becoming too adventurist in foreign policy for the comfort of his colleagues and allies.

The Brezhnev–Kosygin leadership was quick to reassure the leaders of the people's democracies that there would be no changes in Soviet policy. Gomułka's relations with them soon became cordial, but at an early stage he realized that the Kremlin's ideas on economic integration differed from his own. By the mid-1960's he had become convinced that the world had entered a new era of technological progress and that without economic integration Eastern Europe would reap no advantages. Gomułka believed that the scarce Western currency resources of the Soviet bloc ought to be used for the benefit of the bloc as a whole by a system of centrally planned investment, regulation of intra-Comecon trade balances in convertible currency and the joint financing of production among Comecon members. Instead of medium-sized factories, giant enterprises based upon the most advanced Western technology ought to be built to serve the entire Soviet bloc, with each country specializing in certain areas of production. After consultations with the other Comecon countries and, as he claimed in September 1967, with the prior support of Eastern Germany and Bulgaria, Gomułka put foward a proposal for the reform of Comecon at a meeting of communist leaders in Moscow, assembled in November 1967 to celebrate the fiftieth anniversary of the Bolshevik revolution. He spoke with force of the technological revolution of the twentieth century and the need of the socialist countries to follow the capitalist example on the road to integration.[15] Brezhnev's response was cool. In his view the problem was one which required long-term planning. Nothing therefore was done until April 1969, when the Comecon council ordered a survey to be made of the problems of closer economic relations and agreed to establish a Comecon Investment Bank. During 1970 the executive council of Comecon under the chairmanship of Jaroszewicz prepared a scheme of gradual integration, which was eventually adopted in 1971. Gomułka regarded integration as a matter of urgency and hoped to reap the benefits in the Polish plan for 1971–5. In his disappointment he abandoned multilateralism and sought in a tour of the Comecon capitals in 1970 to increase bilateral exchanges and secure markets for the products of Polish factories to be built in the 1970's, but his efforts were of small avail, except in the case of Romania, which agreed to increase her trade with Poland by 50 per cent. This agreement marked an improvement in Polish–Romanian relations which had been placed under strain by Romania's independent course in foreign policy.

The problem of relations with Czechoslovakia gave Gomułka cause for concern in the late 1960's and disrupted more than his plans for Comecon. There was some sympathy at first for Czechoslovakia's retreat from stalinism, but it quickly turned to hostility when the Czechoslovak reform movement widened its scope. The reforms advocated by the Polish revisionists in 1956–7 were freely discussed in Czechoslovakia and more and more put into effect. Gomułka feared the repercussions on Poland, and the Warsaw students in March 1968 clearly manifested their sympathy for Dubček. The situation was aggravated by the protest against anti-semitism in Poland made by leading Czechoslovak reformers. In May the PZPR was secretly briefed that the revisionist and counter-revolutionary forces were gaining the upper hand in Czechoslovakia, to which the rest of the Soviet bloc could not remain indifferent. On 15 July the Soviet bloc leaders met in Warsaw and drew up a strongly worded letter to the Czechoslovak communist party, urging that a curb be imposed upon the reform movement. There is evidence that behind the scenes Gomułka was a leading proponent of a tough course.[16] Poland eventually took part in the invasion of Czechoslovakia on 21 August. The fate of Czechoslovakia did not stir Poland as much as the Hungarian uprising of 1956, but Polish participation in the invasion had little public support. Party propaganda declared that the motive of the Czechoslovak movement was a desire for a rapprochement with Western Germany and an injection of German economic aid. The danger of 'another Munich' with Czechoslovakia leaving the Warsaw Pact was a theme of Polish leaders' speeches and of a brochure prepared for use in the Polish army by the Ministry of Defence. The Czechoslovak reform movement was declared to be part of the same international Zionist conspiracy and West German revisionism which had caused the events of March 1968 in Poland.[17] Only those few intellectuals who were already alienated from Gomułka expressed their shame at Polands' participation in the invasion.

One outstanding success of Gomułka in the field of international relations was his securing the recognition of the Oder–Neisse line by the Federal Republic of Germany. The two states had been at loggerheads on this subject, but some confidential discussions had taken place as early as 1960 concerning the establishment of diplomatic relations.[18] In 1963 the two countries exchanged trade missions. Fear of weakening the Polish position in future negotiations perhaps explains the fury of the Polish government when Cardinal Wyszyński proposed a Polish–German rapprochement at the end of 1965. The West German attitude was that, pending the decisions of a peace conference, the frontiers of Germany were those of 1937, and that the Federal Republic was the only legally constituted German state. This view was modified in March 1966, when without prejudice to the frontier question the Federal Republic proposed to Poland, Czechoslovakia, the USSR and other Eastern European countries that they should renounce the use of force. Only Romania accepted this offer and established diplomatic relations with Western Germany. Poland and the other countries of the Soviet bloc stood aloof. When the German Social Democratic leader, Willy Brandt, became vice-chancellor and minister of foreign affairs in the 'grand coalition' of Christian Democrats and Social Democrats at the end of 1966, a more conciliatory attitude towards Eastern Europe became apparent, a policy which was maintained when Brandt became chancellor in the socialist–liberal coalition government formed in the autumn of 1969.

The Polish government insisted upon the finality of the Oder–Neisse frontier as fixed by the Potsdam Conference in 1945 and also upon recognition of the German Democratic Republic as an equally legally constituted state. On 17 May 1969 Gomułka suddenly proposed to the Federal Republic a treaty based upon the recognition of the Oder–Neisse frontier alone. The GDR was not unnaturally displeased by Poland's dropping the second condition of recognition and East German leaders vented their disapproval in public during the celebrations on the 25th anniversary of People's Poland in July 1969. Gomułka's proposal had followed close upon the deferment of his plan for integration by the Comecon executive council. It is possible that failure by the East German leaders to give his plan support was one reason for the change in the Polish attitude. The response of the Brandt government to Gomułka's proposal was favourable, and discussions on the normalization of relations began in February 1970. At the same time the Federal Republic was engaged in talks with the USSR and the GDR. A treaty between the USSR and the Federal Republic of Germany was signed on 12 August 1970, by which the two parties renounced the use of force and accepted the existing frontiers of all European states. Agreement between the Federal Republic and Poland took longer and the complicated issues of repatriation of Polish citizens of German origin to the Federal Republic and compensation for Nazi war crimes were not resolved until 1973. Nevertheless, on 7 December 1970 Chancellor Brandt and his minister of foreign affairs, Scheele, signed a treaty in Warsaw. Its three fundamental articles confirmed the Oder–Neisse line as the western frontier of Poland, pledged respect for the existing frontiers of the two states and renounced all territorial claims. As a mark of his sincerity Brandt laid a wreath at the monument of the Jewish victims of Nazism and knelt before it as a gesture of expiation. Ratification was delayed until May 1972 owing to opposition in the Western German parliament in Bonn, but for practical purposes the treaty of December 1970 marked the effective settlement of the problem of the western frontier, which had been a bone of international tension since the breakdown of the unity of the wartime Allies in 1945.

The treaty was greeted with relief and enthusiasm by Western opinion which had long sympathized with the Polish claim, but Western governments, out of loyalty to their German ally, had never supported Poland officially. This was not quite true of France, which showed interest in strengthening ties with Poland after 1965. A series of agreements and President de Gaulle's visit to Poland in September 1967 reflected this new attitude. British–Polish relations in the middle and late 1960's were confined to trade, which expanded steadily. Britain was Poland's largest trading partner in the non-communist world. Only Polish–American relations deteriorated during the period. The Polish government's hostility to American policy in Vietnam and later its virulent anti-Israeli stand antagonized Congress and the Administration. United States' economic help ceased and credits which the Poles needed to finance imports dried up without American government backing. It was the task of Gomułka's successor to improve Polish–American relations in the new situation of détente in the early 1970's.

Economic problems and attempted reforms

The last two years of the 1961–5 plan, during which investment was scaled down to the 1963 level, saw a general relaxation throughout the economy, helped by a considerable improvement in agricultural production after the two disastrous years 1962 and 1963. Industrial production rose again and

Table 18. *Basic targets of the 1961–5 plan and their fulfilment*

	Planned increase (1960 = 100)	Percentage fulfilment
National income produced	140.6	135.2
Real earnings	123.0	108.0
Consumption	130.6	128.0
Global industrial production	150.4	150.9
Group A	157.2	159.5
Group B	144.3	137.1
Global agricultural production	122.2	114.5
Employment (persons)	692,000	1,276,000

Source: Jezierski, *Historia gospodarcza*, p. 251.

the market equilibrium was restored. But the results of the plan, when all the data had been released, were far from successful. Only one target, that of industrial production, was adequately met and here again there was a failure of Group B (consumer goods) to meet its share of the target. Moreover, much of the industrial production consisted of stocks rather than directly usable goods.[19] The enormous expansion of the labour force destroyed all hope of increased productivity and prolonged the extensive growth of the economy, which the planners had hoped to reverse. The annual increase in industrial production per worker dropped from 7.5 per cent per year between 1956–60 to 4.2 per cent during 1961–5.[20] Yet despite the high rate of accumulation and employment, the dynamism of economic growth declined in comparison with the previous period. This is well illustrated by table 19. The decline affected both consumer- and producer-goods industries. In the former the average annual growth rate dropped from 18.8 per cent during 1950–8 to 4.5 per cent during 1959–67. In the machine industry the growth rates for the same periods were 23.3 and 14.5 per cent respectively.[21] In terms both of its ability to improve the standard of living of the population and to catch up with Western industrial countries, the Polish economy was becoming less rather than more efficient.

The lessons of the over-ambitious 1961 plan and the state of the economy in general were reviewed by Gomułka and the politburo's economic advisers during 1964–5. They were extensively discussed before and during the Fourth Party Congress at the Fourth Plenum in July 1965, which finalized the targets of the new plan for 1966–70, but in the discussion only the voices supporting Gomułka were tolerated. The views of the world-famous economist Kalecki, who criticized the plan for its

Table 19. *Average yearly growth of industrial production (per cent)*

| 1950–5 | 18.0 | 1961–5 | 8.5 |
| 1956–60 | 9.9 | 1966–8 | 8.2 |

Source: Karpiński, *Polityka uprzemysłowienia*, p. 31

neglect of the standard of living and suggested ways of relaxing the investment drive for the sake of consumption, met with ridicule and abuse at a Warsaw Party conference.[22] Compared with 1959 the approach was more cautious and the percentage increases planned for the key areas of the economy were largely the same as those actually achieved under the revised version of the 1961–5 plan,[23] but there was to be no significant improvement in consumption or any relaxation of the industrial effort. As a justification, the need to provide jobs for 1.5 million young people who would enter the labour market during the five years was stressed in official publications and pronouncements. The emphasis in investment was to change from energy and raw materials to chemicals and machinery, which represented a trend towards modernization of the industrial structure.

Foreign trade and agriculture, the weak points of the economy in the previous plan, received special attention. Two plenary Central Committee sessions in 1965 were concerned with foreign trade and the Fifth Plenum in December marked a turning point by its explicit recognition that Poland's industrial development required a rapid expansion in the volume of foreign trade, especially with capitalist countries, which so far had accounted for only about one third of Polish foreign trade. Without giving up the profitable agricultural exports, which still paid for the majority of industrial imports from the West, a drive was to be made to improve the export of machinery, which formed a small fraction of Polish trade with the West. Much more attention was henceforth devoted to the directions, proportions and profitability of foreign trade, but the expansion of trade with the West was hampered by the progress of European economic integration, the unwillingness of Western countries and firms to offer long-term credits to Poland, and by the Polish concern with the short-term balance of payments. The Polish hope to alleviate this by a reform of the Comecon met with no success. The inability to import advanced Western equipment and technology on a large scale remained a major brake on Polish economic development for the rest of the Gomułka period.

In agriculture the turning point was a joint resolution of the PZPR politburo and the ZSL presidium in March 1965, which established the principle of the parity of investment in agriculture and the rest of the

Table 20. *Investment outlays on agriculture 1956–70 in million zł.*
at 1961 prices

	1956–60	1961–5	1966–70
Total	69,457	102,710	172,797
of which			
Farm buildings	19,881	29,243	59,766
Mechanization	20,153	33,889	50,357
Soil drainage	5,716	12,694	19,457

Source: *Rocznik Statystyczny (1971)*; quoted in *Poland: A Handbook* (Warsaw, 1974), p. 265

economy. From now on agriculture was to receive roughly the same share of productive investment as its share of the national income. The production and import of fertilizers went up strikingly. By 1968 the quantity of artificial fertilizers used in Poland trebled in comparison with 1958, and there was an important increase in the use of quality seed and agricultural machinery. The expanding outlay on agricultural production is illustrated by table 20.

Two-thirds of the machinery, however, still went to state farms, collective farms and the agricultural circles rather than to the private farmers. In general private agriculture received less than half of the total investment outlay, although it contributed over 80 per cent of total farm production. Prices paid to individual farmers were kept low; nor was there any modification of the unpopular compulsory deliveries. According to the Party's programme, private agriculture was doomed to extinction, although this was less emphasized as the time went on, and the way it was to come about remained unclear. Disillusionment with the agricultural circles as a school of socialism, and the increasing abandonment of farming by elderly peasants, conjured up another possibility, the gradual takeover of private by state farms,[24] but the cost of the takeover was enormous and its speed slow. Thus production was bound to suffer in the meantime. A great mistake of Gomułka in the realm of agricultural production in the late 1960's was to restrict and, by 1970, completely abolish the import of grain necessary to feed the livestock. In the context of the whole policy, Polish agriculture simply could not step up the domestic production sufficiently, and when a bad harvest occurred, as it did in 1969, the results were catastrophic. The combined effect of the various policies was to reduce the average yearly increase of all agricultural production during the 1966–70 period to 1.8 per cent, which was exactly the average annual increase during the disastrous years of the Six Year Plan, and half the rate of increase of the 1961–5 period.[25] Legislation passed in 1963 and 1968 attempted to limit the subdivision of farms and to facilitate their amalgamation and compusory acquisition, with some compensation by the state.

The economic difficulties following the 1962–3 crisis made the Party leadership aware that some reforms of the planning and management system were inevitable, and these were discussed and approved by the Fourth Plenum in July 1965, and the Sixth Plenum in April 1966. Their thrust was a better calculation of economic costs, a more rational system of financing of investment, including charging a rate of interest on capital, and a greater use of prices and incentives instead of directive in guiding production. Reforms, however, were not based on any consistent and comprehensive blue-print and proved generally incompatible with the dominant heavily centralized economic system. They proved no more effective than the half-hearted reforms of the 1956–64 period.[26]

Even more than in the early Gomułka period, the problems of the economic plans, changes in targets, new methods of planning and management dominated the activity of the PZPR at all levels and also that of trade unions, youth organizations, the allied parties, the sejm and provincial and local people's councils. The provincial Party committees were urged to take an ever increasing interest in the development of their areas and to devote most of their time to production. Between the Third and the Fifth Party Congresses of 1959–68 only 4 out of 16 plenary meetings of the PZPR Central Committee were devoted predominantly to other than economic matters, of which 2 were given over to ideology, 1 to sejm and local elections, and 1 to education. The rest were wholly or mainly taken up with economic issues as were the Party congresses in 1959, 1964 and 1968. Even more than during the stalinist period the task of 'building socialism' in Poland was in practice equated with rapid industrialization. The one-sided character of this economic offensive and the lack of striking results in both production and consumption produced a growing dissatisfaction in the country and the Party.

The view that the Polish economy needed much more drastic reorientation than the piecemeal reforms and adjustments of the previous ten years became at last the belief of the Party leadership by the time of the Fifth PZPR Congress in November 1968. While again rejecting the idea of market socialism as 'revisionist',[27] the congress approved the principle of supplementing the central planning and management mechanism with a far larger number of economic incentives and of enlarging the scope of decision-making at the enterprise level. A general move towards realistic costing and pricing was to be encouraged, and managers and workers were to be stimulated to a far greater effort to improve the quality, profitability and efficiency of production by a new system of premiums and bonuses which accurately reflected the degree of actual improvement. The overall objective was to break once and for all with the extensive form of economic growth which depended on continued expansion of capital and labour instead of its rational utilization.[28] The details of the reform were worked out during 1969 and 1970. A second major change approved by the congress concerned the direction of industrial development. The heavy investment in raw material extraction, including copper, sulphur, lignite, coke and natural gas, under the current plan was to continue, but other investment in the 1971–5 period was to be concentrated on industries where advanced Western technology could be readily applied and contribute to the modernization of the economy as a whole. The industries chosen for this treatment were machine-building, electrical and electronic, chemical and non-ferrous metal processing. This strategy of selective growth, as it came to be known, reflected the belief that investment could benefit the national economy more if it were concentrated on a narrow range of objectives in a planning period rather than thinly spread throughout the economy. It dovetailed with Gomułka's idea for a greater specialization of production within Comecon.

At the time of the congress the Comecon was still making up its mind about integration, and the PZPR leadership hoped that some of the new investment would be financed jointly and the production of the new, large and technologically advanced factories absorbed by Poland's Comecon partners within the scheme urged by Gomułka.[29] This might have lessened somewhat the burden of the industrial effort and freed some extra resources for consumption. When it became clear in the following spring that nothing concrete could be achieved in 1971–5 and that Comecon integration would be at best a slow, long-term process, the consequences of the ambitious programme of economic modernization became very serious for the Polish consumer. Not only were the targets bearing on his welfare, consumption, housing, social and community services, fixed low in the 1971–5 plan. Serious economies had already been made during the last two years of the 1966–70 plan in preparation for the next five-year plan. The cost of living during 1969–70 rose by over 8 per cent and the yearly increase in real wages in 1968, 1969 and 1970 was merely 1.3, 1.7 and 1.3 per cent respectively.[30] Housing and community construction was slowed down in 1969 and frozen in 1970. The average waiting period for accommodation for a newly-married couple lengthened to seven years. Expenditure on work safety, sanitary installations and social facilities in factories was halted and the funds diverted to production purposes, just as happened during the Six Year Plan. The economies were an acceleration of the trend, which had begun already in the early 1960's, towards shifting the burden of financing certain kinds of social expenditure from the state to private individuals. Housing in cities, which the state had supplied for low rent in the 1950's, was increasingly financed out of individual savings through the so-called housing co-operatives. The shortage of schools was met by the 'thousand schools for the millenium' campaign, with money raised by voluntary contributions from local residents and the public. The improvement of roads in the countryside and various village amenities were financed on a fifty-fifty basis by the state and local voluntary effort. These were odd policies for a socialist state to follow.

The material incentive scheme, designed to intensify industrial growth, and worked out in detail during 1969 and 1970, also had serious anti-consumption implications which spread gloom and dissatisfaction in the industries worst affected by it. Special commissions examined the records of all factories to verify their actual economic performance in 1970, which was to be the base year for calculating future productivity bonuses and premiums. The performance of every enterprise was calculated at the end of each year and paid out as quarterly additions to basic earnings in the following year. Since the first extra payments under the scheme would have been made in April 1972, this amounted to a general income freeze of fifteen months. In industries where prospects for improvement were poor or where 1970 was an unfavourable year, the material incentive scheme amounted to a five-year income standstill. In some cases only a drastic reduction of the labour force could improve productivity and the earnings of remaining employees. It was afterwards alleged that the 1971–5 plan assumed a pool of unemployed differently estimated at between 350,000 and 700,000 by the end of the period, which was probably the first time in the history of a communist economy that unemployment was actually planned for. The prospect of unemployment, income stagnation and discrimination against the traditional industries alienated not only workers and managers from the new reforms and their promoters, but also government and Party officials responsible for those industries or the regions and localities where they were situated.

Doubting the ability of the government economic apparatus to prepare and implement the new reforms, Gomułka induced the Fifth Congress to approve setting up an economic commission of the Central Committee headed by Bolesław Jaszczuk, one of his wartime associates and after 1956 for a number of years the Polish ambassador in Moscow. He was elected secretary of the Central Committee and member of the politburo at the congress, and became Gomułka's closest economic advisor and the real director of the economy. Armed with this authority, assisted by his Central Committee staff and economic secretaries in the regional Party *apparat*, and personally overbearing towards colleagues and subordinates,[31] Jaszczuk carried out his task with great energy and speed. No public criticisms were tolerated. If any private complaints actually reached him, he paid little attention and certainly did not pass them on to Gomułka. The ranks of Gomułka's opponents among the Party elite, consisting of the Partisan Faction and Gierek's supporters, were by the end of 1970 swollen by government and Party officials antagonized by the post-1968 economic reforms and by Jaszczuk's ruthless methods.

One must not judge the Gomułka–Jaszczuk proposals too harshly. They were very complex, perhaps technically imperfect and hastily prepared, but they embodied reforms which were long overdue and widely recognized as essential. They were the nearest approach to a 'grand design' for the remodelling of the economy which the Polish economic reformers had advocated in the late 1950's. They did not go as far and quite in the same direction, but they were the most radical approach to the problem agreed by the Party leadership. Had they been adopted ten years earlier, when the political and economic climate was completely different, they would have done much to streamline the economy and eventually earn Gomułka praise and gratitude. In the late 1960's the situation was unfavourable to reform. After ten lean years the people were unwilling to tighten their belts. The vested interests of groups adversely affected by the reforms needed strong pressure to bring them into line. Gomułka was a discredited leader and the ruling elite were at loggerheads. The judgement of a leading student of the Polish economy that strong political authority is a necessary prerequisite to economic reform seems wholly correct.[32]

The fall of Gomułka

Smouldering discontent ended in a political explosion in the middle of December 1970. After three good harvests the bad weather conditions in 1969 and 1970 severely reduced agricultural output and the amount of foodstuffs for domestic consumption and export. At the same time, imports of grain to feed livestock virtually ceased as a result of Gomułka's decision that by 1970 Poland ought to become self-sufficient in animal fodder. The cattle and pig numbers fell drastically and, as in 1959 and 1965, a steep rise in the price of meat became necessary if the already heavy government subsidies on food were not to be increased still further. This time it was decided to increase prices on a wide range of consumer goods and simultaneously to reduce prices on consumer durables as part of a general regulation of prices. There had been some discussion among the economists about the need to restructure and modernize consumer expenditure, almost half of which was still on foodstuffs, and this provided the government with an additional justification. On 13 December the new prices were published in the form of a Council of Ministers' decree. Overnight and shortly before the traditional heavy Christmas expenditure, prices of basic consumer goods went up by an average of 8 per cent and in some cases by a far greater percentage.

On 14 December, a week after the signing of the Polish–West German treaty, the PZPR Central Committee met for a plenary session and approved both the treaty and the regulation of prices. On the same morning shipbuilding workers in Gdańsk went on strike in protest against the new prices and staged a political demonstration in the city centre.[33] After clashes with the police the mood of the crowd became violent, and public buildings, including the voivodship headquarters of the Party, were attacked and set on fire. The following day the disorders continued and spread to the neighbouring city of Gdynia, also a harbour and shipbuilding centre. That day an informal meeting of Party and government leaders authorized the use of firearms by the police and the employment of army units to quell the disorders. The army, equipped with tanks, went into action that night. On 16 December the disturbances spread to Elbląg in the same region, and on the following day strikes and violent demonstrations broke out in Szczecin, at the western extreme of the Baltic coast. It was only on 17 December that the national press first admitted the outbreak of disturbances, and a Council of Ministers' decree declared a state of emergency, the only time this had occurred in People's Poland. Although the army had restored order in the coastal cities by the end of 18 December, the situation was not wholly under control. The ruthless use of force and Gomułka's blank refusal of any dialogue with the strikers, whom he considered 'counter-revolutionary', had enraged workers in Warsaw and the other industrial cities, caused much disruption of work and led to a show of sympathy with the coastal workers after the weekend.

Gomułka's colleagues demanded a meeting of the politburo to discuss the crisis. They may have been encouraged in their stand by the knowledge that the Soviet leaders were in favour of settling the conflict in the quickest and most peaceful way. Jaroszewicz, deputy premier and deputy member of the politburo, returned to Warsaw from a Comecon executive council meeting in Moscow on 18 December. A stormy confrontation took place on the evening of the same day. In the course of it Gomułka suffered a minor stroke and was taken to hospital. On 19 December the politburo met under the chairmanship of Cyrankiewicz and, after a seven-hour meeting, voted by majority to demand Gomułka's resignation and to appoint Gierek as first secretary. On 20 December, a Sunday, a special plenary session of the Central Committee formally elected Gierek first secretary and approved a major reshuffle of the politburo and the secretariat. Gomułka and his closest associates in the leadership, Jaszczuk, Kliszko, Spychalski and Strzelecki, but not for the time being Loga-Sowiński, found themselves excluded. Their places as full politburo members were taken by Babiuch and Szydlak, closely associated with Gierek, while Jaroszewicz, Moczar and Olszowski, Cyrankiewicz, Jędrychowski, Kruczek, Tejchma and Kociołek remained in the new politburo. Jagielski, Jabłoński, Jaruzelski and Kępa were deputy members, the last three being newcomers. In the evening, Gierek broadcast to the nation and asked for a return to work, criticizing the previous leadership for ill-conceived policies and for being out of touch with the working class. The change of leadership relaxed the tension. Two days later, probably after a meeting between Gierek and Brezhnev, the Soviet Party leaders officially welcomed the changes in Poland. On the following day, 23 December, the sejm met briefly to approve a number of government changes, of which the most important were the replacement of Spychalski by Cyrankiewicz as head of state and of Cyrankiewicz by Jaroszewicz as the chairman of the Council of Ministers. The transfer of power to the new leadership thus acquired constitutional validity.

The long period of Gomułka's political domination thus came to a tragic end in December 1970. After just over fourteen years, his personal popularity and authority dissolved in an atmosphere of universal hostility and general desire to see him go. He came to power during a crisis which he handled most skilfully. The triple conflict between the reformists and the conservatives within the Party, between the Party and the nation, and between Poland and the Soviet Union was substantially settled in the space of one year. He lost power in a fresh crisis, of his own creation, in which his policies set the working class against the Party.

In October 1956 Gomułka embodied the hopes of his countrymen for a better future, offering a freer society, greater participation in government, economic prosperity, national identity and dignity. At first he seemed to meet them, but in the end he bitterly disappointed those hopes. Although the climate in the Soviet bloc was favourable to reform in the early 1960's, Gomułka was too cautious, too unimaginative and too traditionalist to see the necessity for radical change. In some respects his career had striking parallels with that of Piłsudski.[34] In others it was the opposite of that of the Hungarian leader Janos Kadar, who came to power at the same time as Gomułka as a despised Russian puppet, but who outlived him politically as an enlightened, reformist and universally respected statesman.

It is probably too early for a balanced judgement on Gomułka. The events of March 1968 and December 1970 tend to cast a shadow on his earlier career and distort our perspective. One must beware of blaming all his failures on the man himself instead of on the system of which he was a part. Gomułka's tragedy was in not seeing that his ends, which were often good, could not be reached through the means he controlled. He blamed his colleagues, the Party and national character for what were really the faults inherent in the system itself, a system he inherited and did not believe needed major change. There were other important constraints, but the constraints of the system itself were the greatest of all.

The redeeming features of Gomułka's career were his patriotism, courage, personal integrity, modesty, common sense and moderation. His devotion to socialism and to his country's welfare, as he understood them, was unquestionable. He never abused political power for personal ends, though he became a virtual autocrat.[35] He came to distrust the opinion of others and to rely primarily on his own judgement. The politburo lost all vestiges of its collective deliberative function and during the last years of Gomułka's leadership ceased to meet regularly. The circle of his confidants and advisers shrank to a handful, and even they dared not oppose him on issues on which he felt strongly. He became isolated from the nation at large, from the rank and file of the Party and its ruling elite. The continued sacrifice of current consumption and welfare for the sake of industrial growth and its benefits in some remote future eventually became unbearable. Inability to achieve balanced economic development and to solve other problems discredited Gomułka as a statesman. Even his middle-of-the-road and pragmatic attitude to political issues in the end produced widespread dissatisfaction. He became a symbol of economic, political and cultural stagnation and an obstacle to radical changes, on the nature of which Poles were by no means agreed, but for which they seemed ready by the end of the 1960's.

16

Poland under Gierek

The passing of Gomułka and his group marked the end of an era in post-war Polish history. A group of leaders, formed in the pre-war and wartime underground, passed from the stage. They left behind a political and economic system purged of the worst features of stalinism, but still over-centralized, run by a narrow political elite, and open to police arbitrariness. As a system acceptable to the Soviet Union, and yet containing features that made it possible for the population to see it as in some sense 'Polish', it enjoyed genuine, if limited, popular legitimacy. At the same time this legitimacy was weakened by widespread popular frustration, which increased greatly in the later years of the Gomułka leadership. The main source of the frustration was the failure of the standard of living of the bulk of the working class, white-collar workers and peasants to rise.

The period which began with the assumption of leadership by Edward Gierek was still, at the beginning of 1978, rather an open one, and the final judgement on it would have to wait till it was complete. The last chapter of the history of post-war Poland cannot be more than an epilogue. It might, however, be possible to list the criteria by which the Gierek period is likely to be judged. People's Poland can take just pride in the fulfilment of several vital national tasks: the recovery from war damage, the assimilation of the Western Territories, the development of industry, the ending of mass unemployment in towns and under-employment in the country, the expansion of opportunities for social advance, and the support for the development of national culture. It is, however, clear that the communist system has created just as many problems as it has solved, and it is the solution of these problems by which the adequacy of any communist party leadership must be judged.

These outstanding problems can be reduced to six major ones. First, the reconciliation of economic growth and current consumption into a reasonable degree of harmony. Second, the narrowing of the gap between the dynamic development of industry and the still largely stagnant agriculture, and generally fitting a host of small independent producers into the system of a centrally planned economy. Third, combining the advantages of central planning and direction with the initiative, experimentation and energy of individuals and groups acting spontaneously, in other words achieving a proper balance between bureaucracy and participation. Fourth, the creation of a permanent dialogue between the rulers and the ruled which would reduce political tension and eliminate periodic crisis. Fifth, the reconciliation of the Party's ideological commitment to a secular society with the reality of a Roman Catholic church enjoying the allegiance of the bulk of the population; similarly the reconciliation of a commitment to socialism in culture and marxism in science with the desire of the artistic, intellectual and scientific community for untrammelled activity. Sixth and last, the retaining of the goodwill of a proud, patriotic and historically conscious nation without ceasing to be acceptable to the leaders of the Soviet Union. The bare list of these problems suggests both how vital and how difficult they are. Indeed many would regard them as insoluble within the framework of a communist system. But this is too pessimistic. Some of the problems were partially solved already during the Gomułka period, and one could reasonably hope that Gierek would learn from the mistakes and failures of his predecessor.

The aftermath of the December riots

The new Party leaders hoped that the personnel changes in the politburo and the government, the promise of a new style of leadership and the overhaul of Gomułka's economic policies would be sufficient to pacify the workers and restore normal working in industry. They merely increased the wages of the lowest paid workers and the welfare benefits for old-age pensioners and children, and promised to keep the prices of foodstuffs unchanged during 1971 and 1972. This proved a serious underestimate of the strength of the discontent. Early in the new year the unrest revived. On 12 January the Warsaw correspondent of *L'Unità* reported that Poland had become one huge Hyde Park. In the Gdynia shipyard alone, 21 meetings were held in the first fortnight in January. On 22 January the Szczecin shipyard workers struck again, despite a visit of two politburo members and the dismissal of Walaszek, the hated provincial Party secretary. The occupation of the shipyards was followed by that of 36 other enterprises in the city. This time the army and the police were ordered by the government to stay away, while the workers set up a co-ordinated network of strike committees and virtually took over the running of the city. The shipyard strike committee formulated eleven basic demands and demanded talks with the Party leaders. The demands were headed by a return to the prices of 12 December, and included an unprecedented political item: free and secret elections to the factory Party and trade-union committees. After two days Gierek, accompanied by Jaroszewicz, Jaruzelski and Szlachic, the new minister of the interior, arrived at the gate of the shipyard. During a stormy meeting with the workers' delegates, the leaders listened to a litany of grievances and promised to meet some of them, while insisting that there were absolutely no resources for improving wages. At 2 a.m., after ten hours of talks, the strikers agreed to resume work.[1] The leaders then travelled to Gdańsk, where, during another mammoth meeting with the local workers' delegates, similar grievances were voiced and the same answers given. It was felt, however, that a major concession was needed to calm the workers, so on 23 January in Gdańsk Jaroszewicz announced the indefinite suspension of the Jaszczuk incentive scheme. The confrontations proved a great political success for Gierek. He found he could tame hostile audiences by giving the impression of honest effort to cope with great difficulties and obtain promises of help and trust. Persuasion and dialogue with the workers, which Gomułka had ruled out in December 1970, were shown to work successfully in settling a strike. Gierek's popularity became an immense asset to the Party, which had temporarily lost the ability to command.

The Szczecin and Gdańsk meetings brought about a measure of political stabilization. On 6 and 7 February the Eighth Central Committee Plenum met to receive the politburo's report on the December events. The report contained a statement of human and material losses and an analysis of the causes of the December and January riots. Gomułka, Kliszko and Jaszczuk were now severely blamed for mishandling the December crisis and for the neglect of the standard of living in the 1966–1970 plan which had caused it. They were said to have brought the country to the verge of catastrophe, from which it had been saved at the very last moment by the healthy elements in the Party leadership. The atrophy of collective leadership and the autocratic domination of the politburo by Gomułka also came in for much criticism, especially in the discussion of the report. Gomułka, who could not defend himself at the meeting because of illness, was suspended in his membership of the Central Committee, while Kliszko and Jaszczuk were expelled. Three other members, Loga-Sowiński, Kociołek and Walaszek, resigned at the plenum. The resolutions passed by the plenum promised more contacts between the politburo and the Party *aktiv*, greater workers' and local activists' participation in Party organizations, more consultation with workers and the intelligentsia before decisions, the revitalization of trade unions and workers' self-government, and greater provision for welfare in the current plan and budget. A long-term plan for the reform of the economic and political system was to be prepared by a Party–government commission, and the date of the next Party congress was advanced from the autumn of 1972 to the end of 1971.[2] The words had a familiar ring, and recalled many of the promises of the 1955–7 period. No fault was found with the heavily bureaucratic and centralized political system itself, only with the ways it was misapplied during the last five years or so. It was yet another exercise in 'restoring the leninist norms of party and state life' so typical of communist systems in crises, but at least it looked like the beginning of a programme rather than the continuation of *ad hoc* measures.

The need for the latter was not quite over. Strikes and factory meetings, although more sporadic, went on, and so did the search for economies in the central government budget in order to increase consumption and social welfare. An additional 5 milliard *zł.* were found, the equivalent of a rise in nominal wages by 4.2 per cent instead of the planned 1.2 per cent, which was the greatest annual jump in earnings since 1956. The sejm on 13 February approved changes in the national economic plan and the budget, and ratified extensive changes in the composition of the sejm authorities, the State Council, and the economic ministries, especially in the Planning Commission. As a gesture to working-class feelings, taxes on private entrepreneurs were increased. In his exposé of the government measures Jaroszewicz insisted again that this was the absolute limit of financial concessions and that no further resources for improving the standard of living existed.

Even as he spoke the women workers of thirteen textile factories in Łódź came out on strike, declared a lockout, and demanded a 15 per cent wage rise. Starved of investment for years and condemned to continued stagnation under the Jaszczuk selective growth policy, the textile industry was notorious for bad working conditions and low earnings, being 1,000 *zł.* below the average shipyard monthly wage, according to official statistics. Jaroszewicz, Szydlak, Tejchma and Kruczek, Loga-Sowiński's successor as chairman of the CRZZ, travelled to Łódź to face the workers' delegates on 14 February. At first the leaders refused any concessions, but a tour of some of the cotton mills and exposure to a hysterical mob of angry women changed their mind. In the evening of the 15th Jaroszewicz announced on television the annulment of the December price increases. Since the lower prices of industrial goods remained in force, the concession raised the total of extra money given to the population since December to the huge sum of 60 milliard *zł.* This completed the retreat from the objectionable measures of the Gomułka period and the workers' victory over the Party leadership. There was no precedent in the history of communism for such prolonged industrial action with such spectacular consequences. The Poznań riots of June 1956 were limited in scope and due to a local grievance. The 1970–1 strikers questioned a general government policy and wrung out far-reaching concessions through persistent pressure. Their actions seemed to open a new stage in the political awareness of the Polish working class. Polish sociologists were quick to point out their historical and theoretical significance and draw the conclusion that the new political maturity ought to express itself in institutional reforms giving the workers a greater influence over political and economic life.[3]

Jaroszewicz was in fact right that the government had no resources at its disposal to meet any additional consumer spending. But they could be obtained from abroad. Already in early January, after a visit of Gierek and Jaroszewicz to Moscow, the Soviet Union, which had refused to supply grain to Gomułka, agreed to sell 2 million tonnes to his successors. Now additional credits in Western currency were granted by the USSR to Poland. With these credits Polish emissaries toured the capitals of Western Europe buying up available food surpluses. The Gomułka régime in October 1956 had been established in defiance of the Soviet Union and, at least in its early stages, had drawn its strength from popular support for what had been believed to be its anti-Russian stand. The Gierek régime, on the contrary, had to seek Soviet help in order to stabilize the system and its own position. There was in Moscow perhaps also an element of mistrust towards the new Polish first secretary, which might account for the fulsomeness of his references to the Soviet Union. It was a paradox that the internal improvements brought about by the strikes were accompanied by increased dependence of Poland on the Soviet Union.

Although increased consumption was the chief means by which the Gierek leadership brought the industrial unrest under control, they used other means as well. The first was rapprochement with the Catholic church, which paralleled that of 1956–7. Although the church submitted a long list of grievances, only two concessions were originally made: a government mission was sent to the Vatican for exploratory talks, and the church was at last granted full legal title to property in the former German territories. On their part, the hierarchy appealed for social peace, return to work, the end of recriminations and trust in the new leadership, but they could not forbear condemning the use of force and reminding church-goers that fundamental human rights, the rights of the church and the principles of democracy were still largely denied in Poland.[4]

The new leadership tried also to win over the intellectuals, many of whom had become deeply alienated during the second half of the Gomułka period. In January Gierek met the representatives of writers, artists, scientists, film and theatre producers, and later the economists, and stressed the value of their contribution to Poland's development. A noticeable cultural 'thaw' followed the meeting. Creative intellectuals who had been dismissed from their posts or silenced under Gomułka, like Kisielewski and Słonimski, resumed working and publishing, but no reference to the March 1968 events was officially made by the new leadership, and the victims of the 'Zionist' and 'revisionist' purge were not rehabilitated. The presence of two of its main instigators, Moczar and Kępa, in Gierek's politburo and the strength of the 'Partisan Faction' in the Central Committee made any step in that direction most unlikely. In a skilful bid for national popularity Gierek announced on 20 January 1971 the decision to rebuild the Warsaw Royal Castle, destroyed by the Germans between 1939 and 1944. The government was to give substantial aid to the costly project, but voluntary subscriptions were to be the main source of funds. On this issue the new Party leadership also sought to enlist the help of Poles living abroad. Perhaps because of Gierek's own émigré background, the developing contacts with the Polonia became a prominent policy of the Polish government in the 1970's.

The new PZPR leaders emerged in three stages: 20–23 December 1970, 9–14 February 1971 and at the end of the Party congress held 6–11 December 1971. As long as the workers' unrest continued, changes in the Party and government leadership were largely confined to the purge of the inner group of Gomułka's lieutenants in the politburo and secretariat. The Central Committee and the provincial committees remained much the same till the congress, and the most influential group among them consisted of the supporters of General Moczar, who had been so clearly in the ascendant at the time of the previous congress in 1968. For rather obscure reasons, perhaps associated with an upheaval in the Ministry of the Interior in June 1971, which involved the dismissal of several of its prominent officials and the trial of some,[5] Moczar during the year lost his place in the secretariat and the politburo and the chairmanship of ZBoWiD. ZBoWiD lost further significance when its welfare activities were transferred to a new Ministry of Veteran Affairs. But another man with 'partisan' background and a career in the security police, Franciszek Szlachcic, quickly emerged to take Moczar's place. By the December 1971 Party congress he had been promoted to the politburo and the secretariat, where he seemed to eclipse Szydlak as the most important man after Gierek. The politburo consisted of the following full members: E. Babiuch, E. Gierek, H. Jabłoński, the new head of state, M. Jagielski, chairman of the Planning Commission, P. Jaruzelski, minister of defence,

W. Kruczek, chairman of the CRZZ, S. Olszowski, minister of foreign affairs, F. Szlachcic, J. Szydlak and J. Tejchma. K. Barcikowski, Z. Grudzień, Gierek's successor in Katowice, S. Kania and J. Kępa, the Warsaw Party secretary, were deputy members. When Barcikowski and Tejchma, young men promoted in the last years of Gomułka, took up governmental posts, the secretariat came to be dominated by equally young men, Babiuch, Kania, Kowalczyk and Łukaszewicz, who owed their position to Gierek's patronage. Although Gierek exercised undisputed authority, only a small minority could be said to be 'his men' in the leadership. The leading team as a whole was younger and better educated than under Gomułka, and except for Szlachcic and Kępa lacked men with any pronounced ideological orientations. At the Party congress the Central Committee was enlarged from 87 to 115 full members, of whom almost two-thirds were new men; almost three-quarters of the 93 candidate members were newly elected.[6] Twelve voivodship secretaries were replaced by Gierek in the first two years, but a more extensive shake-up of the territorial Party apparatus took place only on the eve of the next Party congress in 1975. Between December 1970 and June 1971 there were also a number of changes in the composition of the State Council and the government. This was the team which planned and executed the policy changes during the first five years of Gierek's leadership.

The new first secretary was in several ways a different leader from Gomułka. His formative years were not spent in revolutionary underground activity in Poland, but working as a miner and then communist trade-union organizer in France and Belgium. He returned to Poland when communist rule was firmly established, and spent two decades working in the Party apparatus in the highly industrialized Silesia and in Warsaw. He was not compromised by the excesses of stalinism, but neither was he prominent in the campaign for democratization during the 1955-7 period. Gierek was primarily an *apparatchik*, yet with a thorough experience of industrial problems and strong contacts with both the working class and the technical intelligentsia. He was known to demand hard work from his subordinates, but to look after their conditions well. He preferred to encourage rather than to bully. He liked living well and seeing others prosper. He had tact, self-control, presence and personal charm, but not the toughness of character of Gomułka. He preferred compromise to confrontation, and was skilful at political manoeuvring. He had an open mind, ready to receive ideas, and sympathetic to intellectuals, but not an original intellect or a mind thinking in broad, long-term strategic categories.

The emergence of a new programme

The February Central Committee plenum authorized the preparation of a new programme of policies and reforms for the Party and the government, and the industrial peace which finally followed the repeal of the December price increases allowed the leadership to plan the future instead of living from hand to mouth. Contrary to expectation, Gierek did not have any ready-made programme when he came to power, nor even any fundamental principles to guide its construction. The programme emerged in practice by tackling those parts of the Gomułka legacy which had blocked the path to increased consumption and industrial growth.

The greatly increased purchasing power of the blue- and white-collar workers required an increased supply of food, still nearly 50 per cent of an average family's budget, and hence a new policy towards the peasants. The policy of compulsory deliveries at low prices was well known to hamper production, but it had continued unchanged since 1950 and was only partially modified in 1957. After consulting the ZSL leaders, the PZPR politburo decided in April 1971 on a number of radical measures: all compulsory deliveries were abolished and replaced by government contracts, the land tax was lowered and reformed to encourage more intensive cultivation, and legislation concerning land use and the protection of farming land and forestry was brought up to date. The selling of farm machinery to private firms was at last allowed. Other state deliveries for agricultural production were guaranteed, the procurement and processing of farm products became more efficient, and the whole peasant population, amounting to 6.5 million persons, was for the first time included in the national health insurance system. Helped by good weather conditions, there was an immediate improvement in agricultural investment, production and sales, and the earnings of the farming community rose dramatically. At long last the peasants reached something like a parity of rights with the workers in the system which theoretically had always been based on the principle of worker–peasant alliance.[7]

Despite an oft-repeated slogan of Gierek 'let the Party lead and the government govern', the PZPR politburo firmly occupied the centre of the stage during 1971. It met every week and the subject of its deliberations was announced in the press. The announcement in June 1971 about the re-examination of the use of foreign licences in the machine and chemical industry was the harbinger of one of the most important policy decisions of the year, which was not given very much publicity: the negotiation with Western firms for large-scale manufacture of their products under licence. One of the first contracts, signed in October 1971, was with the Italian

FIAT company for the production of one of its small models in Poland and comprehensive co-operation in spare-parts production. It became increasingly common to purchase on long-term credit technically advanced Western manufacturing equipment in order to develop or modernize certain branches of Polish industry. The need to make dynamic foreign trade an integral part of economic development had been clearly recognized by Gomułka, but only after the change of leadership did it become an essential feature of Polish economic policy.[8] An element of luck played a large role here. Gomułka had sought, but had not been able to obtain, long-term credits or find capitalist partners for co-operation. Gierek was fortunate in that the change in the economic climate in the West and the progress of détente during the 1970's changed the attitude of Western businessmen and their governments towards trading with communist countries. The politburo's decision to borrow massively from the West was a major cause of the initial success and eventual difficulties of the economic plan for 1971–5.

After scrapping the Gomułka plan, the politburo instructed the government and the Planning Commission in April 1971 to take as its fundamental goals the socially perceptible improvement in the living standard of the working people, the rational utilization of the rapidly rising labour force, due to an upward demographic curve, and the acceleration of the economic growth rate. The preparation of the plan coincided with that of the new Party congress, and its guidelines became part of the new Party programme. A set of 'directives' for the congress were prepared by the Congress Commission and submitted for all-party and national discussion. The leadership were probably still not certain about a number of problems, hence they preferred to keep their options open as long as possible. The traditional report of the Central Committee on the Party's activities between the two congresses (1968–71), not exactly a shining record, was placed before a plenum of the Central Committee in November. This left the congress itself, held between 6 and 11 December, free to deal with the future rather than the past. When the congress was meeting, full results of the policies developed in the course of the year were still unknown, but it was clear that the year would end successfully, with industrial production, despite early disruption, at a respectable level and an unprecedented improvement in consumption. In the course of exactly one year the PZPR had surmounted the worst crisis in its history, set the country on a new course, and created a mood of confidence within its ranks and guarded optimism among the population.

The PZPR programme adopted by the congress covered all aspects of national life. It acknowledged the systematic improvement of the material standard of living of the population as the end of the socialist economy. In concrete terms consumption was to increase by 33 per cent per head and real earnings in the socialist sector by 17–18 per cent between 1971 and 1975. Simultaneously, a high level of investment was postulated to modernize the economy and to strengthen heavy industry and raw materials extraction, as well as those branches of the economy (agriculture, consumer goods and housing) which directly contributed to the standard of living. The other main goals of the Party were to be the extension of secondary education to all young people by 1980, the improvement in the quality and deployment of administrative and technical cadres, a better implementation of democratic centralism in all spheres of organized activity, and a conscious and systematic propaganda of socialist values and attitudes, especially among young people, to keep pace with the changes in the material bases of society. Externally, the PZPR was to pursue the goals of strengthening Poland's links with the Soviet Union and the socialist commonwealth, solidarity with countries of the third world and peaceful co-operation with capitalist countries. In his address to the congress, Gierek went out of his way to stress the importance of Polish–Soviet co-operation in words that Gomułka would not have naturally used and which must have grated on the ears of the Polish population. Perhaps they were meant to reassure the Soviet leaders that the expansion of economic relations with the capitalist West would not lead to any weakening of political and ideological ties with the USSR: 'The perspectives of Poland's further development, the possibility of fulfilling the basic aspirations of the Polish nation, especially its young generation, have a chance of full realization only within the framework of co-operation with the Soviet Union and thanks to this co-operation. It is the chief principle of our national policy.'[9] These sentiments, frequently repeated by Gierek and other leaders in subsequent years, were paralleled in the Polish press, which reached levels of servility unknown since stalinism. The effect on the population was probably the reverse of what was intended.

The two years following the Sixth PZPR Congress saw the strikingly successful implementation of the parts of the Party programme dealing with consumption, social welfare and economic development. In accordance with the new emphasis they were hence referred to as the new 'socio-economic policy' of the Party while the Five Year Plan was renamed 'socio-economic plan'. Soon after the congress Jaroszewicz addressed the first plenary meeting of the new Central Committee on the economic results of 1971 and tasks for 1972. Despite the massive disruption of work at the beginning of the year, production had gone up by 8 per cent compared with 1970, and all the other main targets of the plan had been exceeded. When three months later the plan for the rest of 1971–5 was submitted to the Central Committee and the sejm, the successful results of the preceding twelve months made it possible to raise some of the targets above those laid down in the congress resolution. In 1972 the plan was overfulfilled again, all along the line. National income grew by 10 per cent instead of the 6 per cent assumed in the plan, and money earnings of the population by 15 per cent instead of 8.5 per cent, while living costs actually fell slightly. Industrial production grew faster than in the last twelve years and the plan was overfulfilled by 5 per cent (60 milliard zl.). For the first time for years the growth rate of B group production (consumer goods) was faster than that of A group (production goods). Agricultural production was also higher than planned, and contributed significantly to the overall growth rate of the economy. A real break-through was achieved by the state farms whose production was 50 per cent more than planned. Import of consumer goods increased again, but the really significant increase was in the import of capital goods from capitalist countries. The excess of imports over exports increased the disposable national income and made possible a big rise in investment, especially in industry (34.6 per cent), construction (38.5 per cent) and distribution (38.6 per cent).

The economic achievements were even greater in 1973 and beat a number of economic records. National income rose faster than at any time between 1950 and 1972 and put Poland among the three fastest growing economies in the world beside Japan and Romania. As food prices remained frozen for the year, there was a further big jump in real wages, amounting to 11 per cent in one year, whereas the plan had envisaged 18 per cent in five years. Peasants' income grew equally fast. Agricultural production slowed down a little, but was still high, with cattle and pig production reaching the highest level in Polish history during the period. Industrial production grew by 11 per cent and, as employment rose less rapidly, productivity improved. The growth of B group production remained high. Investment grew by 25 per cent, a faster rate than in all the other socialist countries and in West Europe. In the one year, 1973, the volume of investment in 1971 prices was greater than all the investment of the whole Six Year Plan. In October 1973 the leadership called a National Party Conference, in fact an informal Party congress, to review progress for the 1971–3 period and the tasks for 1974–5. Although various strains caused by the rapid development were admitted, it was decided to raise many targets still further. These targets were in most cases exceeded by a wide margin.

Table 21. *Poland's economic development between 1971 and 1975*

	Resolution of the 6th Congress PZPR	Five Year Plan	Resolution of the 1st National Party Conference	Fulfilment
National income produced (1970 = 100)	138–139	139	155	162
General consumption (1970 = 100)	138–139	139	149–150	155
Real wages (1970 = 100)	117–118	118	138	140
Industrial production	148–150	150	166	173
Agricultural production (1970 = 100)	118–21	119–121	125.5	127
Export (1970 = 100)	—	155	202	253
Import	—	159	—	296
Increase in employment (thousands)	1,700–1,800	1,800	—	1,850
Total investment (thousand million *zł.*; 1966–70 = 100)	1,430 142	1,454 145	1,900+ 179+	1,900 189
Industrial investments (thousand million *zł.*)	—	627	777	839
Agricultural investments (thousand million *zł.*)	—	204	217	258
Supply of goods to the market (1970 = 100)	141	143	163	179

Poland's economic development between 1971 and 1975, and the extent of its acceleration, was statistically summarized in a table published in the report of the Central Committee on the eve of the Seventh PZPR Congress in December 1975 (see table 21).

Not reflected in these figures is the increased state expenditure on housing, community services, social services, and leisure and cultural activities, which further improved the standard of living. The target of over 1 million flats in the period, set by the Sixth Congress, was met with a surplus of 50,000, and the standard of the dwellings was somewhat higher than in previous years, but the share of housing in total state outlay actually dropped compared with the end of the Gomułka period. In the countryside, however, the housing programme was not realized, and the attempt to meet a higher overall housing target set by the Party conference failed. In 1972 the Central Committee and the sejm approved a long-term housing plan extending up to 1990, designed to guarantee every Polish family a flat or house of its own by that date. The completion of new dwellings was to rise to over 4 million in the last decade as a result of the high investment in the construction industry. It was an ambitious programme, but judging by past performance somewhat unrealistic. State investment in community services (water, gas, electricity, transport) doubled during 1971–5 and the planned targets were overfulfilled after 1973. The improvement of social services was speeded up at the beginning of 1974. Old age pensions, invalid pensions, sickness and family benefits were raised; in cash terms the benefits doubled between 1971 and 1975. A National Health Protection Fund, financed partly by individual contributions, and a long-term plan to improve national health services were initiated at the beginning of 1974. State expenditure on health and social welfare nearly doubled between 1970 and 1975. Considerable sums were also spent on sport, tourism and culture.[10]

The contrast between the last five years of Gomułka's rule and the first five years of Gierek's was simply enormous. How was this rapid rate of economic development, nicknamed by some Poles 'a little economic miracle', possible? In the official comments on the achievements of the 1971–5 period the emphasis is laid on the creation of a new atmosphere in which appeals for greater productive efforts met with better response than in the past, the improvement in material incentives for harder work, the rise in productivity and in employment, and the effect of reforms in the planning and management system. Doubtless these factors all played an important part. The new agricultural policy certainly showed that reserves were present in the private farming sector. In the new atmosphere considerable reserves in industry, disguised in the past from the planners, must also have come to light. The new industrial equipment installed in factories was operated largely by the existing crews rather than extra workers. Industrial production was also stimulated by the introduction of so-called Great Economic Organizations (Wielkie Organizacje Gospodarcze – WOG). There were 24 of them in 1973 and the number rose to 110 in 1975, when they employed 61 per cent of all the labour force and produced 67 per cent of the industrial output.[11] They were great multi-enterprise corporations, grouping similar factories on a branch basis (horizontal integration), which proved difficult to control centrally. They acquired considerable autonomy through the introduction of a new financing system. Its effect was to reduce the amount of directives and especially the central control over the wage fund. The danger of the system, as the leaders were aware, was that the WOGs' monopolistic position would allow them to expand profits by changing to more expensive types of production.[12]

There was also another vital factor in the 'economic miracle', namely

Table 22. *Polish imports from Comecon and select capitalist countries*
(in million zł.)

	1970	1975		1970	1975
Bulgaria	318.2	616.5	Austria	246.8	1,528.2
Czechoslovakia	1,241.5	2,711.8	Belgium	115.9	1,006.8
GDR	1,598.6	3,130.5	France	352.1	1,986.9
Hungary	554.1	880.6	FRG	572.5	3,359.5
Romania	285.9	671.6	Great Britain	763.6	2,226.7
USSR	5,445.0	10,556.8	Italy	293.0	1,388.7
			Sweden	150.8	1,430.8
			Switzerland	149.7	1,636.9
			Japan	83.4	966.5
			USA	233.0	1,958.6

Source: *Mały Rocznik Statystyczny (1977)*, pp. 200, 201. (There were further substantial increases in imports in 1976 from France, West Germany and the USA.)

the fast expansion of industrial equipment imports, primarily from the West. While the imports of Western machinery into Poland amounted to about $100 million per annum during the last Five Year Plan under Gomułka, their volume rose to $700 million in 1972, about $1,300 million in 1973 and about $1,900 million in 1974. This caused a dramatic change in the pattern of Polish foreign trade, especially imports (see table 22). The proportions of foreign trade under Gomułka were roughly one-third with the USSR, one-third with other communist countries and one-third with the rest of the world. By 1975 almost a half of Polish foreign trade was with the advanced Western nations, although the Soviet Union remained Poland's most important single partner. Trade with the Comecon remained more or less in balance, but Poland had no hope of stepping up her exports to the West. The balance of payments deficit which was only $60 million in 1970 and $166 million in 1971 rose to $1,430 million in 1973 and $2,050 million in 1975. The original targets for annual foreign-trade turnover growth were 9.2 per cent for exports and 9.7 for imports. The actual annual rise of the two was 20 per cent for exports and 24 per cent for imports. This meant that the Polish balance of trade deficit steadily worsened. The total foreign debt of Poland, which stood at about $700 million at the end of 1971, rose to $6,352 million by the end of 1975. It was believed to be about $12,000 million in the spring of 1977.

This expansionist foreign-trade policy, so markedly different from Gomułka's cautious approach, had a number of beneficial results. It produced a quick growth of industrial capital. The value of fixed assets in 1975 in 1971 prices was one-third higher than in 1970. It also enabled Polish industry to be extensively modernized in a short time. By 1975 half of fixed assets in the manufacturing industry were new plants, commissioned in the 1971–75 period.[13] Most of this modernization occurred in the electromachine and chemical industries, but motor, light, food and consumer-durables industries also benefited. The third benefit was the making up of the neglect of those branches of the economy which are particularly important for the standard of living. The greatest benefit, however, was that this 'import-led growth policy'[14] enabled productive potential to be built up and modernized rapidly without the need to curtail current consumption or expenditure on housing and social services. Beneficial though it was, Gierek's economic manoeuvre contained certain inherent difficulties. Clearly the policy of large-scale borrowing from abroad could not be pursued indefinitely. Foreign credits had to be sooner or later repaid from current production and this might mean curtailing domestic consumption or consumption imports drastically. Foreign creditors nevertheless showed little reluctance to stop lending to Poland, presumably because the large Polish raw material resources, especially coal, sulphur and copper, furnished an ultimate guarantee of repayment. Even more serious were the general consequences of the 'overheating' of the economy caused by an investment boom and domestic inflation. The 1970's were a period of world inflation and the more Poland was integrated ·into the world economy, the more inflation was imported into the country. Despite warning signs in 1973, no steps were taken to control the situation in time, and foreign borrowing went on unchecked and probably resulted in some unnecessary and ill-conceived investment. Although the need to increase central control over investment and to reduce borrowing was recognized in the documents of the Seventh PZPR Congress in December 1975, the dominant tone of the congress documents and the Party propaganda in the preceding four years was boastful pride in the achievements of the Gierek leadership and immoderate optimism about the future. A dangerous gulf arose between the real feelings of the population and the official tone of Party and government communiqués and mass-media comments. The fund of popular goodwill accumulated in the early 1970's was dissipated by 1975, and when harsh measures became inevitable in the following year, working-class hostility once more erupted in a violent way.

Institutional reforms

Compared with the dynamism and innovation in the field of socio-economic policy, institutional changes under Gierek were much less striking. In the aftermath of the riots the new leaders frequently stressed the need of reforms which would make the recurrence of a similar crisis impossible in the future. At the February 1971 Central Committee Plenum the first secretary said: 'The further development of socialist construction in Poland is inseparable from the development of socialist democracy...Our Party is determined to follow this road, to secure the conditions for the functioning of socialist democracy in all spheres of life. One must create indispensible guarantees in all the organizations and institutions of social life for a widening and deepening of the active participation of the working class, the peasants, the intelligentsia, the youth, all men of good will.'[15] Yet as the socio-economic policies produced their unexpectedly gratifying results, and as consumption rose and popular discontent decreased, the new ruling group seemed to lose interest in structural changes. There was much less emphasis on socialist democracy in the Sixth Congress resolutions, and as time went on participation was shelved and emphasis put simply on administrative and managerial efficiency. The Szydlak Commission on the Modernization of the System of the Functioning of the Economy and the State produced only an interim report and then stopped activities. The widespread hopes that Gierek, unlike Gomułka, would prove a thorough reformer remained unfulfilled.

At best there was only a change in the style of governing. The PZPR Central Committee began to meet more frequently, generally four times instead of twice a year, and the agenda of meetings was better planned and announced beforehand. Several national *aktiv* conferences and the first ever National Party Conference increased the amount of consultation within the Party elite. Similar developments took place at the lower levels of Party organization. The changes in the Party statutes at the Sixth Congress confirmed this tendency, demanded more sensitivity to public opinion and bureaucratic phenomena, and gave greater care to the admission of new members. Exchanges of Party cards became a regular practice in order to keep a check on the members' activeness. The recruitment drive continued and between 1970 and 1976 the Party membership increased by another quarter of a million.

The December crisis, like that of October 1956, galvanized the sejm into more intensive activity. It met more often during 1971 than during the previous two years, passed a large number of bills and debated them more thoroughly. The sejm committees equally increased their work. The activities of the sejm and the PZPR Central Committee became more closely linked. The sessions of the former immediately followed the latter and gave them legal validity and the appearance of national support. Nevertheless the Party leadership felt it needed a parliament with a fresh mandate and renewed membership. By passing a constitutional amendment, the sejm cut short its life in February 1972 by a year and a half before its normal term. The new sejm was elected in March 1972. The electoral statistics were not significantly different from those of the previous election. The proportions of PZPR, ZSL, SD and non-party deputies were the same as in 1969. The composition of the new sejm by age and education was again more or less the same, but only 40 per cent of its former members were re-elected. The new sejm saw the passing of Józef Cyrankiewicz from the political stage. He was succeeded as chairman of the Council of State by Professor Henryk Jabłoński, also an ex-socialist, and previously minister of education. Piotr Jaroszewicz was re-elected chairman of the Council of Ministers and the composition of the government was not significantly altered.

An important reform of the people's councils completely recast the structure of local government. The reform started at the bottom, in the countryside, and gradually extended upwards. In January 1972 the basic unit of local government became the *gmina*, a larger community than the previous *gromada*, which in some cases now included or consisted of a small country town. There were to be 2,381 *gminy* instead of 4,313 *gromady*, with roughly double the territory and population. The *gminy* were said to be 'socio-economic micro-regions', furthering the development of the area. The head of the *gmina* administration was to be a centrally appointed chief (*naczelnik*). The *gmina* people's council became a purely representative body and its presidium lost executive authority. The reform enabled the PZPR to have a Party organization with a full-time secretary in each commune and thus to bring the whole of the country at last within its scope.[16] Nevertheless, the political effect of the reform was to strengthen the influence of the state bureaucracy, at the expense of party bureaucracy, in local government. In later years the number of *gmina* officials was reduced and their salaries and qualifications raised, while the *gmina* office took over some functions of the abolished *powiat*. The next step was taken at the National Party Conference in October 1973 and in the sejm legislation of the following November. The presidia of the higher councils also lost executive authority to a centrally appointed official (*naczelnik* in districts, towns and city boroughs, 'president' in cities and *wojewoda* in voivodships). The council in each area became a deliberative and controlling body, approving the budget and plan, checking their execution, supervising the work of the local administration and all institutions and organizations within the area. To raise its authority it became a convention that the chairmen of the different councils were the first secretaries of the PZPR in the area, while their deputies were local ZSL or SL leaders. The executive heads supervised not only their own area officials but also the lower level executives, central-government administrators and directors of economic organizations in their areas. In this way it was claimed that a better representation of local society's interests and views was combined with a stronger, more effective and more centralized administration.[17] The qualifications of district and voivodship officials were raised and the council offices streamlined. The third stage of the reform occurred in May 1975 when the districts, emasculated by previous reforms, and the old voivodships were abolished. The boundaries of the latter were redrawn to produce a larger number of small voivodships, amounting to 46 instead of 17, with the authority divided between a centrally appointed *wojewoda* and a locally elected voivodship people's council. Of the five large cities which had the status of voivodships before the reform, Warsaw, Łódź and Cracow became separate metropolitan areas and Poznań and Wrocław were combined with the surrounding voivodships. The official reason for the third reform was simplifying the administration and getting rid of the *powiat* level, on which many functions had been devolved since 1958, but which in many cases remained too small and economically weak to do the job well. The new system created units which were not too remote from the citizens, yet had the necessary powers and resources to deal effectively with problems of their area. The second and third stage of reorganization enabled poorly qualified staff to be dismissed or demoted. Under the 1971–5 socio-economic plan, the activities of local and regional government expanded considerably. Their budgets increased and their economic and cultural development were stimulated by the inclusion of at least one important town in each new voivodship.

The concern for simplicity and administrative efficiency was no doubt one of the reasons for the reform of local administration. But there was another one, and it was spelled out by Gierek at the *aktiv* conference of September 1971, summoned to discuss the guide-lines for the Sixth Party Congress. He told the meeting, which included the leading territorial Party officials, that the development of each branch of the economy and region must be in harmony with the interest of the whole nation. Poland was not a 'sum of voivodships and *powiaty*' but a single social and political organism. In the same speech he promised to remedy the stagnation of the cadre policy, in other words to promote and demote officials according to qualifications and achievements.[18] The power of district and voivodship

Party secretaries was notorious under Gomułka, as was the low calibre of most of them. The reorganization of the voivodships must have helped to get rid of much dead wood and to break up many local coteries and cliques. The reforms enabled Gierek at one stroke to raise the quality of the local administrators and to reduce the power of the local Party bosses. There was another aspect of the reform. Local government, like the central Party *apparat*, had been since the mid-1960's an important preserve of the Partisan Faction. The administrative reorganization enabled Gierek's cadre secretary, Babiuch, to conduct a disguised purge and promote reliable new men. It thus strengthened the influence of the Gierek group in the Party against the only other group with some unity and cohesion.

The elections to the people's councils of all levels took place in December 1973, just after the second stage of reform. When the third stage came, there were no new elections. The district and voivodship deputies were then redistributed, according to their place of residence, between the new voivodships and the *gminy*. There must have been considerable uncertainty and confusion about the functioning of the new councils, both among officials and deputies. In March 1976 the councils of the new voivodships were elected once again at the same time as the sejm, but the elections to the lower authorities had to wait till February 1978. There is no evidence that the local government reform significantly increased popular participation, especially of non-party men, in the government. The officials of regional and local government remained predominantly members of the PZPR, with the other two parties having a small share of posts, and the non-party men hardly any. The leading role of the PZPR in the country's government, for long an established fact, acquired a legal basis in the electoral law for the people's councils elections passed by the sejm in 1973. Nor did non-party men become more numerous in representative bodies. Governmental power remained the prerogative of the members of the PZPR and the two minor parties. They consulted the ordinary citizens more and listened more carefully to complaints. They had better qualifications and earned higher rewards for efficient work. Their lines of responsibility to the centre were clearer and more strictly enforced. This is what Gierek's socialist democracy came to mean in practice.

No structural changes occurred in the trade-union organization or the institutions of workers' self-government, despite the fact that during the months of unrest in the winter of 1970–1 they were heavily criticized at workers' meetings and at subsequent trade-union conferences. Perhaps in order to allow the workers' feelings to calm down, the trade-union congress, originally promised for the middle of 1971, was postponed until November 1972. In the end only the hierarchy of individual unions was simplified by removing the intermediate level between the national and the enterprise councils, resulting in a substantial reduction of the number of full-time officials. The unions in fact tended to lose their welfare functions to government departments as state expenditure on social services increased. Much greater care was paid to workers' grievances and they were permitted freely to sue managers for breaches of factory health and safety legislation. In the spring of 1974 the sejm passed a Labour Code which brought together all existing regulations, laid down precise rights and duties of employees, and created a logical legal framework for all relations within socialist enterprises. Production nevertheless remained the unions' main concern, and the orthodox stalinist past of the CRZZ chairman, W. Kruczek, guaranteed that the unions would retain their traditional character. The institution of workers' self-government seemed to atrophy and its activities became increasingly less mentioned by the press or in trade-union conferences. By 1977 it was said that in many factories democratically elected workers' councils in fact ceased to exist.[19]

Some reform resulted from the attention given to the problem of young people by the Gierek leadership. These problems were discussed at the Seventh Central Committee Plenum in November 1972 and a National Youth *Aktiv* Conference in February 1973, after which the sejm passed a resolution on the tasks of the nation and state in the education of young people and their place in socialist construction. In 1975 the government prepared a comprehensive plan of policies, reforms and expanded facilities for young people and set up a Council for Education to co-ordinate all central- and local-government activities concerning young people. Another result of the Seventh Plenum and the *aktiv* conference was the amalgamation of existing youth organizations into an all-embracing Federation of Socialist Unions of Polish Youth (Federacja Socjalistycznych Związków Młodzieży Polskiej – FSZMP). During February and March 1973 the various youth organizations held their congresses, declared support for the idea of a federation, and in some cases changed their name. Thus the Union of Rural Youth became a Socialist Union of Rural Youth, the Union of Polish Students became the Socialist Union of Polish Students and the Circles of Military Youth, created in July 1958, the Socialist Union of Military Youth. Then at a joint meeting of the presidia of these organizations, of the Union of Socialist Youth, and the Polish Scout Organization, the new federation was formed on 11 April 1973. Just before the creation of the FSZMP the membership of its constituent organizations was as shown in table 23 (no data available for military youth circles). A recruiting drive took place afterwards in all the organizations and by the end of 1975 the federation had almost 5 million members. The amalgama-

Table 23. *Membership of Youth Organizations*

Name of organization	No. of members	No. of circles, groups, etc.
Union of Socialist Youth (ZMS)	1,296,636	53,179
Union of Rural Youth (ZMW)	1,041,573	34,030
Union of Polish Scouts (ZHP)	2,056,602	63,004
Union of Polish Students (ZSP)	192,287	8,747

Source: B. Hillebrandt, in *Pokolenia* [Generations] vol. 12, no. 2 (April–June 1974), p. 29.

tion and the change of name seemed to suggest a tightening up of the PZPR's ideological control. But from the specific tasks laid down for the federation it was clear that the Party wished them above all to be a way of mobilizing young people for current practical tasks, then of acquiring organizational experience useful afterwards in Party and governmental work, and finally of counteracting non-socialist tendencies among the young from revisionism on one hand to political apathy, 'bourgeois attitudes' and clericalism on the other. Sport, tourism, cultural and other leisure activities of the organizations were also developed to make membership more attractive.

The massive involvement of young people in the 1970 Baltic coastal riots had been a reminder that all was not well with Polish youth and that the Party's influence over it was very weak. The problem was discussed already in Gomułka's days, especially after the March 1968 events, but political and economic issues prevented proper attention being given to the matter. The other problem concerning young people was the efficiency of the existing educational system, originally estblished during the Six Year Plan, in the changed social and economic conditions twenty years later. With his belief in integrated planning of different social and economic problems, Gierek raised the matter of education early. The teaching profession was made more attractive and the training and remuneration of teachers improved by a number of government measures, which culminated in the passing of the Charter of Teachers' Rights and Duties by the sejm in April 1972. Even earlier, at the end of 1971, the politburo set up a committee of experts to prepare a report on the state of education in Poland. The committee was meant to express the trust of the new leadership in the intellectuals and their contribution to national life. Its chairman was the noted sociologist Professor Jan Szczepański, thought to be close to Gierek at that stage, who tackled the problem from a broad sociological perspective.[20] The Szczepański committee recommended the adoption of a universal system of national education lasting 11 years from the age of 7 to 18 and divided into three stages: 3-year local primary school; 5-year general secondary school; and 3-year specialized secondary school preparing pupils for different careers or higher education. The Party and government authorities accepted a slightly less ambitious variant of a 10-year school with the last stage lasting only two years. The bill establishing the new system was passed by the sejm on 13 October 1973, the two-hundredth anniversary of the shortlived National Education Commission which was the first Ministry of Education in Europe. The reform modernized the Polish school system, incorporated up-to-date educational knowledge and adapted the system to the needs of a more advanced industrial society.

The détente, Poland and the USSR

The signing of the treaty with the Federal Republic of Germany in December 1970 and its ratification by the West German and Polish parliaments in May 1972 opened the gates to Poland's diplomatic offensive towards the West. Following in Brezhnev's footsteps, the new Polish first secretary played a dominant role in international exchanges, eclipsing the chairmen of the Council of State and the Council of Ministers who had traditionally represented Poland in diplomacy. In 1972 Gierek visited France and was received like a head of state by President Pompidou. There followed his visits to Belgium (November 1973), the United States (October 1974), Sweden (June 1975) and the Federal Republic of Germany (June 1976). He was host to President Nixon (May–June 1971), President Giscard d'Estaing (June 1975) and President Ford (July 1975), when they visited Poland. These were not mere courtesy visits. An important trade and cultural agreement was concluded with France. The stumbling blocks to the full normalization of relations with West Germany were the repatriation of people of German and mixed origin and the compensation for Poles who worked as forced labourers in Germany during the war, but these were removed by direct talks between Gierek and Chancellor Schmidt during the Helsinki Conference. A rapid expansion of Polish–West German trade followed immediately. Polish–American relations took a dramatic turn for the better under Gierek, and their tangible result was the extension to Poland of the US Export–Import Bank guarantee and large-scale credits for financing Polish imports from the USA.[21] In these areas of Polish diplomatic activity and some others, such as Italy and Britain, the preparatory work had been done by the new foreign minister,

Stefan Olszowski. It was Olszowski who was received by Pope Paul VI in November 1973 during a visit to Rome and who established regular consultations between Poland and the Vatican, which became an important part of Polish diplomacy.[22] The visit excited speculation as to whether Gierek himself might visit the Pope on a future occasion and whether a new concordat between Poland and the Vatican might not after all be possible.

These bilateral contacts with Western countries were accompanied by strong Polish support for an all-European conference on security. It was the previous Polish foreign minister, Rapacki, speaking at the United Nations in December 1964, who apparently first suggested such a conference. The initiative received the powerful backing of Brezhnev, who at the XXIV CPSU Congress (March–April 1971) suggested a comprehensive programme for the normalization of relations between East and West and the relaxation of tension. Poland and the whole Soviet bloc strongly approved the initiative, which at first was rather coolly received in the West. The signing of a strategic arms limitation treaty between the USA and the USSR in May 1972, the end of US involvement in Indo-China early in 1973, and the exchanges of visits between Nixon and Brezhnev were important steps on the way to the 35-nation conference which took place in Helsinki in July 1975 and resulted in the signing of agreements on European security, economic, scientific and cultural co-operation, and human rights. It is still too early to understand Soviet motives behind the détente policy or to appraise its results. Talks on reduction in military forces were initiated in Vienna, without substantial progress being made towards disarmament. Nevertheless, some relaxation resulted from the formal acceptance in Helsinki of the *status quo* in Eastern Europe by Western Europe, Canada and the United States. For almost three decades after the Second World War the frontiers of some communist states and the legitimacy of all their governments had been questioned in one way or another. After Helsinki, communism in Eastern Europe became treated by the West as a permanent phenomenon. This attitude, helped by the first serious economic recession in the West since the war and the search for new markets, paved the way to the rapid expansion of trade and economic and other co-operation between Western and Eastern European countries from which Poland benefited so much under Gierek. The flagging economies of the Soviet bloc received a welcome boost, and the technological gap, which so worried Gomułka in the mid-1960's, was partially closed. The cynics might regard this as perhaps the main motive behind the Soviet interest in détente.

Improved relations with the West and the revision of the image of

'Western imperialism' forever plotting the destruction of communism carried certain risks for the Soviet bloc. The level of military contributions of the people's democracies to the Warsaw Treaty Organization could now obviously be questioned and the need for a close political and economic integration of the Soviet bloc might seem rather less evident. Economic dependence on the West could introduce new constraints in foreign policy. Western methods, ideas and attitudes might weaken socialist ideology, especially in countries like Poland, where it had not been very strongly rooted. One can imagine hard-liners and the guardians of orthodoxy in the propaganda and other *apparats* raising doubts of this kind, and there is evidence that they have been raised in Poland.[23] Without such a hypothesis it is hard to explain certain puzzling developments in the Soviet bloc which have accompanied détente and rapprochement between East and West. Détente brought no loosening up of the Soviet bloc. In Poland there was no absolute decline of trade with the Soviet Union or the rest of the bloc. On the contrary, its turnover doubled between 1970 and 1975, although this was less spectacular than the fourfold increase in the turnover with the developed capitalist countries.[24] Economic co-operation and integration within Comecon developed steadily. A new giant Polish steelworks near Katowice started during the 1971–5 period was based on Soviet technical know-how while Poland was contributing capital and equipment to such joint projects as a natural gas pipeline from Siberia. Nevertheless, more was thought to be necessary by the Soviet leaders. The amount of consultation within the Soviet bloc, through the Consultative Political Committee of the Warsaw Treaty Organization, communist party conferences, and summer gatherings of leaders of the bloc parties in the Crimea increased noticeably in quantity. There were also what a Polish writer in 1975 described as 'qualitative changes' in the sphere of socialist integration. The most likely meaning of this phrase is the growing emphasis on the ideological unity of the Soviet bloc which became increasingly noticeable after 1971 and developed into a veritable ideological offensive in December 1973.[25] The ideological training of PZPR members was intensified, as was the academic development of marxism–leninism. The renaming of the Polish youth organizations as socialist was clearly a part of the offensive. The Poles were frequently reminded that the Russian revolution and Soviet experience had decisive importance for the building of socialism in Poland. In his speeches Gierek took a leading role in emphasizing the points and extolling the CPSU and the USSR. In 1974, on the fiftieth anniversary of the formation of the USSR, he described the friendship with the Soviet Union as the keystone of Polish ideological education and the strengthening of ideological and political unity between

Poland and the USSR as the PZPR's most important task. Other leaders stressed the point that imperialism was still a danger, that détente required continued ideological struggle against capitalism abroad and bourgeois influences at home, and that reactionary influences in Polish culture and Catholicism were still very strong. The concept of the Polish road to socialism, which at least in an attenuated form continued to be part of the PZPR's doctrine during the Gomułka period, was dropped and Gomułka himself seemed to have been reduced in stature. His place in the history of the Polish communist movement was greatly minimized and that of his rival Bierut subtly rehabilitated.[26]

In a country so sensitive to national issues there was bound to be a reaction. In 1974 the intellectuals who had been silenced in March 1968 resumed political protest. In a letter handed by Słonimski to the minister of culture, J. Tejchma, fifteen well-known intellectuals inquired why Poles in the Soviet Union were not allowed to establish links with the mother country or to enjoy full cultural and religious freedom. In September 1975 Kisielewski denounced the treatment of history in Poland as 'Orwellian' in a *Kultura* publication in Paris. Cardinal Wyszyński in a series of sermons preached in 1974 vigorously protested against the internationalist trend in the Party's propaganda and demanded fidelity to Polish national culture as the country's highest value after God.[27] The protests escalated when at the end of 1975 the PZPR leadership announced an impending revision of the constitution and published a draft which included an affirmation of the socialist character of the Polish state, a reference to the guiding principles of the October revolution, an assertion of the leading role of the PZPR in the state, and a phrase about Poland's unshakeable fraternal bonds with the Soviet Union. As soon as the changes were announced, fifty-nine intellectuals headed by the elderly Professor Edward Lipiński submitted to the sejm a petition demanding the inclusion of the democratic rights recognized in the Helsinki Declaration in the new constitution. Subsequently, a few hundred people wrote open letters to the sejm protesting about the changes and supporting the petition of the fifty-nine. The outburst took the Party leaders aback and made them tone down the objectional phrases. The official description of Poland as a people's republic remained, although the Polish state was also declared to be a socialist one (Article 1). The PZPR was described as 'the leading political force of the society in the building of socialism' (Article 3), which did not confer on it quite so explicitly a monopoly of governmental power. The strengthening of friendship and co-operation with the Soviet Union replaced 'unshakeable fraternal bonds' and the phrase about the October revolution disappeared. A paragraph about citizen's rights depending on their fulfilment of civic duties, which came under particularly heavy criticism, also disappeared. In several respects the new Polish constitution anticipated the new Soviet constitution, which was not, however, to be adopted until October 1977; had this been realized at the time the protests might have been even stronger. After the adoption of the constitution the episcopate publicly expressed its disapproval of the changes. Intellectuals' protests and polemics with the Party continued and circulated through the country in a *samizdat* form. Edward Lipiński for example declared himself in favour of the pluralist type of socialism, advocated by the Italian and French communists, rather than the Soviet model to which Poland adhered. In its eagerness to carry the ideological offensive into the constitutional area, the Polish politburo overreached itself and provoked an unnecessary conflict with the intellectuals and the church. The conflict was a symptom of an underlying political malaise. As in 1964, the intellectuals and the church raised their voices when the economic offensive had run into difficulties and when widespread shortages of consumer goods created a mood of despondency and exasperation in the country. It was a clear sign that the Party leadership had lost much of its original popularity.

The political and economic impasse

The Seventh Congress of the PZPR (8–12 December 1975) took place almost exactly five years after the fall of Gomułka. The new leadership had many reasons to be proud of the progress achieved during a short time. The euphoric and optimistic tone of the congress speeches and resolutions suggested that Gierek and his group could take good care of any problem. The ruling group itself was enlarged from 11 to 14 full politburo members and three deputies. S. Kania, in charge of security affairs and public administration generally, became a full politburo member at the congress as also did Z. Grudzień, J. Kępa, and S. Kowalczyk, minister of the interior. Łukaszewicz and Wrzaszczyk became deputy members, and there were some promotions in the secretariat. The leading members of the Party leadership were Babiuch, Kania, Szydlak, all in the secretariat and close to Gierek, and Jaroszewicz, the prime minister, whose power base was in the governmental apparatus. It was a faceless inner group. The only man beside Gierek with a marked personality and independent Party support, Szlachcic, had been demoted in 1974 and was dropped from the Central Committee at the congress. This was followed by a purge of his associates, and the influence of the former Partisan Faction shrank still further. When Kępa lost his secretaryship of the Warsaw Party organization in the spring of 1977 the former Partisans had no longer an organizational base. Gierek's political eminence at the congress was outstanding and his hold over the Party was consolidated by a further enlargement of the Central Committee from 115 to 140 full members and 93 to 111 candidate members. Three quarters of the former and almost all of the latter were men promoted since he assumed office and among them the province of Katowice, Gierek's original power base, was strongly represented.[28] The ruling elite was more monolithic and less faction-ridden than at any time since 1949, but for that reason it seemed to be devoid of controversial ideas, new conceptions or a clear vision of the socialist Poland that was the Party's acknowledged goal. It seemed to have no aims beyond continued economic development, the modernization of the state and increased managerial efficiency. This lack of political vision was not a handicap in a situation of success but it was unlikely to be a source of strength in a period of stress and crisis.

The substance of the congress directives was the guidelines of the 1976–80 economic plan. It was presented to the delegates as a continuation of the road travelled so successfully after 1971, but in fact it was different. In virtually all respects the targets were scaled down and made less ambitious. The planned percentage increases on the 1975 level were to be as follows (the actual 1971–5 increases are in brackets): national income 40–42 (62), consumption 27 (55), real earnings 16–18 (40), industrial output 48–50 (73), agricultural output 15–16 (27), industrial investment 1 per cent (66). Only in housing was investment to remain high. The virtual freezing of industrial investment meant that productivity was to be the primary source of growth in the period. The main reason for the reduction in both investment and consumption rates was the need to increase exports in order to repay some of the huge foreign debts contracted between 1971 and 1975. Borrowing for capital imports and industrial modernization, however, was to continue, subject to the availability of credits. The plan seemed realistic, although in the past productivity had always proved much more difficult to increase than investment, and the envisaged steep increase in export had no precedent in the past performance of the Polish economy. The plan was an implicit admission that the stresses caused by the 1971–75 plan had to be alleviated urgently.

Stresses in the economy became obvious in 1974 and increased during the following two years. The cause was clearly the unprecedented investment boom, which forced up the growth of investment to 89 instead of the planned 45 per cent. Poland's past economic experience, especially the over-ambitious Gomułka plan of 1961–5, had shown the disadvantages of accelerated investment, including an eventual growth rate lower than might have been achieved with less ambitious targets.[29] The reasons for this propensity in communist economies to over-invest are not clear. Explanations range from the preferences of the planners and the faults of the management mechanism,[30] to pressure of economic and political group interests combined with the unrealistic or non-existent cost of capital to socialist enterprises.[31] The creation of WOGs (Great Economic Organizations) certainly stimulated the over-investment tendency. As semi-autonomous business corporations, with a built-in expansionist tendency, they were able to lobby effectively for the allocation of easily available Western investment credits. As had so often happened before, the final cost of investment, in terms of imports, home equipment, energy, raw materials and construction, exceeded estimates, overheated the economy and caused various dislocations.

Under the economic reform, the WOGs acquired considerable power over the level of wages of their employees, which they could raise if extra production justified it. Many of them did it freely and caused wage inflation. Although considerable disparities between different industries and WOGs existed, the general level everywhere tended to rise. The economy was not geared to this sudden increase. While investment in light and consumer goods industries was being stepped up, the results were bound to take some time to materialize. The possibilities of consumption imports were limited by the need to conserve foreign currency to met debt charges. Terms of trade, which had favoured Poland in 1971–2, turned against her and made such imports more expensive. Already at the National Party Conference in October 1973 an 'acute shortage' of furniture, domestic electrical equipment, high quality clothing and shoes was reported.[32] In 1974 meat became scarce and the shortage proved long-lasting. The peasants, whose incomes had increased in 1971, fell considerably behind the wage and salary earners by 1974 and lost the incentive to produce. Costs of imported feeding stuffs, fertilizers and fuel rose steeply, while the prices the state paid for their produce remained stationary. Poor harvests in 1974 and 1975 reduced domestic feeding stuffs and contributed to a decline in pig production. Owing to bad weather the sugar-beet crop failed, and sugar had to be rationed in 1976. Fruit and vegetable supplies were much scarcer than in the previous five years. The problem of what to spend money on became acute for the average Pole. When visas for travel to East Germany were abolished, the number of Poles visiting the country jumped from 142,000 in 1970 to almost 7 million in 1974. These, indeed, were no ordinary tourists but people in search of goods which were unobtainable in Poland. The gap between purchasing power and available goods forced up personal savings from 3,515 zł. per person in 1970 to 9,675 zł. per person in 1976.[33] The proportion of average income saved rose during the period from 2.3 to about 10 per cent.

The absorption of this huge purchasing power became a major concern of the economic authorities. The rational solution of the problem was to raise prices. The prices of petrol, alcohol, cigarettes and some household utensils were raised in 1974 and 1975. In addition, massive hidden price increases began to take place in 1975, through the withdrawal of articles and the introduction of supposedly better and more expensive ones. These changes hit the poorer section of the population hardest and were bitterly resented. They also artificially increased the profits of some of the WOGs and led to a round of wage increases. All this time the basic prices of foodstuffs, the largest item in household budgets, remained unaltered at the original 1970 level, which itself had not changed since 1963–4. The freeze, introduced after the coast strike of December 1970, was to have lasted only two years, but was continued year by year. The Party leadership was caught between two alternatives, a brake on the money earnings or the end of the price freeze, but knowing both to be unpopular they took no action.

By 1976 the situation had become untenable and it was decided to raise prices. To make up for past delay, and in the belief that one sharp increase was preferable to a number of smaller ones spread over a period, the increases were substantial. There was no warning or consultation with the workers. On 24 June Premier Jaroszewicz announced in the sejm that basic food prices would be raised on an average by 60 per cent as from 27 June. Sugar was to rise by 100 per cent, meat by an average of 69 per cent, and butter and cheese by 30 per cent. Monthly bonuses were promised to compensate low-wage earners and old-age pensioners for the rise. Substantial increases in prices paid to farmers for the produce were announced at the same time. The following day, almost exactly the twentieth anniversary of the Poznań riots, workers all over Poland stopped work in protest. In a small number of cases more violent protest took place. The employees of the Ursus tractor factory near Warsaw tore up a railway track and stopped traffic. The workers of the petrochemical complex at Płock held a public meeting which was dispersed by the police. In the city of Radom there were large-scale street demonstrations, many shops were looted and the Party's provincial office was set on fire. In the evening Jaroszewicz announced the withdrawal of the increases, 'pending consultations with the workers'. Simultaneously, the authorities, or some hard-line elements among them, reacted with fury against the violent protesters. They were bitterly condemned at specially summoned meetings and rallies all over Poland. The police rounded up the rioters of Ursus and Radom by the hundred. They were maltreated under arrest and afterwards prosecuted and sentenced to imprisonment in a summary fashion. Dozens were dismissed from their jobs. Subsequently, however, many sentences were reduced on appeal and a sweeping amnesty in July 1977 led to the release of most offenders.

The June events were a traumatic experience for the PZPR leadership and elite. They showed that the politburo was once more seriously out of touch with working-class opinion and had forfeited the trust established in 1971. The inept handling of the price rise and the defeat of the leadership on a major issue brought a heavy loss of face to those responsible for it. Gierek and, even more, Jaroszewicz lost popularity in the country and prestige in the Party. Some observers of the political scene considered Jaroszewicz's position fatally weakened, though in fact he survived the calamity. The events of the winter 1970–1 acquired retrospectively an increased significance. The Polish working class appeared to have gained a permanent consciousness of its economic interests, and a readiness to stand up for them. The threat of further workers' protests was so strong that, although moderate price increases were promised after June 1976, none had been implemented as late as the spring of 1978. Owing to artificially low price levels, supply could not balance the demand, especially for meat. Shortages, queues, frustration and discontent became a permanent feature of the market and everyday life.

The June crisis brought the Catholic church once more into the political arena. In a letter to the Polish government, drawn up by Cardinal Wyszyński in July 1976, and subsequently approved by the episcopate, the church appealed for the respect of civic rights, a real dialogue with the nation and the freeing and re-employment of workers penalized for the June protest. Nevertheless, the episcopate emphasized equally that the good of the country required internal peace and order, and in effect supported the government's effort to restore political stability. From the standpoint of barely disguised hostility to the whole communist system, which characterized the church's official pronouncements in the 1960's, the cardinal and the episcopate moved to a position of constructive criticism of particular policies, combined with a large measure of consensus with the Party and state authorities about the national interest. The authorities publicly expressed their appreciation of the church's role. In an important speech at Mielec in September 1976, Gierek declared that the state and the church in Poland were not in conflict and could fruitfully co-operate in many fields. In October the first personal meeting between Wyszyński and Gierek took place. Informal contacts and frequent consultations over a wide range of issues became adopted practice and certain concessions with regard to building permits for new churches followed. A hundred parishes in new urban areas were established between 1975 and 1977. There was, however, no change in the basic Party line towards religion and the participation of practising Catholics in the exercise of political power.

The aftermath of the June events excited vigorous protests also outside the church. University professors and intellectuals signed open letters asking for a parliamentary committee of inquiry, and there were letters signed by large groups of Ursus and Radom workers in defence of their persecuted workmates. In September the most active group of protesters formed a Workers' Defence Committee (Komitet Obrony Robotników – KOR), which eventually had twenty-four members from a wide range of well-known dissenters such as E. Lipiński, J. Andrzejewski, J. J. Lipski, J. Kuroń and A. Michnik. The names and addresses of the committee were communicated to the authorities and all its subsequent activities were conducted studiously in public. KOR collected money for the defence of arrested workers and assistance to their families. The committee sent observers to their trials, gathered evidence of police brutality and sought to inform public opinion through the publication of 'information bulletins', a dozen or more of which were published during the one year of KOR's existence.[34] It gradually widened its activities to the whole field of human rights. Although the impact of its activities on the workers was unknown, KOR acquired a network of associates among the academic and creative intelligentsia, many of them veterans of the 1968 events, and numerous sympathizers among the new generation of students in Warsaw and other large cities. The authorities showed a surprising tolerance of the committee, containing its activities by harassment, but stopping short of complete suppression. In May 1977, following an outbreak of public student protest in Cracow, the most active younger members of KOR were arrested and threatened with trial, but were released in July.

In October 1977 KOR renamed itself Committee for Social Self-Defence and sought a new political role. A large group of its members and supporters issued a signed 'Declaration of Democratic Movement', calling on the Polish government to fulfil the human-rights treaties and to restore the freedoms of belief, speech and information, association and assembly, and wage bargaining. Alleging that the Party leadership showed incapacity to solve the political, economic and social crisis in the country, the declaration called for the informal organization of citizens in all walks of life to discuss remedies, infiltrate official bodies, assert their constitutional and statutory rights and press for their extension. Unlike the revisionism of the 1950's and 1960's the 'democratic movement' did not seek to influence the Party from within, but rather to stimulate ideas and action outside it in order to alter the country's whole political environment. This was a highly ambitious, not to say utopian goal, given the 'democratic movement's' lack of resources. Apart from the appearance of unauthorized study groups and seminars, the only observable effect of the declaration was the increase in the number of unofficial publications. By January 1978 over ten periodicals were appearing more or less regularly, together with collections of censored or confiscated articles[35] and book-length publications. Again, the authorities restricted themselves largely to the confiscation of duplicating machines, and made no attempt to suppress the publishing movement through wholesale arrests of those involved in it. There was even little propaganda activity against the dissidents. The Party leaders referred to them only occasionally as an insignificant group of the opponents of socialism without real influence on the working class and the nation as a whole.

The lack of a proper historical perspective and direct evidence permits only some tentative hypotheses about the reasons for this extraordinary liberalism, without parallel in communist East Europe and unprecedented in Poland after 1948. One need only recall Gomułka's harsh treatment of Kuroń and Modzelewski for their 'open letter' of 1964. It seems highly probable, however, to appreciate the difference between the two situations, that the liberalism was connected with the détente policy which Poland strongly supported during 1977. The Polish delegation participated actively in the Belgrade conference on human rights and the Polish government expressed satisfaction with its results. More significantly, the year saw a number of high-level diplomatic exchanges, in which the first secretary of the PZPR played a leading role. Gierek visited India, France and Italy and while in Rome had a meeting with the pope to discuss church–state relations in December 1977. It was another milestone in the acceptance of the communist government as the legitimate government of Poland and an important step towards fully normal relations between Poland and the Vatican. Also in 1977 Gierek received visits from five foreign personages: Willy Brandt, King Baudouin of the Belgians, the Shah of Iran, Chancellor Helmut Schmidt and, at the very end of 1977, President Carter. President Carter's visit was particularly significant. The Carter Administration had taken a strong line on the human-rights issue, and the fact that Poland was the only communist state included in the president's world tour was a conscious demonstration of American approval of Polish liberalism. In fact, during a press conference given in Warsaw, the US President publicly praised the Polish stand on human rights and religious freedom. At the same conference he announced additional credits of $200 million, in addition to $300 million already granted, for the purchase of food and animal fodder. The need to maintain good relations with the Carter Administration and to preserve the goodwill of American and Western European opinion was dictated by Poland's foreign-trade situation. Poland had to solve the urgent problem of repaying the huge Western credits received in the early 1970's. The optimistic expectation of repaying them out of current income had been dimmed by the perennial problem of making the new factories and equipment fully operative on time, and by the continuing economic recession in the West, which kept down the volume of imports from East Europe. Poland had, therefore, to renegotiate the terms of repayment of existing credits or obtain additional loans to meet her current liabilities. The toleration of dissent among the intellectuals was a small price to pay to improve the climate for the negotiations and in general to maintain the impetus of détente.

The June 1976 events were manifestly a grave political crisis, the first such crisis caused directly by the policies of the Gierek team, unlike the early 1971 events which could still be attributed to the faulty policies of its predecessor. The Gierek team nevertheless chose to regard the crisis as an economic one, and to respond to it by changes in the economic strategy. The need for such changes was becoming obvious well before the middle of 1976, but, as so often in the past, the political difficulties hastened unwelcome decisions. The first was the curtailment of investment from 35 per cent of the national income in 1976 to about 30 per cent in 1978. Not only were resources released for consumption, but the structure of investment itself was also modified to give housing and consumer goods clear priority over everything else. Increasing emphasis in non-priority investment was on the modernization of existing plants rather than the much more expensive new projects which had been favoured during 1971–6. The chief goals of what became known as 'the economic manoeuvre' were defined in 1977 as the improvement of the market situation, the development of foodstuff production, the intensive development of dwelling construction, and the increase in export. The last goal was made difficult by an unfavourable turn of the terms-of-trade, but in 1977 exports rose twice as fast as imports. The basic target of 1,575,000 dwellings in the 1976–80 plan, which looked increasingly unrealistic, was sustained by a 6 per cent reduction in the industrial building programme. The improvement in the market situation was seen to be a long-term process, largely dependent on the success of the new agricultural policy. Large imports of meat and animal fat from the West, which took place at the turn of 1976–7, could not be continued, but there were to be increased imports of industrial consumer goods from Comecon countries. Services and goods produced internally were to increase twice as fast as the increase of money earnings.

The agricultural policy was the most important aspect of the 'economic manoeuvre'. The drastic measures taken were dictated by a 3.5 per cent drop in agricultural production in 1977 due to yet another bad grain and potato harvest. Fifteen million tonnes of grain and feeding materials had to be imported in 1977–8 at the cost of $2 billion, which was a record sum in Polish economic history. The flight from the countryside was halted; 5,000,000 qualified men were to be directed to agriculture during the 1976–80 period. One-fifth of all investment in the plan was earmarked for agriculture. The annual outlay was 50 per cent more than during the 1971–5 period, and three times more than during the last decade of the Gomułka era. The bulk of the resources was at last going to the private farmers, who still farmed three-quarters of the total agricultural land in Poland. The eventual takeover by the state of all private land remained the official policy of the Party, but a medium-term programme emerged in 1977. In February 1977, at a little publicized Central Committee Plenum, qualified private farmers were to be permitted to buy or lease land from the state, and with the help of machinery to farm it individually. Financial incentives were intensified to encourage specialization in one line of production instead of the traditional mixed farming. Necessity seemed to have persuaded the Party leaders that the quickest method to increase food production was by backing the efficient medium-size private farmer rather than by creating large state or collective farms.[36] Ninety per cent of Polish farms in 1978 were under 10 hectares. According to West European experience, 20 hectares (50 acres) was the minimum capable of supporting the application of modern farming methods.[37] The concrete objective was to create, in addition to the state and co-operative farms, 800,000 to 1 million individual farms of 20–30 hectares each.[38] They would cover about 60 per cent of arable land. An important law, hailed as 'a measure of historic significance, almost comparable to the agrarian reform of 1944',[39] was enacted by the sejm at the end of 1977 to provide for a system of retirement pensions or annuities for old farmers willing to pass on their holdings to their heirs or surrender them to the state. The immediate effect of all these measures was nevertheless slight, and at the second National Party Conference (10 January 1978) Prime Minister Jaroszewicz warned that a 2.2 per cent increase in food and meat production was all that could be hoped for in 1978, and that there was a long way to go before the supply of meat met demand.

The Party conference was a very sober occasion, concerned with entrenchment and consolidation rather than expansion, and strikingly different in mood from the First Party Conference held in January 1973. In addition to the difficulties already mentioned, Jaroszewicz announced the need for energy conservation, for better use of shrinking new labour resources, declining from 270,000 employees in 1976 to 160,000 in 1980, and for combatting growing absenteeism. Gierek's speech to the Party conference gave a more detailed analysis of achievements and problems to be solved. He was able to announce a small number of popular measures, including a continued rise in earnings, an increase in minimum wage, greater state expenditure on social welfare, and a long-term plan for the reduction of working time. Gierek referred also to the need for consultation with the masses, strengthening the representative role of the sejm and the people's councils, reactivating the conferences of workers' self-government, and creating a system of committees of social control attached to the people's councils to investigate complaints against bureaucracy. There was also a mention of planned changes in the management system to streamline the nationalized industry, but these items did not seem to play an important part in his speech. The solution of the various economic problems with regard to increased food production, market equilibrium, more effective use of manpower, equipment and energy, improved quality of export goods clearly constituted for him the way out of the impasse caused by the collapse of the investment boom and the June 1976 events. Neither he nor Jaroszewicz suggested any measures for the elimination or reduction of the vast state subsidies on consumption. These at the end of 1977 were said to amount to 126 milliard *zł.* on food alone and 270 milliard *zł.* on all consumer goods and utilities, amounting altogether to one-third of the total state budget. It was believed that the state added to 70 *zł.* subsidy to every 100 *zł.* spent on food by the consumer. The solution of this problem was perhaps the most important and urgent economic task facing the government.

It was clear that the successful tackling of this task, and perhaps also of some others, depended on a significant change in the political climate. Unpopular policies can be either imposed by force, as they often are in non-democratic systems, or put through with the consent or acquiescence of the people. The events of 1970–1 and 1976 showed that the scruples of the communist elite and the militancy of the workers ruled out the first option in Poland, but the second seemed also to be difficult to obtain, owing to the mood of disillusionment and distrust among wide sections of the workers, the peasants and the intelligentsia. The popular confidence which the Gierek team so skilfully won after 1971 evaporated during 1975 and 1976 as a result of servility to the Soviet Union, the constitutional conflict, the worsening market situation and finally the handling of the food prices and its aftermath. There seemed to be no capital of political trust left on which the Gierek group could draw to secure the acceptance of an obviously necessary sacrifice.

A drastic way to alter the political climate would be to change the ruling group again, as happened in October 1956 and December 1970, but communist systems find it hard to do that except in an acute crisis situation when the alternative to inaction seems worse than a leadership change. There was, moreover, no obvious successor to Gierek within the narrow circle of politburo members, and no latter-day Gomułka awaiting restoration to power. However, if another serious confrontation with the working class were to occur in the future, a split in the ruling elite and a change of leadership might be a possibility. A less drastic way to improve the climate would be for the Party leaders to make some large-scale political concessions or to devise a 'package deal' of political reforms and economic austerity.

Such reforms would, no doubt, be strongly disapproved of by the Soviet leaders and most of Poland's communist neighbours, whose fear of instability and contagion in the bloc is very strong. They would also be opposed by important sections of the power elite within Poland, both on traditional and ideological grounds. For these reasons the Party leadership would be unlikely to attempt reforms except under strong pressure from another quarter. There was little hard evidence in early 1978 of a reformist tendency within the PZPR elite, similar to the democratization movement which emerged in 1954. The resignation of Barcikowski as minister of agriculture in December 1977 and Tejchma as minister of culture in January 1978 was not a good omen because both men enjoyed relatively liberal reputations, but there were some signs that moderate reformism had a certain appeal to sections of the elite. Among the sociologists and political scientists the problem of 'socialist democracy', which was widely discussed in the early 1970's, became popular again after 1976. The clear lesson of the June events, as in December 1970, was that the political system had no means of revealing to the policy-makers what the consequences of their policies were likely to be. Although the amount of consultation within the elite, among the leaders of the different institutional groupings, had grown considerably under Gierek, there was really no genuine system of consultation with 'the masses', especially the workers who were the backbone of the socialist system economically, politically and ideologically. Empirical research into the changing composition of the working class in the 1970's, its greater affluence, improved education and higher aspirations,[40] the rising technological level of Polish industry and need for workers with higher qualifications,[41] and a greater degree of social integration as manifested in the diminishing subjective sense of class difference in incomes[42] all created, in the opinion of many leading social scientists, the basis for a significantly greater participation of the working class in the communist political system. Another possible straw in the wind was an article by M. F. Rakowski, published in *Polityka* (no. 45, 1977), and the reactions to it. Rakowski pointed out several disadvantages of 'centralism' inherent in the Polish system and pleaded for decentralization of decision-making in order to increase its effectiveness. For this he was strongly attacked in *Życie Warszawy* (Life of Warsaw) for allegedly undermining the Party's sacred principle of democratic centralism and hence the socialist system itself. At the National Conference Rakowski's ideas received considerable support from the delegates. The future would show how strong was the support for, and opposition to, political reforms within the PZPR elite, how much influence these tendencies had on the Polish Party leadership, and how the restoration of popular confidence in the Gierek leadership, if it survived, would be achieved.

Polish society, 1945–75

The problems of Poland's political and economic life should not obscure the fact that profound changes have occurred in Polish society. The period of most rapid change took place during the Six Year Plan, especially in the years 1951–3, when Poland was under the influence of stalinism. Thereafter social change was less dramatic. The Poland which emerged from the Second World War was substantially different from the Poland of 1939. According to the census of 1931, the population amounted to 32,107,000, which rose by the end of 1938 to 34,849,000. On 14 February 1946, when the first post-war census was carried out, the population within the new frontiers was 23,930,000. The area covered by the Polish state had fallen from the 388,600 sq. km of 1938 to 311,700 sq. km as a result of the loss of 179,700 sq. km in the east and the gain of 102,800 sq. km in the north and west. The 1946 census showed that the population consisted of 20,520,000 Poles, 2,288,000 Germans, 390,600 persons of other nationalities and 417,000 whose nationality was said to be 'in the course of verification'. During the years 1946–9 virtually all the Germans were expelled from the north and west, with the result that native Poles became the overwhelming majority of the population.[1] Over 1 million so-called 'autochthons' of Polish or Slav descent, who had to some extent been Germanized, remained behind in the new territories. After 1956 and again after 1971 many of them were allowed to emigrate to Germany to join their relatives. No official nationality statistics are published in People's Poland, but one sociologist has estimated that in 1961–2 among the main national minorities in Poland there were 180,000 Ukrainians, 165,000 Byelorussians, 23,000 Czechs and Slovaks, 19,000 Russians, 12,000 Gypsies, 10,000 Lithuanians and 10,000 Greeks and Macedonians.[2] There were also 31,000 Jews, but their numbers declined to about 10,000 after the exodus of 1968. The number of Germans was put at 3,000, but this figure seems too low. An article in *Polityka* of 30 October 1965 gave the figure as 140,000. There is probably no objective means of determining the number of Germans, which may fluctuate according to the changing moods of the 'autochthons'. The minorities thus now form no more than 2 per cent of

Table 24. *Religious denominations*

Churches and religious denominations	Parishes, congregations, etc.	Churches, chapels, prayer houses	Priests, ministers
Roman Catholic	6,716	14,039	19,456
Polish Orthodox	233	301	216
United Evangelical	207	65	206
Polish Baptists	127	53	60
Seventh Day Adventists	124	126	66
Augsburg-Evangelical	122	356	100
Jehovah's Witnesses	108	18	305
'Epiphany' Movement	80	146	405
Other national Christian sects	149	169	180
Other international Christian sects	146	80	84
Jewish	16	24	—
Mohammedan	6	2	6

Source: *Rocznik Statystyczny (1977)*, p. 23.

the population, with the result that Poland is ethnically one of the most homogeneous countries in the world.

Because Poles have always been for the most part Roman Catholic there is an equal homogeneity with regard to religion. No statistics for religious observance have been published since the war, but an impression of the Roman Catholic church's strength may be obtained from figures for 1976 shown in table 24. How many Poles are practising churchgoers cannot be determined on the basis of available evidence, but surveys conducted in 1964 and 1966 revealed that 81–72.5 per cent of the urban and 90.1–82.8 per cent of the rural population regard themselves as believing Catholics. A survey of 'middle-level intelligentsia' in 1971 showed that 64.8 per cent considered themselves believers.[3] Statistics for Roman Catholic baptisms, confirmations, church weddings and children attending religious instruction might throw light on this problem if they were available.[4]

The rapid growth of Poland's population since the Second World War has caused important changes in its social composition (see table 25). The population increase was most striking in the Western Territories, amounting to 35 per cent between 1950 and 1961, which was twice the national rate. In this area the increase was welcome because the departure of Germans had left it underpopulated, but elsewhere the high birth rate was of questionable value. When capital was scarce the rapid expansion of the labour force assisted economic growth, but in the long run it created serious social and economic problems. Despite the Roman Catholic

Table 25. *Population growth and pattern*

Specification	1946	1950	1955	1960	1965	1970	1975	1980 (fore-cast)
Population (millions)	23.6	25.0	27.6	29.8	31.6	32.7	34.2	35.8
Population of working age (millions)	—	14.5	15.6	16.3	17.1	18.3	20.0	21.3
Population in towns (percentage)	32.6	36.0	43.5	48.0	49.5	52.1	55.3	58.2
Population not deriving a living from agriculture (percentage)	—	52.9	—	61.6	—	70.2	74.3	—
Natural increase (per 1,000)	16.0	19.1	19.5	15.0	10.0	8.5	10.2	—

Source: *Mały Rocznik Statystyczny (1977)*, pp. xxiv, xxv.

church's opposition, the government sought with some success to discourage a high birth rate by birth-control propaganda and allowing easy abortion. An important aspect of post-war social developments was the growth of the urban population. Within thirty years the country people declined from 67.4 to 44.7 per cent of the whole. The decline was rapid between 1950 and 1955, but slowed down after 1960. To some extent this decline was a result of the extension of the administrative boundaries of towns and cities, but the prime cause was the large-scale movement from the countryside to the towns which accompanied industrialization. In absolute figures the urban population increased between 1946 and 1976 from 8,000,000 to 19,500,000, whereas the rural population remained static at the level of 15,600,000 in 1946, 15,400,000 in 1960, and 15,000,000 in 1976. The natural increase in the countryside was thus absorbed by the towns. It is estimated that 20 per cent of the inhabitants of Warsaw were born in the countryside, and in Wrocław no less than 40 per cent. In other towns in the Western Territories and new towns like Nowa Huta the proportion is even higher. Polish sociologists refer to this phenomenon as the 'ruralization of the towns',[5] or the 'ruralization of the working class',[6] because the bulk of the migrants from the country became workers. A survey of 1970 showed that 63 per cent of blue-collar workers and 37 per cent of white-collar workers, who had taken up residence in towns in the preceding decade, had come from the rural areas.[7] These figures do not reflect the true extent of urbanization. As can be seen in table 25, a far greater number of persons work in occupations other than agriculture than actually live in towns. In 1950 22.7 per cent of the rural population

Table 26. *Social structure of Poland's population in 1931 and 1970*
(percentages)

Social categories (with dependants)	1931	1970
Capitalists, landlords, petty bourgeoisie	10.7*	—
Workers	28.6	49.8
Peasants	51.8	25.1
Clerical workers	5.5	22.4
Others	3.4	2.7
Total	100.0	100.0

* The insignificant percentage of petty bourgeoisie in 1970 is included under the category of 'others'.

Source: M. Anasz and W. Wesołowski in *Przemiany struktury społecznej w ZSRR i Polsce*, p. 46.

did not make a living from agriculture, but the percentage rose to 30.9 in 1960 and 43 in 1970.[8] These figures may be explained in part by the number of so-called worker–peasants, but the main reason is the category of people, fully employed in towns, who commute to work, owing to the urban housing shortage. This phenomenon has been termed 'the functional (or professional) urbanization of the countryside'. The result is that urban outlooks and habits are more widespread in the country than figures would seem to indicate.

The degree of urbanization varies from region to region. It is high in the Western Territories but low in the eastern and central provinces. In 1976 after the administrative reform the most urbanized voivodships, if Warsaw, Łódź and Cracow are omitted, were Katowice with 85.9 per cent, Gdańsk with 75.9, Szczecin with 72.5, Wałbrzych with 71.8 and Wrocław with 70.8. On the other hand the figure for Zamość is 20.2, for Siedlce 24.3, for Ostrołęka 25.6 and for Biała Podlaska 26.6.[9]

During thirty or more years a fundamental transformation has taken place in the social and occupational structure of the country. The change can be illustrated by different statistics depending on one of three possible criteria: social class, or 'stratum membership', a term used by marxists; employment within and without the public sector; and membership of certain occupational groups. Analysis by social class produces the figures in table 26. The striking feature of these figures is the reversal of the place of the workers and peasants in the social structure and the rise of a large

Table 27. *Population according to source of livelihood from work and social assistance (in percentages; for 1974 also in absolute figures)*

Year	Industry	Construction	Agriculture	Transport and communication	Distribution	Science and education	Health service	Others	Pensioners, etc.
1950	20.9	4.8	47.1	5.2	5.4	2.2	1.2	9.2	4.0
1960	25.0	6.3	38.4	6.1	4.9	2.8	1.8	8.4	6.3
1974 (%)	28.3	7.1	27.1	6.3	5.2	3.9	2.4	7.5	12.2
1974 (million)	9.5	2.3	9.1	2.1	1.7	1.3	0.8	2.5	4.1

Source: *Rocznik Statystyczny (1977)*, p. 32.

Table 28. *Individual farms according to general censuses*
(in thousands: figures in parentheses are percentages of total)

Year	Total no. of holdings	0.5–2 ha	2–5 ha	5–7 ha	7–10 ha	10–15 ha	15–20 ha	Over 20 ha
1950	2,949.8	602.6 (20.4)	991.8 (33.6)	477.5 (16.2)	499.0 (16.9)	246.3 (8.3)	92.7 (3.2)	39.9 (1.4)
1960	3,216.0	801.7 (24.9)	1,091.9 (33.9)	475.7 (14.8)	462.0 (14.4)	283.6 (8.8)	66.6 (2.1)	34.5 (1.1)
1970	3,006.8	742.7 (24.7)	967.5 (32.3)	442.3 (14.7)	444.0 (14.8)	276.0 (9.8)	77.4 (2.6)	39.6 (1.2)

Source: *Rocznik Statystyczny (1977)*, p. 223.

white-collar element. The second index is the proportion of the working population employed by state or socialized organizations like co-operatives. In 1950 already about half, or 4,800,000 out of 10,000,000, worked in the public sector, but by 1970 the number had risen to two-thirds, or 10,300,000 out of 15,000,000. By 1976 the figures were 12,300,000 out of 17,000,000.[10] The third index of social change is shown by the numbers for particular branches of the economy. The trend has been a movement from agriculture to industry, but it should be noted that peasants and their families still formed the largest single group in the economy until the early 1970's. Only in 1974 did industry overtake agriculture as the largest source of employment.

Certain trends appear more clearly if the three main social groups of peasants, manual workers and clerical workers are examined separately. According to the *Rocznik Statystyczny 1977* agriculture employed in 1976 5,235,000 persons, of whom 4,246,000 were individual peasant farmers and only 73,400 belonged to collective farms. By Western European standards peasant farms are very small. There was little change in the various categories of farms in the period 1950–70. Larger farms tended to decline up to 1960 owing to subdivision to escape punitive taxation, but this tendency was subsequently reversed. The smallest farms in the main belong to worker–peasants and play only a small part in the agrarian system. After 1970 there was a tendency for these small farms to decline as their owners handed over their land to the state and for the number of larger farms to increase. Since 1976 the government has given its attention to farms over 20 hectares in size, the number of which it intends to increase until they employ one-fifth of all workers in agriculture. On the other hand the size of the average state farm rose from 510 hectares in 1960 to 1,316 hectares in 1976, but their number fell in the same period from 5,734 to 2,895.

Table 29. *Working population according to major social-occupational groups and age (percentages)*

| | Years of age | | |
Groups	Up to 24	25–49	50 or more
Total working population	20.4	55.5	24.1
All manual workers	26.7	58.7	14.8
Industry and construction	29.4	58.3	12.3
Farming and forestry	23.4	60.9	15.7
All clerical workers	20.9	66.6	12.5
Individual farmers	13.0	43.2	43.8

Source: K. Zagórski in Szczepański, *Narodziny socjalistycznej klasy robotniczej*, p. 217.

Polish agriculture has certain peculiar features. Many peasants supplement their income from farming by working in building and industry. In the years 1965–6, about 10,000,000 persons drew a living from farming, but of them 2,900,000 had other occupations, while 2,700,000 relied wholly on other sources of income than their farms. Women are responsible for the farms if their husbands have other employment. It is calculated on the basis of the 1970 census that the ratio of men to women in peasant farming is 60:100, whereas, it is 46:100 for the country as a whole and 31:100 for manual workers. Peasant–farmers are older than persons employed elsewhere, for which reason transfer of land to heirs or the state may be very rapid as a result of the new pension law for farmers. Educational attainment among peasant farmers is low, but some improvement occurred in the 1970's. Figures for the rural community as a whole illustrate the general situation. In 1960 only 30 per cent of persons over 15 years had completed primary education, while 64.3 per cent had not completed it or had no education at all. In 1970, however, the respective figures were 36 and 38 per cent.[11]

The definition of a worker is by no means as precise as the identification of a peasant or individual farmer. A worker may be employed in agriculture, industry and building construction. In a broad sense the workers and their dependants amounted to 16,000,000 persons, who constituted a half of the population, or, if dependants are deducted, 41.6 per cent. In an analysis of all manual workers, published in 1973 on the basis of the census of 1970, K. Zagórski stressed the difficulty of defining the manual workers as a social group and indeed of distinguishing them from clerical workers and peasants. In his view 4,100,000 persons in 1970, or 25.3 per cent of the manual-working population, were employed in industry, building and similar occupations. A further 361,000, or 2.2 per cent, were employed in unskilled work in industry and construction, while 719,000 (4.3 per cent) worked in transport and communications. Skilled manual work in the wholesale and retail trades, warehousing and other non-industrial occupations absorbed 980,000 (6 per cent). A further 455,000 (2.8 per cent) were employed in unskilled work in distribution. In some of these categories work can be said to contain a clerical element.[12]

Industrial workers constituted about 15 per cent of the working population in 1976. At the end of the Six Year Plan in 1955 they numbered 2,000,000, expanding to 2,700,000 in 1965 and 3,500,000 in 1976.[13] The largest single concentrations were in mineral extraction, coal mining, the electro-mechanical industries, textiles and food processing. The figures in table 29 show that the industrial working class is very young, a quarter to a third being younger than twenty-four years. One Polish sociologist has pointed to a 'triple youth' in the working class: demographic, sociological and technical.[14] About one-third has moved from a peasant environment to industry, in which they find themselves required to obtain higher qualifications, especially in the machine, electrical and chemical industries. The technical training of the working class is still low. A study of 1968 classified 19 per cent of the industrial working class as highly skilled, 30 per cent as skilled and 35 per cent as semi-skilled, the rest being unskilled.[15] Another investigation showed that 20–24 per cent of industrial workers had not completed their primary education.[16] These workers were clearly recruited from the countryside in the early stages of industrialization. After 1965 attendance at primary and secondary trade schools was expanded and most young workers today have been educated in them. There are nevertheless wide regional variations. Three times as many workers have more than a basic education in Poznań than in Łódź. Many workers still maintain their links with the countryside. In 1968 10 per cent of industrial and building workers and 15 per cent of transport workers were part-time farmers, while 22.5 per cent of workers in industry, 28 per cent in construction work and 31.7 per cent in transport commuted to work from the countryside.[17] One-sixth of all country people were industrial or construction workers.

Clerical workers are a social group which has grown most rapidly since the Second World War, expanding in the years 1958–74 from 1,980,000 to 3,934,000 and rising from 31.2 per cent to 35.4 per cent of the working population.[18] These figures assume a wide definition of clerical work, but, if secondary education or above is used as a criterion, this group falls to 28.1 per cent of the working population, which in this narrower sense is generally described as the 'intelligentsia' in Poland. In 1970 one-fifth of

Table 30. *White-collar workers in Poland, 1970*

	Total	Percentage of working population
Administrative-economic and office employees	1,418,000	8.6
Higher level	146,000	0.9
Lower level	1,272,000	7.7
Technical specialists	662,000	4.0
Directors and managers	153,000	0.9
Others	509,000	3.1
Non-technical specialists	763,000	4.7

Source: K. Zagórski in Szczepański, *Narodziny*, p. 210.

the wider group were under 24 years and two-thirds between 25 and 49 years of age. Women formed one-third of all clerical workers, while in warehousing and distribution the ratio of women to men was as high as 67:100. The educational qualifications of this group have improved, with the percentage of persons with higher education rising from 12.1 per cent in 1958 to 16.7 per cent in 1973, while those with a secondary technical education rose from 21 to almost 40 per cent. Whereas in 1945 there were only 100,000 people with higher and secondary education and 250,000 with technical second education, by 1973 there were over one million in the former and just under one million in the latter category. Even more than the manual workers, clerical workers are a heterogeneous category, being stratified by income, social status and influence. In 1965 J. Szczepański divided them into 50,000 'creative intellectuals', 65,000 'experts and managers', and 1,300,000 'administrative and office employees'.[19] The census of 1970 assesses clerical workers differently (table 30). By comparison with the manual workers, clerical workers have a depressed economic status. Between 1937 and 1963 their standard of living fell by about 25 per cent, while that of the manual workers rose by 45 per cent. The comparative income levels of an average clerical and an average manual worker, according to M. Kalecki and L. Beskid, show the following changes: 2.26:1 (1937); 1.12:1 (1960); 1.22:1 (1967); and 1.23:1 (1972). In 1972 about 68 per cent of both clerical and manual workers were in the same middle-income bracket. There was a marked differentiation only in the lowest income bracket, which embraced 7.2 per cent of manual and 1.2 per cent of clerical workers, while in the top bracket there were 24.2 per cent of manual workers as compared with 30.8 per cent of clerical workers.[20] This equalization, which reached its peak in 1960, is probably

Table 31. *Students and graduates in higher education*

	1946	1956	1966	1976
Students (total)	86,000	170,000	274,000	491,000
Students per 10,000 population	36.5	60.7	86.3	142.2
Graduates (total) in that year	3,900	21,700	26,700	62,900

Source: *Rocznik Statystyczny (1977)*, pp. xliv, xlv.

unique by Western European standards. It must be said, however, that within the class of white-collar workers are some of the most highly paid persons in Polish society.

Before the war private trade and handicrafts were a major part of the economy. In 1937 1,373,000 people were employed in the private retail and wholesale trade, and 1,794,000 in handicrafts. By 1976 only 31,600 persons were employed in the private retail trade and catering, while 241,620 worked in private handicrafts, of whom about 100,000 were hired labour. Both groups tended to grow after 1956, but there is little likelihood that they will play a significant role in the economy.

An important aspect of social change in Poland has been the rising standard of education, though the effect is spread unevenly in the three main social groups. Before the war in 1937-8 only 14 per cent of young people between the ages of 14 and 17 years were attending school, but this was increased to 40.7 per cent in the school year 1949-50, rising to 56 per cent in 1959-60. In 1975-6 80 per cent of young people between the ages of 15 and 18 years were receiving education. Progress in the field of higher education is shown in table 31. In the 1970's Poland was among the leading states of the world in respect of secondary vocational and higher education, but with regard to general secondary education achievement was modest. The figures in table 32 show the social distribution of higher education among sections of the population. The intelligentsia continues to be the main source of students in higher education and postgraduates, especially in full-time day studies prior to taking up employment, and has even increased its share of places since 1960. The proportion of full-time working-class students, however, is reasonably high, while in part-time higher education they are the predominant element. On the other hand, a worrying social aspect is the declining number of peasant students, especially in day and evening studies. What is clear from table 32 is the determination of young people to continue their education, whether secondary or higher, after taking up work. A study made in 1968 showed that one-fifth of all persons employed outside

Table 32. *Students and graduates in higher education according to social origin (in percentages)*

Type of higher study and social origin	Students				Graduates	
	Total		First year			
	1960–1	1974–5	1960–1	1974–5	1960–1	1974–5
Day studies						
Worker	26.9	30.0	26.2	30.9	31.6	31.7
Peasant	20.0	13.1	18.3	11.2	23.9	16.5
Intelligentsia	48.0	53.2	49.1	54.4	40.7	48.3
Other	5.6	3.7	6.4	3.5	3.8	3.5
Evening studies						
Worker	54.5	57.8	60.3	59.3	52.6	58.1
Peasant	20.5	14.4	20.3	14.5	21.0	15.7
Intelligentsia	23.7	26.8	18.8	25.4	24.3	25.2
Other	1.3	1.0	0.6	0.8	2.1	1.0
External studies						
Worker	41.9	45.8	45.2	46.9	38.7	46.0
Peasant	31.1	30.7	29.9	30.9	35.8	32.4
Intelligentsia	23.2	21.8	21.4	20.8	22.2	20.1
Other	3.8	1.7	3.5	1.4	3.3	1.5

Source: J. J. Wiatr, *Przemiany społeczne w Polsce* [Social Transformations in Poland] (Warsaw 1976), p. 47.

agriculture continued their education after starting work. About half of clerical workers, who had begun life as manual workers or farmers, completed their education while at work.[21] Higher and secondary education, both full-time and part-time, has been the most important factor in promoting social mobility in People's Poland. The social advance of individual groups is well illustrated by a survey of 1968. Among technical specialists 28.8 per cent had fathers who were peasants or agricultural workers, while 38.5 per cent had fathers who were non-agricultural manual workers. For non-technical specialists the proportions for the same categories were 35.5 and 22.6 per cent, and for administrative and office workers 21.7 and 42.5 per cent.[22] In the three white-collar occupations, where it might be expected that the majority of workers came from the same background, in fact only between one-quarter and one-third did so. Examination of the social origins of particular elites is very revealing. A survey of 1969 showed that the permanent members of the presidia of people's councils at regional and local levels were on average 33 per cent of working-class origin and 61 per cent from the peasantry. At the level of the voivodship, county town and district councils the proportion of

Table 33. *Population of working age according to sectors of national economy (percentages)*

Country and year	Working population (million)	Percentage of total population	Outside agriculture and forestry	Industry	Construction	Transport and communications	Distribution	Agriculture and forestry
Poland (1974)	17.5	52.0	65.4	30.2	7.1	5.8	6.8	34.6
Britain (1971)	25.7	46.3	97.5	35.6	6.7	6.3	14.8	2.5
FRG (1975)	26.8	43.4	93.6	37.1	7.7	5.7	14.0	6.4
France (1975)	21.8	41.3	89.2	28.1	8.6	5.4	15.7	10.8
Italy (1976)	20.3	36.3	84.9	32.3	8.8	5.5	13.2	15.1
Spain (1975)	13.3	37.6	77.7	26.6	9.9	5.1	16.0	22.3
Japan (1975)	52.7	47.6	87.5	26.1	9.0	6.2	21.1	12.5
USA (1975)	94.8	44.5	96.2	24.8	6.2	5.0	20.0	3.8

Source: *Rocznik Statystyczny (1977)*, p. 459

Table 34. *Select indices of the standard of living in Poland and advanced Western countries*
(*Figures per 1,000 inhabitants, except for dwellings and books*)

Country	Dwellings (people per room)		Radio licences		Television licences		Telephones		Books and brochures published (titles)		Daily newspapers (copies)		Motor cars	
	Year	No.	1960	1975	1960	1975	1960	1974	1960	1974	1960	1974	1960	1974
Poland	1974	1.3	176	238	14	189	30	71	6,879	10,749	145	237	4	32
Britain	1971	0.6	×	750	211	315	157	366	23,783	×	514	443	108	252
FRG	1971	0.7	287	312	83	284	113	302	21,103	29,200	307	389	81	291
France	1968	0.9	241	324	41	235	93	236	11,872	26,247	257	220	121	289
Italy	1971	0.9	162	228	43	213	78	246	8,111	9,443	101	126	40	270
Spain	1960	0.9	90	229	8	174	59	200	6,085	24,085	70	96	9	136
Japan	1973	1.1	133	658	73	233	59	356	23,682	32,378	396	526	5	145
USA	1970	0.6	941	1,895	310	571	411	677	15,012	81,023	326	293	340	495

N.B. Not all data are strictly comparable (e.g. the size of rooms is not stated). In some cases the nearest available year was used in the source. (×, no data available.)

Source: *Rocznik Statystyczny (1977)*, pp. 509, 511, 519, 524, 525.

intelligentsia was higher, but never exceeded 20 per cent.[23] Of the managers of nationalized industries 60.6 per cent came from working-class families and 18.6 per cent from the peasantry. One-quarter of the managers had begun work as manual labourers.[24] The intelligentsia is more strongly represented in other professions, but the political and industrial elites are today dominated by people of worker and peasant origin.

Polish sociological literature tends to compare the present with the past. The communist leaders in Poland have sought to raise the country from the backwardness inherited from the epoch of foreign occupation and the failures of the inter-war years, but a different perspective may be obtained by comparing Poland with other countries. It will be seen from table 33 that Poland does not differ greatly, except in as far as a low proportion of the population is employed in distribution and a very much higher proportion in agriculture.

Broad access to education and high social mobility are abstract concepts if unaccompanied by some relation of the standard of living enjoyed by that society to standards prevailing elsewhere. Table 34 provides that comparison and indicates the rate of growth.

The achievements of People's Poland set out in a statistical form are ample illustration of the stresses and strains imposed upon the country. What is clear is that the Poland of today has to a great measure overcome the disadvantages inherited from the partitions. It remains to be seen whether current difficulties will slow down the rate of development.

Epilogue: The rise and fall of Solidarity

The 'serious confrontation with the working class' predicted in chapter 17 duly occurred in the summer of 1980. In late 1978 the Polish Cardinal Karol Wojtyla was elected Pope and his visit to his native country in June 1979 produced an upsurge of national pride and unity. The party leader Gierek hoped to reap some popularity from the visit but the grim economic reality and the government's apparent powerlessness had made his leadership completely discredited in the country and the party. By mid-1980 the economic problems of the country had become so serious, with hard-currency indebtedness above $21,000 million, that a new austerity programme could no longer be postponed. An increase in the price of meat introduced on 1 June was the beginning of it and led to protests and strikes which at first lacked clearly defined political objectives; however, four years of political agitation since the upheavals of 1976 had made an impact. When the Gdańsk shipyard workers went on strike in mid-August, they very quickly formulated a mixture of economic and political demands, calling among other things for the setting up of independent trade unions with the right to strike and demanding the restriction of censorship to state secrets of a military or economic nature and that appointments be made purely on merit. Similar demands were put forward by the Szczecin shipyard strikers. The Gdańsk strike also threw up, in the person of Lech Wałęsa, an electrician who had been fired from the shipyards for his earlier political activities, a leader with remarkable skills both in oratory and in negotiation and a person who seemed to a great many Poles to embody and articulate their political and social aspirations. The authorities initially attempted to placate the Gdańsk workers with costly economic concessions and by sacrificing some of the more unpopular members of the government, but after two extremely tense weeks they gave way.

The acceptance by the government of the principal demands of the strikers in the agreements signed at Gdańsk, Szczecin and Jastrzębie (with miners' representatives) aroused widespread hopes that a new era had dawned in Poland. Within a few weeks, free trade unions had mushroomed all over the country and quickly established a nationwide organization 'Solidarity' which claimed a membership of nearly 10 million. It was very loosely structured and highly democratic, and though dominated by the workers of the main industrial centres contained a broad spectrum of the population with diverse interests and political attitudes. A million PZPR members also joined Solidarity. The reformists in the party believed that they could harness the national mood for change generated by Solidarity and use it to carry through those institutional and economic reforms which they had long regarded as overdue. The rebuff the workers had given the party created the most serious political crisis in the more than 30 year history of People's Poland, and to overcome it the party leadership would have to be bold and experiment with new solutions. The man who had precipitated the crisis by his policies, Edward Gierek, was replaced as party first secretary in early September by Stanisław Kania, a little known individual who had previously been responsible for security, the military and also religious affairs in the Secretariat of the Central Committee.

The new party leadership did not rise to the challenge, however. The first few months of the existence of Solidarity, during which some sort of partnership could have been achieved, were consumed in fruitless wrangling. After grudgingly allowing legal recognition of Solidarity in November the government seemed more concerned to contain the union and to assert its authority in the country than to press ahead with reforms or establishing a working relationship with the new body. The radicals in Solidarity, convinced that the government had only made concessions under threat of force, were determined that all clauses of the Gdańsk agreement should be implemented to the letter, even on issues like the abolition of Saturday working which it was very doubtful that the country could afford. Throughout these months, the hostility of the more conservative elements in the PZPR to the changes brought by Solidarity was made manifest and it was intensified by the fact that on every occasion when the authorities tried to resist the demands of the union, they were, in the end, compelled to give way. Since changes in the provinces were coming slowly and other forms of pressure on the authorities were unavailable, the strike became a political weapon, freely used in local and regional conflicts.

The hardliners attempted to precipitate an open confrontation with Solidarity in March 1981 in Bydgoszcz where the security police beat up three Solidarity activists. Solidarity responded by calling for those responsible to be brought to justice and threatening a general strike if they were not. A majority of the Politbureau seems to have favoured a tough line, but Kania, supported by the new prime minister General Wojciech

Jaruzelski, the minister of defence, was able to hold a policy of negotiation by shifting the focus of decision to the more liberal central committee and eliciting the support of the reformist PZPR branches in the large factories. After several days of tense negotiations, in which the Church played a key mediating role, a new agreement was reached, after which Lech Wałęsa came in for severe criticisms from Solidarity radicals for being too accommodating. Its main result was that private farmers were allowed to form an independent union which called itself 'Rural Solidarity'.

The March confrontation hardened the attitude of the Kremlin and the hardliners within the Polish party to Solidarity. Within the party, Kania's victory also spurred on a grass roots movement which demanded greater democratization and more control over the leadership by rank and file. This movement gathered momentum during the preparations for the party congress which was to be held in the summer and it deeply troubled the Soviet leaders, perhaps raising disturbing memories of the Prague Spring of 1968. Although they failed to oust Kania as first secretary in early June, their pressure alarmed many members of the party and influenced the party congress held in mid-July. The proceedings, marked by great frankness of debate and secret ballot voting, elected a centrist rather than reformist central committee and though it adopted a comprehensive programme of economic and political reforms it failed to grant Solidarity a significant place in the political system. This failure of the PZPR to take over the drive for change emanating from Polish society probably averted direct Soviet military intervention, but it had the effect of creating a political vacuum, as the party became increasingly paralysed and incapable of decisive initiative. As a consequence, Solidarity, which had up to now ostensibly sought to avoid a directly political role, found itself sucked into the vacuum and apart from concern with specific policies proceeded to elaborate its own programme of basic economic, social and political reforms which included workers' control over management in state industry. The inertia of the party was made still more ominous by the serious deterioration of the economic situation from the summer. The shortage of hard currency needed to buy spare parts and raw materials for the factories bought in the west during the Gierek era, as well as grain, which had already been causing problems before mid-1980, was exacerbated by the fall in exports, above all of coal, as a result of the ending of Saturday working and the hated four-shift system in the mines. The wage increases rashly promised by the government in the summer of 1980 in order to forestall political demands now had the effect of creating a vastly inflated demand for low-priced subsidized goods, including basic foodstuffs, many of which effectively disappeared from the shops.

The political and economic situation was thus already critical when Solidarity's national conference took place in September. It proved to be prolonged, extremely critical of the government's policies and the Communist system and confident that only its own remedies could work. By dint of a great effort at persuasion, Wałęsa was able to induce the conference to adopt the principle that political power should be shared. The government would still make the final decisions, but would consult first with the Church and Solidarity over all aspects of policy. However, there was no question of the PZPR being willing to agree to this concept. General Jaruzelski, who in mid-October became party first secretary while retaining the offices of prime minister and minister of defence, was willing to make use of the Church and Solidarity to persuade the country to accept the now clearly inevitable austerity programme, but he was not prepared to share power and made reforms dependent on Solidarity renouncing the strike weapon and agreeing to economic sacrifices. The two sides tried fitfully to reach agreement, but they lacked any real common ground. The radicals in Solidarity were now convinced that the weakness of the government would compel it to yield to their main demands. This was a serious miscalculation. The government had effectively decided on repression and was only waiting to choose the right moment to strike. It came on 13 December when martial law was proclaimed, trade unions and other organizations suspended, severe restrictions on all kinds of activity imposed, and over 5,000 people including the entire Solidarity leadership were arrested and interned. The blow was so heavy that only sporadic resistance was offered to the army and the police.

In taking this action, General Jaruzelski aimed at bringing to an end a threat to Communist power in Poland which he believed could only provoke Soviet intervention. He hoped to use the minimum of force so that he would be able to reach agreement with the more moderate elements in Solidarity and the country, and continue those aspects of the policy of reform which he felt would not undermine the authority of the government. He hoped also to use the powers conferred on him by martial law to introduce a drastic economic stabilization plan and believed that this would induce western bankers and governments to overlook the repressive side of his actions and provide new credits and economic assistance to Poland.

His hopes have only partially been realized. The amount of force used and the demands of the security apparatus made any immediate compromise with sections of Solidarity and above all with Lech Wałęsa himself impossible. After May street demonstrations against martial law and in support of Solidarity began to erupt in various Polish cities, leading to violent clashes with the police and souring the atmosphere. It was thus almost inevitable that the Church's attempt to mediate in the spring and summer of 1982 and to achieve a compromise which would allow the re-emergence of a Solidarity shorn of its political objectives and its radical advisers would fail and that Solidarity should finally be banned in October. Equally, though martial law did enable drastic price increases in consumer goods to be introduced and also led to significant rises in the output of the mines, above all the coalmines, it fell far short of resolving the country's economic problems. With a cessation of new western credits industrial recovery proved virtually impossible and the economic reform had to be diluted, while a truculent and hostile work force has obviously not helped either. Official estimates now concede that the country can only hope in favourable conditions to reach the level of consumption of the late 1970's in 1990.

A year after the introduction of martial law, on 13 December 1982, General Jaruzelski announced his intention of suspending its operation. This was preceded by the government's agreement to a postponed visit by Pope John Paul II in the summer of 1983 and by the freeing of Lech Wałęsa from internment. After the failure of demonstrations and strikes called for by the underground Solidarity leadership for 10 November (but advised against by the Church) the government seems to have decided that the situation in the country was sufficiently stable to permit such liberalization. Time will show whether this is the case and whether the liberalization will prove a decisive step towards reconciling the population to the authorities' economic policies and to the long promised 'renewal' of the communist system. In achieving this national reconciliation a vital role will have to be played by the Catholic church, a major force for moderation in contemporary Polish politics, which has already saved the country from major upheavals in 1956 and 1970–71 and which has played an important role in most recent developments. A failure to reach national agreement would undoubtedly herald further dangerous stagnation and might well precipitate a new confrontation which would have disastrous consequences not only for Poland but for the whole of Europe.

Notes

CHAPTER 1

1 *The Tehran Yalta and Potsdam Conferences – Documents* (Moscow, 1969), p. 50.
2 *Ibid.*, p. 330.
3 W. Kula, *Théorie économique du système féodale – Pour un modèle de l'économie polonaise 16ᵉ–18ᵉ* (Paris–The Hague, 1970), chapter IV, 'La dynamique de la longe durée', pp. 89–126.
4 Cf. R. F. Leslie, *Polish Politics and the Revolution of November 1830* (London, 1956).
5 The best account of the Poznanian movement is S. Kieniewicz, *Społeczeństwo polskie w powstaniu poznańskim 1848 roku* [Polish Society in the Poznań Uprising of 1848] (new edition, revised, Warsaw, 1960).
6 R. F. Leslie, *Reform and Insurrection in Russian Poland, 1856–1865* (London, 1963) deals with this problem.
7 Cf. A. F. Smirnov, *Revolyutsionniye svyazi Rossii i Pol'shi 30–60 gody XIX veka* [The Revolutionary Connections of the Peoples of Russia and Poland from the 1830's to the 1860's] (Moscow, 1962); V. D. Korolyuk and I. S. Miller (eds.), *Vosstaniye 1863 g. i russko-pol'skiye svyazi 60-kh godov* [The Uprising of 1863 and Russo-Polish Contacts in the 1860's] (Moscow, 1960). Cf. also V. A. Dyakov and I. S. Miller, *Revolyutsionnoye Dvizheniye i Vosstaniye 1863 g.* [The Revolutionary Movement in the Russian Army and the Uprising of 1863] (Moscow, 1964).
8 Cf. I. Koberdowa, *Polityka Czartoryszczyzny w okresie powstania styczniowego* [The Policy of the Czartoryski Party during the January Insurrection] (Warsaw, 1957).
9 An English version was published by the London branch of the Society in 1837.
10 For a biography see J. Zdzitowiecki, *Xiążę-Minister Franciszek Xawery Drucki-Lubecki, 1778–1846* (Warsaw, 1948).
11 Cf. W. Jakóbczyk *Studia nad dziejami Wielkopolski w XIX w. – Dzieje Pracy Organicznej* [Studies in the History of Wielkopolska in the Nineteenth Century – The History of Organic Work] (Poznań, 1951), I (1815–50); and *Doktor Marcin – Jan Karol Marcinkowski, 1800–1846* (Poznań, 1946).
12 His correspondence with Cracow in 1863 has been edited by S. Kieniewicz, *Listy Leopolda Kronenberga do Mieczysława Waligórskiego z 1863 roku* [Letters of Leopold Kronenberg to Mieczysław Waligórski, 1863] (Wrocław, 1955).
13 S. Kieniewicz, *Ruch chłopsaki w Galicji w 1846 roku* [The Peasant Movement in Galicia in 1846] (Wrocław, 1951), p. 300.
14 *Ibid.*, pp. 301–2.
15 *Ibid.*, p. 355:

> Pamiętoś ty Panie rok śtyrdziesty szósty,
> Jak cię chłopy biły kijami w zapusty?

There are other versions of this song to traditional peasant airs.
16 Cf. S. Kieniewicz, 'Galicja w latach 1846–1848' [Galicia in 1846–8], in Natalia Gąsiorowska *et al.* (eds.), *Wiosna ludów na ziemiach polskich* [The Springtime of the Peoples in the Polish Lands] (Warsaw, 1848), pp. 300–1.

17 M. Tyrowicz (ed.), *Galicja od pierwszego rozbioru do Wiosny Ludów 1772–1849* [Galicia from the First Partition to the Springtime of the Peoples 1772–1849] (Wrocław, 1956), pp. 211–16.

18 For the career of the younger Sapieha see S. Kieniewicz, *Adam Sapieha (1828–1903)* (Lwów, 1939).

19 For the text see M. Bobrzyński, W. L. Jaworski and J. Milewski, *Z dziejów odrodzenia politycznego Galicji* [On the History of the Political Renaissance in Galicia] (Warsaw, 1905), pp. 69–80. The franchise law is also reproduced in this work.

20 *Ibid.*, pp. 120–2.

21 *Ibid.*, pp. 150–3.

22 J. Szujski, *Kilka prawd z dziejów naszych ku rozważaniu w chwili obecnej* [Some truths from our history to consider at the present moment] (Cracow, 1867), published in his *Dzieła* (Cracow, 1885), I, pp. 278–86.

23 In Austria a *mórg* was the equivalent of 0.55 hectares, whereas the English acre is 0.404686 hectares.

24 S. Kieniewicz, *The Emancipation of the Polish Peasantry* (Chicago, 1969), p. 213, cautiously states that 'the tendency towards polarization (*rozwarstwienie* [differentiation]) was much less visible in Galicia than elsewhere'.

25 The most exhaustive analysis of this is the work of the late Wincenty Styś, *Współzależność rozwoju rodziny chłopskiej i jej gospodarstwa* [The Interrelation of the Development of the Peasant Family and its Farm] (Wrocław, 1959), which is a development of his earlier study of his native village of Husów in Galicia. What Styś wrote of Galicia is convincing, but it has yet to be established whether the same rules apply elsewhere in Poland.

26 The memoirs of Stapiński have been edited by K. Dunin-Wąsowicz as. Jan Stapiński: *Pamiętnik* (Warsaw, 1959).

27 Cf. M. Kniat, *Dzieje uwłaszczenia włościan w Wielkim Księstwie Poznańskim* [The History of the Emancipation of the Peasants in the Grand Duchy of Posen] II (Poznań, 1949), passim.

28 Cf. J. Marczewski, *Narodowa Demokracja w Poznańskiem 1900–1914* [National Democracy in Poznańia, 1900–14] (Warsaw, 1967).

29 A. V. Fedorov, *Russkaya armiya v 50–70 gg. XIX v.* [The Russian Army in the period 1850–70] (Leningrad, 1959), pp. 34–40.

30 S. Kieniewicz and I. Miller (eds.), *Korespondencja Namiestników Królestwa Polskiego z lat 1816–1863 – Perepiska Namiestnikov Korolevstva Pol'skogo 1816–1863* [Correspondence of the Viceroys of the Kingdom of Poland, 1861–3] (Wrocław–Moscow, 1973), pp. 160–2.

31 A. Chrząszczewski, 'Pracodawcy i pracownicy na roli', *W naszych sprawach – Szkice w kwestjach ekonomiczno–społecznych* ['Employers and labourers in agriculture', *On Our Affairs – Essays on Economic and Social Questions*] (Warsaw, 1899–1902), III, p. 55.

32 I. Spustek, *Polacy w Piotrgrodzie, 1914–1917* [Poles in Petrograd, 1914–17] (Warsaw, 1966), pp. 26–7.

33 For a minute discussion of the problem see K. Groniowski, *Realizacja reformy uwłaszczeniowej 1864* [The Realization of the Emancipation Reform of 1864] (Warsaw, 1963); and *Kwestia agrarna w Królestwie Polskim 1871–1914* [The Agrarian Question in the Kingdom of Poland, 1871–1914] (Warsaw, 1966). Cf. also H. Brodowska, *Ruch chłopski po uwłaszczeniu w Królestwie Polskim 1864–1914* [The Peasant Movement in the Kingdom of Poland after emancipation, 1864–1914] (Warsaw, 1967).

34 *Rocznik Statystyczny Królestwa Polskiego* [The Statistical Yearbook of the Kingdom of Poland], Rok I (1913), p. 304.

35 For an English account of this movement see L. Blit, *The Origins of Polish Socialism: The History and Ideas of the First Polish Socialist Party, 1878–1886* (Cambridge, 1971).

36 For his recollections of this period see B. Limanowski, *Pamiętniki* [Memoirs] (3 vols., Warsaw, 1957–61], I and II, covering the years from 1835 to 1907.

37 The text is reproduced in A. Molska (ed.), *Pierwsze pokolenie marksistów polskich* [The First Generation of Polish Marxists] (Warsaw, 1962), I, pp. 5–9, dated September 1878.

38 *Ibid.*, I, pp. 375–424, where the speeches of Diksztajn, Dłuski and Waryński are reprinted.

39 *Ibid.*, I, pp. 573–9.

40 'Odezwa komitetu robotniczego Socjalno–Rewolucyjnej Partii Proletariat' [The Manifesto of the Workers' Committee of the Social–Revolutionary Party Proletariat], *ibid.*, II, pp. 7–16.

41 For the exchange of letters of 1 February and 1/13 March 1884 see *ibid.*, II, pp. 135–43.

42 This periodical has been reproduced as *Proletariat–Organ Międzynarodowej Socjalno–Rewolucyjnej Partii, Warszawa, 1883–1884* [Proletariat – The Organ of the International Social–Revolutionary Party, Warsaw, 1883–4] (Warsaw, 1957).

43 For a Polish account of early socialism see F. Perl, *Dzieje ruchu socjalistycznego w zaborze rosyjskim do powstania PPS* [The History of the Socialist Movement in Russian Poland to the Foundation of the Polish Socialist Party] (new edition, Warsaw, 1958).

44 For an account of this movement see S. Kozicki, *Historia Ligi Narodowej (Okres 1887–1907)* [History of the National League, 1887–1907] (new edition, London, 1964).

45 *Tajne dokumenty rządu rosyjskiego w sprawach polskich* [Secret Documents of the Russian Government on Polish Affairs] (London, 1898).

46 The standard account of the Łódź uprising is A. Próchnik, *Bunt łódzki w roku 1892* [The Łódź Rising of 1892] (new edition, Warsaw, 1950).

47 Perl, *Dzieje ruchu socjalistycznego*, pp. 474–5.

48 For the proceedings of the meeting see H. Buczek and F. Tych (eds.), *Socjaldemokracja Królestwa Polskiego i Litwy – Materiały i dokumenty* [The Social Democracy of the kingdom of Poland and Lithuania – Materials and Documents], I, *1893–1903*, part i, *1893–1897* (Warsaw, 1957), pp. 174–91.

49 J. P. Nettl, *Rosa Luxemburg* 2 vols (London, 1966) deals thoroughly with the Polish aspects of her career.

50 Buczek and Tych, *Socjaldemokracja Królestwa Polskiego i Litwy*, I, part ii, *1899–1901*, nos. 90–1, pp. 436–50.

CHAPTER 2

1 An exhaustive study of the economic problem is provided by I. Pietrzak-Pawłowska, *Królestwo Polskie w początkach imperializmu 1900–1905* [The Kingdom of Poland in the Early Stages of Imperialism 1900–5] (Warsaw, 1955).

2 K. Kelles-Krauz, 'Niepodległość Polski w programie socjalistycznym' [The independence of Poland in the Socialist programme], *Pisma Wybrane* [Collected Works] (Warsaw, 1962), II, part ii, pp. 147–8, reprinted from *Krytyka*, 1866.

3 An acute analysis of the divisions in the PPS is the work of A. Żarnowska, *Geneza rozłamu w Polskiej Partii Socjalistycznej 1904–1906* [The Origin of the Split in the Polish Socialist Party, 1904–6] (Warsaw, 1965).

4 Buczek and Tych, *Socjaldemokracja Królestwa Polskiego i Litwy*, II, part ii, p. 221.

5 E. Mendelsohn, *Class Struggle in the Pale: The Formative Years of the Jewish Workers' Movement in Tsarist Russia* (Cambridge, 1970), pp. 4–8.

6 V. I. Lenin, *Collected works*, VI, January 1902 to August 1902 (3rd printing, Moscow, 1974), pp. 455–61.

7 Buczek and Tych, *Socjaldemokracja Królestwa Polskiego i Litwy*, ii, part ii, p. 369. Cf. also Nettl, *Rosa Luxemburg*, i, pp. 269–83.

8 Z. Balicki, *Egoizm narodowy wobec etyki* [National Egoism and Ethics] (new edition, Lwów–Warsaw, 1914), p. 58.

9 *Ibid.*, p. 60.

10 L. Kulczycki, *Narodowa Demokracja* [National Democracy] (Warsaw–Lwów, 1907), p. 23.

11 *Ibid.*, p. 27.

12 For a minute analysis of the development of National Democratic ideology see S. Kalabiński, *Antynarodowa polityka Endecji w rewolucji 1905–1907* [The Anti-national policy of National Democracy in the Revolution of 1905–7] (Warsaw, 1955), chapter i.

13 For details of his plan see J. Piłsudski, *Pisma Zbiorowe* [Collected Works] (Warsaw, 1937), pp. 249–58.

14 H. Rappaport (ed.), *Narastanie rewolucji w Królestwie Polskim 1900–1904* [The growth of revolution in the Kingdom of Poland, 1900–4] (Warsaw, 1960), no. LXIX, pp. 856–64.

15 *Ibid.*, no. LXXIV, pp. 868–73.

16 F. Tych (ed.), *PPS–Lewica 1906–1918: Materiały i dokumenty* [The PPS–Left, 1906–18: Materials and Documents (Warsaw, 1962), i, (1906–1910), no. 1, pp. 3–4.

17 S. Kalabiński and F. Tych, *Czwarte powstanie czy pierwsza rewolucja: Lata 1905–1907 na ziemiach polskich* [The Fourth Uprising or the First Revolution: The Years 1905–7 in the Polish Territories] (Warsaw, 1969), p. 81.

18 S. Kalabiński (ed.) *Carat i klasy posiadające w walce z rewolucją 1905–1907 w Królestwie Polskim: Materiały Archiwalne* [Tsardom and the Propertied Classes in Struggle with the Revolution of 1905–7 in the Kingdom of Poland: Materials from the Archives] (Warsaw, 1956), no. 16, pp. 16–17.

19 *Ibid.*, no. 20, p. 20; no. 25, p. 22.

20 S. J. Brzeziński, *Polski Związek Ludowy* [The Polish People's Union] (Warsaw, 1957), pp. 237–327.

21 Cf. Żarnowska, *Geneza rozłamu w Polskiej Partii Socjalistycznej*, chapters IV and V.

22 Tych, *PPS–Lewica*, i, no. 2, pp. 4–6.

23 *Ibid.*, ii, no. 4, pp. 13–14.

24 Kalabiński, *Carat i klasy posiadające*, no. 187, pp. 230–1.

25 Kalabiński, *Antynarodowa polityka Endecji*, pp. 133–204.

26 For a contemporary account see *Polsko-rosyjski zjazd w Moskwie* [The Russo-Polish Conference in Moscow] (Cracow, 1905).

27 For an account somewhat critical of the Social Democrats see J. L. Keep, *The Rise of Social Democracy in Russia* (Oxford, 1963), pp. 216–303.

28 For the reply of the left-wing socialists see Tych, *PPS–Lewica*, i, no. 16, pp. 66–80.

29 Z. Łukawski, *Koło Polskie w roysyjskiej Dumie Państwowej w latach 1906–1909* [The Polish Circle in the Russian State Duma, 1906–9] (Wrocław–Warsaw–Cracow, 1967), pp. 13–15.

30 Kalabiński, *Antynarodowa polityka Endecji*, pp. 359–95.

31 Łukawski, *Koło Polskie*, pp. 60–4.

32 P. Korzec, *Pół wieku dziejów ruchu rewolucyjnego Białostocczyzny (1864–1914)* [Half a Century of the History of the Revolutionary Movement in the Region of Białystok] (Warsaw, 1965), chapter VII, p. 259 ff.

33 P. Korzec, *Walki rewolucyjne w Łodzi i okręgu łódzkim w latach 1905–1907* [The Revolutionary Struggles in Łódź and its region, 1905–7] (Warsaw, 1956), chapter IX, p. 239 ff. deals with this bloody episode in Łódź.

34 Marczewski, *Narodowa Demokracja w Poznańskiem 1900–1914*, pp. 277–85.

35 J. Myśliński, *Grupy polityczne Królestwa Polskiego w Zachodniej Galicji (1895–1904)* [Political Groups of the Kingdom of Poland in Western Galicia, 1895–1904]

(Warsaw, 1967) reveals the extent to which the politics of Russian Poland were linked with those of Galicia.

36 J. Buszko, *Sejmowa reforma wyborcza w Galicji 1905–1914* [Electoral Reform for the Regional Parliament in Galicia, 1905–14] (Warsaw, 1956) examines the repercussions of general electoral reform at the local level.

37 W. Najdus, *Szkice z historii Galicji* [Essays on the History of Galicia] (2 vols, Warsaw, 1958–60) covers the problems of Galicia in the period 1900–7.

CHAPTER 3

1 A recent study of the general problems of Russian planning for war is N. Stone, *The Eastern Front 1914–1917* (London, 1975).

2 M. Wierzchowski, *Sprawy Polski w III and IV Dumie Państwowej* [The Affairs of Poland in the Third and Fourth State Dumas] (Warsaw, 1966) should be consulted. Cf. also E. Chmielewski, *The Polish Question in the Russian State Duma* (Knoxville, 1970), which is somewhat less extensive in its treatment of the problems of Poland.

3 The speakers of Marchlewski at the opening and close of the congress makes no mention of the PPS–Left. Cf. J. Marchlewski, *Pisma Wybrane* [Selected Works] (Warsaw, 1952–6), II, pp. 410–13.

4 Tych, *PPS–Lewica 1906–1918*, I, nos. 68–71, pp. 383–408.

5 S. Kieniewicz (ed.), *Galicja w dobie autonomicznej (1850–1914)* [Galicia in the period of autonomy, 1850–1915], a collection of documents, (Wrocław, 1952) gives the text of the bishops' declaration, printed in *Czas*, 17 April 1913, pp. 360–6.

6 S. Arski and J. Chudek (eds.), *Galicyjska działalność wojskowa Piłsudskiego 1906–1914* [The Military Activity of Piłsudski, 1906–14] (Warsaw, 1967), no. 1, pp. 443–4.

7 *Ibid.*, no. 95, p. 613.

8 S. Migdał, *Piłsudszczyna w latach pierwszej wojny światowej* [Piłsudski and his followers in the years of the First World War] (Katowice, 1961), p. 25.

9 This organization is the subject of A. Garlicki, *Geneza legionów: Zarys dziejów Komisji Tymczasowej Skonfederowanych Niepodległościowych Partii* [The Origin of the Legions: An Outline History of the Temporary Commission of Confederated Independence Parties] (Warsaw, 1964).

10 Cf. J. Kirchmayer, *1939 i 1944 – Kilka Zagadnień polskich* [1939 and 1944 – Some Polish Problems] (4th edition, Warsaw, 1959), pp. 47–8.

CHAPTER 4

1 L. Grosfeld, *Polityka Państwo Centralnych wobec Sprawy Polskiej w latach 1914–1918* [The Policy of the Central Powers with regard to Poland, 1914–18] (Warsaw, 1962), pp. 33–4.

2 B. Hutten-Czapski, *60 Jahre Politik und Gesellschaft* (Berlin, 1936), II, p. 145.

3 F. Fischer, *Germany's Aims in the First World War* (London, 1967), p. 104.

4 Cf. I. Geiss, *Der Polnische Grenzstreifen, 1914 1918* (Lübeck Hamburg, 1960), p. 150 ff.

5 A. Dallin, 'The future of Poland', in H. L. Roberts (ed.) *Russian Diplomacy and Eastern Europe, 1914–1917* (New York, 1963), p. 12.

6 J. Rzepecki, *Sprawa Legionu Wschodniego 1914 roku* [The Affair of the Eastern Legion, 1914] (Warsaw, 1966), pp. 158–82.

7 Cf. V. Chernov, *Pered Burii* [Before the Storm] (New York, 1953), pp. 295–304.

8 According to the estimate of Gottlieb von Jagow, the German secretary of state. Cf. Fischer, *Germany's Aims*, p. 204.

9 Fischer, *Germany's Aims*, p. 243.

10 Dallin, 'The Future of Poland', p. 34.

11 For details of the difficulties under which left-wing parties worked cf. B. Radlak, *SDKPiL w latach 1914–1917* [The Social Democracy of the Kingdom of Poland and Lithuania 1914–17] (Warsaw, 1967).

12 J. Holzer and J. Molenda, *Polska w pierwszej wojnie światowej* [Poland in the First World War] (2nd edition, Warsaw, 1967), p. 197.

13 W. Pobóg-Malinowski, *Najnowsza Historia Polityczna Polski, 1864–1945*. [A Contemporary Political History of Poland, 1864–1945] (2nd edition, London, 1967), II, p. 197.

14 Dallin, 'The Future of Poland', p. 74.

15 M. Wrzosek, *Polskie korpusy wojskowe w Rosji w latach 1917–1918* [Polish Military Formations in Russia, 1917–18] (Warsaw, 1969), p. 123.

16 Holzer and Molenda, *Polska w pierwszej wojnie światowej*, p. 297.

17 J. Piłsudski, *Pisma Zbiorowe*, IV, p. 171

18 H. Roos, *A History of Modern Poland* (London, 1966), p. 23.

19 Holzer and Molenda, *Polska w pierwszej wojnie światowej*, p. 297.

20 Fischer, *Germany's Aims*, p. 459.

21 M. Leczyk, *Komitet Narodowy Polski a Ententa i Stany Zjednoczone 1917–1919* [The Polish National Committee and the Entente and the United States, 1917–19] (Warsaw, 1966), pp. 200–1.

22 Pobóg-Malinowski, *Najnowsza Historia Polityczna Polski*, II, p. 127.

23 For a critical view of the situation in November–December 1918 see H. Jabłoński, *Polityka Polskiej Partii Socjalistycznej w czasie wojny 1914–1918* [The Policy of the Polish Socialist Party during the War of 1914–18] (Warsaw, 1958), pp. 499–508. Cf. also H. Jabłoński, *Narodziny Drugiej Rzeczpospolitej (1918–1919)* [The Birth of the Second Republic, 1918–19] (Warsaw, 1962).

24 Pobóg-Malinowski, *Najnowsza Historia Polityczna Polski*, II, p. 146.

25 Leczyk, *Komitet Narodowy Polski*, p. 265.

26 *Ibid.*, p. 279.

27 *Głos Narodu* [The Voice of the Nation], 18 December 1918.

28 This assertion was made by the conservative journalist, Stanisław Mackiewicz, in his *Historia Polski od 11 listopada 1918r. do 17 września 1939r.* (London, 1941), p. 86.

29 *Gazeta Warszawska*, 19 January 1919.

30 *Biblioteka Jagiellońska: Papiery Stanisława Kozickiego* [Papers of Stanisław Kozicki], R. Dmowski to Z. Wasilewski, 25 January 1920, Algeria.

31 For a critical view of Poland's real position see J. Lewandowski, *Imperializm słabości: Kształtowanie się polityki wschodniej piłsudczyków, 1921–1926* [The Imperialism of Weakness: The Shaping of the Concepts of the East Policy of the Piłsudski-ites, 1921–6] (Warsaw, 1967), chapter 1.

32 T. Jędruszczak, *Polityka Polski w sprawie Górnego Śląska 1918–1922* [The Policy of Poland towards the Question of Upper Silesia] (Warsaw, 1958), p. 387. Cf. also J. Przewłocki, *Międzysojusznicza Komisja Rządząca i Plebiscytowa na Górnym Śląsku w latach 1920–1922* [The Inter-Allied Control and Plebiscite Commission in Upper Silesia, 1920–2] (Wrocław–Warsaw–Cracow, 1970), pp. 140–8.

33 M. Nowak-Kiełbikowa, *Polska–Wielka Brytania w latach 1918–1923* [Poland and Great Britain, 1918–23] (Warsaw, 1975), pp. 102–3.

34 N. Davies, *White Eagle, Red Star – The Polish–Soviet War, 1919–1920* (London, 1972), p. 66.

35 A. Leinwand, *Polska Partia Socjalistycza wobec wojny polsko–radzieckiej 1919–1920* [The Polish Socialist Party and Polish–Soviet War, 1919–20] (Warsaw, 1964), chapter III, pp. 88–138.

36 *Documents on British Foreign Policy*, first series, II, p. 782.

CHAPTER 5

1 F. Zweig, *Poland between Two Wars* (London, 1944), p. 13.
2 For all figures relating to land distribution see *Rocznik Statystyki Rzeczypospolitej Polskiej* [Statistical Yearbook of the Polish Republic], IV (1926–6), pp. 34, 106–9.
3 A. Ajnenkiel, *Od 'rządów ludowych' do przewrotu majowego* [From 'Popular Government' to the May Coup] (Warsaw, 1964), p. 18.
4 Z. Landau and J. Tomaszewski, *Zarys historii gospodarczej Polski 1918–1939* [An Outline of the Economic History of Poland, 1918–39] (Warsaw, 1962), pp. 17–18.
5 *Mały Rocznik Statystyczny (1931)*, table 11.
6 C. Poralla, 'Die Wirtschaft zwischen den beiden Kriegen', in *Osteuropa-Handbuch – Polen* (Cologne, 1959), p. 79.
7 L. Landau, J. Pańska and E. Strzelecki, *Bezrobocie wśród chłopów* [Unemployment among Peasants] (Warsaw, 1939), p. 146.
8 'Wielka własność rolna' [Large agricultural properties], *Statystyka Polski*, V (1925), p. viii.
9 S. Svennilson, *Growth and Stagnation in the European Economy* (Geneva, 1954), p. 250, table A, XIX.
10 *Mały Rocznik Statystyczny (1931)*, table 11; table XXI.
11 R. Gradowski, *Polska 1918–1939 – Niektóre zagadnienia kapitalizmu monopolistycznego* [Poland 1918–39 – Some Problems of Monopoly Capitalism] (Warsaw, 1959), p. 10.
12 Zweig, *Poland between Two Wars*, pp. 102–3.
13 H. Mianowski, 'O rzemiośle' [On handicrafts], *Dziesięciolecie Polski Odrodzonej* [A Decade of Reborn Poland] (Warsaw, 1928), pp. 183–6.
14 *Mały Rocznik Statystyczny (1931)*, table IV.
15 Svennilson, *Growth and Stagnation in the European Economy*, p. 305, table A, LXVI (100 is the average annual production for 1925–9).
16 J. Żarnowski, *Społeczeństwo Drugiej Rzeczypospolitej* [The Society of the Second Republic] (Warsaw, 1973), pp. 279–80.
17 J. Giertych, 'O rodzicach Dmowskiego' [On the parents of Dmowski], in *Słowo Narodowe* [The National Word] (14 January 1939), quoted in I. Wolikowska, *Roman Dmowski – Człowiek, Polak, Przyjaciel* [R. Dmowski: The Man, Pole and Friend] (Chicago, 1961), pp. 226–8.
18 Żarnowski, *Społeczeństwo Drugiej Rzeczypospolitej*, p. 32.
19 W. Thomas and F. Znaniecki, *The Polish Peasant in Europe and America* (Boston, Mass., 1918), I, p. 159.
20 Żarnowski, *Społeczeństwo Drugiej Rzeczypospolitej*, p. 114.
21 *Ibid.*, p. 264.
22 *Ibid.*, p. 191.
23 *Świat pojęć* [The World of Concepts] (Warsaw, 1939), pp. 117–18.
24 Żarnowski, *Społeczeństwo Drugiej Rzeczypospolitej*, pp. 228–30.
25 A. Tartakower, 'Zawodowa i społeczna struktura Żydów w Polsce odrodzonej' [The Professional and Social Structure of the Jews in Poland], in *Żydzi w Polsce Odrodzonej* [Jews in Reborn Poland] (Warsaw, 1931), II, p. 557.
26 Żarnowski, *Społeczeństwo Drugiej Rzeczypospolitej*, p. 230.
27 *Ibid.*, p. 32.
28 *Rocznik Statystyki Rzeczypospolitej Polskiej*, IV, p. 26, table V; *Statystyka Polski*, ser. C, XCIV a (1938), table X.
29 F. Beranek, 'Das Judentum in Polen', in *Osteuropa-Handbuch: Polen* (Cologne, 1959), p. 120.
30 R. Mahler, 'Jews in Public Service and the Liberal Professions in Poland, 1918–1939', in *Jewish Social Studies*, VI (4), pp. 313–14.
31 Tartakower, 'Zawadowa i społeczna struktura Żydów,', pp. 366–7.

32 S. Thugutt, *Wybór pism i autobiografia* [Collected Works and Autobiography] (Glasgow, 1943), p. 109.
33 A. Belcikowska, *Stronnictwa i związki polityczne w Polsce* [Parties and Political Alliances in Poland] (Warsaw, 1935), p. 16.
34 *Wyzwolenie* [Liberation], 27 July 1924.
35 *Statystyka Polski*, ser. C, xciv a (1938), table xvi, pp. 60–73.
36 Landau and Tomaszewski, *Zarys historii gospodarczej Polski*, pp. 63–4.
37 *Rocznik Statystyki Rzeczypospolitej Polskiej*, ii (1920–2), p. 248.
38 For this affair, see U. Bazylowski, 'Sprawa Dojlid jako przyczynek do przeprowadzenia reformy rolnej na początku ii Rzeczypospolitej' [The Dojlidy Affair as a factor in carrying out Agrarian Reform at the beginning of the Second Republic], *Dzieje Najnowsze Polski* [History of Contemporary Poland] (1st series), viii (1964), pp. 19–50. 39. Mackiewicz, *Historia Polski*, p. 34.
40 According to one of their spokesmen, Adam Uziembło, they had recognized the need for 'struggle against Russia', unlike those 'who through passive waiting had hoped to make possible victory over the Central Powers'. *Głos Prawdy* [The Voice of Truth], 6 September 1924.
41 W. Stpiczyński, 'Po dsiesięciu lat' [After Ten years], *Głos Prawdy*, 9 August 1924.
42 Zweig, *Poland between Two Wars*, p. 35.
43 *Ibid.*
44 A. Ajnenkiel, *Od 'rządów ludowych' do przewrotu majowego* [From the 'Popular Government' to the May Coup] (Warsaw, 1964), pp. 227, 234.
45 Quoted in J. Malicki, *Marszałek Piłsudski i Sejm* [Marshal Piłsudski and the Sejm] (Warsaw, 1936), p. 276.
46 W. Witos, *Czasy i Ludzie* [Times and Men] (Tarnów, 1926), p. 15.

CHAPTER 6

1 J. Piłsudski, 'Przemówienie do przedstawicieli stronnictw semjmowych (29.v.26)' [A Speech to representatives of the parliamentary parties, 29 May 1926], *Pisma Zebrane*, ix, p. 33.
2 J. Piłsudski, 'Wywiad z korespondentem "Le Matin" (25.v.26)' [An interview with the Correspondent of *Le Matin*, 26 May 1926], *Pisma Zebrane*, ix, p. 22.
3 W. Baranowski, *Rozmowy z Piłsudskim, 1916 r.–1931 r.* [Conversations with Piłsudski, 1916–31] (Warsaw, 1938), pp. 205–6.
4 *Ibid.*
5 *Archiwum Akt Nowych*: Zespół Prezydium Rady Ministrów, Protokoły posiedzeń Rady Ministrów (afterwards cited as PPRM).
6 For the speech in the sejm see *Sprawozdanie Stenograficzne Sejmu Rzeczypospolitej* [Parliamentary Debates], 19 July 1926, cols. 13–31; for the senate speech see *Sprawozdanie Stenograficzne Senatu Rzeczypospolitej*, 30 July 1926, cols. 38–53.
7 *Archiwum Akt Nowych*: Zespoły Szczątkowe, Akty Sprawy Świtalskiego, sygn. ii/88, Dn. 15 listopada 1935 r. Rozmowa z Prezydentem (afterwards cited as ASS).
8 *Messager Polonais*, 9 July 1926.
9 Taking the 1925–9 index of industrial production as 100, cf. Svennilson, *Growth and Stagnation in the European Economy*, table A.66, pp. 304–5.
10 PPRM, 16 June 1926, item 4.
11 Baranowski, *Rozmowy z Piłsudskim*, p. 198.
12 J. Piłsudski, 'Wywiad z redaktorem *Głosu Prawdy* (1.vii.28)' [An Interview with the Editor of *Głos Prawdy*], *Pisma Zebrane*, ix, p. 116.
13 J. Piłsudski, 'Z przemyśleń Naczelnika Państwa' [From the Reflections of a Head of State'], *Pisma Zebrane*, ix, p. 130.
14 *Robotnik*, 8 February 1929.

15 Pobóg-Malinowski, *Najnowsza Historia Polityczna Polski*, II, p. 515.

16 PPRM.

17 J. Piłsudski, 'Dno oka' [The Bottom of the Eye], *Pisma Zebrane*, IX, p. 153.

18 *The National Income of Poland*, Birmingham Information Service on Slavonic Countries, monograph no. 4 (Birmingham, 1937), pp. 5–7.

19 Svennilson, *Growth and Stagnation in the European Economy*, pp. 304–5.

20 Instytut Spraw Społecznych, *Młodzież sięga po pracę* [The Youth seeks Work] (Warsaw, 1938), p. 87.

21 *Mały Rocznik Statystyczny* (1939), table VIII.

22 *Archiwum Akt Nowych*: Zespół Prezydium Rady Ministrów, sygn.22, file 127, Stenogram konferencji premiera Świtalskiego z posłami i senatorami B.B., 17.X.1929.

23 *Robotnik*, 3 December 1929.

24 *Polonia*, 10 December 1929.

25 *Ilustrowany Kurier Codzienny*, 25 December 1929.

26 *Gazeta Warszawska*, 21 June 1930.

27 W. Witos, *Moje Wspomnienia* [My Recollections] (Paris, 1965), p. 183.

28 *ASS* Konferencja u Pana Przedenta w składzie: Prezydent, Sławek, i Beck w dniu 18 listopada 1930 r. [*ASS* Conference with the President. Present: President Sławek and Beck, 18 November 1930].

29 *ASS* Narada u Belwederze dnia 29 kwietnia 1931 r. [*ASS* Conference at the Belvedere Palace, 29 April 1931].

30 *ASS* Rozmowa z Komendantem dnia s.v.33. W Belwederze o godz. 4 pop. Obecni Sławek i ja. [*ASS* Conference at the Belvedere Palace with the Commander, 2 May 1933. Present: Sławek and myself].

31 *Mały Rocznik Statystyczny (1936)*, table x.

32 *Ibid.*, (1939), table VIII.

33 Svennilson, *Growth and Stagnation in the European Economy*, pp. 304–5.

34 M. Drozdowski (Ed.), 'Bezrobocie w Polsce w latach 1925–1936' [Unemployment in Poland. 1925–36], in *Najnowsze Dzieje Polski*, IV (Warsaw, 1969), pp. 211–38.

35 R. Gradowski, *Przyczynek do zagadnienia kapitału państwowo-monopolistycznego w Polsce, 1918–1939* [A Contribution to the Question of State Monopoly Capitalism in Poland, 1918–39] (Warsaw, 1965), p. 24.

36 *ASS* Konferencja u Komendanta w składzie: Sławek i ja. 31 stycznia 1934 r. godz. 17.30. [*ASS* Conference with the Commander, 2 May 1933. Present: Sławek and myself, 17.30 hours, 31 January 1934].

37 *Sprawa brzeska* [The Brześć Affair] (London, 1941), p. 27.

38 Quoted in Roos, *A History of Modern Poland*, p. 122.

39 Pobóg-Malinowski, *Najnowsza Historia Polityczna Polski*, II, p. 719.

40 *International Press Conference*, 5 November 1931.

41 *Gazeta Polska*, 10 January 1931.

42 J. Beck, *Dernier Rapport: Politique polonaise, 1926–1939* (Neuchâtel, 1951), pp. 8–10.

43 J. Laroche, *La Pologue de Pilsudski: Souvenirs d'une ambassade 1926–1935* (Paris, 1953), p. 113.

CHAPTER 7

1 Quoted in Pobóg-Malinowski, *Najnowsza Historia Polityczna Polski*, II, p. 773.

2 S. Kot to I. Paderewski, 3 November 1935, quoted in T. Jędruszczak, *Piłsudczycy bez Piłsudskiego* [Piłsudski-ites without Piłsudski] (Warsaw, 1963), p. 29.

3 For these figures see *ABC*, 12 September 1935.

4 *ASS*, Rozmowa z Prezydentem dn. 1 listopada 1935 r.

5 As in the article entitled 'Żołnierz polski w ruchu reformy socjalnej' [The Polish Soldier in the Movement of Social Reform], *Kurier Poranny* [Morning Courier], 5 January 1936.

6 *Sprawozdanie Stenograficzne Sejmu Rzeczypospolitej* [Parliamentary Debates], 4 June 1936.

7 Pobóg-Malinowski, *Najnowsza Historia Polityczna Polski*, II, p. 788.

8 *Ibid.*

9 R. Wapiński, 'Niektóre problemy ewolucji ideowo–politycznej Endecji w latach 1919–1939' [Some problems of the ideological and political evolution of the National Democrats], in *Kwartalnik Historyczny*, LXXIII (1966), p. 874.

10 For the programme see *Gazeta Polska*, 22 February 1937.

11 These were the words of M. Kukiel, *Strajk chłopski w 1937 r. – dokumenty archiwalne* [The Peasant Strike of 1937 – Documents from the Archives] (Warsaw, 1960), I, p. 212.

12 Cf. E. D. Wynot, *Polish Politics in Transition* (Athens, Georgia, 1974), pp. 160–8.

13 *Gazeta Polska*, 1 July 1939.

14 J. Żarnowski, *Polska partia socjalistyczna w latach 1935–39* [The Polish Socialist Party, 1935–9] (Warsaw, 1965), p. 330.

15 *Materiały źródłowe do historii polskiego ruchu ludowego* [Source Materials on the History of the Polish Peasant Movement] (Warsaw, 1966), III, p. 407.

16 *Robotnik*, 4 June 1939.

17 Svennilson, *Growth and Stagnation in the European Economy*, table A 66, pp. 304–5. The method of assessing the index changed during this period. The index also fails to indicate the rise of certain industries and the decline of others. It should be treated as only a very general indication of economic trends. See Landau and Tomaszewski, *Zarys historii gospodarczej Polski 1918–1939*, pp. 240–2.

18 M. Drozdowski, *Polityka gospodarcza rządu polskiego, 1936–39* [The Economic Policy of the Polish Government, 1936–9] (Warsaw, 1963), p. 96.

19 *Mały Rocznik Statystyczny (1939)*, table XXV, p. 268.

20 Drozdowski, *Polityka gospodarcza rządu polskiego*, p. 200.

21 O. Janowsky, *People at Bay: The Jewish Problem in East Central Europe* (London, 1938), pp. 92–3.

22 J. Szembek, *Diariusz i teki Jana Szembeka* [The Diary and Papers of Jan Szembek] (edited by T. Komarnicki, London, 1966), p. 197.

23 P. Reynaud, *La France a sauvé l'Europe* (Paris, 1947), I, p. 587.

24 Cf. A. M. Cienciala, *Poland and the Western Powers, 1938–1939* (London, 1968), pp. 149–76. Cf. also M. Wojciechowski, *Stosunki Polsko–Niemieckie 1933–1938* [Polish–German Relations, 1935–8] (Poznań, 1965), pp. 503–20.

25 S. Newman, *March 1939: The British Guarantee of Poland* (Oxford, 1976), p. 173.

CHAPTER 8

1 A. J. P. Taylor, *The Second World War* (London, 1975), p. 36.

2 J. R. Butler, *The Grand Strategy, September 1939–June 1941* (London, 1957), pp. 11–12.

3 J. C. Fest, *Hitler* (London, 1974), p. 602.

4 J. Jaklicz, 'Żołnierz 2-giej Rzeczpospolitej' [The Soldier of the Second Republic], in *Zeszyty Historyczne*, no. 35 (1976), p. 145.

5 *Encyklopedia Drugiej Wojny Światowej* [An Encyclopaedia of the Second World War] (Warsaw, 1975), pp. 671, 721.

6 Butler, *The Grand Strategy*, p. 57.

7 S. Rowecki, *Wspomnienia* [Recollections] (Warsaw, 1957), p. 103.

8 Cf. R. M. Kennedy, *The German Campaign in Poland* (Washington, 1956) for details.

9 N. Bethell, *The War Hitler Won* (London, 1972), pp. 32–3.

10 S. Mikolajczyk, *The Pattern of Soviet Domination* (London, 1948), pp. 5–6.

11 Z. Załuski, *Przepustka do historii* [A Permit to History] (Warsaw, 1963), pp. 234–6.

12 *Encyklopedia Drugiej Wojny Światowej*, pp. 670, 381.

13 E. L. Woodward, *British Foreign Policy in the Second World War* (London, 1962), pp. 29–30.

14 R. Coulondre, *De Staline à Hitler: Souvenirs de deux ambassades (1936–1939)* (Paris, 1950), p. 165.

15 Taylor, *The Second World War*, p. 41.

16 A. Korbonski, *Politics of Socialist Agriculture in Poland, 1945–1960* (New York and London, 1965), pp. 33 ff.

17 E. Duraczyński, *Wojna i Okupacja* [War and Occupation] (Warsaw, 1974), p. 82.

18 S. Piotrowski, *Hans Frank's Diary* (Warsaw, 1961), pp. 42–5.

19 Duraczyński, *Wojna i Okupacja*, p. 58.

20 I. Trunk, *Judenrate* (New York, 1972), pp. 5–6.

21 K. Iranek-Osmecki, *He Who Saves One Life* (New York, 1971), pp. 20–1.

22 Duraczyński, *Wojna i Okupacja*, p. 69.

23 Piotrowski, *Hans Frank's Diary*, p. 99.

24 Duraczyński, *Wojna i Okupacja*, p. 102.

25 Iranek-Osmecki, *He Who Saves One Life*, pp. 28–9.

26 *Ibid.*, pp. 281, 291.

27 M. R. D. Foot, *Resistance: An Analysis of the European Resistance to Nazism, 1940–1945* (London, 1976), p. 293.

28 Duraczyński, *Wojna i Okupacja*, p. 64.

29 Piotrowski, *Hans Frank's Diary*, pp. 142–3.

30 *Pravda*, 18 September 1939.

31 R. Conquest, *The Great Purge* (London, 1968), p. 532.

32 M. Turlejska, *Prawdy i Fikcje* [Truths and Fictions] (Warsaw, 1968), pp. 308–10.

33 *Ibid.*, pp. 277–8.

34 *Ibid.*, p. 309.

35 *Ibid.*, pp. 503 ff.

36 R. F. Leslie, *Reform and Insurrection in Russian Poland, 1856–1865* (London, 1963), p. vii.

37 For details see J. M. Ciechanowski, *The Warsaw Rising of 1944* (Cambridge, 1974), pp. 69 ff.

38 *Ibid.*, pp. 69–83.

39 For details see *Polskie Siły Zbrojne w drugiej wojnie światowej* [The Polish Armed Forces in the Second World War], II – *Kampania na obczyźnie* [The Campaign Abroad], part i (London, 1959), pp. 37 ff.

40 *Polskie Siły Zbrojne*, II(i), pp. 195 ff. Cf. also B. Wroński, *Poza krajem – Za ojczyznę* [Beyond the Country – For the Fatherland] (Osny, 1974), pp. 36 ff.

41 A. Polonsky (ed.), *The Great Powers and the Polish Question 1941–45* (London, 1976), p. 17, Document 7, pp. 73–4.

42 *Ibid.*, p. 16.

43 For details see H. Mitchell, *The Second World War* (London, 1975), pp. 138 ff.

44 E. Raczynski, *In Allied London* (London, 1962), p. 52; *Polskie Siły Zbrojne*, II(i), pp. 195 ff., and Wroński, *Poza krajem – Za ojczyznę*, pp. 35 ff.

45 W. T. Kowalski, *Walka dyplomatyczna o miejsce Polski w Europie (1939–1945)* [The Diplomatic Struggle for the place of Poland in Europe, 1939–45] (2nd edition, Warsaw, 1967), pp. 73–4; Raczynski, *In Allied London*, pp. 56 ff.

46 J. Cynk, *The History of the Polish Air Force, 1918–1968* (Reading, 1972), pp. 170–4.

47 J. Retinger, *Memoirs of an Eminence Grise* (London, 1972), p. 94.

48 *Ibid.*, pp. 109–11.

49 Kowalski, *Walka dyplomatyczna*, p. 95.

50 E. J. Rozek, *Allied Wartime Diplomacy: A Pattern in Poland* (New York, 1958), p. 61.

51 Mikolajczyk, *The Pattern of Soviet Domination*, p. 15.

CHAPTER 9

1 Kowalski, *Walka dyplomatyczna*, pp. 118–30.
2 M. K. Dziewanowski, *The Communist Party of Poland* (2nd edition, Cambridge, Mass., 1976), pp. 149–54. Cf. also Conquest, *The Great Purge*, pp. 433–5.
3 For a detailed account of the party's origins see M. Malinowski, *Geneza PPR* [The Genesis of the Polish Workers' Party] (Warsaw, 1972), *passim*.
4 Cf. E. W. Wiśniewski, T. Rawski, Z. Stąpor and J. Zamoyski (eds.), *Wojna wyzwoleńcza narodu polskiego w latach 1939–1945* [The War of Liberation of the Polish Nation, 1939–45] (Warsaw, 1966), pp. 342–7.
5 For the correspondence of Beneš and Sikorski see *Studia z Najnowszych Dziejów Powszechnych* [Studies in General Contemporary History], IV, (1963), pp. 280–318.
6 Kowalski, *Walka dyplomatyczna*, pp. 131–43. Cf. also P. S. Wandycz, *Czechoslovak–Polish Confederation and the Great Powers, 1940–1943* (Bloomington, 1956); and E. Taborsky, 'A Polish–Czechoslovak Confederation – a story of the first Soviet veto', in *Journal of Central European Affairs*, IX (1950).
7 Ciechanowski, *The Warsaw Rising*, pp. 115 ff.
8 T. Bór-Komorowski, *Armia podziemna* [The Underground Army] (London, 1967), p. 136.
9 Ciechanowski, *The Warsaw Rising*, pp. 120–1.
10 For details see J. Garlinski, 'The Polish Underground State', in *The Journal of Contemporary History*, VIII (1975), pp. 219 ff., and S. Korboński, *Polskie państwo podziemne* [The Polish Underground State] (Paris, 1975).
11 For a full discussion of the relations of the pro-London parties see E. Duraczyński, *Stosunki w kierownictwie podziemia londyńskiego 1939–1943* [Relations in the Leadership of the London Underground Movement, 1939–43] (Warsaw, 1966). For the evolution of the National Democrats see J. J. Terej, *Rzeczywistość i Polityka – Z studiów na dziejami najnowszymi Narodowej Demokracji* [Reality and Policy – Studies in the Contemporary History of National Democracy] (Warsaw, 1971).
12 Korboński, *Polskie państwo podziemne*, p. 56.
13 Ciechanowski, *The Warsaw Rising*, pp. 98 ff.
14 *Ibid.*, pp. 132 ff.
15 K. Macksey, *The Partisans of Europe in World War II* (London, 1975), p. 175.
16 *Encyklopedia Drugiej Wojny Światowej*, pp. 676–9.
17 Cf. A. Seaton, *Stalin as War Lord* (London, 1976), p. 175.
18 *DOSPR* [Documents on Polish–Soviet Relations], I, no. 283, pp. 469–73.
19 For details of the Katyn affair see J. K. Zawodny, *Death in the Forest* (London, 1971).
20 *DOSPR*, I, no. 312, pp. 532–3.

CHAPTER 10

1 Raczynski, *In Allied London*, p. 154.
2 J. Rzepecki, *Wspomnienia* [Recollections] (Warsaw, 1956), pp. 257 ff.
3 Ciechanowski, *The Warsaw Rising*, pp. 101 ff.
4 Wiśniewski, *Wojna wyzwoleńcza narodu polskiego*, p. 366.
5 Ciechanowski, *The Warsaw Rising*, pp. 132 ff.
6 For details see J. Garlinski, *Poland, SOE and the Allies* (London, 1969), pp. 235–8, and Ciechanowski, *The Warsaw Rising*, pp. 46–7.
7 Pobóg-Malinowski, *Najnowsza Historia Polityczna Polski, 1864–1945*, III, p. 470.
8 *The Memoirs of Cordell Hull* (London, 1948), pp. 1315–16.
9 Polonsky, *The Great Powers*, Document 91, pp. 189–91, reproduced from *Stalin Correspondence*, I, no. 250.

10 *Ibid.*, Document 92, F.O.371. C.430/8/55, Minute of Roberts, 27 March 1944.

11 Ciechanowski, *The Warsaw Rising*, pp. 190–203; A. Skarzyński, *Polityczne przyczyny powstania warszawskiego* [The Political Reasons for the Warsaw Uprising] (Warsaw, 1964), pp. 181–92.

12 A. Skarzyński, *Polityczne przyczyny powstania warszawskiego*, pp. 73–7.

13 *Stalin Correspondence*, II, nos. 203, 206.

14 Kowalski, *Walka dyplomatyczna*, pp. 406–25.

15 W. Góra, *Powstanie władzy ludowej w Polsce* [The formation of Popular Government in Poland] (Warsaw, 1972), pp. 101, 146.

16 Wiśniewski, *Wojna wyzwoleńcza narodu polskiego*, p. 498.

17 Ciechanowski, *The Warsaw Rising*, pp. 177 ff.

18 *Ibid.*, pp. 195 ff.

19 *Ibid.*, pp. 177 ff.

20 Skarzyński *Polityczne przyczyny powstania warszawskiego*, pp. 197–200.

21 *Polskie Siły Zbrojne*, III, pp. 623 ff.

22 Cynk, *History of the Polish Air force*, pp. 156 ff.

23 Wiśniewski, *Wojna wyzwoleńcza narodu polskiego*, p. 463.

24 Cf. *Polski czyn zbrojny w II wojnie światowej* [Polish Armed Action in the Second World War] (Warsaw, 1975), III (Ludowe wojsko polskie, 1943–1945 [The People's Army, 1943–5]), pp. 25 ff.

25 Ciechanowski, *The Warsaw Rising*, pp. 236 ff.

26 W. A. Harriman and E. Abel, *Special Envoy to Churchill and Stalin 1941–1946* (New York, 1975), pp. 34–8.

27 A. Korbonski, 'The Warsaw Uprising Revisited', *Survey*, no. 2 (1970), p. 96.

28 Garlinski, 'The Polish Underground State' pp. 167 ff.

29 Ciechanowski, *The Warsaw Rising*, pp. 281 ff.

30 Foot, *Resistance*, p. 299.

31 *Polskie Siły Zbrojne*, III, p. 824.

32 Harriman and Abel, *Special Envory to Churchill and Stalin*, p. 349.

33 Dziewanowski, *The Communist Party of Poland*, p. 177.

34 W. Góra, *Polska Rzeczpospolita Ludowa 1944–1974* [The Polish People's Republic, 1944–74] (Warsaw, 1974), pp. 82–3.

35 *Ibid.*, p.83.

36 Korbonski, *Politics of Socialist Agriculture in Poland*, pp. 67 ff.

37 Góra, *Polska Rzeczpospolita Ludowa*, p. 74.

38 Polonsky, *The Great Powers*, Documents 105, 109.

39 *Ibid.*, Document 111.

40 Harriman and Abel, *Special Envoy to Churchill and Stalin*, p. 346.

41 Ciechanowski, *The Warsaw Rising*, pp. 212 ff.

42 Harriman and Abel, *Special Envoy to Churchill and Stalin*, pp. 339–40.

43 *Ibid.*, p. 359.

44 For a summary of negotiations and the draft proposals see Polonsky, *The Great Powers*, Document 112.

45 Harriman and Abel, *Special Envory to Churchill and Stalin*, p. 361

46 A. Przygoński, *Z zagadnień strategii Frontu Narodowego PPR 1942–1945* [Questions of the National Front Strategy of the PPR, 1942–5 (Warsaw, 1976), p. 327.

47 For the British andAmerican replies to the Polish government see Polonsky, *The Great Powers*, Documents 113, 114.

CHAPTER 11

1 For the final communiqué of the Yalta Conference in respect of Poland see Polonsky, *The Great Powers*, Document 130. Cf. also *ibid.*, Documents 122–9 for other important documents concerning Poland.

2 Rozek, *Allied Wartime Diplomacy*, pp. 350–2.

3 Mitchell, *The Second World War*, p. 787.

4 Korbonski, *Politics of Socialist Agriculture*, p. 107.

5 *Ibid.*, p. 108.

6 *Ibid.*, pp. 110–15.

7 For an extensive discussion of the Polish Question at Potsdam see Kowalski, *Walka dyplomatyczna o miejsce Polski w Europie*, pp. 615–62.

8 Cf. E. Wiskemann, *Germany's Eastern Neighbours* (London, 1956), passim.

9 *Dziennik Praw Rzeczypospolitej Polskiej* [The Statute Book of the Polish Republic] (1947), no. 35.

10 Cf. K. Kersten, *Repatriacja ludności polskiej po II wojnie światowej* [The Repatriation of the Polish Population after the Second World War] (Wrocław, 1974), pp. 19 ff.

11 Korbonski, *Politics of Socialist Agriculture*, pp. 67 ff.

12 Z. Brzezinski, *The Soviet Bloc* (Cambridge, Mass, 1971), pp. 12–14.

13 Dziewanowski, *The Communist Party of Poland*, p. 200.

14 *Ibid.*, pp. 198–201.

15 Korbonski, *Politics of Socialist Agriculture*, p. 119.

16 *Ibid.*, p. 119.

17 M. Turlejska, *Spór o Polskę* [The Struggle for Poland] (Warsaw, 1972), pp. 293–308.

18 T. Walichnowski, *U źródeł walk z podziemiem reakcyjnym w Polsce* [At the Source of the Struggle with the Reactionary Underground in Poland] (Warsaw, 1975), p. 175.

19 Korbonski, *Politics of Socialist Agriculture*, pp. 119–20.

20 *Ibid.*, p. 124.

21 B. Syzdek, *Polska Paria Socjalistyczna w latach 1944–48* [The Polish Socialist Party, 1944–8] (Warsaw, 1947), pp. 345 ff.

22 Korbonski, *Politics of Socialist Agriculture*, pp. 124–5.

23 *Ibid.*, pp. 126–8.

24 Turlejska, *Spór o Polskę*, pp. 308–9.

25 Korbonski, *Politics of Socialist Agriculture*, pp. 129–30.

26 A. Ulam, *Titoism and the Cominform* (Cambridge, Mass., 1952)., pp. 146 ff. Dziewanowski, *The Communist Party of Poland*, p. 209.

27 Dziewanowski, *ibid.*, p. 208.

28 M. Djilas, *Conversations with Stalin* (London, 1962), p. 117.

29 N. Bethell, *Gomulka* (London, 1972), p. 139.

30 'Premówienie tow. Wiesława na plenarnym posiedzeniu KC PPR w dniu 5 czerwca 1948 r.' [The Speech of Comrade Wiesław (i.e. Gomułka) at the plenary session of the Central Committee of the PPR, 5 June 1948], in *Zeszyty Historyczne*, no. 34 (1975), pp. 34 ff.

31 Dziewanowski, *The Communist Party of Poland*, pp. 2–10.

32 *Ibid.*, p. 215.

33 *Ibid.*, pp. 216–19.

34 'VIII Plenum Komitetu Centralnego PZPR 19–20 x 1956 r.' [The Eighth Plenum of the Central Committee of the Polish United Workers' Party, 19–20 December 1956], in *Nowe Drogi* [New Roads], no. 10 (Warsaw, 1956), p. 40.

CHAPTER 12

1 Góra, *Polska Rzeczpospolita Ludowa 1944–1974* pp. 284 ff. Fifty-five per cent of village communes afterwards lacked any PZPR organization and much of the rest was rather nominal.

2 J. Malara and L. Rey, *La Pologne d'une occupation à l'autre (1944–1952)* (Paris, 1952), pp. 207 ff.

3 B. Bierut, *Zadania Partii w walce o nowe kadry* [The Party's Tasks in the Struggle for New Cadres] (Warsaw, 1950), p. 58.

4 *Rzeczpospolita* [The Republic], 7 November 1949.

5 E. Crankshaw (ed.), *Khrushchev Remembers: The Last Testament* (London, 1971), p. 176.

6 J. Wiatr in J. van Doorn, *Armed Forces and Society* (The Hague–Paris, 1968), p. 229.

7 O. Halecki (ed.), *Poland* (New York–London, 1957), p. 158.

8 Halecki, *Poland*, p. 156.

9 Defence budget grew from 1 milliard to 6.6 milliard new *zł.* per annum between 1948 and 1952. Malara and Rey, *La Pologne*, p. 201.

10 See Berman's memorandum at the October 1956 Central Committee plenum published in the *Nowe Drogi* issue for that month.

11 The text of the address, subsequent speeches and resolutions was published as a special issue of *Nowe Drogi*, under the title 'III Plenum Komitetu Centralnego Polskiej Zjednoczonej Partii Robotniczej' [Third Plenum of the Central Committee of the Polish United Workers' Party] (Warsaw, 1949).

12 Z. K. Brzezinski, *The Soviet Bloc: Unity and Conflict* (Cambridge, Mass., 1960), pp. 91–7.

13 Góra, *Polska Rzeczpospolita Ludowa*, pp. 287, 365–7.

14 Bierut, *Zadania Partii*, pp. 70, 72.

15 A. B. Ulam, *Expansion and Coexistence: the History of Soviet Foreign Policy from 1917–1967* (London, 1968), p. 466.

16 This expansion is illustrated by the following figures, giving public security appropriations in the state budget in millions of *złotys*:

	1946	1947	1948	1949	1950
Ministry of Public Security	4 0	17 0	23 0	37 0	44 0
Territorial UB Offices	0.7	1.8	2.6	8.3	21.9

These figures give only a partial picture since many UB agents were nominally on the staff of other institutions or enterprises and paid from their budgets. Source: Halecki, *Poland*, p. 166, where fuller figures are given.

17 These and other details of the work of the Tenth Department were revealed by its ex-deputy chief, Col. Józef Światło, who defected to the West in 1953. There is a summary of his broadcasts on Radio Free Europe in 'The Światło Story', *News from Behind the Iron Curtain*, IV, 3 (March, 1955).

18 This was admitted in a Central Committee plenum resolution of 24 January 1955. *Uchwały Komitetu Centralnego Polskiej Zjednoczonej Partii Robotniczej od II do III Zjazdu* [Resolutions of the Central Committee of the Polish United Workers' Party from the Second to the Third Congress] (Warsaw, 1959), pp. 46–7.

19 Góra, *Polska Rzeczpospolita Ludowa*, pp. 288–93, 370–2.

20 The number of forced labour camps in Poland was estimated to be over forty and their inmates about 50,000 in 1954. This was less than in other people's democracies. Halecki, *Poland*, p. 479.

21 The government presidium was first given an official status by a Council of Ministers' resolution of 30 June 1969.
22 *Polska 1944–1965* [Poland 1944–65], I, 1944–55 (Warsaw, 1966), p. 345.
23 The following table is revealing of the sejm's inactivity:

Year	Statutes passed	Decrees approved	Days in session
1952	3	6	3
1953	I	52	5
1954	5	31	4
1955	2	26	5

Source: *Rocznik Statystyczny (1972)*, quoted in Góra, *Polska Rzeczpospolita Ludowa*, p. 362.
24 Malara and Rey, *La Pologne*, p. 186.
25 *Plan 6-letni* [The Six Year Plan] (Warsaw, 1950).
26 A. Jezierski, *Historia gospodarcza Polski Ludowej 1944–1968* [Economic History of People's Poland 1944–68] (Warsaw, 1971), pp. 141, 142.
27 K. Ryć, *Spożycie a wzrost gospodarczy Polski 1945–1970* [Consumption and Poland's Economic Growth 1945–70] (Warsaw, 1968), pp. 66, 67.
28 A. Karpiński, *Zagadnienia socjalistycznej industrializacji Polski* [Problems of Socialist Industrialization of Poland] (Warsaw, 1958), p. 123.
29 H. Jędruszczak, *Zatrudnienie a przemiany społeczne w Polsce w latach 1944–1960* [Employment and Social Transformations in Poland in the Years 1944–60] (Warsaw, 1972), pp. 154 ff.
30 Jezierski, *Historia gospodarcza*, pp. 218, 219, 221, 223.
31 H. Minc's speech at the VIII Central Committee Plenum, published in *Nowe Drogi*, October 1956.
32 Karpiński, *Zagadnienia industrializacji*, passim.
33 Halecki, *Poland*, p. 472.
34 *Ibid.*, p. 481.
35 Malara and Rey, *La Pologne*, pp. 275, 362–3.
36 B. Bierut, *O umocnienie spójni między miastem i wsią* [For the Strengthening of the Bond between Town and Country] (Warsaw, 1952), p. 46.
37 Malara and Rey, *La Pologne*, pp. 278, 364.
38 Halecki, *Poland*, p. 193.
39 Karpiński, *Zagadnienia industrializacji*, p. 200; Halecki, *Poland*, p. 286.
40 Halecki, *Poland*, p. 430.
41 Jezierski, *Historia gospodarcza*, p. 200.
42 The progress of collectivizatioi. in Poland is the subject of a detailed and authoritative study: Korbonski, *Politics of Socialist Agriculture in Poland*, pp. 169 ff.
43 Bierut in June 1952 insisted on a middle path between forcing the pace through administrative pressure and simply waiting for the peasants' change of heart. Bierut, *O umocnienie*, pp. 85, 86.
44 Ryć, *Spożycie a wzrost*, pp. 84–6.
45 This point was heavily stressed by Gomułka at the VIII Central Committee Plenum. English translation in P. E. Zinner (ed.), *National Communism and Popular Revolt in Eastern Europe* (New York, 1956), p. 202.
46 Gomułka's speech at the VIII Plenum, translated in Zinner, *National Communism*, p. 200.

47 Jezierski, *Historia gospodarcza*, p. 209.
48 Gomułka's speech at the VIII Central Committee Plenum, in Zinner, *National Communism*, p. 200.
49 *Kultura: II Numer Krajowy* [Culture: Second Homeland Number] (Paris, 1952), pp. 119 ff.
50 *Kultura: III Numer Krajowy* [Culture: Third Homeland Number] (Paris, 1952), p. 214.
51 *Ibid.*, p. 291.
52 *Kultura: II Numer Krajowy*, p. 132.
53 Halecki, *Poland*, p. 205.
54 F. Fejtö, *A History of the People's Democracies* (London, 1974), pp. 14 ff.
55 Brzezinski, *The Soviet Bloc*, p. 171.
56 Korbonski, *Politics of Socialist Agriculture*, p. 218 ff.
57 R. Hiscocks, *Poland, Bridge for the Abyss?* (London, 1963), pp. 172 ff.
58 'The Światło Story', *News from Behind the Iron Curtain*, March 1955.
59 Ochab's expression used at the VIII Central Committee Plenum, *Nowe Drogi*, October 1956.
60 Private information.
61 *Uchwały Komitetu Centralnego PZPR od II do III Zjazdu*, pp. 50 ff.
62 Korbonski, *Politics of Socialist Agriculture*, pp. 230 ff.
63 Zinner, *National Communism*, pp. 40 ff.
64 Private information.
65 *Po Prostu 1955–6* [Plain Speaking 1955–6: selection of articles] (Warsaw, 1956).
66 Jezierski, *Historia gospodarcza*, p. 146.
67 Karpiński, *Zagadnienia industrializacji*, p. 69.
68 *Ibid.*, p. 73.
69 Jędruszczak, *Zatrudnienie a przemiany*, p. 198.

CHAPTER 13

1 W. Leonhard, *The Kremlin since Stalin* (London, 1960), pp. 120 ff.
2 Text and documents on the reactions to the speech in *The Anti-Stalin Campaign and International Communism: A Selection of Documents*, Russian Institute, Columbia University (New York, 1956).
3 H. Rechowicz, *Bolesław Bierut 1892–1956* (Warsaw, 1977), p. 260.
4 F. Lewis, *The Polish Volcano* (London, 1959), pp. 101–7.
5 Albrecht had been a colleague of Gomułka in the communist underground in occupied Poland. Gierek had joined the communist party as an émigré in Belgium, and was active in the trade-union and resistance movement there during the war. With Ochab they represented the three main sections of the Polish communist elite.
6 Hiscocks, *Poland, Bridge for the Abyss?*, pp. 189 ff.
7 See La Documentation Française. Notes et Etudes Documentaires, no. 2.306, *La periode 'stalinienne' en Pologne à la lumière des écrits polonais (1949–1956)*. Présidence du Conseil – Secretariat Géneral du Gouvernement (Paris, 1957).
8 The fullest account of the Poznań events is by E. Wacowska in *Poznań 1956 – Grudzień 1970* [Poznań 1956 – December 1970] (Paris, 1971), pp. 153–216.
9 Zinner, *National Communism*, pp. 131 ff.
10 Leonhard, *The Kremlin since Stalin*, p. 209.
11 The most important were the formal dismissal of Berman from the politburo, the co-option of Gierek, Roman Nowak and Adam Rapacki as its full members, and Stefan Jędrychowski and Eugeniusz Stawiński as deputy members.
12 English text in Zinner, *National Communism*, pp. 145 ff.
13 *Nowe Drogi*, July–August 1956. Later references to the July plenum proceedings and

numerous rumours confirmed this. The plenum debates were less concerned with the merits of the specific measures than with recriminations about the past and speculation whether the Soviet leaders would permit reforms. See Lewis, *The Polish Volcano*, pp. 164 ff; K. Syrop, *Spring in October: The Polish Revolution of 1956* (London, 1957), pp. 55 ff; K. S. Karol, *Visa for Poland* (London, 1959), pp. 136 ff.

14 Syrop, *Spring in October*, pp. 71 ff.

15 Lewis, *The Polish Volcano*, pp. 166 ff.

16 Lewis, *The Polish Volcano*, pp. 205 ff; Syrop, *Spring in October*, pp. 90 ff.

17 Gomułka's views were publicized earlier in the year by his friend W. Bieńkowski in a series of articles in *Nowa Kultura*. They were reprinted in Bieńkowski, *Rewolucji ciąg dalszy* [The Revolution Continued] (Warsaw, 1957), pp. 41–96.

18 English text in Zinner, *National Communism*, pp. 197–238.

19 *Ibid.*, pp. 239 ff.

20 i.e. Albrecht, Gierek, Jarosiński, Matwin and Ochab.

21 Accounts in Brzezinski, *The Soviet Bloc*, chap. 10 and Fejtö, *A History of the People's Democracies*, chap. 5.

22 Zinner, *National Communism*, pp. 440 ff.

23 For text *ibid.*, pp. 485–9.

24 For text of communiqué *ibid.*, pp. 306–14.

25 The exact figure was 224,000, according to Góra, *Polska Rzeczpospolita Ludowa*, p. 401. Many Poles decided to remain, despite the possibility of repatriation. According to *Izvestia* on 15 January 1959, there were 1,380,000 Poles inhabiting the Soviet Union, mainly Byelorussia, the Ukraine and Lithuania. 45.5 per cent gave Polish as their mother tongue in the census returns from which the figures were derived. Cf. *Polska–ZSRR* [Poland–USSR], (Warsaw, 1960), p. 238.

26 Brzezinski, *The Soviet Bloc*, p. 296.

27 *Ibid.*, chap. 12.

28 *Zeszyty historyczne* [Historical Notebooks], no. 4, (Paris, 1963), p. 15.

29 Formed in 1949 by a merger of a number of separate bodies and dormant during stalinism.

30 A. Bromke, *Poland's Politics: Idealism vs. Realism* (Cambridge, Mass., 1970) chaps. 11, 12.

31 Korbonski, *Politics of Socialist Agriculture*, p. 251.

32 W. Gomułka, *Przemówienia 1956–1957* [Speeches 1956–7] (Warsaw, 1957), pp. 63 ff.

33 *Zeszyty historyczne*, no. 4, p. 9.

34 In the end the PZPR had only 51 per cent of candidates, the ZSL 25 per cent, the SD 8 per cent, while non-party candidates made up the remaining 16 per cent. Z. A. Pelczynski, 'Poland 1957' in D. E. Butler (ed.), *Elections Abroad* (London, 1959), p. 143.

35 Pelczynski 'Poland 1957', p. 165. Full text in Gomułka, *Przemówienia*, p. 209.

CHAPTER 14

1 Bromke, *Poland's Politics* (Cambridge, Mass., 1967), p. 261.

2 For example F. Gibney, *The Frozen Revolution. Poland: A Study in Communist Decay* (New York, 1959); S. L. Shneiderman, *The Warsaw Heresy* (New York, 1959); Hiscocks, *Poland, Bridge for the Abyss*; H. Stehle, *The Independent Satellite: Society and Politics in Poland since 1945* (London, 1965; original German edition, Frankfurt-am-Main, 1963).

3 *Uchwały KC PZPR od II do III Zjazdu* [Resolutions of the Central Committee of the PZPR from the Second to the Third Congress], pp. 468 ff.

4 W. Gomułka, *Przemówienia: wrzesień 1957 – grudzień 1958* [Speeches: September 1975–December 1958] (Warsaw, 1959), p. 36.

5 Brzezinski, *The Soviet Bloc*, chap. 13; Fejtö, *A History of the People's Democracies*, pp. 138 ff.

6 Gomułka, *Przemówienia 1957–1958*, pp. 15 ff.; Karol, *Visa for Poland*, pp. 235 ff.

7 Hiscocks, *Poland, Bridge for the Abyss*, pp. 267 ff.

8 Korbonski, *Politics of Socialist Agriculture*, pp. 297 ff.

9 Stehle, *The Independent Satellite*, pp. 80 ff.

10 *Ibid.*, p. 68.

11 Z. A. Pelczynski, 'Parliamentarism in Poland', in *Parliamentary Affairs*, x, 3, (London, Autumn 1957).

12 *United States Overseas Loans and Grants and Assistance from International Organizations* (Special Report Prepared for the House Foreign Affairs Committee), p. 12.

13 Hiscocks, *Poland, Bridge for the Abyss*, p. 269.

14 A. Karpiński, *Polityka uprzemysłowienia Polski w latach 1958–1968*. [The Policy of the Industrialization of Poland in the Years 1958–68] (Warsaw, 1969), p. 104.

15 Jezierski, *Historia gospodarcza*, p. 248.

16 Stehle, *The Independent Satellite*, pp. 38 ff.

17 M. Kaser, *Comecon: Integration Problems of the Planned Economies* (2nd ed., Oxford, 1967), pp. 107 ff.

18 Stehle, *The Independent Satellite*, pp. 222 ff., 324 ff.

19 *Ibid.*, pp. 254 ff.

CHAPTER 15

1 *Twenty Years of the Polish People's Republic* (Warsaw, 1964), p. 7.

2 Góra, *Polska Rzeczpospolita Ludowa*, pp. 466, 480.

3 See Stehle, *The Independent Satellite*, pp. 57, 342, 343, and Bromke, *Poland's Politics*, pp. 198 ff. for an account of the group and its leading members.

4 Bromke, *Poland's Politics*, p. 203.

5 W. Bieńkowski, *Motory i hamulce socjalizmu* [The Engines and Brakes of Socialism] (Paris, 1969), chap. 3.

6 Bromke, *Poland's Politics*, pp. 190 ff.

7 L. Blit, *The Eastern Pretender: Bolesław Piasecki: His Life and Times* (London, 1965), p. 214, for the beginning of expansion.

8 *Dokumenty: Dialog polsko-niemiecki w świetle dokumentów kościelnych* [Documents: Polish–German Dialogue in the Light of Church Documents] (Paris, 1966), and A. Liebich, 'La lettre des évêques: une étude sur les réactions polonaises à l'Ostpolitik de la RFA', in *Etudes Internationales*, vi, 4 (Quebec, December 1975).

9 J. Kuroń and K. Modzelewski, *List otwarty do partii* [Open Letter to the Party] (Paris, 1967).

10 *Dokumenty: Wydarzenia marcowe 1968* [Documents: March Events 1968] (Paris, 1969); *Polskie przedwiośnie: Dokumentów marcowych tom II – Czechosłowacja* [Polish Early Spring: volume ii of March Documents – Czechoslovakia] (Paris, 1969).

11 For a more balanced analysis of the Jewish question in the Polish communist movement see Bieńkowski, *Motory i hamulce*, chap. 6.

12 Bethell, *Gomulka*, p. 269.

13 For a fuller analysis see Z. A. Pelczynski, 'The Downfall of Gomulka' in A. Bromke and J. W. Strong (eds.), *Gierek's Poland* (New York, 1973).

14 Bethell, *Gomulka*, pp. 238 ff.

15 *Rocznik polityczny i gospodarczy 1967* [Political and Economic Yearbook 1967] (Warsaw, 1967), pp. 764, 765.

16 Bethell, *Gomulka*, p. 264.

17 *Aktualne problemy Czechosłowacji i nasze stanowisko* [Current Problems of Czechoslovakia and our Position] (Warsaw, September 1969).

18 Stehle, *The Independent Satellite*, pp. 256 ff.
19 J. G. Zielinski, *Economic Reforms in Polish Industry* (London, 1973), p. 301.
20 Ryć, *Spożycie a wzrost*, p. 177.
21 Karpiński, *Polityka uprzemysłowienia*, pp. 33, 35.
22 W. Bieńkowski, *Socjologia klęski (dramat gomułkowskiego czternastolecia)* [The Sociology of Disaster (The Drama of Gomułka's Fourteen Years)] (Paris, 1971), pp. 110–14.
23 Jezierski, *Historia gospodarcza*, p. 252.
24 W. Bieńkowski, *Kryzys rolnictwa czy kryzys polityki rolnej?* [Crisis of Farming or Crisis of Farming Policy?] (Paris, 1970), p. 31.
25 Z. Grochowski (ed.), *Rolnictwo polskie w latach 1971–1975 i aktualne problemy jego rozwoju* [Polish Farming in the Years 1971–5 and Topical Problems of its Development] (Warsaw, 1976), p. 20. Another expert opinion (D. Gałaj's) gives the 1966–70 rate of increase as 1.4 rather than 1.8 per cent. Cf. *Village and Agriculture*, I (Warsaw, 1975), p. 24.
26 Zielinski, *Economic Reforms*, pp. 298–303.
27 *V Zjazd Polskiej Zjednoczonej Partii Robotniczej: 11–16 listopada 1968 r.* [Fifth Congress of the Polish United Workers' Party: 11–16 November 1968] (Warsaw, 1968), pp. 4, 236.
28 Zielinski, *Economic Reforms*, p. 18.
29 *V Zjazd*, p. 41, 57, 247, 316.
30 *For Further Development of People's Poland. 6th Congress of the Polish United Workers' Party, December 6–11, 1971. Basic Documents* (Warsaw, 1972), pp. 34 ff. According to calculations of a Western economist, real earnings actually decreased by 2.3 per cent in 1969 and rose only by 0.45 per cent during 1970.
31 He was heavily criticized for his behaviour and officially censured at the February 1971 plenum. Pelczynski, 'The Downfall of Gomulka', p. 7.
32 Zielinski, *Economic Reforms*, p. 21.
33 Pelczynski, 'The Downfall of Gomulka', pp. 1 ff.
34 A. Bromke, 'Beyond the Gomulka Era', *Foreign Affairs*, XLIX, no. 3 (April, 1971).
35 Bethell, *Gomulka*, pp. 250–2.

CHAPTER 16

1 The transcript of the proceedings, secretly recorded on tape, has been published in the West. E. Wacowska (ed.) *Dokumenty: Rewolta szczecińska i jej znaczenie* [Documents: the Szczecin Revolt and its Significance] (Paris, 1971).
2 The proceedings of the VIII Plenum were published in an edited form as a special issue of *Nowe Drogi* in May 1971. Cf. summary in Pelczynski, 'The Downfall of Gomulka', pp. 4–9.
3 Cf. J. Szczepański's articles in *Życie Warszawy*, 10–11 January 1971, and *Nowe Drogi*, no. 4, 1971, and J. J. Wiatr's in *Nowe Drogi*, nos. 1 and 3, 1971.
4 *Dokumenty: Poznań 1956–grudzień 1970* [Documents: Poznań 1956–December 1970] (Paris, 1971), pp. 133 ff.
5 A. Bromke, 'Poland under Gierek: A New Political Style', in *Problems of Communism*, no. 5 (Sept.–Oct. 1972).
6 Figures from V. C. Chrypiński, 'Political Change under Gierek', in Bromke and Strong, *Gierek's Poland*, pp. 36 ff.
7 Lipski, 'Changes in Agriculture', *ibid.*, pp. 103 ff.
8 W. Trzeciakowski, 'Foreign Trade: A Retrospective View', *ibid.*, pp. 71 ff.
9 *Rocznik polityczny i gospodarczy 1972* (Warsaw 1972), p. 221.
10 Figures based on *Report of the Central Committee of the PZPR covering the period between the 6th and the 7th Congress* (in English, Warsaw, December 1975), passim.

11 *Mały Rocznik Statystyczny 1977* [Little Statistical Yearbook 1977] (Warsaw, 1977), p. 122.

12 *For Further Development of People's Poland: 6th Congress of the Polish United Workers' Party December 6–11, 1971: Basic Documents* (Warsaw, 1972), p. 148.

13 *Report of the Central Committee...between the 6th and 7th Congress*, p. 12.

14 The technical aspect of this process is analysed in S. Gomulka and J. Sylwestrowicz, 'Import-led Growth: Theory and Estimation' in F. L. Altman (ed.), *On the Measurement of Factor Productivities* (Göttingen–Zurich, 1976).

15 *Rocznik polityczny i gospodarczy 1971* (Warsaw, 1971), pp. 47, 48.

16 Bromke and Strong, *Gierek's Poland*, pp. 108 ff.

17 *Rocznik polityczny i gospodarczy 1974* (Warsaw, 1974), pp. 133 ff.

18 *Rocznik polityczny i gospodarczy 1972* (Warsaw, 1972), p. 160.

19 Private information.

20 Bromke and Strong, *Gierek's Poland*, pp. 134 ff.

21 A. Bromke, 'Polish Foreign Policy in the 1970s' in Bromke and Strong, *Gierek's Poland*, pp. 198 ff.

22 M. F. Rakowski, *The Foreign Policy of the Polish People's Republic (Sketches from Thirty Years of History)* (Warsaw, 1975), pp. 203 ff.

23 Bromke and Strong, *Gierek's Poland*, pp. 210, 202.

24 The increases (in million *zł.*) were from 18,103 to 37,711 for Comecon countries and 7,749 to 31,307 for developed capitalist countries. *Mały Rocznik Statystyczny 1977* (Warsaw, 1977), p. 199.

25 A. Bromke, 'A New Juncture in Poland', in *Problems of Communism*, xxv, no. 5 (September–October 1976), pp. 8 ff.

26 Cf. H. Rechowicz's biography, *Bolesław Bierut* (Katowice, first published in 1974, 2nd edition 1977).

27 Bromke, 'A New Juncture in Poland', p. 11.

28 *Ibid.*, pp. 7, 8.

29 Zielinski, *Economic Reforms*, chap. 2.

30 *Ibid.*, pp. 40 ff.

31 J. Pajestka, *Czynniki i współzależności rozwoju społeczno-gospodarczego kraju* [Factors and Correlations of the Socio-economic Development of the Country] (Warsaw, 1975), pp. 270 ff.

32 *I Konferencja Krajowa PZPR 22–23 października 1973 r.: Podstawowe dokumenty i materiały* [First National Conference of PZPR 22–23 October 1973: Basic Documents and Materials] (Warsaw, 1973), p. 126.

33 *Mały Rocznik Statystyczny 1977*, p. 291.

34 The early ones were published in *Aneks*, nos. 13–14 (London, 1977). Cf. also an account of KOR activities up to May 1977 issued in Warsaw and republished in London by *Aneks* as a brochure *Wypadki czerwcowe i działalność Komitetu Obrony Robotników* [The June Events and the Activity of the Workers' Defence Committee] (n.d.).

35 The first collection was republished in Polish by Index on Censorship as *Zapis 1* (London, May 1977).

36 This was in fact advocated by Bieńkowski in *Kryzys rolnictwa* before the end of the Gomułka period.

37 A. Woś (ed.) *Osiągnięcia i problemy rozwojowe polskiego rolnictwa* [Achievements and Developmental Problems of Polish Agriculture] (Warsaw, 1975), p. 74.

38 Z. Szeliga, 'Agriculture', in *Polish Perspectives*, xxi, 3 (Warsaw, March 1978), p. 33.

39 W. Zujewicz, 'Turn-of-the-year observations', in *Polish Perspectives*, xxi, 1 (Warsaw, January 1978) p. 13.

40 M. Anasz and W. Wesołowski, 'Przemiany struktury społecznej w Polsce Ludowej' [Transformations of Social Structure in People's Poland], in M. W. Rutkiewicz *et al.*

(eds.), *Przemiany struktury społecznej w ZSRR i Polsce* [Transformations of Social Structure in the USSR and Poland] (Warsaw, 1976).

41 W. Wesołowski, 'Rola klasy robotniczej na obecnym etapie (kilka refleksji)' [Role of the working class in the present stage (a few reflections)] in J. Szczepański (ed.), *Narodziny socjalistycznej klasy robotniczej* [The Birth of The Socialist Working Class] (Warsaw, 1974).

42 W. Wesołowski and J. J. Wiatr, 'Nowe aspekty struktury społecznej jako podstawa rozwoju demokracji socjalistycznej' [New aspects of the social structure as a foundation for the development of socialist democracy], *Nowe Drogi*, September 1977.

CHAPTER 17

1 A. Sarapata (ed.), *Przemiany społeczne w Polsce Ludowej* [Social Transformations in People's Poland] (Warsaw, 1965), p. 89.

2 A. Kwilecki, quoted in J. J. Wiatr, 'Polish Society', in *Poland: a Handbook* (Warsaw, 1974), p. 131.

3 A. Podgórecki, 'The global analysis of Polish society (a sociological point of view)' *The Polish Sociological Bulletin*, no. 4 (Warsaw, 1976), p. 25.

4 Such statistics and estimates compiled by church authorities are known to exist, but have not been made public.

5 S. Nowakowski in Sarapata, *Przemiany społeczne*, p. 162.

6 J. Szczepański, *Zmiany społeczeństwa polskiego w procesie uprzemysłowienia* [Changes of Polish Society in the Process of Industrialization] (Warsaw, 1973), p. 67.

7 K. Zagórski in Szczepański, *Narodziny*, p. 228.

8 *Ibid.*, p. 249.

9 *Rocznik Statystyczny (1977)*, pp. xxx, xxxi.

10 L. Zieńkowski (ed.), *Struktura gospodarki narodowej* [The Structure of National Economy] (Warsaw, 1969), p. 34.

11 Anasz and Wesołowski in Rutkiewicz, *Przemiany struktury*, p. 65.

12 Zagórski in Szczepański, *Narodziny*, pp. 208–212.

13 *Rocznik Statystyczny (1965)*, p. 148; *Rocznik Statystyczny (1977)*, p. 132.

14 Wesołowski in Szczepański, *Narodziny*, p. 60.

15 W. Wesołowski (ed.), *Struktura i dynamika społeczeństwa polskiego* [The Structure and Dynamics of Polish Society] (Warsaw, 1970), p. 22.

16 Wesołowski in Szczepański, *Narodziny*, p. 49.

17 M. Jarosińska and J. Kulpińska in Rutkiewicz, *Przemiany struktury*, pp. 119, 120.

18 W. Makarczyk and J. Bluszkowski in W. Wesołowski (ed.), *Kształt struktury społecznej* [The Shape of Social Structure] (Wrocław–Warsaw, 1977), p. 181.

19 Sarapata, *Przemiany społeczne*, p. 33.

20 Anasz and Wesołowski in Rutkiewicz, *Przemiany struktury*, p. 54.

21 K. Zagorski 'Social Mobility in Poland', in S. Nowak (ed.), *Polish Sociology* (Wrocław, 1974), p. 156.

22 *Ibid.*, p. 147.

23 *Ibid.*, p. 157.

24 *Ibid.*, p. 159.

Select bibliography

This bibliography is limited to principal works in English relating to Poland since the uprising of January 1863, whereas reference is made to Polish sources and secondary works in the endnotes. Most of the works listed here contain extensive bibliographies.

Alton, T. P., *Polish Postwar Economy* (New York, 1955)

Bethell, N., *Gomułka, His Poland and His Communism* (London, 1969)

Benes, V. and Pounds, J. G., *Poland* (London, 1972)

Blit, L., *The Origins of Polish Socialism: The History and Ideas of the First Polish Socialist Party, 1878–1886* (Cambridge, 1971)

    The Eastern Pretender: Bolesław Piasecki: His Life and Times (London, 1965)

Bromke, A., *Poland's Politics: Idealism vs. Realism* (Cambridge, Mass., 1967)

Bromke, A. and Strong, J. W., *Gierek's Poland* (New York, 1973)

Budurowycz, B., *Polish–Soviet Relations 1932–1939* (Columbia, 1963)

Chmielewski, E., *The Polish Question in the Russian State Duma* (Knoxville, 1970)

Ciechanowski, J. M., *The Warsaw Rising of 1944* (Cambridge, 1974)

Cienciala, A. M., *Poland and the Western Powers, 1938–1939: A Study in the Interdependence of Eastern and Western Europe* (London, 1968)

Cottam, K. J., *Boleslaw Limanowski (1835–1935) – A Study in Socialism and Nationalism* (New York, 1978)

Davies, N., *White Eagle, Red Star – The Polish–Soviet War, 1919–1920* (London, 1972)

Dębicki, R., *The Foreign Policy of Poland, 1919–1939* (New York, 1962)

Dziewanowski, M. K., *Joseph Piłsudski: A European Federalist, 1918–1922* (Stanford, 1968)

    The Communist Party of Poland: An Outline History (Cambridge, Mass., 1959, new ed. 1977)

    Poland in the Twentieth Centry (New York, 1977)

Gibney, F., *The Frozen Revolution. Poland: A Study in Communist Decay* (New York, 1959)

Gieysztor, A., with S. Kieniewicz, E. Rostworowski, J. Tazbir and H. Wereszycki, *History of Poland* (Warsaw, 1968)

Gross, F., *The Polish Worker: A Study of a Social Stratum* (New York, 1944)

Gross, J. T., *Polish Society under German Occupation – The Generalgouvernement, 1939–1944* (Princeton, 1979)

Hiscocks, C. R., *Poland, Bridge for the Abyss? – An Interpretation of Developments in post-war Poland* (London, 1963)

Jordan, Z., *The Oder–Neisse Line: A Study of the Political and European Significance of Poland's Western Frontier* (London, 1952)

Kaeckenbeeck, G., *The International Experiment of Upper Silesia: A Study of the Workings of the Upper Silesian Settlement, 1922–1937* (London, 1942)

Karol, K. S., *Visa for Poland* (London, 1959)

Kieniewicz, S., *The Emancipation of the Polish Peasantry* (Chicago, 1969)

Kolankiewicz, G. and Taras, R., 'Poland: Socialism for Everyman', in *Political Change in Communist States*, edited by A. Brown and J. Gray (London, 1977)

Komarnicki, T., *The Rebirth of the Polish Republic: A Study in the Diplomatic History of Europe, 1914–1920* (London, 1957)

Korbel, J., *Poland between East and West: Soviet and German Diplomacy towards Poland, 1919–1933* (Princeton, 1963)

Korbonski, A., *Politics of Socialist Agriculture in Poland, 1945–1960* (New York and London, 1965)

Kulski, W. W., *Germany and Poland* (Syracuse, New York, 1976)

Lane, D. and Kolankiewicz, G., *Social Groups in Poland* (New York, 1973)

Leslie, R. F., *Reform and Insurrection in Russian Poland, 1856–1865* (London, 1963)

Lewis, F., *A Case of Hope* (New York, 1958)
    The Polish Volcano. A case history of hope (London, 1959)

Macartney, C. A. and Palmer, A. W., *Independent Eastern Europe – A History* (London, 1962)

Montias, J. M., *Central Planning in Poland* (New Haven, 1962)

Morrow, I. F. D., *The Pace Settlement in the German–Polish Borderlands* (Oxford, 1936)

Narkiewicz, O. A., *The Green Flag: Polish Populist Politics 1867–1970* (Totowa, New Jersey, 1976)

Nettl, J. P., *Rosa Luxemburg*, 2 vols. (London, 1966)

Newman, S., *March 1939: the British Guarantee to Poland* (Oxford, 1976)

Polonsky, A., *Politics in Independent Poland 1921–1939* (Oxford, 1972)
    The Great Powers and the Polish Question 1941–45 (London, 1976)

Raina, P., *Political Opposition in Poland 1954–1977* (London, 1978)

Rakowski, M. F., *The Foreign Policy of the Polish People's Republic (Sketches from Thirty Years of History)* (Warsaw, 1975)

Riekhoff, H. von, *German–Polish Relations 1918–1933* (Baltimore, 1971)

Roos, H., *A History of Modern Poland* (London, 1966)

Rosenthal, H., *German and Pole: National Conflict and Modern Myth* (Gainesville, 1976)

Rothschild, J., *Pilsudski's Coup d'Etat* (New York, 1966)

Rozek, E. J., *Allied Wartime Diplomacy: A Pattern in Poland* (New York, 1958)

Seton-Watson, G. H. N., *Eastern Europe between the Wars, 1918–1941* (Cambridge, 1946)
    The East European Revolution (London, 1956)

Shotwell, J., and Laserson, M., *Poland and Russia, 1919–1945* (New York, 1945)

Stehle, H., *The Independent Satellite: Society and politics in Poland since 1945* (London, 1965)

Staar, R. F., *Poland, 1944–62: The Sovietization of Captive People* (Baton Rouge, 1962)

Svennilson, S., *Growth and Stagnation in the European Economy* (Geneva, 1954)

Syrop, K., *Spring in October: The Polish Revolution of 1956* (London, 1957)

Taylor, J., *The Economic Development of Poland, 1919–1950* (Ithaca, New York, 1952)

Thomas, W. and Znaniecki, F., *The Polish Peasant in Europe and America*, 5 vols. (Boston, Mass., 1918)

Tims, R., *Germanizing Prussian Poland* (New York, 1941)

Wandycz, P., *France and her Eastern Allies, 1919–1925: French–Czechoslovak–Polish Relations from the Paris Peace Conference to Locarno* (Minneapolis, 1962)

Soviet–Polish Relations, 1917–1921 (Cambridge, Mass., 1969)

The Lands of Partitioned Poland, 1795–1918 (Seattle, 1974)

Czechoslovak–Polish Confederation and the Great Powers, 1940–1943 (Bloomington, 1956)

Wellisz, L., *Foreign Capital in Poland* (London, 1938)

Wiskemann, E. *Germany's Eastern Neighbours: Problems relating to the Oder–Neisse Line and the Czech Frontier Region* (London, 1956)

Wynot, E. D., *Polish Politics in Transition: The Camp of National Unity and the Struggle for Power* (Athens, Georgia, 1974)

Zawodny, J. K., *Death in the Forest: The Katyn Massacre* (Notre Dame, Indiana, 1962)

Nothing but Honour: The Story of the Warsaw Uprising (London, 1978)

Zielinski, J. G., *Economic Reforms in Polish Industry* (London, 1973)

Zweig, F., *Poland between Two Wars: A Critical Study of Social and Economic Change* (London, 1944)

Index

488